Acquisition and Loss of Nationality

Policies and Trends in 15 European States

Volume 2: Country Analyses

IMISCOE (International Migration, Integration and Social Cohesion)

IMISCOE is a European Commission-funded Network of Excellence of more than 350 scientists from various research institutes that specialise in migration and integration issues in Europe. These researchers, who come from all branches of the economic and social sciences, the humanities and law, implement an integrated, multidisciplinary and internationally comparative research program that focuses on Europe's migration and integration challenges.

Within the program, existing research is integrated and new research lines are developed that involve issues crucial to European-level policy making and provide a theory-based design to implement new research.

The publication program of IMISCOE is based on five distinct publication profiles, designed to make its research and results available to scientists, policymakers and the public at large. High-quality manuscripts written by IMISCOE members, or in cooperation with IMISCOE members, are published in these five series. An Editorial Committee coordinates the review process of the manuscripts. The five series are:

1. Joint Studies
2. Research
3. Dissertations
4. Reports
5. Textbook

More information on the network can be found at: www.imiscoe.org.

IMISCOE **Research** includes publications resulting from research of IMISCOE members like research monographs and edited volumes.

Acquisition and Loss of Nationality

Policies and Trends in 15 European States

Volume 2: Country Analyses

edited by
Rainer Bauböck
Eva Ersbøll
Kees Groenendijk
Harald Waldrauch

IMISCOE Research

AMSTERDAM UNIVERSITY PRESS

This publication is based on research funded by the Community's Sixth Framework Programme and cofunded by the Austrian Federal Ministry for Education, Science and Culture.

Cover illustration: © The Scotsman Publications Ltd. / Donald Macleod
Muhammed Maqsood and children during first citizenship ceremony (photo *The Scotsman* 20 January 2005)

Cover design: Studio Jan de Boer BNO, Amsterdam
Lay-out: Fito Prepublishing, Almere

ISBN-13 978 90 5356 949 8 (both volumes)
ISBN-10 90 5356 949 9

ISBN-13 978 90 5356 920 7 (volume 1)
ISBN-10 90 5356 920 0

ISBN-13 978 90 5356 921 4 (volume 2)
ISBN-10 90 5356 921 9

NUR 741 / 763

Contents

Tables

Preface

Bernhard Perchinig and Rainer Bauböck

From summer 2004 to the end of 2005 an international network of researchers analysed the rules and practices regulating the acquisition and loss of nationality in the fifteen 'old' EU Member States. The results of this EU-funded project with the acronym NATAC (The acquisition of nationality in EU Member States: rules, practices and quantitative developments) are published in two volumes. The first volume consists of comparative reports on specific modes of acquiring and losing nationality, on nationality statistics, on European trends in nationality legislation and on statuses of 'denizenship' and 'quasi-citizenship'. It also contains an account of the comparative methodology that has been developed specifically for this project, a chapter on international and European law and an assessment of the implementation of nationality law from the perspective of NGOs counselling immigrants who apply for naturalisation. The second volume consists of chapters that provide in-depth analyses of each country in our sample. In addition to these two volumes, we make available statistical data, the answers to our questionnaires and more extensive versions of several comparative chapters on the internet at www.imiscoe.org/natac. We hope that this material will be widely used for further research.

Whereas Volume 1 focuses on cross-country comparison, the country chapters collected in Volume 2 analyse the internal dynamics of nationality policy in each Member State and inform about the national background of legislative trends.

The authors of these country reports were involved in the development of the common conceptual framework and analytical instruments of the project. Their chapters are structured according to a common grid in order to facilitate comparative analyses. In this way, the present volume is the result of a stronger collaborative effort than previous collections of case studies on nationality law and policies.

The introductory part in each chapter gives an overview of the development of nationality law and the administrative practice of granting and withdrawing nationality, with particular emphasis on the period since 1985 and the political motives and objectives behind the amendments.

The chapters then describe the main historical changes in nationality law followed by a detailed analysis of the specific modes of, and conditions for, acquiring and losing nationality under current regulations. Here the focus is on the rules for acquisition of nationality by birth and after birth (naturalisation), on specific regulations for spouses and children, and on the modes of facilitated naturalisation for various other groups. In this context, the authors also discuss rules governing the status of quasi-citizens, expatriates or co-nationals abroad. Other features covered in this part are the framework for political decision-making, the application of nationality law in practice and political motives behind reforms.

A further section deals with statistical developments and provides figures and trends. Statistics on naturalisation are collected in different ways and there is a strong variation with regard to detail and availability of data. As pointed out in Chapter 6 of Volume 1, comparison across countries is therefore very difficult. Since each state's citizenship policies also determine who will enjoy the privileges of Union citizenship in all other Member States, the lack of common standards for data-gathering and statistical evaluation is not only a concern for academic research, but also for policymaking at both national and European levels.

Finally, each chapter discusses the institutional arrangements for lawmaking and implementation of nationality legislation. Here the authors analyse the impact of the framework for decisionmaking on nationality policies and the role of the bureaucracy in implementation, e.g. with regard to the duration of the naturalisation process or regional differences in the application.

In current academic debates on citizenship some authors assume that the legal status of nationality has lost in importance due to the development of human rights, a denizenship status and European Union citizenship. Contrary to this hypothesis, our study has found a growing density of legal regulation and an escalation of political debates on nationality policies since the 1990s. Naturalisation and loss of nationality are still at the core of sovereignty of the nation state, with only limited influence of international conventions and EU citizenship. Although these developments have diminished gaps in the legal position and rights of citizens and aliens, absolute security of residence, the right to vote and an unrestricted right to family reunification and free movement in the European Union are still a privilege of nationals of the Member States. Immigrants falling under the remit of the EU directive on the status of long-term, resident third country nationals[1] have to be granted equal treatment with nationals with regard to access to the labour market and working conditions, education and training, health and access to goods, services and housing, but access to this status may be made conditional on the fulfilment of integration conditions. Third country nationals with less than five years of residence in one Member State, or those who per se cannot accede the status due to lack of legal residence (e.g., rejected asylum seekers who cannot be deported), still face unequal treatment and insecurity of residence.

Nationality legislation, which has been a 'dormant' political field characterised by a high degree of stability and few major changes in legislation up to the 1990s, is now a strongly contested policy field in many Member States. Although the development of nationality legislation over time has not been the main focus of the project, the country reports clearly document a general growth of politicisation of nationality and a resulting volatility of policies that has also increased the impact of party composition of governments on the direction of nationality reforms. Brubaker's (1992) argument that nationality regimes are inherently stable since they reflect specific paths of nation-building and constructions of national identity seems to have become less salient in contemporary Europe. Our study provides the evidence but does not fully explore the reasons for this development. This will be a task for further in-depth comparison that correlates our data with independent variables such as changes in government.

One obvious reason for the return of nationality regulations into politics is the growing importance of the linkage between immigration and naturalisation, which has profoundly affected traditional conceptions of national membership and belonging. Meanwhile, all fifteen states in our sample are countries of immigration, and naturalisation is seen as an element in a process of immigrants' integration. The connection made between integration and naturalisation, however, differs considerably among the Member States, ranging from an understanding of naturalisation as a tool for integration to perceiving the acquisition of nationality as a reward for successful integration. Conditions for naturalisation for the first, second or third generation, the acceptance of multiple nationality or the specific combination of ius soli and ius sanguinis vary widely, and there are no clear trends across all Member States. Clusters of 'liberal' and 'restrictive' Member States can be identified with regard to different dimensions of nationality legislation, but these clusters do not form a coherent and stable picture. For example, in Germany a major liberal reform in 1999 was followed a few years later by new restrictions through naturalisation tests introduced in 2006. Mediterranean countries with similar traditions of emigration and recent experiences of large inflows have lately diverged strongly in their nationality laws. Portugal adopted a very liberal reform in February 2006, while Italy, Spain and especially Greece have, for the time being, retained restrictive legislations. In 2000, Belgium introduced much easier access to its nationality, while its northern neighbour has since moved in the opposite direction.

Although there is neither direct harmonisation of nationality laws in Europe, nor a clear overall trend towards convergence, Member States' legislations are to a certain degree influenced by other countries' policies. First, there are clear hints that legislation has often been influenced by concepts and practices developed in other EU Member States. This is particularly visible in the field of language requirements and naturalisation tests, which have become a common feature of naturalisation in Europe in recent years. Apart from such borrowing across state borders within the European Union, there is also a much more direct impact of sending states on regulations and reforms in the receiving states. The best example for this is the interplay between Turkish and German policies. In 1995, Turkey introduced the so-called 'pink card' granting former Turkish nationals rights to inherit and own property, to return to and to take up residence in Turkey as well as other citizenship rights apart from the franchise. The 'pink card' was introduced as an incentive for Turkish immigrants to formally renounce their Turkish nationality in order to naturalise in Germany. When it turned out that many immigrants were nevertheless unwilling to pay this price for naturalisation, Turkey simplified the reacquisition of Turkish nationality after naturalisation in another country. However, the 1999 reform in Germany removed a clause that had precluded the withdrawal of German nationality from residents in the country. Shortly before the provincial and federal elections of 2005, German authorities started to enforce the ban on dual nationality by declaring null and void the German nationality of up to 50,000 persons who had reacquired Turkish nationality since 2000.

As this example shows, nationality is re-entering the political arena not only in response to immigration but also to emigration. Many Member States privilege emigrants or people they deem to be 'co-ethnics' with regard to access to or retention of nationality or grant nationality iure sanguinis to their descendants. In order to maintain ties with their emigrants, some Member States allow them to naturalise abroad without losing their nationality of origin, while in others acquisition of a new nationality leads to automatic loss of the previous one. Special citizenship rights of expatriates include today, in twelve of the states in our sample, voting rights in home country elections and in a few cases (France, Italy and Portugal) even reserved seats in parliament to represent the external electorate.

These developments, which are described in Volume 1, also raise important questions with regard to the normative foundations of democracy and nationality: Over how many generations shall emigrants be allowed to transfer their nationality of origin to their descendants, even if these do not have genuine ties with that country, and how does this privilege compare with the reluctance of many Member States to grant voting rights to third country nationals who have resided in their territory for many years? Are we witnessing a deterritorialisation of nationality and a re-emergence of a quasi-feudal model of political representation? Will the inclusive dynamics of citizenship be once again superseded by its function as a boundarymarker for national communities?

Holding the nationality of one Member State does not only guarantee a set of core rights in that state, but also entails access to Union Citizenship, which includes freedom of movement and residence and the right to vote in local elections and European Parliament elections in other Member States. Despite this European dimension of Member State nationality, there is still no common understanding of the concept at the European level, and the regulation of access to nationality remains the exclusive prerogative of the Member States. The conditions for access to the common status of Union Citizenship therefore vary considerably across states.

This lack of common standards is not only questionable from a normative point of view, but might even impede access to Union Citizenship by mobile individuals: residence periods for naturalisation vary greatly from Member State to Member State and are not added up. Third country nationals residing consecutively in several Member States, without reaching the required period of residence in any one country, might stay for years in the European Union without having opportunities of access to Union Citizenship. Although nationality law clearly lies in the competence of the Member States, these problems show the need for future action. The institutions of the Union have recognised the need to exchange information and to promote good practices in this area, but there has been no follow-up action.[2]

Empirical research within the project has centred on several main questions. One is the relation between ius sanguinis and ius soli. As the chapters in this volume show, there has never been a clear-cut distinction between ius soli and ius sanguinis regimes; most countries have made use of both approaches during the last sixty years, and the often-proclaimed trend towards strengthening ius soli elements (e.g. Hansen & Weil 2001; Joppke 2003) has not yet reached several of the more peripheral European countries.

The continued dominance of ius sanguinis is also reflected in specific regulations for expatriates and their descendants, which can be found in nearly all countries and which grant these groups facilitated naturalisation, double nationality or iure sanguinis transmission of nationality abroad across several generations. In five states (Germany, Greece, Ireland, Portugal and Spain), preferential regulations even give access to citizenship to co-ethnic diasporas or descendants of former citizens who reside abroad. These tendencies have been interpreted as indicating a new trend towards the 're-ethnicisation' of citizenship in liberal democracies that counterbalances a more general trend towards de-ethnicisation in the admission of immigrants (Joppke 2003, 2004). Such mixed models of collective belonging challenge the widespread idea that nationality in Europe has become a formal legal expression of a universalistic conception of citizenship.

A further focus of the chapters concerns the toleration of multiple nationality. In contrast to the assumption of a clear trend towards acceptance of multiple nationality, our reports show a more wavering attitude, with phases of growing and of declining acceptance, depending on changes in government and political climate. As with the aforementioned topics, the country studies can be seen as a caveat against overgeneralisation and hasty conclusions about general tendencies. Politics does also matter in nationality policies, and apparently clearly established lines of development may be turned around under changing circumstances.

The legislative process and the implementation of nationality legislation by public administrations show an even broader variety. Whereas in some countries policy-making in this field is restricted to the political parties, in others churches, social partners or non-governmental organisations are also involved. Although our research did not include a systematic comparison of the policy making process, the chapters in the present volume show the decisive influence of national patterns and a strong impact of public administrations on policy outcomes. In this respect, the reports draw specific attention to widespread regional differences in the implementation of nationality laws not only within federal states, which creates the same normative problem of unequal conditions of access to a common status that we have already discussed with regard to European Union citizenship.

It is astonishing to see how little effort the analysed states put into encouraging their potential citizens to naturalise and informing them on how to do so. This lack of promotion of new citizens contrasts sharply with the prevailing attitude in traditional immigration countries such as the USA, Canada or Australia, which provide targeted information to applicants for naturalisation and generally regard high naturalisation rates as indicators of successful integration.

The ongoing debate about convergence or divergence in nationality law cannot easily be settled. Convergence has partly been initiated by international conventions, particularly the Council of Europe's Convention on Reduction of Cases of Multiple Nationality and Military Obligations in Cases of Multiple Nationality of 1963 and the European Convention on Nationality of 1997. The European Union has not played an important role in the development of the nationality policies of its

Member States yet, and the decisions of the European Court of Justice covering the topic (see Chapter 1 in Volume 1) have hardly had a significant impact on policy developments in the Member States. Nationality policies still seem to be an exclusive matter of the nation-state, constrained to a certain extent only by international, but not yet by European Union law.

Nationality law reform has become a conflict-loaded issue in many countries. As the reports in this volume show, the development of nationality legislation reflects societal conflicts about national self-understanding as well as about immigrant integration and thus cannot be understood without knowledge of the historic context. The thick history of nationality policies in the Member States and the growing dissent between political actors over their future also casts doubts on extrapolations of short term trends into the future. In the area of citizenship, the nation-state still defines the most important aspects for policy development. A thorough understanding of citizenship policies in Europe thus requires both comparative analyses across countries and historically grounded thick descriptions of national traditions and contemporary politics. We believe therefore that the chapters collected in this volume provide not merely background material that complements the core results of our project presented in Volume 1. They are also important starting points for future projects that attempt to compare the trajectories of citizenship in particular European states.

Notes

1 Council Directive 2003/109/EC of 25 November 2003 Concerning the Status of Third-Country Nationals who are Long-term Residents.
2 See the Presidency Conclusions of the Tampere European Council in October 1999 and the Communications by the Commission COM (2000) 757 and COM (2003) 336.

Bibliography

Brubaker, R. (1992), *Citizenship and Nationhood in France and Germany*. Cambridge, MA: Harvard University Press.

Hansen, R. & P. Weil (eds.) (2001), *Towards a European nationality: citizenship, immigration and nationality law in the EU*. Basingstoke: Palgrave.

Joppke, C. (2003), 'Citizenship between De- and Re-ethnicization (I)', *Archives Européennes de sociologie* 44: 429-458.

Joppke, C. (2004), 'Ethnic Diversity and the State', *British Journal of Sociology* 55 (3): 451-463.

1 Austria

Dilek Çinar and Harald Waldrauch

1.1 Introduction

The acquisition and loss of Austrian nationality are regulated by the Federal Law on Austrian Nationality 1985,[1] which was last amended in 2005; the new provisions came into force in March 2006.[2] Because the period of investigation of this book ends with mid 2005, this chapter primarily covers the legal status after the amendment to the nationality law in 1998, which came into force in January 1999.[3] Nevertheless, the conclusions contain a summary of the current legal status as of March 2006. The Nationality Law of 1985 is based on five principles (Mussger, Fessler, Szymanski & Keller 2001: 26ff). First, according to the principle of ius sanguinis, a child born in wedlock acquires Austrian nationality by birth if one of the parents is an Austrian national. According to the same principle, children born abroad to Austrian expatriates acquire Austrian nationality by birth. Second, the Nationality Law of 1985 contains certain provisions to avoid statelessness. The third principle characteristic of the Austrian Nationality Law is the ban on multiple nationality. The fourth principle of individual autonomy provides for equality between men and women. Finally, the law contains several provisions to ensure that members of a family share the same nationality. Although these principles have been characteristic of the Austrian nationality legislation for many decades, the priority attached to the different principles has changed over time. In particular, the principle that members of a family should have a common nationality has become less important, because of legislative reforms to achieve gender equality with respect to the acquisition and loss of Austrian nationality (Mussger et al. 2001: 28).

Since the introduction of legal provisions concerning Austrian nationality in the nineteenth century, the principle of ius sanguinis has been predominant in Austrian nationality legislation. Although Austria has been transformed from an emigration country to an immigration country over the last decades, Austrian Nationality Law still does not contain provisions based on the principle of ius soli. Thus, birth in Austria does neither entail automatic acquisition of the Austrian nationality nor does it constitute a legal entitlement to naturalisation for the children of immigrants during minority or upon reaching majority.

The main modes of acquisition *after birth* are discretionary naturalisation and legal entitlement to be granted Austrian nationality. Naturalisation by discretion requires at least ten years of residence, the absence of criminal convictions, sufficient income, sufficient knowledge of German (since 1999), an affirmative attitude toward the Republic and renunciation of the original nationality. The requirement of ten years of residence may be reduced to four or six years for 'special reasons'. This applies to recognised refugees, minor children and EEA-nationals, who may acquire Austrian nationality after four years of residence; persons born in Austria, persons who can prove their 'sustainable integration', persons who are former nationals and persons recognised for special achievements may be naturalised after six years of residence. Different groups of foreign nationals who enjoy legal entitlement to the acquisition of Austrian nationality include, among others, (1) spouses and children of Austrian nationals, (2) spouses and children of applicants for naturalisation who will be granted Austrian nationality (extension of naturalisation), (3) long-term residents, i.e., persons who have been resident in Austria for fifteen years and can prove their sustainable integration and (4) persons who have been resident in Austria for 30 years or (5) stateless persons.[4]

According to art. 11 (1) of the Constitution, nationality legislation is a federal matter, whereas the execution of the law is a matter of the nine federal provinces. The government of the respective federal province is the highest executive authority. As there are no official guidelines concerning the implementation of legal provisions, the authorities have a wide margin of interpretation in discretionary naturalisation, and decisions on matters of nationality are frequently subject to judicial review by the Administrative Courts. The administration of nationality legislation by the federal provinces was a major source of anomalies in the past, especially with respect to naturalisations after at least four years and less than ten years of residence for 'special reasons'. The law did not lay down the special reasons justifying the reduction of the residence requirement of ten years until the reform of 1998. The province of Vienna made use of this clause from the late 1980s until the mid-1990s in order to facilitate the naturalisation of immigrants and of their family members. At the same time, profound changes in the legal framework regulating the entry, residence and employment of foreign nationals made the option of naturalisation for many immigrants increasingly attractive. While during the 1980s between 8,000 and 10,000 persons were naturalised annually, in the following years the number of naturalisations increased steadily.

Until the mid-1990s the amendment of the Nationality Law was not on the political agenda. Since then the continuous growth of the number of persons granted Austrian nationality has met with resistance from the right-wing Freedoms Party (FPÖ) and the Christian Democratic People's Party (ÖVP), the then coalition partner of the Social Democrats (SPÖ). Between 1996 and 1998, the amendment of nationality legislation became a hotly debated issue. While the FPÖ and the ÖVP insisted on the introduction of further assimilation or integration requirements, the Green Party and the Liberal Party (LIF) proposed the reduction of the general residence requirement to five years, the introduction of the principle of 'double' ius soli, i.e., acquisition at birth in the territory if one parent was also born in the territory, and toleration of dual nationality.

In 1998, the two governing parties SPÖ and ÖVP reached agreement on amending the conditions for facilitated naturalisation. Except for former Austrian nationals, recognised refugees and EEA-nationals, this mode of acquisition was made dependent on at least six years of residence and proof of the applicant's 'sustainable integration'. Acquisition of Austrian nationality by discretionary naturalisation or by legal entitlement was made conditional upon sufficient knowledge of the German language. The official aim of the reform of 1998 was to 'harmonise' the administration of the nationality legislation across the country and to restrict the possibility of facilitated naturalisation.

The statistical developments since the entry into force of the new provisions in January 1999 show, however, that the restrictions did not have an impact on the total number of naturalisations. Contrary to the government's expectation that the reform of 1998 would lead to a decrease in the number of naturalisations, roughly 25,000 persons acquired Austrian nationality in 1999. In 2003 and 2004, more than 40,000 persons were granted Austrian nationality. There are two major factors that explain the surge in naturalisations since the mid-1990s. First, Turkish nationals, who represent one of the major immigrant groups in Austria, do not suffer serious disadvantages anymore when they renounce their Turkish nationality. Accordingly, the naturalisation of immigrants with Turkish nationality has been increasing significantly over the last decade. Second, more and more immigrants become eligible to apply for naturalisation after at least ten years of residence.

In September 2005, the Ministry of the interior proposed a bill in order to further restrict access to Austrian nationality. The ministerial draft bill gave rise to manifold criticism by legal scholars, the bar association, the UNHCR and other stakeholders. Upon revision of some of the contested provisions, the Council of Ministers of the governing coalition parties BZÖ[5] and ÖVP approved the governmental draft bill on

15 November 2005. The proposed amendment of the Nationality Law of 1985 will be discussed in the concluding section of this contribution.

1.2 Historical development

1.2.1 *Developments 1811-1945*

Legal provisions concerning the acquisition and loss of Austrian nationality were introduced in the early nineteenth century and remained effective in the Austrian part of the Habsburg Empire until the end of the First World War. According to § 28 of the Civil Code of 1811, acquisition of Austrian nationality by birth was based on the principle of ius sanguinis. Children born in wedlock acquired Austrian nationality if the father was an Austrian national; children born out of wedlock became Austrian nationals irrespective of the nationality of the father or the child's place of birth if the mother held Austrian nationality (Goldemund, Ringhofer & Theuer 1969: 473f). Children born out of wedlock to an Austrian father became Austrian nationals upon legitimation. Another automatic mode of acquisition concerned foreign women who acquired their husband's Austrian nationality upon marriage. Foreigners without familial ties to Austrian nationals became Austrian nationals *ipso iure* either upon entry into the civil service or after ten years of uninterrupted residence. As the automatic naturalisation of foreign nationals after ten years of residence gave rise to diplomatic disputes, this provision was amended in 1833 to allow for discretionary naturalisation by application (Heinl 1950: 33). Finally, foreign nationals could be naturalised by application if they could prove 'good manners' and sufficient income; a certain period of residence in the country prior to application was not required, but in this case naturalisation was ultimately an act of 'grace' (Thienel 1989: 41).

The relevant legal source concerning the loss of Austrian nationality was the *Auswanderungspatent* 1832 (Emigration Law). Emigration of Austrian nationals was subject to authorisation. Austrian nationals who intended to live abroad permanently had to apply for release from Austrian nationality prior to emigration in order not to incur a penalty. According to § 9 of the Emigration Law, the loss of the status as an Austrian 'subject' became effective after departure from Austria. Austrian nationals were granted the right to leave the country without prior authorisation in 1867, but emigration continued to provide a ground for loss of nationality (Brandl 1996: 62). The Emigration Law was not only relevant for Austrian nationals who went abroad, but also with respect to the nationality status of women. According to § 19 of the Emigration Law Austrian women lost their status as 'female subjects' upon marriage to a foreigner (Goldemund et al. 1969: 474).

Although Austrian nationality granted unlimited access to civil rights, the right to unconditional residence and public assistance for the poor was dependent on having the so-called *Heimatrecht*, i.e., the right of abode in a municipality. Austrian nationals living in a municipality where they did not enjoy the *Heimatrecht* were liable to deportation if they became a public burden. The right to unconditional residence and public assistance was acquired either automatically by descent, marriage, practising of certain professions or by legal entitlement after ten years of residence in the respective municipality. The naturalisation of foreigners was, among other things, dependent on a municipality's willingness to grant a foreigner *Heimatrecht*.

After the end of First World War and the collapse of the Austro-Hungarian monarchy in 1918, the *Heimatrecht* was decisive for the reassignment of former nationals to one of the successor states. According to the Treaty of Saint-Germain-en-Laye, which came into force in July 1920, the acquisition of Austrian nationality was conditional upon having *Heimatrecht* in a municipality within the new borders of the Republic of *Deutsch-Österreich* and not holding the nationality of another state (Brandl 1996: 63; Bauböck & Çinar 2001).[6]

The new Constitution of 1920 introduced two important elements in matters of nationality. First, legislation concerning the acquisition and loss of nationality was declared a matter of the federal state (*Bund*) and administration of the legal provisions one of the federal provinces (*Länder*) (Brandl 1996: 65). Second, a separate provincial citizenship (*Landesbürgerschaft*) was created for each of the nine Austrian federal provinces. According to the Nationality Law of 1925, acquisition of Austrian nationality was henceforth conditional upon holding or acquiring the citizenship of a federal province. Persons who were Austrian nationals and had *Heimatrecht* in a municipality were declared citizens of the respective federal province (*Landesbürger*). Children of Austrian nationals acquired provincial citizenship and Austrian nationality according to the principle of ius sanguinis. Foreigners could already acquire provincial citizenship after four years of residence in Austria (de Groot 1989: 150), if they could prove that a municipality would grant them *Heimatrecht* and if they gave up their previous citizenship. Other modes of acquisition of the provincial citizenship and the Austrian nationality concerned the automatic acquisition of nationality by professors upon taking office at an Austrian university, by a foreign woman who married an Austrian national and by the children of foreign nationals who obtained the Austrian nationality. However, after 1933, the naturalisation of foreigners was possible only in individual cases if granting Austrian nationality served the interests of the government (Goldemund et al. 1969: 409).

Following the annexation of Austria to Nazi Germany in 1938, all persons holding Austrian nationality were declared nationals of the Third Reich. Simultaneous to the abrogation of the Nationality Law of 1925 in July 1939 the provisions of the German Nationality Law of 1913 became effective in Austria (Heinl 1950: 48f).

1.2.2 *Developments 1945-1985*

After the reestablishment of Austria as an independent state, the German Nationality Law of 1913 was abrogated in April 1945. A few months later, the Law on the Transition to Austrian Nationality (*Staatsbürgerschaftsüberleitungsgesetz*) and the Nationality Law of 1945 came into force. All persons who held Austrian nationality on 13 March 1938 or would have acquired it until 1945 on the basis of the Nationality Law of 1925 were declared Austrian nationals. However, persons who were considered to have fulfilled a condition that would have entailed the loss of Austrian nationality between 1938 and 1945 were excluded. According to § 7 of the Nationality Law of 1925, persons who acquired a foreign nationality as well as women marrying foreign nationals lost Austrian nationality. Thus the Austrian nationality of persons who had to leave the country during the Nazi regime was restored automatically only if they did not hold another nationality (Burger & Wendelin 2004: 2). Persons who had acquired a foreign nationality could regain Austrian nationality by declaration until July 1950 if they could prove that they had had their habitual residence in Austria since January 1919.[7] In this case, applicants did not have to renounce a foreign nationality acquired abroad.

The Nationality Law of 1945 was based on the Nationality Law of 1925, but provincial citizenship and *Heimatrecht* were not reintroduced. Due to numerous amendments of the transitional provisions between 1945 and 1949 the Nationality Law of 1945 was republished in 1949. Although the Nationality Law of 1949 was basically in line with the legal provisions in force since 1925, the law also contained some changes. First, according to § 9 of the Nationality Law of 1949, women who acquired a foreign nationality automatically upon marriage could henceforth apply for permission to retain their Austrian nationality. Second, naturalisation of foreign nationals was made more difficult and different waiting periods were introduced. § 5 of the Nationality Law of 1949 provided that foreign nationals could acquire Austrian nationality after four years of residence only if the naturalisation of the applicant would benefit the interest of the federal state. After ten years of residence naturalisation by discretion was possible if the applicant fulfilled the general conditions. Foreign nationals who had resided in Austria for 30 years and fulfilled the general conditions had a legal entitlement to naturalisation. This latter provision was a reformulation of the legal entitlement to naturalisation of persons who could prove to have had their habitual residence in Austria since January 1919 (Heinl 1950: 125). The general conditions to be fulfilled were, among other things, the renunciation of the previous nationality, absence of a relationship with the home country that could damage the interests of Austria and absence of a criminal record. These different waiting periods introduced in 1949 are still part of the current law that regulates the naturalisation of foreign nationals.

Between 1945 and 1950 roughly one million 'displaced persons' from Eastern Europe and the former Soviet Union, among them more than 300,000 so-called *Volksdeutsche* (ethnic Germans), had become stranded in Austria (Fassmann & Münz 1995: 34). While many displaced persons stayed in Austria temporarily, about 530,000 settled permanently. Between 1954 and 1956, displaced persons of German descent who were either stateless or whose nationality status was unclear were granted the right to acquire Austrian nationality by declaration.[8] Until 1958, roughly 230,000 *Volksdeutsche* acquired Austrian nationality. In contrast, displaced persons who were not ethnic Germans had to apply for discretionary naturalisation (Stieber 1995: 149).

During the first half of the 1960s reform, discussions concentrated on domestic as well as international issues in nationality matters, namely the need for a register of Austrian nationals (*Staatsbürgerschaftsevidenz*) and the adoption of the UN Convention on the Status of Married Women, the UN Convention on the Reduction of Statelessness, and the Convention of the Council of Europe on the Reduction of Multiple Nationality (Thienel 1989: 95). A new nationality law was passed in 1965, which came into force in July 1966.[9] Again, the Nationality Law of 1965 maintained on the one hand the basic principles of nationality legislation as it had developed since 1925, on the other hand several changes were introduced in order to eliminate the discrimination of women in matters of nationality. The most important changes in this respect were:

- Children born in wedlock could acquire the Austrian nationality of their mother if they would otherwise be stateless (§ 7).
- Automatic loss of Austrian nationality by marriage to a foreign national was abolished (§ 26).
- Automatic acquisition of nationality by marriage to an Austrian national was transformed into a right to naturalisation by declaration (§ 9).
- Automatic granting of nationality to a foreign woman whose husband acquired the Austrian nationality was transformed into a legal

entitlement to the extension of naturalisation upon application (§ 16).

Two further changes were introduced with respect to the ban on multiple nationality and the loss of Austrian nationality. First, according to § 10 of the Nationality Law of 1965, recognised refugees were explicitly exempt from the requirement to renounce their previous nationality in order to be granted Austrian nationality. Second, with an aim to strengthening the principle of individual autonomy, § 37 of the Nationality Law of 1965 provided, for the first time, for the loss of nationality by *voluntary* renunciation (Thienel 1989: 95).

Until the mid-1980s, the Nationality Law of 1965 was amended with regard to the naturalisation of foreign nationals, the reacquisition of nationality and the nationality status of men and women (Mussger et al. 2001: 22f). The amendments of 1973 and 1983 deserve special attention. While the latter reform eliminated still existing inequalities between men and women, the original aim of the amendment in 1973 was, among other things, to facilitate the naturalisation of the so-called 'guest workers' (Novak 1974: 589).

Until the early 1960s, Austria was an emigration country. Germany and Switzerland were the main destination countries for many Austrian labour migrants. The aggregate migration balance between 1951 and 1961 amounted to –129,000 (Waldrauch 2003). When Austria started facing labour shortages during the economic boom of the late 1950s, the Austrian Economic Chamber entered into negotiations with German and Swiss companies to stop the recruitment of Austrian workers (Münz, Zuser & Kytir 2003: 21). As these negotiations were not successful, the Social Partners reached an agreement to recruit workers from Mediterranean countries. Recruitment agreements were concluded with Spain (1962), Turkey (1964) and former Yugoslavia (1966), which led to an increase of the share of foreign workers from 1.6 per cent in 1965 to 7.2 per cent in 1975 (Waldrauch 2003). The share of foreign nationals living in Austria increased from 1.4 per cent in 1961 to 2.8 per cent in 1971 (Münz et al. 2003: 38). It is against this background that the amendment of Nationality Law 1973 was supposed to liberalise the conditions of naturalisation.

Until the reform of 1973, § 10 (4) of the Nationality Law of 1965, which is a constitutional provision, stated that foreigners could be granted Austrian nationality irrespective of some of the general conditions for naturalisation in case their 'extraordinary achievements' would serve the interests of the Republic. Thus, the draft version of the government bill allowed for 'ordinary' achievements to be a sufficient reason in order to waive the requirements of ten years of residence, sufficient income, and renunciation of the original citizenship. The intention was to remove the most important obstacles to the naturalisation of so-called 'guest workers' and their descendents. However, in the preliminary stages of the parliamentary procedure the government was accused of just 'fishing for voters' (Novak 1974: 590). In addition, the proposed amendment would have required a two-thirds majority vote by the parliament to amend a constitutional provision, which may explain the reluctance of the Constitutional Committee that eventually rejected the proposed amendment. Instead, the Constitutional Committee agreed on abolishing the requirement of a certain period of residence in the country for minors with a foreign nationality. As, according to § 17 of the Nationality Law of 1965, minor children already had a legal entitlement to be granted Austrian nationality together with their parents without having to fulfil any residence requirements, this amendment had hardly any impact in practice.

The reform of 1973 also brought changes with regard to survivors of the Holocaust, political emigrants and expatriates (Novak 1974). The time limit for applications for the reacquisition of Austrian nationality by former nationals who had had to leave the country to escape political persecution between 1933 and 1945 was extended until December 1974 (§ 58 in the version of 1973). The same group of people was granted the right to reacquire Austrian nationality by notification (*Anzeige*) to the authorities of the re-establishment of their habitual residence in Austria, if they had been Austrian nationals for at least ten years, were entitled to permanent settlement and fulfilled the general conditions for naturalisation (§ 58c). Finally, the permission to retain Austrian nationality when acquiring a foreign nationality was made conditional on 'future achievements' for the benefit of the Republic instead of 'extraordinary' achievements (§ 28).

A profound change of nationality legislation in the mid-1980s brought about full equality between men and women.[10] Most importantly, the gender inequality with respect to the acquisition of nationality by children born in wedlock was eliminated. Since September 1983, children born in wedlock acquire Austrian nationality by birth if one of the parents is an Austrian national. Minor children born before September 1983 who could not acquire Austrian nationality because their father was not an Austrian national were given the option upon declaration to obtain the Austrian nationality from their mother until December 1988.[11]

However, the gender equality reform also eliminated a 'female privilege' (Bauböck & Çinar 2001). Until then, women married to an Austrian national could acquire their husband's nationality by simple declaration without having to fulfil any other conditions. Since the reform of 1983, persons married to Austrian nationals have to fulfil the general conditions of naturalisation.

1.3 Recent developments and current institutional arrangements

The Nationality Law of 1965 was reissued in 1985[12] and has been amended several times since then. The most important amendments between 1985 and 1998 concerned (1) the relationship between nationality of the Federal Republic (*Bundesbürgerschaft*) and 'citizenship' of the federal provinces (*Landesbürgerschaft*), (2) the reacquisition of Austrian nationality and (3) the naturalisation of foreign nationals.

According to art. 6 (1) of the Constitution of 1929, each federal province had its own 'provincial citizenship' (*Landesbürgerschaft*), which was declared a prerequisite for the acquisition of 'federal citizenship' (*Bundesbürgerschaft*). Although art. 6 (1) also provided that the acquisition and loss of the citizenship of each federal province took place under uniform conditions, no federal law was introduced to regulate these conditions. The provisional Constitution of 1945 and the Nationality Law of 1949 declared that, subject to further constitutional amendments, this subdivision of Austrian nationality into provincial and state citizenship was suspended (Mussger et al. 2001: 20). It was only in 1988 that the principle of a 'uniform' Austrian nationality was laid down in the Constitution. Although the citizenship of the federal provinces was maintained, the amended art. 6 (2) of the Constitution reversed the relationship between the *Bundesbürgerschaft* and *Landesbürgerschaft*. Persons holding Austrian nationality were henceforth considered 'citizens' of the federal province where they have their main residence.[13]

Another important development with respect to rights of Austrian nationals occurred in 1990, when a number of laws that regulate the eligibility of voters in national elections and referenda were amended (see BGBl. 148/90). Since then, Austrian nationals living abroad enjoy full voting rights in parliamentary and presidential elections as well as in national referenda, if they are included in the register of voters in a municipality. The registration requires an application by Austrian expatriates and needs to be renewed every ten years.

As mentioned above, survivors of the Holocaust and political emigrants were granted the right to reacquire nationality by notification (*Anzeige*) in 1973, but they had to re-establish their habitual residence in Austria and to meet, with some exceptions, the general conditions for naturalisation. The amendment of 1993, finally, liberalised the conditions for the reacquisition of nationality by persons who had had to leave the country before 1945.

The Nationality Law of 1985 was last amended in 1998 with the aim of eliminating differences in the administration of the law by the federal provinces with respect to the facilitated naturalisation of immigrants. The reform of 1998 also introduced for the first time language proficiency as an explicit condition for naturalisation. The political background of this reform and current debates about tightening certain conditions for naturalisation will be described in sect. 1.3.2. The next section describes the current modes of acquisition and loss. Provisions amended by the reform of 1998 that came into force in January 1999 are indicated in brackets. Further changes proposed by a draft governmental bill in November 2005 will be discussed in the concluding sect. 1.4.

1.3.1 Main modes of acquisition and loss of nationality

1.3.1.1 Acquisition of Austrian nationality

The Nationality Law of 1985 provides, together with the Decree on Nationality, the main source of legal provisions currently regulating acquisition and loss of Austrian nationality.[14] Austrian nationality is either acquired by (1) descent, i.e., *by birth* (§§ 7, 7a, 8), or *after birth* by (2) the granting of nationality (or extension of the granting) (§§ 10-24), (3) *ex lege* by taking office as a professor at an Austrian university, the Academy of Arts in Vienna or an Austrian Arts College (§ 25 (1)),[15] (4) by declaration (§ 25 (2)) or (5) by notification (§ 58c).

(1) Acquisition at birth: As already mentioned, Austrian nationality legislation is based on the principle of ius sanguinis. While birth in Austria does not constitute a claim to the acquisition of citizenship at birth by descendents of immigrants,[16] Austrian nationality is attributed to children of Austrian nationals living abroad by virtue of descent. With respect to the attribution of nationality iure sanguinis to children born abroad, Austrian nationality legislation does not contain any restrictions, so that Austrian nationality may be indefinitely attributed to descendents of Austrian emigrants. This intergenerational transmission will only be prevented if parents of Austrian origin have renounced their Austrian nationality before the birth of the child in order to acquire the nationality of their (foreign) country of residence. Since 1999 retaining Austrian nationality has been made easier so that we can expect more iure sanguinis acquisitions abroad as a consequence. If the first generation retains Austrian nationality, then all subsequent generations can pass on their nationality acquired at birth to their own children.

Children born in wedlock acquire Austrian nationality by birth if one of the parents is or was until his or her death an Austrian national (§ 10 (7)). Children born out of wedlock acquire the nationality of their Austrian mother. If the father of a child born out of wedlock is an Austrian national, the child receives the nationality of the father upon legitimation (i.e., through the marriage of the parents or by declaration of a child as legitimate by the Federal President) (§ 10 (7a)).[17] Since 1985, automatic acquisition by legitimation requires the consent of a child above the age of fourteen and of his or her legal agent, as the Constitutional Court declared automatic naturalisation by legitimation a violation of the principle of equality (Thienel 1989: 146). The Court argued that this *automatic* and *compulsory* mode of acquisition amounts to unequal treatment of children who acquire Austrian nationality *after birth* by extension of their parents' naturalisation and by legitimation, respectively. In the first case, the child of a person who acquires Austrian nationality does not become an Austrian national automatically, as the extension of the granting of Austrian nationality to a child requires an application filed on a voluntary basis. In contrast, the Nationality Law of 1965 (§7 Abs (4)) provided for the automatic acquisition of Austrian nationality by an illegitimate child of an Austrian father upon marriage of the parents. Neither the child nor the parents could object to acquisition of Austrian nationality. Against this background, the Court argued that children who acquire Austrian nationality after birth and sometimes against their will are being treated unequally compared to children who also acquire it after birth, but only on the basis of a voluntary act.

Foundlings up to the age of *six months* are considered Austrian nationals by descent (§ 10 (8) 1).

(2) General conditions for acquisition after birth: Foreign nationals may acquire Austrian nationality either by discretionary naturalisation or by naturalisation through legal entitlement based on long-term residence or familial ties. As a general rule, foreign nationals seeking naturalisation must have had their principal residence in Austria without interruption for ten years (§ 10 (1)). In addition, the following requirements have to be met:

- The applicant must not have been convicted, by an Austrian or foreign court, to imprisonment of more than three months (*before 1999:* six months) because of one or more intentional crimes including 'youth crimes', or by an Austrian court to imprisonment of more than three months (*before 1999:* six months) because of a fiscal offence (§ 10 (2) and (3)).
- There must be no criminal proceedings pending for an intentional crime or fiscal offence that may be punished with imprisonment (§ 10 (1) 4).
- There must be no ban on the applicant's residence (*Aufenthaltsverbot*) in Austria and no proceedings pending to terminate the residence of the applicant (§ 10 (5)).
- The applicant must have an 'affirmative attitude towards the Republic of Austria', which is to be judged on the basis of his or her past behaviour, and he or she must not represent a danger to public law, order and security including any other public interest that is cov-

ered by art. 8 (2) of the European Convention for the Protection of Human Rights and Fundamental Freedoms (§ 10 (1) 6).
- The applicant must have sufficient income unless the applicant is not responsible for his or her own financial upkeep (§ 10 (1) 7).
- The applicant must not have relations to a foreign state, which could damage the interests or the reputation of Austria (§ 10 (1) 8).
- The applicant must undertake steps to be released from his or her previous nationality if this is possible and reasonable (§ 10 (3)).
- The applicant must have knowledge of the German language at a level that corresponds to his or her social circumstances (*since 1999*) (§10a).

Fulfilment of the general conditions for naturalisation does not automatically result in the granting of Austrian nationality. In exercising their discretion authorities have to take into consideration the common good, public interests and the extent of integration of the applicant (§ 11). In this context, authorities may base their decision on additional criteria such as 'work ethics' or compliance with legal requirements concerning road safety (Mussger et al. 2001: 80; Thienel 1990: 204f). However, authorities are obliged to justify the way they make use of their discretion.

(2.1.) *Facilitated naturalisation*: Austrian nationality may be granted after four or six years of residence if the general conditions for naturalisation are fulfilled and if there is a reason deserving special consideration (*besonders berücksichtigungswürdiger Grund*) (§ 10 (4) and (5)). Since 1999, the law states that Austrian nationality may be granted after four years of residence if the applicant is an EEA-national or a recognised refugee (§ 10 (5) 4-5). Other applicants may be granted Austrian nationality after six years of residence
- if they are former Austrian nationals, unless nationality was lost by withdrawal (§ 10 (5) 1), or
- if they can prove that their personal and professional integration is 'sustainable' (§ 10 (5) 3), or
- if they were born in Austria (§ 10 (5) 6), or
- because of their special achievements in the arts, economy, science or sports (§ 10 (5) 2).

Minors who fulfil one of these conditions may be naturalised after four years of residence. As the reasons for facilitated naturalisation enumerated by the law are not exhaustive, authorities may apply additional criteria in practice.

With the reform of 1998, birth in Austria has, for the first time, been specified by law as a reason for facilitated naturalisation. However, birth in Austria still does not constitute a legal entitlement to the acquisition of Austrian nationality, and in practice the overwhelming majority of minors acquire Austrian nationality together with their parents rather than because of birth in Austria (Waldrauch & Çinar 2003: 274). The main categories of foreign nationals who have acquired Austrian nationality according to the new provisions for facilitated naturalisation are recognised refugees after four years of residence and foreign nationals who have lived in Austria for at least six years and were able to prove their 'sustainable integration'.

Foreign nationals who have attained and are expected to attain 'extraordinary achievements' may be naturalised without having to meet any residence requirement, if the granting of Austrian nationality benefits the interests of the Republic. In this case, neither proof of sufficient income nor renunciation of the original nationality is necessary (§ 10 (6), constitutional provision).[18]

Finally, persons who acquire Austrian nationality by *grant (Verleihung)* (or extension of grant) have to take the following oath:

'I swear that I will be a loyal citizen of the Republic of Austria, that I will always conscientiously abide by the laws and that I will avoid everything that might harm the interests and the reputation of the Republic.'

Usually persons who are granted Austrian nationality have their principal residence in Austria. However, in a few cases application for acquisition of Austrian nationality may be filed abroad. This includes persons married to an Austrian national for at least five years (§ 11a (1) b), the extension of naturalisation to children and spouses (after five years of marriage) (§ 17), the naturalisation of children of Austrian nationals (§ 12 (4)) and former Austrian nationals who have lost Austrian nationality because of marriage to a foreign national within five years after divorce (§ 13).

(2.2.) *Legal entitlement*: Several provisions of the Nationality Law of 1985 confer to certain groups of foreigners legal entitlement to acquire Austrian nationality. Privileged groups of foreign nationals include family members of an Austrian national or a reference person who is about to be granted Austrian nationality, long-term residents, stateless persons and former Austrian nationals.

(2.2.1.) *Family members*: The most important group of foreign nationals who enjoy a right to acquisition of Austrian nationality consists of family members of Austrian nationals or of a reference person who is about to be granted Austrian nationality. The foreign spouse of an Austrian national has a legal entitlement to obtain Austrian nationality after four years of marriage if he or she has lived in Austria for at least one year or after three years of marriage and residence in Austria for at least two years (§ 11a). The residence requirement is dispensed with, if the marriage has been maintained for at least five years and the Austrian spouse has held Austrian nationality for at least ten years. Since 1999, the couple must live in the same household.

A foreign child of an Austrian national has a legal entitlement to be granted Austrian nationality (the mother's or the father's), if the child is a minor, unmarried and born in wedlock (§ 12 (4)). If the child was born out of wedlock, the legal entitlement is dependent on the mother holding the Austrian nationality. If the relevant Austrian parent is the father, the transfer of nationality by legal entitlement presupposes the proof of paternity, and the father must have custody over the child. Except for the residence requirement of ten years, foreign family members of Austrian nationals must fulfil the general conditions of naturalisation in order to make use of legal entitlement.

The acquisition of Austrian nationality by a foreign national has to be extended to his or her spouse (§ 16) and children (§ 17) upon application if they fulfil the same requirements as foreign family members of Austrian nationals (see above 2.2.1).

(2.2.2.) *Long-term residents*: Austrian nationality may be obtained by legal entitlement if a foreign national has had his principal residence in Austria for at least 30 years (§ 12 (1) a). Since 1999, foreign nationals who have had their principal residence in Austria for at least fifteen years also have a legal entitlement to acquisition of Austrian nationality if they can prove their sustainable personal and professional integration ((§ 12 (1) b)). In both cases applicants have to meet the requirements for discretionary naturalisation as described above (see 2.1.).

(2.2.3.) *Stateless persons*: Persons born in Austria who have been stateless since birth have a legal entitlement to acquisition of Austrian nationality if they have had their principal residence for a total of ten years in the country. The applicant must not have been convicted by an Austrian court for the violation of 'national security' as defined by the UN Convention on the Reduction of Statelessness of 1961[19] or to imprisonment of five years or more. The application has to be filed within two years after reaching the age of 18 (§ 14). The 'lack of protection by the country of origin' was declared in a report of the Constitutional Committee a 'special reason' for facilitated naturalisation after less than ten years of residence. However, the Administrative Court argued in several decisions that even if statelessness entails the lack of protection by the country of origin, statelessness alone is not a sufficient condition for facilitated naturalisation; the Court found furthermore that statelessness is not an indicator of 'advanced assimilation' that would justify the reduction of the general residence requirement of ten years.[20] In this context, it is important to note that Austria has made the granting of nationality to stateless persons dependent upon all of the conditions permissible according to art. 1 (2) of the Convention on the Reduction of Statelessness 1961. The aim of the legislator was to make use of permissible restrictions to the greatest extent possible (Thienel 1990: 242). Similarly, with respect to art. 6 (par. 4) of the European Convention on Nationality of 2000, Austria declared to retain the right not to facilitate the acquisition of its nationality for stateless persons (and recognised refugees) for this reason alone.[21]

(2.2.4.) *Former nationals*: Reacquisition of Austrian nationality by legal entitlement is possible for different groups of former nationals (§ 12 (2) and (3)). First, persons who have been Austrian nationals for at least ten years and who have not lost Austrian nationality by withdrawal or renunciation have a right to reacquire Austrian nationality after one year of residence in Austria (§ 12 (2)). Second, persons who have lost Austrian nationality at a time when they did not yet have full legal capacity have a right to be granted Austrian nationality if the application is filed within two years upon gaining full legal capacity, unless loss of nationality was based on withdrawal (§ 12 (3)). Third, persons who have lost Austrian nationality because of automatic or voluntary acquisition of a foreign nationality following marriage are entitled to reacquire Austrian nationality if the application is filed within five years after the dissolving of the marriage (§ 13). In all of these cases, apart from the residence requirement of ten years, applicants have to fulfil the general conditions for naturalisation.

While in respect of discretionary naturalisation, the authorities have to consider the common good, public interests and the extent of the applicant's integration by taking account of his or her 'general conduct' (§ 11), this provision does not apply in cases where foreign nationals have a legal entitlement to naturalisation (§ 11a-17).

(2.3.) *Acquisition by notification*: Since the amendment of 1993, survivors of the Holocaust and political emigrants reacquire Austrian nationality by simple notification (*Anzeige*) addressed to the authorities about having left the country before 1945 due to political persecution (§ 58c). There are no other conditions attached to reacquisition of Austrian nationality by notification. Granting of nationality is free of charge and renunciation of previous nationality is no longer required. To be sure, the reacquisition of Austrian nationality by political emigrants is numerically not significant, but has above all symbolic and political importance. Still, it is noteworthy that between 1993 and 2001, approximately 1,800 political emigrants regained Austrian nationality, whereas the number of political emigrants who reacquired Austrian nationality between 1965 and 1992 amounted to roughly 350 (Burger & Wendelin 2004: 6).

1.3.1.2 *Loss of Austrian nationality*

The main modes of loss of Austrian nationality are laid down in §§ 26-38 of the Nationality Law of 1985, which enumerate different reasons for loss of nationality. First, the acquisition of a foreign nationality provokes the loss of Austrian nationality, if an Austrian national expresses his or her 'positive intention' (*positive Willenserklärung*) to obtain the nationality of another state (§ 27). Submitting an application, making a declaration or explicitly giving one's consent in order to receive a foreign nationality is considered expression of such positive intent. Austrian nationality is not lost, however, if a foreign nationality is acquired because the Austrian national did not object to the *automatic* acquisition, even if the right to object to it is prescribed in foreign law (Mussger et al. 2001: 117). In addition, neither does a declaration of intent targeted not primarily at the acquisition of a foreign nationality (e.g., marriage with a foreign national) lead to the loss of Austrian nationality, even if the Austrian national was aware that he or she would acquire the foreign nationality automatically. The loss of nationality is extended to the reference person's minor children unless the other parent retains Austrian nationality.

In order to prevent the loss of Austrian nationality when acquiring the nationality of another state, Austrian nationals have to apply for permission to retain their Austrian nationality (§ 28). If the conditions laid down by the law are fulfilled, authorities have to approve the retention of Austrian nationality. However, authorities have almost unlimited leeway, as the requirements to be met are defined very vaguely (Thienel 1990: 302). The law merely states that retention of Austrian nationality has to be approved if the applicant has performed 'special achievements' in the past and is expected to do so in the future, or if there is another reason that deserves 'special consideration'. In both cases, retention of Austrian nationality has to benefit the interests of the Republic. In addition, the foreign state must not object to the retention of Austrian nationality, and the Austrian national has to fulfil some of the general conditions for acquisition of Austrian nationality such as the absence of criminal convictions.

With the amendment of the Nationality Law in 1998, a new provision was introduced to allow for retention of Austrian nationality, even if the applicants cannot prove that acceptance of dual nationality would benefit the public interest. Since 1999, retention of Austrian nationality is to be approved if the applicant can show that there is a special reason related to his or her private or family life justifying dual nationality (§ 28 (2)). According to the explanatory notes to the draft government bill, the easing of the rather demanding conditions with regard to retention of Austrian nationality aims at the avoidance of severe 'adverse effects' that a person would suffer from loss of the Austrian nationality. According to information given by some provincial authorities, such adverse effects include severe financial disadvantages, loss of inheritance rights in another state or loss of employment in both countries. The new possibility of retention is, however, restricted to persons who have acquired Austrian nationality by *descent*.[22]

The government bill of November 2005 aims to further facilitate the retention and reacquisition of Austrian nationality. Both provisions are likely to have the effect of increasing the number of Austrian expatriates who may also hold a foreign nationality and can, thus, transmit Austrian nationality iure sanguinis to children born abroad.

Second, persons who *voluntarily* enter into the military service of a foreign state lose Austrian nationality automatically (§ 32), even if they thereby become stateless.[23] However, if the person concerned is a dual national and performs military service in the country of which he or she is a national, Austrian nationality does not lapse, unless performance of military service is prolonged voluntarily or extended to include, for example, voluntary weapon drill (Mussger et al. 2001: 127).

Third, Austrian nationality has to be revoked if a person who has acquired Austrian nationality by grant (or extension of the grant) has retained his or her prior nationality for more than two years since acquisition (§ 34). As a general rule, the granting of Austrian nationality depends on the renunciation of the previous nationality where this is legally possible and reasonable. In order to facilitate renunciation of the previous nationality, Austrian authorities issue an assurance (*Zusicherung*) stating that Austrian nationality will be granted if the applicant can prove the renunciation of his or her previous nationality within two years. If, however, a person cannot give up his or her previous nationality without having acquired the nationality of another state, Austrian nationality is granted under the condition that the renunciation of the previous nationality will be proven within two years following acquisition of Austrian nationality. Deliberate non-compliance with this obligation is a reason for deprivation of Austrian nationality, of which the authorities have to notify the relevant person six months in advance. However, deprivation of Austrian nationality because of retention of the previous nationality is not permissible if the relevant person has acquired Austrian nationality more than six years previously.

Finally, the law provides for loss of Austrian nationality by *renunciation* (§ 37). An Austrian national may renounce nationality if he or she also holds the nationality of another country and has had his or her principal residence abroad for five years. Dual nationals, who have their principle residence in Austria have to fulfil further conditions: (1) Renunciation of nationality is not possible if there are criminal proceedings pending because of a crime carrying a sentence of more than six months imprisonment, or if the execution of such a sentence is pending. (2) A male national between the ages of sixteen and thirty-six can renounce Austrian nationality only if he has been either declared unfit for military service or alternative civilian service, or if he has performed military or alternative service in another country of which he holds the nationality and is released from military or alternative service on the basis of a bilateral or international agreement. In all circumstances, a written declaration of renunciation has to be filed with the responsible authority.

1.3.2 *Political analysis*

According to the census of 2001, roughly 710,000 foreign nationals make up 8.9 per cent of Austria's population (8,032,926). Nationals of former Yugoslavia (322,261) and Turkey (127,226) are the two biggest groups who account for 63 per cent of the total foreign population. It should be noted that these figures include foreign nationals born in Austria. The share of foreign nationals born in the country is the highest among nationals of Turkey (26.4 per cent), Croatia (20.7 per cent), Serbia and Montenegro (18.2 per cent) and Bosnia-Herzegovina (16.4 per cent) (Waldrauch 2003: 2). The number of persons who were born abroad and live in Austria is much higher than the number of foreign nationals. Roughly 1,000,000 residents or 12.5 per cent of the population are foreign-born. Thus, the share of the foreign-born population in Austria is higher than in the USA (Jandl & Kraler 2003). However, unlike the USA and like many other European countries, Austria's self-image is not that of an immigration country.

The legal framework with regard to the entry, residence and employment of foreign nationals, which was based since the early 1960s on the principle of the temporary admission of 'guest workers', remained in place until the early 1990s. In this period, the Law on the Employment of Aliens of 1975 (*Ausländerbeschäftigungsgesetz*), together with the Law on the Aliens Police (*Fremdenpolizeigesetz*), was the main instrument to safeguard a tight link between the development of the economic cycle and the employment of foreign workers. In other words, migration to Austria was regulated indirectly either by exerting strict control over the employment of foreign nationals or by adopting a laissez-faire approach in times of accelerated economic growth (Davy & Gächter 1993: 159). Accordingly, the main authority responsible in the area of migration policy was the Ministry of Social Affairs. In line with the 'guest worker' approach, the integration of foreign workers and of their family members was hardly on the political agenda until the mid-1990s. In the years following the fall of the Iron Curtain, a series of legislative reforms were undertaken by the coalition government of SPÖ and ÖVP (Social Democratic Party and People's Party) to reduce the number of applications for asylum, prevent illegal migration, restrict the number of foreign workers as well as to introduce an immigration policy based on annual quotas.

According to the census of 1981, the share of foreign nationals in Austria's population was 3.9 per cent (291,448 persons). Ten years later, this ratio has increased to 6.6 per cent (517,690 persons). The growth of the foreign population occurred mainly between 1989 and 1993 (+ 338,050 persons). Although the public and political discourse focused almost exclusively on the growing number of applications for asylum (1988: 6,718; 1992: 24,361) and the accommodation of asylum seekers, the rapid increase in the foreign population was primarily triggered by the economic boom of the late 1980s and early 1990s (Bauböck 1996: 20; Davy & Gächter 1993: 173; Zuser 1996:18). The share of foreign workers employed in Austria increased from 5.4 per cent in 1988 to 9.0 per cent in 1992. The two traditional sending countries, i.e., (former) Yugoslavia and Turkey, played an important role in satisfying the demand for foreign workers during this economic growth. Migrant workers from both countries accounted for 60 per cent of the increase in the number of foreign employees between 1988 and 1992. In response to this development, a quota was introduced in 1990 to restrict the share of foreign workers to 10 per cent of the workforce. In 1993, this quota was reduced to 8 per cent of the workforce (Davy & Çinar 2001: 594, FN 228).

More radical steps were taken with regard to the entry and residence of foreign nationals in 1992/93. The new *Residence Law,* which came into force in July 1993, introduced annual immigration quotas for the first time (it was in force until mid-1995 and also applied to foreign children born in Austria!). Although the Residence Law was designed to regulate the admission of *new* immigrants, it had a profound impact on the status of legally admitted immigrants, particularly of those who did not hold an unlimited residence permit. Due to new and rigid provisions concerning the renewal and withdrawal of residence permits, legally resident immigrants were faced with the risk of losing their right to residence. In fact, after the Residence Law came into force, several immigrants and/or family members became illegal residents and had to reapply for admission from abroad under the new quota system (Waldrauch 2003: 6; Bauböck 1996: 22).

The harshness of the new provisions gave rise to widespread and sustained criticism. The appointment of a new Minister of the Interior by the SPÖ, Caspar Einem, led to an amendment of the Residence Law in 1995, which removed some of the most contested provisions. In the same year, the Ministry of the Interior announced a profound reform under the slogan 'integration before new immigration' (*Integration vor Neuzuwanderung*). The most important change implemented by the Aliens Act of 1997 was the principle of 'consolidated residence' (*Aufenthaltsverfestigung*), which provided for increased security of residence and protection against expulsion after five, eight and ten years of residence. The expulsion of the so-called 'second generation' was declared unlawful altogether. However, as called for by the Federation of Trade Unions and the Chamber of Labour, access to legal employment for family members was made conditional upon four to eight years of residence in Austria. The Aliens Act of 1997 also made it possible to expel foreign nationals if they had spent less than eight years in Austria and faced unemployment lasting for one year. The so-called 'integration package', which came into force in January 1998, was based on a compromise between the coalition parties SPÖ, ÖVP and the social partners. Part of this compromise was an agreement on what the next reform step would be, namely amendment of the Nationality Law of 1985.

Between 1980 and 1990, the number of persons granted Austrian nationality remained more or less stable at between 8,000 and 10,000. The naturalisation rates of nationals of former Yugoslavia (1990: 1.7 per cent) and Turkey (1990: 1.1 per cent) were particularly low. Starting in 1991, the number of persons granted Austrian nationality increased steadily. This applies particularly to nationals of Turkey: While in 1989, roughly 700 applicants with Turkish nationality were naturalised, the number of former Turkish nationals who acquired Austrian nationality amounted to 3,200 in 1995 and 7,500 in 1996.

This rapid growth of the number of persons applying for Austrian nationality is due to different factors. The rise of an anti-immigrant discourse in the early 1990s triggered by the FPÖ as well as by the SPÖ (Zuser 1996: 64-70), which was followed by a rigid legislation in the early 1990s that gravely impaired the legal resident status of even long-term immigrants and of their family members, transformed the option of naturalisation into an 'escape route' (Bauböck & Çinar 1999). In addition, in the province of Vienna, where acquisition of nationality has always been easier than in other Austrian provinces the naturalisation of immigrant families was encouraged and facilitated particularly between 1989 and 1994. The Viennese authorities made use of the possibility of granting Austrian nationality after four years and less than ten years of residence due to 'special reasons'.

Until the reform of 1998, the Nationality Law did not stipulate the special reasons. In practice, authorities could take into account an applicant's status as a (1) recognised refugee or (2) a stateless person as well as (3) birth in Austria, (4) 'complete' linguistic and cultural assimilation or (5) employment in a 'shortage occupation'. In 1989, the following special reasons were added to the list by the Viennese authorities: (6) the applicant has a close family member who is an Austrian national, (7) the applicant has a satisfactory record of employment of four years and (8) the applicant lives with his or her spouse in Vienna where the children attend school (Çinar 1999: 147). Between 1989 and

1994, the number of persons granted Austrian nationality by Viennese authorities for special reasons rose from 735 to 2,028. In the same period, roughly 63 to 80 per cent of all facilitated naturalisations took place in Vienna. A major side effect of this practice was that under certain conditions the granting of Austrian nationality had to be extended to family members upon application (§§ 16 and 17 of the Nationality Law of 1985). Therefore, the total number of acquisitions of Austrian nationality increased considerably between 1989 and 1994.

Although the Viennese practice became more restrictive in the following years, as the minimum residence requirement was raised from four to six years and facilitated naturalisation was made dependent on sufficient knowledge of German, this had no impact on the upward trend in naturalisations. Two factors explain the continuous surge in naturalisations since the early 1990s. First, each year more and more immigrants become eligible to acquire Austrian nationality on the basis of at least ten years of residence. Second, since June 1995, Turkish emigrants who naturalise abroad can keep their citizenship rights in Turkey (aside from their political rights). To this end, a so-called 'pink card' has been introduced which can be obtained by persons who acquired Turkish nationality by birth and who have been given permission by the Council of Ministers to be released from Turkish citizenship. The 'pink card' provides former Turkish nationals with the rights to residence, employment, acquisition of real estate, inheritance, etc.[24] In addition, the amendment of 1995 abolished a provision according to which voluntary expatriation required compliance with military obligations. In other words, male Turkish citizens at the age when they can be drafted may 'opt out' of Turkish citizenship in order to naturalise abroad without having to first serve in the Turkish army. Both amendments had a significant impact on the naturalisation patterns of immigrants with Turkish citizenship.

Against this background, the FPÖ, followed by the ÖVP, started campaigning against the 'premature' granting of Austrian nationality. In 1996 and 1997, all of the parties apart from the SPÖ repeatedly introduced draft bills to amend the 1985 Nationality Law. While the SPÖ remained silent for a long time, the ÖVP rapidly became the key player in the political debate. The ÖVP argued that Austrian nationality is a 'valuable good', which should not be given away to foreign nationals who lack the 'will to integrate'.[25] According to the proposal of the ÖVP presented in autumn 1996, the authorities responsible for naturalisation should, in exercising their discretion, consider whether the applicant meets the following requirements: (1) fifteen years of residence, (2) sufficient integration, (3) German language skills and (4) participation in integration courses to be offered by the federal provinces on the political and legal system of Austria and the history and culture of Austria and Europe. In addition, the ÖVP proposed that persons married to an Austrian national as well as family members of a person who is about to acquire Austrian nationality should be naturalised by discretion instead of by legal entitlement.

According to the FPÖ proposal, a new constitutional provision should be introduced into the Nationality Law stating that Austria is not an immigration country. Austrian nationality should be granted only if this would benefit the interests of the Republic. The annual number of naturalisations in each federal province should not exceed 0.5 per cent of the local population. The integration of foreign nationals (i.e., knowledge of German and of the legal system of Austria) applying for naturalisation should be ascertained by an official decree by the respective federal government. Finally, each Austrian national should be given the right to raise objections regarding the required integration of the applicant.

The proposals of the Greens and the Liberal Party, which was founded by a former member of the FPÖ in the early 1990s, went in the opposite direction. Both parties proposed the introduction of the principle of 'double ius soli', the reduction of the general residence requirement from ten to five years and the abolishment of the requirement to renounce the original nationality (Greens) or tolerance of dual nationality with respect to applicants from countries that did not have a ban on dual nationality (Liberals). While the proposal of the Liberals included basic knowledge of the German language to be taken into account in discretionary naturalisations, the proposal of the Greens did not make naturalisation conditional upon language proficiency.

As mentioned above, the SPÖ did not introduce a draft bill. However, the city councillor of Vienna in charge of integration matters, Renate Brauner (SPÖ), argued in favour of tolerating dual nationality for the so-called 'second generation' until the age of majority. The ÖVP vehemently objected to the toleration of dual nationality and argued that there could not be 'dual loyalties'. The then Minister of the Interior, Karl Schlögl (SPÖ), declared that the reduction of the general waiting period to eight years might be a reasonable amendment, but that dual nationality should only be tolerated in exceptional cases. The Minister of the Interior also rejected the introduction of comprehensive assimilation requirements (Bauböck & Çinar 2001).

The SPÖ-ÖVP coalition government eventually reached an agreement in May 1998 and presented a joint draft bill, which left the traditional cornerstones of Austrian nationality legislation untouched, i.e., the predominance of the principle of ius sanguinis, the avoidance of multiple nationality and the principle that acquisition of Austrian nationality is the final step of a 'successful' integration process.[26] The compromise between the two ruling parties was to 'harmonise' the administration of the law by the authorities of the federal provinces, especially with regard to facilitated naturalisations because of special reasons, and to make the granting of Austrian nationality dependent on knowledge of the German language.

The statistical developments since the entry into force of the new provisions in January 1999 show that the restrictions did not have an impact on the increasing number of naturalisations. In 1999, roughly 25,000 persons acquired Austrian nationality. In 2003, roughly 45,000 persons were naturalised. This development has again provoked claims by representatives of the two ruling parties BZÖ and ÖVP that the conditions for naturalisation should be further tightened. The proposed amendments will be discussed later (see sect. 1.4 below).

1.3.3 *Statistical developments*

Austrian naturalisation statistics cover three different ways of acquisition, namely acquisition by grant (§§ 10-14) or extension of grant (§§ 16-17), by declaration (§ 25 (2); Art. I/II from 1983-88) and by notification (§ 58c). In other words, acquisitions by descent (§ 7, § 8) and legitimation (§ 7a) and automatic acquisitions upon taking office as a professor at an Austrian university (§ 25 (1)) are not covered.

Absolute numbers: From 1946 until the end of 2004, 1,031,456 persons were naturalised in Austria; 25,785 (2.5 per cent) of them had their residence abroad. However, roughly 48 per cent of all naturalisations already occurred in the 1940s and 1950s, when a large number of ethnic Germans ('Volksdeutsche') and other refugees from Central and Eastern Europe were granted nationality. In the three decades that followed the absolute number of naturalisations was considerably lower than in the 1940s and 1950s: in the 1960s a total of 50,984 persons was naturalised, in the 1970s 66,719 and in the 1980s 87,431. Since 1990, however, the immigration of the past decades has left its mark on the naturalisation statistics: in the 1990s a total of 154,363 persons was naturalised, and in the five years since then already 180,393.

From 1985 to 1990 between 8,000 and 10,000 persons were naturalised each year. In the following years the number of naturalisations rose, almost without exception, from about 11,500 in 1991 to 18,500 in 1998. After that, the number of naturalisations surged steeply from around 25,000 in 1999 to over 45,000 in 2003, only to drop slightly to about 42,000 in 2004.

Legal basis: The surge of naturalisations over the last twenty years was mainly due to the increase – in absolute and relative terms – of naturalisations of foreign nationals after ten years of residence and of extensions of grants to their family members: the share of grants after ten years (§ 10 (1)) was only 13 per cent in 1985, but reached 35 per cent in 2003 (for absolute numbers, see Table 1.1). Parallel to that the proportion of spouses to whom the grant was extended (§ 16) rose from 7 per cent in 1985 to a high of 13.5 per cent in 1999/2000, and the one of grant extensions to children (§ 17) from 17 per cent in 1985 to almost 38 per cent in 2003. Grants to spouses of Austrian nationals (§ 11a), in contrast, made up a steady 12-17 per cent of all naturalisations between 1987 and 1998, but dropped to less than 7 per cent in 2003. The same development can be observed with respect to naturalisations on the basis of 'reasons deserving special consideration' (§ 10 (4) 1 in combination with § 10 (5); until 1998: § 10 (3))[27] or achievements for Austria (§ 10 (6); until 1998: § 10 (4)) (the latter being much less important): whereas until 1998 12-17 per cent of all naturalisations were due to special reasons or achievements, their share dropped below 4 per cent in 2004!

All other naturalisations combined were only significant numerically in the 1980s, which was mainly due to naturalisations on the basis of the transitional Art. I/II: This regulation allowed for acquisition of nationality by declaration of children born to Austrian mothers before September 1983, who did not acquire Austrian nationality by descent due to the law in force at that time. Between 1985 and 1989, naturalisations of children of Austrian parents amounted to a minimum of 16 per cent and a maximum of 36 per cent of all naturalisations. This contrasts starkly with the picture since 1990, where the proportion of all naturalisations, besides the ones mentioned in the previous paragraph, never exceeded 8 per cent.

One of the main motives for the reform of Austria's nationality law in 1998 was to lay down clearer rules for the naturalisation of persons with special reasons after less than ten years of residence. Before 1999, the different Austrian provinces made use of the respective regulations in very different ways and to very diverging extents. Naturalisations on the basis of the old § 10 (3) and (4) were especially frequent in the province of Vienna: 16 to 26 per cent of all naturalisations in Austria's capital between 1985 and 1998 occurred because of special reasons or achievements. This is in stark contrast to the rest of Austria, where the percentage of these early naturalisations only ranged between 9 and 17 per cent. The 1998 reform had a strong impact on naturalisations because of special reasons or achievements: in Vienna they now account for only between 13 per cent (2000) and 4 per cent (2003) of all naturalisations, and even in absolute numbers they fell way below the average for the years 1985-98. In all other provinces combined, the percentage range of these kinds of naturalisations in 1999-2004 was about the same (13-3 per cent); however, their absolute number increased considerably in 1999-2001, only then to drop to a level which is below the one for the years immediately before 1999.

Table 1.1: Naturalisations by legal basis of acquisition in Austria

	10 years residence	*Special reasons / achievements*	*15 or 30 years residence*	*Extension of grant to spouses*	*Extension of grant to children*	*Spouses of Austrian nationals*	*Former Austrian nationals*	*Children of Austrian nationals*	*Other*	**Total**
1985	1139	1192	130	585	1468	870	85	2987	32	**8488**
1986	1156	1504	120	742	1740	1067	96	3581	9	**10015**
1987	1070	1270	97	659	1670	1042	77	2209	18	**8112**
1988	1265	1391	107	717	1963	1132	75	1565	17	**8232**
1989	1622	1191	81	698	2201	1222	59	1390	6	**8470**
1990	1983	1535	85	845	2764	1530	78	368	10	**9198**
1991	2707	1913	91	1036	3426	1745	103	360	13	**11394**
1992	2719	1989	64	1102	3934	1671	100	325	16	**11920**
1993	3254	2389	79	1414	4648	2100	109	398	11	**14402**
1994	3234	2694	72	1763	5245	2039	874	343	6	**16270**
1995	3276	2322	76	1636	4535	2382	504	556	22	**15309**
1996	3717	1998	56	1811	5748	2141	384	378	10	**16243**
1997	3283	2650	66	1844	5203	2594	198	434	2	**16274**
1998	3825	2714	77	2245	5905	2919	143	483	10	**18321**
1999	5456	3083	955	3358	8922	2825	111	303	19	**25032**
2000	6021	3067	692	3276	8532	2547	99	389	22	**24645**
2001	9336	2703	856	4042	11856	2715	92	470	10	**32080**
2002	12017	1879	1041	4313	13747	2610	71	692	12	**36382**
2003	15835	1666	1549	4868	17008	2964	84	1124	14	**45112**
2004	13961	1610	1529	4145	15674	3646	73	1523	13	**42174**

Source: Statistics Austria, own calculations. ***Legal basis of modes of acquisition***: * Ten years residence: § 10 (1); * Special reasons / achievements: § 10 (6), § 10 (4) 1 in combination with § 10 (5), except former Austrians, i.e., § 10 (5) 1; * Fifteen or 30 years residence: § 12 (1) b+a (before 1999: only § 12 a = 30 years of residence); * Extension of grant to spouses: § 16; * Extension of grant to children: § 17; * Former Austrian nationals: § 10 (4) 1 in combination with § 10 (5) (before 1999: § 10 (3)+(4)) 1 (since 1999), § 12 (2)+(3) (before 1999: § 12 b+c), § 13, § 58c (since 1993); * Children of Austrian nationals: art. I/II (1983-1988), § 12 (4) (before 1999: § 12 d); * Other: § 10 (4) 2 (since 1999), § 14, § 25 (2) 1+2.

With the reform of 1998, the 'reasons deserving special consideration' were spelt out explicitly in § 10 (4) 1 and § 10 (5) of the law for the first time, although not exhaustively. From 1999 to 2004, 42 per cent of all naturalisations on the basis of these sections in the law occurred because of 'effective personal and professional integration' (§ 10 (5) 3). The only other explicitly mentioned special reason with a significant share (22 per cent) in this period is being an accepted refugee (§ 10 (5) 4). All other exemplarily listed reasons (former Austrian nationals; birth in Austria; past and future achievements besides those of § 10 (6); EEA-nationality) together account for only 7 per cent of all grants on the basis of § 10 (4) 1 and (5). The remaining 28 per cent are naturalisations based on unspecified special reasons.

Former nationality: In 1985, 37 per cent of all naturalisations concerned nationals of the fourteen countries that were members of the EU before the latest round of accessions in 2004. In the twenty years that followed, however, not only the share of naturalised EU nationals decreased dramatically to 0.5 per cent or less in 2002-2004, but also their absolute number shrank to about one-fifteenth of the 1985 numbers (see Table 1.2). Nationals of the two most important sending countries of migrant workers to Austria, (the former) Yugoslavia and Turkey, accounted for only 17 per cent and 3 per cent of all naturalisations in

Table 1.2: Naturalisations by former nationality in Austria

	Ex-YU	*Turkey*	*EU15*	*Ex-com. CEE*	*Other Europe*	*Africa*	*America*	*Asia*	*Austral., Oceania*	**Total**
1985	1449	296	3103	1368	141	269	345	1252	23	**8488**
1986	1463	334	3519	2192	197	256	416	1389	39	**10015**
1987	1416	392	2179	1847	103	274	379	1307	20	**8112**
1988	1731	509	1633	1986	120	260	248	1501	19	**8232**
1989	2323	723	1387	1665	116	262	354	1437	31	**8470**
1990	2641	1106	712	2121	62	436	206	1732	7	**9198**
1991	3221	1809	692	2416	96	555	207	2247	15	**11394**
1992	4337	1994	589	1852	115	559	220	2090	8	**11920**
1993	5791	2688	638	1933	171	720	255	2054	8	**14402**
1994	5623	3379	508	2657	140	735	344	2677	17	**16270**
1995	4538	3209	360	2588	430	841	471	2654	18	**15309**
1996	3133	7499	294	2086	171	628	411	1847	14	**16243**
1997	3671	5068	282	2896	190	957	441	2544	13	**16274**
1998	4151	5683	245	3872	211	1209	453	2356	14	**18321**
1999	6745	10350	151	3590	93	1078	366	2499	11	**25032**
2000	7576	6732	144	4924	82	1400	357	3267	11	**24645**
2001	10760	10068	165	5156	63	1822	374	3521	6	**32080**
2002	14018	12649	149	4202	50	1555	364	3298	5	**36382**
2003	21615	13680	154	4253	24	1807	376	3032	22	**45112**
2004	19068	13024	209	3498	51	2077	507	3563	16	**42174**

Source: Statistics Austria, own calculations.

1985, whereas in 2004, their combined percentage was 76 per cent (45 per cent and 31 per cent). In absolute numbers this corresponds to an increase by a factor of 13 and 44 respectively! Over the same period, the number of naturalisations of nationals from (ex-)communist countries in Central and Eastern Europe more than doubled, and those of Africans increased by a factor of almost 8, those of Asians nearly tripled, and those of Americans 'only' increased by a factor of 1.5.

Province and country of residence: In the early 1990s, roughly 70 per cent of all naturalisations took place in Vienna. However, since the year 2000, the percentage of naturalisations in Austria's capital dropped to about 40 per cent. Lower and Upper Austria alone accounted for more than 10 per cent each of all Austrian naturalisations at any time since 1985, but hardly ever for more than 15 per cent. From 1985-89, the percentage of naturalisations of persons with residence abroad ranged between 11 and 20 per cent, which was mainly due to naturalisations based on the transitional art. I/II mentioned above. From 1990-1998, between 2 to 6 per cent of all naturalised persons had residence abroad, with peaks in 1994 and 1995 (6 per cent) caused by a surge of applications based on § 58c, which was introduced in 1993. Since 1999, the share of persons naturalised abroad hovers around the 1 per cent mark.

Country of birth: A large number of persons are naturalised every year who were already born in Austria and who (in most cases) do not have to go through naturalisation procedures in other countries with ius soli regulations in place. While their percentage reached 23-28 per cent in the late 1980s and early 1990s, native-born persons account for 29-33 per cent of all naturalised since 1999. Most persons born in Austria are naturalised by way of extension of a grant to a parent.

Sex and age: For a number of years now, almost exactly the same number of men and women have been naturalised in Austria. The proportion of persons naturalised who were below and above the age of majority has also been uniform: since 2001 the proportion is 41 per cent to 59 per cent.

1.3.4 Institutional arrangements

1.3.4.1 The legislative process

According to art. 11 (1) of the Constitution, nationality legislation is a federal matter. Parliament is vested with federal legislative powers. The National Council (*Nationalrat*) and the Federal Council (*Bundesrat*) form the two chambers of Parliament. The Federal Council represents the interests of the nine federal provinces. A draft bill may be introduced to the National Council by the federal government, members of the National Council and the Federal Council or by popular referendum (*Volksbegehren*).[28]

Most frequently, a draft bill is prepared by the legislative department of the Ministry in charge of the respective area of law, i.e., the Ministry of the Interior in the case of nationality legislation. Usually the Social Partners (Chamber of Commerce, Chamber of Labour, Federation of the Trade Unions, etc.) as well as other interest groups are asked to give their expert opinion on the ministerial draft bill (*Ministerialentwurf*). The round of consultations may lead to the revision of some provisions. The draft bill is then introduced to the Council of Ministers for approval as a draft government bill (*Regierungsvorlage*). A draft government bill will be 'read' three times in the National Council, which means that the draft bill will be assigned to a parliamentary committee at the first reading. After the deliberations and possible changes proposed by the parliamentary committee the draft bill will be 'read' a second time in the National Council in a general debate, followed by a special debate in which amendments may be requested. At the second reading the National Council may decide either to re-assign the bill to the parliamentary committee or to vote on the bill.

Decisions require a simple majority of votes unless the amendment includes constitutional provisions, in which case participation of 50 per cent of the members of the National Council and a majority of two-thirds of the votes in favour of the bill are required. If the bill gets approved at the third and final 'reading' by the National Council, it will be sent to the Federal Council for approval. Except for constitutional provisions that affect the competence of the federal provinces, the Federal Council has only a 'suspensive' veto right in matters of nationality, i.e., the National Council can vote a second time and approve the bill by a simple majority.

Although the role of the Federal Council as the representative body of the federal provinces is restricted in the legislative process, civil servants responsible for the execution of nationality legislation in the different provinces do have an impact on the preparation of legislative reforms. For example, the last amendment of the Nationality Law was based to a great extent on a draft bill by the ÖVP. The draft bill by the ÖVP was in turn in accordance with several provisions of a proposal, which was prepared by the responsible authorities of the federal provinces.

1.3.4.2 The process of implementation

Whereas nationality legislation is a federal matter, the federal provinces are vested with the power to administer the law. The government of the respective federal provinces is the highest executive authority (§ 39). However, the Ministry of the Interior may lodge an appeal with the Administrative Court if it considers the decision of a provincial government unconstitutional (Mussger et al. 2001: 138). Applicants can either appeal to the Administrative Court or to the Constitutional Court.

Representatives of the federal government and federal provinces meet regularly to exchange experiences and address administrative problems, but there are no common guidelines for the implementation of legal provisions[29] allowing the authorities a wide margin of interpretation in *discretionary* naturalisations. While nationality legislation is seldom subject to judicial review by the Constitutional Court, administrative acts in matters of nationality are frequently subject to review by the Administrative Court. There are numerous decisions by the Administrative Court that address the implementation of the indeterminate legal provisions contained in nationality legislation. This applies particularly to questions as to whether an applicant represents a danger to public order and security or whether the applicant qualifies for facilitated naturalisation or whether the applicant's professional and personal integration is sufficient and 'sustainable'.

There is no definition of 'sustainable integration' in the Nationality Law of 1985. According to the explanatory notes of the draft government bill of 1998, the applicant must have the right to permanent residence and a work permit valid for at least two years. In addition, the applicant must live together with his or her family in Austria (Mussger et al. 2001:77).[30] According to the Administrative Court, particularly good knowledge of the German language may also be considered an indicator of sufficient integration and may justify facilitated naturalisation by reducing the requirement of ten years of residence.[31]

The indeterminacy of the integration requirement is certainly a source of diverging implementation practices across the country. For example, in Lower Austria authorities also take into account whether the applicant makes an effort to adapt to the 'Austrian way of life' and participates in the activities of local associations that benefit the common interest of the municipality.[32] Neither the adaptation to the Austrian way of life nor participation in local associations is mentioned in the explanatory notes to the draft bill. However, the Administrative Court argued that the responsible authorities might consider additional factors to judge the extent of integration of an applicant.[33]

Since the introduction of sufficient knowledge of German as a condition for naturalisation, the Administrative Court repeatedly dealt with the required level of language proficiency. The Court argued that applicants should have basic or minimum knowledge of German to master everyday life and that it is not necessary to have an 'easy' communication with the applicant.[34] The Court also decided that lack of German language skills by family members of the applicant or communication within the family in another language are not sufficient reasons to conclude that the applicant is not integrated (Feik 2003: 4).

Another difference between the federal provinces concerns the fees for acquisition of Austrian nationality. Applicants have to pay a federal fee, which amounts to 768 euros for discretionary naturalisation, and provincial fees that differ widely across the federal provinces. The acquisition of Austrian nationality by a family with one child may cost roughly 1,400 euros in the province of Vienna, whereas the same family would have to pay up to 3,000 euros in Upper Austria, Styria or Vorarlberg (Waldrauch & Çinar 2003: 275f). The reform of the nationality legislation that came into force in early 2006 raised the fees even further by € 175.

There are no public outreach programs to encourage immigrants to naturalise.

1.4 Conclusions

Austrian Nationality Law was amended repeatedly since 1945. From the early 1960s until 1985, the adoption of international conventions made changes to the law necessary.[35] The most important driving factor with respect to legislative reforms in this period, was the elimination of gender inequalities where the acquisition and loss of Austrian nationality was concerned. Conditions relevant to the acquisition of nationality by immigrants and their descendents, however, remained basically the same until the late 1990s. The last amendment of the Nationality Law in 1998 aimed at making acquisition of Austrian nationality by immigrants more difficult. This is in stark contrast to developments in several other Western European countries that have become more tolerant towards the incidence of dual nationality and have granted a legal entitlement to acquisition of nationality by children of immigrants (Hansen & Weil 2001; Çinar 1994). How can we explain the persistence of Austria's highly reluctant approach towards the integration of immigrants and their descendents as citizens?

A first simple hypothesis is that Austria has not developed a self-understanding as an immigration country, despite the permanent settlement of post-war migrants and their family members, but has retained 'guest worker' approach. Yet, other European countries with inclusive citizenship policies also do not regard themselves as countries of immigration, and Austria no longer pursues 'guest worker' policies. On the contrary, Austria is the first European country that adopted an immigration policy based on a quota system in the early 1990s. However, this shift in immigration policy, i.e., the establishment of strict immigration controls, did not entail a shift in 'immigrant policies' (Hammar

1985) in terms of an active policy of integration, for example, by facilitating the acquisition of nationality by immigrants and their descendents. Restrictions with respect to immigrants' access to social rights and benefits, as well as to political rights were maintained, and the conditions for naturalisation became more demanding in the late 1990s.

A second hypothesis is that the history of Austrian citizenship policy reflects the perception of the Austrian nation as a 'community of descent'. The conception of the nation in terms of descent and ethnicity does not in principle allow immigrants or their descendents to easily become members of the national community. The exclusivity of the principle of ius sanguinis in Austrian nationality law since the nineteenth century seems to support this hypothesis. However, despite the predominance of the principle of ius sanguinis, Austrian nationality legislation, until recently, was not characterised by sweeping requirements for assimilation as one might have expected from a society in which the self-image is based on common descent and ethnicity. For example, until the reform of 1998, Austrian Nationality Law did not contain proficiency in the German language as a condition for naturalisation. This does not mean that in practice knowledge of German was irrelevant with respect to the acquisition of the Austrian nationality. In a few traditionally conservative federal provinces, like Vorarlberg and Tyrol, the granting of Austrian nationality was always dependent on proof of language proficiency. However this practice had no legal basis.

It is noteworthy that until the mid-1990s there were no major political debates about Austrian national identity and Austrian Nationality Law. After 1945, Austria could not afford to reconstruct its political self-image on the basis of traditional German nationalism. Yet, neither was the reconstruction of the 'Second Republic' connected to the multiethnic and multilingual composition of the Habsburg Monarchy, nor did it build upon a republican understanding of political belonging and membership (Bauböck & Çinar 2001). In the post-war period, the vacuum of national identity was filled mainly by referral to music, arts and landscape rather than common descent, ethnicity and language. With respect to nationality legislation, the political 'emptiness' of Austrian national identity produced a peculiar framework: the principle of ius sanguinis was reaffirmed after 1945, but requirements of cultural assimilation were not part of nationality legislation. From the mid-1980s, however, Austria's political landscape – dominated by Conservatives and Social Democrats – underwent a major transformation due to the rapid rise of the right-wing Freedom Party as well as increasing support for the Greens. The impact of this reconfiguration was, among other things, the politicisation of questions related to immigration, identity and citizenship. The steady growth of voters opting for the

Freedom Party combined with the federal structure of the Austrian political system eventually triggered a political competition among the federal provinces to be more restrictive with respect to the naturalisation of immigrants (Bauböck & Çinar 2001). While the Social Democratic Party failed to participate with self-confidence in the debate on the meaning of citizenship and the conditions for membership in the Austrian polity, their then coalition partner, the Conservatives, successfully enforced the claim for a more restrictive naturalisation policy and the introduction of German language proficiency as a condition for naturalisation.

The most important factor, however, that led to calls for a restrictive administration of nationality legislation was the surge in naturalisations since the early 1990s. Despite demanding conditions for naturalisation, a steadily increasing number of immigrants acquired Austrian nationality as they fulfilled the general residence requirement of ten years. Thus, more and more immigrants could escape the legal restrictions imposed on third country nationals with respect to access to the labour market, social rights and benefits and political participation. In the province of Vienna, where access to municipal housing was for a long time exclusively reserved for Austrian nationals, this development led to growing resentments about the allocation of municipal housing to (naturalised) 'foreigners'. Already before the amendment of the nationality legislation in 1998, the Viennese authorities responded by making facilitated naturalisations dependent on more restrictive conditions. The example of Vienna shows that a restrictive naturalisation policy is not necessarily the expression of an assimilationist approach. Rather, it can be argued that restrictions in nationality legislation have more to do with the wish to constrain immigrants' access to the labour market, social benefits, political rights and family reunion, and less with an ethnic conception of Austrian national identity. In the case of Austria, this latter point is of particular importance. Contrary to the well-known arguments about the 'denationalisation' of citizenship rights (Soysal 1994), acquisition of Austrian nationality still matters a lot with respect to immigrants' security of residence, access to the labour market and social and political rights.

This fact is clearly reflected in the continuous surge in naturalisations over the last decade, despite the fact that the reform of 1998 made acquisition of Austrian nationality dependent on proof of sufficient knowledge of the German language and increased the residence requirement for facilitated naturalisations of third country nationals (except for recognised refugees) from four to six years. The tightening of the conditions for facilitated naturalisation did not produce the result that the government intended to achieve with the reform of 1998, i.e., gaining control over the increasing numbers of persons naturalised, as the proportion of foreign nationals who have lived in the country for at least ten years has grown considerably since the last major immigration wave of the 1990s. Thus, in order to effectively restrict the number of naturalisations, the general conditions for naturalisation and, in particular, family-based modes of acquisition would rather have to be made more difficult.

In its government programme of 2003, the Austrian government already expressed its intentions to further restrict the possibility of naturalisation of immigrants after less than ten years of residence, while at the same time removing certain conditions of naturalisation for former Austrian nationals.[36] An extensive amendment to the law was finally passed on 6 December 2005.[37] The new provisions came into force in March 2006. The most important changes can be summarised as follows:

- *General conditions for discretionary naturalisation*: Under current legislation, naturalisation is possible after ten years of uninterrupted and registered 'principal residence'. Henceforth, only periods of 'legal' residence will count and applicants must be 'settled' for at least five years under the *Law on Settlement and Residence of 2005*.[38] Naturalisation of foreign nationals, who cannot obtain a settlement permit (e.g. asylum seekers who are not granted refugee status but enjoy subsidiary protection) will now require a minimum residence of fifteen years. The duration of legal residence will be interrupted by residence abroad that exceeds 20 per cent of the required time of residence in Austria. Any prison sentence for an intentional crime or a fiscal offence as well as any conviction for an offence specified in the *Aliens Police Law* of 2005 shall preclude the granting of nationality.[39] In addition, serious and repeated violations of administrative regulations, especially concerning road safety, will also prohibit naturalisation. According to a new provision Austrian nationality must not be granted to foreigners if they have a 'close relation' with an extremist or terrorist group. The new law no longer allows the granting of nationality if the applicant has a lack of financial means, even if this is due to circumstances beyond the applicant's control, and it rules out recourse to provincial welfare benefits (*Sozialhilfe*) for the three years preceding naturalisation.
- *Language proficiency and knowledge of the country*: Stricter conditions will apply for knowledge of the German language irrespective of whether nationality is to be granted by discretion or legal entitlement. Henceforth, applicants for naturalisation have to comply with the requirements of the 'integration agreement' regulated by § 14 of the Law on Settlement and Residence of 2005, i.e., they must either attend a 'German integration course' of at least 300 hours or otherwise prove knowledge of German at the proficiency level A-2 of the

Common European Framework of Reference. Certain categories of applicants, including former nationals, survivors of the Holocaust, and persons who are not able to comply with the requirement of language proficiency because of old age, lasting illness or lack of legal capacity, will be exempted. No proof of language proficiency is required from minor children attending a primary school (generally from ages six to ten). However, those in secondary school (ages eleven to fourteen) must obtain a passing grade in the subject of German language. In addition, applicants must prove basic knowledge of the 'democratic order and history of Austria and the respective federal province' by taking a multiple-choice test.[40]

- *General integration clause*: The new law also adds a clause that all decisions on naturalisation have to take into account the applicants' 'orientation towards social, economic and cultural life in Austria and towards the basic values of a European democratic state and its society'.
- *Conditions for facilitated naturalisation by legal entitlement*: Three groups of foreign nationals who could be naturalised by discretionary decision after four years of residence under the old law will instead be granted legal entitlement to acquisition of Austrian nationality after six years, if they comply with the general conditions for naturalisation, i.e. (1) recognised refugees, (2) nationals of EEA-states and (3) persons born in Austria. Birth in Austria will thus for the first time establish a legal claim to the acquisition of nationality. However, this move towards ius soli is, seriously called into question by the many conditions for naturalisation that apply to these native-born persons as they do to immigrants.
- *Conditions for naturalisation of foreign spouses*: Naturalisation of foreigners married to Austrian nationals will become much more difficult. The required duration of uninterrupted and legal residence will be raised from three or four to six years and the duration of marriage from one or two to five years.
- *Facilitating reacquisition and retention of Austrian nationality*: Some minor changes will make it easier for certain groups (especially minors) to reacquire Austrian nationality or to retain it when naturalising abroad. Similar reasons for retaining a previous nationality will still not be accepted for immigrants who naturalise in Austria.
- *Higher fees*: Federal fees for acquiring nationality will be raised drastically. Provincial fees that are added to federal ones are also likely to rise to compensate for the costs of the newly introduced exams on provincial history. Fees for naturalisation in Austria will in most cases then be the highest among the fifteen 'old' EU states.

This recent amendment of Austrian nationality legislation is inspired by the principle of 'integration before new immigration' which has been asserted in domestic politics since the late 1990s. The first major step to establish this principle in the law was taken in 2002 when the Aliens Law was amended to introduce an obligation for persons who entered the country since 1998 onwards to comply with a so-called 'integration agreement', i.e., to attend German integration courses of 100 hours. The second step consists of a new regulation that came into force in January 2006, which raised the duration of the compulsory integration courses to 300 hours. The amendment of Austrian nationality legislation is the third step in the process of redefining integration as a task to be accomplished by immigrants before they can be granted secure residence or full citizenship rights. While its traditionally restrictive approach towards the legal integration of immigrants as citizens during the previous two decades as citizens made Austria appear as an 'outsider', or at least a latecomer, in terms of the integration of immigrants, the recent domestic reforms of immigration and nationality legislation are in line with similar restrictive reforms in a number of other European immigration countries, and they may thus have changed Austria's position to that of a 'trend setter'.

Chronological table of major reforms in Austrian nationality law since 1945

Date	Document	Content
27 April 1945	Law 1/1945 (StGBl. 1/1945)	Proclamation of Independence of Austria.
1 May 1945	Law 4/1945 (Verfassungs-Überleitungsgesetz; StGBl 4/1945)	Restoration of the Austrian Constitution of 1920, in the version of 1929.
29 May 1945	Notification (Kundmachung StGBl. 16/1945), entry into force: 10 June 1945	Notification on the abolishment of acts and decrees of the German Reich concerning nationality within the territory of Austria.
10 July 1945	Law on the re-establishment of Austrian nationality (Staatsbürgerschafts-Überleitungsgesetz, StBGl. 59/1945), entry into force: 15 July 1945	
10 July 1945	Law on acquisition and loss of Austrian nationality (Gesetz über den Erwerb und Verlust der österreichischen Staatsbürgerschaft – Staatsbürgerschaftsgesetz 1945, StBGl. 60/1945), entry into force: 15 July1945	
4 November 1949	Law 276/1949 (Staatsbürgerschaftsgesetz 1949 and Staatsbürgerschafts-	Re-announcement due to numerous amendments between 1945 and 1949 of the re-

Date	Document	Content
	Überleitungsgesetz 1949, Constitutional Provisions on Nationality concerning the treatment of National Socialists, BGBl. 276/1949), entry into force: 31 December 1945	establishment of Austrian nationality law on acquisition and loss of Austrian nationality and of constitutional provisions concerning the treatment of National Socialists with regard to Austrian nationality.
2 June 1954	Law 142/1954 (Bundesgesetz betreffend den Erwerb der Staatsbürgerschaft durch Volksdeutsche, BGBl 142/1954), entry into force: 6 August 1954	Law on the acquisition of nationality by 'Volksdeutsche' (defined as German-speaking persons, who are stateless or whose nationality is unclear).
26 October 1958	Law 214/1958 (BGBl. 214/1958)	Ratification of the protocol concerning military obligations in certain cases of double nationality.
6 November 1958	Law 45/1959 (BGBl. 45/1959)	Agreement between Austria and Germany on exchange of information concerning naturalisations and dual nationality.
17 July 1963	Law 40/1964 (BGBl. 40/1964)	Agreement between Austria and Denmark on exchange of information on naturalisations.
10 September 1964	(BM.f. I.-Zl. 220-275-32/65)	Agreement between Austria, Belgium, Germany, Greece, France, Italy, Luxemburg, the Netherlands, Switzerland and Turkey on exchange of information on naturalisations.
15 July 1965	New codification and re-announcement of the Federal Law on Austrian Nationality 1965 (Staatsbürgerschaftsgesetz 1965, BGBl. 250/1965), entry into force 1 July 1966	Comprehensive amendment of automatic modes of acquisition and loss of nationality in preparation of Austria's accession to international conventions; abolishment of automatic acquisition of nationality by women marrying Austrian nationals.
19 January 1968	Law 238/1968 (BGBl.238/196)	Accession to the Convention on the Nationality of Married Women
11 July 1973	Federal Law amending the Nationality Law 1965 (BGBl. 394/1973), entry into force 1 January 1974	Facilitation of naturalisation of minor children; adaptation to reform of the law on elections to federal parliament and law on deletion of criminal record 1971; facilitation of the retention of Austrian nationality when naturalising abroad; introduction of new modes of acquisition for expatriates and former Austrian nationals.

Date	Document	Content
7 November 1974	Federal Law amending the Nationality Law 1965 (BGBl. 703/ 1974), entry into force 1 January 1975	Adjustment to reform of criminal law.
22 September 1972	Law 538/1974 (BGBl 538/1974), entry into force: 1 September 1975	Ratification of the Convention on the Reduction of Statelessness 1961.
31 July 1975	Law 471/1975 (BGBl. 471/1975), entry into force: 1 September 1975	Ratification of the Convention on the Reduction of Cases of Multiple Nationality and on Military Obligations in Cases of Multiple Nationality.
1 January 1981	Law 450/1981 (BGBl. 450/1981)	Agreement between Austria and Argentina concerning military obligations of dual nationals.
3 March 1983	Federal Law Amending the Nationality Law1965 (BGBl. 170/ 1983), entry into force 1 September 1983	Granting Austrian women the right to pass their nationality on to their children born in wedlock upon declaration within three years after the entry into force of the amendment; further equalisation of the conditions of voluntary acquisition of nationality to be fulfilled by men and women.
27 September 1984	Constitutional Court Decision (VfGH VfSlg 10.036, BGBl 375/ 1984)	Concerning automatic acquisition of nationality upon legitimation by a child of an Austrian father.
9 May 1985	Federal Law amending the Nationality Law 1965 (BGBl 202/ 1985), entry into force 1 June 1985	Extension of co-determination rights of minors above the age of fourteen concerning acquisition and loss of nationality.
19 July 1985	Federal Law on Austrian Nationality 1985 (Staatsbürger-schaftsgesetz 1985, BGBl 311/ 1985), entry into force 31 July 1985	Re-announcement of the Nationality Law 1965 including all amendments since 1965.
3 July 1986	Federal Law amending the Nationality Law 1985 (BGBl 386/ 1986), entry into force 1 September 1986	Extension of the right of Austrian mothers to pass on nationality to their children born before 1983 until 31 December 1988.
29 November 1988	Law 685/1988 (BGBl 685/1988), entry into force 1 January 1989	Constitutional Amendment anchoring the uniformity ('Einheitlichkeit') of Austrian nationality in the Constitution and adjustment of the Nationality Law 1985.
14 March 1990	Law 148/1990 (BGBl 148/1990), entry into force 15 March 1990	Amendment of the legal regulations on voting rights.
30 July 1993	Amendment of Nationality Law 1985 (BGBl 521/1993), entry into force: 31 July 1993	Facilitation of reacquisition of Austrian nationality by former nationals who suffered persecution by organs of the

Date	Document	Content
		NSDAP or the authorities of the Third Reich.
8 July 1994	Law 505/1994 (BGBl 505/1994), entry into force: 1 January 1995	Adjustment of the Nationality Law 1985 to terminology of the Law on Principal Residence (Hauptwohnsitzgesetz).
19 August 1997	Law 109/1997 (BGBl 109/1997)	Adjustment of the Nationality Law 1985 to the amendment of the Law on Civil Service and the Law on the Organisation of Universities concerning foreign university or college professors.
17 September 1998	Law 39/2000 (BGBl. III Nr. 39/ 2000), entry into force: 1 March 2000	Ratification of the European Convention on Nationality.
1 January 1998	Law 30/1998 (BGBl. 30/1998)	Adjustment of terminology to the amendment of the Law on Training of Women in the Federal Armed Forces (Gesetz über die Ausbildung von Frauen im Bundesheer.
1 July 1998	Law 123/1998 (BGBl 123/1998)	Adjustment of Nationality Law 1985 to the amendment of the Law on Civil Service (1. Dienstrechts-Novelle 1998).
14 August 1998	Amendment of the Nationality Law 1985 (Staatsbürgerschaftsgesetz-Novelle 1998, BGBl 124/1998), entry into force: 1 January 1999	Among other things introduction of sufficient knowledge of German as a condition for naturalisation; amendment of the conditions for 'facilitated' naturalisation; introduction of a legal entitlement to naturalisation after 15 years of uninterrupted residence in case of proof of 'lasting integration'.
19 March 1999	Law III Nr. 214/2000 (BGBl. III Nr. 214/2000), entry into force: 1 January 2001	Agreement between Austria and Switzerland concerning military obligations of dual nationals (a dual national shall fulfil his military obligations in the country of habitual residence).
6 December 2005	Amendment of the Nationality Law 1985 (Staatsbürgerschaftsgesetz-Novelle 2005, BGBl 37/2006), entry into force: 23 March 2006	Longer residence periods for acquisition through marriage and facilitated naturalisation; stricter requirements of clean criminal record and sufficient financial means; standardised German language test and new societal knowledge test; increase of fees.

Notes

1 Federal Law on Austrian Nationality 1985, Staatsbürgerschaftsgesetz 1985, BGBl. 311/1985, entry into force 31 July 1985.
2 Bundesgesetz, mit dem das Staatsbürgerschaftsgesetz 1985 (StbG), das Tilgungsgesetz 1972 und das Gebührengesetz 1957 geändert werden (Staatsbürgerschaftsrechts-Novelle 2005), BGBl. I Nr. 37/2006.
3 Amendment of Nationality Law 1985, Staatsbürgerschaftsgesetz-Novelle 1998, BGBl. 124/1998, entry into force: 1 January 1999.
4 For a detailed description of the conditions for naturalisation by legal entitlement see sect. 1.3.1.1.
5 The Freedom Party, who joined the ÖVP-led government in 2000, split in spring 2005. The FPÖ ministers and members of Parliament then formed the BZÖ (Alliance for the Future of Austria).
6 For a detailed discussion of the Treaty of Saint-Germain and bilateral treaties see Thienel (1989: 49-60).
7 For persons who had to flee Austria because of political persecution, the time spent abroad was put on par with residence in Austria.
8 Law 142/1954, Bundesgesetz betreffend den Erwerb der Staatsbürgerschaft durch Volksdeutsche, BGBl. 142/1954, entry into force: 6 August 1954.
9 New codification and re-announcement of the Federal Law on Austrian Nationality 1965, Staatsbürgerschaftsgesetz 1965, BGBl. 250/1965, entry into force 1 July 1966.
10 Federal Law Amending the Nationality Law1965, BGBl. 170/1983, entry into force 1 September 1983.
11 BGBl. 170/1983, art. I/II; Federal Law amending the Nationality Law 1985, BGBl. 386/1986, entry into force 1 September 1986, art. I/II.
12 Federal Law on Austrian Nationality 1985, Staatsbürgerschaftsgesetz 1985, BGBl. 311/1985, entry into force 31 July 1985.
13 Law 685/1988, BGBl. 685/1988, entry into force 1 January 1989.
14 See BGBl. 311/1985 in the version of BGBl. I Nr. 124/1998 (Nationality Law 1985) and BGBl. 329/1985 in the version of BGBl. 660/1993 and 982/1994 (Decree on Nationality).
15 Since 1998, this provision applies only to persons who are not EEA-nationals. Spouses and minor children of the respective persons acquire Austrian nationality by declaration (§ 25 (2)).
16 The amendment that came into force in March 2006, however, introduced for the first time a legal entitlement to naturalisation for foreign nationals born in Austria after six years of residence (see sect. 1.4).
17 The formal recognition of paternity by the father is not sufficient, as such recognition does not establish a marital father-child bond (Thienel 1990: 150).
18 The residence requirement of ten years may be waived also in the case of a person who, prior to 1945, had the nationality of one of the successor states of the Austro-Hungarian Monarchy or was stateless, had his or her principal residence in the federal territory and had to leave the country because of political persecution (§ 10 (4) 2).
19 The Convention came into force in Austria in December 1975 (See BGBl. 538/1974). Austria made two reservations to art. 8, § 3 (a), (i) and (ii) of the Convention. First, Austria declared that it retains the right to deprive a person of his nationality if such a person enters the military service of a foreign State of his own free will. Second, Austria retained the right to deprive a person of his nationality, if such person being in the service of a foreign State, acts in a manner seriously prejudicial to the interests or to the prestige of the Republic of Austria.

20 E.g., VwGH 94/01/0744 and 93/01/1255.
21 See Reservation concerning art. 6 (1) lit.b of the European Convention on Nationality, BGBl. III 39/2000.
22 In this context, it is noteworthy that according to Chapter II art. 5 (2) of the European Convention on Nationality 1997, to which Austria is a Contracting State, each State Party should be guided by the principle of non-discrimination between its nationals, whether they are nationals by birth or have acquired its nationality subsequently. Although Austria did not make any reservations to Chapter II art. 5 (2) of the Convention, the explanatory notes to the draft proposal of the Austrian government state that the principle of non-discrimination between nationals is not a binding provision, but still contain a declaration of intent to eliminate such discriminatory provisions in matters of nationality law (see RV 1089, AB 1319 BlgNR, XX. GP).
23 See note 20 above concerning Austria's reservations to the Convention on the Reduction of Statelessness 1961.
24 See art. 2 of Law no. 4112 and Dogan (2002: 127-130).
25 *Der Standard*, 12/13 October 1996: 27.
26 Regierungsvorlage, 1283 BlgNR 20.GP.
27 For the purposes of this overview we excluded the special reason former Austrian nationality (§ 10 (5) 1) here and rather grouped it together with other modes of acquisition targeting former Austrian nationals; for details see the note to Table 1.1.
28 Para. 69 Geschäftsordnungsgesetz, BGBl. 10/1975 in the version of BGBl. I Nr. 163/ 1998.
29 Information provided by the Ministry of the Interior, 10 February 2005.
30 1283 BlgNR 10.GP.
31 VwGH 2000/01/0081.
32 Information provided by the Nationality Department of the Federal Government of Upper Austria, 29 April, 2005 (on file with the authors).
33 VwGH 2000/01/0277.
34 VwGH 2002/01/0147 and VwGH 2002/01/0186.
35 Austria is party to the UN Convention on the Status of Married Women (BGBl. 238/ 1968), the Convention on the Elimination of all Forms of Discrimination against Women (BGBl. 443/1982), the UN Convention on the Reduction of Statelessness (BGBl. 538/1974), the Convention of the Council of Europe on the Reduction of Multiple Nationality and Military Obligations in Cases of Multiple Nationality(BGBl. 471/1976), the Protocol on Military Services in cases of Multiple Nationality (BGBl. 214/1958), and the European Convention on Nationality (BGBl. III 39/2000).
36 See Chapter 4 of the 'Regierungsprogramm der österreichischen Bundesregierung für die XXII. Gesetzgebungsperiode' (on file with the author).
37 See Amendment of Nationality Law 1985, Staatsbürgerschaftsgesetz-Novelle 2005, BGBl. 37/2006, entry into force: 23 March 2006.
38 Applicants who have resided in Austria for at least 30 years are exempted from the requirement of 'legal' residence.
39 Such offences include (among other things) prostitution and procurement, human trafficking, provision of false information, marriages of convenience, illegal employment, etc.
40 The Ministry of the interior and the provincial governments shall regulate the content of the test on the basis of the curriculum for the final grade of secondary school (*Hauptschule*). Topics to be covered are the structure and relevant institutions of the Republic of Austria, basic civil rights and liberties, possibilities of legal protection, electoral rights, and the history of Austria and the respective province.

Bibliography

Bauböck, R. (1996), *'Nach Rasse und Sprache verschieden': Migrationspolitik in Österreich von der Monarchie bis heute*. Reihe Politikwissenschaft 31. Vienna: Institut für Höhere Studien.

Bauböck, R. & D. Çinar (2001), 'Nationality Law and Naturalisation in Austria', in R. Hansen & P. Weil (eds.), *Citizenship, Immigration and Nationality Law in the European Union*, 255-272. New York: Palgrave.

Burger, H & H. Wendelin (2004), *Staatsbürgerschaft und Vertreibung. Bericht über ein Projekt der österreichischen Historikerkommission*. www.kakanien.ac.at/beitr/fallstudie/HBurger_HWendelin1.pdf

Brandl, U. (1996), 'Austrian Nationality Law', in B. Nascimbene (ed.), *Nationality Laws in the European Union*, 61-93. Milano: Butterworths.

Çinar, D. (1999), 'Die neuen Einwanderer Europas: Fremde auf Dauer?' (unpublished dissertation), University of Vienna.

Davy, U. & D. Çinar (2001) 'Österreich', in U. Davy (ed.), *Die Integration von Einwanderern. Rechtliche Regelungen im europäischen Vergleich*, 567-708. Frankfurt: Campus Verlag.

Davy, U. & A. Gächter (1993), 'Zuwanderungsrecht und Zuwanderungspolitik in Österreich', Teil I, *Journal für Rechtspolitik* 1: 155-174.

De Groot, G.R. (1989), *Staatsangehörigkeitsrecht im Wandel. Eine rechtsvergleichende Studie über Erwerbs- und Verlustgründe der Staatsangehörigkeit*. Cologne: Carl Heymans Verlag.

Dogan, V. (2002), *Türk Vatandaslik Hukuku*. Ankara: Yetkin Basimevi.

Fassmann, H. & R. Münz (1995), *Einwanderungsland Österreich?* Wien: J&V-Dachs Verlag.

Fassmann, H. & I. Stacher (ed.), *Österreichischer Migrations- und Integrationsbericht*. Klagenfurt/Celovec: Drava Verlag.

Feik, R. (2003), 'Sprachkenntnisprüfungen und Staatsbürgerschaft', paper presented at the symposion 'Sprachenreche und Migration', 6- 8 March 2003, University of Vienna (on file with the authors).

Goldemund, I., K. Ringhofer & K. Theuer (1969), *Das österreichische Staatsbürgerschaftsrecht*. Wien: Manzsche Verlags- und Universitätsbuchhandlung.

Hansen, R. & P. Weil (2001), 'Introduction: Citizenship, Immigration and Nationality: Towards a Convergence in Europe?', R. Hansen & P. Weil (eds.), *Towards a European Nationality. Citizenship, Immigration and Nationality Law in the EU*, 1-23. New York: Palgrave.

Hammar, T. (1985), *European immigration policy. A comparative study*. Cambridge, MA: Cambridge University Press.

Heinl, A. (1950), *Das österreichische Staatsbürgerschaftsrecht*. 3rd edition. Vienna: Manzsche Verlags- und Universitätsbuchhandlung.

Jandl, M. & A. Kraler (2003), *Austria: A Country of Immigration?*, Migration Information Source. www.migrationinformation.org.

König, K. & B. Perchinig (2003), 'Österreich', in J. Niessen. Y. Schibel & R. Magoni (eds.) *EU and US approaches to the management of immigration*, 1-28. Brussels/Vienna: Migration Policy Group.

Mussger, H., P. Fessler, W. Szymanski & C. Keller (2001), *Österreichisches Staatsbürgerschaftsrecht*. 4th edition. Vienna: Juridica Verlag.

Münz, R., P. Zuser & J. Kytir (2003), 'Grenzüberschreitende Wanderungen und ausländische Wohnbevölkerung: Struktur und Entwicklung', in H. Fassmann & I. Stacher (eds.), *Österreichischer Migrations- und Integrationsbericht*, 20-86. Klagenfurt/Celovec: Drava Verlag.

Novak, R. (1974), 'Die Staatsbürgerschaftsgesetz-Novelle 1973', *Österreichische Juristen-Zeitung* 29 (22): 589-593.
Soysal, Y. (1994), *Limits of Citienship. Migrants and Postnational Membership in Europe.* Chicago: University of Chicago Press.
Stieber, G. (1995), 'Volksdeutsche und displaced persons', in G. Heiss & O. Rathkolb (eds.), *Asylland wider Willen*, 140-156. Vienna: Dachs Verlag.
Thienel, R. (1989/1990), *Österreichische Staatsbürgerschaft.* Vol. I and II. Vienna: Staatsdruckerei.
Waldrauch, H. (2003), *Country profile Austria: Immigration and integration of foreign nationals: flows, stocks and policies.* Report prepared for the Forum Internazionale ed Europeo di Ricerche sull'Immigrazione (FIERI), July 2003. Vienna: European Centre for Social Welfare Policy and Research.
Waldrauch, H. & D. Çinar (2003), 'Staatsbürgerschaftspolitik und Einbürgerungspraxis in Österreich', in H. Fassmann & I. Stacher (eds.), *Österreichischer Migrations- und Integrationsbericht*, 261-283. Klagenfurt/Celovec: Drava Verlag.
Zuser, P. (1996), *Die Konstruktion der Ausländerfrage in Österreich. Eine Analyse des öffentlichen Diskurses.* Reihe Politikwissenschaft 35. Vienna: Institut für Höhere Studien.

2 Belgium

Marie-Claire Foblets and Sander Loones

2.1 Introduction

The provisions of the Code of Belgian Nationality[1] regarding the grounds for acquisition or loss of nationality constitute a complex legal puzzle. With a view to offering as clear an analysis of this puzzle as possible, we will focus in this introduction on the main modes of acquisition and loss of Belgian nationality today, and on the principles on which the logical and internal consistency of the legislation is based. In the second part we provide the historical background and list the main developments up to 1984 with regard to nationality law in Belgium (sect. 2.2). We will also discuss at length the current modes of acquisition and loss of nationality and the political discussions that have accompanied the developments in nationality law throughout. Some statistical data will be provided before referring to the principal institutional arrangements that have been introduced to improve the implementation of the nationality legislation (sect. 2.3). We will end by formulating a number of conclusions that may serve as a synthesis of all three parts of the analysis (sect. 2.4).

Since 1984, Belgian nationality legislation has been based on a few clear principles (Closset 2004: 83-107; Verwilghen 1980: 46-48). *Firstly*, the CBN favours ius sanguinis as the criterion for attributing nationality by virtue of parentage, but adds to it ius soli, i.e., the criterion of birth in Belgium.

The Code, *secondly*, allows for broad access to nationality in order to facilitate the integration of foreigners into society. It therefore provides, amongst others, for different modes of acquisition of nationality based on residence.

Thirdly, Belgian nationality law is especially concerned about the respect for equality between all nationals (especially between men and women and between all children, whether born in wedlock or not) and has therefore abandoned the system whereby uniformity of nationality was ensured within one family. Henceforth a foreigner who marries a Belgian or whose partner becomes a Belgian citizen does not necessarily become Belgian her- or himself (art. 16 CBN) and both the mother and the father now transmit their Belgian nationality to their children.

Moreover, these measures also serve as a means of realising the *fourth* principle of nationality law: combating certain forms of fraud, especially sham marriages and the 'legal kidnapping' of children, i.e., the situation in which a parent takes out of the country a child thus separating it from the spouse or partner who has been granted custody. By conferring on the child its Belgian parent's nationality, be it the father or the mother, the Belgian authorities are offered more possibilities to negotiate the return of the child, since the Belgian child enjoys diplomatic protection (Fulchiron 2005).

Finally, the CBN has sought to avoid statelessness, but contains hardly any provisions likely to prevent the accumulation of nationalities. For example, the provisions of art. 8 and 9 of the CBN relating to the attribution of Belgian nationality to a child on the grounds of parentage, or by reason of adoption by a Belgian, have led since their introduction to an impressive increase in the number of dual or multiple nationals (see sect. 2.3.1.1).

As mentioned above, an overview of the current modes of acquisition and loss of Belgian nationality will be provided in sect. 2.3. However in order to illustrate the logic behind some of the principles of the CBN, the most important modes are briefly discussed here.

As for the first principle, the combined application of the ius sanguinis and ius soli principles, it should be noted that the legislator, without jeopardising the primacy of ius sanguinis, gives special treatment to children born in Belgium.

Thus, the Code grants Belgian nationality not only to children born in Belgium to a Belgian parent (art. 8 CBN), but also to children born in Belgium to a foreign parent or to parents whose legal status is unknown (art. 10, 11 and 11bis CBN). However, whereas children born in Belgium to a Belgian parent acquire nationality automatically, children born in Belgium to a foreign parent can obtain Belgian nationality only under certain strict conditions: the child's foreign parent should him- or herself have been born in Belgium and/or have lived there for some time (art. 11 and 11bis); the (adopted) child must have had his or her main residence in Belgium since his or her birth (art. 11bis, 12bis, para. 1, 1° and 13, 1°). Furthermore, if these conditions are not met, in particular in the case where a child does not have a parent born in Belgium, Belgian nationality can only be obtained by declaration. This declaration has to be made by the (adopting) parents before the child reaches the age of twelve (art. 11bis CBN) or by the adult target person him- or herself (art. 12bis, para. 1, 1° and 13, 1°). The declaration is submitted for verification to the Public Prosecutor's Office and, in the event that the latter opposes it, to a judge or the Chamber of Representatives.

Respect for ius sanguinis, however, remains a basic principle in Belgian nationality law: the CBN grants Belgian nationality to children who were born abroad, on condition that they were born to a Belgian parent. The acquisition is automatic when a child does not possess any other nationality at the time of birth (art. 8 para. 1, 2°, c CBN) and is provided by registration (art. 8 para. 1, 2°, b CBN) or by declaration (art. 13, 3° CBN) in other cases. Other examples would be the transfer and the extension of the newly acquired Belgian nationality to the (adopted) children (art. 9, 12, 12bis, para. 1, 2° and 13, 2° CBN).

The acquisition of nationality on the basis of the principle of ius sanguinis has an important consequence: Belgian nationals who derive their nationality from a Belgian parent at birth cannot be stripped of their Belgian nationality (art. 22 para. 1, 7° and 23 para. 1 CBN). However, after the modifications made by the law of 13 July 1991,[2] this protection was extended to children born in Belgium to a foreign parent who was also born in Belgium and has had his or her main residence there for at least five of the ten years preceding the birth (art. 11 CBN).

As stated above under the second principle, the two most important ways to acquire Belgian nationality today are (partially) residence-based modes of acquisition: acquisition by declaration and by 'naturalisation'.

Since the coming into force of the law of 1 March 2000,[3] the procedure relating to nationality by declaration (art. 12bis CBN) applies to foreigners who have reached the age of eighteen and who meet the following conditions: first, a foreigner is eligible if he or she was born in Belgium and has had his or her legal and main residence there since birth. Second, the declaration can be made by a foreigner who was born abroad to a parent (at least one) who at the time of the declaration had Belgian nationality. Finally the procedure also applies to foreigners who have had their main legal residence in Belgium for at least seven years at the time of declaration and who have been authorised to reside in the country pursuant to the provisions of the law on residence of foreigners of 15 December 1980.[4]

The flexibility of the legislator towards the acquisition of nationality since 2000 has been made apparent by giving the last two groups of foreigners the possibility of becoming Belgian through a mere declaration. In previous legislation only those foreigners who were born in Belgium, were between the ages of eighteen and 30 and had established their main residence in Belgium since birth were eligible to obtain nationality by declaration. Birth in Belgium is henceforth no longer required; the duration of the stay is eliminated for the second group, and is reduced to a period of seven years for the third group. The increase in flexibility is also apparent from a study of the statistics: the number of foreigners who applied for nationality by declaration rose from about 5,250 in 1999 to more than 25,500 in 2000 and more than 27,500 in 2001, to about 21,250 in 2002 and about 14,500 in 2003.

Apart from acquisition of nationality by declaration, Belgian nationality can be obtained as the result of a discretionary procedure conducted by the Chamber of Representatives on the basis of a voluntary act by a foreigner who did not have any prior close ties to Belgium by birth, parentage or residence at an early age (art. 18-21 CBN). In this context, the specific term 'naturalisation' is used. Naturalisation thus is not an act of the executive branch of Government, but of the legislative authority (Nuyts 2001: II.4-11-15).

The naturalisation procedure can currently be used by foreigners who have reached the age of eighteen and have established their main residence in Belgium for three years (instead of five years, as was the case before the law of 2000), or two years for refugees (i.e., people who were granted the status of refugee) and stateless people (until 2000, three years).

As far as the loss of Belgian nationality is concerned, there are no systematically kept statistics. It should however be mentioned that the procedure by which nationality can be forfeited in case of serious violations of the obligations of a Belgian citizen, is not applied in practice (art. 23 CBN).[5] Furthermore, Belgian nationality can only be lost if the person acquires another nationality (art. 22 CBN).

2.2 Historical development

2.2.1 *Nationality law in Belgium from 1804 up to 1909: The move to Belgian independence*

Belgium became an independent country in 1830. Previously, the territory had been successively under the spheres of influence of the French and the Dutch.

After the Belgian provinces were annexed by France in 1795, Napoleon's *Code civil* which regulated French nationality came into effect there in March 1803. More specifically, the principles of nationality law can be found in art. 9, 10, 12, 17 and 19 of the Napoleonic Code and can be summarised as follows (Gérard 1859: 12):

- Nationality was granted at birth, following the principle of *ius sanguinis paterni*: a child whose father was French had French nationality, even if it was born abroad (art. 10 *Code civil*). This mode of acquisition was legitimised by the nationalist conviction that nationality cannot simply follow from accidentally having been born in a certain territory, but has to be seen as the heritage of a people, which is made up of individuals who together form a sovereign nation (Verwilghen 1985: 18; Closset 1984: 782).
- If a foreigner was born in France, he or she could nevertheless voluntarily opt for French nationality by making a *déclaration de domi-*

ciliation (declaration of domicile) within one year after reaching the age of 22 (art. 9 *Code civil*). By means of this policy, the theory of J. J. Rousseau was put into practice, according to which the acquisition of nationality constitutes a contract to which an individual can voluntarily choose to adhere.
- The principle of unity of nationality within the family was also stressed (art. 12 and 19 *Code civil*). Up until 1985, the Belgian legislation would continue to be based largely on this principle: a married woman followed the nationality status of her husband and so did the children born in wedlock.
- The loss and re-acquisition of French nationality were regulated in art. 17 and 20 of the *Code civil*. French nationality was withdrawn from a person who acquired a foreign nationality or who settled abroad and did not show any evidence of a desire to return. These modes of loss have also been incorporated into the current CBN (art. 22, para. 1, 1° and 5° CBN).

During the Dutch-Belgian union from 1815 to 1830, the Napoleonic Code remained in effect,[6] for the most part, but was supplemented by some provisions of the *Loi fondamentale* of 24 August 1815 concerning public offices and services. Thus, certain principles of ius soli were reintroduced, such as the granting of Dutch nationality to everyone born in the Kingdom or in the colonies and whose parents were residents there (Closset 2004: 36-41).

Upon Belgium's independence in 1830, an amalgam of old and new legislation determining nationality was enacted. Thus the above-mentioned articles of the *Code civil* remained in effect and the Constitution created transitional measures to guide the move to independence (art. 133). It also regulated essential principles of nationality law (art. 8 and 9). It introduced, for instance, naturalisation by an act of Parliament as a specific mode of acquisition.[7]

In sum, the legislation remained basically unchanged from 1831 up to 1909: the importance of ius sanguinis was confirmed, but supplementary legislation was passed making it possible to acquire nationality by naturalisation. Moreover, the fact that the legislation was spread over multiple sources of law meant that the jurisprudence had great practical impact (Verwilghen 1985: 23; Gérard 1859: 12).

After 1931, several provisions were added to the *Code civil*: beside the rules regulating the modes of voluntary acquisition of Belgian nationality by option and by naturalisation,[8] other provisions stipulated that Belgian nationality was granted to certain categories of persons, more specifically to those people born in Belgium of legally unknown parents.[9] Still other provisions regulated the re-acquisition of Belgian nationality, particularly when this nationality had been lost on a voluntary basis.[10] Finally, several laws were passed that entailed the approval of a number of international conventions.[11]

2.2.2 *The nationality law of 1909: A first liberalisation*

As the practical application of the *Code civil* appeared more and more difficult, and the fact that the legislation was spread over several sources of law came under increasing criticism, the call for new nationality legislation grew louder. This tendency was reinforced by the rising social, legal and political interest in the ius soli principle as a result of several conflicts over territory caused by the transition to Belgian independence (Closset 2004: 42).

The law of 1909 thus abrogated the provisions of the *Code civil* and of certain specific laws,[12] and introduced a whole new set of rules. This law is now considered to have been at the time of its promulgation a liberal one, as it provided that beside the conservation of ius sanguinis, the ius soli principle would apply. More precisely, nationality was also granted to every child born in Belgium of parents with an undefined nationality (art. 4) and to all persons turning 23, who had lived in Belgium during their 22nd year and did not indicate a desire to retain their foreign nationality and who were born in Belgium of foreign parents, at least one of whom was also born in Belgium or had resided there continuously for ten years.

2.2.3 *The nationality law of 1922 and the law of 1932: Towards a concise nationality legislation*

The liberal legislation of 1909 would soon come to an end. The desire for protectionism and greater restriction in granting Belgian nationality to foreigners formed the basis of the law of 15 May 1922, which completely repealed the law of 1909 and brought the fundamental provisions in the nationality legislation together in one text. This law was characterised by a radical return to the primacy of the ius sanguinis principle and introduced the acquisition of nationality by 'possession of Belgian status' (*possession d'état de Belge*). The latter is the acquisition of Belgian nationality by a person who acted for many years (at least ten years) in good faith as a Belgian national and/or was presumed to be a Belgian national.

However, some further modifications proved necessary in order to address certain lacunae in the law. Thus the law of 4 August 1926 specified the term within which persons who had been unable because of war to opt in due time for Belgian nationality could still do so; the law of 30 May 1927 provided for a system of publication of the House of Representatives' decisions on naturalisation; and the law of 15 October

1932 tightened both the rules intended to prevent the existence of statelessness as well as the conditions required in order to be naturalised by a parliamentary act.[13]

The laws of 1922, 1926, 1927 and 1932 were finally grouped by the Royal decree of 14 December 1932 known as the 'law on acquisition, loss and re-acquisition of nationality'.[14] In its general terms, this text remained in force up to the introduction of the new Nationality Code in 1984.

The most essential principles of the aforementioned law of 1932 can be summarised as follows:

- The strict application of the ius sanguinis principle was confirmed. Furthermore, ius sanguinis was once again applied only with the father as the reference person, at least as far as legitimate filiation was concerned. A legitimate child, i.e., born in wedlock, could thus acquire Belgian nationality only through a Belgian father, so that the child of a stateless father and a Belgian mother was also deemed stateless. *Ius sanguinis paterni* was defined in such a way that even foundlings in Belgium were presumed to have been born to a Belgian father and were thus presumed to be Belgian (Closset 2004: 47). Only in the case of so called natural children[15] was a limited opening left for the acquisition of nationality by means of filiation through the mother. Such children were considered Belgian if maternal filiation was known with certainty before the paternal one and if the mother was Belgian (art. 2).
- The principle of unity of nationality within the family was considerably weakened. It became possible for a woman who married a Belgian or whose partner acquired Belgian nationality by option to refuse the Belgian nationality which she thereby would have acquired automatically. To do so, she had to make a declaration to this effect within six months (art. 4). A similar regulation existed for the children of a foreigner who voluntarily became Belgian: they could relinquish Belgian nationality before they reached the age of 23 (art. 6).
- The policy decision to balance out the freedom of changing one's nationality and the desire to prevent statelessness and multiple nationality found concrete expression. An illustration of the latter: Belgian nationality could not be acquired by naturalisation by a parliamentary act if the legislation of the country of origin allowed for the (voluntary) retention of the first nationality (art. 14). An example of the desire to prevent statelessness: a Belgian woman who married a foreigner, or whose partner no longer remained Belgian, lost her Belgian nationality only if she acquired the new nationality of her husband (art. 18, 2°).

2.2.4 *The law of 28 June 1984: Introduction of the new Code of Belgian Nationality (CBN)*

In the course of time, especially since the stabilisation of post-war immigration, the legislation governing Belgian nationality has grown into a central instrument of policy in matters of integration and migration. This applies in particular since the 1990s.

The discussions in Parliament illustrate, however, that not everybody shares the same views. If some consider that a host country like Belgium should show openness and a readiness to evolve into a multicultural society, notably by setting a minimum number of requirements for foreigners who wish to adopt the nationality of their country of residence, others continue to oppose this and insist upon the necessity of strict nationality legislation.

On the whole though, one may say that since the early 1980s, the policymakers proceed to conceive of Belgian nationality as one of the main instruments of their integration policy – hence their unremitting efforts to lend more substance to this policy in the matter of the nationality law.

The law of 28 June 1984 introduced an entirely new Code, which replaced the previous law of 1932 and substantially modified the rules governing the attribution, acquisition, loss and re-acquisition of Belgian nationality. More specifically, a number of elements are new (Closset 2004: 49-53; Heyvaert 1986; Liénard-Ligny 1984-1985; Mignon 1989a; Mignon 1989b; Verwilghen 1985: 52-138):

- The principle of ius sanguinis as the main criterion since 1922 for the granting of Belgian nationality was amended, giving way on the one hand to an adjustment of that criterion,[16] and on the other hand to ius soli, with a view to facilitating the integration of immigrants and stateless people.
- The evolution of family law has contributed to the further weakening of the previously generally accepted principle of the unity of nationality within the family. That principle was no longer compatible with the evolution of family law, both domestic and international, towards equal treatment within the family. The inequality of sexes and discrimination suffered by adoptive children and by children born out of wedlock were no longer considered acceptable.
- With respect to the possession of multiple nationalities, the legislator has adopted a twofold attitude: after having made possible numerous cases of dual nationality,[17] the 1984 Code multiplied the cases in which Belgian nationality can be lost, and furthermore required the loss of that nationality by an adult in case of dual or multiple nationality.

- While under the previous legislation, the conditions and procedures for acquiring Belgian nationality considerably limited the foreigner's right to become Belgian, the new Code has simplified these conditions and procedures in order to facilitate the integration – via nationality – of foreigners who have settled in Belgium.

Nevertheless, the legislation did not break completely with the past on numerous points, and the 1984 Code continues to be rooted in the ancient law: if it is no longer the sole criterion for the acquisition of nationality, ius sanguinis has not been abandoned; the conditions and procedures for opting for Belgian nationality and for naturalisation, although relaxed and simplified, for the most part look very much like those provided by the law of 1932; the distinction between the system applicable to adults and to minors has been maintained; the system of loss of nationality has remained unchanged; the principle of non-retroactivity of the granting, acquisition, loss and recovery of nationality has been maintained and the notion of being Belgian by birth has not been abandoned by the Code.[18]

Unlike the former nationality laws, however, that evoked only moderate political interest, the CBN has been modified repeatedly since 1984. The text of the law of 1 March 2000, better known by the public as the 'quickly-Belgian-law', represents, after the laws of 13 June 1991, 6 August 1993, 13 April 1995 and 22 December 1998, the fifth modification of a Code in hardly twenty years' time.[19] The basic intention underlying these reforms of the CBN has remained unchanged: facilitating the integration of foreigners into society.[20]

In the next chapter the current modes of acquisition and loss of nationality and the political discussions that have accompanied the developments in Belgian nationality law since 1984 will be discussed.

2.3 Recent developments and current institutional arrangements

2.3.1 *Main modes of acquisition and loss of nationality*

2.3.1.1 *Acquisition of Belgian nationality*

The CBN makes a distinction between automatic (*toekenning – attribution*) and non-automatic (*verkrijging – acquisition*) modes of acquiring nationality. Whereas the second type requires an explicit expression of intent by the target person, the automatic modes of acquisition provide *ex lege* access to nationality.

Filiation to a Belgian parent does not always automatically lead to the acquisition of Belgian nationality. The CBN requires, moreover, a minimal territorial link with Belgium and thus avoids the possibility of generations of persons who no longer have any genuine link with Belgium passing on their nationality. Thus the following persons are considered Belgian: children born in Belgium of a Belgian parent and children born abroad of a Belgian parent who was him- or herself born in Belgium. If both child and parent were born abroad, however, the parent must make a statement before the child reaches the age of five requesting that Belgian nationality be granted to the child. This mode of acquisition, which is defined by the Belgian legislation as automatic, is known as acquisition by registration (art. 8 CBN). If no such statement was made, the child can still acquire Belgian nationality by option between the ages of eighteen and 22 (art. 13, 3° CBN).

The law of 13 June 1991 that came into force on 1 January 1992 has definitely confirmed this determining role of the place of birth in Belgian nationality law (ius soli) and has also simplified the possibility of acquiring Belgian nationality for second and third generation immigrants. Belgian nationality can thus also be acquired by a minor child who is found in Belgium (art. 10, para. 2 CBN) or who is born in Belgium and would be stateless if Belgian nationality were not awarded (art. 10, para. 1 CBN).[21] Third generation foreigners, that is children who are born in Belgium from parents of whom at least one was also born in Belgium, can now acquire Belgian nationality in a simple manner. One parent is required to have resided in Belgium during five of the ten years before the birth and the child must be formally registered (art. 11 CBN). A specific system of acquisition of nationality was also developed for second-generation foreigners, i.e., foreign children born in Belgium. If a child has lived in Belgium since its birth, (adoptive) parents who have already resided in Belgium for ten years can make a statement at the registrar (art. 11bis CBN).[22] This mode of acquisition is defined by Belgian law as an *ex lege* mode, since the registrar cannot on his own initiative prevent the registration of the child as a Belgian national. However the public prosecutor can, within a period of one month, refuse the acquisition if the statement was not made 'in the interest of the child'. A refusal may be appealed before the court. The immediate consequence of the changes made by the law of 1991 was the granting, by full force of law, of Belgian nationality to several thousand young foreigners (Closset 2004: 57-59; Lambein 1991-1992; Liénard-Ligny 1991).

Furthermore, minor children whose father or mother acquires Belgian nationality are, by extension, also entitled to automatic acquisition of nationality (art. 12 CBN). The other parent who retains his or her foreign nationality cannot prevent this. However, if a child has multiple nationalities it may renounce the Belgian one after the age of eighteen (art. 22, para. 1, 2° CBN).

Finally, nationality can also be acquired by an adopted child. Just as in the cases above, a territorial link with Belgium is required, so that the adoption of a minor by a Belgian father or mother is not in itself a sufficient basis for the acquisition of nationality. In this way, a system similar to that of ordinary filiation was established. If the adopted child or the adopting parent was born in Belgium, the child acquires nationality automatically. If not, the adopting parent must register the adoption within five years (art. 9 CBN).

In order to ensure equality between men and women, the Code has since 1984 abandoned the system whereby children only acquired the nationality of the father (see sect. 2.2.3). Both the mother and the father now transmit their Belgian nationality to their children. In addition, the Code also eliminated the old distinction between legitimate children and children born out of wedlock and has thus anticipated the later reform of the legislation relating to parentage, and drawn the consequences of the *Marckx* case as judged by the European Court of Human Rights condemning Belgium for being discriminatory towards natural children.[23] Legitimate parentage and natural parentage are henceforth governed by an identical system.

The acquisition of nationality by declaration is a mode by which foreigners who were born in Belgium can acquire Belgian nationality without, in principle, having to go through any procedure. Moreover, by the law of 1 March 2000, access to this mode of acquisition was made more flexible. Thus, for example, it is no longer required that a foreigner makes the declaration between the age of eighteen and thirty, since the upper age limit has been removed. As of 2000, any foreigner over the age of eighteen who satisfies the conditions can make such a declaration. To be able to make the declaration of nationality, a foreigner (1) must be born in Belgium and have had his or her main residence there since birth, either (2) must be born abroad to a parent who at the time of the declaration has Belgian nationality,[24] or (3) must have been authorised to reside in the country pursuant to the provisions of the law on residence of foreigners and have had his or her main residence in Belgium for at least seven years (art. 12bis CBN).

According to the Statement of Reasons accompanying the law of 1 March 2000, the notion of 'main residence' refers to a legal residence on the basis of various sorts of residence permits.[25] A main residence in Belgium that is not founded on a legal residence permit does, in principle, not offer the possibility to a foreigner to acquire Belgian nationality by declaration.[26] In the circular letter of 25 April 2000,[27] the Minister confirmed that position. However, one should note that the law clearly mentions 'main residence', and not legal residence. The Court of Cassation (Supreme Court) thus stated that it is not relevant whether the foreigner disposed of a legal residence permit in the country throughout the entire required period, as long as his or her main residence was established for a sufficiently long time in Belgium and he or she has a legal right to reside there at the time of the declaration.[28] With the law of 27 December 2004, however, the legislator confirmed the interpretation according to which legal residence is required.[29] The Court of Cassation has in the meantime changed its juriprudence accordingly.[30] It would perhaps have been preferable to speak of a 'residence based on legal authorisation' wherever the expression 'legal residence' is used in the CBN. This would have prevented the risk of misunderstanding.[31]

After the declaration has been made, the public prosecutor has to give an advice concerning the acquisition of nationality. In the case of a negative advice a judicial appeal procedure may be initiated; if no appeal is introduced, the case is transformed into a naturalisation case that is dealt with by the Chamber of Representatives.

In this respect, the law of 2000 has also redefined the competences of the Public Prosecutor's Office in order to expedite the procedure. Firstly, the time limit within which the Prosecutor's Department has to provide its advice is now uniformly reduced to one month.[32] Secondly, the public prosecutor can henceforth issue a negative advice only when there is an impediment 'on account of important facts pertaining to the individual applicant'[33] and when the basic conditions of the procedure are not met: duration of residence, main residence, age requirement(s), etc. The prosecutor can no longer do so if he or she deems that the applicant does not show sufficient willingness to integrate. This willingness is assumed to exist solely by virtue of the declaration of Belgian nationality.

Belgian nationality can also be obtained as the result of a procedure involving the Chamber of Representatives. As mentioned above, the specific term 'naturalisation' is used in this context. Access to this procedure was facilitated consecutively by the laws of 13 April 1995, 22 December 1998 and 1 March 2000. Since 2000, the naturalisation procedure is free of charge.

In order to apply for naturalisation, a foreigner has to meet the following conditions: he or she should have reached at least the age of eighteen and should have had his or her main residence in Belgium for three years. The period is reduced to two years for a foreigner whose status as a refugee or stateless person is recognised in Belgium. The person concerned should, in principle, maintain his or her main residence in Belgium throughout the procedure[34] and, according to the jurisprudence of the Chamber's Commission for Naturalisation, which handles the applications, the main residence must be based on a residence permit of unlimited duration in Belgium. Persons who only stay temporarily in Belgium cannot, in principle, have recourse to this mode of acquisition.

In practice, a foreigner has to submit a motivated application which, since 2000, no longer asks for evidence of integration, but must contain the following handwritten declaration: 'I declare that I wish to become a Belgian national and that I shall comply with the Constitution and the laws of the Belgian people and the European Convention for the Protection of Human Rights and Fundamental Freedoms.'

The application for naturalisation is in principle addressed either directly to the Chamber or to the registrar of births, deaths and marriages of the place where the applicant has his or her main residence, who sends the application to the Chamber.[35] The Chamber then forwards the application to the public prosecutor who has to issue an advice within one month.[36] Here too, since the law of 2000, negative advice can only be based on important facts pertaining to the individual applicant and not on a lack of willingness to integrate. The Chamber of Representatives can also ask other authorities to launch a specific investigation. More specifically, the Office of Foreigners' Affairs and National Security are in most cases asked for their advice.[37]

Eventually the Commission for Naturalisation of the Chamber examines the file and the Chamber approves, postpones or rejects the application. Traditionally the Belgian nationality law provided for two types of naturalisation: ordinary and full naturalisation. Only full naturalisation placed the person concerned on a completely equal footing with other Belgians in terms of political rights. Ordinary naturalisation, by contrast, did not grant those political rights for which the Constitution or other legislation required full naturalisation (e.g., the right to vote).[38] Since the modification of the Constitution in 1991, the difference between full and ordinary naturalisation has been abandoned.[39] With the law of 6 August 1993, this difference has also been removed from the CBN and from other laws, so that there now remains only one type of naturalisation.

The Chamber retains a discretionary power in the matter of naturalisation. Therefore, naturalisation is a favour and not a right and there is henceforth no appeal against a negative decision. Furthermore, given the principle of separation of powers, the judicial power has no authority to overrule a naturalisation act. In this regard, the Court of Arbitration (Constitutional Court) ruled, for instance, that even though it has the fundamental competence to review formal laws such as the naturalisation laws, it would not be able to do so without calling into question another fundamental principle of the Constitution, namely the sovereign competence of the legislature to decide in this case.[40]

The possibility of opting for Belgian nationality is reserved to persons who have a strong link with Belgium by their birth, their filiation or their residence in Belgium at a young age. Particular application of this procedure is made in the case of marriage with a Belgian, possession of Belgian status (*possession d'état de Belge*) and re-acquisition of Belgian nationality.

More specifically, four categories of foreigners having a special connection with Belgium qualify: (1) a child born in Belgium (who does not qualify for acquisition by declaration because the main residence in Belgium has been interrupted); (2) a child born abroad and who was adopted by a Belgian; (3) a child born abroad whose (adopting) parent (s) had Belgian nationality before or at the time of the birth of the child (and who did not acquire Belgian nationality *ex lege* because a territorial link with Belgium is lacking); and (4) a child who before the age of six has had his or her main residence in Belgium for at least one year together with a parent or legal guardian (art. 13 CBN).

By the law of 22 December 1998, this procedure was made almost entirely equivalent to the simple mode of acquisition by declaration. Here too, the willingness to integrate is presumed to be present by sole virtue of making the declaration of option. The only difference between the two procedures lies in the conditions regarding age and residence requirements. The foreigner must opt for Belgian nationality between the age of eighteen and 22 and he or she must have had his or her main residence in Belgium during the twelve months preceding the declaration, and also during at least nine years or continuously from the age of fourteen to eighteen (art. 14 CBN).

A particular form of acquisition by option is the one applied to the foreign spouse of a Belgian national (art. 16 CBN). As already mentioned, Belgian nationality law has since 1984 abandoned the system whereby solely the foreign woman automatically acquired her husband's Belgian nationality. It now provides that marriage does not have an automatic effect on either of the spouses' nationality. Instead, it introduces a distinction based on the type of residence status available to the foreign spouse: the foreigner who has a right to reside legally and with no time restraints in Belgium on grounds other than his or her marriage, and who thus cannot be suspected of contracting the marriage for nationality purposes, can begin the procedure of acquiring Belgian nationality by option after six months of cohabitation. By contrast, the foreigner who has permission to stay in Belgium only because of his or her marriage with a Belgian national must wait three years before being able to file such an application. No minimum or maximum age is required and since 1 June 2003 the homosexual spouse of a Belgian national can also make use of this mode of acquisition.[41]

A further category of foreigners who can use the procedure of acquisition by option is made up of those persons who have erroneously been considered Belgian by the Belgian authorities for a continuous period of at least ten years. The person concerned must be able to prove his or her Belgian status (inclusion in electoral rolls, completion of military service, uninterrupted possession of Belgian identity papers, etc.) and make the declaration within one year of the date on which he or she was officially notified that he or she does not actually hold Belgian nationality (art. 17 CBN).[42]

Finally, the procedure of acquisition by option is open to any person who lost his or her Belgian nationality by a means other than by forfeiture (art. 23 CBN)[43] and who wishes to re-acquire Belgian nationality (art. 24 CBN). Before they can acquire nationality by option they must, in principle, be at least eighteen years old and have had their main residence in Belgium at least during the year preceding the declaration.

2.3.1.2 *Loss of Belgian nationality*

Just as with the acquisition of Belgian nationality, different modes of loss can be distinguished according to whether or not the loss is the consequence of an action by the person concerned. A special mode of loss is the forfeiture of nationality.

The adult person who acquires a foreign nationality on his or her own initiative will legally lose Belgian nationality (art. 22, para. 1, 1° CBN). Consequently, the loss must result from a formal act by the person concerned (e.g., he or she submits an application, signs a document indicating acceptance of a foreign nationality, makes an oath or signs a declaration). Nationality cannot be lost without a prior legal act or if the other nationality is acquired only indirectly (e.g., through marriage).

In this regard one should also note the asymmetry of the Belgian provisions concerning the effect that acquiring another, elected nationality has on nationality by right of birth: while the Code provides for the automatic loss of Belgian nationality by someone who, after the age of eighteen, voluntarily acquires a foreign nationality (art. 22, para. 1, 1° CBN), there is no similar requirement that someone who voluntarily acquires Belgian nationality must renounce his or her original nationality by birth. Legal action is underway to end this discrimination. More specifically, several bills were introduced to modify art. 22 CBN in such a way that someone who voluntarily acquires a foreign nationality can retain the Belgian nationality.[44]

The renunciation of Belgian nationality constitutes the second mode of loss (art. 22, para. 1, 2° CBN). Belgian nationality will be lost if a declaration is made to this effect and if the person concerned proves that he or she already has a foreign nationality or will acquire a foreign nationality by making the said declaration renouncing Belgian nationality.

A minor whose (adoptive) parent(s) lose(s) their Belgian nationality, or who is adopted by a foreigner, will also lose his or her Belgian nationality if he or she acquires or already possesses another nationality (art. 22, para. 1, 3° and 4° CBN).

A fourth mode consists in the loss of Belgian nationality by failure to declare one's intention to retain it, in cases where such a declaration is required (art. 22, para. 1, 5° CBN). A person who was born abroad, and who never had his or her main residence in Belgium between the ages of eighteen and 28, must declare his or her intention to retain Belgian nationality before turning 28. Otherwise Belgian nationality is lost. Furthermore, such a declaration must be renewed every ten years. It should be remembered that Belgian nationality can in that case easily be re-acquired by means of the procedure of acquisition by option (art. 24 CBN).[45]

The last mode of loss is the forfeiture of nationality (art. 22, para. 1, 7° and 23, para. 1 CBN). The nationality of Belgians who did not acquire their nationality from a Belgian parent at the time of their birth or from a foreign parent who was likewise born in Belgium and had his or her main residence there for at least five of the ten years preceding the birth (art. 11bis CBN) may be declared forfeit by virtue of a judgement handed down by the Court of Appeal. This is possible when such individuals are seriously in breach of their obligations as Belgian citizens. It should, however, be mentioned that this procedure is no longer applied in practice.[46]

2.3.2 *Political analysis*

It seems that in the course of drafting the nationality regulations of 2000, a new vision of citizenship and membership in society has played an increasingly important role. One that is optimistic about the potential of nationality as a means of integration. However, idealism cannot be taken as the sole explanation for the fact that the CBN was amended and made more flexible on several occasions. In the final section, we shall examine a few bottlenecks that have resulted from the consecutive amendments to the law. Regarding these matters, we shall go back to the parliamentary discussions relating to the amendments of 2000, since these reforms may be considered to constitute the most far-reaching reforms since 1984 as far as the relaxation of the conditions for access to the various procedures for acquiring nationality is concerned (Foblets 2000-2001; Foblets 2003: 261-275; Guillain 2002; Stockx 2000).

The Minister of Justice's commentary on the bill preceding the aforesaid amendments of 2000 reveals the following underlying optimistic approach: a foreigner wishing to acquire Belgian nationality is seen as a citizen of the world, with a positive attitude to a variety of cultures and ready to co-invest in the future of the multicultural society. But for a few exceptions, the foreigners seeking to obtain Belgian nationality are people willing to contribute to the success of (the future of) society.[47]

The series of measures approved in 2000 are therefore to be seen against the background of that idealistic vision of membership in society.

The opposition though voiced strong criticism of the governmental proposals, considering them to have been inspired less by idealism than, for the most part, by political pragmatism and the lack of a sense of reality. We shall now look in greater detail at a few of these criticisms. In particular, we will point out the so-called 'instrumentation' of the nationality rules, and the three different functions that the amendments voted in 2000 attribute to the concept of nationality.

The federal legislature has tried to ascribe various roles to the acquisition, possession and loss of Belgian nationality since 1984. Some have used the expression 'instrumentation' of the CBN to describe this type of legislative policy. One might also speak of pragmatism on the part of the legislator. Three functions attributed to nationality are now of particular importance: nationality as facilitator of the integration of foreigners into the life of society, nationality as guarantor of parliamentary democracy, opening up the citizen's political participation at all levels, and nationality as guardian of the laws on immigration. We shall try to show how since 1984 the Belgian legislator has constantly relied on the CBN and its various provisions to play these three specific roles, either simultaneously or in turn.

The history of the concept of nationality in Belgian law has already been described repeatedly (Carlier & Goffin 1996; Closset 2004: 31-59; De Valkeneer 1984; Foblets & Foqué M. Verwilghen 2002; Liénard-Ligny 1985: 222; Louis 1995; Maeckelberghe 1989: 146; Marescaux & Taverne 1984; Verschueren 1995; Verwilghen 1984; Verwilghen 1992). Different phases may be distinguished in the evolution of Belgian nationality law throughout the twentieth century.

The law of 1909 provided that beside the conservation of the principle of ius sanguinis, the ius soli rule would be applied. The rules of 1932 relied, as we have indicated above, almost exclusively on the principle of ius sanguinis. In the 1980s, more particularly through the CBN and its successive amendments, the principle of ius soli was reintroduced whereby people who were born in Belgium of foreign parents could henceforth acquire Belgian nationality. However, the basic logic behind the nationality rules remained untouched, providing a greater claim to the right to acquire Belgian nationality as there are indications that a foreigner has become integrated into Belgian society or at least is presumed to be willing to integrate.

The consistency with which the aforementioned basic rationale has been followed for decades has, however, notably weakened under the law of 2000. The possibility for the authorities to keep control over the applications for Belgian nationality has declined or at least become more difficult for mainly two reasons: on the one hand, the different modes of acquisition hinge more and more exclusively on the applicant's duration of residence and, on the other hand, the legislator has radically eliminated from all procedures the requirement to show sufficient willingness to integrate.

Certainly several authors had, already prior to the amendments of 2000, suggested eliminating the willingness to integrate as a basic condition for acquiring Belgian nationality, since it was the subject of a very divided, often contradictory, jurisprudence (De Decker & Suykerbuyk 1993; de Moffarts 1987; de Moffarts 1995; Lambein 1993: 513; Sluys 1991; Verhellen 1998; Walleyn 1989). One of the main criticisms of the text of the law of 2000 was, however, that the new CBN not only eliminates all considerations of integration, but also all incentives to integration, reducing the concept so to say to insignificance. Under the previous law, for instance, at least within the Naturalisation Commission of the Chamber of Representatives, the prevailing opinion was that the criterion of willingness to integrate was an important condition for justifying the rejection or postponement of applications for naturalisation.[48] Postponement was intended to motivate applicants to learn (at least) one of the national languages, and possibly to make the necessary efforts to integrate in their milieu. In the debates with a view to the legal amendments in 2000, it was therefore suggested that removing integration as a condition for naturalisation calls into question the efforts of many years of integration policy.

But the problem also lies elsewhere. The elimination of all considerations linked to integration is even more radical since the CBN does provide no procedure for reversing acquisition in cases of abuse or fraud that would, for instance, make it possible to strip someone of Belgian nationality, possibly with retroactive effect. As a result of the discussions on the CBN in 2000, the question arose whether one could refer in this issue to art. 23 of the Code, which provides for the forfeiture of nationality. The problem is that art. 23 would have to be amended if the intention were indeed to use this provision as the legal grounds for authorising the withdrawal of Belgian nationality from naturalised foreigners (Belgians) who (continue to) show obvious unwillingness to integrate. This solution would be unfortunate for, in its *ratio*, art. 23 aims especially at cases of violation of the domestic and international security of the State (high treason), which cannot simply be compared with a lack of willingness to integrate. To illustrate this, according to reports, there have been in total only 38 Belgians whose nationality has been forfeited, four before and 34 after the Second World War (see 2.3.1.2).[49]

The conclusion is obvious: once foreigners have acquired Belgian nationality, the authorities can no longer motivate this category of citizens to integrate. This would in any case be contrary to the Constitution and to a series of binding international human rights treaties which demand that once a foreigner has acquired nationality, he or she is considered formally equal and is to be treated on an equal footing with other nationals.[50] Obliging only a specific group of (new) nationals to complete extra integration requirements could be considered discriminatory.

From a cursory comparison, it appears that the acquisition of Belgian nationality is nowadays so greatly simplified that since 1 May 2000 the Code ranks among the most flexible in Europe. The reasons for the extreme ease of acquisition of Belgian nationality are also to be sought elsewhere. They are linked to the second function of nationality in Belgian law: giving people access to political citizenship.

The issue of foreigners' voting rights is not new in Belgium, but arose with the stabilisation on the national territory of the post-war waves of migration. It is tied to the question whether the legislator can continue to exclude entire communities of foreigners from voting for the sole reason that they do not (yet) hold Belgian nationality, in some cases voluntarily in other cases because they are bound by a foreign law forbidding them to renounce their first nationality by right of birth. Since the 1990s, the question has become all the more burning, as very often such communities had settled in the country for many years.

The subject has been discussed extensively and was first resolved for European Union nationals. Their right to vote and eligiblity for municipal elections are recognised since the amendment of the Constitution on 11 December 1998 (art. 8 Constitution).[51] However, for years, the granting of voting rights to non-EU nationals remained an extremely sensitive issue, especially in Flanders. This was also the case for the Flemish Liberals (the VLD), one of the largest political parties in the country and a member of the coalition in 2000, which was reluctant to grant voting rights to non-EU nationals. To break the deadlock, the government had chosen not to grant voting rights to these foreigners, but to pass the law of 1 March 2000, aimed at further relaxing the conditions for acquiring Belgian nationality, in this case, in order to encourage access to political citizenship.

Eventually, the granting of voting rights to non-EU nationals and their eligibility to stand in municipal elections was discussed again and voted on in Parliament in the course of 2004.[52] Since then, foreigners who are registered, have had their main residence in Belgium for five years and have filed an application to obtain the status of voter have the right to vote in municipal elections. They also have to declare that they will comply with the Constitution, the Belgian laws and the European Convention for the Protection of Human Rights and Fundamental Freedoms.

This legislative pragmatism is not without its dangers. While trying to resolve the question of the political rights of foreigners in Belgium the legislator has made access to Belgian nationality so much easier that its possession might end up serving purposes other than to gain political citizenship. We shall come back to this further on in this contribution. Yet the third function that the Belgian legislator has sought, since 1985, to ascribe to some provisions of the CBN still needs to be illustrated.

Concerning this third function of the CBN, namely that of guardian of the laws on immigration, the amendment of art. 16 CBN by the law of 6 August 1993 is particularly noteworthy. As mentioned above, this modification was intended to further combat so-called 'nationality marriages' (sham marriages).

Henceforth, a foreigner who marries a Belgian partner and who comes to settle in Belgium as a consequence of his or her marriage is bound to wait a period of three years before being authorised to make a declaration of option for nationality. This period does not apply to a foreigner who, at the time of marriage, was already authorised to stay in Belgium on a permanent basis: for him or her, the waiting period is only six months. This different treatment of two categories of marriage partners in Belgian nationality law is to be attributed to the third function of nationality: the acquisition of Belgian nationality is encouraged, but not to the detriment of the Belgian immigration policy. The foreigner who might use marriage to a Belgian national as a way of gaining not only easier access to the territory of the country, but also to acquire nationality, will have to show more patience.

Making the CBN simultaneously play various roles currently leads to the loss of its coherence, because, on the one hand, inconsistencies are being created in the legislation and, on the other hand, the roles which the various branches of the law ascribe to nationality are not necessarily compatible.

The inconsistencies are internal as well as external. Internal inconsistency means that the provisions of the Code lack compatibility in their mutual relationships. The external inconsistencies relate to contradictions between various provisions of the CBN and other legislation. Some types of nationality acquisition neutralise, or even damage the effects the legislator has tried to achieve by other legislation, in this case concerning the foreigners' access to the territory and residence in Belgium. Thus one observes counterproductive effects.

We shall limit ourselves to one example, which demonstrates both these internal and external inconsistencies: art. 12bis, para. 1, 2° CBN was introduced by the law of 2000 and provides adult foreigners who were born abroad and who have a Belgian parent with the possibility of acquiring Belgian nationality by declaration. They do not have to fulfil any residency requirements except that the declaration itself must be made in Belgium, which presupposes that the person concerned resides there at least temporarily. Moreover, there are no conditions regarding the parents' mode of acquisition of Belgian nationality. Even a recently acquired nationality is sufficient.[53]

While passing this mode of acquisition, the legislator in 2000 does not seem to have realised that it has introduced a difference in treatment between biological and adopted children, that certain categories of children born in Belgium are thereby disadvantaged in comparison to those who were born abroad, and that indirectly the law grants a right of residence to foreigners who according to Belgian immigration laws would not be entitled to long-term residence (Renauld 2005: 35-38).

Firstly, adopted children who are born abroad and who have a Belgian adopting parent can only acquire nationality by option (art. 13, 2° CBN). In this respect they still have to satisfy an age and residency requirement: they can opt for Belgian nationality between the age of eighteen and 22 if they had their main residence in Belgium during the twelve months preceding the option and also during at least nine years or continuously from the age of fourteen to eighteen (art. 14 CBN). Biological children who are born abroad and have a Belgian parent can, however, make use of the simple procedure of acquisition by declaration, which only requires that the child has reached the age of eighteen. Thus, rules for granting nationality to the adopted child are clearly more restrictive than for a child whose origin can be determined by other means.[54]

A further internal inconsistency follows from the observation that the acquisition of nationality by declaration provided for in art. 12bis, para. 1, 2° CBN concerns only children who were born abroad. Although the foreigners who were born in Belgium are usually able on other legal grounds to acquire Belgian nationality by simple declaration, it appears that this is not always the case. Thus, a foreigner who was born in Belgium but grew up abroad, and of whom one parent acquires Belgian nationality, cannot acquire Belgian nationality by simple declaration but only by option, which requires that the child fulfils the restrictive conditions regarding age and residency of art. 14 CBN, whereas if he or she had been born abroad, he or she would not be required to meet these conditions. Such differential treatment, dealing less favourably with those who were born in Belgium than with those born abroad, does not seem to be consistent with the logic of the CBN.

A question was put to the Court of Arbitration concerning the here afore mentioned inconsistencies. The Court however qualified the petitions as inadmissible.[55]

Finally, we wish to point out an external inconsistency. Whereas the legislator opted not to grant certain categories of foreigners a right to residence on the basis of restricting of new immigration, the same legislator judged that foreigners might nevertheless be indirectly granted a right to residence via the nationality legislation. For art. 10, para. 1, 2° and 15 of the law on residence of foreigners provides for the right of residence to be granted to foreigners who fulfil the legal conditions for acquiring Belgian nationality by declaration (e.g., art. 12bis, para. 1, 2° CBN) or by option. They are fully entitled to reside in the country, without having to seek prior authorisation from the Minister or the Office of Foreigners' Affairs, and without having to make a formal declaration to acquire nationality. This combined reading of two legal texts leads to the conclusion that, when a foreigner acquires Belgian nationality, any children born abroad, even if they are now adults, are also entitled to nationality and to residence. This is clearly inconsistent with the legislation relating to immigration and family reunification: parents of foreign nationality who would like their grown-up children living abroad to join them, are not authorised to do so by the law on residence of foreigners. Now the simplified access to Belgian nationality provides them with the solution.[56]

These internal and external inconsistencies demonstrate that making access to Belgian nationality easier can have spread effects, it undermines or at least neutralises the very impact for which certain provisions have been written and passed. The other effect of such a policy, on which we shall conclude here, concerns the different roles nationality (still) occupies in various fields of our law, and which are not always compatible with the gradual relaxation of the criteria for its acquisition.

Extensive simplification of access to nationality, as is the case in Belgium since 2000, might cause nationality no longer to play its traditional role as the criterion for one's identity. The Code now allows for broad access to nationality in order to facilitate the integration of foreigners into society. However, it does so without any longer requiring any (objective) proof of willingness on the part of the foreigner to effectively integrate: all requirements, apart from length of stay in Belgium, have been abandoned.

The traditional role of nationality, in the sense of offering a criterion for one's identity, is currently still supported in the recent codification of Belgian private international law,[57] which provides that the national law of a person applies, at least in areas of one's personal status (e.g., the national law is applied in matter of determining someone's full name, in defining the relevant basic conditions for the validity of a marriage, and in cases of (adoptive) filiation). It thereby considers that the sense of identity will be better respected through the recognition of a person's foreign nationality.

Since 2000, however, the CBN seems to be according a new role to the concept of nationality, whereby nationality is closely linked to one's residence on the territory and not as much to one's integration into a society. Or, to put it another way, the legislation takes as its point of departure the view that the foreigner is already integrated solely by virtue of having resided on the state's territory for a certain number of years.

Neither of these two different roles is, however, sufficient in itself, since, on the one hand, easy access to nationality is not necessarily contradicted by the principle of recognition of a foreign affiliation used in private international law and, on the other hand, an individual settling in a new environment does not necessarily facilitate the harmonious integration of that person into the host society, even when this settlement alone suffices to allow someone to acquire – after a certain time – the nationality of the place of his or her new residence.

In order that both roles might be fulfilled at the same time, it is essential that they at least balance each other out. However, by radically opting for a residence-based concept of nationality, which does not require the person concerned to prove he or she is willing to integrate or even has a basic knowledge of the local language, this balance seems to be lacking.

Moreover, restricting the conditions for acquiring nationality to mere residence requirements clashes with certain principles of private international law, since various elements of connectedness lie behind the reference rules which private international law provides.[58] Restricting these links to the question whether the ordinary residence of the person concerned is in a certain country considerably limits the meaning of the principle of the 'closest connection', on the basis of which private international law was developed; on the basis of this principle one seeks always to identify the core interests of an individual in a certain context and to ascertain the degree of integration within a social and legal system before determining which law is applicable in any given case (Erauw 2002: 414-423; Meeusen 1997: 110). The possession of a nationality indicates the presence of a diversity of significant links between a particular individual and the country of which he or she carries the nationality.

It does not, then, seem reasonable to have recourse to the integrative purpose of nationality without taking into account sociological parameters other than the duration of residence as conditions for acquisition of nationality. More specifically, a sufficient basic knowledge of one of the three national languages (Dutch, French and German) and, possibly, proof of the intention to continue residing on the territory should, for instance, be seen as more solid requirements.

Furthermore, the knowledge of the language of the country of residence is a condition that one finds in most legislation currently in force in the various European countries regarding the acquisition of nationality (D'Hondt 2002: 270-277). It might therefore come as a surprise that it was precisely on this issue that the Belgian legislator in 2000 demonstrated such laxity. In Flanders, the legislation has opted for a different policy. A few years ago, the Flemish Parliament passed the so-called *Vlaams Inburgeringsdecreet* ('Flemish Decree on Integration').[59] Its purpose is to set up training programs for new immigrants, providing them with the necessary knowledge that will subsequently allow them to participate as citizens in the life of society. Making access to Belgian nationality too easy brings such initiatives into disrepute: the foreigner who acquires Belgian nationality is not obliged to know the language of the place of residence, while the immigrant who is a newcomer in Flanders is subject to such an obligation.

2.3.3 *Statistical developments*

As demonstrated above, the policy adopted with respect to Belgian nationality has been modified various times in the course of the years. It might therefore be useful to complete the analysis by looking at the statistical impact of the different amendments to the CBN.

Special attention goes to the impact of the law of 1984 introducing the new CBN, of the law of 1991 extending the modes of acquisition of nationality by ius soli and of the law of 2000, which substantially relaxed the conditions of access to the various procedures for acquiring nationality (Verschueren 1995; Bietlot, Caestecker, Hardeman & Rea 2002).

The introduction of the new Code of 1984 was intended to make the acquisition of Belgian nationality easier, especially for second- and third-generation immigrants. In practice, however, the code did not have the intended long-term effect. On 1 January 1985, the date that the CBN came into force, a large number of children from mixed marriages did at once become Belgian (about 60,000). However, the acqui-

Table 2.1: Acquisition of Belgian nationality

1985	63,824	1990	8,612	1995	26,109	2000	61,878
1986	8,477	1991	8,418	1996	24,552	2001	62,982
1987	8,341	1992	46,308	1997	31,598	2002	46,417
1988	8,330	1993	16,348	1998	33,918	2003	33,709
1989	8,768	1994	25,766	1999	24,119		

Source: National Institute for Statistics (NIS)

sition of nationality via other ways did not meet with great success. Generally speaking, between 1986 and 1991, just over 8,000 foreigners acquired Belgian nationality per year (Dumon & Adriaensens 1989: 24).

The causes of this limited long-term success are to be found in a number of administrative and legal barriers such as the high costs and the lengthy duration of the different procedures. The disbelief of foreigners that the acquisition of Belgian nationality would be a solution to their precarious social situation may be a second explanation.

The first fundamental changes to the CBN were made in 1991. The most important amendment, as we have already mentioned, was the extension of the types of acquisition based on the ius soli principle.

As a consequence, in the year 1992 approximately 46,000 foreigners gained Belgian nationality. About 38,500 of them made use of the new modes provided for in the Code: the acquisition of Belgian nationality by mere registration when third-generation immigrants are concerned (new art. 11 CBN) and by declaration in case of second-generation immigrants (new art. 11bis and 12bis CBN). In 1993, the number of acquisitions of nationality was also higher than in the years preceding the amendment of 1991. The total number was about 16,000, of which half were obtained by second-generation immigrants.

From the figures of 1992 and 1993, it is evident that third-generation immigrants from EU countries in particular made use of the easy access to Belgian nationality by registration,[60] while mostly non-EU nationals benefited from the measures concerning second-generation immigrants[61] (Poulain 1994: 13-14, 47-49; Verschueren 1995: 250-251).

Finally, we turn to the statistical impact of the law of 2000. At the initiative of the administration, especially the Ministry of Justice, the effectiveness and efficiency of this law was investigated one year after it came into force (Bietlot et al. 2002). Before lingering on the numerical data provided in the aforementioned study, it might be useful to point out the remarks raised by the investigation regarding the availability and relevance of the then existing statistics.

The authors of the study observe that the study in question could not be exhaustive, since no central authority had at the time organised a complete and precise system of registration of applications for nationality, neither by place and date of filing of the application, nor by the profile of the applicants. This would be necessary because different authorities intervene in the process of nationality acquisition. Furthermore, the data collection has highlighted discrepancies in the figures according to the source consulted (municipalities, prosecutors' departments, Office of Foreigners' Affairs or National Security). Finally, the data of the National Institute on Statistics, which makes use of the national register to determine the number of foreigners who have acquired Belgian nationality and the legal procedure by which they have done so, are available only with some delay.

Notwithstanding the lack of an exhaustive data entry system and the discrepancy between the sources, the authors made clear with their study that by facilitating the conditions of access to Belgian nationality and simplifying the steps to be taken, the law of 2000 caused a significant increase in applications for and acquisitions of Belgian nationality.

More specifically, an average of between 1,000 and 2,500 applications for nationality (all procedures combined) were filed every month before May 2000. After the law of 2000 entered into force, the number of applications fluctuated between 6,000 and 8,000, and has, in December 2000, stabilised to around 4,000 applications per month, which is about twice the average observed before the law of 2000.

One should also note that in 2000, 7.2 per cent of the foreign adult population living in Belgium applied for Belgian nationality and that, since the new law, nationality is mostly acquired by declaration of an adult foreigner who has his or her main residence in Belgium for at least seven years and who is authorised to stay in Belgium for an unlimited time (art. 12bis, para. 1, 3° CBN).

Finally, it can be pointed out that the law of 2000 had an impact especially on the number of acquisitions of nationality in the years 2000 and 2001. From 2002 on, the growth seems to have diminished and current statistics are likely to show a stabilisation.[62]

2.3.4 *Institutional arrangements*

2.3.4.1 *The legislative process*

Belgium is a federal State comprised of regions and communities, which each have their own legislative powers, executive powers and administrations (art. 1 Constitution).[63] The regions have been assigned the competence to deal mostly with economic matters, while the communities regulate culture, education and personal affairs, such as the reception and integration of immigrants.[64] The federal legislative authority retains, however, the competency for nationality, immigration and political rights (Van de Putte & Clement 2000: 22-24; Alen 1995: 368, 471).

The federal competence in the matter of nationality legislation is based on the Constitution, which requires that the federal legislative power decides who can call him- or herself a Belgian, on the one hand, by establishing the general rules governing nationality and, on the other hand, by granting naturalisation in individual cases (art. 8 and 9 Constitution).

The Federal Chamber of Representatives and the Senate, both acting on an equal footing, must formulate the general legislation governing nationality. These rules can, except for a number of special principles embedded in the Constitution, in principle be modified by a simple majority both in the Chamber and in the Senate. Individual decisions on naturalisation are, however, taken by the Chamber of Representatives without intervention by the Senate. Naturalisation by a parliamentary act requires that a special procedure be followed.

The federal authority also has competence regarding the laws on political rights. Only the federal legislator can grant foreigners active and passive voting rights for the elections of the European, federal, community and regional parliaments as well as for provincial councils, municipal councils and district territorial bodies (art. 8 and art. 41, para. 2 Constitution). As mentioned above, the right to vote in municipal elections has over the last years been granted to both EU nationals and eventually also to third-country nationals.

Generally speaking, it can finally be noted that the matter of nationality is within the remit of the Minister of Justice, while the Minister of the Interior collaborates in drafting the policy relating to foreigners' residence in the territory.

2.3.4.2 *The process of implementation*

Various bodies play a role in the different procedures for acquisition and loss of nationality. Besides the intervention of the registrar, in certain cases the prosecutor's department, the courts and the Chamber of Representatives also have a task to fulfil. We shall focus briefly on these bodies and in particular on certain tensions existing between them (Bietlot et al. 2002: 159-185; Caestecker, Bietlot, Hardeman & Rea 2001: 255).

- The civil registrar must check the documents submitted to him or her at the time of the application for nationality. Although it is clear in the preparatory work to the law of 2000 and the circular letter of 2 July 2000 that in the case of a dispute concerning these documents are concerned, the competent official has to accept a replacement document, it seems that he or she often claims an exclusive right to assess the validity of the birth certificate or similar document. The assessment thereof belongs, however, to the judicial power or, should the case arise, to the Naturalisation Commission in the Chamber of Representatives.
- Various bodies then intervene in the handling of the application. Although they all have to acknowledge receipt of the file immediately, it seems that no precise deadlines were set for this purpose. For example, even though the law of 2000 does formally establish the one-month deadline within which the public prosecutor should offer advice, evaluations of this law point out that this deadline is not met in practice. The delay can be explained by the fact that the

clock only starts running from the moment that receipt of the file has been acknowledged by the public prosecutor, which does not always occur immediately, but varies between one week and six months. The large prosecutor's offices, like those in Brussels and Antwerp, show the most delays (Bietlot et al. 2002: 159-185). However, the circular letter of 25 April 2000 states in this respect that the terms 'immediately' and 'without delay' used in the CBN reflect the legislator's will to see the obligations pertaining to the registrar and to the public prosecutor fulfilled without delay.[65]
- Even though the law of 2000 suppresses the obligation to consult with the Office of Foreigners' Affairs and with National Security regarding procedures of acquisition by declaration and by option, the aforementioned circular letter of 25 April 2000 states that the registrar should forward a copy of the file not only to the prosecutor's office, but also to the Office of Foreigners' Affairs and to National Security, while specifying that these should send their remarks, if any, to the public prosecutor. The advice of the Office of Foreigners' Affairs limits itself to communicating the administrative situation of the person concerned without, as was the case in the past, commenting on the desirability of the acquisition of nationality. National Security has to communicate remarks only if there is a problem.
- Within the framework of a procedure of acquisition by declaration or by option, the public prosecutor can offer positive or negative advice. In a case where advice is not provided within the one-month period,[66] the advice is deemed to be positive.

When the public prosecutor concludes that there is no reason to give a negative advice, he or she sends a statement to this effect to the registrar, who immediately has to register it in the ad hoc registers. The same applies when no advice has been given by the expiry of the one-month period. The person concerned becomes Belgian from the moment of registration.

When negative advice is given the case can be brought before the courts (which happens in one out of every four applications). The court summons the person concerned and listens to him or her. A substantiated verdict is then given on the legitimacy of the negative advice. An appeal can be filed against that verdict with the Court of Appeal. If the person concerned does not bring the matter before a court, the file is sent to the Chamber of Representatives where it will be considered as if it were an application for naturalisation by an act of Parliament.

2.4 Conclusions

The idea of making integration easier for foreigners through the acquisition of nationality is certainly not new. The Belgian legislators have pursued this notion ever since the early 1980s.

However, making access to nationality easier should not be pushed so far that it might later slow down the integration of those who would have been ready to meet a number of reasonable conditions for adapting to the society of their new place of residence. That is the risk some new nationals currently face, more so due to a number of measures relaxing Belgian nationality law which came into force on 1 March 2000.

There are obviously other instruments that facilitate the promotion of integration of foreigners and people of immigrant origins into society. One thinks in particular of the intensified struggle against discriminatory treatment,[67] the effective penalising of racist behaviour or some form of training programmes for newcomers, as are currently set up in the Netherlands and in Flanders (see 2.3.2). Would it not be far better if the legislation in general, including nationality law, were to reflect a more consistent view of membership of a state, a nation, a community at large?

It is up to the legislator to determine which rules govern state membership. If this is not done in a clear and consistent way, some foreigners will take advantage of the situation, while others who were hoping to acquire nationality in order to effectively participate in the life of the society of their new homeland will be left aside. Though nationality cannot have as its sole objective the final evidence of the integration process, one should not fall into the opposite extreme, and reduce it to a mere confirmation of one's residence. One could legitimately argue that this is, however, what has happened to Belgian nationality since 2000.

Nowhere in Europe are the conditions for the granting of nationality to foreigners as flexible as in Belgium. As long as the European Member States retain sovereignty over the granting and/or loss of their own nationality, discrepancies between national legislations in this regard cannot be excluded (de Groot 2004). But one should also be ready to accept the consequences. Flexible rules inevitably have the effect of drawing people in. This is all the more so when European citizenship is also tied to the acquisition of nationality. By means of a flexible nationality law, Belgium is giving European citizenship to foreigners who would not qualify for this in any of our neighbouring countries. Sooner or later this sort of situation is going to add a new argument to the discussion of whether the rights tied to European citizenship can still be made dependent – mainly, if not exclusively – upon the possession of the nationality from one of the Member States.

Chronological table of major reforms in Belgian nationality law since 1945

Date	Document	Content of change
14 December 1932	Royal Decree, Belgian Official Gazette, 17 December 1932 (Koninklijk besluit van 14 december 1932 houdende coördinatie van de wetten op de verwerving, het verlies en de herkrijging van de Belgische nationaliteit, Belgisch Staatsblad 17 december 1932)	Consolidation of nationality laws of 15 May 1922, 4 August 1926, 30 May 1927 and 15 October 1932.
21 May 1951	Law, Belgian Official Gazette, 30 May 1951 (Wet van 21 mei 1951 waarbij bepaald wordt dat alleen het beschikkend gedeelte van sommige vonnissen dient overgeschreven, Belgisch Staatsblad 30 mei 1951)	Directives to registrar concerning final court decision attributing nationality.
30 December 1953	Law, Belgian Official Gazette, 17 January 1954 (Wet van 30 december 1953 betreffende het verval van de Belgische nationaliteit uit hoofde van een veroordeling bij verstek wegens een misdrijf tussen 26 augustus 1939 en 15 juni 1949 tegen de uitwendige veiligheid van de Staat gepleegd, Belgisch Staatsblad 17 januari 1954)	Forfeiture of Belgian nationality because of a conviction by default on the basis of a criminal offence against the safety of the State in the exterior and committed between 26 August 1939 and 15 June 1949.
21 June 1960	Law, Belgian Official Gazette, 30 June 1960 (Wet van 21 juni 1960 houdende statuut van de militairen die tijdens de oorlog 1940-1945 in de Belgische Strijdkrachten in Groot-Brittannië gediend hebben, Belgisch Staatsblad 30 juni 1960)	Special conditions on acquisition of nationality by armed forces in the Second World War.
27 June 1960	Law supplementing the Law of 30 December 1953, Belgian Official Gazette, 12 July 1960 (Wet van 27 juni 1960 ter aanvulling van de wet van 30 december 1953 betreffende het verval van de Belgische nationaliteit uit hoofde van een veroordeling bij verstek, wegens een misdrijf gepleegd tussen 26 augustus 1939 en 15 juni 1949 tegen de uitwendige veiligheid van de Staat, Belgisch Staatsblad 12 juli 1960)	Further specifications on forfeiture of nationality because of a conviction by default on the basis of a criminal offence against the exterior safety of the State committed between 26 August 1939 and 15 June 1949.
22 December 1961	Law, Belgian Official Gazette, 8 January 1962 (Wet van 22	Nationality provisions after independence of the Republic of

Date	Document	Content of change
	december 1961 betreffende de verwerving of herkrijging van de Belgische nationaliteit door de buitenlanders die geboren zijn of hun woonplaats hebben op het grondgebied van de Republiek Congo of door de Congolezen die hun gewone verblijfplaats in België hebben gehad, Belgisch Staatsblad 8 januari 1962)	Congo.
30 March 1962	Law, Belgian Official Gazette, 13 April 1962 (Wet van 30 maart 1962 betreffende het verval van de Belgische nationaliteit ten gevolge van de besluitwet van 20 juni 1945, Belgisch Staatsblad 13 april 1962)	Conditions on reacquisition of nationality after nationality was forfeited (Second World War).
17 March 1964	Law, Belgian Official Gazette, 24 March 1964 (Wet van 17 maart 1964 op de naturalisatie, Belgisch Staatsblad 24 maart 1964)	Modification conditions of naturalisation by a Parliamentary act.
3 December 1964	Law, Belgian Official Gazette, 4 December 1964 (Wet van 3 december 1964 tot wijziging van artikel 4 van de wet van 30 december 1953 betreffende het verval van de Belgische nationaliteit, Belgisch Staatsblad 4 december 1964	Modifications procedure forfeiture of nationality.
2 April 1965	Law, Belgian Official Gazette, 21 April 1965 (Wet van 2 april 1965 tot wijziging van artikel 22 van de op 14 december 1932 gecoördineerde wetten op de verwerving, het verlies en de herkrijging van de nationaliteit, Belgisch Staatsblad 21 april 1965)	Procedure of acquisition of nationality by declaration.
10 October 1967	Law, Belgian Official Gazette, 31 October 1967 (Wet van 10 oktober 1967 houdende het Gerechtelijk Wetboek, Belgisch Staatsblad 31 oktober 1967)	Jurisdiction in nationality cases.
28 June 1984	Law, Belgian Official Gazette, 12 July 1984 (Wet van 28 juni 1984 betreffende sommige aspecten van de toestand van de vreemdelingen en houdende invoering van het Wetboek van de Belgische nationaliteit, Belgisch Staatsblad 12 juli 1984)	Introduction of new nationality Code – simplification acquisition of nationality, especially for second and third generation migrants.
18 July 1984	Royal Decree, Belgian Official Gazette, 4 August 1984 (Koninklijk	Determining the date of entry into force of the Law of 28 June 1984.

Date	Document	Content of change
	besluit van 18 juli 1984 tot vaststelling van de datum van inwerkingtreding van de wet van 28 juni 1984 betreffende sommige aspecten van de toestand van de vreemdelingen en houdende invoering van het Wetboek van de Belgische nationaliteit, Belgisch Staatsblad 4 augustus 1984)	
22 December 1989	Law, Belgian Official Gazette, 29 December 1989 (Wet van 22 december 1989 houdende fiscale bepalingen, Belgisch Staatsblad 29 december 1989)	Naturalisation procedure made more accessible by reducing the costs.
1 February 1991	Constitutional change, Belgian Official Gazette, 15 February 1991 (Grondwetsherziening van 1 februari 1991, Belgisch Staatsblad 15 februari 1991)	Elimination of the distinction between full and ordinary naturalisation.
17 April 1991	Constitutional change, Belgian Official Gazette, 3 May 1991 (Grondwetsherziening van 17 april 1991, Belgisch Staatsblad 3 mei 1991)	Further elimination of the distinction between full and ordinary naturalisation.
22 May 1991	Law, drafted in Strasbourg on 24 November 1977, Belgian Official Gazette, 6 July 1991 (Wet van 22 mei 1991 houdende goedkeuring van volgende Internationale Akten : (1) Overeenkomst betreffende de beperking van gevallen van meervoudige nationaliteit en betreffende militaire verplichtingen in geval van meervoudige nationaliteit, opgemaakt te Straatsburg op 6 mei 1963; (2) Protocol houdende wijziging van de Overeenkomst betreffende de beperking van gevallen van meervoudige nationaliteit en betreffende militaire verplichtingen in geval van meervoudige nationaliteit, opgemaakt te Straatsburg op 24 november 1977; (3) Aanvullend Protocol bij de Overeenkomst betreffende de beperking van gevallen van meervoudige nationaliteit en betreffende militaire verplichtingen in geval van meervoudige nationaliteit, opgemaakt te	Approval of the following International Acts: (1) The agreement concerning the limitation of cases of multiple nationality and concerning the military obligations in case of multiple nationality, drafted in Strasbourg on 6 May 1963; (2) The protocol concerning the alteration of the Agreement concerning the limitation of cases of multiple nationality and concerning the military obligations in case of multiple nationality, drafted in Strasbourg on 24 November 1977; (3) The additional protocol to the agreement concerning the limitation of cases of multiple nationality and concerning the military obligations in case of multiple nationality.

Date	Document	Content of change
	Straatsburg op 24 november 1977, Belgisch Staatsblad 6 juli 1991)	
13 June 1991	Law, Belgian Official Gazette, 3 September 1991 (Wet van 13 juni 1991 tot wijziging van het Wetboek van de Belgische nationaliteit en van de artikelen 569 en 628 van het Gerechtelijk Wetboek)	Simplification of the acquisition of nationality, especially for second and third generation migrants (e.g., acquisition ius soli).
6 August 1993	Law, Belgian Official Gazette, 23 September 1993 (Wet van 6 augustus 1993 tot wijziging van het wetboek van de Belgische nationaliteit en van de wetten betreffende de naturalisatie, Belgisch Staatsblad 23 september 1993)	Adaptation Code to Constitutional changes of 1991 – tightening regulation nationality acquisition after marriage.
17 February 1994	Coordinated Constitution, Belgian Official Gazette, 17 February 1994 (Gecoördineerde Grondwet van 17 februari 1994, Belgisch Staatsblad 17 februari 1994)	Insertion part 'Belgians and their rights' and principle of equal protection of foreigners and Belgians.
13 April 1995	Law, Belgian Official Gazette, 10 June 1995 (Wet van 13 april 1995 tot wijziging van de naturalisatieprocedure en van het Wetboek van de Belgische nationaliteit, Belgisch Staatsblad 10 juni 1995)	Change of the naturalisation procedure: sole competence of House of Representatives.
13 December 1995	Royal Decree, Belgian Official Gazette, 16 December 1995 and 20 January 1996 (Koninklijk besluit van 13 december 1995 tot bepaling van de inhoud van het aanvraagformulier inzake naturalisatie en de bij het verzoek om naturalisatie en bij de nationaliteitsverklaring te voegen akten en stavingstukken en tot vaststelling van de datum van inwerkingtreding van de wet van 13 april 1995 tot wijziging van de naturalisatieprocedure en van het Wetboek van de Belgische nationaliteit, Belgisch Staatsblad 16 december 1995 en 20 januari 1996)	Determining the contents of the application form concerning naturalisation and the documents and substantiates to be added to the application and determining the date of entry into force of the Law of 13 April 1995 changing the naturalisation procedure and the Code on Belgian nationality.
22 December 1998	Law, Belgian Official Gazette, 6 March 1999, ed. 2 (Wet van 22 december 1998 tot wijziging van het Wetboek van de Belgische nationaliteit wat de	Different modes of acquisition simplified and harmonised.

Date	Document	Content of change
	naturalisatieprocedure betreft, Belgisch Staatsblad 6 maart 1998, ed. 2)	
13 June 1999	Royal Decree, Belgian Official Gazette, 3 August 1999 (Koninklijk besluit van 13 juni 1999 tot wijziging, wat betreft de bijlage, van het koninklijk besluit van 13 december 1995 tot bepaling van de inhoud van het aanvraagformulier inzake naturalisatie en de bij het verzoek te voegen akten en stavingsstukken en tot vaststelling van de datum van inwerkingtreding van de wet van 13 april 1995 tot wijziging van de naturalisatieprocedure en van het Wetboek van de Belgische nationaliteit, Belgisch Staatsblad 3 augustus 1999)	Changes to the Royal Decree of 13 December 1995.
1 March 2000	Law, Belgian Official Gazette, 6 April 2000, ed. 2 (Wet van 1 maart 2000 tot wijziging van een aantal bepalingen betreffende de Belgische nationaliteit, Belgisch Staatsblad 6 april 2000, ed. 2)	Radical simplification of nationality acquisition (elimination of integration test, reduction of demanded residence in Belgium, introduction of free naturalisation procedure).
16 April 2000	Royal Decree, Belgian Official Gazette, 27 April 2000 (Koninklijk besluit van 16 april 2000 tot wijziging van het koninklijk besluit van 13 december 1995 tot bepaling van de inhoud van het aanvraagformulier inzake naturalisatie en de bij het verzoek te voegen akten en stavingstukken en tot vaststelling van de datum van inwerkingtreding van de wet van 13 april 1995 tot wijziging van de naturalisatieprocedure en van het Wetboek van de Belgische nationaliteit, Belgisch Staatsblad 27 april 2000)	Changing the Royal Decree of 13 December 1995.
4 October 2000	Royal Decree, Belgian Official Gazette, 24 October 2000 (Koninklijk besluit van 4 oktober 2000 tot wijziging van het koninklijk besluit van 13 december 1995 tot bepaling van de inhoud van het aanvraagformulier inzake naturalisatie en de bij het verzoek om naturalisatie en bij de	Changes to the Royal Decree of 13 December 1995.

Date	Document	Content of change
	nationaliteitsverklaring te voegen akten en stavingstukken en tot vaststelling van de datum van inwerkingtreding van de wet van 13 april 1995 tot wijziging van de naturalisatieprocedure en van het Wetboek van de Belgische nationaliteit, Belgisch Staatsblad 24 oktober 2000)	
27 December 2004	Law, Belgian Official Gazette, 31 December 2004, ed. 2 (Programmawet van 27 december 2004, Belgisch Staatsblad 31 december 2004, ed. 2)	Main residence (art. 12bis, para. 1 CBN) must be covered by legal residence.

Notes

1 Law of 28 June 1984 dealing with certain aspects of the requirements for foreigners and the introduction of the Code of Belgian Nationality (hereafter named Code of Nationality, Code or 'CBN'), *Belgian Official Gazette*, 12 July 1984.

2 Law of 13 June 1991 changing the Code on Belgian Nationality and art. 569 and 628 of the Judicial Code, *Belgian Official Gazette*, 3 September 1991.

3 Law of 1 March 2000 modifying a series of provisions relating to Belgian nationality, *Belgian Official Gazette*, 6 April 2000.

4 Law of 15 December 1980 concerning access to the territory, residence, establishment and removal of foreigners, *Belgian Official Gazette*, 31 December 1980 as amended. Hereafter named 'law on residence of foreigners'.

5 At the end of May 2006, the Belgian government approved a draft law which gives an answer to a number of points of criticism we raise in this article as well as filling in a number of lacunae. Since at the time when this article was completed the draft law was not yet definitive, we decided not to include its contents in the main body of the text, but rather to refer to it in the notes systematically as 'draft law of 2006'.
As regards art. 23, the draft law provides the possibility for a Belgian citizen to lose his or her nationality not only in case of serious violations of the obligations of a Belgian citizen, but also in cases of fraud, deceit or false statements.

6 Only art. 9 was repealed.

7 A distinction was then made between ordinary and full naturalisation, whereby only the latter conferred the right to enjoy all political rights. This distinction would remain in effect until the amendment of the Constitution in 1991.

8 In this regard, see especially the laws of 27 September 1935 and of 6 and 7 August 1881 concerning naturalisation. The law of 1 April 1879 determined the period of time after which nationality by option could be granted (art. 9).

9 Law of 15 August 1981 attributing Belgian nationality to children born in Belgium of legally unknown parents, *Belgian Official Gazette*, 18 August 1881.

10 Law of 21 June 1865, *Belgian Official Gazette*, 24 June 1865, and Law of 25 March 1894 concerning acquisition of Belgian nationality, *Belgian Official Gazette*, 1 April 1894.

11 Law of 11 July 1869 approving the Convention concluded at Brussels on 16 November 1868 between Belgium and the United States of America to regulate the nationality of migrants and military service, *Belgian Official Gazette*, 15 July 1869; Law of 30 December 1891 approving the Convention between Belgium and France of 30 July 1891 concerning military service, *Belgian Official Gazette*, 30 January 1892; Law of 19 May 1898 approving the article added to the declaration signed on 11 December 1897 and concluded on 15 January 1898 between Belgium and Portugal concerning military service, *Belgian Official Gazette*, 30 July 1898.

12 Other laws were, on the other hand, retained, such as the law of 6 August 1881 on naturalisation.

13 These laws were published in the *Belgian Official Gazette*, respectively on 9 and 10 August 1926, on 4 June 1927 and on 4 December 1932.

14 *Belgian Official Gazette*, 17 December 1932.

15 Children born out of wedlock.

16 The CBN no longer grants Belgian nationality in all cases to a Belgian parent's child. Distinctions are made depending on whether or not the child or its parent was born in Belgium.

17 Especially through the attribution of Belgian nationality to a child born to a Belgian mother and a foreign father (see 2.3.1.1).

18 The concept of being 'Belgian by birth' was, however, suppressed by the law of 6 August 1993 because it had become largely irrelevant: at that time the Parliament had already approved two amendments to the Constitution that removed the difference between full and ordinary naturalisation (see 2.3.1.1).

19 Law of 13 June 1991 changing the Code on Belgian nationality and art. 569 and 628 of the Judicial Code, *Belgian Official Gazette*, 3 September 1991; Law of 6 August 1993 changing the Code on Belgian nationality and the Law regarding naturalisation, *Belgian Official Gazette*, 23 September 1993; Law of 13 April 1995 changing the naturalisation procedure and the Code on Belgian nationality, *Belgian Official Gazette*, 10 June 1995; Law of 22 December 1998 changing the naturalisation procedure of Code on Belgian nationality, *Belgian Official Gazette*, 6 March 1999, ed. 2 and Law of 1 March 2000 changing certain provisions regarding Belgian nationality, *Belgian Official Gazette*, 6 April 2000, ed. 2.

20 The same underlying philosophy is also maintained in the draft law of 2006 (see note 46).

21 In order to prevent fraudulent use of this possibility, the draft law of 2006 (see note 5) provides that Belgium nationality will only be granted if the child's statelessness does not result from the parents' unwillingness to have the child registered with the diplomatic or consular representatives in the country of ordinary residence.

22 The draft law of 2006 (see note 5) foresees that only the years of residence covered by a permit for an unlimited period count towards the ten years.

23 European Court of Human Rights, 13 June 1979, www.curia.eu.int. However, Closset states that the Code creates an inequality among children from another point of view: the law had not previously made any distinction in the modes of acquisition of Belgian nationality by right of birth according to the place of birth. The present Code makes such a distinction (art. 8 and 9 CBN) and children born in Belgium now enjoy Belgian nationality under more flexible conditions than those born abroad (Closset 2004: 99).

24 Only the biological parent(s) is (are) concerned. In case of adoption by a Belgian parent, the procedure of acquisition by option has to be followed.

25 The different sorts of residence permits are: authorisation to settle, authorisation or permission to stay for an unlimited duration, or authorisation or permission to stay for a limited duration.

26 Chamber of Representatives 1999-2000, Parl. St. 0292/001 and 0293/001, 10-11.
27 *Belgian Official Gazette*, 6 May 2000.
28 Court of Cassation, 16 January 2004, www.cass.be.
29 *Belgian Official Gazette*, 31 December 2004, ed. 2.
30 Court of Cassation, 20 June 2005, www.cass.be.
31 In order to avoid all misunderstanding, the draft law of 2006 (see note 5) limits main residence to the cases in which the person concerned holds a valid residence permit for a limited or unlimited period, other than for a short stay.
32 The draft law of 2006 (see note 5) provides for an extension of this deadline of one month, which in practice has proven impracticable (see note 65).
33 The term 'important facts pertaining to the individual applicant' was explained in the Circular letter of 6 August 1984 (*Belgian Official Gazette*, 14 August 1984) and in the Circular letter of 8 November 1991 (*Belgian Official Gazette*, 7 December 1991). In the Circular letter of 20 July 2000 (*Belgian Official Gazette*, 27 July 2000, ed. 2) the Minister of Justice recalled the fact that 'not every criminal conviction constitutes an important fact pertaining to the individual applicant. Thus if a conviction happened a long time ago, involved a minor offence, or if there were any mitigating circumstances, this may mean that the conviction is not considered serious enough to affect an individual's application. Conversely, an impediment may exist even without any criminal conviction: for example, if the person has previously received an expulsion order from the Belgian territory. Similarly, acts of serious delinquency – whether or not a person has been convicted for them – violations of state security, terrorist activities, espionage or pronounced refusal to live by the Belgian laws can serve as grounds for refusal. Furthermore, a foreign conviction can also be taken into account.'
34 A period of residence abroad can possibly be given the same consideration as residence in Belgium, if the foreigner demonstrates that he or she retained real ties to Belgium during the time required by the law (art. 19 CBN).
35 In the context of the procedures of acquisition of nationality by declaration (art. 12bis CBN) or by option (art. 15 CBN), the case can also be converted into an application for naturalisation before the Chamber of Representatives if the public prosecutor gives a negative advice and if the foreigner does not initiate a judicial appeal against this negative advice.
36 On this deadline and the amendments as foreseen by the draft law of 2006 (see note 5), see note 65.
37 Circular letter of 25 April 2000 concerning the law of 1 March 2000, *Belgian Official Gazette*, 6 May 2000. Concerning the respect of the deadline also see 2.3.2.2.
38 The right to vote was granted after the modification of the Electoral Code by the law of 5 July 1976. The persons who were not 'Belgian by birth' or by full naturalisation remained however excluded from the following political rights: the right to be a minister or a secretary of state; a deputy, a senator; a member of the Flemish Council, of the Council of the French-speaking Community and the Walloon Regional Council; a member of the Flemish Executive or the Executive of the French-speaking Community or the Executive of the Walloon Region; or a member of a provincial council (see respectively: art. 86 and 91bis (old) Constitution; art. 50 (old) Constitution and art. 223 of the electoral Code currently repealed; art. 56 (old) Constitution and art. 224 of the Code of Elections currently repealed; art. 24 of the special law of 8 August 1980 on institutional reforms; art. 23 of the organic law of 19 October 1921 concerning the provincial elections).
39 Amendment to the Constitution of 1 February 1991, *Belgian Official Gazette*, 15 February 1991 (suppression of art. 5 para.2; modification of art. 50 and 86 relating to eligibility for the Chamber of Representatives and ministerial offices); amendment to the

Constitution of 17 April 1991, *Belgian Official Gazette*, 3 May 1991 (modification of art. 56 relating to eligibility for senator).

40 Judgement of the Constitutional Court (Arbitragehof) n° 75/98 of 24 June 1998.

41 Law of 13 February 2003 making marriage to persons of the same sex possible and changing a number of provisions of the Civil Code, *Belgian Official Gazette*, 28 February 2003.

42 The one-year deadline will be extended to the age of nineteen if the target person was a minor when it was ascertained that he or she was not Belgian.

43 A person who lost Belgian nationality as a result of it being declared forfeit, can only reacquire it through naturalisation by a parliamentary act.

44 Proposal of Mahoux and Istasse, Doc.parl.Senate., extr. sess. 2003, n° 3-11/1; Proposal of Roelants du Vivier, Doc. parl. Senate., extr. sess. 2003, n° 3-42/1; Proposal of de Bethune, Doc. parl. Senate., extr. sess. 2003, n° 3-146/1; Proposal of Milquet and Viseur, Doc. parl. Ch.Repr., extr. sess. 2003, n° 510061/004; Proposal of Collard and Bellot, Doc.parl.Ch.Repr., extr. sess. 2003, n° 510105/001.
The asymmetry between the prohibition against retaining the first (Belgian) nationality and the absence of that prohibition if the first nationality is a foreign one and therefore does not present an obstacle to obtaining Belgian nationality, will be rectified in the application of the draft law of 2006 (see note 5). Henceforth, Belgians will also be allowed to obtain a foreign nationality without thereby automatically losing their Belgian nationality.

45 The requirement of renewing the declaration is eliminated in the draft law of 2006 (see note 5).

46 Chamber of Representatives, Questions and answers: Question n° 46 of 22 September 1999, QRVA 50 006, DO 0000199950254; Question n° 463 of 3 December 2004, QRVA 51 063, 10177, DO 20042005002806. Senate, Questions and answers: Question n° 3-929 of 19 October 2004, QRVA1593. The absence of a legal provision that punishes cases of fraud, deceit or false statements with the loss of Belgian nationality is remedied in the draft law of 2006 (see note 5). If the bill is approved, foreigners who are guilty of any of these acts may, even without serious breach of their obligations as Belgian citizens, lose their nationality.

47 Chamber of Representatives 1999-2000, Parl. St.,plen. 034, 11 and 31-32.

48 From the statistics made available by the Naturalisation Commission of the Chamber of Representatives concerning the applications for naturalisation since the coming into force of the law of 13 April 1995 which changed the procedure, it does indeed appear that since that time no less than 45 per cent of the applications adjourned were on grounds of insufficient integration.

49 The situation will change once the amendments contained in the draft law of 2006 come into effect, for they also punish fraud, deceit and false statements (see also notes 5, 62 and 87).

50 Art. 10 of the Constitution states that all Belgians are 'equal before the law'. This being said, the status of all Belgians is not identical in every respect: some categories continue to be subject to special rules: Belgians of foreign origin can, for instance, in times of war be the object of special measures restricting their rights.

51 *Belgian Official Gazette*, 15 December 1998.

52 Law of 19 March 2004 granting the right to vote at the municipal elections to foreigners, *Belgian Official Gazette*, 23 April 2004. The Law of 23 December 2005 specifying various provisions, *Belgian Official Gazette*, 30 December 2005, 2nd edition, states explicitly that the condition regarding principal residence should be understood as meaning 'legal main residence'.

53 The draft law of 2006 (see footnote 5) stipulates that parties will have to prove that they remained in contact with each other. The draft law provides that in this respect a declaration by the parent who has obtained Belgian nationality would be sufficient.

54 The preparatory stages of the law of 2000 indicate that the legislators wished in this way to rule out sham adoptions: 'Abuses of the procedures would indeed be a risk if adoption by a Belgian was in itself sufficient to allow a foreigner adopted as an adult by a Belgian to become a Belgian by declaration' (Doc. Parl. Chambre, 1999, n° 50-0292/001, 10).

55 Judgement of the Constitutional Court n° 93/2005 of 25 May 2005. The Constitutional Court also noted, however, that: 'B.3. It is true that the option offered to an adult foreigner born abroad, and who has at least one parent who at the time of the declaration holds Belgian nationality, to acquire Belgian nationality subject only to the conditions of Article 12bis, §1, 2°, is not justified if one compares his or her situation to that of other categories of foreigners mentioned in the preliminary question and who are required to have their principal residence in Belgium. Nevertheless, it is up to the legislator to put an end to this discrepancy.' In the draft law of 2006 (see footnote 5), the discrepancy is eliminated by extending the provision of art. 12bis, para. 1, 2° to children born in Belgium and to foreigners adopted by Belgians. For the latter category, this would apply on condition that the adoption took place while the child was a minor, in order to avoid sham adoptions.

56 The draft law of 2006 does not make any change to this inconsistency. On the contrary, article 12bis, para. 1, 2° is extended in its scope to (adult) foreigners born in Belgium and (adult) foreigners adopted by one or two Belgians.

57 Law of 16 July 2004 concerning the code of private international law, *Belgian Official Gazette*, 27 July 2004.

58 On the other hand, there would also be a violation of Belgian international private law if every reference to the place of residence (e.g., birth on the territory of the person concerned or of a reference person) were eliminated while determining someone's nationality.

59 Decree of 28 February 2003 on the Flemish integration policy, *Belgian Official Gazette*, 8 May 2003. On 19 May 2006 the Flemish government submitted a draft decree to parliament amending the Decree of 18 February 2003 (Item 850 [2005-2006] – No. 1). The intention of the proposal is to define the target group more clearly and more broadly: All newcomers – with the exception of non-Belgian EU citizens – who wish to settle permanently in Flanders, as well as certain already-established groups of immigrants, will be required to follow a training programme.

60 In 1992, 60 per cent of the foreigners who acquired nationality by registration seemed to be former EU nationals.

61 It is significant that, in 1993, of the 16,000 persons who became Belgian, more than 9,000 were former Turkish or Moroccan nationals.

62 Global statistics for the year 2006 are, however, not yet available.

63 Respectively the Flemish, Walloon and Brussels regions and the Flemish, French and German-speaking communities.

64 Art. 5 para. 1, II, 33 Special law of 8 August 1980 reforming the institutions, *Belgian Official Gazette*, 15 August 1980.

65 The draft law of 2006 takes into account the difficulty in practice of honouring this very short deadline of one month. If the amendments are approved, the deadline will be extended to four months. In order to ensure that this extension does not clash with the interests of the foreigner, the bill also stipulates that the deadline must be calculated at the latest from the date the file is submitted.

66 See note 65.

67 The law combating discrimination, amending the law of 15 February 1993 and creating a Centre which monitors the equality of opportunities and the fight against racism was adopted, *Belgian Official Gazette*, 17 March 2003.

Bibliography

Alen, A. (1995), *Handboek van het Belgisch Staatsrecht*. Deurne: Kluwer Rechtswetenschappen België.

Bietlot, M., F. Caestecker, F. Hardeman & A. Rea (2002), 'Evaluation de l'application de la loi du 1er mars 2000', in M.-C. Foblets, R. Foqué & M. Verwilghen (eds.), *Naar de Belgische nationaliteit / Devenir Belge*, 147-186. Brussels/Antwerp: Bruylant/Maklu.

Caestecker, F., M. Bietlot, F. Hardeman & A. Rea (2001), *Effectivité et efficience de la loi sur la nationalité du 1er mars 2000*. www.ulb.ac.be.

Carlier, J.-Y. & S. Goffin (1996), 'Le droit belge de la nationalité', in B. Nascimbene (ed.), *Le droit de la nationalité dans l'Union européenne / Nationality Laws in the European Union*, 95-167. London : Butterworths.

Closset, C.-L. (1984), *Nationalité et statut personnel*. Brussels: Bruylant.

Closset, C.-L. (2004), *Traité de la nationalité en droit belge*. Brussels: Larcier.

De Decker, M. & M. Suykerbuyk (1993), 'Nationaliteit en integratiewil', in *Recht en verdraagzaamheid in de multiculturele samenleving*, 283-302. Antwerp/Apeldoorn: Maklu.

De Groot, G.-R. (2004), 'Ontwikkelingen inzake het nationaliteitsrecht in Europa', in J. Meeusen, M.-C. Foblets & B. Hubeau (eds.), *Migratie- en Migrantenrecht. Deel 10*, 323-365. Bruges: Die Keure.

De Moffarts, G. (1987), 'Betekenis van de "integratiewil" in het Wetboek van de Belgische nationaliteit', *Tijdschrift voor Vreemdelingenrecht* 43: 27-31.

De Moffarts, G. (1995), 'L'option de nationalité, la "volonté d'intégration" et la connaissance de la langue de la région', *Revue du droit des étrangers* 84: 311-312.

De Valkeneer, R. (1984), 'Condition des étrangers et Code de la nationalité belge', *Revue du notariat belge* 2739: 389-419.

D'Hondt, S. (2002), 'Het integratiecriterium: hoe is de toets aan de integratie geregeld in de wetgeving van de Europese lidstaten?', in M.C. Foblets, R. Foqué & M. Verwilghen (eds.), *Naar de Belgische nationaliteit / Devenir Belge*, 245-293. Brussels/Antwerp: Bruylant/Maklu.

Dumon, W. & G. Adriaensens (1989), *OCDE – Système d'observation permanente de migrations Belgique 1990*. Leuven: Sociologisch Onderzoeksinstituut (S.O.I.).

Erauw, J. (2002), 'De nationaliteit en de toepassing van de nationale wet van de persoon', in M.-C. Foblets, R. Foqué & M. Verwilghen (eds.), *Naar de Belgische nationaliteit / Devenir Belge*, 411-441. Brussels/Antwerp: Bruylant/Maklu.

Foblets, M.-C. (2000-2001), 'Een nieuw nationaliteitsrecht? De Wet van 1 maart 2000 tot wijziging van een aantal bepalingen betreffende de Belgische nationaliteit', *Rechtskundig Weekblad* 31: 1145-1165.

Foblets, M.-C. (2003), 'Le parcours mouvementé du Code de la nationalité belge: rétrospective (1985-2003)', *Annales de droit de Louvain* 63: 259-276.

Foblets, M.-C., R. Foqué & M. Verwilghen (eds.) (2002), *Naar de Belgische nationaliteit / Devenir Belge*. Brussels/Antwerp: Bruylant/Maklu.

Fulchiron, H. (2005), 'La responsabilité parentale dans l'espace européen', inD. Gadbin & F. Kernalguen (eds.), *Le statut juridique de l'enfant dans l'espace européen*: 173-188. Antwerp: Bruylant.

Gérard, P.A. (1859), *Code civil expliqué par la jurisprudence des cours et tribunaux en Belgique et à l'étranger*. Brussels : Libr. Rozez.

Guillain, C. (2002), 'La Loi du 1 mars modifiant certaines dispositions relatives à la nationalité belge: un nouveau pas vers la citoyenneté?', *Revue du droit des étrangers* 120: 603-616.

Heyvaert, A. (1986), *De Belgische nationaliteit. Korte commentaar op het Wetboek van de Belgische nationaliteit.* Antwerpen: Kluwer rechtswetenschappen.

Lambein, K. (1991-1992), 'De wet van 13 juni 1991 tot wijziging van het Wetboek van de Belgische nationaliteit', *Rechtskundig Weekblad* 16: 548-550.

Lambein, K. (1993), 'De nationaliteit', in *Overzicht van rechtspraak (1985-1992). Internationaal privaatrecht en nationaliteitsrecht, Tijdschrift voor privaatrecht* 2: 513-669.

Liénard-Ligny, M (1984-1985), 'À propos du Code de la nationalité belge', *Revue belge de droit international* 2: 649-671.

Liénard-Ligny, M (1985), 'Nationalité belge et statut personnel depuis la loi du 28 juin 1984', *Annales de droit de Liège* 2: 195-236.

Liénard-Ligny, M (1991), 'Nationalité belge: les lois de 1991', *Revue du droit des étrangers* 65: 325-335.

Louis, B. (1995), 'La nationalité et la citoyenneté à l'aune des droits de l'homme. À propos de quelques propositions de loi', *Revue du droit des étrangers* 82: 14-27.

Maeckelberghe, J. (1989), 'L'officier de l'état civil face aux nouvelles législations engendrées par l'évolution du droit familial: Le Code de la nationalité belge', *Mouvement communal*: 146-161.

Marescaux, M-H. & M. Taverne (1984), 'Le droit des étrangers, moteur du Code de la nationalité', *Journal des tribunaux* 5312: 625-636.

Meeusen, J. (1997), *Nationalisme en internationalisme in het internationaal privaatrecht : analyse van het Belgische conflictenrecht.* Antwerpen: Intersentia.

Mignon, E. (1989a), 'L'acquisition de la nationalité belge: quelques remarques sur l'application du Code de la nationalité belge 4 années après son entrée en vigueur', *Revue du droit des étrangers* 53: 67-71.

Mignon, E. (1989b), 'Verwerven van de Belgische nationaliteit: enkele bemerkingen bij de toepassing van het nieuwe nationaliteitswetboek, 4 jaar na de inwerkingtreding', *Tijdschrift voor Vreemdelingenrecht* 56: 26-33.

Nuyts, D. (2001), 'Nationaliteit', *Administratieve wegwijzer Vreemdelingen, Vluchtelingen, Migranten* 2003: 195-279.

Poulain, M. (1994), *Migrations internationales, migrations en Belgique* (1993). Rapport SOPEMI 1994. Louvain-la-Neuve: UCL.

Renauld, B. (2005), 'Le Code de la nationalité belge. Présentation synthétique et développements récents', in J.-Y. Carlier & S. Saroléa (eds.), *Droit des étrangers et nationalité*, 9-75. Brussels: Larcier.

Sluys, E. (1991), 'Het gerechtelijk toezicht op de nationaliteitskeuze', *Tijdschrift voor privaatrecht* 4: 1089-1137.

Stockx, R. (2000), 'De snel-Belg-wet of de Wet van 1 maart 2000 tot wijziging van een aantal bepalingen betreffende de Belgische nationaliteit', *Administratieve wegwijzer Vreemdelingen, Vluchtelingen, Migranten* 71: 68-81.

Van de Putte, M. & J. Clement (2000), *Bevoegdheidsverdeling in het federale België.* Bruges: Die Keure.

Verhellen, J. (1998), 'De nationaliteit', in *Overzicht van rechtspraak. Internationaal privaatrecht en nationaliteitsrecht (1993-1998), Tijdschrift voor privaatrecht* 4: 1378-1389.

Verschueren, H. (1995), 'De ontwikkelingen in de Belgische nationaliteitswetgeving belicht vanuit het Europese en internationale recht', in K. De Feyter, M.-Cl. Foblets & B. Hubeau (eds.), *Migratie- en Migrantenrecht. Deel 1*, 241-263. Bruges: Die Keure.

Verwilghen, M. (1980), 'Conflits de lois relatifs à la protection de la personne des mineurs', *Revue trimestrielle de droit familial* 1: 5-51.

Verwilghen, M. (1984), 'Nationalité et statut personnel dans les projets de réforme du droit de la nationalité belge', in M. Verwilghen (ed.), *Nationalité et statut personnel*, 351-441. Brussel/Paris: Bruylant/L.G.D.J.

Verwilghen, M. (1985), *Le code de la nationalité belge*. Brussels: Bruylant.

Verwilghen, M. (1992), 'Le nouveau visage de la nationalité belge', *Journal des tribunaux* 5615 : 2-12.

Walleyn, L. (1989), 'Nationaliteitskeuze en beoordeling van de integratiewil', *Tijdschrift voor Vreemdelingenrecht* 55: 43.

3 Denmark

Eva Ersbøll

3.1 Introduction

Unlike many other European countries, Denmark did not reform its nationality law at the beginning of the new millennium, and Denmark has not followed the European trends in nationality law of facilitating naturalisation, extending entitlement to nationality, accepting multiple nationality and introducing ius soli elements into its nationality law. Far from providing for easier access to nationality, Denmark has made the conditions for the acquisition of nationality stricter over the last six years. Existing nationality legislation is generally based on Danish nationality traditions.

Danish nationality law has its origin in political conditions, which go back to the eighteenth century. Foreigners, especially Germans, at the time had a strong influence in the state administration which in 1776 made the Danish autocratic King promulgate an act on *Indfødsret* or *Ius Indigenatus* according to which access to public positions in the Kingdom became the prerogative of native-born subjects and those who were considered equal to them.

The Act on *Indfødsret* was not a nationality law in the current sense of the word, but it had many of the characteristics of a nationality law. The acquisition of the status of 'native-born' was, in principle, based on ius soli, but soon ius sanguinis became important, as only children born on the state's territory of Danish parents acquired *indfødsret* at birth, while children born on the territory of alien parents had to remain in the Danish Kingdom in order to fulfil the acquisition criteria. The only way for immigrants to acquire a status equal to that of native-born people was through naturalisation by the King.

When Denmark became a democracy in 1849, the King lost his exclusive authority to grant naturalisation, as the Constitution stated aliens could only henceforth acquire *indfødsret (ius indigenatus)* by statute. Around this time, *indfødsret* was increasingly seen as a citizenship or nationality concept, as political rights became attached to this status.

Apart from its provisions on naturalisation, the 1776 Act was in force until 1898, when Denmark adopted its first general nationality law: The Law on the Acquisition and Loss of *Indfødsret*. The law changed the fundamental acquisition principle from ius soli to ius sanguinis. A nationality law reform took place in 1925 and again in 1950, when gender equality was introduced as a principle (some inequality still exists even today, as only children with a Danish mother and not children with a Danish father acquire Danish nationality *ex lege* at birth, if they are born abroad and out of wedlock). The nationality law in force at present is the 1950 Act, although amended several times, especially over the last ten years.

Since the late 1890s, Danish nationality law has been based on Nordic cooperation. Until recently, the Nordic nationality laws have been almost identical. The differences regarding naturalisation stem to a large extent from the Danish constitutional requirement on aliens' acquisition of Danish nationality by statute, which means that decisions on naturalisation are made by the legislative power in acts granting nationality, mentioning each of the applicants by name etc.

The end of Nordic homogeneity regarding nationality law has, among other things, been triggered by some of the Nordic countries' changed attitudes on the toleration of multiple nationality. Traditionally, all Nordic countries disapproved of this status; nationals lost their nationality in cases of voluntary acquisition of another nationality and in cases of naturalisation, applicants were normally required to renounce their former nationality. However, since toleration of multiple nationality was made acceptable by the 1997 European Convention on Nationality, Sweden, Finland and Iceland have reformed their nationality laws and introduced toleration of multiple nationality as the main principle, while Denmark has strongly rejected changing its traditionally negative attitude towards this status.

Denmark has also responded differently in other respects to new challenges stemming from globalisation and immigration by, among other things, increasing its already relatively high barriers to naturalisation. Thus, Denmark is the only Nordic country with a general residence requirement of nine years (eight years for refugees and stateless persons) and a conduct requirement excluding aliens from naturalisation on a permanent basis (in so far as they have been sentenced to imprisonment for eighteen months or more). The Danish language requirements have also been made more stringent, first in June 2002 and later in December 2005. The effect was a sharp fall in the number of naturalisations from 2002 to 2003, and a comparable fall is to be expected in 2007 when the new language requirements begin to apply. The fall may even be sharper due to a new provision according to which applicants for naturalisation must be self-supporting in the sense that they cannot have received social benefits for more than an aggregate period of one year within the last five.

The high barriers to naturalisation for long-term immigrants do not apply to nationals from the Nordic countries. Traditionally, Denmark has facilitated the acquisition of nationality for Nordic nationals. In the aftermath of the Second World War, the Nordic countries discussed the introduction of a common Nordic citizenship; however the issue was set aside for more urgent matters. Instead, a Nordic agreement was concluded, entitling nationals from the Nordic countries to privileged acquisition of nationality through notification/declaration and facilitated naturalisation. Today, the residence requirement for naturalisation of Nordic nationals is two years, and since 2004, only second-generation immigrants from other Nordic countries can be granted Danish nationality by entitlement.

Ethnically, Denmark has had a homogeneous population since 1864, and even though the country has now, like other European countries, become a country of immigration, it has not identified itself as such. On the other hand, Denmark has not given much consideration to its own emigrants either, and the approximately 25,000 Danes who have emigrated annually over the last fifteen years have also faced some problems.

One problem has been a lack of voting rights in Danish parliamentary elections due to a Danish constitutional condition requiring residence in Denmark. Expatriates have tried to have the interpretation of the residence requirement softened through the political system, but so far it has been the general understanding that an amendment of the constitution is necessary in order to extend expatriates' electoral rights.

Another problem has been the legislative barriers for expatriates wishing to settle in Denmark with their foreign families due to an amendment of the Danish Aliens Act in 2002. The purpose of the act was to curb immigrants' rights to family reunification with spouses from their country of origin, however, based on the consideration that many immigrants have acquired Danish nationality, the law was changed, and Danish nationals as well as non-nationals had to meet the same requirements: among others, in order to settle in Denmark with a foreign spouse, the couple's aggregate ties to Denmark had to be stronger than the couple's aggregate ties to another country. This 'attachment requirement' prevented many expatriates from resettling in Denmark with their foreign families. Strong public criticism of the arrangement forced the government to change the law again in 2004 and since then, Danish nationals who have held Danish nationality for 28 years or more no longer have to fulfil the attachment requirement. The amendment has, however, created a new problem of discrimination among Danish nationals, depending on the length of time they have been nationals.

The fact that Danish nationality law has the highest barriers for naturalisation among the Nordic countries may not only be a matter of Danish history and tradition but may also be because of the special Danish procedural arrangement for naturalisation and the fact that criteria for naturalisation are not adopted by law, but negotiated and agreed upon in camera by political parties representing a majority in Parliament. Making naturalisation criteria a matter of agreement between political parties may have curbed more in-depth considerations on the meaning of nationality and its influence on immigrants' integration into Danish society.

3.2 Historical development

3.2.1 Pre-constitutional time

The Danish state has been a Kingdom since approximately 900 A.D. Due to its favourable geopolitical position at the entrance to the Baltic Sea, the Danish monarchy was able to exercise hegemony over Northern Europe since the late middle ages. The Danish state has been described as a composite state stretching from the North Cape to Hamburg. However, in the middle of the seventeenth century, Denmark lost its hegemony over Northern Europe to the newly established Swedish empire around the Baltic (Østergaard 2000: 147).

In 1660, the Estates handed over the realm as a kingdom of inheritance to the King, and an absolute monarchy came into being. The Royal Act of 1665 allowed the King to freely choose his 'servants'. Those of noble birth lost their privileges, and the King invited foreigners, especially German aristocrats, to serve as high officials in order to exclude the Danish nobility from re-gaining political influence. In the eighteenth century, public discontent with the German influence in state administration erupted. A growing nationalism was fuelled by J. F. Struensee's regime from 1770-1772. Struensee was German speaking and considered a foreigner, and he ruled the country via his cabinet orders on behalf of the King. After his regime was brought down, a Danish-minded government became a necessity and the Act on *Indfødsret* (*Ius Indigenatus*) supported Danish national politics.

The title of the 1776 Act was 'Indfødss-Retten, according to which all public positions in his Majesty's Kingdom are exclusively reserved for native-born subjects and those who are respected as equal to them'. In the preamble, the arrangement was reasoned by fairness: it was considered reasonable and fair that 'the children of the country should enjoy the bread of the country and that the advantages of the state should fall to the lot of its citizens'. For the first time, the subjects of the state were acknowledged as the citizens of the state. It is worth noting, however, that the *Indfødsret* Act was not Danish as such, as the Danish state at that time consisted of the Kingdoms of Denmark and Norway and the duchies of Schleswig and Holstein,[1] and all residents in the multinational state were considered the King's subjects.

The aim of the act was to secure public positions for native-born subjects. Therefore, the first section of the act stated that in order to obtain a public position, a person should be born in the states or born to native-born parents who were travelling or serving the King abroad. However, public positions could also be offered to those who were considered equal to native-born people, especially those who served the King and wealthy estate owners. In order to achieve such an equal status, a letter of naturalisation was required from the King.

The legal status of foreigners and their children was otherwise regulated in sect. 9 of the act. According to this provision, all foreigners who were not considered equal to native-born persons (through naturalisation) would have the same freedom to reside and work in the Kingdom and the same protection by the government as formerly. Furthermore, it was established that foreigners' 'children who are born in the Danish State one and all shall be respected and regarded completely as native-born if they remain in the State'. This provision was, after a while, interpreted as limiting the ius soli principle in the first section of the act such that only children born of native-born parents acquired *indfødsret* at birth. For other children, the acquisition was conditional upon their staying in the country. It seems fair to suggest that all children born in the territory were considered native-born, but children born of foreign parents would only acquire the rights attached to the status if they remained in the realm; if, eventually, this condition was not fulfilled, the *ius indigenatus* would lapse.

3.2.2 *The first Danish Constitution, 1849*

During the Napoleonic wars, Denmark-Norway and Sweden were on opposite sides. After Napoleon's defeat, the Danish King was, as a result of his alliance with Napoleon, compelled to cede Norway to Sweden in 1814; 'in return' for Norway, the King received the Duchy of Lauenburg. This altered the balance between the Nordic and the German populations in the composite state. With the duchies, Schleswig and Holstein and Lauenburg, as part of the realm, approximately one-third of the population became German; the Dual Monarchy gave way to the so-called *Gesamtstaat* ('*Helstat*' or United Monarchy) (Østergaard 2000: 155).

Separate Schleswig-Holstein and Danish movements evolved and demanded, on the one hand, German unification and, on the other hand, Nordic unity. The revolutions abroad influenced the national movements, and the Three-Year War between Prussia and Denmark broke out in 1848. At that time, the Danish King had appointed a new, national-liberal government to draft a constitution. For the drafters of the constitution, the Belgian Constitution became an important model, which among others is reflected in the Constitution's provision according to which no alien in the future could acquire *indfødsret* 'except by statute'. During the discussions on this provision, there were political disagreements between the Eider-Danish National Liberals, who wanted Schleswig incorporated in Denmark (and the Southern border of Denmark at the River Eider between Schleswig and Holstein), and the supporters of the multinational united monarchy (Østergaard 2000: 157). On one side, a Scandinavianist, the famous Danish minister and poet, N. F. S. Grundtvig, suggested that nationals from Sweden and Norway should be entitled to *indfødsret* after a certain period of residence in Denmark. On the other side, an influential supporter of the united monarchy and future Prime Minister, A. S. Ørsted, was completely opposed to proper Danish legislation on the acquisition of *indfødsret* as long as uncertainties existed about the duchies' relations with Denmark.

The first Danish constitution was adopted on 5 June 1849. It did not contain any provision on nationality or citizenship, but some provisions dealt with the concept of *indfødsret*; apart from the provision for aliens' acquisition of *indfødsret* by statute, the Constitution contained provisions on having *indfødsret* as a condition for appointment as civil servant and for electoral rights at parliamentary elections.

As the June Constitution was adopted at a time of uncertainty as to the duchies' attachment to Denmark, it only applied to the Danish Kingdom. However, when in 1851 the Three-Year War ended and the united monarchy lived on it became necessary to adopt a common constitution for the entire monarchy. By the new Constitution of 1855, *indfødsret* became a common matter for the whole Kingdom. Still, problems amongst the pro-German and the Danish population continued, and in 1858 the Constitution was annulled for Holstein and Lauenburg. In 1863, Denmark tried to tie Schleswig to the Kingdom through a new common Eider-Danish Constitution, but this provoked the German powers, and in 1864, Prussia and Austria declared war on the Danish state. Eventually Denmark suffered a 'self-inflicted defeat' and had to cede Schleswig, Holstein and Lauenburg in 1864. (Østergaard 2000: 156). As a result, Denmark became a 'nation state' with an ethnically homogeneous population, and more than 150,000 Danes ended up living outside the Danish state (Lundgreen-Nielsen 1992: 145). According to the Vienna Treaty of 1864, art. XIX, they could retain their status as Danish subjects provided they moved to Denmark within a six-year time limit. Thousands of people used this opportunity each year until 1872, when the new German Empire changed its legislation in such a way that those concerned could stay in Germany as Danish subjects.

3.2.3 *Danish emigration*

Around the mid nineteenth century, Denmark emerged as a country of emigration. Factors like a growing population, poverty, low income, high prices for land, unemployment and better possibilities for transportation made many, especially young Danes, emigrate overseas, first and foremost to America. Danish emigration was also stimulated by the loss of Northern Schleswig in 1864. Although the more than 150,000 Danes who then came under the German regime were able to opt for Denmark, many of them considered America to be a more attractive alternative. Danish emigration culminated in the 1880s, when around 80,000 Danes left their native country (Stilling & Olsen 1994: 30).

Danish-Americans considered it important to become American citizens. The concept of *indfødsret* had increasingly become the legal expression of being 'Danish', but the 1776 Act did not include provisions for renunciation or loss of *indfødsret*. This legal situation was impractical, as foreign states could require the renunciation of all legal connections with the country of origin as a condition for naturalisation. In practice, Denmark would release a person from his or her status as a Danish subject, but this would not lead to the loss of Danish *indfødsret*. Therefore in 1871, an act on loss of *indfødsret* was adopted (Act No. 54 of 25 March 1871 including an Addition to the Act on *Indfødsret* of 15 January 1776).

According to this law, Danish native-born subjects who were naturalised as foreign citizens could no longer enjoy the rights attached to Danish *indfødsret* and neither were they under any obligations stemming from the *indfødsret*. However, upon taking up residence in Denmark again, their subjecthood might change; if they had not yet been released from subjecthood to the foreign state they could notify the Minister of the Interior of their wish to be released and if they stayed in Denmark for two years or more, they were presumed to have resigned from their foreign subjecthood (unless this was counteracted by international treaty).[2]

Still, from a nationality law perspective, the legal situation was chaotic. Even though *indfødsret* was considered a nationality concept, another Danish nationality concept also existed at the same time. The Danish Ministry of the Interior described the difference between the two concepts by pointing out that Danish *indfødsret* was inalienable, while this was not the case with Danish nationality: 'anyone who by taking up habitual residence in Denmark has entered into a permanent subjecthood to the Danish state is without any formal act considered a Danish national... hence it follows that reckoned among the Danish subjects are also persons without Danish *indfødsret*. It may frequently happen that Danish subjects are released entirely from their subjecthood by a formal act, especially when this is necessary for becoming naturalised in a foreign state, but such release does not lead to the loss of a person's *indfødsret*.'[3]

The legal uncertainty as to who were nationals and who were foreigners became increasingly intolerable. In other countries at the time the distinction between the two concepts had become clearer and consistency between the national and international perceptions of the nationality concept was achieved, exept in Denmark. A Danish nationality law reform became therefore imperative.

3.2.4 The 1898 nationality law reform

During the nineteenth century, citizens began to increasingly participate in public life, public authorities assumed more functions, social assistance was developed, access to international communication and travel became increasingly easy, and international cooperation was strengthened. These developments contributed to making the national/foreigner distinction more relevant, and it became natural to introduce fundamental nationality principles, such as the principles of ius sanguinis and family unity into Danish nationality law (Larsen 1948a: 118).

Moreover, in 1888, Denmark and Sweden ratified a bilateral agreement on poverty relief and repatriation, which also made it clear that more uniform nationality law reforms were necessary. The two countries prepared a provisional draft recognising that the Danish provisions were based on principles 'from times past', and that an amendment was necessary with a view to international cooperation.[4] Denmark and Sweden wanted Norway to participate in a common nationality law reform, and a commission with delegates from the three countries was set up to work out draft acts.

In 1890, the draft was finished.[5] Norway had already adopted a new nationality act in 1888. In Sweden, a new act (the first Swedish act on nationality) was passed in 1894; like the Norwegian act, it was based on the ius sanguinis principle, confirming the former Swedish customary rules. A similar bill on Danish *indfødsret* was presented to the Parliament in 1896 equating '*indfødsret*' with 'nationality' (with brackets round 'nationality'). According to the preparatory work, the reason for granting a person *indfødsret*, and thereby political rights etc., was that said person was affiliated to the state as a citizen/national; furthermore, by using the word *indfødsret* synonymously with nationality in the new act, an amendment to the Danish Constitution became unnecessary.

In Parliament, however, there were hesitations as to whether it was a proper solution to abruptly replace the old nationality concept with a new one, which should only be granted to native-born people. The result would be that those affiliated to the Danish state through many years of residence could claim diplomatic protection from foreign states, and Danish expatriates without *indfødsret* could become 'stateless'.

Consequently, the bracketed word 'nationality' was removed, and it was emphasised in the act that it did not change the legal status of those who had become Danish nationals by taking up residence in Denmark. With this amendment, the new act was adopted as Act No. 42 of 19 March 1898 on the Acquisition and Loss of *Indfødsret.*

The act introduced, as already mentioned, ius sanguinis as the fundamental acquisition principle. According to the first section, a child born in wedlock acquired Danish *indfødsret,* if the father had Danish *indfødsret,* and it was emphasised that this applied irrespectively of whether the child was born in the country or abroad. Sect. 9 regarding children born out of wedlock stated that an illegitimate child would acquire Danish *indfødsret* if the mother had Danish *indfødsret.* However, if the mother's nationality status was changed due to her marriage with another man than the child's father, there would be no change to the child's *indfødsret.* Furthermore, sect. 10 contained the well-known rule of presumption establishing that children who are found in the realm and whose nationality cannot be ascertained are considered nationals until the contrary has been established.

It was underlined in the preparatory work that the recognition of the ius sanguinis principle and the introduction of conferring *indfødsret* by descent should not exclude other modes of 'conferring *indfødsret* without the will of the individual', which would lead to the malpractice known from France, where foreigners in accordance with the principle of descent had been able to transfer their foreign nationality to their offspring during an indefinite number of generations. A solution to this problem could have been to introduce a rule of presumption similar to the French double ius soli principle, but this idea was given up, as a complete socialisation was considered to occur normally with the first generation of foreigners born and brought up in the territory. Instead, the act stated in sect. 2 that a person born and raised in Denmark would acquire Danish *indfødsret ex lege* at the age of nineteen, unless said person already had a foreign nationality and within the previous year had declared his or her wish not to acquire Danish *indfødsret.* Children of foreigners who had themselves retained a foreign nationality this way could not give such a declaration. Danish *indfødsret* acquired by a man via this mode would be extended to his wife and children. The provision in sect. 2 resembled sect. 9 in the 1776 Act, as it had been interpreted in practice by 1898.

At that time, most countries followed the principle of family unity as to nationality, and due to the husband's principal status, a foreign woman acquired her husband's nationality by marriage. This principle was also codified in the new act, sect. 3. By such a marriage also the couple's children would acquire Danish *indfødsret,* if they were less than eighteen years old and unmarried. The provision caused some concern, but it was considered to be in harmony with liberal ideas on the right to respect for family life without interference from the authorities.

It was incontrovertible that it should continue to be possible to acquire Danish *indfødsret* through naturalisation, however the naturalisation requirements were not laid down in the new act, which in sect. 4 confined itself to refer to the constitutional provision, according to which no alien could acquire *indfødsret* except by statute. In addition, it was stated that naturalisation of a man also included his wife and children unless otherwise decided. Hitherto, it had been a precondition for naturalisation that all persons to be naturalised were explicitly mentioned by name in an act on acquisition of *indfødsret,* but as a consequence of the recognition of the principle of family unity, Parliament agreed upon a rule of presumption, according to which it normally would be in the best interest of all parties that wife and children acquired *indfødsret* with the husband.

In a time of emigration, it was natural to legislate regarding loss of *indfødsret,* as renunciation of a former nationality was often made a condition for naturalisation abroad. Therefore, according to sect. 5, a Dane who acquired a foreign nationality would lose Danish *indfødsret,* and if said person was a married man, and the foreign nationality was extended to his wife and children, they would also lose their *indfødsret,* unless they stayed in Denmark. This new rule applied regardless of whether the person in question acquired the foreign nationality voluntarily or not.

Another innovative rule was contained in sect. 5, para. 2, which stated that a person who wished to become a foreign national could be released from his or her nationality relationship to Denmark by a royal resolution, conditioned by said person's acquisition of a foreign nationality within a certain time limit.

As to a Danish woman's loss of *indfødsret* by marriage to a foreigner, the act also established that the couple's children born before the marriage would lose their *indfødsret* upon the parents' marriage, if the children were under majority and unmarried – even if they became stateless.

Furthermore, the law contained provisions for the suspension of *indfødsret* for persons who resided abroad continuously during a period of ten years. These rules were considered an alternative to rules on loss of nationality by expatriation, but they were repealed in 1908, before they had any legal effect. Like larger emigration countries, Denmark recognised the importance of emigrants being able to retain their original nationality and the importance to the Danish state of emigrants being affiliated to Denmark.

When the First World War began, many Danish subjects and persons with Danish *indfødsret* lived in Northern Schleswig with an unclear legal status. The provision on *ius indigenatus* in the Vienna Peace Treaty of 1864, art. XIX, para. 5, was interpreted differently in Denmark and Prussia. The primordial French text stated that '(l)e droit d'indigénat, tant dans le Royaume de Danemarc que dans les Duchés, est conservé à tous les individus qui les possèdent à l'époque de l'échange des ratifications du présent Traité' (Larsen 1948a : 54). Denmark understood the term '*indfødsret*' to mean the same as the German term 'Staatsangehörigkeit', but in German law 'Staatsangehöriger', Unterthan' and 'Staatsbürger' were analogous terms (national, subject and citizen), and the Prussian government considered an option for subjecthood to be decisive for the option of 'indigenat', whereas Denmark considered it to be possible for a person with *indigenat/indfødsret* to be released from his or her subjecthood while still retaining *indigenat/indfødsret* and 'nationality rights', with, among others, the right to remain in and return to the country of nationality/*indfødsret* (Matzen 1907: 4).

This legal uncertainty created many problems for those who had opted for Denmark, but had remained in Schleswig. Prussia had promised not to expel those who had opted for Denmark from Germany, and in 1914 they were ordered to do German military service, although many of them had already done or were doing their military service in Denmark. This made the Danish government pass an act granting *indfødsret* to such persons. The events illustrate which problems the unique peculiarity of Danish nationality law created, and within the following years it was accepted in Danish law and practice, that Danish *indfødsret*, subjecthood, nationality and citizenship were to be seen as synonymous concepts.

In 1916-18, the extension of the Danish realm changed again. Denmark transferred the West Indian Islands to the USA and recognised Iceland as an independent state. According to the Act of the Danish-Iceland Federation, Icelandic nationals in Denmark were granted equal rights to those of Danish nationals, and vice versa. Another important change of the area of the realm took place at the end of the First World

War, when it was decided by the Treaty of Versailles that Germany should cede parts of Southern Jutland to Denmark. Following a referendum, the Northern part of Schleswig was reunited with Denmark in 1920, and all inhabitants in this area acquired Danish nationality and lost their German nationality, however with the possibility to opt differently within a two-year period.

3.2.5 *The 1925 nationality law reform*

The First World War and the general social development led to a new reform of the nationality laws. Again, Sweden invited Denmark and Norway for talks, and this time the crucial question was the status of married women. Women were gaining civil and political rights equal to men, and women's organisations lobbied for equality regarding nationality rights as well. The question of gender equality was controversial, but eventually, in 1924-25 Denmark, Norway and Sweden adopted new nationality laws based on a new common Nordic report.[6]

It turned out that the time was not yet ripe for giving married women independence in terms of nationality. In many other countries, the nationality law still provided for the loss of a woman's nationality with her marriage to a foreigner, and consequently, it was considered necessary to let foreign women married to Danish men acquire their husband's nationality by marriage, disregarding the inconvenience created by this arrangement. Therefore, the new Nationality Act's sect. 3 contained a provision that was almost similar to sect. 3 of the 1898 Act on automatic transfer of Danish nationality to a foreign woman by her marriage to a Danish man – and likewise to the couple's unmarried children under eighteen years of age.

Furthermore, the new law continued the former provision on automatic acquisition of nationality at birth, *ex lege*, by descent. A child born in wedlock acquired Danish nationality, if the father was a Danish national, and a child born out of wedlock acquired Danish nationality if the mother was a Danish national. (The new law placed both rules in sect. 1.) The 1898 Act's acquisition modes for foundlings (sect. 1(2)) and second and third generations of immigrant descent (sect. 2) were also extended as was the naturalisation rule (sect. 4).

Delegates from the Nordic countries had suggested in their common report that the Swedish and Norwegian provisions on naturalisation should attach importance to the applicant's age, residence and period of residence in the country in question, conduct and ability to provide for his or her family plus loss of a former nationality. Such conditions were also part of Danish naturalisation practice, according to which the residence requirement was fifteen years for aliens in general, and less for nationals from Norway and Sweden (ten years, since 1914).[7] There was a requirement of 'honest and sober conduct'. Crimes committed which were considered degrading resulted in a waiting period of 25 years and rehabilitation was required, while imprisonment with hard labour excluded naturalisation. Only those who could provide for themselves and their family could gain nationality. Applicants should master the Danish language, and their children should enjoy a Danish education and attend Danish schools.

When someone who was granted naturalisation had a wife and unmarried children younger than eighteen years of age, they were naturalised simultaneously unless otherwise decided (sect. 4 (2)). However, in terms of loss of nationality, a significant change was introduced for married women and their children, as their loss of Danish nationality was made conditional on them acquiring a new nationality (sect. 5). Thus, if the man was stateless, or if the law in his country did not transfer his nationality to his wife and children, they would keep their Danish nationality. In Parliament, there was even a wish to couple the loss of nationality to *voluntary* acquisition of a new nationality, but opposition towards dual nationality hindered this solution. Another innovation was a provision, according to which the loss of a nationality acquired by birth only became effective upon emigration from Denmark (sect. 5, last sentence). This rule has been called a modern 'adscription' (Larsen 1948a: 344).

A new rule on loss of Danish nationality due to birth and residence abroad was introduced (sect. 6). According to this new rule, a Danish man or an unmarried Danish woman who was born abroad and had never resided in Denmark would lose Danish nationality upon reaching 22 years of age. Nationality could however be retained by means of a royal resolution. If a married man lost his nationality via this mode, the loss would include his wife and children born during the marriage. The same rule on loss applied to a woman and her children born out of marriage.

The 1925 Law was in force until 1950, but the Second World War led to some amendments. The rule on loss of Danish nationality due to birth and residence abroad was suspended at the outbreak of the war, and after the end of the war certain other provisions on automatic acquisition of nationality were suspended regarding German nationals and persons of German origin including Danish women married to Germans, due to shattered preconditions.

One of the suspended rules was the socialisation-based mode of acquisition for second generation of immigrant descent. The rule was based on an assumption of integration, which could not be taken for granted in relation to second generation of German origin after the German occupation of Denmark, 9 April 1945, where Germans had settled in Denmark and endeavoured to strengthen resident Germans'

German-national sentiment. Neither could it be presumed that a marriage between a Danish man and a German woman was entered into without regard to the woman's future nationality status. The third group whose right to Danish nationality was suspended was that of Danish women married to Germans. These women could no longer retain their Danish nationality, irrespective of whether they had acquired it at birth and still lived in Denmark. This suspension in particular was considered problematic, and it was only in force until 1947, while the other suspensions lasted until 1948. In the interim period, individuals from the groups excluded from obtaining Danish nationality in accordance with the suspended provisions might acquire Danish nationality through naturalisation based on the legislature's individual assessment of their case. The government regretted this arrangement, but due to the constitutional requirement on aliens' acquisition of nationality by statute it was impossible to leave any discretion to administrative authorities.

3.2.6 *The 1950 nationality law reform*

During the Second World War, the desire for further Nordic cooperation arose, and the introduction of a common Nordic nationality was discussed. A Danish nationality expert, the head of the Nationality Office, Knud Larsen, drew up a booklet on Nordic nationality of May 1944. He presented the idea of establishing a union citizenship common for all citizens of the Nordic union and 'no one else'. The common Nordic nationality should be attached to the internal nationality of each member state; he concluded that, as a consequence, the countries would need uniform nationality legislation (Larsen 1944: 39). Naturalisation would, one way or another, be a matter of common interest, as it would bring with it rights in other member states. Therefore, in cases of naturalisation, a hearing procedure amongst the countries should be established (Larsen 1944: 77).

Apart from the question of a common Nordic nationality, it was especially the unsatisfactory nationality status of married women that made a nationality reform necessary. In a common Nordic report of 1949, Nordic delegates pointed out that the principle of equality as well as the states' interest in being able to control their citizenry made a nationality law reform necessary.[8] Nevertheless, the unity of the family should be taken into consideration. If spouses in mixed marriages had different nationalities then a married woman might lose her unconditional right to stay in her husband's country and her social citizenship rights. Therefore, the Aliens Acts should be administered in such a way that a wife would not be separated from her husband, unless a pressing social need necessitated her expulsion, and the social welfare system should be reconsidered. Moreover, a foreign spouse to a Danish national should be able to acquire Danish nationality under favourable conditions.

As the Nordic delegates feared that the introduction of a common Nordic nationality would postpone the general nationality law reforms, they could not recommend the introduction of such a status at once. Instead, they recommended that rules illustrating the mutual connection between the Nordic states should be adopted. Among other things, each of the Nordic states should grant nationals from the other Nordic states an optional right to their nationality, and residence in another Nordic state should to a certain extent be considered equal to residence in the state granting its nationality. Finland and Iceland did not participate in the negotiations, but the rules on preferential treatment for Nordic nationals should also come into force in these countries by an agreement between the countries.

The bill introduced in the Danish Parliament in 1950 was in complete conformity with the delegates' recommendations. Apart from the suggestions on gender equality and the special rules for Nordic citizens, it contained a provision on natural-born Danish nationals' reacquisition of a lost Danish nationality and a provision on deprivation of Danish nationality due to violation of the Danish Criminal Code's parts 12 and 13 on gross disloyalty towards the Danish state.[9] Except for the provision on deprivation of nationality, the bill was adopted in 1950 (as Act No. 252 of 27 May 1950 on Danish Nationality). This act is still in force today, but has been subject to several amendments.

The 1950 Act continued the 1925 Act's provisions on acquisition of Danish nationality through descent at birth (ius sanguinis), but despite the introduction of the principle of gender equality as to granting women an independent nationality, it did not give a married woman the right to pass her nationality on to her children. The reason for this omission was animosity toward dual nationality. As an exception, a married woman could (only) pass her nationality on to the children in cases where the husband was a stateless person or where the child would not acquire the nationality of the father at birth (sect. 1). As to a child born out of wedlock of a Danish father and an alien mother, the principle of transfer of the father's nationality to the child by the parents' marriage (legitimation) was re-enacted, among other things, in order to achieve equality among siblings born before and after the marriage (sect. 2).

Concerning the second generation of immigrant descent, it was indisputable that those born and raised in the country should have an unconditional right to Danish nationality, but the provision on this mode of acquisition (sect. 3) was reformulated due to the fact that in many countries the automatic acquisition of nationality as applied until then would not lead to the loss of the former nationality, and neither would the acquisition of a new nationality before the age of 21. Therefore, the second generation immigrant offspring's acquisition of nationality was made dependent on making a declaration to that effect between the ages of 21 and 23 (addressed to the county governor or other relevant authority). A person who was stateless or who would lose his or her foreign nationality by the acquisition of Danish nationality could already make the declaration once having attained the age of eighteen. Furthermore, based on experiences from the war, a new provision was introduced excluding nationals from an enemy state from the scope of the provision.

Another novelty was the introduction of the right to reacquisition of nationality, already known from the Norwegian and Swedish nationality law. Although the right only applied to persons with a genuine link to Denmark – as only natural-born Danish nationals with residence in Denmark until attaining the age of eighteen were covered – and although there was a two years' residence requirement, the rule caused misgivings in Parliament. The reactions had to do with Denmark's frontier with Germany. There were objections to the fact that while young German-minded persons from Northern Schleswig having acquired German nationality during the World War were able to reacquire Danish nationality from the perspective *ubi bene, ibi patria*, elderly, Danish-minded persons born in the region while it was in German hands, would fall outside the scope of the provision requiring the declaring person to be a natural-born Danish national. Eventually the rule was included in the Danish nationality law (sect. 4) driven by a wish for Nordic legal unity.

The new provision on naturalisation (sect. 6) was identical to the traditional Danish naturalisation rule, but it originated from the gender equality principle that a wife was no longer part of her husband's naturalisation. It was, however, assumed that a married woman should be able to acquire her husband's nationality under favourable conditions (more favourable than those applying to a husband applying for his wife's nationality). Children should still be included in the acquisition of a nationality by their parents, either by declaration (sect. 5) or naturalisation (sect. 6 (2)).

It had hitherto been the rule that any acquisition of a foreign nationality would lead to the loss of Danish nationality, regardless of whether the acquisition was voluntary or involuntary. This would no longer be the case. According to the 1950 Act's sect. 7(1), (2) and (3), Danish nationality will be lost by (1) any person who acquires a foreign nationality upon application or with his or her express consent, (2) any person who acquires a foreign nationality by entering the public service of another country and (3) an unmarried child under eighteen years of age who becomes a foreign national by the fact that either parent holding or sharing custody of the child acquires a foreign nationality in the manner indicated in para. 1 or 2 hereof, unless the other parent retains Danish nationality and shares custody of the child.

Furthermore, according to sect. 8, Danish nationality may be lost due to permanent residence abroad. Any person, born abroad and who has never lived in Denmark nor been staying abroad under circumstances indicating some association with the country will lose his or her Danish nationality on attaining the age of 22. Furthermore, if such a person has a child who has acquired Danish nationality through him or her, the child will also lose its nationality. In 1950, the loss would occur regardless of whether it created statelessness, but this is no longer the case (see sects. 3.2.6.1 and 3.3.1). There is also a provision to grant an application for retention, submitted before the applicant's 22nd birthday.

Sect. 9 contains a provision on voluntary renunciation of Danish nationality, following an application and conditioned by the acquisition of another nationality within a certain time limit.

Finally, the 1950 Act introduced specific rules as to nationals from the Nordic countries. Under a Nordic agreement, the King could decide that one or more of the rules in sect. 10 A-C should be applied. According to the rule under A, birth in an agreement country was equivalent to birth in Denmark, and residence in an agreement country until the declaring person's twelfth birthday was equivalent to residence in Denmark; the reason for this was the close relationship between the Nordic countries regarding language, culture and way of life.[10] According to the rule under B, a national from an agreement country who had acquired his or her nationality by another mode of acquisition than naturalisation could, after ten years of residence in Denmark, acquire Danish nationality by making a declaration if between the ages of 21 and 60 years; a precondition was, however, that the person concerned had not been sentenced to imprisonment or any measure equivalent to imprisonment. This rule was not only seen as a confirmation of the close relationship between the countries, it was also meant to ease the pressure on the countries' naturalisation systems. According to the rule under C, a person who had lost Danish nationality and had subsequently remained a national of a Nordic country could recover his or her Danish nationality by submitting a declaration to that effect to a county governor or other relevant authority after having taken up residence in Denmark. The aim of this provision was to facilitate movement across the Nordic borders.[11]

3.2.6.1 *The 1968 change to the Act on Danish Nationality*

Apart from legislation passed as a consequence of the German occupation and the gender equality principle, the first substantial amendment of the 1950 Act was made in 1968. It was brought about by a recommendation from the Nordic Council on easing the existing rules on access to nationality for Nordic nationals and the adoption of the 1961 UN Convention on the Reduction of Statelessness. Denmark was reluctant to ratify the 1961 Convention due to its art. 8 (3) allowing a contracting state to retain provisions on deprivation of nationality for nationals who had acted inconsistently with their duty of loyalty towards the state.[12]

However, the Nordic countries agreed to amend their nationality laws in order to follow the Convention's requirements on the reduction of statelessness and the Nordic Council's recommendations on facilitating the acquisition of their nationality for nationals from the other Nordic countries. The Danish Nationality Act was changed by Act No. 399 of 11 December 1968 amending sect. 3 in such a way that birth on Danish territory was no longer a requirement for second generation immigrant descendants' acquisition of Danish nationality; instead they could acquire nationality by making a declaration to that effect between the ages of 21 and 23 years, insofar as they had lived in Denmark for at least five years before the age of sixteen and permanently between the ages of sixteen and 21. The right also applied to those aged eighteen who had lived in the country permanently for the previous five years and prior to that for a total of at last five years if they were stateless or would automatically lose their former nationality as a result of the acquisition of the new nationality.[13] In general, being raised in Denmark was considered sufficient to create the link necessary for acquisition of nationality.

Furthermore, the Nationality Act's sect. 8 (2) was brought into conformity with the 1961 Convention's art. 6, according to which a child's extended automatic loss of nationality shall be conditional upon the possession or acquisition of another nationality, and in agreement with the recommendation from the Nordic Council, residence in another Nordic country for an aggregate period of not less than seven years should be considered equivalent to residence in Denmark (in which case the provision on loss due to permanent residence abroad, see sect. 8 (1), would not be applicable). Lastly, the period of ten years required before a Nordic national could acquire Danish nationality by declaration, see sect. 10 B, was reduced to seven years, and the residence requirement for Nordic nationals in regard to naturalisation was reduced to three years.

3.2.6.2 The 1978 change to the Act on Danish Nationality

Since the recognition of a married woman's right to an independent nationality, Parliament has several times discussed the question of a married woman's right to pass her nationality on to her children. It was agreed that a solution should be found within the framework of the Nordic cooperation, but in 1969 and 1972 the question came up again in Parliament due to the many 'foreign workers' who had arrived in Denmark and the increasing number of mixed marriages. Again, the question was referred to the Nordic Council, but in 1977 a private bill was passed and adopted, amending sect. 1 of the Nationality Act by granting a child born in wedlock Danish nationality at birth if at least one of the child's parents was a Danish national.

At the same time, a new provision, sect. 2 A, was included in the law, granting a foreign adopted child under the age of seven a right to Danish nationality by declaration if the child resided in Denmark with the adoptive parents both being Danish nationals. Again here, the dislike of dual nationality led to choosing the acquisition mode of 'declaration' instead of automatic acquisition, *ex lege*, by adoption.[14]

Furthermore, sect. 9 on the renunciation of nationality was changed by the inclusion of a new para. 2 according to which a foreign national permanently resident in a foreign country cannot be denied release from his or her (additional) Danish nationality. This amendment was brought about by the European 1977 protocol (amending the 1963 Convention on reduction of multiple nationality, which was ratified by Denmark in 1972), stating in art. 1 that a contracting state may not withhold its consent to release if the applicant has his or her ordinary residence outside the territory of the state.

Finally, the 1978 amendment contained a new rule on loss of nationality by residence in an agreement country and a transitional rule on acquisition of Danish nationality by a person born in wedlock of a Danish mother between 1 January 1961 and 1 January 1979 by the mother submitting a declaration in this regard between 1 January 1979 and 31 December 1981.

3.3 Recent developments and current institutional arrangements

3.3.1 Political analysis

Since the First World War, Denmark had pursued a rather restrictive immigration policy, but the years 1969-1971 marked an exception. In Denmark as well as other European countries with full employment, migrant workers were recruited as 'guest workers', and Denmark had a net immigration of approximately 20,000 foreigners from non-EC and non-Nordic countries. However, in 1973 things changed (Ersbøll 2001:

246). The oil-crisis contributed to bringing an end to immigration, Denmark joined the EC, and a landslide election changed the party-political structure; support for the 'old parties' fell, and new parties entered Parliament, among them the Progress Party fighting high taxation and a large public sector. The composition of the different governments became more complex and their parliamentary base narrower (Rerup & Christiansen 2005). The political climate changed, and the changes influenced the parliamentary debates on naturalisation.

Traditionally, naturalisation acts had been adopted without discussion in Parliament, but this practice changed gradually in the 1970s and 1980s. In 1976, a member representing the Progress Party in the Parliamentary Committee on Nationality suggested a bill on naturalisation to be amended by the exclusion of an applicant. The reason for this proposal, which was criticised as something historically unique, was that the applicant did not fulfil the normal criteria (of a consecutive residence period) for naturalisation, and the Progress Party was unwilling to grant him Danish nationality in order to make it possible for him to become a Danish civil servant. In 1978, Members of the Progress Party declared their general discontent about the naturalisation of applicants who had sold or used drugs, and in 1981, they proposed to exclude three applicants from a bill, as they were against granting Danish nationality to those who had committed a crime within the required residence period of seven years; this proposal also met with strong opposition from the other parties, and in order to protect the applicants' right to privacy, two parties, the Centre-Democrats and the Socialist People's Party, tried to get the doors closed during the parliamentary reading of the bill. Nevertheless, the naturalisation criteria were tightened when a new circular on naturalisation was published in 1981 in order to implement a recommendation from the Nordic Council on the reduction of the residence requirement for Nordic nationals to two years and on naturalisation of men and women in mixed marriages on equal terms.

In the following years, there was no disagreement on nationality law (apart from an incident on naturalisation of a sportsman in order to allow him to play for the national team), but strong disagreement arose in 1983 regarding the new Aliens Act. The Social Democrats had relinquished power in 1982. A new coalition government came into office under the leadership of a Conservative prime minister, and issue arose when the opposition managed to get the new Aliens Act adopted with very liberal admission criteria. In the late 1980s, elections were called at short intervals, and refugee and immigration issues moved into the centre of the political debate.

By Act No. 159 of 18 March 1991, the Minister of the Interior was authorised to issue regulations regarding fees for application for naturalisation. A fee of DKK 3000 (around 400 Euro) was suggested, but the political parties disagreed as to the fairness of requiring a fee from applicants without any certainty of being naturalised. However, following re-election of the government, the Minister of the Interior agreed to reduce the fee to DKK 1000 (approximately 135 Euro), and the proposal was adopted.

In 1993, the longest-reigning Prime Minister since the end of the Second World War had to step down following an inquiry into the Conservative Minister for Justice's illegal inactivity concerning the handling of applications from Tamil refugees on family reunification (the so-called 'Tamil case'). This paved the way for a new Social Democratic government (Rerup & Christiansen 2005). The political atmosphere was severely affected by the preceding events. Customarily, the Progress Party suggested amendments to the bills on naturalisation, which were then passed three times a year. The party disagreed with the naturalisation criteria agreed upon by a majority of the political parties, and the Party's representatives on the Parliamentary Standing Committee on Nationality proposed that a number of applicants who fulfilled the naturalisation criteria nevertheless be excluded due to crimes, public debt or 'insufficient knowledge of the Danish language'. The proposals were formulated in such a way that the applicants in question could be identified by name through their number in the bill. Questions were raised as to the legality of this practice, which seemed to violate the right to privacy, but since the Ministry of Justice did not confirm its illegality, the practice continued (until recently).

During the debate on fees for applications for naturalisation, the Progress Party raised the question of the introduction of rules for the deprivation of nationality, and in the following years the party put forward several proposals for parliamentary resolutions on tightened requirements for the acquisition of Danish nationality. Almost identical proposals were put forward again and again for several years, not only on strengthening the requirements for naturalisation, but also on the introduction of a quota system for naturalisation (maximum 1000 naturalisations per year).

In 1994, the Liberals and the Conservatives also put forward a proposal for a parliamentary resolution on more rigorous requirements for naturalisation. They regarded Danish nationality as a 'seal of approval' which should be deserved, and therefore, applicants should be able to read and write Danish to a reasonable extent, and they should not have any public debt. Furthermore, they should have been free of crimes for a number of years, and serious crimes should prohibit naturalisation. This proposal was also reintroduced during the following three years, and in the wake of all the proposals, naturalisation practice changed further.

Previously, only members of the Progress Party had proposed amendments to the bills on naturalisation with a view to excluding applicants with a criminal record, public debt etc., but after 1994, members of the Liberals (with one exception) and the Conservatives also stated their wish to make it more difficult for foreigners with criminal records and public debts to acquire Danish nationality, and later the Liberals also proposed amendments to the bills suggesting that a number of applicants be excluded.

Subsequently, the Social Democratic government came to an agreement with the Liberals and the Conservatives on a tightening of the criteria for naturalisation. However, already one year later, new disagreements arose after the Parliamentary Standing Committee on Nationality had decided to include some applicants in a bill on naturalisation against the wish of Liberal committee members. After that, both the Liberals and the Conservatives proposed that a number of applicants should be excluded from the bills, although in far fewer numbers than those proposed by the Progress Party and the Danish People's Party (a new party formed by a breakaway group from the Progress Party, which had split into two sections in 1995). Like the Progress Party, the Danish Peoples Party made several proposals for parliamentary resolutions on tightening the requirements for naturalisation etc.

In 1997-1998, the parliamentary debate on nationality quietened down. The Commissioner of the Council of the Baltic Sea States on Democratic Institutions and Human Rights, including the Rights of Persons belonging to Minorities, had published his report from 1996 on Criteria and Procedures for Obtaining Citizenship in the CBSS Member States, and representatives of the Socialist People's Party approached the Minister for Justice for an interpellation on the government's intention to follow the recommendations. With the exception of the Progress Party and the Danish People's Party, all political parties agreed to a parliamentary resolution in which Parliament stressed the importance of considering the acquisition of Danish nationality as a crucial positive element in the process of foreigners' integration in Denmark.

For a short period it seemed as if the political debate on nationality would be more harmonious. The Act on Danish Nationality was amended in 1997 in order to implement the Hague Convention on the Protection of Children and Cooperation in Respect of Inter-country Adoption (1993)[15] and in 1998 in order to implement the European Convention on Nationality (1997).[16] With the 1998 amendment, children born out of wedlock were granted equal rights with children born in wedlock to acquire either of the parents' Danish nationality, with the exception of children born abroad to a Danish father and a foreign mother. Furthermore, an alien child, under twelve years of age, adopted through a Danish adoption order or a decision on adoption taken abroad and valid under the Danish Act on Adoption will become a Danish national if adopted by a married couple where at least one of the spouses is a Danish national, or by an unmarried Danish national. The rules on second generation acquisition of Danish nationality were made more flexible by allowing the last five-year period to be spent in Denmark within a six-year period, among other things in order to give these young people the same opportunity as other young people to spend one year abroad before starting an education, without hampering their entitlement to Danish nationality. Finally, it was made a condition for loss of nationality due to permanent residence abroad that the person in question did not thereby become stateless.

Soon, however, new political disagreements cropped up. Among the proposals for parliamentary resolutions from the mid-1990s there had been a proposal from the Liberals and the Conservatives to make the mode of acquisition of nationality by declaration for second-generation offspring of immigrant descent conditional on the absence of a criminal record. This proposal was reintroduced in 1999 and followed by proposals from the Danish People's Party and Freedom 2000 (a new party formed by members of the then dissolved Progress Party). Both parties wanted the declaration mechanism to be abolished. In their opinion it would be more in harmony with the Constitution's sect. 44 (1) on aliens' acquisition of nationality by statute to let the democratically elected politicians consider all applications for nationality through the naturalisation procedure. As a result, the Minister for Justice (at that time responsible for nationality matters) introduced a bill on making second-generation immigrant descendants' access to nationality by declaration conditional on the absence of a criminal record. The bill was introduced even though the Minister in 1996 had defended the existing declaration rule as fair and moreover based on the Nordic Agreement. The amendment was adopted within about one week.[17]

In the autumn of 2001, the Minister for Justice introduced a bill on amendment of the Nationality Act making deprivation of nationality possible for persons who have acquired Danish nationality by fraudulent acts. A general election was called for 20 November 2001 and in the light of the terrorist attacks on the World Trade Center on 11 September 2001, the election campaign was supposed to centre on Denmark's role in the fight against terror, instead refugee and immigration issues took centre stage. The Social Democrats and the left-wing parties lost many of their mandates, and the Liberals became Denmark's largest political party. Together with the Conservatives they formed a government with parliamentary support from the Danish People's Party (Rerup & Christiansen 2005).

The Liberals had promised to strengthen the immigration and asylum policy and to carry through a better integration of foreigners into Danish society before the elections, and a Ministry for Refugee, Immigration and Integration Affairs (the Ministry for Integration) was subsequently established to implement this policy. This Ministry became responsible for nationality issues, and the new Minister for Integration reintroduced the bill (annulled due to the elections) on deprivation of nationality, which was adopted on 19 March 2002 (as sect. 8 A).

At almost the same time the Minister introduced another bill including two different proposals for changes. The first proposal implied that persons acquiring Danish nationality according to the special rules for Nordic nationals should prove that they thereby lose their former nationality. Even though Denmark has constantly wished to avoid multiple nationality, such a provision had not before then been necessary as all the Nordic countries had provided for loss of their nationality *ex lege* in cases of voluntary acquisition of a foreign nationality; but the situation changed when Sweden accepted dual nationality, and by making Nordic nationals' acquisition of nationality by declaration conditional on proof that any other nationality will thereby be lost, the new provision (adopted as sect. 4 A) neutralised the effects of Sweden's toleration of multiple nationality.[18] The other amendment was a rule divesting a marriage contracted by a person already married of legal effects under the Nationality Act as long as both (bigamous) marriages subsist (adopted as sect. 2 B). Consequently, children born in the second marriage are considered to be born out of wedlock. This change does not affect the nationality of children born in Denmark, since all children born in Denmark (whether in or out of wedlock) are given equal nationality rights; but this equality of status does not apply to children born abroad, and whereas children born in a bigamous marriage from a nationality point of view are considered to be born out of marriage, such children with a Danish father and an alien mother will not acquire their father's Danish nationality *ex lege* at birth. The reason for this amendment was that the government considered it offensive that Danish nationality could be acquired automatically on the basis of someone's several – co-existing – marriages.[19]

As the Liberals, the Conservatives and the Danish People's Party form a majority in Parliament, the three parties are able to decide the nationality policy among themselves, and in May 2002, the three parties entered into an agreement on new strengthened requirements for naturalisation. The agreement was transformed into a new circular on naturalisation, No. 55 of 12 June 2002. It was agreed that in future only two bills on naturalisation should be presented in Parliament annually. As a new condition for naturalisation, the applicants must sign a declaration concerning faithfulness and loyalty to Denmark. The residence requirements were increased by two years (nine years for aliens with no special status, eight years for refugees and stateless persons and from six to eight years for spouses of nationals – depending on the length of their marriage). The rules on conduct were strengthened, i.e., a sentence to imprisonment between one and two years implied a waiting period of eighteen years, and a sentence of more than two years excluded from naturalisation forever. Also overdue debt to the state precludes naturalisation. Lastly, an examination certificate was required as documentation of the applicants' knowledge of the Danish language, society, culture and history, and furthermore, the former exception for persons over the age of 65 was repealed, which was heavily criticised by the opposition.

By this amendment, most of the Danish People's Party's proposals for changes to the nationality law were adopted. Among what was left was the proposal to repeal second-generation immigrant descendants' entitlement to Danish nationality by declaration and the proposal to introduce a rule on deprivation of nationality due to committed crimes. In 2003, the Danish People's Party entered into an agreement with the government on carrying through such rules, and in 2004, a bill was presented to Parliament to fulfil the agreement.

Following the change, only second-generation immigrant descendants from the Nordic countries have access to nationality by declaration; furthermore, a condition is included that the declarants must prove that the acquisition of Danish nationality will cause them to lose their former nationality. The ground given for the amendment was that the actual composition of the Danish population no longer affords the necessary certainty as to the requisite integration of persons from non-Nordic countries falling under the declaration rule (sect. 3). It was mentioned in the explanatory notes that the existing provision entitling the second generation of immigrant descent to acquire Danish nationality (sect. 3), aimed at fulfilment of Denmark's obligations resulting from the UN Convention of 30 August 1961 on the Reduction of Statelessness as to persons born in the realm without a nationality. The proposed limitation of sect. 3 implied that these obligations should be fulfilled in another way. Therefore, the Ministry of Integration should – after having informed the Parliamentary Standing Committee on Nationality – include applicants covered by the 1961 Convention in a bill on naturalisation;[20] other stateless persons who had fallen under the declaration-rule even though they were not covered by the 1961 Convention would in the future be treated in accordance with the normal guidelines for naturalisation.

It was taken into consideration that the state according to the European Convention on Nationality (1997) shall facilitate the acquisition of its nationality for those born and/or lawfully and habitually resident in its territory for a period of time beginning before the age of eighteen. But since it was already provided for in the normal guidelines that some Danish-born persons may be granted facilitated naturalisation and that persons who arrive in Denmark before the age of fifteen may apply for naturalisation at the age of eighteen, it was considered that the Danish obligations pursuant to the 1997 Convention were fulfilled.[21]

Also deemed to be in accordance with the 1997 Convention was a new provision (sect. 8 B) on deprivation of nationality due to certain crimes against the state included in the Criminal Code's Parts 12 and 13. The explanatory notes state that nationality and citizenship rights presuppose loyalty to Denmark and the vital interests of the Danish society, and if a person is convicted for crimes against the state, said person has, according to the view of the government and the Danish People's Party, shown such a lack of loyalty that there ought to be a possibility for deprivation of nationality. The provision on deprivation of nationality applies to all Danish nationals regardless of whether they are nationals by birth or have acquired their nationality subsequently and therefore it is considered to be in harmony with art. 5 (2) of the 1997 Convention prohibiting discrimination between nationals. Furthermore, as the provision does not authorise deprivation of nationality if that will make the person concerned stateless, the provision is considered in accordance with Denmark's international obligations to avoid statelessness.[22]

The amendment of the Nationality Act was adopted by a narrow majority by the votes of the Liberals, the Conservatives and the Danish People's Party (61) against the votes of the Social Democrats, the Socialist People's Party, the Social Liberals, the Red-Green Alliance and the Christian People's Party (50).

In contrast to several other European countries, Denmark has not had a general approach to the promotion of the acquisition of nationality. The present government has declared that 'one shall deserve becoming a Danish national'.[23] It has been the wish of the government to strengthen the conditions for acquisition of nationality in order to make them 'respond more precisely to the society's expectations of the individual making an effort to become part of Danish society'. The Social Democrats consider an application for Danish nationality as a desire for further integration in Danish society. The left-wing parties and the Social Liberals have welcomed foreigners applying for Danish nationality considering access to nationality as part of the integration process and crucial for integration, for which reason they want relaxed criteria for naturalisation. The most deliberate and goal-oriented naturalisation policy has been pursued by the Danish People's Party – with a view to reducing the overall number of naturalisations. Spokesmen for the party reject the idea of access to nationality as a means of integration; they consider Danish nationality as the most precious gift from the Danish people to foreigners who apply for it and deserve it – after having completed a process of integration. Before the general election in 2001, a spokesman of the party warned against 'replacement' of the Danish population and the creation of a 'multi-ethnic society'; in particular, he warned against the fundamentalist tendencies within Islam. Furthermore, with regard to the Danish Constitution, the party considers a reduction of the numbers of applicants to be necessary in order for the Members of Parliament to be able to 'know and control' the applicants included in the bills on naturalisation.[24] The party's ideal is an annual quota of 2,000 in order to prevent the number of naturalisations being a menace to the Danes' birthright to their own country.

In 2002, the government expressed a wish to sharpen the conduct and language requirements, among other things because the naturalisation criteria were seen as instrumental in the process of integration. Danish nationality was seen as something to strive for: a 'carrot' for foreigners to adapt to Danish society, be independent, learn Danish and be able to socialise with the Danes. When it turned out that the 2002 language requirements did not prevent an increasing number of applicants from applying for naturalisation, the Danish People's Party made demands for a language test comparable to the school leaving examination of the public lower secondary school to be passed with a mark of nine (above average). The former Minister for Integration rejected the demand, which would imply that two thirds of the applicants would be excluded from being naturalised. Due to this disagreement the minister opened the way for negotiations on new naturalisation criteria with political parties other than The Danish People's Party, notably the Social Democrats, but also the Social Liberals. The Social Democrats had by and large accepted the existing requirements, while the Social Liberals' and other opposition parties' main objections regarded the diminished possibilities for dispensation from the demands on skills in the Danish language and knowledge of the Danish society.

In the parliamentary elections of 2005, the Danish People's Party was strengthened and in early summer 2005 the party declared that it was time for the second phase of the aliens policy; among the initiatives announced was a requirement that an applicant for naturalisation had to be self-supporting for at least ten years. The Party was again involved in the negotiations on new naturalisation criteria while negotiations with the Social Democrats and the Social liberals failed, and on 8 December 2005, a new agreement was concluded between the government parties and the Danish People's Party.

The new agreement, which entered into force 12 December 2005, has been transformed to a new circular on naturalisation, No. 9 of 12

January 2006. It stipulates that applicants for nationality must declare that they have not committed any crimes dealt with in the Criminal Code's Parts 12 and 13 (sect. 19 (1)). The rules on conduct have been further strengthened, i.e., a sentence to a term of imprisonment of more than 60 days for violations of the Criminal Code's Parts 12 and 13 as well as a sentence to a term of imprisonment of more than eighteen months now exclude naturalisation forever (sect. 19(2)).[25] As a new condition, the applicants must be self-supporting in the sense that they must not have received social benefits according to the social assistance law or the integration law for more than one out of the last five years (sect. 23). Another novelty is a nationality test by which the applicants shall demonstrate their knowledge of Danish culture, history and society (28 out of 40 questions shall be answered correctly); the test will be made on the basis of a textbook. In addition, the Danish language skill requirements have been raised considerably from 'Test in Danish 2' to 'Test in Danish 3'. While the target group of Danish Education 2 is persons with relatively short-term school attendance, the target group of Danish Education 3 is persons with an average or long-term school attendance, i.e., a vocational education, upper-secondary school or a long-term higher education. The language schools have reported that on a national basis only around 25-30 per cent of all participants are referred to Danish Education 3. Exemption from the new language requirements is possible only under very special circumstances, such as documented very severe physical or psychological disease resulting in the applicant not being able to fulfil the language requirements. In a note to the provision on exemption (sect. 24) it is made clear that the Ministry of Integration is presumed to submit the cases for exemption to the Parliamentary Committee on Nationality where the applicant has a severe physical handicap (such as mongolism), is brain-injured, blind or deaf, or has severe psychological diseases such as (paranoid) schizophrenia, a psychosis or a severe depression. It adds that the Ministry is presumed to refuse applications for exemption of those suffering from PTSD (Posttraumatic stress disorder) – 'even if the condition is chronic and this is documented by a medical declaration'. The Minister for Integration has explained that the reason for the exclusion is that PTSD 'is not a mental disease of such a severe nature that it as such can form the basis for submission to the Committee on Nationality'.[26]

The new agreement will prevent many foreigners from acquiring Danish nationality. Especially severely traumatised persons with chronic PTSD will not be able to fulfil the new language requirements as they are lacking the ability to learn a new language and many will not be able to hold a job; to exclude them from seeking exemption seems discriminatory. The agreement has therefore given rise to severe criticism from different organisations and institutions, language teachers, doctors and private persons; even demonstrations have been arranged. But so far, the agreement still stands.

3.3.2 Statistical developments

At the beginning of 2005, the Danish population comprised almost 5.5 million inhabitants with 4.9 per cent foreigners. The rest (95.1 per cent) are Danish nationals. Among them are 119,162 immigrants and 72,758 second or third generation 'immigrants' (see Table 3.1).

Approximately 43 per cent of all immigrants and descendants have acquired Danish nationality. From 1985 to 1997, the number of persons who acquired Danish nationality by other modes than by descent increased from more than 3,000 to more than 5,000. Most of the shifts occurred through naturalisation, while approximately 1,000 shifts per year occurred via the declaration/notification procedure and adoption. Since 1998, the total number of shifts increased to more than 10,000 per year, in 2000 the number of shifts was 18,811 and in 2002 it was 17,300. The annual number of declarations was at that time approximately 1,000, and the number of foreign adopted children amounted to around 600 per year (most of whom will have acquired Danish nationality by the adoption order) (see Table 3.2).

In 2002, only 1,045 persons out of 17,727 had their case dealt with after the new 2002 Circular entered into force. Therefore, only the statistics for 2003 demonstrate the impact of the 2002 Circular's strengthened criteria for naturalisation; it appears clear that the strengthened criteria resulted in a decline in naturalisations, but so far it seemed reasonable to expect that the decline was temporary (see the 2004 statistics) as it was, to a large extent, caused by the new language requirement which forced many applicants to put their applications on hold until they had passed a language exam (see Table 3.3 on the number of and reasons for refusals of naturalisation). However, with the new 2005 language and financial requirements there is reason to suppose that the decline will be more permanent, see below.

The figures demonstrate that so far the most important change has been the strengthening of the language requirement. As mentioned above, the 2002 requirements resulted in a delay in naturalisations,

Table 3.1: Composition of the Danish population

Year	*Danish by origin*		*Danish by acquisition (Immigrants and descendants)*		*Foreigners*		*Total*
2004/05	4,959,310	91.6 %	191,920	3.5 %	267,604	4.9 %	5,411,405

Source: Statistics Denmark, Nyt fra Danmarks Statistik, www.dst.dk/nyt.

Table 3.2: Shift to Danish nationality

Year	*Total*	*Declaration*	*Number of persons included in acts on naturalisation*[27]	*Adoption*[28]
1985	3,309		1,894	460
1986	3,622		2,143	662
1987	3,763		2,047	535
1988	3,744		2,269	455
1989	3,258		2,363	399
1990	3,028		1,823	352
1991	5,484		3,837	551
1992	5,104		2,789	475
1993	5,037	377	3,132	442
1994	5,736	369	2,430	511
1995	5,260	486	2,630	567
1996	7,281	471	4,917 (including children)	524
1997	5,482	590	3,532 (including children)	591
1998	10,262	683	10,113 (including children)	684
1999	12,416	1601	11,759 (including children)	638
2000	18,811	1500	15,925 (including children)	681
2001	11,902	868	8,484 (including children)	636
2002	17,300	901	17,727 (including children)	587
2003	6,583	1,134	6,184 (including children)	594
2004	14,976	810	9,485 (including children)	457

Sources: The total numbers of shifts and the numbers of adoptions stem from Statistics Denmark (Statistiske Efterretninger); the numbers of declarations have been supplied by the Ministry of Integration and the numbers of persons included in the naturalisation acts stem from the acts (accessible via the website of the Parliament: www.ft.dk)

especially for applicants without a Danish school education who would have to complete a language course. This problem could, however, to a large extent have been solved as time went by and applicants finished their courses, but with the 2005 requirements the prospects are no longer the same. Many immigrants have no ties to the labour market and the required language skills are now set so high that certain groups may be unable to fulfil them – even if they do their utmost. No groups are generally exempted from the tests; unlike before, all applications for exemption shall now be submitted to the Parliamentary Standing Committee on Nationality that makes its decisions in camera. The Committee's practice in respect of granting exemption from the language requirements became much more restrictive during the last year. In 2004, the Committee refused to grant Danish nationality to 168 persons on the ground of insufficient skills in the Danish language etc. due to physical or mental illness; 107 persons were exempted from the language requirement. Thus, in 2004, exemption from the language requirement was granted in approximately 39 per cent of the cases referred to the Committee. However, in February 2005 at the first meeting in the present Committee on Nationality,

Table 3.3: Refusals of naturalisation in Denmark (including dropped cases)

Reason for refusal	*1999*	*2000*	*2001*	*2002*	*2003*	*2004*
Has not issued solemn declaration (see 2002 Circular para. 2, 20, 23 and 24)				129	261	153
Unwilling to renounce a former nationality	2	6	6	6	12	18
Residence period too short or no residence in Denmark	70	222	246	962	716	592
Age requirement not fulfilled	3	13	14	7	9	13
Committed crimes	358	516	489	551	460	555
Due public debt	230	168	276	191	142	159
Lack of Danish language proficiency	537	840	778	504	2507	1632
Shelved cases (left the country, disappeared, dead)		218	169	187	133	143
Total	**1200**	**1983**	**1978**	**2537**	**4107**	**3122**

Source: Ministry of Integration

which was set up after the last election, it was decided to tighten the interpretation of the exemption rules. The result was that in the period from 17 March to 30 September 2005, 209 persons had their applications turned down and only fourteen were granted dispensation from the language requirement, meaning that dispensation was only granted in 6 per cent of the cases.[29] In future, even fewer persons may be granted exemption, since applicants suffering from PTSD have been excluded from being granted exemption (due to this disorder).

The Committee's restrictiveness is also illustrated by its practice regarding stateless applicants. In 2002, applications from 74 stateless persons were presented to the Committee, which decided that the applicants' Danish language skills constituted a hindrance to naturalisation in 21 cases. In 2003, 74 cases were presented to the Committee and in 53 of these cases exemption from the language requirements was rejected. In 2004, fourteen applicants out of 25 had their applications for exemption from the language requirements rejected.[30]

There are no Danish statistics on cases of dual nationality. Refugees and immigrants from countries where release from nationality is impossible or very difficult are not required to renounce their previous nationality. The Ministry of Integration has drawn up a list of such countries (up to 20). In practice, a large number of applicants are exempted from the requirement of renunciation of a former nationality, maybe up to 40 per cent.[31]

Denmark has only a small net immigration. In 2004, the number of persons who immigrated to Denmark was 49,859 while the number of emigrants was 45,017. Among the immigrants were 17,737 Danish nationals, while 20,741 Danish nationals emigrated.

3.3.3 *Special categories and quasi-citizenship*

Since 1776, Danish nationality law has applied to all parts of the Danish realm (see the Nationality Act, sect. 14). All Danish nationals have the same kind of nationality regardless of whether they are born in Denmark, the Faroe Islands or Greenland. There are no specific statistics for different parts of the realm.

As to quasi-citizenship, such a status is not a familiar concept within Danish nationality law. However, a few Icelandic nationals (at the most 37 people) have a similar status: the Danish Constitutional Act, sect. 87, states, that nationals of Iceland who are equal in rights to Danish nationals in accordance with the Act to Repeal the Act on the Danish-Icelandic Federation (Act No. 205 of 16 May 1950) retain the constitutional rights tied to Danish nationality. Thus, said Icelandic nationals may during residence in Denmark enjoy voting rights for national elections and other rights guaranteed by the Constitution for Danish nationals.

This special status was created when Iceland gained independence in 1918 (see the Act No. 19 of 30 November 1918 on the Danish-Icelandic Federation). After the Federation had been brought to an end, it was decided by Act No. 205 of 16 May 1950 that Icelandic nationals with habitual residence in Denmark on 6 March 1946 or during the preceding ten years retained the right to live or take up residence in Denmark and there enjoy equal rights with Danish nationals.

3.3.4 *Institutional arrangements*

3.3.4.1 *The legislative process*

Like most European democracies, Denmark has a tripartition of power: the legislative, executive and judicial branches (see sect. 3 of the Constitutional Act of Denmark (1953)). The legislative authority is conjointly vested in the King (the government) and the Parliament (the Folketing). The only constitutional provision on acquisition of nationality is sect. 44 (1), according to which 'no alien shall be naturalised except by statute', instituted by the first Danish Constitution (1849). The idea was to transfer the competence of granting *indfødsret* from the (former) sovereign King to the King and the Parliament (the legislature). As already mentioned, the model for the rule was a similar provision in the Belgian Constitution. The Constituent Assembly considered such a provision to be rooted in 'general constitutional concepts'. The aim was to prevent the King (the administration) from being the sole grant-awarding authority; instead, the legislature should grant naturalisation either by a general or a personal (singular) act. There was no further indication as to how the legislature should deal with naturalisation matters.

When the new Parliament (the *Rigsdag*) read the first bill on naturalisation (of ten applicants), there were different opinions on the procedure to be followed. The Three-Year War and the national division between the supporters of the Eider policy and the united monarchy (*helstats-*) policy influenced the debate; among other things it was discussed whether nationals from the Nordic countries and nationals from Germany should be dealt with in the same way.

A practice soon developed, however, according to which the Ministry responsible for the *indfødsret*-legislation (under the June Constitution the Ministry of the Interior) drafted bills on naturalisation including applicants whom the Ministry presumed fulfilled the legislature's requirements for naturalisation. At first, it was assumed that the 1776 Act's conditions on acquisition based on special achievement for the country should be taken into consideration, but in practice affiliation to 'the people' became decisive. Among the crucial elements from the beginning was knowledge of the Danish language; in addition, a long period of residence on the state territory and good conduct were necessary preconditions. A bill on naturalisation contained the names of the individual applicants, small biographies and information as to whether the local authorities could recommend their naturalisation. Over time, general guidelines from the Parliament to the Ministry were given in the form of circulars,[32] and personal sensitive information regarding the applicants was removed from the bills.[33]

Bills on naturalisation are, like other bills, subject to three readings in the Chamber. After the first reading, the bill is referred to a committee, which since 1953 has been the Standing Committee on Nationality (the *Indfødsretsudvalg*) composed of 17 Members of Parliament representing the major parties. The Standing Committee on Nationality may receive confidential information on the applicants' conduct, language ability etc. and ask questions of the relevant minister. When the Committee has dealt with the bill, it submits a report to the Parliament. Traditionally, as practice developed, the Parliament felt a kind of obligation to grant nationality to all persons included in a bill on naturalisation,[34] but since the late 1980s, this practice changed and several amendments for exclusion of certain applicants from the bills have, as already mentioned, become a common feature of the committee report. This may, however, now change as it appears from the introduction to the 2005 agreement that the political parties behind the agreement, which includes the Danish People's Party, will (now) vote on the government's bill on naturalisation.[35]

Over the course of time, an increasing number of foreigners have applied for naturalisation. From 1 January 1850 to 31 December 1914, a number of 11,495 foreigners were naturalised,[36] which is less than the number of naturalised persons within each year from 1999 to 2004 (except for 2003). It is evident that it is no longer possible for the Standing Committee on Nationality to deal with each applicant's case. The examination is left to the relevant ministry, now the Ministry of Integration. However, doubtful cases are referred to the Committee, which decides whether an applicant is to be included in a bill.

In general, the legislative naturalisation process is out of step with present day conditions. The naturalisation criteria, which were earlier agreed upon by the members of the Standing Committee, have now been decided by three of the Parliament's seven political parties. There is no in-depth public discussion on the criteria in Parliament. Applicants who fulfil the criteria may count on being naturalised, but they have no legal guarantee; the criteria may be amended at relatively short intervals and even retroactively, and there is no accessible regulation on doubtful cases and exemptions from the general criteria, which seems inconsistent with the rule of law (Ersbøll 1997: 202). It has been the general perception, as naturalisation is based on the discretion of the Parliament, that no one has *a right* to Danish nationality. In principle, there are no restraints on the Parliament's and the Standing Committee's discretionary powers other than the limitations which follow from international agreements and conventions ratified by Denmark (Kleis & Beckman 2004: 106). During the reading of the bills there has been division in Parliament, causing much discussion, often during all three readings. The legislative treatment of the naturalisation cases leads to delays for even obvious cases – as most of the cases are.[37] In general, it is detrimental to the applicants' protection of due process, while lacking in possibilities for appeal.[38]

A more up-to-date arrangement might be brought about in three different ways. For several reasons the best solution would be to repeal the Constitution's sect. 44 (1), however amending the Danish Constitution is very difficult. The Constitutional Act's sect. 88 firstly requires that Parliament pass a bill for the purpose of a new constitutional provision; secondly, that writs shall be issued for the election of a new Parliament and that the bill shall be passed un-amended by the new Parliament; subsequently, the bill shall, within six months after its final passage, be submitted to the electors for approval or rejection by direct voting. In order for the bill to come into force it is required that a majority of those taking part in the voting and at least 40 per cent of the electorate vote in favour of the bill. The last requirement is considered particularly difficult to fulfil.[39]

Another solution may be to adopt a general act on naturalisation, authorising the administration to grant naturalisation by entitlement if and when the conditions in the act are met. In order to comply with the Constitutional Act, such an act must contain completely distinct naturalisation criteria. The text must not leave any room for discretionary administrative decisions and must not include vague clauses. The only task which may be left to the administration is to ascertain whether the applicants meet the act's criteria whereby they will have acquired nationality (directly) 'by statute'. Consequently, (discretionary) decisions on dispensation from the general criteria must still rest with the legislature. The adoption of such a general act on naturalisation by entitlement was discussed in Parliament at the beginning of the twentieth century. Recently, a similar proposal has been advocated in the Danish literature (Koch 1999: 35), but it is at present rather unlikely that the Parliament will vote for this solution.

However, some members of Parliament, the Social Liberals, have suggested a third solution, the adoption of a general act on naturalisation containing the naturalisation criteria while still leaving the competence of granting naturalisation to Parliament. While such a procedure would ensure an open parliamentary debate on the criteria and allow the participation of all Members of Parliament it would not solve the problems of delays, lack of review possibilities, etc. And the proposal has not gained support in Parliament; the view being that as long as Parliament (in principle) can naturalise on the basis of different criteria each time a bill is to be passed, it is useless to adopt a general law containing the naturalisation criteria.

Under the present system, the police receive application forms and check formalities, e.g. whether they have been correctly filled in and all the required documentation has been submitted.[40] Thereafter, the individual cases are sent to the Ministry of Integration, which after a waiting period of sixteen to eighteen months checks whether the naturalisation criteria are met and, if so, it includes the applicants in a bill on naturalisation. Such bills are introduced in Parliament in April and October; the reading of the bills normally takes two to three months, and after their adoption the Ministry of Integration will notify the persons included and send them proof of their Danish nationality. Persons whose naturalisation is conditioned by their release from a former nationality will receive proof of their Danish nationality only after they have documented their release. The Presidium of the Parliament has decided to invite new Danish nationals to an official welcoming celebration; on 26 March 2006 a nationality day was arranged in Parliament for all new nationals naturalised during the preceding year. Thereafter, it will be decided whether or not to make such a celebration a traditional practice.[41]

The (general) Act on Danish Nationality (1950) was adopted and is amended in the same way as other acts, and as with many other (general) acts, there will normally be a hearing procedure among different ministries, institutions and organisations before the bill's introduction in Parliament.

3.3.4.2 *The process of implementation*

While the Ministry of Integration and the Parliament (and the police) share responsibility for the implementation of the rules on naturalisation of foreigners, the Ministry of Integration alone is responsible for decisions about whether a Danish national with permanent residence abroad may keep his or her Danish nationality (sect. 8 (1)) and for making decisions on release from Danish nationality (sect. 9).

Regional authorities like the county governor, the Prefect of Copenhagen, the High Commissioner of the Faroe Islands and the High Commissioner of Greenland are responsible for the implementation of the provisions on acquisition of nationality by declaration (by entitlement, see sects. 3 and 4). Persons entitled to Danish nationality may submit a declaration to these authorities, and once a declaration is received it cannot be withdrawn. If the conditions specified in the relevant provision of the Nationality Act are met by the date on which the declaration is received, nationality is acquired and effective from that date, and a nationality certificate is subsequently issued to the declarant person. The process of implementation shall, in principle, be uniform, as the Constitution's sect. 44 (1), as mentioned earlier, leaves no room for discretionary decisions; the task of the authorities is merely to ascertain whether the unambiguously formulated conditions are met, in which case nationality is acquired *ex lege* (by statute).

The competence to make decisions on deprivation of nationality due to fraudulent conduct during the procedure of acquisition of Danish nationality (sect. 8 A) or due to violation of part 12 and 13 of the Danish Criminal Code (sect. 8 B) lies with the courts of justice (normally the district court where the person concerned lives or resides). It is up to the prosecutor, at the request of the Ministry of Integration, to institute proceedings for deprivation of nationality. Proceedings are governed by the rules for the administration of criminal justice.

The Ministry of Integration has published information on the conditions for acquisition and loss of nationality etc. Such information is also accessible on the Ministry's homepage, which furthermore contains the answers to frequently asked questions on nationality (in Danish and English), but there are no public outreach programs encouraging immigrants to naturalise (or expatriates to reclaim Danish nationality).

While as a rule the legislature's decisions on naturalisation cannot be appealed, the regional authorities' decisions may be appealed to the Ministry of Integration and the Ministry's decisions may be brought before the Parliamentary Ombudsman and/or a court of justice.

3.4 Conclusions

Denmark was originally a rather typical nation-state consisting of several entities; however, after having been defeated in its wars, Denmark had lost most of its territories. In the nineteenth century, Denmark evolved into a homogeneous nation-state with a political culture and identity based on an interaction between language, people, nation and state (Østergaard 2000: 143). It has been pointed out that Danish national identity and political culture combine features of what is often referred to as East European integral nationalism typical of smaller, recently independent nation-states and the patriotic concept of citizenship in the older West European state nations, and that the explanation for this apparent paradox is that Denmark belongs to both families (Østergaard 2000: 144).

Danish nationality policy should be seen in a broad historical perspective including Denmark's geopolitical position. When it comes to the naturalisation of foreigners, Denmark has pursued a more exclusive policy than its Nordic neighbouring states, especially by setting up requirements for longer periods of habitual residence in its territory. Historically, during parliamentary debate on nationality issues it has been indicated that Denmark has had an immigration different from the other Nordic countries. One of the reasons may have been that the Danish capital is located at the edge of Denmark very close to Sweden. For instance, around the beginning of the First World War, Members of Parliament were concerned about the fact that ten times as many Swedish nationals moved to and were naturalised in Denmark, compared with Danish nationals who moved to and were naturalised in Sweden. They argued for more restrictive naturalisation criteria asserting that the Swedish applicants were motivated by the Danish social welfare system, although the Minister for the Interior suggested that the attractive Danish capital close to the Swedish hinterland could be part of the explanation. An even more influential factor has probably been the fact that the only neighbouring country connected to Denmark is Germany, which historically has had a strong influence on Denmark, and for a long time immigrants from Germany formed another major part of the applicants for naturalisation.

During the last decades another influential factor may have been that the legislature has continuously demonstrated that it is divided on matters of immigration and nationality; this disagreement may curb any interest in a reform of the more than fifty-year-old nationality act. However, first and foremost, the party composition of the legislature during these last decades seems to have been decisive. The Social Democrats have not been able to agree on a common immigration policy, and the leaders of the party have been weakened by this internal disagreement. In their turn, the Danish People's Party has succeeded in carrying through the policy which members of the Party have advocated since the party came into existence, and it has been implemented to a large extent while the Danish People's Party has acted as a supporting party to the Liberal-Conservative government. In this course, many former social democratic voters have voted for the Danish People's Party. The Social Democrats have during the last years not had much political influence. The newly elected chairman of the party has promised to 'work the government out of office' by coming to terms with it, but as long as the government's policy is carried out with the support of the Danish People's Party, the Social Democrats' influence may be limited to concessions.

As matters stand, the present Act on Danish Nationality dates from 1950 and no regular reform has been discussed – in spite of the increasing immigration to Denmark and an almost comparable Danish emigration. On the contrary, while other countries tend to tolerate dual nationality, Denmark stands firm on its traditional opposition to this status,[42] and while other countries tend to replace discretionary naturalisation by entitlement to nationality for certain groups, Denmark has repealed its traditional provision granting second generations of immigrant descent a right to Danish nationality.

Thus, while Denmark had a nationality law in line with many other European and especially the Nordic countries in the twentieth century, this has changed – not only due to the tougher criteria for acquisition and loss of nationality, but maybe even more because some of the other countries have provided easier access to their nationality. Insofar as there has been a converging development this can to some extent be traced to international agreements and conventions, which have set some standards as well as some limitations.

Over the last years, there has not been a general perception of *the right to a nationality* as a means of integrating foreigners into the social and political life of Denmark or as a desirable goal in itself. Instead, *the strengthening of the criteria* for acquisition of nationality has been seen as a means of fulfilling the visions and strategies of the government regarding the integration of foreigners. The abolition of (non-Nordic) second-generation immigrant descendants' rights to Danish nationality is aimed at ensuring 'that the possibility of acquisition by declaration cannot be used in situations where the persons concerned have had their habitual residence in another country as children, during the most important years for integration'. Based on a presumption of immigrants' desires to acquire Danish nationality under certain conditions, the achievement of Danish nationality has been seen as an incentive for them to comply with the sharpened requirements on conduct, Danish language abilities etc.; thus, (a better) integration is seen as a kind of *quid pro quo* for the acquisition of nationality.

Furthermore some politicians have used the traditional interpretation of the constitutional provision on foreigners' acquisition of nationality by statute to justify repealing the second generation immigrant descendants' right to nationality in a way that seems to be unfounded. When the constitution of 1849 was adopted, it was the general idea that persons born and brought up in Denmark were 'Danish' as a matter of fact. Repealing their entitlement to nationality seems to be out of line with both past and present considerations towards integration.

Chronological table of major reforms in Danish nationality law since 1945

Date	Document	Content of change
27 May 1950	Act No. 252 on Danish Nationality (Lov om dansk indfødsret), in force, since 1 January 1951	Gender equality; facilitated access to nationality for Nordic nationals.
24 March 1952	Circular No. 51 on naturalisation (Cirkulære vedrørende meddelelse af dansk indfødsret)	Normal residence requirement reduced from 15 to 10 years (7 for Nordic nationals).
5 June 1953	Constitutional Act No. 169 (Danmarks Riges Grundlov) in force	Sect. 44 (1) maintaining the former Constitution's sect. 50 (1) stating that 'No alien shall be naturalised except by statute'.
23 June 1956	Circular No.108 on naturalisation (Cirkulære vedrørende ændring af indenrigsministeriets cirkulære af 24. marts 1952 om meddelelse af dansk indfødsret)	Residence requirement for adopted children of school age 1½ years; less for pre-schoolers.
6 June 1968	Circular No. 126 on naturalisation (Cirkulære om meddelelse af dansk indfødsret (naturalisation))	Normal residence requirement reduced to 7 years (3 years for Nordic nationals); eased conduct rules.
11 December 1968	Act No. 399 amending the 1950 Law (Lov om ændring af lov om dansk indfødsret)	Persons between 21 and 23 entitled to nationality, if they had resided in Denmark for 5 years before the age of 16 and permanently between the age of 16 and 21.
29 March 1978	Act No. 117 amending the 1950 law (Lov om ændring af lov om indfødsret)	Gender equality as to transfer of nationality to children in wedlock; nationality by declaration for adopted children under 7 years.
21 May 1981	Circular No. 77 on naturalisation (Cirkulære om meddelelse af dansk indfødsret (naturalisation))	Gender equality as to facilitated naturalisation for spouses (3 years of marriage, 4 years of co-habitation in Denmark); residence for Nordic nationals 2 years.
1 June 1983	Circular No. 69 on naturalisation (Cirkulære om meddelelse af dansk	Tightening language requirement; elaborating residence rules as to

Date	Document	Content of change
	indfødsret (naturalisation))	socialisation-based acquisition.
4 June 1986	Act No. 326 amending the 1950 law (Lov om ændring af lov om indfødsret)	Automatic acquisition by adoption for children under 12 years.
2 February 1990	Circular No. 17 on naturalisation (Cirkulære om dansk indfødsret (naturalisation))	More explicit conditions for naturalisation.
18 March 1991	Act No. 159 amending the 1950 law (Lov om ændring af lov om indfødsret)	Fee for discretionary naturalisation.
6 February 1992	Circular No. 11077 on naturalisation (Cirkulære om dansk indfødsret ved naturalisation)	Right to naturalisation for a stateless child born and residing in Denmark.
21 December 1994	Act No. 1097 amending the 1950 Law (Lov om indfødsrets meddelelse og om ændring af lov om dansk indfødsret)	Statutory basis for naturalisation fee of 1000 Danish Crowns (approximately 135 Euro); information on applicants may be collected by authorities.
2 April 1997	Act No. 233 amending the 1950 Law (Lov om ændring af adoptionsloven, indfødsretsloven og navneloven)	Ratification of Hague Convention on the Protection of Children and Cooperation in Respect of Intercountry Adoption (1993).
3 October 1997	Circular No. 132 on naturalisation (Cirkulære om dansk indfødsret ved naturalisation)	Elaborating requirements, among others by stating that residence periods shall be counted from the granting of a permanent residence permit (already in practice for some years).
23 December 1998	Act No. 1018 amending the 1950 Law (Lov om ændring af (bl.a.) lov om dansk indfødsret)	Ratification of the European Convention on Nationality (1997): Equal rights to children born in and out of wedlock, with the exception of children born abroad; equal rights to adopted and biological children; prevention of statelessness.
16 June 1999	Circular No. 90 on naturalisation (Cirkulære om dansk indfødsret ved naturalisation)	Relaxed calculation of residence period; stateless persons 6 years; 'princess rule'; disadvantaged groups exempted from language requirement.
29 December 1999	Act No. 1102 amending the 1950 Law (Lov om ændring af lov om indfødsret)	Second generation's entitlement to nationality conditional on absence of criminal record.
5 April 2002	Act No. 193 amending the 1950 Law (Lov om ændring af indfødsretsloven og udlændingeloven)	Loss of nationality due to fraud.
6 June 2002	Act No. 366 amending the 1950 Law (Lov om ændring af indfødsretsloven)	A marriage contracted by a person already married has no consequences regarding nationality.

Date	Document	Content of change
12 June 2002	Circular No. 55 on naturalisation (Cirkulæreskrivelse om nye retningslinier for optagelse på lovforslag om indfødsrets meddelelse)	Oath of loyalty; increased residence requirements (normally 9 years); strengthened rules on conduct, debts and language (formal certification, knowledge of society, culture and history, repealed exception for the elderly).
5 May 2004	Act No. 311 amending the 1950 Law (Lov om ændring af lov om indfødsret)	Repealed second generation's entitlement to nationality, with the exception of Nordic nationals; introduced loss of nationality due to conviction of crimes directed against the vital interests of the state.
7 June 2004	Consolidated Act No. 422 on Danish Nationality (Bekendtgørelse af lov om dansk indfødsret)	
8 December 2005	Circular No 9 of 12 January on Naturalisation (Cirkulæreskrivelse nr. 9 af 12. januar 2006 om naturalisation)	Declaration on (absence of) crimes against the state, strengthened rules on conduct and language, naturalisation test, self-support (no reliance on social benefits for more than one year out of five); no exemption from language requirements for those with PTSD.

Notes

1 In addition, the state comprised the Atlantic dependencies of Iceland, the Faroe Islands and Greenland plus colonies in the West Indies, West Africa and India.

2 The so-called Bancroft Treaties (1868-1874) between the United States and a number of other states illustrate another effort to solve the problems connected to migration and naturalisation. The important consideration was to achieve an arrangement for the migrants' military obligations making it possible for the state of emigration to consider the naturalisation lapsed if an emigrant returned to his native country. A Danish-American convention in this respect was signed 20 July 1872.

3 Letter of 18 September 1875 (1332/1875) to the Ministry of Foreign Affairs (Larsen 1948b: 47).

4 Provisional draft of a legislation as uniform as possible for Denmark and Sweden concerning acquisition and loss of nationality *(Foreløbigt udkast til en saa vidt muligt ensartet Lovgivning for Danmark og Sverige angaaende Erhvervelse og Fortabelse af Statsborgerret)* (1888).

5 Draft Law on Acquisition and Loss of Nationality, prepared by commissioners for Denmark, Sweden and Norway *(Udkast til Lov om Erhvervelse og Tab af Statsborgerret, udarbejdet af Kommitterede for Danmark, Sverige og Norge)* (1890).

6 New draft nationality laws, prepared by delegates from Denmark, Norway and Sweden, 1921 (Udkast til nye Statsborgerretslove, udarbejdede af Delegerede for Danmark, Norge og Sverige, 1921).

7 The general residence period suggested in the Norwegian and Swedish draft Acts was five years.
8 Report including new draft nationality laws for Denmark, Norway and Sweden, prepared by delegates from the three countries. (Betænkning med udkast til nye statsborgerretslove for Danmark, Norge og Sverige, afgivet af delegerede for de tre lande) (1949).
9 According to the bill, it was a precondition for deprivation of nationality that said person had been sentenced to imprisonment for at least one year. The proposal on expatriation had its background in situations of treason during the Second World War, but was rejected by Parliament for several reasons.
10 By limiting the age to twelve, it was intended to secure that the declaring person had attended Danish school for a period of two to three years.
11 On 21 December 1950, Denmark, Norway and Sweden agreed to implement the provisions mentioned under A-C.
12 The Convention was ratified by Denmark ten years later.
13 The provision should fulfil the requirements in art. 1 of the 1961 Convention as to a contracting state's granting of its nationality to persons born on its territory who would otherwise be stateless, see art. 1 (1) (b) and 1 (2). It comprised any foreigner born on the state territory, as it was often difficult to prove whether a person was stateless or not.
14 It was only in 1986 that the provision changed in order to grant foreign adopted children Danish nationality automatically by virtue of the adoption order.
15 Act No. 233 of 2 April 1997.
16 Act No. 1018 of 23 December 1998.
17 Act No. 1102 of 29 December 1999.
18 The proposal was based on a new Nordic Agreement on Nationality (of 14 January 2002).
19 See Act No. 193 of 5 April 2002.
20 Problematic with respect to an effective implementation of the entitlement to nationality (for persons who fulfil the 1961 Convention's requirements) is that it has not found expression in any Danish regulation, including the new 2005 agreement, see below.
21 A general facilitated acquisition of nationality for second and third generations of immigrant descent seems to be lacking, insofar as persons belonging to these groups can only be granted naturalisation independently at the age of eighteen where many of them will fulfil the normal residence requirement of nine years and no further facilitation will thus apply (generally speaking).
22 See the 1997 Convention, art. 7 recognising deprivation of nationality without creating statelessness in cases of conduct seriously prejudicial to the vital interest of the state party (including treason and other activities directed against the vital interests of the state but not criminal offences of a general nature according to the explanatory report).
23 'The Liberals' programme (Time for change)'.
24 The spokesman has often referred to the Constitution and the naturalisation requirements decided by the first parliamentary committee on nationality and the 1776 Act stating that the children of the country should enjoy the bread of the country.
25 There are other intensifications, i.e., any fine for violation of the Criminal Act's chapters 12 and 13 incur a waiting period of 6 years, and imprisonment of up to 60 days for such violations leads to a waiting period of 12 years from when the sentence is served.

26 Letter of 20 January 2006 to the Rehabilitation and Research Centre for Torture Victims.
27 The number of people included in the two or three annual naturalisation acts does not correspond to the total number of shifts to Danish nationality, as naturalisation by statute in many cases is made conditional on the applicant's release from a former nationality by a certain day (typically by two years), and in practice, naturalisation will only take place if and when the applicant is released from the former nationality. Furthermore, it should be noted that the number of children naturalised together with their parents has only since 1996 been mentioned in the general notes to the bills.
28 The statistics are estimated numbers of acquisition by adoption. From 1990 the numbers cover adopted children under the age of twelve to whom Danish nationality since 1986 is normally transferred automatically by the adoption order. Statistics before 1990 cover adopted children under the age of fourteen and some of them, probably less than 5 per year, may have acquired Danish nationality by declaration and should in principle not be counted in this column.
29 www.ft.dk/samling/20051/almdel/IFU/spm/2/svar/endeligt/20051114/index.htm (Reply to question 2 of 13 October 2005).
30 www.ft.dk/Samling/20031/udvbilag/IFU/Almdel_bilag71.htm (Reply to question 6 of 18 February 2004).
31 See Official Norwegian Reports (Norges offentlige utredninger) (NOU) 2000:32, Law on Acquisition and Loss of Nationality (*Lov om erhverv og tap av norsk statsborgerskap*), p. 79. See further the introduction to the Danish 2005 agreement where it is stated that the agreement parties have decided to initiate an analysis as to the possibilities of adjusting practice with a view to reduce (the number of cases of) dual nationality.
32 Only recently have all the criteria been published; until 1997 the more detailed guidelines were contained in a confidential 'office circular'.
33 At present, the applicants' name, municipality, year of birth, country of origin and former nationality are published in the bills on naturalisation. Confident information as to residence, language abilities, public debt and possible punishable acts are given to the Parliamentary Standing Committee on Nationality.
34 For a long period there were amendments to include additional applicants, but the only applicants to be excluded would be those who had died or withdrawn their application.
35 So far, the Danish People's Party has proposed amendments, which could not be agreed upon, and the Party was not put under an obligation to vote for the government's bill. In future, the only amendments for exclusion to be expected will be the Minister for Integration's own amendments concerning applicants whose conditions have changed in the period between their inclusion in the bill and its reading in Parliament.
36 Alphabetic list of names of persons naturalised in the years 1850-1915, drawn up by the Ministry of the Interior (1916).
37 Under all circumstances applicants who fulfil the criteria after a bill has been introduced will have to wait at least half a year for another bill to be introduced (as only two bills are introduced per year, one in spring and one in autumn).
38 As a consequence of the Constitution's sect. 44 (1), Denmark has made a reservation to the European Convention on Nationality, art. 12 on the right to an administrative or judicial review. In the reservation it states that the legislature grants naturalisation and as the legislature is not bound by the general rules of administrative law, no rights exist for an administrative review. Nothing is mentioned regarding the possibilities of judicial review, which cannot be totally excluded.
39 Since 1849, the Constitution has only been (substantially) amended four times.

40 As it has not been discussed whether to transfer this task from the police to other local authorities; however this question seems likely to be raised with an amendment of the present naturalisation system.

41 The initiative comes from the Social Liberals following American and Canadian models.

42 The new Minister for Integration, in a newspaper article of 6 April 2005, declared that nationality is not a 'grab-bag', and that the answer to globalisation is not that anybody can have a wallet full of different passports; nationality means something and it is important to avoid that a person, through dual nationality, has for instance electoral rights in more than one country. Nationality should be chosen by 'the heart'.

Bibliography

Bjørn, C. (2005), *Denmark – History* - 6.6, 6.7, 6.8, 6.9 and 6.10. www.um.dk.

Ersbøll, E. (1997), 'Retten til at have Rettigheder', in M. Kjærum, K. Slavinsky & J. Vedsted-Hansen (eds.), *Grundloven og menneskerettigheder i et dansk og europæisk perspektiv*, 183-210. Copenhagen: Jurist- og Økonomforbundets Forlag.

Ersbøll, E. (2001), 'Nationality Law in Denmark, Finland and Sweden', in R. Hansen & P. Weil (eds.), *Towards a European Nationality: Citizenship, Immigration and Nationality Law*, 230-254. New York: Palgrave.

Ersbøll, E. (2003), 'Statsborgerskab – medborgarskap – europæisk konvergens – nordisk divergens?' *Mennesker og Rettigheter, Nordic Journal of Human rights* 21: 147-164.

Feldbæk, O. (2005), *Denmark – History* -6.5. www.um.dk.

Kleis, B. & N. Beckman (2004), *Indfødsretsloven med kommentarer*. Copenhagen: Jurist- og Økonomforbundets Forlag.

Koch, I. E. (1999), 'Retssikkerhed i forbindelse med erhvervelse af indfødsret ved lov', *Juristen* 1: 26-42.

Larsen, K. (1944), *Nordisk Statsborgerret*. Copenhagen: Foreningen Norden.

Larsen, K. (1948a), *Indfødsretslovene I, Lovtekster og Kommentarer*. Copenhagen: Ejnar Munksgaard.

Larsen, K. (1948b), *Indfødsretslovene II, Cirkulærer og Afgørelser*. Copenhagen: Ejnar Munksgaard.

Lundgreen-Nielsen, F. (1992), 'Grundtvig og danskhed', in *Dansk Identitetshistorie 3, Folkets Danmark 1848 - 1940*. Copenhagen: C. A. Reitzel.

Matzen, H. (1907), *Indfødsretten i Wienerfreden*. Særtryk af 'Sønderjydske Aarbøger'. Aabenraa: Hejmdal's Trykkeri.

Østergaard, U. (2000): 'Danish Nationality Identity: Between Multinational Heritage and Small State Nationalism', in H. Branner & M. Kelstrup (eds.), *Denmark's Policy towards Europe after 1945: History, Theory and Options*, 139-184. Odense: University Press.

Rerup, L. & N. F. Christiansen (2005), *Denmark – History*, 6.17 and 6.18. www.um.dk.

Rerup, L. (2005), *Denmark – History*, 6.11, 6.12, 6.13 and 6.14. www.um.dk.

Stilling, N. P. & A. L. Olsen (1994), *A New Life, Danish Emigration to North America as described by the emigrants themselves in letters 1842-1946*. Aalborg: Danes Worldwide Archive.

Trommer, A. (2005), *Denmark – History*, 6.15. www.um.dk.

Zahle, H. (1996), 'Danish Nationality Law', in B. Nascimbene (ed.), *Nationality Law in the European Union*. London: Butterworths.

4 Finland

Jessica Fagerlund

4.1 Introduction

In January 2003, the city of Turku, honoured, as the first city in Finland, the new Finnish nationals by inviting them to a nationality party (Anon 2005). This celebration can be seen as an effort to strengthen the feeling of kinship for the new Finnish nationals, and the intention was to make a tradition out of this celebration. This comes as a timely encouragement for all those immigrants wishing to become naturalised in Finland at a time when Finland is introducing somewhat stricter requirements for the acquisition of Finnish nationality.

Finland adopted a new Nationality Act in 2003. The main principles embedded in the Act are the acceptance of multiple nationality, prevention of statelessness and gender equality. The provisions for naturalisation have become more detailed and new modes of acquisition for certain groups of persons have been introduced.

Finnish nationality law has traditionally been based on the principle of ius sanguinis while ius soli has had a limited application in Finnish legislation. Children acquire Finnish nationality at birth as a consequence of their parents' Finnish nationality. Men and women are placed in an almost equal position, as a child will acquire Finnish nationality both from a Finnish mother and a Finnish father. Acquisition at birth of a parent's nationality is automatic in all cases except when the child is born abroad, out of wedlock, by a Finnish father and a foreign mother. An occasion of ius sanguinis after birth is at hand when a child is born out of wedlock by a Finnish father and a foreign mother and the parents later get married; then the child will automatically acquire Finnish nationality through the parents' marriage.

Ius soli practices for certain children born in Finland have evolved as the Finnish nationality legislation has developed and the prevention of statelessness has become an important consideration within nationality law. Foundlings and other children whose nationality is unknown or who cannot acquire their parents' nationality acquire Finnish nationality automatically at birth.

Finland has traditionally held a critical position as regards multiple nationality, but as the international trend lately has been moving towards a more positive attitude to the acceptance of multiple nationality, Finland has consequently revised its position on the matter. On 1 June 2003, when the new Nationality Act came into force, toleration of multiple nationality was introduced as a major principle. A Finnish national acquiring a second nationality no longer automatically loses his or her Finnish nationality. Nor is it a requirement for a foreign national who acquires Finnish nationality to renounce his or her former nationality. Before this change came about the principal rule was that anyone acquiring a second nationality automatically lost his or her Finnish nationality, and a condition for acquisition of Finnish nationality was that any other nationality was renounced.

Gender equality has gradually been introduced into Finnish nationality law. Since 1968, a foreign woman will no longer automatically acquire her Finnish husband's nationality upon marriage. As of today women and men have an almost equal position in nationality matters, as explained above.

Discretionary naturalisation, i.e., acquisition by application, is the main mode of acquisition of Finnish nationality for persons who have not acquired Finnish nationality as a consequence of the ius sanguinis or ius soli principles. The barrier for acquiring Finnish nationality by discretionary naturalisation cannot be considered as exceptionally high, even though the normal residence requirement in the new Act was raised from five to six years of continuous residence in Finland. In contrast to the old Nationality Act, the requirement for a guaranteed livelihood was abolished in the new Act and language proficiency has been specifically included.

A number of exceptions apply with regard to the conditions for discretionary naturalisation, in particular as far as the required period of residence in Finland is concerned. Groups to whom exceptions apply are refugees, stateless persons, spouses, former Finnish nationals, Nordic nationals, co-applicants and children of Finnish nationals.

Finnish nationality can also be acquired by declaration. This possibility applies to certain groups of persons under specific conditions, e.g., former Finnish nationals, Nordic nationals and young persons who have lived in Finland for a long time.

Finnish nationality may be lost for a limited number of reasons, but it is noteworthy that Finnish nationality may never be lost if such loss would lead to statelessness. False or misleading information given in order to acquire Finnish nationality may lead to the loss of Finnish nationality for a main applicant as well as for a co-applicant child. Furthermore, a person may lose his or her Finnish nationality if it is granted on the basis of the father's nationality and paternity is later annulled. A person will also automatically lose his or her Finnish nationality upon turning 22 years of age, if he or she has insufficient connection to Finland. Finally, a child who has acquired Finnish nationality as a foundling or as a person with an unclear nationality automatically loses his or her Finnish nationality if his or her foreign nationality is established before he or she turns five years of age.

The rules on acquisition and loss of nationality that apply to nationals living in Finland also apply to expatriates, if not stated otherwise in the law. Loss of Finnish nationality at the age of 22 due to insufficient connection to Finland is of relevance to expatriates' descendents. Children born out of wedlock by a Finnish father and a foreign mother are treated differently depending on whether they are born in Finland or abroad (see above). Furthermore, spouses of expatriates do not benefit from the favourable naturalisation rules for spouses of Finnish nationals as a consequence of the requirement of at least the last two years of habitual residence in Finland.

Nordic cooperation in the field of nationality legislation can be traced back to the late nineteenth century. The object of the cooperation was to harmonise the legislation and later on in the process also to place all nationals from the Nordic countries on an as equal a footing as possible (Ersbøll 2003). The abolishment of the passport requirement for Nordic nationals travelling within the Nordic countries and the exemption from the requirement of residence, study and work permits for Nordic nationals working, studying or taking up residence in another Nordic country are examples of what the cooperation has accomplished.

The Nordic countries have agreed on reciprocal rules on facilitated acquisition and reacquisition of nationality. The Nordic Agreement of 1950 contained rules on, e.g., reacquisition of nationality by declaration when taking up residence again in the former state of nationality. Finland acceded to the Nordic Agreement in 1969, after an introduction of the declaration procedure in the Finnish Nationality Act of 1968 had made the accession possible.[1]

The Nordic countries have tried to achieve uniformity with regard to nationality rules since the cooperation started. However lately, there has been a change in this approach, and the Nordic countries seem now to be going different ways. Finland and Iceland have followed Sweden as to full acceptance of multiple nationality, while Denmark and Norway have stuck to the traditional principle of avoiding this status.

The Nordic Agreement was amended in 1977, 1998 and 2002. The last amendment was made after requests from states not in favour of accepting multiple nationality. The amendment introduces the possibility for member states to make the loss of former nationalities a condition for acquisition of their nationality.

The Province of Åland is a region of specific interest with regard to nationality matters in Finland. This province consists of a group of about 6,500 islands, located in the Baltic Sea, between Finland and Sweden. The province was subject to a territorial conflict between Sweden and Finland after Finland's independence from Russia in 1917. Both countries wished to have Åland as part of their territory. This resulted in, among other things, a regional nationality for the Ålanders called 'right of domicile'. Besides being Finnish nationals the majority of the inhabitants of the Åland Islands also possess this right of domicile. There are strict rules regulating who is in possession of this right and who may acquire it.

4.2 Historical development

4.2.1 Nationality in Finland before independence

Finland was part of the Swedish Kingdom between the fourteenth century and 1809. Persons residing in Finland at that time were consequently subjects of the Swedish King. Persons residing within the Swedish territory enjoyed the civil rights regulated in the Swedish National Law Code of 1734. Moving abroad led to the loss of these rights. Women and minor children derived their rights from their husband/father (Rosas & Suksi 1996: 268).

At that time, only people born in Sweden or Finland could be appointed to certain governmental offices. The Swedish monarch could, however, appoint foreigners to such offices on grounds of special achievements for the state. This can be regarded as a first kind of naturalisation arrangement (Rosas & Suksi 1996: 269).

As a result of the war between Sweden and Russia in 1808-1809, Sweden was forced to relinquish Finland to Russia. From 1809 to 1917, Finland was an autonomous Grand Duchy within the Russian Empire. The Russian tsar assumed the position of Grand Duke of Finland, but the law applicable within the Grand Duchy was still the old Swedish law, most notably the 1772 Constitution and the 1789 Act of Union and Security.

It was clear from the beginning of the Grand Duchy period that Finns had a special position compared to other subjects of the Russian Empire. The use of the Russian, Swedish and Finnish languages, as well as decrees and acts applicable in Finland imply that being a Finnish subject was something else than being merely a Russian subject (Jussila 1978: 7). Finns were in a sense both Russian and Finnish subjects, while other subjects of the Russian governorate were merely considered subjects of the Russian Empire, and they did not enjoy civil rights in Finland. If they wished to enjoy such rights in Finland they had to become naturalised Finnish citizens. Finns, on the other hand, were not regarded as foreigners in the rest of the Russian Empire where they enjoyed all the same privileges as any other Russian subject (Screen 1978: 21). Foreigners who moved to Finland and became subjects under the Russian Empire were at the same time guaranteed civil rights in Finland, while foreigners moving to the territory of the Russian governorate did not automatically benefit from civil rights in the Grand Duchy of Finland (Jussila 1978: 9).

At the end of the nineteenth century, Russian law did not recognise nationality as a legal concept. The legislation did not talk about nationals; it only mentioned subjects of the Russian Empire (Jussila 1978: 5). However, nationality was not an unknown concept for the Russians. This is evident from the expression used by the Grand Duke already in 1809: he referred to nationals of Finland by using the French expression *'citoyens de la Finlande'* when granting the regulations for the Finnish Governmental Council. Furthermore, Finnish nationality and naturalisation possibilities were mentioned in a number of regulations thereafter (Rosas & Suksi 1996: 270).

In 1858, a Decree was promulgated in Finland and Russia simultaneously regarding the registration in Finland of Russian subjects and foreigners residing in Russia.[2] The Decree introduced a kind of naturalisation possibility by codifying customary procedures for the application for civil rights in Finland. First, an individual application had to be made to the governor. The governor gave his opinion on the application and sent it to the Department of Economy at the Senate. After the Department had delivered its opinion, the application was decided upon by the Grand Duke. If the application was accepted, the applicant was registered in the parish where he wished to reside, and he then enjoyed most of the same rights as a Finnish subject born in Finland. The Russian nobility did, however, not enjoy the same rights as the Finnish nobility; instead they maintained their nobility rights in Russia (Jussila 1978: 14f). The main rule was that if an applicant had had his permanent residence in Finland for the last three years, had a good reputation, and was able to support himself he could be naturalised in Finland. Naturalisation was extended to his wife and minor children. Ius sanguinis was the principle followed for persons born in Finland, but Finnish nationality was only derived from a Finnish father, not from a Finnish mother. A Finnish national who took up residence abroad lost his Finnish nationality (Rosas & Suksi 1996: 270f).

4.2.2 *The first Finnish constitution and the first nationality laws of the Republic of Finland*

In 1917, Finland declared itself an independent state. The Constitution of 1919 (*Regeringsformen 1919*) was its first constitution as independent Finland. According to sect. 4, a child born by Finnish parents acquired Finnish nationality at birth. In addition, this section provided for legislation on naturalisation of foreigners. Spousal transfer of nationality was explicitly mentioned, i.e. Finnish nationality was automatically transferred from a Finnish man to his foreign wife upon marriage. Transfer of nationality was not possible the other way round, meaning that a Finnish woman could not pass her nationality to a foreign husband. The President of the Republic was given the authority to grant and to release a person from Finnish nationality (sect. 31).

The first Nationality Act[3] was adopted in 1920 and regulated naturalisation of foreign nationals. A person who had lived for the last five years in Finland, had a good reputation and was able to support himself and his family could upon application acquire Finnish nationality, provided that he lost or was freed from his former nationality (sect. 1). A wife and minor children would automatically acquire Finnish nationality together with the husband/father (sect. 2). A person who acquired Finnish nationality would only be regarded as a Finnish national after he or she had taken an oath of allegiance before the county governor (sect. 6).

The 1920 Nationality Act did not contain any provisions on loss of nationality. Emigrated Finnish nationals consequently often ended up with dual nationality or were not able to acquire the nationality of their new country if the new country did not accept dual nationality. Therefore in 1927, this Act was complemented with an Act on the Loss of Finnish Nationality.[4] Acquisition of a foreign nationality when taking up residence abroad thereafter resulted in the loss of the Finnish nationality (sect. 1). A person without any close connections to Finland also lost his or her Finnish nationality at the age of 22 (sect. 2). The Act furthermore opened up the possibility for Finnish nationals to apply to the President for release from their Finnish nationality (sect. 4).

4.2.3 *Nationality legislation in one single Act*

In 1941, provisions on acquisition and loss of nationality were included in one Act, the 1941 Act on Acquisition and Loss of Finnish Nationality.[5] This Act was more detailed than its predecessors and was influenced by the nationality laws of the Nordic neighbours, as well as the 1930 Hague Congress on the Codification of International Law. Prevention of multiple nationality and statelessness were the principal aims of the Act, and the first small step towards gender equality was made: children born out of wedlock and children born to stateless fathers acquired Finnish nationality from their mother (sect. 1), and facilitated naturalisation of foreign men marrying Finnish women was introduced (sect. 4 (2)). Foundlings were, for the first time, mentioned in the Act (sect. 2), and the oath of allegiance was finally abolished.

4.2.4 Consequences of the First and Second World Wars on nationality

The territorial adjustments made with regard to the Finnish-Russian/Soviet border after the First World War as well as after the Winter War 1939-1940 and the Continuation War 1941-1944 had consequences for those living in the affected area. The Peace Treaty of Tartu in 1920 had resulted in the Petschenga area becoming part of the Finnish territory. As a consequence, a number of Russians became residents of Finland. The Peace Treaty of Tartu contained a provision regulating the status of these persons, automatically making them Finnish nationals. Those who had reached eighteen years of age could opt for keeping their Russian nationality and freely move to Russian territory. Persons who made use of this option were not deprived of their property rights in Petschenga (Rosas & Suksi 1996: 274).

After Finland had lost the Winter War against Russia, persons resident in the territories that in accordance with the Peace Treaty of Moscow were ceded to the Soviet Union were regarded as having lost their Finnish nationality. During the Continuation War, Finland temporarily reacquired areas that had been occupied by the Soviet Union during the Winter War. An Act was consequently adopted in order to make it possible for people who had remained in the occupied areas to regain their lost Finnish nationality by declaration.[6] Those who had in the meantime been moved to the territory by the Soviet Union were treated as foreigners and did not benefit from the right to facilitated acquisition of Finnish nationality by declaration.

During the Second World War when Finland fought the Winter War and the Continuation War against Russia, the Russians captured part of the Finnish territory in the East of the country. As a consequence of the Winter War a number of refugees from two areas that were captured, Ingria and East Karelia, found their way back to Finnish territory. A peculiarity within the 1941 Nationality Act were the special regulations that applied to children of refugees of Finnish descent from Ingria and East Karelia who acquired Finnish nationality by declaration (sect. 13). For them the requirement of being able to support themselves and their families did not apply. This is the only time that ethnicity has been of significance within Finnish nationality law.

4.2.5 *Gender equality and Nordic influences*

In 1967, the constitutional provision in sect. 4 on acquisition of Finnish nationality was amended and another step towards gender equality in nationality law was made when equality between spouses regarding the acquisition of Finnish nationality was introduced in the Act amending sect. 4 clause 1 of the Constitution.[7] The rule on automatic acquisition of Finnish nationality by a foreign woman marrying a Finnish national was finally abolished. While Finland is seen as a pioneer of women's rights being the first European country to accept women's right to vote in 1906, it is remarkable that Finland was one of the last European countries to introduce gender equality in this regard.

The 1968 Nationality Act,[8] which replaced the previous Act on Acquisition and Loss of Finnish Nationality of 1941, also introduced the possibility of facilitated discretionary naturalisation for spouses of Finnish nationals, regardless of gender (sect. 4). The provision was very vague as to what was required from the spouse in order to qualify for facilitated discretionary naturalisation. It merely stated that naturalisation could be approved despite normal requirements not being fulfilled. In 1968, normal requirements included five years of habitual continuous residence in Finland, that the applicant was eighteen years of age or older, and that he or she was living a respectable life and had a secure income. The Act further promoted equality between men and women, as women would no longer lose their Finnish nationality when marrying a foreign man. The 1968 Act also facilitated acquisition of Finnish nationality for women who had lost their Finnish nationality due to marriage with a foreign man or because their spouses had acquired a foreign nationality (sect. 15). For these women a declaration within five years of the entry into force of the Act was sufficient in order to reacquire Finnish nationality. These amendments made the Finnish accession to the United Nations Convention on the Nationality of Married Women (1957) feasible. Finland acceded to the Convention on 15 May 1968.

The prevention of statelessness was also taken one step forward by the 1968 Nationality Act. Children born in Finland who would otherwise become stateless now automatically acquired Finnish nationality at birth (sect. 1 (1)(4)). Although Finland has not ratified the Convention on the Reduction of Statelessness (1961), the basis for this change is found in this Convention.

The legal effort to prevent statelessness provided for Finnish accession in October 1968 to the United Nations Convention relating to the Status of Stateless Persons (1954), which states in art. 32 that the 'Contracting States shall as far as possible facilitate the [...] naturalization of stateless persons'. Due to cooperation with the other Nordic countries on nationality matters, Finland made a general reservation to this Convention still allowing nationals of the Nordic countries to receive special rights and privileges.

Prior to the enactment of the 1968 Nationality Act a renunciation of Finnish nationality was conditioned on the person in question moving abroad. In the new Act this condition was abolished. Furthermore, the right to facilitated acquisition of Finnish nationality for descendents of refugees from Ingria and East Karelia was abolished.

Following a recommendation of the Nordic Council (no. 1-1964), facilitated acquisition of Finnish nationality for Nordic nationals was introduced in the 1968 Nationality Act. The purpose was to provide for Finnish accession to the Nordic Agreement in 1969. As a consequence of this change, the normal requirement of five years of habitual residence was not applicable to nationals of the other Nordic countries who wished to be naturalised in Finland (sect. 4 (2)). No specific time of habitual residence was mentioned in the law for Nordic nationals, but in practice two years was sufficient. Furthermore, the declaration procedure was made applicable to nationals of the other Nordic countries who for the past seven years had had their habitual residence in Finland (sect. 10 (4)). Acquisition of nationality by declaration for former Finnish nationals who in the meantime had been nationals of another Nordic country was also facilitated. These former nationals acquired Finnish nationality immediately when they resettled in Finland (sect. 10 (5)).

A new provision in the 1968 Act stipulated that former Finnish nationals who had been continuously resident in Finland until the age of eighteen could reacquire their Finnish nationality by declaration after two new years of residence in Finland (sect. 6). The Nordic Agreement was also of significance with regard to this provision, as it stated that habitual residence in one of the other contracting states before the age of twelve should count as residence in Finland (sect. 10 (3)).

The rules on acquisition of Finnish nationality by declaration for second-generation immigrants can also be traced back to the Nordic cooperation in 1968-1969; for this group of immigrants habitual residence in another Nordic country is regarded as equal to residence in Finland provided that such residence took place before the age of sixteen and more than five years before the declaration is made (sect. 5 (1) and 10 (2)).

A major change that the 1968 Nationality Decree[9] brought about at this point in time was that the Ministry of the Interior became the main authority involved in decisions on acquisition and loss of Finnish nationality. Nevertheless, the President of the Republic remained the formal decision-making authority.

4.2.6 *Major amendments to Finnish nationality legislation in 1984*

The 1968 Nationality Act became the subject of major amendments in 1984.[10] Again, gender equality was taken one step further as parents were put on a more equal footing than before. Previously, the main principle was that children born in wedlock derived their nationality from their father. From this point on however, a Finnish mother would always pass her Finnish nationality to her children (sect. 1). Gender equality was consequently a reality for children born in wedlock. This amendment made possible the Finnish ratification of the International Convention on the Elimination of all Forms of Discrimination against Women on 4 September 1986.

Adopted children were mentioned for the first time in Finnish nationality legislation in 1984. The amended Act introduced the possibility for adopted children to acquire Finnish nationality by declaration (sect. 3b). Such a declaration could be made immediately after a child had been adopted, provided that the adoption was valid in Finland and that at least one of the adoptive parents was a Finnish national. Furthermore, the Act elaborated on the prevention of statelessness by making it a condition for being released from Finnish nationality that said person would not become stateless (sect. 9). Finally, the amendments introduced a new practice with regard to children of fifteen years or older, as these could no longer acquire or be released from their Finnish nationality against their will (sect. 12a).

In 1985, a new Nationality Decree[11] was consequently promulgated following the amendments of the 1968 Nationality Act. This Decree included mainly procedural provisions and did not introduce any new features. However, the provisions were slightly more detailed than in the previous Nationality Decree of 1968 and the language was modernised.

4.3 Recent developments and current institutional arrangements

4.3.1 *Political analysis*

In 2003, a new Nationality Act was adopted in Finland, repealing the old Nationality Act of 1968 with amendments. A new Nationality Decree complementing the new Act was approved in 2004. The new Act and the new Decree spell out the modalities with regard to acquisition and loss of Finnish nationality and they regulate the mandate and duties of the responsible authorities. They give an in depth meaning to the main principles mentioned in the constitutional provision on acquisition of Finnish nationality, and they make up the core of Finnish nationality legislation.

The political intentions behind the new Nationality Act of 2003 have been manifold. Acceptance of multiple nationality, prevention of statelessness, and gender equality are among the principal considerations behind the Act. The need for a more detailed law reducing the different possible interpretations of the old Act was also a factor of significance in the work towards a new Nationality Act. Another intention behind the new Act was that Finland should be able to ratify the European Convention on Nationality without making any reservations.

As the new Nationality Act has only been in force since 1 June 2003 it is difficult to provide a thorough analysis of the impacts of the Act at this time. Nor is it feasible this early to conclude whether the Act has achieved its intended effects. The statistics for 2003 does, however, indicate that the Act at least partly has had the expected impact of increasing the number of declarations handed in to the Finnish Directorate of Immigration following the acceptance of multiple nationality (see sect. 4.3.2).

A principal consideration behind the reform was that the old Nationality Act was deficient and partly outdated. There were major inadequacies with regard to the legal safeguards and definitions of the requirements for naturalisation as the provisions of the old Act had a rather general character. The requirements for acquiring Finnish nationality were not clear enough for an applicant to know beforehand whether he or she would be granted Finnish nationality upon application. The shortcomings of the Act were largely compensated by the 1985 Nationality Decree and various ministerial briefs. The Finnish Constitution does however state in its art. 5 that the rules for acquisition and loss of Finnish nationality shall be stipulated in a Parliamentary Act, making the above mentioned practice with decrees and ministerial briefs not legally satisfactory. Furthermore, the legal safety of an individual applicant was not satisfactorily guaranteed, as the mandates and duties of the authorities involved in the procedure were not clearly stipulated. This indeed had a negative impact on the efficiency and expediency of the procedure.[12]

When the previous Nationality Act was passed in 1968, the immigrant population was small, and it was mostly foreign spouses of Finnish nationals who were naturalised. In the 1990s, the picture had changed and more often foreign families took up residence in Finland and wished to be naturalised. The number of foreigners residing in Finland had increased a remarkable 56 per cent between 1995 and 2003. In 1995, there were 68,600 foreign nationals residing in Finland as opposed to 107,100 in 2003 (Statistics Finland 2005). The increase in the number of applications for naturalisation and resulting acquisitions of Finnish nationality has directly reflected this increase. Between 1991 and 1995, on average only 854 foreigners were granted

Finnish nationality each year, whereas in the year 2000 alone 2,977 foreign nationals were naturalised in Finland (Directorate of Immigration 2005). It was evident that the rules on acquisition and loss of Finnish nationality had to be adapted in order to reflect this change in the immigration pattern.

Discussions on a new Nationality Act started already at the beginning of the 1990s. They evolved largely around the issue of multiple nationality. A reform of the old Nationality Act was however not initiated until 1997 under a coalition government led by the Social Democratic Party. The Ministry of the Interior in charge of nationality matters was at that time headed by Jan-Erik Enestam, a minister from the Swedish People's Party, a party mainly representing the Swedish-speaking population of Finland. He expressed resistance to accepting multiple nationality and referred to the ongoing debate in the other Nordic countries on the issue. Work on the reform was consequently temporarily interrupted that year in order to follow the developments in the other Nordic countries that had likewise started revising their nationality legislation (Peltoniemi 2003).

The Finland Society[13] and the Finnish Expatriate Parliament[14] were among the driving forces initiating and supporting legislation that would accept multiple nationality. The Finnish Expatriate Parliament has ever since it was established in 1997 had the acceptance of multiple nationality as a central goal (Peltoniemi 2003). In December 1999, the Social Democrat Riitta Prusti presented an initiative according to which multiple nationality would be accepted.[15] It was signed by 103 of the 200 Members of Parliament from the whole spectrum of parties represented in Parliament. This initiative was later included in the proposition for a new Nationality Act. As a result of the intense lobbying work of the Finnish expatriates the political parties were to a large extent in agreement on accepting multiple nationality. The political debate on the issue was therefore rather tame.[16]

There seems to have been a general acceptance between the political parties with regard to all issues regulated in the new Nationality Act. As mentioned above, only the introduction of multiple nationality caused some political debate. The intense lobbying work by the Finnish expatriates for acceptance of multiple nationality contributed to a great extent to the broad political support for the matter. All other matters, for example the introduction of a language requirement in the Act and the strengthened residence requirement (from five to six years) were not debated at all, but tacitly accepted.[17] In contrast to for instance the recent comprehensive Dutch debates on nationality matters, the Finnish political debate has been almost non-existent. This can be explained by the fact that these two countries have very different migration patterns. Out of a Dutch population of roughly 16 million people,

3 million are first- or second-generation immigrants (Council of Europe 2003). In Finland with a total population of 5.2 million, less than 110,000 have a foreign nationality.[18] Consequently, a new Nationality Act in Finland with the introduction of somewhat stricter requirements for acquisition of Finnish nationality will not give rise to a political debate of the same intensity as in a country like the Netherlands where similar changes will have consequences for a much larger group of persons.

In April 2000, the work on the reform of the nationality legislation was resumed at the Ministry of the Interior, now headed by a minister from the National Coalition Party, but still under a coalition government headed by the Social Democratic Party.[19] The Act was drafted in cooperation with the Directorate of Immigration. The Bill for the new Nationality Act was introduced in Parliament in 2002. The sole entity with critical remarks about the Bill was the Ministry of Defence that drew attention to the risk to national security that multiple nationality might cause, e.g., by making espionage easier. On 24 January 2003, still under the same government as in April 2000 when work on the Act was resumed, the Finnish Parliament passed the new Nationality Act. The Act was backed by all the major political parties.

The main novelty in the Nationality Act of 2003 is the acceptance of multiple nationality. As mentioned in the introduction, loss of Finnish nationality is no longer a consequence of the acquisition of a foreign nationality. Nor does the new Act include a requirement of renunciation of former nationalities when acquiring Finnish nationality. The new Act furthermore facilitates the reacquisition of Finnish nationality by persons who have lost their Finnish nationality due to the earlier prohibition of multiple nationality.

In Finland, multiple nationality has been considered problematic with regards to voting rights, military service, consular assistance and the security of the republic. A main argument against multiple nationality was that it was not considered expedient that a person who took up residence abroad would retain his or her Finnish nationality when acquiring a foreign nationality. Nor was it considered expedient that Finnish nationality would be passed on from one generation to another for those with little or no connection to Finland. Security reasons also spoke in favour of non-acceptance of multiple nationality. Due to the risk of loyalty conflicts, it was not considered recommendable that minorities with multiple nationalities should evolve.[20]

The growing tendency internationally and the increasing willingness nationally to accept multiple nationality brought with it that also Finland started to reconsider its views on the matter in the 1990s. The Swedish law reforms in this regard, as well as the Norwegian considerations, have been important for Finland's acceptance of multiple nationality. Sweden, as the country with the greatest number of Finnish expatriates, accepted multiple nationality in 2001, when the new Swedish Nationality Act went into force. When the Finnish Nationality Act of 2003 was adopted, the impression was that Norway which was also working on a new Nationality Act was going to accept multiple nationality as well.[21]

A major argument for accepting multiple nationality were the positive implications for the individual. Another argument was that acceptance of multiple nationality would contribute to preserving contact with emigrant and Diaspora populations abroad. Furthermore, it was now considered to be in the interest of the Finnish Republic that immigrants who had taken up permanent residence in Finland should acquire Finnish nationality. It was considered important that after the integration phase the foreign population would acquire full rights and obligations in order to participate in Finnish society.[22] Despite the arguments against multiple nationality, the overall picture was still that multiple nationality would better serve the interests of Finland.

Prior to the law reform, nationals of certain states had difficulty in acquiring Finnish nationality because the legislation of their state of nationality made renunciation of their nationality impossible. These included nationals of Iran, the former Yugoslavia, and Algeria.[23] In practice, however, such nationals were exempted from the requirement to renounce their former nationality.[24] Even though it was already possible for this group to acquire Finnish nationality prior to the reform, the reform made the exemption procedure superfluous and acquisition of Finnish nationality easier. Other groups benefiting from the acceptance of multiple nationality are former Finnish nationals, descendants of Finnish nationals and descendents of former Finnish nationals who lost their Finnish nationality or were not granted Finnish nationality due to the previous prohibition of multiple nationality. These groups may acquire Finnish nationality by facilitated acquisition (declaration), and it is worth noting that habitual residence in Finland is not a requirement for such former Finns and Finnish descendants in order to (re)acquire Finnish nationality.

Apart from multiple nationality, the new Finnish Nationality Act promotes gender equality as both parents are put in a more equal position in cases where a child's nationality is determined by ius sanguinis (sect. 9). A child will always acquire Finnish nationality from the mother, no matter whether the child is under her custody or not (sect. 9 (1)). The novelty of the new Act is that a child can now always acquire Finnish nationality from a Finnish father provided that paternity has been established. A child born abroad of a foreign mother and a Finnish father can acquire Finnish nationality by declaration (sect. 26). In all other cases where paternity has been established, a child will acquire Finnish nationality automatically at birth from the father (sect. 9 (2)).

By making the acquisition of Finnish nationality possible in cases where either of the parents is a Finnish national, the conditions of art. 6 (1) of the European Convention on Nationality, signed by Finland in 1997 but not yet acceded to, was met. A proposition is underway for the purpose of acceding to the Nationality Convention. The proposition will be discussed in the Parliament at the earliest during the autumn session 2005 (Ministry of the Interior 2005a).

The new Finnish Constitution of 1999 in sect. 5 includes a provision hindering loss or renunciation of Finnish nationality if that leads to statelessness. Consequently, the new Nationality Act has as a major aim the prevention of statelessness. The Act adopts the principle laid down in the new constitution by introducing a provision stipulating that a person cannot lose or renounce Finnish nationality if that would lead to statelessness (sect. 4). Another new provision preventing statelessness is sect. 9, which states that children of refugees or parents granted a residence permit on the grounds of a need for protection will acquire Finnish nationality at birth if they are born in Finland and do not acquire the nationality of their parents. A third provision, sect. 12, stipulates that children are considered Finnish nationals as long as the nationality of their parents are unknown. According to the same section, foundlings who are found on Finnish territory are also considered to be Finnish nationals as long as they have not been established as nationals of a foreign state. The new Nationality Act introduces provisions stating that if such children are found to be nationals of another state they will retain Finnish nationality only after they reach the age of five years (sect. 12).

A further aim of the revision of the Nationality Act was to adapt the legislation with regard to the prevention of statelessness in order for it to exactly correspond to the UN Convention on the Reduction of Statelessness. The intention behind this was to make the accession by Finland to the convention feasible.

While a Finnish national no longer automatically loses his or her Finnish nationality when acquiring another nationality, the new Nationality Act introduces some other new modes for the loss of Finnish nationality.

One provision stipulates that a person who has been granted Finnish nationality upon application or declaration may lose his or her Finnish nationality if he or she has provided false or misleading information to the authorities and the conduct exhibited was decisive to the acquisition (sect. 33 (1)). A child of a person who loses Finnish nationality because of fraud may also lose his or her Finnish nationality transferred or extended by that parent, unless the other parent is a Finnish national (sect. 33 (2)). Finnish nationality will not be lost as a consequence of false or misleading information if more than five years have passed since the nationality was acquired (sect. 33 (4)).

Furthermore, a person may lose his or her Finnish nationality according to sect. 32 if nationality was granted on the basis of the father's nationality and paternity was later annulled. As mentioned above, a foundling or a person with unclear nationality who has acquired Finnish nationality at birth will lose Finnish nationality if he or she is established as a foreign national; but since an age limit has been included in the law, Finnish nationality is retained if the foreign nationality is established only after he or she reaches the age of five.

A Finnish national may be released from Finnish nationality upon application, if he or she is a foreign national or is about to acquire the nationality of another state (sect. 35). A new condition mentioned in the Act is that release is not possible if the applicant is domiciled in Finland and the reason for applying for release is to avoid military service or other citizen's obligations. As already mentioned, loss of Finnish nationality is never possible if it leads to statelessness. However, if acquisition of a foreign nationality is conditioned upon the loss of a previous nationality, a person may be released from his or her Finnish nationality even if that means that he or she will be stateless for a short period of time (sect. 35 (2)).

The new Nationality Act also changed the requirements for discretionary naturalisation. By tradition, Finland is not a country of immigration. A rather limited number of foreigners have settled in Finland, and a comparatively small number of them have been naturalised. As a consequence, there has not been a need to discuss whether to reduce the overall numbers of naturalisations by introducing stricter conditions for immigrants to qualify for Finnish nationality, and the threshold for acquiring Finnish nationality by discretionary naturalisation has therefore been relatively low. However, during the last fourteen years, the number of immigrants has quadrupled, as has the number of applications for naturalisation, and with the adoption of the new Nationality Act in 2003, a change towards slightly more restrictive conditions for naturalisation, including stricter residence and language requirements, could therefore be observed.

The idea behind the required period of residence and the language requirement is that immigrants wishing to be naturalised must be able to take care of themselves in Finnish society and shall accept the legal principles that are considered important in Finland. The number of years of habitual residence required for naturalisation was increased in the new Act from five to six years (sect. 13 (1)(2a)). In the preparatory work comparisons were made of other states' requirements. A six-year period was chosen as a middle course, being neither among the longest nor among the shortest periods of residence required for naturalisation. At the same time an alternative residency requirement was introduced, stipulating that residence in Finland for eight years after the age of fifteen, with the last two years uninterrupted equally qualifies for naturalisation (sect. 13 (1)(2b)).

Other conditions for discretionary naturalisation are that the applicant is eighteen years of age or older (unless married before that) (sect. 13 (1)(1)), and he or she may not have any punishable acts on record, nor any restraining order issued against him or her (integrity requirement) (sect. 13 (1)(3)). Furthermore, he or she must not materially fail to provide maintenance or meet pecuniary obligations under public law (sect. 13 (1)(4)). In addition the applicant must provide a reliable account of his or her livelihood (sect. 13 (1)(5)) and have satisfactory oral and written skills in Finnish or Swedish (sect. 13 (1)(6)).

The integrity requirement is applied rather strictly and includes a wide range of acts. The most common type of punishable acts that lead to a failure to meet the integrity requirement are acts such as speeding and other minor traffic offences. Also in cases where a court has abstained from punishing an accused in spite of he or she having been found guilty, the integrity requirement has been applied in a subsequent nationality case. The administrative practice of the Directorate of Immigration does not demonstrate any relevant differences between different nationalities in terms of satisfying the integrity requirement.[25]

With regard to the requirement that an applicant for Finnish nationality must provide a reliable account of his or her livelihood, it is worth noting that the administrative practice of the Directorate of Immigration has shown that failure to meet this requirement has not been considered a legal obstacle for naturalisation. Failure to meet the required length of residence in Finland has, on the other hand, been applied strictly. The duration of the procedure for naturalisation applications has, however, resulted in this requirement very seldom being an obstacle to naturalisation. It is assumed that the number of applicants failing to fulfil this requirement will increase, as the procedure speeds up.[26]

A number of exceptions apply to the requirements for discretionary naturalisation. Some of the exceptions are new and some have been revised in the new Nationality Act. An exception introduced in the new Act concerns refugees and persons who have achieved residence permits on grounds of the need for protection (sect. 20). For such persons the period of required habitual residence in Finland is shorter, either the last four years of uninterrupted residence in Finland, or a total of six years of residence in Finland since the age of fifteen, with the last two years uninterrupted. Another exception applies to former Finnish nationals and nationals of the other Nordic countries who may be granted Finnish nationality if they have had their habitual residence in Finland for the last two years continuously (sect. 21). For a co-applicant child of fifteen years of age or older, the residence requirement is lowered to the last four years of habitual residence in Finland without interruption or a total of six years since the age of seven, with the last two years uninterrupted (sect. 23 (2)). A co-applicant child under the age of fifteen may be granted Finnish nationality immediately when taking up residence in Finland, notwithstanding the normal requirements for residence and language (sect. 23 (1)). Furthermore, a new provision has been included in the Act stating that a person who acted as a Finnish national in good faith and was presumed to be a Finnish national for at least ten years may acquire Finnish nationality by discretionary naturalisation notwithstanding the normal requirements on residence and language skills (sect. 18 (1)(2c)). The same applies to persons with close connections to Finland or if other strong reasons are present (sect. 18).

Facilitated acquisition is still possible for a foreign spouse of a Finnish national. One requirement under sect. 22 of the new Nationality Act is that the foreign spouse has lived in Finland for the last four years uninterrupted, or for six years since the age of fifteen, with the last two years uninterrupted. In addition, the spouses shall have lived together for the last three years.

The residence requirement is closely connected to the language requirement. It is presumed that the longer the period of residence in Finland is, the better the language skills will be. The preparatory work for the new Act underlines the importance of satisfactory knowledge of the Finnish or Swedish language for successful integration. Sufficient knowledge in one of these languages was considered important by the government in order to be able to act as a Finnish national within Finnish society.[27] Consequently, a requirement of satisfactory oral and written skills in Finnish or Swedish, or similar skills in Finnish sign language was also introduced in the new Nationality Act (sect. 13 (1) (6)).

The 1968 Nationality Act had no rules on required language skills, but the 1985 Nationality Decree included a general requirement of sufficient knowledge of Finnish or Swedish. There were, however, no clear rules on how to prove the language proficiency, and no coherent administrative practice on the type of certificates or tests accepted as sufficient proof of the required language skills.[28]

The major difference compared to the old Act is that the language requirement is now mentioned explicitly and that the new Nationality Decree of 2004[29] exhaustively outlines ways of documenting such knowledge of the language skills (sect. 7). While the old Decree required some kind of documentation of Finnish or Swedish language skills, it did not regulate the type of documentation and the quality of skills required. A language certificate from a teacher was in practice considered as sufficient in order to prove skills in Finnish or Swedish, and civil servants at the Directorate of Immigration experienced that many immigrants who applied for and acquired Finnish nationality had a very poor knowledge of the Finnish and Swedish languages.[30]

The new Nationality Act and Decree lay down detailed rules, by referring to art. 15-17 in the Governmental Decree on the examination of proficiency in Finnish and Swedish within the state administration,[31] on the level of language knowledge required and the documentation accepted as proof of the language skills. An applicant able to provide documentation showing that he or she has passed a general or a national language examination at level three (out of six levels, where six is excellent and three is satisfactory), or that he or she has completed basic education in Finnish or Swedish, will meet the language requirement.

It can generally be assumed that it has become more difficult to fulfil the language requirement. Members of Parliament have criticised the new requirement as detrimental especially to the possibility for elderly immigrants to acquire Finnish nationality. The Act does, however, allow for exceptions from the language requirement for immigrants with long lawful residence in Finland who have reached the age of 65 years (sect. 18 (1)(2b)). Younger persons may also be exempted if there are special and weighty reasons in favour of such an exemption (sect. 18 (2)). It is too early to tell whether the language requirement will generally function as a barrier discouraging acquisition of Finnish nationality, but it is not unlikely that strict application thereof will have that effect.

It may be assumed that the group particularly susceptible to the language requirement are refugee women, whose participation in social life and Finnish society is not encouraged by their ethnic groups, and who either cannot or will not participate in language courses. In fact, the language proficiency requirement has already proved to be an obstacle for Kurds from Iran and Iraq.[32] Furthermore, unemployment among the refugee and immigrant population is high, consequently limiting full participation in Finnish society and therefore limiting opportunities to learn the language in every day social intercourse.

It is noteworthy that a practice has developed favouring Norwegian and Danish nationals as regards the language requirement. According to administrative practice Danish and Norwegian nationals do not have to prove their knowledge of the Swedish or Finnish language (Rosas & Suksi 1996: 289). As both the Danish and Norwegian languages are closely related to the Swedish language this cannot be considered as unreasonable; apart from which, it cannot be expected that a national from one of these countries will be able to speak Swedish within the short period of time required before he or she can be naturalised.

The required period of residence and the strict language requirement makes the acquisition of Finnish nationality a reward for successful integration rather than a means to promote a better integration. The lawmaker has expressly stated in the preparatory works of the new Nationality Act that the intention is that one must be able to function independently in the Finnish society in order to qualify for Finnish nationality.[33]

Apart from naturalisation, Finnish law provides for acquisition of nationality by declaration. This possibility to acquire Finnish nationality was written down in the new constitution (sect. 5 (1)) in 1999, although the declaration procedure was already introduced in the Nationality Act of 1968.

A new category of persons who can acquire Finnish nationality by declaration after the entry into force of the new Nationality Act are persons born in Finland to foreign mothers and Finnish fathers, whose paternity was established after they turned eighteen or after they got married (sect. 26 (1)).

Another group that may acquire Finnish nationality by declaration are former Finnish nationals (sect. 29). If Finnish nationality was lost due to the earlier prohibition of multiple nationality, Finnish nationality may be reacquired by declaration, provided that the declaration is made within five years from the entry into force of the new Nationality Act, i.e., before 1 June 2008 (sect. 60). A person who has lost Finnish nationality due to insufficient connection with Finland and who never received information on the procedure for retaining nationality, and, as mentioned above, a person who after losing Finnish nationality has continuously been a national of another Nordic country will also be able to reacquire Finnish nationality by declaration when taking up residence in Finland (sect. 29 (2) and 30).

Other former Finnish nationals can reacquire their Finnish nationality by declaration by meeting a residency requirement of ten years of habitual residence in Finland with the last two years uninterrupted if they are eighteen years of age and did not lose their Finnish nationality due to fraud (sect. 29 (1)). Nordic nationals can also acquire Finnish nationality upon declaration if they are eighteen years of age, have not acquired their other Nordic nationality through naturalisation, and have lived the last six years in Finland (sect. 30).

There is a possibility for children born abroad and out of wedlock to a foreign mother and a Finnish father to acquire Finnish nationality by declaration (sect. 26). Furthermore, a young person between eighteen and 22 years of age who has had his or her habitual residence in Finland for ten years with the last two years uninterrupted and who has not been sentenced to imprisonment can also acquire Finnish nationality by declaration (sect. 28 (1)). For second-generation immigrants the requirement that the person may have no sentence to imprisonment on his or her record if he or she wishes to acquire Finnish nationality by declaration (sect. 28 (2)) was introduced in the new Nationality Act. The reason for introducing this requirement was that it was considered more appropriate by the legislator that a person who has been sentenced to imprisonment is evaluated in the application procedure, where there is a possibility for the authorities to refuse the granting of Finnish nationality.

Another aim of the new Act was to approximate the rights of an adoptive child to that of a biological child. Adopted children under twelve years of age now automatically acquire Finnish nationality (sect. 10). Adopted children twelve years of age or older may acquire Finnish nationality by declaration (sect. 27). The declaration procedure for adopted children over twelve has little practical use, as it is rather uncommon to adopt older children from foreign countries.

Anyone wishing to acquire Finnish nationality must be able to meet the requirement of established identity in sect. 6. This is a new provision. If a person has been using an identity registered in the population information system for at least ten years, his or her identity is considered to be reliably established in accordance with sect. 6, regardless of whether he or she has used other identities before then.

4.3.2 *Statistical developments*

The number of nationality matters handled by the Directorate of Immigration has increased rapidly since 1995. This is due in particular to the large immigration flows that reached Finland at the beginning of the 1990s. Immigration to Finland started to increase in 1989. At that time 18,000 foreigners were living in Finland. By 2003, the number had increased to 107,000. These immigrants began to meet the requirements for naturalisation in 1995 and after.

In 1998 and 1999, the number of persons naturalised in Finland rose dramatically from less than 1,000 a year to more than 4,000. This rise in the number of naturalised Finnish nationals reflects the rise in the number of asylum seekers that were granted asylum or other types of residence permits at the beginning of the 1990s. At that time the residence requirement for discretionary naturalisation was five years, and the processing time was around three years. The highest number of applications was made to the Finnish immigration authorities in 1997.

Table 4.1 shows that while there has been a moderate increase in the Finnish population since 1990, the foreign population has more than

Table 4.1: Number of the total Finnish population, foreign population in Finland, number of favourable decisions on asylum and naturalisation applications in Finland from 1990-2004

Year	*Total population*	*Foreign population*	*Favourable decisions on asylum applications*	*Naturalisation applications*	*Acquisition of Finnish nationality by naturalisation*
1990	4,998,000	26,300	157	602	899
1991	4,973,936	37,600	1719	744	1236
1992	5,054,982	46,300	576	614	876
1993	5,077,912	55,600	2082	753	839
1994	5,098,754	62,000	316	1340	651
1995	5,116,826	68,600	223	1686	668
1996	5,132,320	73,800	345	2431	981
1997	5,147,349	80,600	281	3353	1439
1998	5,159,646	85,100	379	2837	4017
1999	5,171,302	87,800	496	2239	4730
2000	5,181,115	91,100	467	2323	2977
2001	5,194,901	98,600	813	1933	2720
2002	5,206,295	103,700	591	2499	3049
2003	5,219,732	107,100	494	2630	4526
2004	5,236,118	108,346	800	2004	6880

Sources: Statistics Finland and the Directorate of Immigration

quadrupled in that same period, and so has the number of persons applying for Finnish nationality. Traditionally, Finland has been a country of emigration, not immigration,[34] which is indicated in the same table: foreigners with habitual residence in Finland represent only 2 per cent of the total population and the numbers of favourable decisions on asylum applications are remarkably low both in international terms and in comparison to the total number of persons applying for asylum in Finland.

The rather long processing period for nationality applications makes it difficult to draw any specific conclusion from the yearly naturalisation statistics. The processing time for nationality applications has for the last years been around three years. Nationality declarations have an average processing time that is much shorter. In 2003, the processing of a declaration lasted on average 75 days. A much more secure way to analyse the impact of legislative amendments in nationality law is therefore to look at the annual statistics on numbers of nationality applications submitted to the Finnish immigration authorities.

A factor that to a certain extent has influenced statistics on naturalisations is the change made in the new Nationality Act with regard to acquisition of Finnish nationality for adopted children. As already mentioned, adopted children under twelve years of age now automatically acquire Finnish nationality upon adoption. Children under twelve years of age are therefore no longer included in statistics on nationality declarations. However, as they only account for around 300 adoptions yearly (310 under eighteen years of age in 2004), the change does not have a major impact on the general statistics on the acquisition of Finnish nationality.

Where do the people who acquire Finnish nationality come from? Table 4.2 shows that the majority of those naturalised in Finland are of European origin, and that former Russians make up more than half of them. More than a third of those naturalised in Finland in 2004 were in fact Russians, and these were to a great extent represented by Ingermanlanders.[35] This reflects an amendment made to the Alien's Act in 1993 facilitating the acquisition of residence permits for persons with a connection to Finland.[36]

Other groups with immigration and naturalisation patterns worthy of note are nationals from Somalia and Iraq. For Somalis there was a peak in 1999 when 1,208 persons were naturalised in Finland, while only one person of Somali origin was naturalised three years earlier. This reflects the deteriorating situation in Somalia after the civil war broke out in 1991 and the number of refugees who found their way to Finland during the first half of the 1990s as a result of this conflict. The number of Iraqis who apply for and acquire Finnish nationality has also seen a steady increase, however not yet as drastic as for Somalis. In 2004, 447 Iraqi nationals were naturalised in Finland. This is almost twice as many as in the previous year. Compared to before 1998 this number has increased remarkably, e.g., in 1997 only fifteen Iraqis were naturalised in Finland. The number of Iraqis naturalised in Fin-

Table 4.2: Number of naturalisations in Finland between the years 1990 and 2004 by continent/country of former nationality

	Europe	*Of these: Russia*	*Africa*	*Of these: Somalia*	*America*	*Asia*	*Of these: Iraq*	*Oceania*	*Stateless/ unknown*
1990	554	0	70	0	87	115	5	4	69
1991	736	0	101	0	102	201	4	10	86
1992	507	21	104	0	55	140	2	4	66
1993	450	87	67	0	44	214	11	1	63
1994	342	116	56	1	43	152	6	0	58
1995	335	94	81	1	28	144	4	2	78
1996	365	146	120	1	35	328	7	1	132
1997	509	210	180	10	52	489	15	2	207
1998	1254	666	788	476	77	1299	135	6	602
1999	1612	800	1365	1208	41	696	140	4	1012
2000	1387	666	522	346	81	800	185	1	186
2001	1194	533	406	222	90	829	224	1	200
2002	1419	418	419	204	96	889	217	1	225
2003	3037	1682	403	209	112	861	165	21	101
2004	4449	2313	426	165	242	1517	447	31	215

Source: Statistics Finland

land can be traced back to the unstable situation in Iraq under Saddam Hussein's regime.

Due to the previous non-acceptance of multiple nationality, many people lost their Finnish nationality when they acquired a foreign nationality. For the same reason many immigrants who met the requirements for naturalisation in Finland never applied for Finnish nationality. As the new law accepting multiple nationality entered into force, a remarkable increase in naturalisation applications and declarations was expected. As mentioned above, a former Finnish national has a right to re-acquire his or her Finnish nationality, according to sect. 60, if it was lost due to the previous non-acceptance of multiple nationality. According to this section declarations can be submitted within five years after the new Nationality Act entered into force. It was expected that 5000 declarations based on sect. 60 would be submitted to the Directorate of Immigration each year during this period. During the first year that the new Nationality Act was in force, i.e. from 1 June 2003 until 31 May 2004, the number of declarations made by former Finnish nationals and their descendants was 3011 (UVI 2004b). While the total number of declarations almost quadrupled in 2003 compared to the previous year (see Table 4.3), this number was still not as high as expected.[37] The reason why the number was almost 2000 lower than expected is most likely that the high declaration fee, 300 euros for adults in 2003, was considered by many to be out of proportion.

At the end of 2004, 4,568 former Finnish nationals and their offspring from 78 different states had made declarations in accordance with sect. 60 in order to acquire Finnish nationality. Most of these applications came from the United States, Sweden, Australia, Canada and Switzerland. Of these 4,568 declarations 3,983 had acquired Finnish nationality by the end of the year. 1,569 of these were former Finnish

Table 4.3: Number of declarations for Finnish nationality made from 1995-2003

Year	*Declarations for Finnish nationality*
1995	283
1996	317
1997	378
1998	429
1999	343
2000	436
2001	480
2002	539
2003	2053
2004	2515

Sources: Annual Reports of the Directorate of Immigration and the Bill for the new Nationality Act, HE 235/2002.

nationals and 921 were offspring of current or former Finnish nationals (UVI 2004a: 15).

4.3.3 *The Province of Åland and 'the right of domicile'*

Under sect. 120 of the Finnish Constitution, the Province of Åland constitutes an autonomous part of Finland. The Autonomy Act for Åland[38] includes provisions on 'the right of domicile' in Åland, with amendments. The right of domicile can be described as a regional nationality, which is required in order to own or be in possession of real estate, vote in and stand for elections to the provincial parliament, and conduct a business within the province of Åland. The Provincial Government may grant exemptions from the requirement of right of domicile for persons wishing to acquire real estate or conduct a business in Åland. Acquisition of the right of domicile is regulated in the Autonomy Act adopted by the Finnish Government, while forfeiture of the right of domicile may be regulated in Acts adopted by the Provincial Government of Åland.

The right of domicile follows the principle of ius sanguinis and is acquired at birth if either of the parents is in possession of the right of domicile (Autonomy Act, sect. 6). Others can also acquire the right of domicile if certain requirements are met. According to sect. 7 of the Autonomy Act, a person wishing to acquire the right of domicile in Åland must be a Finnish national, have had his or her habitual residence in Åland for the last five years without interruption, and have adequate knowledge of the Swedish language.[39] A person who has lived outside Åland for more than five years loses the right of domicile.[40] Forfeiture of Finnish nationality also leads to the loss of the right of domicile in the Province of Åland (Autonomy Act, sect. 7).

4.3.4 *Institutional arrangements*

4.3.4.1 *The legislative process*

Enacting legislation is one of the main tasks of the Finnish Parliament. Both the Government and Members of Parliament can submit bills to the Parliament. The Government, through the Ministry of the Interior, plays a vital role in immigration matters in Finland. Revising nationality legislation is one of the Ministry's tasks. The new Nationality Act was consequently drafted by the Ministry of the Interior, with the assistance of the Directorate of Immigration.

The handling of a Governmental bill or a Member of Parliaments' initiative starts with a preliminary debate in plenary session. No decisions are made at this stage of the legislative procedure as the purpose of the debate is merely to provide a basis for the subsequent committee work. The Members of Parliament are given an opportunity to present their views on the bill as a guide to the committee work. At the end of the debate Parliament decides which committee the further preparation of the bill shall be referred to.

During the committee's handling of the bill, which is the next stage in the legislative procedure, there may be hearings of experts, such as officials, representatives of government agencies, organisations and other interest groups who will present their views on the legislative proposal.

The bill is subject to a general debate within the committee where it will be analysed section by section. The committee will present a report with its views and recommendations as to what decision Parliament should take on the bill. The handling of a bill in a committee normally takes a month or two.

Fifty different agencies, organisations, and interest groups were asked to state their views on the Bill for the new Nationality Act. Among these were the Finnish Expatriate Parliament, the Finland Society, the Refugee Advice Centre, relevant ministries, and the administrative courts. A specific statement on multiple nationality and its impact on the various branches of the administration was asked for and given by seventeen different agencies, including the Ministry of Justice, the Ministry of Foreign Affairs, the Ministry of Defence and the Ministry of Labour.

The Nationality Act of 2003 was handled in the Committee for Constitutional Law. This Committee handles all matters concerning constitutional law, but also other related matters such as nationality, language, political parties, and ministerial responsibilities.

Following the Committee's handling, the bill goes through two readings in plenary session of Parliament. In the first hearing the bill will be decided upon section by section. Voting will be conducted if necessary. At least two days have to pass before the second reading of the bill can take place. At the second reading, the bill can no longer be amended and will be either approved or rejected. If a bill is amended during the first hearing it must be referred to the Grand Committee for scrutiny before it can be voted on in the second hearing. Normally a bill is read within two to four months, however, major legislative projects may require considerably more time.

A simple majority of votes is required for approving or rejecting ordinary legislative acts. Amendments of constitutional provisions must first be approved by a simple majority of votes in the second parliamentary reading. The bill will thereafter be left in abeyance until a new Parliament has been elected. The new Parliament must approve the bill by a two-thirds majority in order for it to become law. If declared urgent by a five-sixths majority of the Parliament, amendments of constitutional law may be approved by the same Parliament by a two-thirds majority.

A law approved by Parliament must be sent to the President of the Republic for ratification. If the President does not ratify a law within three months, the law will be returned to Parliament and handled again.[41] If after this handling Parliament approves the law without amendments, the law will enter into force without ratification by the President.

In Finland, legislative acts by Parliament are not subject to judicial review by a constitutional court. Nor does the Supreme Court have an explicit right to declare an act unconstitutional. Instead, the Committee for Constitutional Law has the authority to review the constitutionality of bills and recommend changes. Recommendations of the Committee are not judicially binding, but in practice they are unconditionally followed (Timonen 1993). Consequently, the Constitutional Law Committee may be regarded as fulfilling the tasks of a constitutional court.

4.3.4.2 The process of implementation

The processing of nationality applications and declarations is carried out within the Directorate of Immigration. The Directorate took over the role of the Ministry of the Interior as the new immigration agency when it became operational on 1 March 1995.[42] The Directorate is an administrative agency that processes and decides on matters related to immigration, residence, refugee issues, and Finnish nationality. The Directorate is subordinate to the Ministry of the Interior.

Until 1998, the President was the authority who formally decided nationality matters. The President decided whether a person had a right to acquire Finnish nationality and whether he or she should lose his or her Finnish nationality. Through the amendments to the Nationality Act that were enacted on 15 August 1998 this authority was transferred from the President to the Directorate of Immigration.[43] A major consideration behind this amendment was the need to make the processing of nationality matters more effective.

An *application* for Finnish nationality can only be submitted in Finland and it shall be submitted in person to the district police were the applicant is residing. A nationality *declaration* must be submitted in person to the local police station where the person is residing or to a Finnish diplomatic mission, consulate, or honorary consulate if the person is residing abroad. A declaration can also be sent by post with the attachment of a receipt showing that the handling fee has been paid. The possibility of sending a declaration by post is primarily meant for persons having a long way to travel in order to reach a Finnish diplomatic mission or for persons in countries where Finland does not have such missions.

Applications and declarations shall be made on specific application forms. Such forms are available at the Directorate of Immigration, the District Police and at Finnish missions abroad, as well as on the website of the Directorate of Immigration. Documents shall be attached in accordance with the instructions on the specific form, typically proof of established paternity, copy of passport or identity card and birth certificate. Applicants from countries suffering or recovering from (civil) war often have difficulties providing documents regarding their identity. This concerns nationals from Somalia, Iraq, Afghanistan and Angola in particular. As already mentioned, the identity of a person who has used one and the same identity in the population information system for at least ten years is considered to be established in accordance with the Nationality Act.

There is a fee for both nationality applications and declarations that is regulated periodically by a decree issued by the Ministry of the Interior. There has been a steady increase of the fee due to inflation and the rise in general administrative costs. For all nationality applications, including applications for release from Finnish nationality, the current fee is 400 euros.[44] Dependant applicants, i.e., unmarried children under eighteen years of age, are included in the application of their parents and, thus, exempted from the fee. The fee for a nationality declaration is 300 euros.[45] The declaration fee is reduced for children and for persons who were sent as war children to another Nordic country during the Winter War in 1939-1940 and the Continuation War in 1941-1944. For these two groups the fee is only 100 euros. The declaration fee for persons who are 65 years of age or older is 250 euros. Application and declaration fees must be paid in order for the application or declaration to be processed by the Directorate of Immigration.

The high fee has proven to be a hurdle for some applicants who are dependent on social security benefits. The unemployment rate is significantly higher among refugees than among other immigrants. Among some nationalities, e.g., Somalis, Iranians and Iraqis, the rate is as high as 70 per cent. The monthly social subsistence without housing assistance for unemployed persons without previous work experience is approximately 350 euros per month. This covers only the most necessary monthly costs and saving money for the application fee poses a problem. The social authorities do not generally give additional subsistence to cover a nationality application fee. There is, however, a discrepancy between the practices of various municipalities, as some do pay the fee for their residents.[46]

The problem with the long processing time, as outlined below, has been an underlying reason for the increased fee for nationality applications and declarations. The intention was that the fee should cover the real costs for processing an application or a declaration. The fee has apparently had an unintended effect, as the number of declarations made to the Directorate has been much lower than expected. Worries have consequently been expressed that the high fees constitute a barrier for many immigrants and former Finnish nationals wishing to (re)acquire Finnish nationality.[47] In particular, it has been viewed as unfair that persons who have lost Finnish nationality due to the previous non-acceptance of multiple nationality must now pay such a high fee in order to reacquire Finnish nationality. The Finnish authorities are concerned with the development and need to reconsider the fees and decide whether the reduction in the number of nationality declarations and applications is desirable, which is contra indicated by the moderate annual growth of the Finnish population.

The application or declaration will be processed by the nationality unit of the Directorate of Immigration. The period within which an application or declaration has to be processed has not been legally regulated, leaving it rather unclear for an applicant to know when to expect an answer. After rendering a decision the Directorate notifies the applicant in writing of the result of the application or declaration procedure.

The Directorate of Immigration, the Ministry for Foreign Affairs and Finnish diplomatic missions abroad provide information about the possibilities and procedures for acquisition and renunciation of Finnish nationality. All these authorities have been playing a role in distributing information about the new principle since the acceptance of multiple nationality was introduced in the Nationality Act of 2003. While the goal is to inform Finnish expatriates about the possibility of retaining or reclaiming Finnish nationality, the information about the new Act has not taken the form of a recruitment campaign.

It was recognised early on by the authorities that the procedures took too long and that there was a need to reorganise the Directorate of Immigration and make processing more effective. The number of nationality applications increased remarkably after 1995 as a result of an increasing number of immigrants finding their way to Finland. Due to lack of financial resources within the Directorate, the increase in the number of immigration and nationality cases were not matched by a corresponding increase in personnel. The result has been that processing times have become unacceptably long, at an average of three years for nationality applications. In 1997, the Directorate recruited extra personnel in order to manage the constantly increasing pile of applications. Immigration matters were, however, prioritised, leading to the reallocation of resources within the Directorate from nationality matters to immigration matters.[48]

The long processing times in nationality matters has been the subject of repeated criticism by the public, Members of Parliament and the Parliamentary Ombudsman. The Ombudsman has several times drawn attention to the unreasonably long processing times for nationality applications, and considered this to be in breach of sect. 21 of the Constitution stipulating that cases be processed without unfounded delay. The Ombudsman has considered a processing time of three years to be far beyond acceptable.[49]

It was expected that the amendments in the Nationality Act in 1998[50] when the President of the Republic lost his authority to grant and reject Finnish nationality would lead to a reduction in processing time of 30 per cent. However, the caseload and redirection of capacity within the Directorate prevented this reduction from being realised.

A project was started at the beginning of this decade with an aim to render processing of nationality matters more effective and limit the delays. Processing of nationality cases according to the principle 'first in – first out' has as a result partly been abandoned, and new applications that are considered clearly founded have been processed immediately, at best within a few weeks. Old applications have been grouped in order to process similar cases simultaneously, consequently speeding up the processing time.[51]

Another project, launched in 2004, also aims to shorten processing time within the Directorate of Immigration. A goal of the project is to cut down the average processing time to one and a half years for nationality applications and two months for declarations. This goal has not yet been achieved, but a decrease in processing times could be observed at the end of 2004 as applications then had an average processing time of 2.4 years as opposed to 2.8 years in 2003, and declarations were processed in 2.4 months. Another aim of the project is to delineate factors preventing and delaying the processing of nationality matters and to amend the processing practices in order to overcome problems linked to such factors.[52] As of today, applications are processed immediately and a decision will be made within a few months provided that all necessary documentation is submitted together with the application.[53]

Decisions by the President were not subject to administrative appeal. A person whose application the President had rejected simply had to make a new application in order to get the decision reviewed. However, when the authority to take decisions on nationality declarations and applications was transferred to the Directorate of Immigration, a legal remedy of appeal was introduced.

According to sect. 41 of the Nationality Act, decisions made by the Directorate of Immigration can be appealed to a county administrative court, and decisions made by the county administrative courts can be further appealed to the Supreme Administrative Court (sect. 42). The need to ensure the uniformity of decisions brought about the introduction in 2003 of a possibility for the Directorate of Immigration to appeal a decision that has been reversed or changed by a decision of the county administrative court (sect. 42).

As the new Act has only been in force since June 2003, the administrative and legal practices of the administrative courts and the Supreme Administrative Court have not yet developed.

4.4 Conclusions

'Swedes we are not, Russians we do not wish to be – Let us thus be Finns'[54]

Until recently, Finnish nationality law was influenced by Finland's relation to its two large neighbouring countries, Russia and Sweden. The idea of Finland as a nation emerged in the nineteenth century during the Grand Duchy period under the Russian Empire, and a Finnish nationality was recognised around the middle of the same century.

Ius sanguinis was already the main principle followed in nationality matters during the Grand Duchy period. Habitual residence in Finland was crucial, and moving abroad would normally lead to loss of Finnish nationality. Despite multiple nationality not being accepted, Finnish subjects also had, as a consequence of Finland being part of the Russian Empire, a subject relationship to Russia. Russians, on the other hand, were not considered subjects of the Grand Duchy of Finland, but they could be naturalised in Finland following a period of residence there. For Finnish nationals, the Russian subjecthood was a kind of federal citizenship in the Russian Empire, while the Finnish subjecthood/nationality could be considered as a regional citizenship in the grand Duchy of Finland, relevant for all subjects of Finland.

Parallels may be drawn to the regime governing the Province of Åland today. The *right of domicile* in Åland is a kind of regional nationality with specific rights for those in possession of that right, i.e., mostly ethnic Ålanders. The earlier relationship between Finland and Russia resembles today's relationship between Åland and Finland: Finnish nationals were Russian subjects, like persons with the *right of domicile* in Åland are Finnish nationals. Under the Russian Empire, Finnish subjects benefited from rights both in Finland and in Russia, but were freed from many of the obligations of other Russian subjects. Similarly, persons in possession of the *right of domicile* in Åland benefit from the rights of Finnish nationals, while they are freed from some of the duties. One example is that military service is not obligatory for Finnish nationals who at the same time have the *right of domicile* in Åland.[55]

Åland has always been inhabited by Swedish-speaking people with a culture similar to the Swedish culture. They have in fact always felt a closer affiliation to the Swedes than to the Finns. When the Swedish Kingdom was forced to relinquish Finland to Russia after the 1808-1809 war, Åland was 'part of the package'. As a consequence, Åland became part of the Grand Duchy of Finland. When Finland declared itself independent in 1917, Åland wished to be reunified with the Swedish Kingdom. A majority of the inhabitants of Åland signed a petition to that end, which was presented to the Swedish King and Government. Finland was not prepared to meet this demand. The nationality question of the Ålanders was referred to the newly formed League of Nations in 1921. The issue became one of the few success stories of the League, and the solution was three-fold, giving something to each of the three parties involved in the conflict: Finland was granted sovereignty over Åland, the inhabitants of Åland were guaranteed their Swedish culture, language, local customs and the system of self-government, and Sweden was assured that Åland would never become a military threat to Sweden as the Åland Islands would remain demilitarised and were in addition declared neutral.

Even though Finnish nationality was forced upon the Ålanders almost 90 years ago, still today, they do not perceive themselves as Finns. They speak about 'travelling to Finland' like they were going to another country, and most Ålanders know the city of Stockholm better than they know any Finnish city. The inhabitants of Åland have built up a strong ethnic culture and pride in their identity as Ålanders, and they prefer calling themselves Ålanders, rather than Swedes or Finns. So why not change Russians to Finns and Finns to Ålanders in the slogan at the beginning of this chapter, and it will describe the nationality dilemma of yet another group of persons. For the Ålanders the *right of domicile* has been an effective tool to safeguard their interests and to protect the specific characteristics of the province.

Another group of interest for Finnish nationality legislation are the expatriates. The expatriates have lately had a strong influence on the development of Finnish nationality law. Through the Finland Society and the Finnish Expatriate Parliament, they were the major forces behind the adoption of the principle of multiple nationality in the new Finnish Nationality Act of 2003.

Traditionally there has been a firm political consensus behind the negative position with regard to multiple nationality in Finnish nationality law. Despite this, the principle was adopted without any major political or public debate. Questions that were touched upon were, however, the effect that multiple nationality would have on national identity and loyalty. Furthermore, during the hearing of the new Nationality Act only the Ministry of Defence expressed some criticism, as it feared that multiple nationality could pose a threat to national security, as e.g., espionage would become easier.[56]

Multiple nationality was in fact praised by all of the major political parties. The reason for the rather abrupt change of opinion on this matter and the relatively quiet debate beforehand can be based on a Finnish eagerness to follow international trends, which again can be based on a fear of being isolated as a consequence of the country's geographical position, on the outskirts of Europe. The Swedish acceptance of multiple nationality a few years earlier most likely also contributed to making the decision easier and kept the debate toned down. Considering that the Finnish acceptance of multiple nationality contributed to a Nordic discrepancy in nationality matters, where the aim ever since the end of the nineteenth century has been greater uniformity, it is remarkable that the discussion was not more intense and did not to a greater extent touch upon Nordic cooperation and its future.

Chronological table of major reforms in Finnish nationality law

Date	Document	Content of change
1967	518/1967 Act amending sect. 4 clause 1 of the Constitution (Laki hallitusmuodon 4 §:n 1 momentin muuttamisesta).	Gender equality: no longer automatic acquisition of Finnish nationality by foreign women marrying citizen men.
1968	401/1968 Nationality Act (Kansalaisuuslaki)	Gender equality and prevention of statelessness further promoted. Declaration procedure introduced. Facilitated acquisition introduced for former Finnish nationals and Nordic nationals.
1968	402/1968 Nationality Decree (Kansalaisuusasetus)	Ministry of the Interior becomes the main authority in nationality matters.
1984	584/1984 Act amending the Nationality Act (Laki kansalaisuuslain muuttamisesta)	Finnish nationality always acquired from the mother. Declaration procedure introduced for adopted children. Loss of Finnish nationality at the age of 22 if no close connection. Prevention of statelessness further promoted.
1985	699/1985 Nationality Decree (Kansalaisuusasetus)	Slightly more detailed provisions and modernised language.
1995	155/1995 Act amending the Nationality Act (Laki kansalaisuuslain muuttamisesta)	The Directorate of Immigration becomes the new immigration agency also handling nationality matters.
1995	223/1995 Decree amending the Nationality Decree 699/1985 (Asetus kansalaisuusasetuksen (699/85) muuttamisesta)	The Directorate of Immigration becomes the agency in charge of processing and deciding on nationality issues.
1996	1373/1996 Decree amending the Nationality Decree (Asetus kansalaisuusasetuksen muuttamisesta)	This decree includes only minor amendments to the decree of 1985: it regulates the tasks of the police in nationality matters and allows the

Date	Document	Content of change
		Directorate of Immigration to access information from the social welfare authorities.
1998	480/1998 Act repealing sect. 31 of the Finnish Constitution (Laki Suomen Hallitusmuodon 31 §:n kumoamisesta)	The President of Finland no longer decides on nationality matters. This authority now belongs to the Directorate of Immigration.
1998	481/1998 Act amending the Nationality Act (Laki kansalaisuuslain muuttamisesta)	The Directorate of Immigration takes over the tasks of the President of the Republic. Introduction of appeal to the County Administrative Court against decisions by the Directorate.
1998	482/1998 Decree amending the Nationality Decree (Asetus kansalaisuusasetuksen muuttamisesta)	The Directorate of Immigration takes over the tasks of the Ministry of the Interior and the President of the Republic.
1999	731/1999 Constitution of Finland (Suomen perustuslaki)	Prevention of statelessness: a condition that voluntary or involuntary loss of nationality shall not lead to statelessness.
2003	359/2003 Nationality Act (Kansalaisuuslaki)	Acceptance of multiple nationality. Further promotion of gender equality and prevention of statelessness. Inclusion of language requirement and abolishment of requirement of guaranteed livelihood. Approximation of an adopted child's rights to that of a biological child.
2004	799/2004 Nationality Decree (Valtioneuvoston asetus kansalaisuudesta)	Inclusion of clear rules on how to prove required language skills.

Notes

1 Iceland acceded to the Nordic Agreement in 1998.

2 Förordning om Ryske undersåtares och i Ryssland vistande utlänningars inskrifning i Finland, entry into force 20 March 1858.

3 33/1920 Act on the Acceptance of Foreigners as Finnish Nationals, Lag om utlännings antagande till finsk medborgare.

4 18/1927 Lag om förlust av finskt medborgarskap, entry into force 1 January 1928. An additional reason for urging a legal possibility to renunciate one's Finnish nationality was the new practice in 1922 of the United States prescribing that a foreign woman would no longer automatically acquire the nationality of her American husband upon marriage. As a consequence, a Finnish woman marrying an American man became stateless. By making acquisition of another nationality a condition for losing Finnish nationality when taking up residence abroad, such a situation was avoided.

5 325/1941 Lag om förvärvande og förlust av finskt medborgarskap, entry into force 1 July 1941.

6 838/1941 Lag om medborgarskap för vissa invånare på det med riket återförenade området (Act on the Citizenship of Certain Inhabitants of Areas Returned to the Realm).
7 518/1967 Lag om ändring av 4 § 1 momentet regeringsformen, entry into force 1 July 1968.
8 401/1968 Medborgarskapslag, entry into force 1 July 1968.
9 402/1968 Medborgarskapsförordning, entry into force 1 July 1968
Decrees are legal acts issued on the basis of authority expressly given in the Constitution or in another act. Such decrees could relate to public administration, the implementation of laws, management of public assets, and the organisation of the Council of State and the ministries. After the entry into force of the new Constitution in 1999, the President of the Republic, the Government or a Ministry may issue decrees. Prior to this, the President issued all Nationality Decrees. The latest Nationality Decree was issued by Governmental Decree in 2004.
10 584/1984 Act amending the Nationality Act 401/1968, Lag om ändring av medborgarskapslagen 401/1968, entry into force 1 September 1984.
11 699/1985 Medborgarskopsförordning, entry into force 1 September 1985.
12 HE 235/2002 (HE: Hallituksen esitys: Government Bill), Hallituksen esitys Eduskunnalle kansalaisuuslaiksi, Government Bill to the Parliament proposing a new Nationality Act.
13 The Finland Society, founded in 1927, is an interest group providing expertise and service to Finnish expatriates, and Finns moving abroad. The Society furthermore conveys an up-to-date image of Finland to the outside world and raises awareness in Finland about Finnish expatriates.
14 The Finnish Expatriate Parliament, founded in 1997, is a cooperative forum and promoter of interests for all Finns living abroad. At the Parliament the Finnish expatriates living around the world come together and decide collectively on issues that are of importance for them.
15 LA 180/1999 (LA: Lakialoite: Parliamentary motion), Laki kansalaisuuslain muuttamisesta, Act amending the Nationality Act, Prusti, R / Social Democratic Party.
16 Information provided by researcher Jussi Ronkainen at the University of Joensuu in an e-mail of 7 June 2005.
17 Information provided by Tiina Suominen, nationality division director at the Directorate of Immigration, in a telephone conversation on 15 September 2005.
18 These numbers are not completely comparable, as the number of first- and second-generation immigrants will be a bit higher than the number of persons with a foreign nationality living in a country. There are no statistics available on the number of first and second generation immigrants in Finland. The author finds, however, that this comparison gives an indication of a great difference in the number of immigrants living in Finland and the Netherlands.
19 KK 335/2000 (KK: Kirjallinen kysymys: Written question by a Member of Parliament to the Government), Pohjoismaiden ulkopuolella asuville Suomessa syntyneille myönnettävä kaksoiskansalaisuus, Accepting double nationality for persons born in Finland and residing outside the Nordic countries, Vistbacka R. / True Finns Party.
20 HE 235/2002: 6; KK 335/2000.
21 The Norwegian Parliament adopted the new Norwegian Nationality Act on 8 June 2005. The Act does not accept multiple nationality. Even though the Norwegian Official Report on a new Nationality Act was in favour of multiple nationality, the Ministry of Local Government and Regional Development took a negative view with regard to it. See the proposition to the Odelsting: Ot.prp. nr. 41 (2004-2005) Om lov om norsk statsborgerskap.

22 HE 235/2002: 17.
23 Information provided by the Refugee Advice Centre, a Finnish non-governmental organisation.
24 HE 235/2002: 6.
25 Information provided by the Refugee Advice Centre.
26 Information provided by the Refugee Advice Centre.
27 HE 235/2002: 42.
28 Information provided by the Refugee Advice Centre.
29 799/2004 Statsrådets förordning om medborgarskap, enacted 1 September 2004.
30 Information provided by Tiina Suominen, nationality division director at the Directorate of Immigration, in a telephone conversation on 15 September 2005.
31 481/2003 Statsrådets förordning om bedömning av kunskaper i finska och svenska inom statsförvaltningen, entry into force 1 January 2004.
32 Information provided by the Refugee Advice Centre.
33 HE 235/2002: 12.
34 While Sweden, for example, accepted great numbers of labour immigrants after the Second World War, following its rapidly expanding industrial sector, Finland was struggling with its economy and many Finns emigrated to Sweden in order to be able to support their families.
35 Information provided by the Refugee Advice Centre.
36 639/1993 Act amending the Alien's Act, Lag om ändring av utlänningslagen, entry into force 15 July 1993: sect. 18.
37 The number of nationality applications was not affected in the same way, as the increase was only a moderate 5 per cent.
38 1144/1991 Självstyrelselag för Åland, entry into force 1 January 1993.
39 Swedish is the official language in the Province of Åland.
40 Provincial Act (1993:2) on the Right of Domicile in Åland, Landskapslag om åländsk hembygdsrätt, sect. 4.
41 This veto power of the President is today of minor significance as a tool to halt the legislative work of the Parliament. It is mainly used when there is a need to make technical corrections to a bill after it has been accepted by the Parliament (Timonen 1993).
42 Amendments were made to the 1968 Nationality Act in this regard (see 155/1995 Act amending the Nationality Act 401/1968, Lag om ändring av medborgarskapslagen, entry into force 1 March 1995). A Decree (223/1995 Decree amending the Nationality Decree 699/1985, Förordning om ändring av medborgarskapsförordningen (699/85), entry into force 1 March 1995) with amendments to the Nationality Decree of 1985 was enacted the same year. The amendments were needed as the Directorate of Immigration took over the role as the agency in charge of processing and deciding on nationality issues.
43 480/1998 Act repealing sect. 31 of the Finnish Constitution, Lag om upphävande av 31 § Regeringsformen för Finland, entry into force 15 August 1998; 481/1998 Act amending the Nationality Act 401/1968. Lag om ändring av medborgarskapslagen, entry into force 15 August 1998; and 482/1998 Decree amending the Nationality Decree 699/1985, Förordning om ändring av medborgarskapsförordningen, entry into force 15 August 1998, were amended accordingly.
44 All fees are from the end of 2004.
45 The only changes for 2005 were that the declaration fee was reduced to 240 euros and this reduced fee also applies to those 65 years of age or older.
46 Information provided by the Refugee Advice Centre.
47 AM 89/2003 (AM: Åtgärdsmotion: Parliamentary motion), Avgifterna för beviljande av medborgarskap, Fees for granting citizenship, Biaudet E. / Swedish People's Party.

48 KK 1265/2001, Ulkomaalaisviraston hakemusten käsittelyajat, Processing time for applications within the Directorate of Immigration, Kanerva E. / Social Democratic Party.

49 See in particular the decision of the Ombudsmann on processing times within the Directorate of Immigration for asylum and nationality applications, 16 December 2003, 362/2/03 Ratkaisija: Apulaisoikeusasiamies Ilkka Rautio, Esittelijä: Oikeusasiamiehensihteeri Jari Pirjola, Päätös ulkomaalaisviraston turvapaikka- ja kansalaisuushakemusten käsittelyajoista.

50 Government Bill revoking sect. 31 in the Finnish Constitution and amending the Nationality Act, HE 49/1998, Hallituksen esitys laeiksi Suomen Hallitusmuodon 31 §:n kumoamisesta ja kansalaisuuslain muuttamisesta.

51 KK 1265/2001, Ulkomaalaisviraston hakemusten käsittelyajat, Processing time for applications handed in to the Directorate of Immigration, Kanerva E. / Suomen Sosialidemo-kraattinen Puolue.

52 KK 258/2004, Kansalaisuushakemusten käsittelyajat, Processing time for nationality applications, Holmlund A. / Centre Party; Ministry of the Interior 2005b.

53 KK 58/2005, Kansalaisuushakemusten käsittely, Processing of nationality applications, Essayah S. / Christian Democrats.

54 'Svenskar är vi icke, ryssar vilja vi icke vara – Låt oss alltså vara finnar' (Author's translation to English). This slogan could be heard in Finland during the nineteenth century (Elmgren 2002: chapter 3.3).

55 This is a consequence of the demilitarisation of the Åland Islands, originating in the Peace Treaty of Paris in 1856 after the Crimean War.

56 Information provided by Jussi Ronkainen, University of Joensuu.

Bibliography

Anon (2005), 'Suomen kansalaisuuspäätösten käsittelyaikataulussa suuria eroja', *Turun Sanomat*, 8 March 2005. www.turunsanomat.fi.

Council of Europe (2003), *Demographic Year Book 2003*. www.coe.int.

Elmgren, A. (2002), *Den Allrakäraste fienden*. Lund: Lund University.

Ersbøll, E. (2003), 'Statsborgerskab – medborgarskap. Europæisk konvergens – nordisk divergens', *Mennesker & rettigheter* 21 (2): 147-164.

Jussila, O. (1978), 'Från ryska undersåtar till finländska medborgare – om medborgarbegreppets utveckling under första hälften av 1800-talet', *Historisk tidsskrift för Finland* 1978 (1): 5-20.

Ministry of the Interior (2005a), *Accession to the Council of Europe Convention on Nationality and the United Nations Convention on the Reduction of Statelessness [Sättande i kraft av Europarådets konvention om medborgarskap och Förenta Nationernas konvention om begränsning av statslöshet]*. www.intermin.fi.

Ministry of the Interior (2005b), *Handläggningstiderna vid utlänningsverket förkortades påfallande genom projektet för effektivisering av utlänningsverkets verksamhet*. www.intermin.fi.

Peltoniemi P. (2003), 'Dual Citizenship Possible in June', *Suomen Silta/Finland Bridge* 2003 (2). www.suomi-seura.fi.

Rosas A. & M. Suksi (1996), 'Finnish nationality law', in B. Nascimbene (ed.), *Nationality laws in the European Union*, 267-307. Milano: Butterworths/Giuffrè.

Screen, J. E. O. (1978), 'Undersåte och medborgare: finländska officerare i rysk tjänst', *Historisk tidsskrift för Finland* 1978 (1): 21-29.

Statistics Finland (2005), *Population Structure and Acquisition of Finnish Nationality*. www.stat.fi.

Timonen, P. (ed.) (1993), *Inledning till Finlands rättsordning 2*. Helsinki: Juristförbundets Förlag.
UVI (Directorate of Immigration) (2004a), *Annual Report 2004*. www.uvi.fi.
UVI (Directorate of Immigration) (2004b), *3011 personer önskade återfå sitt finska medborgarskap*. www.uvi.fi.
UVI (Directorate of Immigration) (2005), *Citizenship granted 1991-2000*. www.uvi.fi.

5 France

Patrick Weil and Alexis Spire

5.1 Introduction

France is frequently portrayed as having a strong integrative national identity forged through its revolutionary experience.

French nationality law as it currently exists was essentially established by 1889. Since then French legislation has been a mixture of ius soli and ius sanguinis. Ius sanguinis was a modern tradition invented by France, and it diffused across continental Europe during the nineteenth century. However, despite this strong tradition of ius sanguinis, France was also the first country of immigration in Europe, which led to the reincorporation of ius soli in order to attribute nationality to children of immigrants, even against their will. Today French nationality is attributed at birth if one of the child's parents is French (regardless of place of birth), or if the child is born in France and has one parent already born in France. A person born in France whose parents are neither French nor born in France will automatically become French at age eighteen if he or she still resides in France and does not refuse the citizenship. Immigrants (i.e., foreign residents in France born in a foreign country) may apply for naturalisation. Formally the barriers are very low for ordinary naturalisation: five years of residence is the normal requirement. Furthermore, due to a little known law of 1961, the majority of immigrants have no required period of residence if they come from a former colony or a francophone country: theoretically, they just have to be resident in France at the time of application. However, the naturalisation service does not encourage naturalisation and faces a backlog of applications. The rate of naturalisation nowadays is approximately 5 per cent.

The ease of naturalisation in France is facilitated by a very tolerant position towards dual citizenship. Formally, France signed the 1963 Council of Europe Convention, which attempts to reduce cases of dual citizenship. However, in practice – except for the nationals directly concerned by the 1963 Convention – France has always allowed newly-naturalised citizens to retain their previous citizenship.

In fact, since the First World War, France has always tolerated dual citizenship, but for some extreme cases a provision permits revocation of citizenship for dual citizens (primarily for those who become an enemy of the French state for one reason or another).

Since 1973, French nationals living abroad can transmit their French nationality through an infinite number of generations, as long as the French descendant applies and registers with a French authority. Foreign spouses can acquire French citizenship through marriage and after two or three years of marriage receive citizenship by a declaration that takes effect one year later if the state has not opposed it for some legal reason. Since 1973, there is also total gender equality: both spouses of different nationalities transmit their citizenships to their children, and a foreign spouse (male or female) of a French citizen can become naturalised by a declaration that can be registered after two years of marriage (if they reside in France) and that takes effect after one year. Finally, loss of French nationality can only occur at the demand of the individual who must reside in a foreign country and be a dual national for it to be granted.

5.2 Historical development

Ius soli was the dominant criterion of nationality law in France in the eighteenth century (Sahlins 2004). The French revolution broke from this tradition. Because ius soli connoted feudal allegiance, it was decided, against Napoleon Bonaparte's wishes (Weil 2002), that the new civil Code of 1803 would grant French nationality at birth only to a child born to a French father, either in France or abroad.[1] This principle of ius sanguinis was not ethnically motivated but meant that family links transmitted by the *pater familias* had become more important than subjecthood and that nationality would be transmitted like family names through the father. This approach dominated French national legislation throughout most of the nineteenth century (1803-1889).

5.2.1 *Double ius soli: the heart of French nationality law*

At the end of the nineteenth century, France faced a contradiction between the legal tradition of the Civil Code and the evolution of migration. The majority of individuals born on French territory to foreign parents were not becoming French citizens, even though they belonged to families who had lived on French territory for extended periods of time. The main reason these foreigners were not becoming French was to escape the military draft that accompanied citizenship. Therefore, on 7 February 1851, a law introduced optional double ius soli: an individual born in France to an alien father born in France was a French citizen at the age of the majority except if he or she refused citizenship.

This law was not very successful and therefore repealed by the changes in the 1889 law, that more comprehensively addressed the new reality of France as a country of immigrants. To fulfil the principle of equality of public charges and duties, third generation 'immigrants' were automatically granted French citizenship and drafted (Brubaker 1992). Since then, ius soli has been the heart of French nationality law. It is both a mechanism for granting French nationality automatically to third generation 'immigrants' born in France and the simplest means by which French citizens prove their nationality.[2]

5.2.2 *A century of legislative stability*

For nationality legislation, the 100 years that followed 1889 were a period of legislative stability. After 1889, the most important nationality reform concerned the withdrawal of colonial privileges or inequalities and the equalisation of men and women.

Throughout the First World War, France was highly concerned with newly naturalised people from enemy nations and the difficulty of controlling their mixed loyalties. In response to Germany's Delbruck Law of 22 July 1913 that allowed Germans who were naturalised abroad to retain their original citizenship, France instituted formal procedures for denaturalisation with the laws of 7 April 1915 and 18 June 1917. The procedure was overseen by the *Conseil d'Etat* then by the Judicial Court System. The government's suspicion of naturalised citizens from enemy nations also led to the formation of an agency dedicated to the surveillance of newly naturalised citizens (Weil 2002). This agency was

Table 5.1: Composition of the population in France 1901-1990

Year	*French by birth*		*French by acquisition*		*Foreigners*		*Total*
	In thousands	*%*	*In thousands*	*%*	*In thousands*	*%*	*In thousands*
1901	37,200	96.7	220	0.6	1,030	2.7	38,450
1906	37,600	96.7	220	0.6	1,050	2.7	38,840
1911	37,800	96.4	250	0.6	1,160	3.0	39,190
1921	37,800	95.4	250	0.6	1,530	4.0	38,800
1926	37,600	93.4	250	0.6	2,410	6.0	40,230
1931	38,200	92.5	360	0.9	2,710	6.6	41,220
1936	36,500	93.4	520	1.3	2,200	5.3	41,180
1946	37,250	93.5	850	2.1	1,740	4.4	39,850
1954	39,900	93.4	1,070	2.5	1,760	4.1	42,780
1962	43,000	92.5	1,283	2.8	2,170	4.7	46,460
1968	45,710	92.0	1,320	2.7	2,620	5.3	49,650
1975	47,760	90.8	1,390	2.7	3,440	6.5	52,600
1982	49,170	90.6	1,430	2.6	3,680	6.8	54,280
1990	51,280	90.6	1,770	3.1	3,580	6.3	56,620

Source: French Census

under the authority of the Interior Ministry and created in April 1918, but was quickly disbanded after the armistice of 11 November 1918. As the war ended the political priority also shifted to demographic concerns and to the increase of naturalisations.

With the casualties of the First World War, France was sorely in need of new citizens and therefore encouraged immigration. However, despite population increases throughout the 1920s not enough people were becoming citizens, so in 1927 Parliament took matters into its own hands and adopted the most liberal legislation the French Republic has ever known (Weil 2002).

One of the major goals was to reverse a provision by which a wife took her husband's nationality. This law had resulted in the net loss of 60,000 French women between 1914 and 1927: 120,000 French women had become foreigners through marriage and 60,000 foreign women had become French by marrying a French man. So, starting in 1927 policymakers permitted a French woman marrying a foreigner to keep her nationality and transfer it to her children. Also, under a new naturalisation policy, the residence period imposed on immigrants was reduced from ten years to three.

The effect was immediate: between 1927 and 1930, 170,000 foreigners acquired French nationality through naturalisation compared with 45,000 in the preceding five years. Yet this expansion of French nationality occurred at the same time as the financial crash of 1929, and as the economic crisis worsened, so did the expression of xenophobia. In the 1930s, violent debates erupted between guardians of 'nationality by origin' and those who defended the *français de papier* (foreigners granted citizenship). To placate those who doubted the loyalty of the newly naturalised citizens a law of 1934 delayed their entry to certain professions.

According to a new law passed on 12 November 1938, naturalised citizens could not vote or be elected to public office for five years, and the denaturalisation provisions were strengthened. The latter were activated if a foreigner knowingly made a false declaration, presented a document containing a lie or misinformation or used fraudulent means to obtain naturalisation. Nationality through marriage was limited: foreigners could not marry until they obtained a visa for more than one year. A foreign woman wishing to marry a French man had to submit an application before the marriage, and this application would not be considered if she had received an expulsion order or had had a request for naturalisation rejected.

Some experts proposed adding to these individual or professional restrictions a citizenship criterion that would be based either on ethnic origin or degree of assimilation. George Mauco (who, since 1932 when he published his doctorate on the subject (Mauco 1932), was considered the immigration expert) was one of the principal defenders of this approach.

At the beginning of the Second World War, there were three million foreigners in France, of whom 950,000 were Italian, 600,000 Spanish, 515,000 Polish and 2,450,000 Belgian. In order to make them participate in the war the government accelerated the process of naturalisation: 73,000 foreigners were naturalised or reintegrated in 1939 and 43,000 in the first six months of 1940.

Mauco had proposed in 1939, on the eve of the war, a review of all naturalisations, and between 1940 and 1944 the Vichy Regime, incorporating a Nazi law, revised the naturalisations that had taken place since the passing of the 1927 law, resulting in 15,154 French citizens becoming foreigners. The procedure was aimed at Jews, 6,000 of whom were denaturalised and many of whom were deported to Germany (Weil 2002). However, it is important to note that technically the imposition of collective discrimination based on origin, which often meant the deportation to Germany and extermination of French Jews or those of Jewish origin, was effected without modification of French nationality law.

5.2.3 *Nationality after the Second World War*

After the war, in a speech to the Consultative Assembly on 3 March 1945, General de Gaulle suggested: 'the lack of population and the lack of births are the principle cause of French unhappiness and the main obstacles which prevent French recovery'. He continued: 'to secure the twelve million children that France will need in the next ten years, to reduce our absurd child rate mortality, to secure over the next years, with rigour and intelligence, desirable immigration for the French nation, a great plan is outlined'.

With this goal in mind, the ordinance of 19 October 1945 established a new nationality code. It confirmed an open approach to the integration of immigrants and their children regardless of their country of origin, contrary to the wishes of the proponents of the ethnic approach, led by Georges Mauco, general secretary of the High Committee of Population. However, the duration of required residence was raised from three years to five and the rights of married women were slightly reduced. The system adopted in 1945 tried to maximise the number of women who remained French by restricting the ability of women to choose their nationality after marriage. Foreign women who married French men were automatically French except if they expressed their will not to become so before the marriage, and French women marrying foreigners remained French, unless they declared prior to the marriage that they wished to adopt the husband's nationality.

5.2.4 *Naturalisation policy from 1945 to 1973*

In the years immediately following the Liberation, the French administration gave priority to citizenship cases that had been ignored during the Vichy regime, as part of a public push to increase naturalisations and pursue a 'population growth policy'. However, the rhetoric of aggressively seeking larger population numbers coexisted with a selective preference for foreigners who were considered 'easier' to assimilate.

5.2.4.1 *The new French people are mostly European*

From 1945 to 1963, over 90 per cent of the naturalised French population came from other European countries, reflecting the large European population living in France at the time. In 1946, 39,000 foreigners acquired French citizenship, of which 15,000 were Italian, 6,000 Polish, and 6,400 Spanish. In 1947, the number jumped to 112,000, of which 44,000 (40 per cent) were Italian, 19,000 Polish, and 13,000 Spanish. Naturalisations then began to decline in 1948, going down from 71,000 to 25,000 in 1952. This drop was largely due to a policy of choosing foreigners who would be easiest to 'assimilate'.

This new policy was the idea of Paul Ribeyre, a Christian Democrat known for conservative positions, who in April 1952 distributed a confidential memo that reinstated selection based on ethnic criteria: 'We must avoid naturalising people who will be difficult to assimilate or who will alter the ethnic and spiritual character of the French nation'.

As a result of Ribeyre's instructions, the composition of naturalised citizens changed significantly over the years. For example: in 1946, the population called 'Armenians and Turks' were 7.1 per cent of those nationalised by decree, but in 1953, they were only 5.3 per cent, compared to Polish people, who were 15.9 per cent of those naturalised in 1946 and 26.5 per cent in 1953 (Spire 2005). Naturally this evolution reflected changing demands for naturalisation, but at the same time it would not have been possible without strict selection among the applications: between 1951 and 1953 the naturalisation approval rate[3] fluctuated between 60 and 65 per cent while in previous years it had always been higher than 75 per cent. And these selections were clearly made to favour certain nationalities that were considered 'easier to assimilate' (Weil 1995). By the middle of the 1950s, these restrictions had started to calm down as the economy picked up steam and new staff controlled the Population Ministry. The new direction was evident in the instructions of 22 November 1953 which encouraged 'liberal application of the naturalisation laws' and after about one year this new direction had an impact on the naturalisation statistics (cf. Table 5.2). Up until the end of the 1960s, Italians, Poles, and Spanish people were

Table 5.2: Acquisitions of nationality in France broken down by mode of acquisition

	Total	*Acquisitions by decree*			*Acquisitions by declaration*		
		Naturalisations	*Reintegrations*	*as minors*	*by marriage*	*as minors*	*other declarations*
1945	17,884	3,377	903	703	976	11,282	-
1946	38,869	14,154	744	3,216	5,187	15,088	-
1947	111,736	67,737	1,899	15,607	11,992	14,095	-
1948	70,925	48,955	1,186	9,868	3,269	7,422	3
1949	61,270	41,701	1,411	9,295	479	8,137	26
1950	43,790	27,912	977	7,075	270	7,255	129
1951	25,257	14,897	502	4,063	194	5,386	65
1952	28,139	15,707	493	4,798	211	6,534	20
1953	34,824	19,078	650	6,749	188	7,880	35
1954	39,308	20,410	593	6,883	164	10,992	16
1955	44,972	21,506	452	7,619	248	14,658	27
1956	38,040	17,263	350	7,091	233	12,726	129
1957	36,890	17,620	514	7,456	377	10,549	192
1958	34,452	17,205	458	6,789	702	8,904	217
1959	34,098	17,278	497	7,005	924	8,113	76
1960	29,683	13,192	253	5,763	2,035	8,184	123
1961	25,954	10,774	167	5,011	1,770	7,993	82
1962	28,149	11,120	157	5,617	1,234	9,686	235
1963	30,648	13,443	115	6,749	917	9,167	156
1964	27,289	11,890	147	5,773	764	8,479	160
1965	41,487	20,029	205	10,625	735	9,575	215
1966	30,488	15,652	204	7,018	635	6,707	180
1967	57,231	30,415	222	15,026	668	10,469	326
1968	38,287	19,876	520	9,539	520	7,299	454
1969	38,397	19,457	702	9,957	536	7,556	119
1970	35,000	18,002	784	9,200	372	6,498	92
1971	39,989	20,531	952	11,071	363	6,916	102
1972	35,254	17,235	823	9,793	282	6,945	94
1973	33,662	17,434	761	8,456	464	6,175	326
1974	36,050	16,241	711	7,076	5,984	5,226	745
1975	41,388	18,006	1,021	7,647	8,394	5,348	922
1976	45,131	20,140	1,538	8,989	9,181	4,107	1,133
1977	48,135	21,610	1,676	9,620	9,885	4,198	1,093
1978	50,977	22,439	1,670	9,996	10,849	4,623	1,361
1979	46,810	20,164	1,562	9,256	10,044	4,245	1,519
1980	52,129	20,203	1,977	9,324	13,767	4,836	1,996
1981	54,030	21,541	2,811	10,048	13,209	4,600	1,802
1982	48,835	18,073	2,349	8,037	14,227	4,473	1,668
1983	39,714	13,213	1,557	5,220	13,213	4,793	1,699
1984	35,575	13,635	1,599	4,822	10,279	4,201	1,037
1985	60,688	26,902	2,708	11,978	12,634	5,088	1,367

Sources: Table of persons acquiring French citizenship (Spire & Thave 1999).

over 70 per cent of the newly naturalised French, but they became increasingly outnumbered by migrants from former French colonies.

5.2.4.2 *The impact of decolonisation*

The law of 22 December 1961 modified the 1945 Ordinance that governed the conditions under which former colonial subjects could enter France, which became increasingly relevant as the majority of colonies had achieved independence by 1960. The new law no longer required good health and legal residence. In addition, the law of 1961 increased the possibilities for naturalisation without residence requirements, which benefited migrants from former French colonies or territories. Thus the former colonial population became an increasingly important part of the newly naturalised French population.

After the signing of the 1962 *Evian Accords*, Algerians who wanted to become French were subjected to a unique statute in which they could automatically become French if they lived in France, were over eighteen years old and performed a 'declaration of acceptance' of the French republic. However, in the years following independence the former 'French muslims' who enacted this procedure to become French were very few in number (between 1962 and 1967 the total number of applications was no more than 60,000) because to them it represented a betrayal of Algeria (Sayad 1999: 335-336). So, in 1967, the 'declaration of acceptance' was no longer required and Algerians who wished to become French followed a procedure of 'reintegration by decree' which required residence in France of five years.

5.2.5 *The law of 1973*

The law of 1973 completely equalised the nationality rights for men, women and legitimate children. Specific rights were also granted to citizens from former French colonies: nationality was automatically given at birth to children born in France of parents who had been born in the former colonies or overseas territories (Lagarde 1997).

This liberal legislation was applied in a political context in which the statute of immigration was being called into question. In 1974, confronted with a significant increase in unemployment, the French government halted the immigration of new workers; and in 1984 parliament passed a law creating a ten year residence permit (*titre unique*), which guaranteed the personal security of legal foreign residents whatever their nationality or origin. In the meantime there was an unsuccessful attempt led by President Giscard d'Estaing to forcefully repatriate 500,000 Algerian immigrants (Weil 1995).

Nationality became a divisive issue in the mid 1980s as young people who had been born in France and had been made automatically

French by law were increasingly seen as a problematic 'unassimilated' population. They were 'French without being aware of it or wanting it' ('français sans le savoir et sans le vouloir'). It was true that since 1981 several hundred children who had been born in France to Algerian parents had expressed their desire to renounce their allegiance to France (Brubaker 1992). They had often been made French at birth due to double ius soli: they had been born in France to a parent born in Algeria before 1962, at the time when Algeria was still a French territory divided into three regions (the same was not true, for instance, of Moroccans). For these children, some of whose parents had fought for the independence of Algeria, and above all for the Algerian state, being made French at birth without the possibility of renouncing their French citizenship (a different situation for children born to Moroccan or Portuguese parents) posed a problem. In 1982, Gaston Defferre, socialist Minister of the Interior, attempted to revise the double ius soli rule, in order to respond to the Algerians' demand, but failed (Weil 1995: 164-167).

On the other side of the political spectrum, ius soli, both simple and double, was fundamentally questioned. Some on the right favoured the establishment of strict ius sanguinis accompanied by a process of naturalisation, which would allow new French citizens to be 'selected' according to their capacity for assimilation. On the extreme right, the National Front had been proposing a re-examination of naturalisation since 1974.

5.2.6 *Preserving ties of nationality with French emigrants*

Today the French government allows citizens who reside abroad to acquire a second nationality while retaining their French citizenship. In addition, French citizens living abroad can pass citizenship across generations to their offspring, indefinitely. However, historically, French nationality law has not always been this liberal and in the past was much more restrictive for citizens living abroad.

The 1803 Civil Code allowed French citizens to move abroad and acquire foreign nationality, but in doing so they would lose their French nationality. However, just before the war with Austria, Napoleon ended this freedom and required all French people, even those who had since acquired foreign nationality, to return home. On 26 August 1811 the government then made it illegal for French people to acquire foreign nationality without the permission of the Emperor (Fahrmeir 2000).

The law of 1889 once again allowed French people to take foreign citizenship, but in doing so they would lose French citizenship. The only exception was for men eligible for military service, who were required to seek government permission. The goal was to avoid people changing citizenship in order to escape military service. The law of 9 April 1954 stated again that all men younger than 50 years old who acquired foreign citizenship would remain French unless they specifically requested permission from the French government. But while the goal of the 1889 law had been to prevent people from avoiding military service, the logic of the 1954 law was different (Weil 2002). It was 'essential to allow French people living abroad to retain their French citizenship while in the process of extending French culture and economic strength'. However, there was a troubling inequality in the citizenship law. Legally, a French man who became a citizen of another country would remain French unless he specifically requested the forfeiture of his French citizenship. Women however, would lose their French nationality if they became citizens of another country. The law of 1973 assured absolute equality between men and women and therefore abolished this discrimination.

Starting in 1973, the acquisition of foreign citizenship did not affect French nationality for both men and women. The only way to lose French citizenship was through an explicit request as double nationality is officially recognised by the French state. French people living abroad can transmit French nationality to their children for an infinite number of generations, although the government retains the right to contest citizenship if the person in question has left France for over 50 years (Lagarde 1997).

5.3 Recent developments and current institutional arrangements

5.3.1 *Nationality regulations since 1985*

The economic crisis, rising unemployment, and increasing success of the National Front during the early 1980s made immigration and nationality law reform a major political issue. These debates led to three modifications of French nationality (in 1993, 1998, and 2003), as well as a large national debate on the role of immigration in French society.

5.3.1.1 *Nationality law becomes a political issue (1985-1993)*

Starting in 1985, the extreme right (and shortly thereafter the mainstream right) began publicly attacking the ease with which foreigners became French. As opposed to the 1927 debates, which focused on naturalisation requirements, the 1980s debate centred on the concept of ius soli. Right-wing rhetoric argued that automatic attribution of nationality to foreigners was unfair to the foreigners, but their real motivation was not to help foreigners, but rather to purge France of non-European foreigners and former colonial subjects who were the majority of new French citizens and whom the right wing considered undesirable.

This right wing initiative emerged from the fact that France experienced a rapid increase in requests for naturalisation across all categories at the end of the 1980s. This increase is most likely due to changing attitudes among foreigners who were long-term residents in France. The increasingly strict laws on temporary stays and return visits to home countries gave long term residents the incentive to become French, secure the right to travel as much as possible, and improve their position in an economic marketplace increasingly marked by recession. Thus, regardless of national and social class background, more long-term residents sought French nationality during the period of suspended immigration and economic crisis than during the period of economic growth (Spire 2005). We can therefore understand foreigners' motivations for acquiring French citizenship as a function of the job market and access to travel mobility.

The growing number of foreigners demanding French citizenship during the 1980s and 1990s went hand in hand with an increase in the diversity of national origins, reflecting the various new migration waves that had blossomed since the early 1970s (see Table 5.3).

While Europeans were 95 per cent of the new French during the years immediately following the Second World War, they were only 20 per cent of the new citizens in 1993. The new French citizens came from further and further away, led by the Maghreb (Algeria, Morocco,

Table 5.3: Acquisitions of nationality in France by former nationality (in per cent)

	All modes of acquisition					
	Europe	*Africa*	*America*	*Asia*	*Other*	*Total*
1985	46.8%	26.1%	3.9%	22.2%	1.0%	100%
1986	48.9%	27.0%	4.4%	18.7%	1.0%	100%
1987	45.7%	28.4%	3.9%	20.6%	1.4%	100%
1988	44.0%	31.5%	4.2%	19.5%	0.7%	100%
1989	37.5%	34.5%	4.6%	22.7%	0.7%	100%
1990	31.7%	42.5%	4.6%	20.5%	0.8%	100%
1991	27.0%	48.9%	4.5%	19.3%	0.4%	100%
1992	22.1%	54.2%	4.5%	19.0%	0.2%	100%
1993	20.0%	56.2%	4.4%	18.8%	0.6%	100%
1994	18.4%	58.2%	4.6%	18.1%	0.8%	100%
1995	18.7%	55.1%	5.4%	19.7%	1.1%	100%
1996	17.7%	55.7%	5.1%	20.6%	0.9%	100%
1997	18.1%	56.1%	5.0%	19.8%	1.1%	100%
1998	17.4%	57.6%	5.0%	18.8%	1.2%	100%
1999	15.2%	60.4%	4.8%	18.2%	1.4%	100%
2000	13.6%	61.2%	5.0%	18.6%	1.5%	100%
2001	12.3%	64.0%	4.9%	17.3%	1.5%	100%
2002	12.9%	65.3%	5.3%	16.4%	0.1%	100%
2003	12.9%	66.8%	5.5%	14.8%	0.1%	100%

Source: Ministry of Social Affairs.

and Tunisia), followed by Southeast Asia, and Portugal. Since 1992, Maghrebians represent more than 40 per cent of the new French citizens, which has been of crucial importance in the ongoing debates about access to French nationality.

As the numbers of French citizens with non-European origins increased during a left-wing presidency, the right wing had ammunition to attack the nationality law and the left-wing politicians.

After the legislative elections of March 1986 the right wing returned to power and the newly-appointed Minister of Interior quickly announced a series of immigration-related priorities: restriction of migrant flows, intensification of repatriations of illegal immigrants, and the reform of the nationality code.

On 12 November 1986, the right-wing government of Jacques Chirac proposed a bill that would remove the automatic attribution of citizenship by marriage, and continued the right to citizenship for children born in France with one parent born in France (double ius soli) but made it no longer automatic, instead requiring a declaration of will to become French. However, this proposal was actively contested by left-wing parties as well as various churches (Wayland 1993). The political scene was further complicated by the highly publicised student protests that forced the government to back off from its intended university reform plans. So, fearing even larger mobilisations by the pro-immigrant rights constituency, Prime Minister Chirac scrapped the plans for reforming the nationality code. To avoid the appearance of having given into the left, the government decided to appoint a commission of experts headed by Marceau Long (vice-president of the *Conseil d'Etat*) to study various ways of reforming the nationality code. The commission was formed in June 1987 and in 1988 presented a report entitled 'What it means to be French now and in the future' (Long 1988) which would become the basis for the law of 1993.

5.3.1.2 *Nationality rights become a form of immigration control (1993)*

The law of 22 July 1993 was ostensibly a reform of French nationality law, but was also part of a broader immigration control agenda. At the same time, two other laws were adopted, one that facilitated increased surveillance (the law of 10 August 1993), and another that restricted the conditions of entry into the country (the law of 24 August 1993). The goal was to restrict access to French nationality and to increase the importance of ius sanguinis for foreigners (Lagarde 1993: 556). The law of 1993 was also important because it reintegrated nationality rules into the Civil Code, where they used to be – formally – from 1803 until 1927. In fact, during one century, the location of nationality rules was strongly debated by courts and by scholars: was it part of public or private law? To resolve the problem, starting in 1927, an autonomous *Code de la Nationalité* existed.

Most importantly, the law of 1993 removed the application of double ius soli to children born in France to at least one parent born in a French territory that had become independent. For example: a child born in France to parents from Senegal, Ivory Coast, or Madagascar who were born before 1960 would have been considered French at birth before 1994, but after the new law this child had the same status as anyone born in France to foreign parents.

The second change was that children born in France to parents born in Algeria before independence (1962) could only take advantage of double ius soli if – at the moment of their birth – one of their parents had lived in metropolitan France for five years, despite the fact that before 1962, Algeria was neither a colony nor a territory, but fully part of France and divided into three French departments. This change was hotly contested, and would provoke serious problems of proof for children born after 1 January 1994 when they become adults and apply for a French passport. It therefore seemed to violate the principles of double ius soli.

The most contested part of the law of 22 July 1993 was the reform of simple ius soli. Prior to 1889, a child born in France to foreign parents would become French without any formalities, at age eighteen, if he or she had lived in France for the previous five years. The child also had the right to claim French citizenship, declared by his or her parents, between his or her birth and age eighteen. But, in 1993 these two options were abolished.

Instead one single option was introduced: children born in France to foreign parents could declare their will to become French between sixteen and 21 years of age and have their declaration registered either by a judge, a mayor or a local police officer.

The law of 1993 also shows suspicion of mixed marriages. The law of 9 January 1973 had made men and women equal concerning the effects of marriage on nationality: a foreign spouse, either male or female, could become French with a simple declaration. This provided easy access to French nationality, so the law of 7 May 1984 imposed a six month delay after marriage before the spouse could be naturalised by declaration. Under the pretext of fighting 'marriages of convenience' the law of 22 July 1993 increased the delay to two years. Two new conditions were added: the couple must have been living together continuously during those two years, and the French partner must retain his or her nationality.

The law of 1993 was therefore a serious attempt to restrict access to French nationality from several angles. Nevertheless, it did liberalise access to nationality in one small respect (Lagarde 1993: 559). Whereas previously the administration could reject citizenship applications without justification, it was required to justify its decisions from 1 January 1994 onwards.[4] Therefore government bureaucrats could no longer reject people based on unsubstantiated 'suspicions' and needed to document their decisions.

5.3.1.3 *A compromise between two principles (1998)*

Policymakers on the left expressed their wish to return to the former legislation in the electoral campaigns of 1995 and 1997. After the left's victory in the 1997 elections, a report was commissioned on 'the conditions of the application of the principle of ius soli for the attribution of French nationality' (Weil 1997). The report aimed to find a compromise between the wishes of those politicians who wanted to return to the previous legislation and the jurists, who had reservations about the impact of repeated modifications of the nationality law on the personal status of many second generation immigrants.

The law adopted on 16 March 1998 introduced several significant modifications:

- It re-established the principle that children born in France to foreign parents would be deemed French if they still lived in France at the age of eighteen and had remained in France throughout their adolescence.
- It upheld the need for children between sixteen and eighteen to openly declare their desire to become French, but for children between the ages of thirteen and sixteen the parents could make this declaration, with the child's consent, if the child had lived in France since the age of eight.
- The requirement of five years residence at the moment of acquisition would no longer have to be necessarily continuous.
- The 'double ius soli' rule for children of Algerian parents (but not for children of parents born in Overseas Territories) was re-established.
- The delay for obtaining citizenship by marriage was reduced to one year.

The law of 16 March 1998 thus reformed the most controversial aspects of the 1993 reforms and added a few innovations. Moreover, it intended to overcome several additional shortcomings of the previous legislation:

- Certain young people had difficulties in understanding what was required of them. In addition, they often faced parental constraints; in particular boys were encouraged to apply while girls were not (Weil 1997).

- Adolescents born in France to foreign parents could experience difficulty in proving that they had continuously resided in France for five years before the date of their application to become French citizens. Failure to prove this constituted the main reason for refusal: 42 per cent of all applicants in 1996. After leaving school, at the age of sixteen, young people were often unemployed and therefore unable to prove their link with an institution during that time.
- The tribunals in charge of registering declarations employed different practices in this regard. The refusal rate at the national level had remained stable for two years at 2.6 per cent. Yet, without any coherent explanation, significant differences existed between regions. Three regions had a particularly high refusal rate: Low-Normandy (7 per cent), Lorraine (5.3 per cent) and Brittany (6 per cent). In 1996, seven departments had a refusal rate of over 10 per cent: Morbihan (41.2 per cent), Gers (24.3 per cent), Alpes de Haute Provence (20 per cent) Dordogne (17.5 per cent), Meurthe et Moselle (10.9 per cent), Lot (10.4 per cent). As a result, some tribunals gained a reputation for being restrictive, others for being more liberal.
- The most serious situation resulted from individuals not applying because they believed that they were already French. One study undertaken in Alsace spells this out (Weil 1997). Some young people who had been born in France felt French, and not having been properly informed of their status as a foreigner missed the deadline of 21 years of age without realising it. Information was circulated irregularly, which might explain the significant variations in the rates of nationalisation requests in the same region, for example in Alsace, 68 per cent in Mulhouse as opposed to 42 per cent in Strasbourg. Unequal access to information almost certainly disproportionately affected young people from underprivileged immigrant backgrounds.

The new legislation adopted in 1998 therefore states that children born in France of two foreign-born parents are French if they live in France and have done so throughout their adolescence. Proof of integration is established by non-continuous residence of five years after the age of eleven, and proof of residence is furnished by school certificates.

The new legislation built on a positive aspect of the 1993 law by putting greater emphasis on the autonomy of the child, as the power of parents to declare their child French without the latter's agreement was no longer possible. Between the ages of thirteen and sixteen (with their parent's authorisation) and between the ages of sixteen and eighteen (without such authorisation) young people could express their wish to become French and acquire French nationality before the age of eighteen. In the six months before their eighteenth birthday, and above all during the following year when they became adults, they could declare that they wanted to remain foreign and decline French nationality.

The new legislation also made it easier to prove French nationality. Nationality was now listed on the birth certificates and in the family booklets. Those who wished to become French now had greater resources to support their claim.

5.3.1.4 *New restrictions introduced by the 2003 Law*

When the right wing returned to power in 2002, it attempted to restrict foreigners' access to French visas, as well as their access to French nationality. Whereas prior to the end of the 1980s, these two issues had been separated, they were once again combined politically.

While claiming to fight against supposed 'marriages of convenience' the new government tightened access to French nationality for foreign spouses. While the law of 1998 reduced the delay for access to French citizenship to one year, the new law of 2003 re-established a delay of two years. While the delay was previously waived if the couple had children, this exception was no longer valid. In addition, the delay could be increased to three years mainly for foreign spouses living abroad, if at the moment of declaration the spouse could not prove that he or she had lived in France continuously for the past year. A French language test was also added for the foreign spouse and the prefecture was encouraged to investigate if the couple had truly lived together as a married couple.

Access to nationality for unaccompanied foreign minors has been delayed. Over the years more and more youths have been arriving in France without their parents, and in principle are supposed to be affiliated with the Youth Social Assistance Service (ASE), which caters to their administrative needs during their stay. Previously, these minors, who were often asylum seekers, had access to French nationality upon declaration and without delay. However, the 2003 law imposed a three year delay, required ASE to document the time period, and as such has greatly reduced the number of youths eligible for French citizenship. Only minors who arrive before the age of fifteen and who are affiliated with ASE can qualify, which is less than one quarter of those who arrive in France without parents. The rest of these youths face considerable difficulties for integration and often float between illegal status and general social exclusion.

As early as 1945, assimilation became a condition for naturalisation, as the foreigner had to prove that he or she was sufficiently fluent in the French language. The 2003 law reinforced this condition and added the requirement of proving sufficient knowledge about the rights and responsibilities of French citizenship. The deputies who drafted this amendment stated that it was to ensure that newly naturalised citizens understood the significance of 'becoming a citizen'. The decision of 22 February 2005 goes further and proposes formal procedures for evaluating the 'linguistic assimilation of candidates for French citizenship'. Language competency is now judged in a 20 to 30 minute interview in an office specifically designated as an 'Assimilation Evaluation Office'. It is for the moment however unclear how this new condition will be interpreted and applied by the prefectures and consular services.

These recent modifications to the regulations for access to citizenship have not led to a huge public debate like when the 1993 and 1998 changes were proposed. There are two main explanations for this relative silence. First, the law of November 2003 requires knowledge of the rights and responsibilities of French citizens but did not add much change to the existing clause about assimilation. In addition, the law of 2003 has aspects that are much more restrictive than the requirements for access to citizenship. For example, it extends the minimum waiting period for getting a Permanent Residence Permit from three to five years, and measures of that kind have received more attention from NGOs, left wing activists or political parties.

Finally, the government administration has always been able to revoke French citizenship, under the authority of the *Conseil d'Etat*, if a newly naturalised citizen commits certain crimes during the first ten years of citizenship. Now the government has the power to revoke citizenship for crimes that were committed before the person became a French citizen, but were only recently discovered. This should not however affect many people, as revoking citizenship is rare and occurs only in specific and complicated cases. These days denaturalisation is used on average less than once a year, and only for people sentenced to prison terms of five years or more. However, denaturalisation is still a privilege that the government retains the right to exercise in exceptional circumstances.

5.3.2 *Institutional arrangements: the long road to naturalisation*

In addition to legal obstacles to naturalisation, there are also practical barriers in getting past the numerous bureaucrats charged with administrating the naturalisation process. Generally speaking the naturalisation process can be broken into two main bureaucratic hurdles: first the local bureaucrats at the prefecture and then the central administration charged with applying the rules equally across the country.

5.3.2.1 *Starting with the prefectures*

The first step is for naturalisation applications to be submitted to the prefecture office. While this step is often considered a mere technicality it is in fact a crucial stage, because the prefecture must verify that the foreigner has the right to become French. In the application the candidate must provide paperwork proving his or her residence in France. The candidate is then subject to an investigation by the gendarmes, the police, and finally the mayor's office, before verification that the applicant is eligible is given (Spire 2005).

The investigations into eligibility have always had lots of room for ambiguity and personal interpretation as to how much rigor is required. At times the staff in the prefecture can judge that the applicant is ineligible and immediately refuse the applicant. For example, starting in the mid-1970s the applications of foreign students were systematically refused because their residence in France was not considered sufficiently 'stable'. To avoid overtaxing the naturalisation staff with too many applications the prefectures were encouraged to immediately reject students. This type of behaviour represents an arbitrary power that is difficult to measure but nevertheless very important. Furthermore, this behaviour is far from evenly applied as the judgement as to which applications are 'suitable' changes according to the individual staff at the prefecture.

The importance of civil servants in the process does not stop at determining who is eligible to apply at the prefecture, and there are numerous civil servants who investigate the application and then render their verdict, each constituting a potential veto. For example, the Departmental Office of Social Affairs is often contacted depending on the family situation. A doctor is needed for the medical certificate. There are also forms relating to the professional status of the applicant, and there is the verbal assimilation exam. Finally, the prefect must attach a report on the political, demographic, and professional characteristics of the applicant. The application is then transmitted to the Under Secretary of Naturalisations for the Social Affairs Ministry who is in charge of processing all applications.

5.3.2.2 *Treatment of the applications*

Each application is examined by a staff person who reports, on an 'instruction page'[5], on the most important aspects of the file likely to be analysed during the deliberations. For example, the staff person might highlight the length of residence in France, the opinion of the prefecture, the age of the applicant, his or her profession, his or her family situation. After 1945, this process of highlighting important aspects was performed by an additional agent specifically designated for the task, but, since the 2003 reforms, the applications are only viewed by one person, except in the most difficult of cases where a second agent is required. This change allowed the Under Secretary of Naturalisations to shorten the delays without hiring additional staff. In 2002, the average waiting period for having an application reviewed by the Under Secretary of Naturalisations was sixteen months, and by the end of 2004 this period had fallen to three months (not counting the review time for each prefecture). In difficult cases the application is examined by the head of the office, and if necessary, by the Under Secretary of Naturalisations (Weil 2005). Only in rare cases is the final decision the product of two or three successive opinions.

For an application to be considered 'acceptable' the first criterion is residence in France, i.e. the candidate must have his or her current primary residence in France. The applicant must also justify his or her 'assimilation into the French community, primarily by sufficient knowledge of the French language' (art. 21-24 of the Civil Code). 40 per cent of the applications deemed 'unacceptable' are because of these criteria. During the 1950s when most applicants were European, the criterion of 'assimilation' was rarely used and mainly signified linguistic competence.[6] When the applicants increasingly came from sub-Saharan Africa in the 1970s, this criterion of assimilation became much more important. More than just speaking the language, assimilation also became defined as accepting French values, especially when candidates practiced polygamy or wore Islamic headscarves, despite the fact that administrative tribunals discouraged such approaches.[7] The naturalisation candidate may also have to prove that he or she is a member of society 'in good standing' and without conflicts in the community, although this is rarely pursued.

As soon as the application is considered acceptable, the agents of the Under Secretary of Naturalisation must judge the actual content. These decisions often reflect the broader government policy of the time, but such policies are not publicised and therefore nearly impossible for the applicant to address. These orientations are communicated confidentially within the administration, and are not subject to public scrutiny. Priority is always given to refugees and stateless persons, legionaries, or members of communities that have special relations with France (Christians from Lebanon, Syria, and Egypt, Jewish people from Northern Africa). For each case the administration examines the stability of residence, the amount of connections in France, the individual character, and the degree of assimilation into the French community. Each decision has certain legal constraints, but there is also plenty of room for individual discretion in applying the legal principles.

3.2.3 *Increasing importance of appeals and the role of the Conseil d'Etat*

Since the beginning of the 1980s the number of appeals brought before the *Conseil d'Etat* has consistently risen. When an appeal is brought, the judge must confirm that a factual error, an incorrect application of the law, an incorrect interpretation of the law, or an abuse of legal powers did not take place.[8]

The rise of appeals and consequently the development of the Conseil d'Etat jurisprudence have restricted the room for discretionary decisions on the part of the naturalisation service, framing more and more of its decisions. A circular from 1981 insisted that people be informed of their various rights and options for appeals, and as such more people have dared to appeal each year: 50 in 1981, 550 in 1982, and 650 in 1983.

Recently, the law of 22 July 1993 further restricted the discretionary powers of the administration by requiring written justifications of all refusals of nationality. Bureaucrats who examine and decide on the naturalisation files can no longer merely rely on a hunch. They must present hard evidence to support their decisions, knowing that the evidence may be presented later during an official appeal procedure.

5.4 Conclusions

The full history of French nationality law cannot be understood without also studying developments in other modern states. Nineteenth-century European lawyers in charge of creating citizenship laws all read the same texts and adapted them to their individual countries as they saw fit (Weil 2002: 194). For example, after the Civil Code was adopted, Napoleon ordered, in 1809 just before the war with Austria, the repatriation of all French people, even those who had acquired the nationality of countries at war with France. This clause was inspired by an English law concerning sailors who had become members of foreign navies (Weil 2002: 196). In addition, France's Civil Code influenced European approaches to nationality, most notably the notion of ius sanguinis that became the hallmark of modern nationality law in the majority of European states.

Relative to the rest of Europe, France was the first country to adopt ius sanguinis (in 1803) and was followed by most of the other countries in Europe. As France emerged the only European country of immigration in Europe at the end of the nineteenth century, France was the first state that opted for ius sanguinis, only to reintroduce ius soli in 1889. The latter was then founded on socialisation rather than on the former principle of feudal allegiance. In the latter half of the twentieth century, most of the European countries became, willingly or not, countries of immigration and often followed the path taken by France. And, when European countries that followed the French tradition of ius sanguinis perceived themselves as countries of immigration, important legal changes were soon to follow. Laws that used ius soli to automatically attribute citizenship to grandchildren of immigrants were adopted by the Netherlands in 1953, Spain in 1982, and Belgium in 1992 (Weil & Hansen 1999). Across Europe various other measures have also been taken to ease access to citizenship for children of immigrants. With the exception of Denmark, Greece and Luxembourg, all of the EU-15 Member States allow children of immigrants born or raised on their soil to access citizenship imposing on them all the requirements of the regular naturalisation procedure. So, as more and more countries receive large numbers of immigrants, and in turn switch to more liberal nationality laws, it seems that the borders of nationality law are directly linked with migration flows. Of course, nationality law has several layers, and we must analyse the access for immigrants and their children, the access for spouses, the rules governing denaturalisation, and the rules governing the change from one nationality to another.

But in France, after fifteen years of debate and three legislative changes (1993, 1998 and 2003), the logic of the progressive integration of immigrants and their descendants that was adopted in 1889 does not seem to be in question. In current French nationality law, the longer the link with France the fewer individuals can refuse to be French. French nationality is therefore automatically given to the third generation born in France (double ius soli). Second-generation children are recognised as French at the age of majority, and their agreement is assumed if they do not formally refuse French nationality. For the immigrant generation one needs to follow the impact in practice of new naturalisation conditions. Until now, naturalisation was relatively easy and given to 80 per cent of applicants. France admits dual nationality, albeit not to nationals of countries still adhering to the Council of Europe 1963 Convention. Legally, as a principle of international and national law, people with a second nationality cannot invoke their foreign nationality vis-à-vis the second state of which they are a national. In their relation with the state, the fact that nationals may possess another nationality is not significant. As for cultural integration, a person who has dual nationality only 'practices' the nationality of the country of residence but like the culture of origin, the nationality of origin that is not 'practiced' disappears rapidly with the succession of generations.

Chronological table of major reforms in French nationality law

Date	Document	Content of change
19 October 1945	Ordinance on nationality	Confirms a liberal approach to the integration of the immigrants.
24 December 1945	Decree on naturalisation	The ministry of Population is in charge of the implementation of the naturalisation policy.
23 April 1952	Circular on naturalisation	More explicit conditions for assimilation; the creation of an assimilation report (procès-verbal d'assimilation)
22 December 1961	Law No. 61-408 (Art. 2-6)	No required period of residence for migrants from former French colonies or territories
22 December 1961	Law No. 61-408 (Art. 7)	Good health is no longer a requirement
3 July 1962	Evian Agreements	French muslims born in Algeria while it was a French department are deemed to have relinquished French citizenship if they don't make a declaration recognising French nationality before 27 March 1967.
9 January 1973	Law No. 73-42 on naturalisation	It completely equalises the situation of men and women and that of natural and legitimate children.
8 Décember 1983	Law No. 83-1046	No more discrimination of naturalised citizens: a person who has acquired French nationality enjoys all the rights attached to the status of being a French citizen, from the day of that acquisition.
7 May 1984	Law No. 84-341	This law imposes a six month delay after marriage before the spouse can be naturalised by declaration.
22 July 1993	Law No. 93-933 on naturalisation	Imposing two new conditions for the naturalisation of a spouse: the couple must have been living together continuously during two years, and the French partner must retain his or her nationality.
22 July 1993	Law No. 93-933 on naturalisation	Creation of a mechanism of voluntary declaration between the age of 16 and 21.
16 March 1998	Law No. 98-170 (Art 2)	Suppression of the previous

Date	Document	Content of change
		law: Automatic access to French nationality at 18 for children born in France of two foreign born parents.
16 March 1998 Law No. 98-170 (Art. 6)	Children born in France of foreign parents can declare their desire to become French when between sixteen and eighteen years of age	
16 March 1998 Law No. 98-170 (Art.. 29)	Establishment of a special status for minors ('titre d'identité républicain').	
20 August 1998	Decree No. 98-719	Public information regarding nationality matters
17 October 2000	Circular n°2000/530	Facilitated naturalisation for children who are under six years of age when they arrive in France.
30 December 2000	Law No. 2000-1353	Waiving the fees for naturalisation
26 November 2003	Law No. 2003-119	Access to French nationality by marriage after 2 years in France or 3 years in a foreign country
14 January 2005	Decree 2005-25	New formal procedure for evaluating the 'linguistic assimilation' of candidates for French citizenship'

Notes

1 Ius soli was partially maintained, mainly as a result of a constitutional constraint: a child born in France to foreign parents could claim French nationality at the age of majority if he was resident in French territory.

2 For that purpose they just need to produce their own birth certificate and that of one of their parents.

3 The naturalisation approval rate is the percentage of positively decided cases against the total number of decisions on naturalisation and reintegration applications made during that period by the administration.

4 The administration was also required to justify its decisions concerning cases of loss of French citizenship.

5 This 'pink slip' is filled out by hand by the staff at the office of the Under Secretary of Naturalisations and has no officially required protocol. The comments are

completely up to the agent at hand and are subsequently signed and stamped by this agent.

6 In a decision of 12 March 1953 ('The Spouse Bazso'), the *Conseil d'Etat* overruled a judgement of the administration that had considered an applicant insufficiently assimilated because of ongoing ties with a foreign country.

7 On 9 November 2000 the administrative tribunal of Nantes stated that 'while the headscarf is considered a requirement that expresses religious convictions, it shall not be considered an ostentatious or proselytising symbol' (Morillon 2003: 284).

8 Decision of the *Conseil d'Etat* of 27 May 1983.

Bibliography

Anderson, B. (1983), *Imagined Communities: Reflections on the Origins and Spread of Nationalism*. London: Verso.

Brubaker, R. (1992), *Citizenship and Nationhood in France and Germany*. Cambridge, MA: Harvard University Press.

Fahrmeir, A. (2000), *Citizens and Aliens, Foreigners and the Law in Britain and the German States 1789-1870*, New York: Berghan Books.

Feldblum, M. (1999), *Reconstructing Citizenship. The Politics of Nationality Reform and Immigration in Contemporary France*. Albany, NY: SUNY Press.

Fulchiron, H. (1996), *Etre français aujourd'hui... Premier bilan de la mise en œuvre du nouveau droit de la nationalité*. Lyon: Presses universitaires de Lyon.

Gellner, E. (1983), *Nations and nationalism*. Blackwell: Oxford.

Laacher, S. (ed.) (1987), *Questions de nationalité: histoire et enjeux d'un code*. Paris: L'Harmattan.

Lagarde, P. (1993), 'La nationalité française rétrécie', *Revue critique de droit international privé* 82 (4): 535-563.

Lagarde, P. (1997), *La nationalité française*. Third edition. Paris: Dalloz.

Lebon, A. (1999), *Immigration et présence étrangère en France 1997/1998*. Paris: La Documentation française.

Long, M. (ed.) (1988), *Etre français aujourd'hui et demain. Rapport de la Commission de la nationalité présenté au Premier ministre*. Paris: La Documentation française, Christian Bourgois/UGE.

Mauco, G. (1932), *Les Étrangers en France. Leur rôle dans l'activité économique*. Paris: Armand Colin.

Morillon, A. (2003), *Approche sociologique de la naturalisation en France. Enjeux et signification de l'acquisition de la nationalité française par décret*. Thèse pour le doctorat de sociologie, université de Rennes 2.

Noiriel, G. (1988), *Le Creuset français: Histoire de l'immigration, XIXe-XXe siècles*. Paris: Éditions du Seuil.

Ponty, J. (1992), 'Le problème des naturalisations', *Revue du Nord*, collection Histoire 7: 99-113.

Sahlins, P. (2004), *Unnaturally French: Foreign Citizens in the Old Regime and After*. Ithaca, NY: Cornell University Press.

Sayad, A. (1999), *La double absence. Des illusions de l'émigré aux souffrances de l'immigré*. Paris: Éditions du Seuil.

Silverman, M. (1992), *Deconstructing the Nation: Immigration, Racism and Citizenship in modern France*. London etc.: Routledge.

Spire, A. & S. Thave (1999), 'Les acquisitions de nationalité française depuis 1945', in *Regards sur l'immigration depuis 1945*, 35-57, Paris: Publications de l'INSEE.

Spire, A. (2005), *Etrangers à la carte. L'administration de l'immigration en France (1945-1975)*. Paris: Grasset.
Wayland S. (1993), 'Mobilising to defend nationality law in France', *New Community* 20 (1): 93-110.
Weil, P. (1995), *La France et ses étrangers. L'aventure d'une politique de l'immigration de 1938 à nos jours*. Paris: Folio/Gallimard.
Weil, P. (1997), *Rapport au Premier ministre sur les législations de la nationalité et de l'immigration*. Paris: La Documentation française.
Weil, P. & R. Hansen (eds.) (1999), *Nationalité et citoyenneté en Europe*. Paris: La Découverte.
Weil, P. (2002), *Qu'est-ce qu'un français? Histoire de la nationalité française depuis la Révolution*. Paris: Grasset.
Weil, P. (2005), *Qu'est-ce qu'un français? Histoire de la nationalité française depuis la Révolution*. Paris: Folio/Gallimard.

6 Germany

Kay Hailbronner

6.1 Introduction

The new millennium marked a major change in German nationality law. The nationality law of 1913 (*Reichs- und Staatsangehörigkeitsgesetz*), valid from the German Empire through the 'Third Reich' and the Federal Republic – which was subject to many changes and amendments – was replaced by a new nationality law, the Nationality Act,[1] which entered into force on 1 January 2000. The new nationality law was the result of a highly controversial debate between the major political parties in 1998, preceding federal parliamentary elections. The nationality law (*Staatsangehörigkeitsgesetz)* – although in many respects still based upon the provisions of the law of 1913 – has taken up the trend of some of the more recent European nationality laws by substantially facilitating naturalisation, by including a stronger toleration of dual nationality, by a replacement of discretionary regulations with individual rights, by introducing new modes of acquisition, and in particular by introducing a ius soli element into the nationality law.

A major purpose of the law, supported by the ruling Social Democratic party and the coalition partner *Bündnis 90/Die Grünen* as well as the liberal party, was the promotion of acquisition of German nationality for migrant workers and their second and third generation descendants as an essential prerequisite of their integration into the German society. Until 1 January 2000 one of the predominant features of German nationality law and practice, although not explicitly laid down in the law of 1913, had been that acquisition of German nationality through naturalisation was an exception rather than the rule.

One of the main novelties of the 1999/2000 reform was the introduction of the ius soli principle in para. 4 of the law. Children of a foreign parent acquire German citizenship under the condition that one parent has had a lawful habitual residence in Germany for eight years and that he or she is in possession of a secure residence permit. Since January 2004, the threshold has been raised for the acquisition under ius soli by requiring a settlement permit or in the case of EU citizens a right of free movement. Since the settlement permit requires a higher level of knowledge of the German language than previously and the possession of an unlimited residence permit, which until 2004 had been sufficient for naturalisation, ius soli acquisition will only take place in the case of a higher degree of integration of a foreign parent.

Another major feature has been the facilitation of naturalisation. A foreigner is entitled to naturalisation after a habitual lawful residence of eight years rather than previously fifteen years. In addition, naturalisation depends upon a number of requirements, including a declaration of loyalty to the free and democratic constitutional order, possession of a regular residence permit or freedom of movement as an EU citizen, or an equally privileged right under the EEA-Agreement. In addition, the foreigner has to prove the ability of earning a living without any recourse to social welfare or similar social benefits (unemployment assistance), absence of a criminal record and the renunciation or loss of a previous nationality.

The Immigration Act of 2004 has slightly changed the requirements on naturalisation by declining a right to naturalisation in the absence of sufficient knowledge of the German language and the existence of facts indicating that a foreigner supports or engages in unconstitutional political activities or is subject to expulsion due to a terrorist affiliation.

One of the central issues of the new German nationality law of 1999/2000 was the principle of avoiding dual nationality, which hitherto had been an essential element of the German nationality law.

Following a highly emotional debate on dual nationality, the reform of 1999/2000 maintained the principle of avoiding dual nationality. To a certain extent it takes into account the interests of the immigrant population in maintaining their previous nationality by providing for a large number of exceptions to the requirement of relinquishing a prior nationality. The general rule is that a foreigner is not obliged to renounce his or her previous nationality if renunciation entails serious disadvantages or is dependent upon particularly difficult conditions. Therefore the nationality law closely follows the pattern of other European states by admitting dual nationality more generously.

Due to the fact that children usually acquire the nationality of their parents by descent, the introduction of the ius soli principle will entail at least dual, if not multiple nationalities for foreign children born in Germany. Since the issue of dual nationality has turned out to be a highly controversial concept, the new law uses the 'optional model', which obliges foreign children to decide by the end of their eighteenth year which nationality to keep and which to renounce. If they declare the wish to keep the foreign nationality or if they do not declare anything by the end of their eighteenth year, German nationality will be lost within a specified period of time. If they declare an intention to keep German nationality, however, they are obliged to prove the loss or renunciation of their foreign nationality, unless the German authorities have formally approved the retention thereof. The permission to retain the former nationality will be granted if renunciation of the foreign nationality is either impossible or unreasonable, or if multiple nationality would have to be accepted according to the general rules on naturalisation.

In order to limit dual nationality, further amendments concerning the loss of German nationality have been adopted. The first one affects the abolition of the so-called national clause (*Inlandsklausel*). Since 1 January 2000, the acquisition of a foreign nationality based on an application leads to the automatic loss of German nationality even if the national retains domicile on German territory. In contrast, according to the former legal situation, German nationality was lost only when the national did not keep his or her habitual residence in Germany (cf. sect. 25 para. 1 of the Imperial Nationality Act[2]). Second, automatic loss of German nationality also results from voluntary entry in a foreign army without permission of the German Ministry of Defence, if the national possesses the nationality of this foreign state in addition to his or her German nationality.

Apart from these amendments, the modes of losing German nationality were not affected by the reform of 1999/2000. German nationality is lost by release from citizenship upon request if a person has applied for the acquisition of a foreign nationality and when the conferment of this nationality is assured, by voluntary renunciation of the German nationality by a dual or a multiple nationality, or by adoption by a foreign national if the foreign nationality is thereby acquired.

The traditional modes of acquisition of German nationality have also remained largely unchanged. German nationality is basically acquired by descent from a German mother or a German father, by legitimisation, by adoption or by naturalisation. In the absence of a marriage, descent from a German father requires a formal procedure to determine fatherhood.

Spouses of German nationals are entitled to naturalisation on the condition that they renounce their previous nationality unless there is a reason for acceptance of dual nationality and if certain integration requirements are met. According to the administrative practice a residence of three years is required and a marriage of two years. The applicant must be able to express him- or herself in the German language.[3]

The most important change of the reform legislation can be found in the changed perception of the acquisition of German nationality. Since 1 January 2000, naturalisation and acquisition of the German nationality is considered being in the public interest of Germany rather than an unavoidable fact. The change in nationality law also reflects a substantial change in the perception of migration. The original assumption that the migrant workers recruited in the early 1970s would eventually return to their home countries, has been abandoned. Only about 12,000 to 17,000 persons were naturalised each year from 1974 until 1989, in spite of an increasing number of persons having their permanent residence in Germany. This situation changed substantially with the new Nationality Act giving a legal right to naturalisation if certain conditions were fulfilled. As a result, the number of naturalisations went up substantially since the new law entered into force (see sect. 6.3.2).

With the Immigration Act of 2004 (*Zuwanderungsgesetz*) some amendments have been introduced in order to take account of the new integration requirements introduced by it as well as the security considerations resulting from the anti-terrorism legislation following 11 September 2001. Under sect. 11 StAG the right to naturalisation is precluded if a foreigner does not have sufficient knowledge of the German language and if there are sufficient facts indicating that the foreigner is engaged in or supporting activities directed against the free democratic order or the security of the Federal Republic or a *Land*, or if an applicant is intending unlawful disruption of the functioning of the constitutional organs of the federation or a *Land* or their members, or is endangering by use of force or preparatory actions the external affairs of the Federal Republic of Germany. A similar exclusion clause applies in the case of participation in terrorist organisations or support of terrorist activities.

According to art. 116 of the Basic Law, ethnic Germans expelled as a result of post-war measures as well as their families, relatives and descendants are entitled to privileged acquisition of German nationality. The details are regulated by the Federal Expellees Act (*Bundesvertriebenengesetz*) since 19 May 1953. Between 1950 and 1987, a total of approximately 1.4 million ethnic Germans and their family members entered Germany, mostly without major integration problems.

With the large increase of the number of immigrants of German ethnic origin as a result of the liberalisation and democratisation in the Eastern Bloc, substantial changes were made in the law in order to gain more control over the immigration patterns of ethnic Germans. In 1993, an annual quota of 225,000 was introduced and on 1 January 2000 the quota was reduced to around 100,000 persons, a figure corresponding to the number of ethnic Germans entering Germany in 1998. In addition, prior to entry, a language test was introduced in order to prove that persons are actually ethnic Germans. Until 2000, ethnic Germans possessing the legal status of a German without German nationality under art. 116 para. 1 of the Basic law, were entitled to naturalisation on the basis of their admission to German territory. Since 1 January 2000, repatriate Germans acquire German nationality automatically by entering German territory on the basis of a previous admission title.

After 2000, the composition of the category of repatriate Germans (*Aussiedler*) changed as only a few of the family relatives and their descendants tended to be of German ethnic origin as well. Since family members did not have to prove sufficient knowledge of the German language in the admission procedure, unless they applied for repatriate status themselves, an increasing percentage of repatriate Germans did not have sufficient command of the German language and were therefore subject to social marginalisation. In the new Immigration Act of 2004 the provisions of the Federal Expellees Act were changed by introducing a condition of proof of basic knowledge of the German language for non-German spouses as well as non-German descendants[4] intending to acquire German nationality based upon the special provisions of the Expellees Act and the Basic Law.

6.2 Historical development

6.2.1 German nationality law until 2000

The German Nationality Law (*Reichs- und Staatsangehörigkeitsgesetz*) of 22 July 1913 introduced for the first time a common German nationality for all the nationals of the various states constituting the 'German Reich' of 1870. The German nationality did not fully replace the nationality of each of the states of the federation, but in fact supplemented it. German nationality under the Constitution of 1919 provided that every national of a federal state simultaneously acquired German nationality. Each German was granted the same rights and duties and every German inside and outside the territory of the German Empire was entitled to protection and was not allowed to be extradited to any foreign government for the purpose of punishment or persecution.

Under the rule of the Nazi regime the German nationality law was repeatedly changed, primarily for ideological and racial reasons. One of the first measures was the abolition of the nationality of the *Länder* as a result of the establishment of Germany as a unitary state. The law of 14 July 1933 provided for the withdrawal of naturalisations in the period between 1918 and 1933 and the removal of German citizenship from persons having violated a duty of loyalty to the German Empire or the 'German nation'. According to further regulations, all Jews having their ordinary residence abroad were collectively deprived of citizenship.

As a result of the 'reunification' with Austria and the territorial acquisitions from 1933 until 1941 in Eastern Europe, German nationality was generally granted collectively to persons considered as ethnic Germans living in the territories incorporated into the German Reich or attached as protectorates to the Empire (Hailbronner & Renner 2005: 16 ff). Another reason for collective acquisition of German nationality was the admission to the *Wehrmacht*, SS, police or Nazi organisations, provided that the persons were of German ethnic origin.

The Federal Republic of Germany of 1949 decided to base its nationality law upon the nationality law of 1913, rather than enacting a completely new law. In addition to regulations and changes made by the Allied Powers from 1945-1949, the nationality law of 1913 was substantially changed by three amendments of 1955, 1956 and 1957. The first Act, amending the Nationality Act of 1913, abolished collective naturalisations between 1938 and 1945. The validity of such collective naturalisations had been a matter of dispute in the jurisprudence and literature of the Federal Republic (Hailbronner & Renner 2005: 63; Genzel 1969a: 113; Genzel 1969b: 98). By the second law of 1956 (Makarov 1956: 744), the collective acquisition of German nationality by Austrians was abolished. Austrians, however, could reacquire German nationality by declaration if they had established permanent residence in Germany by that time.

The third law of 1957 and the subsequent legislation of 1969 established equal treatment of men and women in nationality legislation by equal treatment in the acquisition of German nationality by spouses and descendants of German nationals.

Between 1969 and 1990, the debate on German nationality was very much focused upon issues concerning the separation of Germany. While originally the law of the German Democratic Republic provided for a common German nationality, in 1967 with the adoption of the *Staatsbürgerschaftsgesetz* of the GDR the idea of a common German nationality was relinquished and replaced by a separate citizenship of the GDR. The Federal Republic of Germany reacted by insisting upon a common German nationality, based upon the *Reichs- und Staatsangehörigkeitsgesetz* of 1913. Thereby, every German, acquiring German nationality by descent, was still to be considered as a German national, regardless of whether the person had his or her permanent residence in the Federal Republic or the GDR. The legal basis for this position was the insistence upon an inseparable common German nationality attached to the legal continuation of the German Empire.[5] This concept enabled the Federal Republic to issue passports and to claim as German citizens every citizen of the GDR who managed to legally or illegally leave the territory of the GDR and arrive at a consulate or embassy of the Federal Republic of Germany (Hailbronner 1981: 712-713; Vedder 2003: 11 ff.; Klein 1983: 2289).

The Treaty on the Basic Relations between the Federal Republic of Germany and the GDR of 12 December 1972 (*Grundlagenvertrag*) as well as the treaties with the Soviet Union and Poland of 1970 and Czechoslovakia of 1973 left out the controversial issue of German nationality. In a protocol it was explicitly stated in the treaty on the relations between the GDR and the Federal Republic of Germany that the treaty will facilitate a solution of issues of nationality. The Federal Constitutional Court decided that these treaties could not be interpreted as effectuating a loss of nationality of Germans having acquired German nationality under the nationality law of 1913 or under the Basic Law.[6]

After the reunification of Germany on 3 October 1990, the East German laws and regulations on nationality were abolished. With the accession of the GDR to the Federal Republic the nationality legislation valid in the Federal Republic became fully applicable in the territory of the former GDR and in Berlin. A number of questions, however, remained to be solved concerning the effects of naturalisations and other issues related to the effects of the East German nationality legislation (Renner 1999: 230). These issues have not yet been completely solved.

Subsequent changes of the nationality legislation were primarily devoted to a solution of the problem of integration of the immigrant population by facilitating access to German nationality. In the early 1990s a discussion started about the political rights of the immigrant population. By the end of 1998 there were 7.32 million foreign nationals living in Germany, already accounting for 9 per cent of the German population. Most foreigners living in Germany have been living there for a long time. By the end of 1997, approximately 30 per cent of all foreigners had been in Germany for twenty years or more, 40 per cent for at least fifteen years and almost 50 per cent for more than ten years. Almost two thirds of all Turks and Greeks, 31 per cent of Italians and 80 per cent of Spaniards had lived in Germany for more than ten years and 1.59 million (21.7 per cent of all foreigners) had been born in Germany.

The figures show a basic dilemma of German immigration policy: An increasing number of children of migrant workers were born and have grown up in Germany, received their schooling and professional formation in Germany, will eventually work in Germany and yet are children of 'foreign' nationals in Germany, although their nationality has frequently become only an emotional attachment to the home country of their parents, and is sometimes considered a mere reassurance, a sort of 'alternative' nationality. There is in principle no dispute about the need to integrate large parts of the foreign population into Germany by inducing them to become German citizens. All German governments have declared that there is a public interest in the naturalisation of foreigners living permanently in Germany.[7] There is no consensus, however, on the ways and conditions under which German citizenship should be acquired.

The particular issue was the acquisition of German citizenship by birth on German territory, which introduced an element of ius soli into the German concept of citizenship and which has given rise to a heated controversy between the major political parties in recent years.

An attempt to solve the fundamental dilemma arising from the exclusion of a substantial part of the population from political rights by granting limited voting rights at a local level to foreigners in some of the *Länder* failed due to the decision by the Federal Constitutional Court declaring such an attempt to be unconstitutional.[8] The Court stated that the concept of democracy as laid down in the Basic Law does not permit a disassociation of political rights from the concept of nationality. Nationality therefore is the legal prerequisite for the acquisition of political rights, legitimising the exercising of all power in the Federal Republic of Germany. The Court, however, also stated that the only possible approach to solving the gap between the permanent population and democratic participation lies in changing the nationality law, for example, by facilitating the acquisition of the German nationality by foreigners living permanently in Germany and thereby having become subject to German sovereignty in a manner comparable to German nationals.

In the context of the general debate about Germany's immigration policy and its factual change into an immigration country, pressure increased for a reform of German citizenship legislation. There were numerous proposals ranging from simplifying the naturalisation process and increasing the acceptance of multiple nationality to introducing a ius soli principle for third generation foreigners born in Germany (Apel 1992: 99; Blumenwitz 1993: 151; Hobe 1994: 191; d'Oliveira 1990: 114; John 1991: 85; Löwer 1993: 156; Lübbe-Wolff 1996: 57; Mangoldt 1994: 33; Marx 1997: 67; Meireis 1994: 241; Münch 1994: 1199; Predeick 1991: 623; Renner 1994: 865; Schrötter & Möhlig 1995: 437).

The *Bundestag* decided in 1990 to substantially facilitate the acquisition of German citizenship for young foreigners aged sixteen to 23, provided that they renounced their previous citizenship, had lived permanently and lawfully in Germany for eight years, had attended a school in Germany for at least six years and had not been prosecuted for a criminal offence. In addition, the acquisition of German citizenship for the first generation of recruited migrant workers was also facilitated substantially, provided that certain requirements were met:

- legal habitual residence in Germany for fifteen years,
- renunciation of previous nationality;
- absence of criminal conviction;
- ability to earn a living.

Originally, facilitated naturalisation of young foreigners and of long-term residents was granted 'as a rule', i.e., administrative discretion was very limited. Another amendment in June 1993 changed these rules by establishing an individual right entitling every foreigner fulfilling the aforementioned requirements to demand naturalisation (Hailbronner 1999b: 1 ff).[9] Although these provisions of the Aliens Act granting an entitlement to German citizenship provided for a renouncement of the previous nationality, a number of exceptions were made which led in fact to a steadily increasing number of naturalisations with dual nationality. Exceptions were granted for instance if a foreigner could not renounce his or her previous nationality or only under particularly difficult conditions, e.g., if the original home country required military service before giving up nationality.

The general number of naturalisations in 1995 increased to 313,606 compared to 34,913 in 1985 (in 1997, however, the number decreased to 278, 662). However, it must be taken into account that this figure includes a substantial number – up to three quarters – of naturalisations of German repatriates (*Aussiedler*) who acquire German citizenship very easily on the basis of art. 116 of the Basic Law in connection with the Expellees Act, giving them a constitutional right to obtain German citizenship as a refugee or expellee of German ethnic origin or as their spouse or descendant, provided that they had been admitted to the territory of the 'German Reich' within the frontiers of 31 December 1937. Nevertheless, in 1990, naturalisations based upon the provisions of the Aliens Act for the immigrant population increased at a rate of about 35 per cent, in 1994 even at a rate of 54 per cent and in 1996, by 20 per cent compared to the preceding year (Beauftragte der Bundesregierung für Ausländerfragen 1999: 11); in 1997, however, the number of naturalisations decreased by about 4 per cent. With 1.18 per cent of the total foreign population, the rate of naturalisations in 1996 was still relatively small compared to other western European states, although it had quadrupled since 1986.[10] The share of women was substantially higher with 1.37 per cent than that of men with 1.03 per cent.

According to an agreement between the Christian Democratic Party and the Liberal Party of 1994, the introduction of a special nationality (*Kinderstaatszugehörigkeit*) for children of the third generation who were born in Germany was envisaged.[11] In order to be eligible for this special nationality, which was intended to ensure equal treatment between German nationals (issue of German identity card), at least one of the child's parents would have to be born in Germany and both would have to reside lawfully in Germany during the ten years preceding the child's birth. Additionally, both parents would have to be entitled to an unlimited residence permit. The 'quasi-nationality' for children would require an application by parents before the child's twelfth birthday. With the child's eighteenth birthday, the young adult would acquire full German nationality upon renouncing his or her prior nationality. It is very doubtful whether the proposal was practicable and whether a 'quasi-nationality' would have been acceptable in international relations and what effect such a special nationality might have had for instance with regard to the application of international treaties relating to visa and travel documents (Europäisches Forum für Migrationsstudien 1995: 11, 19; Lübbe-Wolff 1996: 57; Ziemske 1995: 380, 381). The proposal was never realised nor any of the other proposals, due to political developments in the *Bundestag* and *Bundesrat*.

Following a shift of power in the *Länder* in 1999, the *Bundesrat*, the upper house of Parliament, representing the German *Länder*, which were then dominated by the Christian Democratic Party, suggested that German nationality would be acquired automatically by a child whose foreign parents were born in Germany and who, at the time of the child's birth, disposed of a residence permit.[12] Children whose parents are in possession of an unlimited residence permit and have been living in Germany for five years were to be given a right to naturalisation. In both cases, the acquisition of German citizenship would be independent of the renunciation of a previous nationality.

The proposals of the Social Democratic Party and the Green Party were going in the same direction. The Social Democratic Party has suggested supplementing the principle whereby German nationality is acquired by descent with the principle of territoriality (ius soli). Children of foreign parents therefore ought to automatically acquire German citizenship as a result of birth on German territory, provided that at least one parent has been born in Germany and has secured his or her permanent residence in Germany. Dual nationality is not to be prevented in such cases. Additionally, for permanent residents, individual rights to the acquisition of German nationality were to be created independently of renunciation of their previous nationality. The draft suggested a facilitation of naturalisation for the following groups of citizens:

- foreigners with a permanent residence permit after eight years of residence,
- foreigners belonging to the so-called second generation aliens who have grown up in Germany,
- spouses of Germans after three years of lawful residence, provided that they have been married for at least two years.

Additionally, the proposal provided for a facilitation of discretionary naturalisation, which should be enabled after a residence of five years and only be dependent upon the capacity to earn a living, absence of a criminal conviction for a serious offence and absence of a reason for expulsion for endangering public safety or violent behaviour.[13]

Following another shift in the distribution of political power in the Federation and the *Länder*, the proposal could not be realised as in the meantime the Christian Democratic Parties had won some state elections and it became uncertain whether the draft bill would receive a majority in the *Bundesrat*. A 'compromise' was worked out by the Liberal Party, which provided for the acquisition of a full nationality by birth on German territory if both parents apply and at least one of the parents does have a right of residence in Germany. The proposal of the Liberal Party suggested a loss of dual nationality by obliging the naturalised person to opt for one nationality once that person has reached the age of 21. If the previous (dual) nationality were not given up, German nationality would be lost.[14]

A renewal of the discussion was provoked when the coalition agreement between the Social Democrats and *Bündnis 90/Die Grünen* of 20 October 1998 was presented to the public. According to the intentions of the coalition, German citizenship should be conferred at birth to children born on German territory if one foreign parent had already been born on German territory or if he or she had entered Germany before the age of fourteen, furthermore providing that, in both cases, he or she at the time of birth is in possession of a residence permit (*Aufenthaltserlaubnis*). Other amendments intended by the coalition were a facilitation of the naturalisation process when applying on the grounds of an entitlement to German citizenship. It was proposed that naturalisation be allowed if a foreigner was able to sustain himself or herself and his or her dependants, if there were no convictions for criminal offences and, finally, if no grounds for expulsion or deportation had arisen; the residence requirement was to be reduced from fifteen to eight years. Other proposed amendments related to a right to naturalisation for minors and a reduction of the residence requirement to three years for spouses of German nationals. Dual or multiple nationality was to be accepted in all those cases (Hailbronner 1999a: 51 ff.).

6.2.2 The nationality law reform of 2000

These proposals met heavy resistance by some of the *Länder*, particularly since the first draft presented by the Ministry of the Interior provided for a broad acceptance of dual and multiple nationality and the introduction of the ius soli principle.[15] Due to changing majorities in Parliament a new proposal was submitted by the Social Democrats, *Bündnis 90/Die Grünen* and the Liberal Party (FDP) comprising not only the introduction of the ius soli principle, but also the insertion of the 'optional model'. Both chambers went on to adopt this draft with minor changes[16] in May 1999.[17] The new law on the reform of the German citizenship law of 15 July 1999 became law on 1 January 2000.[18] In addition, administrative guidelines for its application were to be adopted.

One of the major changes was the introduction of the ius soli principle in art. 4 of the German Nationality Law implying that a child of foreign parents acquires German citizenship under the 'optional model' on the condition that one parent has legally had their habitual residence in Germany for eight years and that he or she has been in the possession of a residence permit, an *Aufenthaltsberechtigung* or an unlimited *Aufenthaltserlaubnis* for three years; the model of the double ius soli in force in some other European states has therefore not been introduced. Foreign children legally residing in Germany were entitled to naturalisation upon their tenth birthday if the above-mentioned conditions were fulfilled at the time of birth (para. 40b StAG; transitional regulation which expired on 31 December 2000). Due to the fact that children usually acquire the nationality of their parents by descent, the introduction of the ius soli principle will entail at least double if not multiple nationalities for foreign children born in Germany. Thus, para. 29 StAG introduced the highly disputed optional model and the obligation to decide upon reaching the age of eighteen which nationality to keep and which to renounce. If the young adult declares that he or she intends to keep his foreign nationality or if he or she does not declare anything on reaching the age of eighteen, he or she will lose his or her German nationality. If, on the other hand, he or she declares an intention to keep German citizenship, the young adult is obliged to prove the loss or renouncement of the foreign nationality (para. 29 (2) StAG) unless German authorities have formally approved that he or she may keep his foreign nationality. According to para. 29 (4) StAG, this permission to retain the former nationality (*Beibehaltungsgenehmigung*) is to be issued if renunciation of the foreign nationality is either impossible or unreasonable or if – in the case of naturalisation – multiple nationality would be accepted according to the general rules.

Aside from the introduction of the ius soli principle the naturalisation process has also been facilitated. The foreigner is entitled to naturalisation after a residence period of eight instead of fifteen years on the condition that he or she declares himself bound to the free and democratic order of the Constitution (*freiheitliche und demokratische Grundordnung*), that he or she is in possession of a residence permit, that he or she is capable of earning a living without any recourse to public assistance or unemployment benefits (except in those cases in which the dependence on those benefits is not attributable to the applicant's fault or negligence), that there is no criminal conviction and, finally, that loss or renunciation of the previous nationality occurs. Dual nationality is accepted in more cases, e.g., if the applicants are elderly persons and dual nationality is the only obstacle to naturalisation, if the dismissal of the previous nationality is related to disproportionate difficulties, and if a denial of the application for naturalisation would constitute a particular hardship; moreover, double nationality is accepted in cases in which the renunciation of the previous nationality entails – in addition to the loss of civil rights – economic or financial disadvantages, or, generally in the case of EU citizens, provided that reciprocity exists.

Due to the fact that the acquisition of German citizenship has been facilitated, some amendments relate to the loss of German citizenship and the limitation of acquisition by descent. Acquisition of German citizenship abroad is excluded if the German parent who has his or her habitual residence abroad was born abroad after 31 December 1999, except in those cases that would result in statelessness. Despite this provision, the acquisition of German citizenship remains possible if both parents are in possession of German citizenship or if the one parent who has German citizenship notifies the competent diplomatic representation at the time of birth.

6.2.3 *Immigration Act of 2004*

The law reform of 1999/2000 was considered as part of a major reform of nationality law. The intention was in a two-phase procedure to make further revisions for adjusting the nationality law to a new comprehensive migration policy and changes in the residence rights of EU citizens. It was also intended to devise a special administrative law for nationality issues and to reform the legislation on repatriate Germans.

The Immigration Act of 2004 made some adjustments to the changes in immigration law but did not yet provide for further changes. One of the major features of the Immigration Act has been the emphasis upon integration requirements. Therefore, integration requirements have been introduced making the right to naturalisation dependent upon a proof of sufficient knowledge of the German language. In addition, the successful attendance of an integration course, consisting of a language course and a course on basic facts of German history and the political system reduces the required time of lawful residence for naturalisation from eight to seven years.

Major points of controversy were again the question of acceptance of dual nationality, the legal status of German repatriates and the conditions for the admission of repatriates, particularly regarding the proof of knowledge of the German language and diverse procedures for consulting with the secret services in the naturalisation proceedings.

Some changes were required by the new system of residence titles introduced by the new Immigration Act. Since the Immigration Act provides for a residence permit and a settlement permit as the only residence titles replacing a number of different titles under the Aliens Act of 1990, the nationality law requirements had to be adjusted to the new system with the requirement of a settlement permit in those cases in which an unlimited residence permit was previously necessary. The Immigration Act has also abolished the EU residence permit. Therefore, the new provision now requires only the right of freedom of movement, which is certified by a formal declaration to EU citizens upon taking up residence in Germany. EU citizens remain privileged with regard to naturalisation. Already under the law of 1999, EU citizens were entitled to naturalisation without renouncing their previous nationality provided that reciprocity was granted. The issue as to under what conditions reciprocity is granted had been a matter of controversy between the *Länder*. Some of the *Länder* have required that reciprocity only be guaranteed if another EU Member State provides the right to naturalisation. Other *Länder* considered it sufficient if a German national was in fact naturalised without the requirement of giving up German nationality. The matter was finally settled by a decision of the Federal Administrative Court deciding in favour of a more liberal interpretation which states that reciprocity does not require a formal similarity in terms of granting an individual right to naturalisation if in fact German nationals will be naturalised without having to renounce their German nationality.[19]

In principle, the provisions on ius soli acquisition have remained largely unchanged. A request by the opposition parties to replace the provisions on ius soli acquisition by a more restrictive rule whereby only children whose parents were born in Germany should be entitled to ius soli acquisition of German nationality, did not receive a majority in the Bundestag.[20]

Naturalisation under Sec. 8 of the nationality law is in principle dependent upon the non-existence of a reason which would justify expulsion or on the capability to earn a living. The Immigration Act has considerably expanded previously existing possibilities for making exceptions to these requirements. Previously, it was only possible to make an exception to the requirement on the capability of earning a living in the case of aliens up to the age of 23 or aliens who were unable to earn a living through no fault of their own. The new provision provides discretionary exceptions for reasons of public interest or to avoid a particular hardship. This enables a considerably larger amount of discretion (Renner 2004:176, 179). The particular hardship clause requires unusual disadvantages or difficulties in the case of non-naturalisation.

Since the new provisions enable a weighing of interests (public interest or particular individual hardships) it will be possible to take into account the reasons for dependence on social benefits and the degree of dependence on social welfare. Similar considerations apply when making an exception to the requirement of the absence of criminal conviction. The discretionary clause, however, applies only if there is no individual right to naturalisation under sect. 10 of the law. Sect. 12a gives an implicit indication the kinds of criminal convictions that will be tolerated.

A declaration of loyalty had already been introduced by the reform of 1999. The new sect. 37 requires that the naturalisation authorities have to submit the personal data of any applicants who have reached the age of sixteen to the secret services.

The law reform of 1999/2000 was accompanied by a political decision to renounce the 1963 Convention on dual nationality, which provides only for a very restricted acceptance of dual nationality. By signing the European Convention on Nationality on February 2002, Germany subscribed to the basic principles of the European Convention on Nationality allowing state parties in art. 14 to provide for dual nationality for children automatically acquiring the nationality of a host state at birth and for married partners possessing another nationality. In addition, art. 15 in other cases leaves it up to the contracting states to admit, under its internal laws, multiple nationality if its nationals acquire or posses the nationality of another state.

With regard to the loss of nationality, the optional model, in the view of the German government, required a reservation whereby Germany declared that loss of German nationality *ex lege* may, on the basis of the option provision in sect. 29 of the Nationality Law (opting for either German or a foreign nationality upon coming of age), be effected in the case of persons who, in addition to a foreign nationality, acquired German nationality by virtue of having been born in Germany. With regard to art. 7 para. 1 lit. f and lit. g Germany has also declared that loss of nationality may occur if, upon a person coming of age, or in the case of an adult being adopted, it be established that the requirements governing the acquisition of German nationality were not met.

6.3 Recent developments and current institutional arrangements

6.3.1 *Political analysis*

Although there was a basic consensus among the major political parties that the integration of the foreign population, recruited in the 1960s as migrant workers, and their descendants, had been largely neglected in the following decades, no agreement could be reached on the role of naturalisation and the acquisition of German nationality in the process of integration. While the ruling Social Democratic Party in 1999 considered the acquisition of German nationality to be an essential instrument in achieving integration, the opposing Christian Democratic Parties (CDU/CSU) argued that naturalisation should complete the process of integration rather than pave the way towards integration. The disagreement focussed upon the issue of dual nationality. While the Social Democratic Party and its coalition partner, *Bündnis 90/Die Grünen*, with the assistance of the Liberal Party advocated a concept of toleration of dual nationality based upon a dual attachment to different nations and dual cultural and political ties, the opposition parties maintained that dual nationality was a typical indication of a lack of integration and an unwillingness to accept requirements of loyalty and identity attached to a more traditional ethno-cultural concept of nationality. The German public appeared deeply divided over the issue. While a clear majority of the mass media as well as the churches and humanitarian organisations were in favour of multiculturalism and dual nationality, the German population became increasingly critical about a substantial increase of dual nationals resident in Germany. Surveys showed that a majority supported easier access to German nationality, but opinions were deeply divided on the issue of whether this should be achieved by introducing elements of ius soli and/or accepting dual nationality.

Against this political backdrop legal disputes arose about the impact of constitutional law and international treaties, such as the Council of Europe Convention on the reduction of dual nationality of 1963. The doctrine of avoiding dual nationality had been frequently put forward as an argument based on constitutional and international law. Although the Constitutional Court stated in its decision on the voting rights of aliens that dual or multiple nationality is regarded as an evil that, if possible, should be avoided or eliminated, in the interest of states as well as in the interest of the affected citizen, the Court clearly had argued on the basis of the then existing law, shared by the obligation of the European Convention on avoiding dual nationality of 1963 as well as by the traditional German concept of nationality. Supporters of a reform legislation have argued that the traditional arguments voiced against dual nationality do not outweigh the need to integrate second and third generation foreigners into the political system of the Federal Republic of Germany. As a more practical argument in favour of dual nationality, one may point to the increasing number of dual nationals, particularly as a result of a large number of mixed marriages and naturalisations, who during the validity of the nationality law of 1913 were in fact living in Germany and have not created any substantial problems in the application of international treaties or in exercising of diplomatic protection. There is in fact no precise account of the exact number of dual nationals who acquired German nationality simply on the basis of descent from a German parent or by naturalisation. One argument put forward in the political debate was that almost all Germans repatriated on the basis of art. 116 of the Basic Law as expelled Germans of ethnic German origin had acquired German nationality, maintaining as a rule their previous nationality of the USSR or the 1990 successor states of the USSR. One could also point to the fact that an original provision on the registration of dual nationality had been given up, obviously for the reason that the number of dual nationals did not create substantial problems in administrative practice.

Against the objection concerning the conflict of loyalties it has been argued that the concept of the German state has, similar to the developments in other European states, undergone substantial changes through the immigration of a large foreign population and the process of European integration. As a *de facto* immigration country, Germany could not ignore the fact that a substantial part of its population consisted of migrant workers and their children. Therefore, the argument was that the basis for German nationality can no longer be seen exclusively from the viewpoint of a nation with a cultural and historical identity primarily transferred by descent. One may note, however, that a common objection against German nationality law, particularly by foreign observers, that German nationality law is ethno-centred and based primarily upon ethnicity was an incorrect interpretation of the existing legislation even before 1990. The privileged treatment of ethnic Germans and their descendants, expelled as a result of post-war measures, does not indicate such a concept. The very basis of art. 116 of the Basic Law is the protection of ethnic Germans and their relatives, who were conceived as victims of post-war measures, although the protection aspect has, in the course of time, and due to the substantial political changes in Eastern Europe, lost most of its validity, particularly if one considers that some of the successor states of the USSR are now EU Member States.

Although there was a general debate on the reform of the German nationality law in the election year 1998, no bill was presented that year. After the Social Democratic Party and the Green Party had won the federal parliamentary elections in September 1998, the new government presented a new nationality law on 13 January 1999. In addition to abandoning the principle of avoiding of plural nationality, the bill introduced an element of ius soli acquisition of German nationality. In the following debate on this bill the issue of ius soli acquisition of German nationality became a predominant topic in the elections in the state of Hessen. The Christian Democratic Party in Hessen very successfully launched a public campaign collecting signatures against the Bill proposed by the Social Democratic Party. The whole topic became extremely controversial and emotional. Proponents of the introduction of ius soli elements argued that problems relating to unequal treatment and growing discrimination could only be solved through automatic acquisition of German nationality for third-generation foreigners born on German territory and that actions like the public campaign against dual nationality were supporting xenophobia and discrimination. On the other hand, it was argued that acquisition of German citizenship on the basis of ius soli had been alien to the German concept of nation, which never considered itself as a country of immigration, unlike traditional immigration countries like the US and Canada which have their very social and political foundation in an open immigration policy. The fact that Germany had become a *de facto* country of immigration did not speak in favour of changing its basic rules as to who should be admitted to German citizenship. From a practical point of view it was argued that ius soli acquisition excluded any examination whether there was a sufficient prospect of integration. Since experience had shown that the fact of being born in Germany could not be considered as a sufficient indicator for integration, ius soli acquisition of German nationality should not be introduced into German nationality law.

When the Christian Democratic Union overwhelmingly won the state election in Hessen, it was at least partly attributed to the campaign against the nationality legislation of the federal government. As a further result the federal government lost its previous majority in the Federal Council (*Bundesrat*), which would have been required in order to pass the bill. Therefore, the federal government withdrew its first proposal and replaced it by a bill that retained the principle of avoiding dual nationality, conceding, however, a number of exceptions in specified situations. The bill, nevertheless, maintained the introduction of the ius soli principle with the so-called optional model in order to avoid permanent dual nationality. A joint proposal of the Social Democratic Party and its coalition partner, *Bündnis 90/Die Grünen*, together with the Liberal Party[21] created the basis for the approval by the *Bundestag* and *Bundesrat* to the law.[22] A draft bill supported by the Christian Democratic Parties[23] did not receive the necessary majority in Parliament. Both bills had been the subject of intense public debate by experts in the competent parliamentary committee.[24] The law entered into force on 1 January 2000, the general administrative guidelines of 13 December 2000 entered into force on 1 February 2001.

Although the adoption of the new Nationality Law in 1999 did not bring to an end the public debate on the concept of German nationality, the emotions were somewhat calmed when it became apparent that a considerably smaller number of foreign nationals were acquiring German nationality under the new ius soli regime or by naturalisation as had been originally envisaged. The Immigration Act 2004, therefore, did not attract much attention in terms of changing the nationality legislation since its focus was on immigration, although an unsuccessful attempt was made to substantially restrict the scope of application of the ius soli rule.

6.3.2 *Statistical development*

It may be somewhat early to try to statistically evaluate whether the nationality reform of 1999/2000 has been a success in terms of achieving the aims of the reform. As far as the ius soli rules are concerned there are a variety of new administrative tasks. It is only beginning in 2008 that the nationality authorities have to deal with the issue of the optional model for a yearly average of 40,000 persons, it is difficult to make any predictions as to the practical operation and legal difficulties that will arise in the relationship to the optional model (for administrative issues see Krömer 2000: 363). An important factor for the operation of the nationality law reform of 1999/2000 is the statistical development of naturalisations. However, one has to be careful when interpreting statistics (see Renner 2004: 176; Göbel-Zimmermann 2003: 65).

The number of naturalisations since the mid-1970s remained fairly constant until the end of the 1980s, between 25,000 and 45,000. From 1981 until 1985, 69,000 foreigners were naturalised by regular procedure (discretion) and 117,770 by the legal right to naturalisation (primarily repatriating ethnic Germans). A significant development can be seen if one looks at the statistics from 1991-1995. In the same period there were 489,004 discretionary and 926,283 obligatory naturalisations (Beauftragte der Bundesregierung für Ausländerfragen 1997: 60). The latter category were mainly ethnic Germans in the sense of art. 116 of the Basis Law, who acquired the status of a German upon admission to German territory, and after August 1999 by a certificate of admission whereby they automatically acquired German nationality for themselves and their descendants.

As a result, they were no longer counted in the statistics on naturalisation after August 1999. This explains why the number of naturalisations, which in 1998 had been at a peak of 291,331 dropped to 248,206 in 1999 and to 140,731 in 2003. Until August 1999, repatriating ethnic Germans accounted for up to two-thirds of the naturalisations. In general, repatriate Germans kept their previous nationality. Dual nationality of repatriate Germans has always been accepted under the respective laws although hardly any Germans knew about this situation. Therefore, the largely theoretical dual nationality of repatriate Germans has never been a subject of public controversy.

The 186,688 foreigners who achieved German nationality by naturalisation in 2000 indicates an increasing willingness of foreigners to become German nationals. Although the numbers in the following years have fallen to 140,000 in 2003, the general assessment is that this cannot be taken as a sign of a failure of the nationality legislation. Different reasons are given for the decline in numbers, one of them being that with the entry into force of the new legislation a number of applications had accumulated which could be granted rather quickly when the new law entered into force.

As a result of new provisions in the German Aliens Act of 1990 (*Ausländergesetz*) which provided for the individual right to naturalisation, the number of naturalisations had already increased in the mid 1990s from 45,000 (1993) to 106,790 (1998). The overall quota of naturalisations rose from 0.46 per cent in 1991 to 2.43 per cent in 2001. The increase in the number of naturalisations of foreigners in 1999 was primarily due to an increase in naturalisations of Turkish citizens. In 1999, former Turkish citizens made up two-thirds of all naturalisations of foreigners.[25] The increase in 2000 of 30 per cent is largely attributed to the ability to deal with problematic applications more quickly as a result of the entry into force of the new provisions of 1 January 2000. As an example, numerous applications by Iranian applicants could be decided positively since the new provisions reduced the required time of habitual residence to eight years and since the new provisions made it possible to accept dual nationality on a much larger scale if an application for renouncement had been communicated to the Iranian authorities. This also explains to some extent the relatively high number of naturalisations without renouncement of a previous nationality of 44.9 per cent in 2000.

The statistics demonstrate a significant impact of the nationality legislation on the acceptance of dual nationality. While in 1998 only 15,006 (19.1 per cent) of 78,474 persons were naturalised under the general provisions of sect. 85 of the Aliens Act and by acceptance of dual nationality, in 2000 as much as 80,856 (44.9 per cent) of 186,688 naturalisations were by acceptance of dual nationality. The interpretative value of this statement must, however, not be overestimated. In many cases acceptance of dual nationality is only temporary. By law the loss of nationality takes place only if a former national has acquired the nationality of a different state, in order to prevent statelessness. In the German administrative practice temporary dual nationality arises as a result of naturalisation on the promise to submit an application for renouncement, which may sometimes take years. Temporary dual nationality is subsequently ended by renouncement of a previous nationality. Therefore, developments like a subsequent loss of a previous nationality cannot properly be taken into account in the statistics. On the other hand, the statistics on acquisition of German nationality by renouncing a previous nationality may lead to a wrong impression of the actual number of dual nationals. Particularly in the case of Turkish citizens where the German nationality was regularly acquired under a legally doubtful procedure of renouncing the former Turkish nationality and with an almost simultaneous re-acquisition of Turkish nationality once the applicants had been naturalised as German citizens. This somewhat strange legal situation was made possible by the provision according to the nationality law valid until the end of 1999 whereby the German nationality was not lost as a result of the voluntary acquisition of a foreign nationality if the German national's permanent residence remained in Germany. Turkish nationals with the silent agreement of the Turkish authorities did in practice almost immediately after formal renunciation of their Turkish nationality re-acquire the Turkish nationality once they had received the German nationality.

Abuse of the law was stopped by the nationality law reform of 1999/2000 providing for a loss of German nationality upon voluntary acquisition of a foreign nationality even in the case of applicants maintaining their permanent residence in Germany. Unfortunately, the legal change was not noticed by many Turkish citizens and obviously not even by the Turkish authorities. Therefore, it is estimated that 40,000 Turks almost unnoticed lost their German nationality after the entry into force of the new nationality law and upon the reacquisition of their Turkish nationality.

The statistics show a substantial difference in acceptance of dual nationality. Nationals of the Iranian Republic, Yugoslavia, Afghanistan, Morocco, Ukraine, Israel, The Russian Federation, Lebanon, Tunisia and Syria are generally naturalised in the range, between 80 and 99 per cent without having to renounce their previous nationality. The general statistics in 2003 show a number of 142,406 naturalisations of which 57,285 were under acceptance of dual nationality.

The naturalisation of Union citizens, however, has been rather insignificant in spite of the privileged possibility to maintain their previous nationality on the basis of reciprocity. In 2003 of 1,849,986 EU citizens, only 4,025 were naturalised as German citizens, of which 3,203 kept their previous citizenship. The number may rise significantly with the EU enlargement with the eastern European states.

In general, the provision on privileged naturalisation which was intended to promote the naturalisation of EU citizens has not had its intended effect. Naturalisations of EU citizens correspond only to 1.83 per cent of the total number of naturalisations in Germany in 2003 (information from the *Statistische Bundesamt* of 20 September 2004); the quota of dual nationals was, at almost 80 per cent, considerably above the average quota of 40.2 per cent of all naturalisations. The statistics indicate that there is no substantial need or interest by Union citizens to acquire German nationality, due to the secure residence status granted by Union citizenship.

As to the practical effects of the reform legislation on ius soli acquisition of German nationality, the statistics show a somewhat diverse picture. The original assumption of the number of ius soli acquisitions (about 100,000 per year; non-recurring 300,000 to 350,000 additional naturalisations based on Sec. 40b of the Nationality Law) had been largely wrong. In 2000, 41,257 children acquired ius soli German nationality by birth on German territory.[26] This number remained more or less constant in the following years with 36,819 persons in 2003. In addition, in 2001 and 2002 approximately 43,700 children were naturalised according to the special provision of sect. 40b of the Nationality Law which, for a limited period, made it possible for children born before the entry into force of the new law to acquire German nationality on the basis of ius soli if they would have fulfilled the requirements of ius soli acquisition had the law been in force at that time. An attempt to prolong this provision beyond the year 2001 was rejected in the *Bundestag*.

The relatively small number of ius soli acquisitions is sometimes attributed to the requirement that one parent must be in possession of an unlimited residence title. This requirement had been fulfilled by slightly less than half of the foreign population living in Germany on 1 January 2004.

6.3.3 *Special categories and quasi-citizenship*

The status of ethnic Germans living in Eastern and Central Europe and presumed to be victims or descendants of victims of expulsion or persecution by post-war measures has been regulated by the Federal Expellees Act (*Bundesvertriebenengesetz*) since 19 May 1953. It was repeatedly amended, for the last time by the Immigration Act of 30 July 2004.[27] Repatriates have a special constitutional position as Germans without German nationality. This means that they are entitled to take up residence in Germany and acquire German nationality. Until 1999, German repatriates who had passed a reception procedure in their country of origin and had received a certificate of admission (*Aufnahmebescheid*) were entitled to naturalisation according to sect. 6 of the *Staatsangehörigkeitsregelungsgesetz* (Peters 2003: 193; Hailbronner & Renner 2005: 451). The nationality reform legislation of 1999/2000 changed the legal situation. Repatriates and family relatives and descendants are automatically granted German nationality by the issuance of a certificate as a German repatriate (*Spätaussiedlerbescheinigung*) according to sect. 15 of the Federal Expellees Act (cf. sect. 7 of the *Staat-*

sangehörigkeitsgesetz). This still requires them to pass the aforementioned admission procedure according to the Federal Expellees Act. To receive the status as a German repatriate it is in principle necessary for persons born after 1923 to prove descent from an ethnic German and adherence to the German nation, which is generally indicated by the acquisition of knowledge of the German language within the family. The Federal Administrative Court decided that the required knowledge of the German language must be achieved by adulthood.[28] The law of 7 September 2001 on German repatriates[29] reacted by clarifying that membership to the German nation must be demonstrated by acquisition of the German language within the family, which means that the applicant is able to have a conversation in German at the time of emigration. (Renner 2003: 913, 923).

Since the entry into force of the Immigration Act 2004 the family relatives and non-German descendants of a German repatriate are only included in a certificate of admission (*Aufnahmebescheid*) upon proof of basic knowledge of the German language. The requirement of basic knowledge of the German language, which until then had not been required, was included in order to promote the integration of the immigrants and incite potential applicants to already learn German in their country of origin. The legislation thereby reacted to the fact that in 2002 only 22 per cent of persons admitted under the provisions were in fact ethnic Germans while 64 per cent were non-German spouses and descendants and other relatives. In most cases the non-German family relatives did not have any knowledge of the German language. It is not altogether clear whether basic knowledge of the German language is equal to the language requirements under the general naturalisation provisions of the Nationality Law.[30]

Since the entry into force of the Immigration Act 2004 German repatriates as well as their family relatives are also entitled to participate in an integration course and to receive further assistance for integration, particularly in order to facilitate professional formation and the education of juveniles.

The procedure for acquiring legal status as a German repatriate is divided into two steps. The first step in the readmission procedure is to find out whether a person meets the basic requirements for admission under the Federal Expellees Act and whether admission is within the quota for admission. A person having passed the admission procedure receives a certificate of admission (*Aufnahmebescheid*), which entitles the person to take up permanent residence in Germany. After entering into Germany a further procedure results in the issuing of a certificate of recognition as a German repatriate (*Spätaussiedlerbescheinigung*) according to sect. 15 of the Federal Expellees Act which states with binding force for all authorities that the person is entitled to all privileges and rights as a German repatriate. The issuance of this certificate leads to the automatic acquisition of German nationality according to sect. 7 of the *Staatsangehörigkeitsgesetz*.

The fact that this occurs in two separate procedures has been subject to criticism. A certain coordination has been achieved by concentrating the authority for both certificates in the *Bundesverwaltungsamt* in Berlin. The certificate of recognition as a German repatriate is issued automatically as the entry into force of the Immigration Act and does not require an application. However, there are a number of unsolved issues relating to the acquisition of German nationality by German repatriates. Restrictions concerning the necessary knowledge of the German language have been generally acknowledged as an essential element of the general integration policy. About 50 per cent of all applicants do not pass the German language test. From an administrative point of view it is envisaged to replace the existing two-step procedure by a single procedure, which terminates in the recognition of the legal status as a repatriate.

As a result of enlargement of the European Union it will be necessary to redefine the concept of a German repatriate. Until now, the Baltic States are still included in the scope of application of the Expellees Act. It is, however, very doubtful whether one can still assume that ethnic Germans or their second- or third-generation descendants in these countries are still in need of special protection by privileged access to the German nationality. There are also good arguments for terminating the special legal status of ethnic Germans expelled after the Second World War and their descendants. After the collapse of the Soviet Union the situation justifying protection has substantially changed and one may well ask whether need for protection still exists.

6.3.4 *Institutional arrangements*

6.3.4.1 *The legislative process*

Under art. 73 of the Basic Law, the Federation has the exclusive power to legislate with respect to citizenship in the Federation. Special authority is granted the Federation by art. 116 of the Basic Law which defines a German as a person who either possesses German citizenship or has been admitted to the territory of the *German Reich* within the boundaries of 31 December 1937 as a refugee or expellee of German ethnic origin or as a spouse or descendant of such persons. Art. 116 para. 1 provides explicitly for further legislation ('unless otherwise provided by a law').

The exclusively federal legislation on nationality means that nationality issues are usually dealt with by the Federal Ministry of the Interior, which is in charge of matters of nationality. However, the law reforms during the last fifteen years have been heavily controversial and frequently accompanied by an emotional public debate. As a result of the development of Germany into a de facto immigration country with a high percentage of immigrants nationality issues have become very closely connected with general migration issues and questions of homogeneity and identity. This explains why naturalisation and toleration of dual nationality have been very closely connected to a general debate on the right concept for integration for foreigners into the German society. While the more conservative parties have maintained that integration cannot be equivalent to a toleration of split loyalties and multiculturalism, the Social Democratic Party and the Greens have very much promoted the idea of a 'republican concept' of nationality, requiring the 'members of the club' to comply with the laws and to respect the basic principles of the Constitution as the only prerequisites for acquisition of nationality. The debate on the term '*Leitkultur*' (guiding culture) has indicated that German society is divided on what the right concept for the integration of foreigners is.

This explains also why German nationality issues have frequently played a dominant role in federal and state elections. The repeated attempts of the Social Democratic Party to reach an informal agreement between the major political parties about leaving controversial issues of nationality law out of the electoral campaigns were therefore never much more than rhetorical.

Due to the exclusive power of the Federation, the *Länder* as single entities do not have a substantial role to play in the legislative process. The Basic Law distinguishes between laws requiring the consent of the *Bundesrat* as the representation of the *Länder* and those laws against which the *Bundesrat* may enter an objection within a certain period, which, however, may be overridden by the *Bundestag*. Nationality law as a rule falls into the category of those laws requiring the consent of the *Bundesrat*. While nationality law as such falls under the exclusive competence of the Federation, the *Länder* have the power to execute federal laws in their own right and may regulate the establishment of the authorities and the administrative procedures if federal laws enacted with the consent of the *Bundesrat* do not otherwise provide. Since nationality law generally requires administrative regulations, any substantial reform of nationality law will usually be dependent upon the consent of the *Bundesrat*.

The history of the Federal Republic has shown that the distribution of political power in federal and state elections does not follow the same pattern. Frequently, in state elections voters decide for a different political composition of the state government in order to achieve a certain distribution of power between the Federation and the *Länder*. This means that in order to pass laws the federal government needs to achieve a consensus amongst the opposition parties representing the majority of the state governments in the *Bundesrat*. To achieve the necessary consent of the *Bundesrat* for nationality laws it has generally been necessary to seek a compromise between the major political parties or to persuade some governments of the *Länder* so that a majority in the *Bundesrat* coud be achieved.

In passing nationality laws the legislative procedure follows the general pattern of a politically controversial law. Generally, the federal government or a state will introduce a bill in the *Bundestag* which shall first be submitted to the *Bundesrat*. If no agreement can be reached, the *Bundesrat* will demand that a committee for joint consideration of bills, composed of members of the *Bundestag* and the *Bundesrat*, be convened. This was the case with the nationality law in 1998/1999 when at first no compromise could be reached. Generally, the legislative process is also accompanied by a hearing of experts in the internal affairs committee. If the committee reaches an agreement and proposes an amendment to the adopted bill, the *Bundestag* will vote on it a second time followed by the consent of the *Bundesrat*.

It is highly controversial to what extent constitutional provisions on the principle of democracy and of art. 116 on nationality provide constitutional limits to the legislative competence of the Federation in nationality matters. Art. 116 para. 1 of the Basic Law provides that no German may be deprived of his or her citizenship. Citizenship may be lost only pursuant to a law and against the will of the person affected only if he or she does not become stateless as a result. Both provisions have been heavily used in order to argue the unconstitutionality of the legislative reform 1999/2000. However, finally no attempt has been made to challenge the nationality legislation in the Constitutional Court. This may be due to the fact that art. 116 of the Basic Law does provide a relatively wide legislative power to define German citizenship by statutory legislation (for an opinion on the constitutional reform see Hailbronner 1999c: 1273).

Recently, the loss of nationality for Turkish citizens, who in ignoring the reform legislation 1999/2000 have reacquired their Turkish citizenship after previously renouncing it, has become the subject of political controversy. Some 40,000 Turkish nationals, who had acquired German nationality, had lost their German nationality as a result of a new provision leading to the loss of German nationality due to the acquisition of a new nationality. They had ignored the change in legislation, which previously had made it possible to retain the nationality of the country of origin in case of naturalisation if the persons concerned had their habitual residence in Germany. The loss of German nationality has led to proposals for a legislative change in order to provide for a facilitated procedure to reacquire the German nationality (upon renouncement of the Turkish nationality). The Immigration Act, however, has provided for a settlement permit for those Germans having lost the German nationality taking into account that German nationals might lose German nationality when the optional model becomes operational. This provision will now be used to also grant a secure residence permit to Turkish citizens who have involuntarily lost their German nationality since they were assuming that they could reacquire their Turkish nationality with the cooperation of the Turkish authorities which readily assisted in circumventing the previous German legislation without any adverse consequences. As a result a number of legal problems have arisen concerning the legal status of former Turkish dual nationals who have lost their German nationality wanting to get back their German nationality by giving up their Turkish nationality (this time not only formally). The federal government so far does not see any need to change the legislation. The opposition parties have claimed that at the last elections at which a substantial number of German nationals of Turkish origin participated may have been influenced by the votes of a substantial number of people who at the time of voting had no political rights.

6.3.4.2 The process of implementation

It is within the competence of the *Länder* to execute federal laws in their own right. Under art. 84 of the Basic Law they are authorised to regulate the establishment of authorities and administrative procedures insofar as federal laws enacted with the consent of the *Bundesrat* do not otherwise provide such. With the consent of the *Bundesrat* the federal government may issue general administrative rules (art. 84 para. 2 of the Basic Law).

It follows that the *Länder* may issue administrative guidelines on their own to the extent that there are no federal administrative rules enacted with the consent of the *Bundesrat*. Since nationality law frequently leaves a wide margin of interpretation, administrative guidelines of the *Länder* may differ substantially according to the different political aims of the *Länder* governments.

Based upon art. 84 para. 2 of the Basic Law and previously sect. 39 of the *Reichs- und Staatsangehörigkeitsgesetz* 1913 authorising the federal government to issue administrative guidelines with respect to the administrative procedures and the cooperation between the various competent authorities, as well as to formal matters, a number of administrative rules have been enacted since 1950 covering matters like

- the exceptional permit to retain German nationality in case of voluntary acquisition of a foreign nationality,
- the acquisition of German nationality by appointment as a German civil servant,

- rules on fees for nationality procedures,
- the type and form of nationality certificates,
- the exchange of information in matters of nationality with other states,
- the rules on the examination of nationality for German repatriates,
- the rules on naturalisation,
- the rules on the acquisition and loss of German nationality by legitimation as child through adoption,
- the rules on naturalisation in case of dependence on social benefits.

In addition to these federal rules, the different *Länder* have adopted a variety of administrative rules supplementing the federal provisions of the law and providing interpretative guidelines for the application of federal provisions (for a comprehensive survey of administrative rules see Hailbronner & Renner 2005: 1242 ff.).

Among the federal administrative rules the administrative circular on naturalisation of 1 September 1977 (Hailbronner & Renner 2005: 1246) has played a large practical role. Rules on exercising administrative discretion were commonly drafted by the *Bund* and the *Länder* in 1977 and were used during the following decades to determine the large scope of discretionary power, which was given by the nationality law on matters of naturalisation. The *Bund* and *Länder* have commonly agreed in principle on rules on the extraordinary retention of the German nationality in case of acquisition of a foreign nationality and rules on the relevance of development aid in naturalisation proceedings. In 1991 the new *Ausländergesetz* 1990 was adopted which provided for some changes in the rules for naturalisation, in particular with respect to the facilitation of dual nationality and the granting of individual rights to naturalisation. The Federation, in order to give some guidance to the *Länder* authorities issued informal non-binding federal administrative guidelines (*Vorläufige Anwendungshinweise*) which were not adopted by the *Bundesrat*. Only between 1995 and 1998 did the Federal Ministry of Interior submit a draft for administrative guidelines to the Aliens Act, which was approved finally by the *Bundesrat* with 159 amendments.[31] The administrative guidelines to the Aliens Act were adopted on 28 June 2000 by the federal government.[32]

After the adoption of the nationality law reform 1999/2000 the draft of the general administrative guidelines was submitted to the *Bundesrat* in December 1999. The *Bundesrat* in April 2000 proposed more than 80 amendments.[33] In January 2001 the administrative guidelines to the new nationality law[34] were proclaimed and entered into force on 1 February 2001.[35] After lengthy negotiations the Federation has managed to agree on common administrative guidelines with the *Länder*, represented by the *Bundesrat*. There are substantial gaps and uncertainties particularly in areas where the Federation and the majority of the *Länder* differ on matters of political importance. Two examples can be quoted to demonstrate this point.

Until 1 January 2005 the practice of the *Länder* with regard to the examination of the constitutional loyalty of applicants for naturalisation differed substantially. Some *Länder*, primarily but not exclusively those *Länder* that had objected to the reform of the nationality law and were ruled by the Christian Democratic Party, made obligatory that before an application for naturalisation was to be granted the security services in charge of the protection of the Constitution (*Verfassungsschutzbehörden*) had to be consulted with a formal request for information.[36] The same procedure was adopted by Bavaria, Saxony and Thuringia. In some other *Länder*, the security services were only consulted in particular cases where there were concrete indications for unconstitutional activities. In another group of *Länder* the practice differed according to the country of origin of the applicants for naturalisation. In Berlin, applicants from a specific list of countries, which was subsequently enlarged, were checked through the security services.

Some *Länder* introduced an obligatory check by the security services after 11 September 2001, while others maintained the practice of consulting with the security services only in cases where there were concrete indications relating to terrorist or unconstitutional activities.

After 11 September 2001, the *Länder* Baden-Württemberg and Bavaria submitted a proposal to change the federal regulations by the introduction of an obligatory referral to the security services for applicants having completed their sixteenth year of age. The federal government refused to accept this amendment. The obligatory referral to the security services for naturalisations has only been included in nationality law because of compromises reached in the Immigration Act 2004. Since 1 January 2005, the naturalisation authorities have to transmit all personal data of applicants for naturalisation and according to the existing rules the security services are obliged to immediately inform the naturalisation authorities about any information regarding unconstitutional or terrorist activities.[37]

A second similarly political issue concerns the administrative rules on sufficient knowledge of the German language. In spite of the general principle that there should be a requirement for knowledge of the German language as a prerequisite for the acquisition of German nationality, there was a substantial disagreement between the Federation and the majority of the *Länder* on the concrete requirements with regard to the level of knowledge and the procedure to be followed for examining the language knowledge. Although one may identify a certain trend whereby the *Länder* ruled by the Christian Democratic Parties appear to be stricter than *Länder* ruled by the Social Democratic Party in coalition with the Greens, the different practices cannot be wholly attributed to political affiliations. There are other factors, like the number of foreigners, the particular integration problems of some *Länder* and different categories of foreigners influencing the general attitude of the *Länder* with regard to the requirement for sufficient knowledge of the German language. Hessen, for instance, having followed a rather strict line in matters of dual nationality, does not require a written test, which has led to a decision by the Administrative Court of Appeal ruling that the practice is not in accordance with federal law.[38] In Bavaria and Baden-Württemberg, Berlin, Brandenburg, Bremen and Saxony, the proof of sufficient knowledge of the German language also requires a written test with varying requirements as to the level of writing.

There are no indications of discriminatory treatment of certain groups of applicants for naturalisation on ethnic or racial grounds. Organisations advocating the rights of immigrants have frequently complained about the bureaucratic nature of naturalisation proceedings, the fees to be paid and the length of the procedure. The complaints by particular groups of applicants for naturalisation, however, cannot be attributed to discrimination on the basis of race or ethnicity. Sometimes, there are particular problems, like in the case of former Yugoslavs, due to the fact that it is frequently unclear which nationality has to be relinquished since attribution of an applicant to a particular successor state may create difficulties. In the case of Kosovo-Albanians administrative difficulties arose due to the fact that the Yugoslavian authorities require a certificate that the applicant does not owe taxes in Albania (Beauftragte der Bundesregierung für Ausländerfragen 2002: 62). It is not known if any of the numerous initiatives, programs or actions against racial and ethnic discrimination in particularly are connected to discriminatory practices related to the acquisition of German nationality.

After the adoption of the reform legislation 1999/2000, the *Länder* have either started or supported to a varying degree programmes promoting naturalisation. Some of the *Länder* like Berlin with an average of 6,500 naturalisations since 2000 have achieved substantial success in higher naturalisation figures. Other *Länder* have had relatively low naturalisation figures. However, comparison is very difficult due to the difference in numbers of foreign residents and the categories of foreign residents. No comparison is possible, in particular, between the new *Länder* and the old *Länder* due to a completely different situation with regard to foreign populations.

Individuals or authorities not involved in a decision on the acquisition of nationality have no right to appeal against decisions by authorities on matters of nationality. According to the German Administrative Court Procedures Act, persons affected by an administrative decision may file an appeal with the administrative court against a negative decision of the naturalisation authorities. A further appeal may be filed with the Administrative Appeal Court and in particular with the Federal Administrative Court, if an appeal is accepted by the Federal Court, or if the Administrative Court of Appeal admits an appeal for the reasons laid down in the Administrative Court Procedures Act.

6.4 Conclusions

The reform of the nationality law in German in 1999/2000 has brought about a substantial change to the traditional German nationality law which was based upon the Nationality Act of 1913. The nationality legislation of 1999/2000 has brought the German legislation very much in line with the predominant pattern of most European nationality laws, providing for easier access for foreigners to the German nationality. The nationality law therefore appears to be a logical consequence of the fact that Germany had in fact become a de facto country of immigration, while at the time neither nationality law nor the immigration law had fully taken account of this development. The nationality law can therefore be considered as a further step towards the adjustment of Germany as a country with a large number of immigrants. Facilitation of the naturalisation of foreigners who have been permanently resident on German territory for a long time not only corresponds to a basic principle of democracy but also reflects the increasing need to integrate foreigners into the social and political life of Germany which is in the interest of the German nation as a whole. In this perspective one can clearly see a connection between the nationality legislation and the Immigration Act of 2004, which also provides for integration of the foreign population by obligatory integration courses and a further facilitation of the acquisition of secure residence status and subsequent naturalisation.

One has to be careful, however, as to whether the nationality legislation has brought about a substantial change in the perception of the German nation. There is clearly a shift in the perception of the inclusion of foreigners into German society. Though one may generally observe that acquisition of German nationality and naturalisation are recognised as not only unavoidable but also desirable effects of the change in composition of the population living permanently on German territory, public opinion as well as the political parties are deeply divided on the fundamental question as to what conditions have to be fulfilled in order to be admitted to the 'club'. The debate on dual nationality has been a significant indicator for the criticism of a large part of the German people against replacing traditional concepts of historical, cultural and ethnic identity by a concept exclusively based upon the observance of the law and certain common constitutional principles. With European citizenship these traditional concepts may gradually become less important. It is, however, an open question as to what extent the traditional concepts of who is to be considered a 'German' will persist.

The nationality law reform of 1999/2000 is only a first step in drafting a new comprehensive nationality legislation. Some changes to the nationality law have been adopted in the Immigration Act 2004. There are, however, a number of further issues which may arise in the future. Legal issues arise particularly regarding the application and implementation of the new nationality provisions, notably how to deal with the duty to opt for or against German nationality between the ages of eighteen and 23, which will arise in 2008, and the fact that aside from some practical problems, this might be the starting point for an ever broader acceptance of double and multiple nationality in those cases. Further reforms will probably be necessary concerning the loss of German nationality when persons having acquired dual nationality return permanently to their country of origin. Issues might also arise with regard to the assertion of minority rights of dual nationals. Until now the international treaties and national provisions on the protection of minorities in Germany have not been applied to immigrants. However, with a substantial part of the German population currently having a different cultural, linguistic and ethnical background, these questions might well arise in the future.

Finally, it will be important to see to what extent citizenship law will influence the integration of foreigners. It should be noted that changes in nationality law have an influence upon integration, but that they are not by themselves a means of integration. The main objective must be the active participation of that part of the German population which is of foreign origin, in the actual political and social life of Germany. Therefore, economic integration and measures against unemployment and a low level of education and professional knowledge of persons of foreign origin, whether German nationals or not, may play a much bigger role than nationality issues.

Chronological table of major reforms of German nationality law since 1945

Date	Document	Content of change
22 February 1955	First Act on Regulation of Questions of Nationality (Erstes Gesetz zur Regelung von Fragen der Staatsangehörigkeit)	Regulations regarding the nationality of persons who became Germans as residents of occupied areas or members of the Wehrmacht during the Second World War. Legal claim for victims of the Nazi Regime to (re)obtain German nationality.
17 May 1956	Second Act on Regulation of Questions of Nationality (Zweites Gesetz zur Regelung von Fragen der Staatsangehörigkeit)	Regulation on the expatriation of Austrians who obtained German citizenship after the annexation of Austria except for some specific cases.
19 August 1957	Third Act on Regulation of Questions of Nationality (Drittes Gesetz zur Regelung von Fragen der Staatsangehörigkeit)	Regulation regarding naturalisation of wives of Germans. Time limit for people to raise their claims according to the law of 1955.
19 December 1963	Amendment of the German Nationality Act (Gesetz zur Änderung des Reichs- und Staatsangehörigkeitsgesetzes)	Regulation of the nationality of the children of German women.
8 September 1969	Amendment of the German Nationality Act (Gesetz zur Änderung des Reichs- und Staatsangehörigkeitsgesetzes)	Provisions regarding the naturalisation of spouses of German citizens.
29 September 1969	Ratification of the Convention on the Reduction of Cases of Multiple Nationality and Military Obligations in Cases of Multiple Nationality of 6 May 1963 (Übereinkommen über die Verringerung der Mehrstaatigkeit und über die Wehrpflicht von Mehrstaatern)	The Convention contains regulations regarding the loss of citizenship in case of obtaining the citizenship of another country by naturalisation. Additionally, it provides that people with multiple nationalities should only serve in the military once.
27 August 1973	Ratification of the Convention on the Nationality of Married Women of 20 February 1957 (Übereinkommen über die Staatsangehörigkeit verheirateter Frauen)	The Convention provides that women may keep their original citizenship despite of marriage or their husband's change of nationality.
20 December 1974	Amendment of the German Nationality Act (Gesetz zur Änderung des Reichs- und Staatsangehörigkeitsgesetzes)	Provisions regarding the nationality of illegitimate children of German women; regulation on the release from German nationality.
12 April 1976	Ratification of the Convention relating to the Status of Stateless	Provisions regarding the legal status of stateless persons; these

Date	Document	Content of change
	Persons of 28 September 1954 (Übereinkommen über die Rechtsstellung der Staatenlosen)	persons obtain a legal status comparable to refugees.
2 July 1976	Amendment of the German Nationality Act provided for by the Act on Legal Adoption (Gesetz über die Annahme als Kind und zur Änderung anderer Vorschriften – Adoptionsgesetz)	Regulation of the naturalisation and expatriation in the case of adoption.
29 June 1977	Act on the Implementation of the Convention on the Reduction of Statelessness of 30 August 1961 and of the Convention on the Reduction of Cases of Statelessness of 13 September 1973 – Act on the Reduction of Statelessness (Ausführungsgesetz zu dem Übereinkommen vom 30.8.1961 zur Verminderung der Staatenlosigkeit und zu dem Übereinkommen vom 13.9.1973 zur Verringerung der Fälle von Staatenlosigkeit – Gesetz zur Verminderung von Staatenlosigkeit)	Regulations in order to reduce the cases of statelessness (e.g., by restrictions regarding the loss of German nationality, or simplification of naturalisation for children).
9 July 1990	German Aliens Act (Gesetz über die Einreise und den Aufenthalt von Ausländern im Bundesgebiet – Ausländergesetz)	Facilitation of naturalisation of long-term residents and of young aliens.
30 June 1993	Amendment of the German Nationality Act provided for by the Act on the Amendment of Regulations on Asylum Procedure, Aliens and Nationality Law (Gesetz zur Änderung asylverfahrens-, ausländer- und staatsangehörigkeitsrechtlicher Vorschriften)	The 1990 facilitations of naturalisation were converted into legal claims.
16 December 1997	Act on the Reform of Legitimation Law (Gesetz zur Reform des Kindschaftsrechts)	Amendment of the regulations on legitimation.
15 July 1999	Act on the Reform of Nationality Law (Gesetz zur Reform des Staatsangehörigkeitsrechts)	Introduction of the acquisition of the German nationality by ius soli, connected with the obligation to opt for one of both nationalities after attaining majority; facilitation of the naturalisation of long-term residents (eight instead of fifteen years of legal habitual residence); new conditions for a claim to naturalisation, e.g., sufficient knowledge of the German

Date	Document	Content of change
		language, protective clause preventing extremist aliens from naturalisation; a few new exceptions to the non-acceptance of dual nationality.
13 December 2000	General Administrative Regulation on Nationality Law (Allgemeine Verwaltungsvorschrift zum Staatsangehörigkeitsrecht)	The Administrative Regulation was enacted in order to ensure that the different authorities enforce the law of 1999 in similar manner.
16 February 2001	Amendment of the German Nationality Act provided for by the Act on Termination of Discrimination of Homosexual Partnerships (Gesetz zur Beendigung der Diskriminierung gleichgeschlechtlicher Gemeinschaften – Lebenspartnerschaftsgesetz)	Facilitation of naturalisation of registered homosexual partners (so-called Lebenspartner).
3 December 2001	Amendment of the German Nationality Act by the sixth Act on the Introduction of Euro (Sechstes Euro-Einführungsgesetz)	Conversion of DM-amounts into Euro.
20 December 2001	Denunciation of the Convention on the Reduction of Cases of Multiple Nationality and Military Obligations in Cases of Multiple Nationality of 6 May 1963 (Übereinkommen über die Verringerung von Mehrstaatigkeit und über die Wehrpflicht von Mehrstaatern)	See above (notification of 29 September 1969).
9 January 2002	Amendment of the German Nationality Act provided for by the Act on Combatting International Terrorism (Terrorismusbekämpfungsgesetz)	Cases of support of international terrorism added to the above-mentioned protective clause.
4 February 2002	Signature of the European Convention on Nationality of 6 November 1997 (Europäisches Übereinkommen über die Staatsangehörigkeit)	Regulation regarding questions of multiple nationality, military obligations and the prevention of statelessness.
21 August 2002	Amendment of the German Nationality Act provided for by the Act on Amendment of Regulations on Administrative Procedure (Gesetz zur Änderung verwaltungsverfahrensrechtlicher Vorschriften)	Exception for procedures regarding nationality while electronic exchange of documents in administrative procedures is generally introduced.
13 May 2004	Act on the European Convention on Nationality of 6. November 1997 (Gesetz zu dem	See above (4 February 2002).

Date	Document	Content of change
	Europäischen Übereinkommen vom 6.11.1997 über die Staatsangehörigkeit)	
30 July 2004	Amendment of the German Nationality Act provided for by the Act to Control and Restrict Immigration and to Regulate the Residence and Integration of EU Citizens and Foreigners – Immigration Act (Gesetz zur Steuerung und Begrenzung der Zuwanderung und zur Regelung des Aufenthalts und der Integration von Unionsbürgern und Ausländern – Zuwanderungsgesetz)	Adaptation of the regulations on naturalisation to the new system of residence permits; introduction of a new regulation on hardship cases concerning naturalisation by discretion; introduction of a standard request for information on any anti-constitutional records prior to the decision on naturalisation.

Notes

1 Staatsangehörigkeitsgesetz (StAG) of 15 July, 1999, Federal Law Gazette, vol. I, p. 1618.
2 Reichs- und Staatsangehörigkeitsgesetz (RuStAG) of 22 July, 1913, Imperial Law Gazette, p. 583.
3 See Decisions of the Federal Administrative Court, vol. 79, p. 94.
4 The status 'ethnic German' according to art. 116 of the Basic Law is not transferred to descendants.
5 Decisions of the Federal Constitutional Court, vol. 36, p. 1.
6 Decisions of the Federal Constitutional Court, vol. 40, p. 141; vol. 41, p. 203.
7 See for example the statement of the Federal Government in: Bundestagsdrucksache (Official Records of the Bundestag), No. 10/2071.
8 Decisions of the Federal Constitutional Court, vol. 83, p. 37, 59 ff.
9 This was part of the so-called *Asylkompromiss*, Bundesgesetzblatt (Federal Law Gazette), vol. I, p. 1062.
10 Ethnic Germans are not included in this rate of naturalisation.
11 As to the coalition agreement see Eylmann 1995: 161, 163; Leutheuser-Schnarrenberger 1995: 81, 85; Ziemske 1995: 380 and the Plenarprotokoll des Deutschen Bundestages (Parliament's Plenary Protocol), No. 13/18, p. 1217.
12 Bundestagsdrucksache (Official Records of the Bundestag), No. 13/9815.
13 Bundestagsdrucksache (Official Records of the Bundestag), No. 13/259.
14 On the optional model see the report by the Reference and Research Services of the Bundestag (eds.), No. WF III-49/99 of 10 October 1996.
15 *Zeitschrift für Ausländerrecht* 1999, 50: ZAR-Nachrichten: 'Zuwanderung, Integration und Reform des Staatsangehörigkeitsrechts'; Barwig, Brinkmann, Hailbronner, Huber, Kreuzer, Lörcher & Schumacher 1999.
16 Bundestagsdrucksache (Official Records of the Bundestag), No. 14/867.
17 Plenarprotokoll des Deutschen Bundestages No. 14/40, p. 3415 ff.; Bundesratsdrucksache (Records of the Bundesrat) No. 296/99; on the consultation of the

Committee on the Interior see Bundestagsinnenausschuss-Protokoll (Protocol of the Committee on the Intererior) No. 12, dated 13 March 1999.

18 Bundesgesetzblatt (*Federal Law Gazette*), vol. I, p. 1618; on the amendments see Hailbronner 1999c; Huber & Butzke 1999: 2769 ff.

19 Judgement of 20 April 2004, *Deutsche Verwaltungsblätter* 2004, vol. 22, p. 1430.

20 Bundestagsdrucksache (Official Records of the Bundestag), No. 15/955, p. 38 ff.

21 Bundestagsdrucksache (Official Records of the Bundestag), No. 14/533; see *Zeitschrift für Ausländerrecht* 1999, 98: ZAR-Nachrichten: 'Neue Gesetzentwürfe zur Reform des Staatsangehörigkeitsrechts'.

22 Plenarprotokoll des Deutschen Bundestages No. 14/40, p. 3415 f.; Plenarprotokoll des Deutschen Bundesrats (Federal Chamber's Plenary Protocol) No. 738; see *Zeitschrift für Ausländerrecht* 1999, 150: ZAR-Nachrichten: 'Reform des Staatsangehörigkeitsrechts verabschiedet').

23 Bundestagsdrucksache No. 14/535.

24 On consultation of the Committee on the Interior (*Innenausschuss*) see Bundestagsinnenausschuss-Protokoll No. 12; see *Zeitschrift für Ausländerrecht* 1999, 150: ZAR-Nachrichten: 'Reform des Staatsangehörigkeitsrechts verabschiedet'.

25 See Press Release Statistisches Bundesamt (Federal Statistical Office Germany) of 28 December 2000: 'Einbürgerungen von Ausländern 1999 gegenüber 1998 um ein Drittel gestiegen'. www.destatis.de.

26 See Bundestagsdrucksache (Official Records of the Bundestag) No. 14/9815, p. 5.

27 Bundesgesetzblatt (*Federal Law Gazette*), vol. I, p. 1950.

28 Federal Administrative Court, *Neue Zeitschrift für Verwaltungsrecht-Rechtsprechungsreport* 2001, vol. 5, p. 342.

29 Spätaussiedlerstatusgesetz of 30 August 2001, Bundesgesetzblatt (*Federal Law Gazette*), vol. I, p. 2266.

30 See Bundestagsdrucksache (Official Records of the Bundestag), No. 15/3479, p. 16, 47.

31 See Official Records of the Bundesrat (Bundesratsdrucksache), No. 350/99.

32 In the meantime, a decision of the Constitutional Court had declared the authorisation of the Federal Minister of Interior unconstitutional, interpreting art. 84 as a competency of the federal government as a whole, Decisions of the Federal Constitutional Court, vol. 100, p. 249.

33 Official Records of the Bundesrat (Bundesratsdrucksache), No. 749/99.

34 Federal Administrative Guidelines on Nationality Law (StAR-VwV).

35 *Bundesanzeiger* No. 21a of 21 January 2001; Hailbronner & Renner 2005: 1250.

36 See for instance StAR-VwV of Baden-Württemberg of 5 January 2001, supplementing No. 86.2 StAR-VwV.

37 According to an analysis of the Bavarian practice, the obligatory consultation of the security services from 1996-1998 provided relevant information in 300 cases of a total of 28,100 naturalisations, corresponding to a quota of 1.07 per cent.

38 Decision of the Administrative Appeal Court of 19 August 2002, *Das Standesamt* 2003, vol. 1, p. 15.

Bibliography

Apel, G. (1992), 'Gedanken zu einem zuwanderungspolitischen Konzept', *Zeitschrift für Ausländerrecht* 3: 99-107.

Barwig, K., G. Brinkmann, K. Hailbronner, B. Huber, Ch. Kreuzer, K. Lörcher & Ch. Schumacher (eds.) (1999), *Neue Regierung – neue Ausländerpolitik?* Baden-Baden: Nomos.

Beauftragte der Bundesregierung für Ausländerfragen (eds.) (1997), *Bericht über die Lage der Ausländer in Deutschland*. Berlin and Bonn. www.integrationsbeauftragte.de.

Beauftragte der Bundesregierung für Ausländerfragen (eds.) (1999), *Daten und Fakten zur Ausländersituation*. Berlin and Bonn. www.integrationsbeauftragte.de.

Beauftragte der Bundesregierung für Ausländerfragen (eds.) (2002), *Bericht über die Lage der Ausländer in Deutschland*. Berlin and Bonn. www.integrationsbeauftragte.de.

Blumenwitz, D. (1993), 'Territorialitätsprinzip und Mehrstaatigkeit', *Zeitschrift für Ausländerrecht* 4: 151-156.

Europäisches Forum für Migrationsstudien (eds.) (1995), *Staatsangehörigkeit und Einbürgerung*. Bamberg: Europäisches Forum für Migrationsstudien.

Eylmann, H. (1995), 'Rechtspolitische Zielsetzungen der CDU/ CSU in der 13. Legislaturperiode', *Zeitschrift für Rechtspolitik* 5: 161-165.

Genzel, H. (1969a), 'Die Staatsangehörigkeit ausgebürgerter deutscher Emigranten', *Das Standesamt* 5: 113-120.

Genzel, H. (1969b), 'Die Staatsangehörigkeit ausgebürgerter Juden', *Juristenzeitung* 3: 98-101.

Göbel-Zimmermann, R. (2003), 'Das neue Staatsangehörigkeitsrecht – Erfahrungen und Reformvorschläge', *Zeitschrift für Ausländerrecht* 2: 65-75.

Hailbronner, K. & G. Renner (2005), *Kommentar zum Staatsangehörigkeitsrecht*. München: C.H. Beck.

Hailbronner, K. (1981), 'Deutsche Staatsangehörigkeit und DDR-Staatsbürgerschaft', *Juristische Schulung* 10: 712-718.

Hailbronner, K. (1999a), 'Doppelte Staatsangehörigkeit', *Zeitschrift für Ausländerrecht* 2: 51-58.

Hailbronner, K. (1999b), *Ausländerrecht, Kommentar*. Heidelberg: C.F. Müller.

Hailbronner, K. (1999c), 'Die Reform des deutschen Staatsangehörigkeitsrechts', *Neue Zeitschrift für Verwaltungsrecht* 12: 1273-1280.

Hobe, S. (1994), 'Das Staatsvolk nach dem Grundgesetz', *Juristenzeitung* 4: 191-195.

Huber, P. M. & K. Butzke (1999), 'Das neue Staatsangehörigkeitsrecht und sein verfassungsrechtliches Fundament', *Neue Juristische Wochenschrift* 38: 2769-2775.

Jessurun d'Oliveira, H. U. (1990), 'Tendenzen im Staatsangehörigkeitsrecht', *Zeitschrift für Ausländerrecht* 3: 114-119.

John, B. (1991), 'Vom Stammesangehörigen zum Clubmitglied – Plädoyer für weitere Einbürgerungserleichterungen', *Zeitschrift für Ausländerrecht* 2: 85-86.

Klein, E. (1983), 'DDR-Staatsbürgerschaftserwerb und deutsche Staatsangehörigkeit', *Neue Juristische Wochenschrift* 41: 2289-2292.

Krömer, K. (2000), 'Der Ius-Soli-Erwerb der deutschen Staatsangehörigkeit und die Aufgaben des Standesbeamten', *Das Standesamt* 12: 363-369.

Leutheuser-Schnarrenberger, S. (1995), 'Liberale Rechtspolitik in der 13. Legislaturperiode', *Zeitschrift für Rechtspolitik* 3: 81-85.

Löwer, W. (1993), 'Abstammungsprinzip und Mehrstaatigkeit', *Zeitschrift für Ausländerrecht* 4: 156-160.

Lübbe-Wolff, G. (1996), 'Entziehung und Verlust der deutschen Staatsangehörigkeit – Art. 16 I GG', *Juristische Ausbildung* 2: 57-64.

Makarov, A. (1955), 'Das Bundesgesetz zur Regelung von Staatsangehörigkeitsfragen vom 22. Januar 1955', *Juristenzeitung* 21: 659-663.
Makarov, A. (1956), 'Das Gesetz über die deutsch-österreichische Staatsangehörigkeit', *Juristenzeitung* 23: 744-749.
Mangoldt, H. von (1994), 'Ius-sanguinis- und ius-soli-Prinzip in der Entwicklung des deutschen Staatsangehörigkeitsrechts', *Das Standesamt* 2: 33-42.
Marx, R. (1997), 'Reform des Staatsangehörigkeitsrechts: Mythische oder rechtlich begründete Hindernisse?', *Zeitschrift für Ausländerrecht* 2: 67-74.
Meireis, R. (1994), 'Aspekte einer Neuregelung des deutschen Staatsangehörigkeitsrechts, Oder ein Versuch, über die Betrachtung von Bäumen den Wald nicht aus den Augen zu verlieren', *Das Standesamt* 8: 241-249.
Münch, I. von (1994), 'Darf es ein bisschen mehr sein?, Gedanken zur Mehrstaatigkeit', *Neue Juristische Wochenschrift* 18: 1199-1201.
Peters, W. (2003), 'Aussiedlerzuzug – Entwicklung und Perspektiven', *Zeitschrift für Ausländerrecht* 5/6: 193-197.
Predeick, H.-U. (1991), 'Staatsangehörigkeitsrecht und Ausländerpolitik, Verfassungsrechtliche Probleme der Einführung des ius-soli-Prinzips', *Deutsche Verwaltungsblätter* 12: 623-631.
Renner, G. (1994), 'Ausländerintegration, ius soli und Mehrstaatigkeit', *Zeitschrift für Familienrecht* 14: 865-872.
Renner, G. (1999), 'Grundgesetz und deutsche Staatsangehörigkeit', *Neue Justiz* 5: 230-234.
Renner, G. (2003), 'Vom Wandel des Staatsangehörigkeitsrechts', in *Festgabe 50 Jahre Bundesverwaltungsgericht*, 913-933, Cologne etc.: Heymann.
Renner, G. (2004), 'Staatsangehörigkeitsrecht – Nach der Reform reformbedürftig?', *Zeitschrift für Ausländerrecht* 5/6: 176-185.
Schrötter, H.-J. & A. Möhlig (1995), 'Staatsangehörigkeit in der Diskussion, Rechtliche Aspekte und politische Ansätze', *Zeitschrift für Rechtspolitik* 10: 374-380.
Vedder, Ch. (2003), 'Kommentierung zu Art. 116 GG', in I. von Münch & P. Kunig (eds.), *Grundgesetz. Kommentar.* 5th edition. München: C.H. Beck.
Ziemske, B. (1995), 'Über den Versuch, sachliche Probleme durch neue Begrifflichkeit zu lösen, Ein Beitrag zur "Kinderstaatszugehörigkeit"', *Zeitschrift für Rechtspolitik* 10: 380-381.

7 Greece

Dimitris Christopoulos

7.1 Introduction

Greek nationality law is based on the principle of origin. Ius sanguinis, i.e., the automatic acquisition of the father's nationality at birth, irrespective of where the child was born, is already identified in the first article of the Code of Greek Nationality in 1856: 'The child of a Greek male [or female] acquires Greek nationality at birth.'[1]

The most significant insertion ever registered in the Greek nationality law is the addition, in 1984, of the word 'Greek female' to the aforementioned article, following the modernisation of the provisions of the Greek Civil Code regarding the implementation of gender equality.

The Greek term for nationality is *ithageneia*. The term *ithageneia* is deeply entrenched in Greek history, as it refers to the comprehensive character of the orthodox *genos*. One may define *genos* as the religious community of the rebel orthodox population within the Ottoman Empire that was gradually transformed into the Greek nation in the course of the nineteenth century.

Differentiating between national and foreigner, the law of Greek nationality draws, with regard to the individual's descent, the additional distinction between members of the Greek-Orthodox *genos*, that is *homogenis*, and persons of different descent, of another *genos*, that is *allogenis*. This additional distinction between the two categories of *homogenis* and *allogenis*, is under continual historical and political negotiation: the most exciting aspects of the history of Greek nationality are related to this negotiation.

In Greece, all combinations of the above-mentioned different meanings are possible. In the firm image of the Greek national *homogenis*, appears the revealing exception of the national *allogenis*, which refers to persons belonging to minorities in Greece or to naturalised foreigners. The rule of foreigner *allogenis* includes the exception of the foreigner *homogenis*, i.e., the Greek from the diaspora, who is either a member of a Greek minority abroad or an emigrant.

The rule for acquiring Greek nationality at birth is accompanied by two regulations relating to persons who, while not having been born with the Greek nationality, wish to acquire it. The first describes the naturalisation procedure for foreigners, which provides for very strict timelines and preconditions, including a ten-years permanent lawful residence in the country before the naturalisation application is submitted. The second, the so-called procedure of nationality definition, is reserved for those who manage to prove to the competent Greek authorities both that they are of Greek descent and that they 'behave as Greeks', as mentioned in the relevant circulars for the implementation of the law. The use of the term 'definition of nationality' shows that, according to the Greek law, all the prerequisites, i.e., Greek descent and national consciousness, exist prior to the procedure of nationality definition. The administration simply ascertains the existence of the specific prerequisites.

According to a Ministerial Circular of 1960: 'irrespective of the historical origin of the content of the term(s), it is necessary to point out that the Ministry, in its interpretation of the terms *homogenis* and *allogenis*, does not consider the racial origin of the individual as a unique criterion [...]. On the contrary, in compliance with the opinion of the Nationality Council and the relevant opinions in the field of theory, the Ministry has always accepted that the main criterion for the distinction between *homogenis* and *allogenis* is national consciousness. [...] The individual's racial origin or the national descent does not define on its own the sense of *homogenis* and *allogenis*, but constitutes a subsidiary element for appraisal in the specific judgement.'[2]

Greek legal order uses the term *homogenis* to define the non-Greek citizen of Greek ethnic origin. As this composite word describes, *homogenis* is a person who belongs to the same *genos* (descent), thus to the same nation, while being a citizen of another country. The principle that lies behind the legal status of *homogenis* is that the individual is of Greek descent. However – and surprisingly enough – what is decisive is the person's 'Greek national consciousnesses'. The latter is defined as the link with the Greek nation in terms of common language, religion, and traditions. In this sense, and if the argument is examined in its extreme version, an individual may be considered and recognised as *homogenis*, even if he or she has no Greek origin through blood parentage. Greek national consciousness would suffice. However, in practice this is never the case. The norm is that the criteria of origin and consciousness are either employed cumulatively or the ethnic origin criterion prevails. In the following, it is mentioned that the administration requires a case-by-case examination in order to determine a sense of belonging and an ethnic membership.

However, recourse to the subjective political criterion related to a national does not only facilitate the acquisition of Greek nationality for *homogenis* foreigners. It also allows excluding from nationality status those Greeks, who are considered not to share Greek national consciousness. In the course of Greek history in the twentieth century, the main target groups for nationality withdrawals have been the Greek left-wing dissidents, as well as individuals belonging to national minorities. The history of Greek nationality has a separate lengthy chapter in legislation and practices for withdrawal of nationality from minorities up to 1998, and from Greek Communists, up to 1974.

Nationality acquisition in Greece clearly depends on whether the person concerned is *homogenis* or not. The number of naturalisations is extremely low. It is rather indicative that less than 15,000 *allogenis* foreigners have been naturalised during the last 25 years. This number includes all potential categories of persons applying for Greek nationality, i.e., spouses of Greek nationals, individuals born and brought up in Greece whose parents did not acquire the Greek nationality, and finally, migrants and refugees. At the same time, the country's population of ten million increased by one million foreigners during the last decade.

In contrast, the time required for *homogenis* to acquire nationality is much less. This procedure refers also to the Greek Pontians (*Efkseinos Pontos* in Greek is the Black Sea) from the former Soviet Union, most of whom acquired nationality through summary procedures during the last decade. The numbers of *homogenis* that acquired Greek nationality via the definition procedure may thus be estimated to be some hundred thousands. Unfortunately, there are no statistical data on the acquisition of nationality of *homogenis*.

At the end of the Cold War, Greek nationality entered the most critical decade ever in its perturbed history. During this decade, changes on the political scene of Eastern Europe created a considerable migration and so-called 'repatriation' inflow towards the country. These new phenomena challenged radically the self-perception of Greek nationhood and consequently the dominant nationality policies. Nevertheless, even after the end of the Cold War the practice of nationality withdrawal, which dominated the state policy until the last decade of the twentieth century, was maintained.

The first decade of this century shows more lively activity by the Greek state, bringing in new laws pertaining to Greek nationality with considerably more new circulars for their application. The successive regulations and adjustments illustrate the reluctance and (to a certain extent) reasonable difficulty of the Greek administration to handle the new challenges in a realistic manner.

The new Code of Nationality, which passed at the end of 2004 (Law 3284), abstains from introducing any new perception that would meet the current challenges. It only offers a legally comprehensive systematisation of the previous regulations and a timid renovation of stereotype views that traditionally have dominated the relevant legislative and administrative discourse.

However, 'changing the boundaries' (Bauböck 1994: 199) of Greek nationality is already on the agenda.

7.2 Historical development

7.2.1 *Greek nationality: from subordination to the orthodox genos to participation in the Greek state*

Since 1864, Greek Constitutions have used the term 'quality' of being Greek,[3] illustrating in an apt way the differentiating functions of the nationality concept.

The focus of Greek nationality on the principle of origin and ius sanguinis runs the major part of its course unchanged. Nonetheless, it experienced a fundamental exception, which is traced to its historic origin. This is not surprising. The newly established – under revolutionary law – state had to create its people in a certain way. Its jurisdiction over persons living in the land where Greek sovereignty lay constituted perhaps the safest criterion, in a first phase. To the extent that the struggle for nation building by the revolting Greeks was in an initial stage, the element of land was in search of the most apposite – in a political sense – alliance with religious faith. 'Greek people are the Christian residents of a state, which has been founded following revolution' (Dimoulis 2001: 96). At the same time, the Constitution of Epidaurus of 1822 provided for two additional categories, 'non-autochthonous' (i.e. people coming from beyond the country's borders) and 'foreigners', who desired to become naturalised.[4] The 'non-autochthonous' people were Christians, non-indigenous, while 'foreigners' were western philhellenes.

This *sui generis* combination of ius soli and *ius religionis*, which determined Greek citizens according to pro-national criteria, was abandoned by the Constitution of 1823. The territorial prerequisite for the acquisition of Greek nationality remained in force under this Constitution;[5] the element of language was introduced for the first time as a prerequisite for the acquisition of nationality by the non-autochthonous population, who now had to 'speak Greek as their mother tongue' (the Greek text uses the term 'father tongue') (para. b). The term 'foreigners' was replaced by the related term 'non-nationals'. Moreover, the conditions for their naturalisation were set out for the first time. These consisted of five years of residence in the territory, accompanied cumulatively by the possession of 'immovable property' and the non-perpetration of criminal offences during the stay (para. l). Alternatively, 'great valour and important services to the homeland's needs, including morality, created sufficient rights for naturalisation'.

The term 'Greek citizens' public right' appears for the first time in the Constitution of Trisina of 1827 and continues to exist until the establishment of the Constitution of 1952. The political, civil and social rights afforded to Greeks constitute the expression of the democratic principle of conferring the status of national, included in the Constitution's section under the term: 'Greek citizens' public right' (Kokkinos 1997: 83). This principle is based on the contradiction which runs through the history of Greek nation-building and, consequently, the law on nationality: At the moment that political sovereignty is pointed out as a guarantee of all the Greeks' Rights without any discrimination on the basis of descent, the status of Greek national is conferred according to ethno-cultural criteria (Liakos 2002: 63-79). The Constitution of 1827 brings in an entire section 'on nationalisation' and paves the way for ius sanguinis: 'Greek is: [...] whoever is born on foreign territory to a Greek father' and not merely a Greek-speaking person, as was provided for earlier.

The Constitution of 1832 proceeds with an extremely detailed regularisation of the prerequisites relating to Greek nationality (art. 13), reflecting a particular political co-existence of all possible criteria for the acquisition of nationality (ius soli, *ius religionis*, ius sanguinis). It introduces, for the first time in Greek constitutional history, a provision, that sets out in detail the reasons for the withdrawal of nationality (art. 15). Finally, the Constitution of 1844 cites the laws which are expected to define the 'attributes' of Greek citizens. All the constitutional instruments of the country adopted this practice from then on.

During that period, Greeks, coming from throughout the Ottoman Empire, the so-called 'non-autochthonous', arrived in the newly established republic. The issue with respect to the rights and privileges of this population in the newly established state was a purely socio-economic conflict between the old inhabitants of the territory and the newcomers. The famous hostility between autochthonous and non-autochthonous Greeks concerned mainly the conflict for the latter's position in the state apparatus (Dimakis 1991). As a result, the autochthonous Greeks contested the Greek quality of the newcomers and they expressed claims for their exclusion from the status of Greek nationality.

The first law on Greek nationality was promulgated in 1835 and signalled the regulatory transition towards the law of origin.[6] It remained in force until 1856 when the Civil Law passed. The provisions of the Civil Law on nationality survived for an entire century; they remained in force even following the promulgation of the Civil Code of 1946, until the promulgation of the first Code of Greek Nationality in 1955. It is of interest to underline that, currently, most of its provisions remain in force and apply to persons born prior to the date of promulgation of the Code of Greek Nationality in 1955.

In the course of this century, the rule of nationality was captured in the following formulation: 'Greek is whoever has been born to a Greek father' (art. 14[a] of the Civil Law). While confirming the absolute prevalence of ius sanguinis, this Law introduced the first exceptions in favour of ius soli as to adopted children or children born out of wedlock or as to individuals of unknown nationality that are born on Greek territory. These persons acquire Greek nationality in deviation from ius sanguinis.

7.2.2 *From the first expansion of the Greek state to its territorial integration*

This period was launched with the promulgation of Civil Law, it continued with the first territorial expansion of the Greek state to the north by the annexation of the regions of Thessaly-Arta and, subsequently, of other territories, and ended with the territorial integration of Greece by the annexation of the Dodecanese in 1947. These successive changes rendered the law of Greek nationality one of the most unapproachable and unreadable parts of Greek legislation. The territorial re-adaptations and major political evolutions, which took place in the course of the hundred years which passed until the adoption of the Code of Greek Nationality (1856-1955), left their traces on the relevant legislation. As a result, the relevant provisions are characterised by absolute inconsistency, incomprehensiveness, and segmentation. The consecutive amendments of these provisions have rendered Greek legislation on nationality an almost inaccessible regulatory volume, which has caused confusion to its implementers, as well as to contemporary scholars.

The international treaties, which accompany the expansion of the Greek state, include rules on the nationality of the persons residing in these regions, in a manner that is either binding or optional subject to a series of prerequisites. The successive annexations of new lands to the Greek territory have always had two main impacts: large numbers of *homogenis* automatically acquired the Greek nationality and the remaining Ottoman subjects were granted a sufficient time limit to stay in the Greek state, after which they had to leave Greek territory unless they converted to Orthodox Christianity. An eloquent example of collective incorporation can be found in the Treaty of 1881 between Greece and the Ottoman Empire following the annexation of Thessaly-Arta, which allowed a time limit of three years for persons wishing to retain Ottoman nationality to leave the country. The Treaty of 1881 did not distinguish between *homogenis* and *allogenis*, which resulted in the collective incorporation of all those who desired to acquire Greek nationality without any differentiation. Nonetheless, this Treaty did not definitively settle the issue of the nationality of the Ottomans of Thessaly. The presence of many Ottomans who remained in Greece because they opted for Greek nationality was a pending matter that was regulated under extremely unfavourable terms for the Greek state, following military defeat by the Ottomans in 1897. In line with the new peace treaty, the muslim residents of Thessaly who had acquired Greek nationality under the terms of the convention of 1881, were again offered the right to opt for Ottoman nationality. This time, they were granted the possibility of remaining in Greece or even returning to Greece, in cases where they had been forced to flee Greek territory following 1881.[7] This historically 'asymmetrical' right of muslims was to last only a few years, since the imminent annexation of a major part of Macedonia and, later on, of Thrace, would reinstall the status of 1881. From then on only those who opted for Greek nationality had the right of residence on Greek territory, while Ottoman subjects were granted a time limit of three years to leave Greek land, unless they converted to Orthodox Christianity and acquired Greek nationality.[8]

Collective incorporation through free option of nationality, which took place in line with the prior treaties, generated a new problem for the expanding Greek state. The traditional divergence between autochthonous and non-autochthonous populations receded. The novel counterpoint, which runs through the history of Greek nationality, is between *homogenis* and *allogenis*. Within this framework, the use of the term *homogenia* and, moreover, the conferment of the status of *homogenis* oriented the Greek irredentist aspirations to its neighbouring countries.

Additionally, the quality of *homogenis* justified discriminatory results in favour of persons under the so-called status, within or without the Greek territory. The heritage of the Ottoman millet, i.e., the self-governed religious community in the Ottoman Empire, certainly offered a number of guarantees for the attribution of this definition. These guarantees were rather instable though, for – as time progressed – the Macedonian landscape kept becoming ethnic moving sand. Nevertheless, it is crucial to underline that the continuous reciprocation of the administrative practice as to the conferment of the status of *homogenis* (or *allogenis*) between 'racial origin' and 'national conscious', which are identified even nowadays, originate from the substantially pro-national character of certification of the Greek *genos*. The certification of an Albanian muslim, a Turkish muslim or of a Jew as *allogenis* was rather easy for the Greek authorities, on the basis of the criterion of exclusion from the orthodox *genos*. The situation however became complicated, when it came to the orthodox populations which had not been assimilated by the Greek nation. This mainly concerned the Bulgarian-Macedonian population of the New Lands and – to a lesser extent – the Aromanians-Vlachs.

In line with the Neuilly Peace Treaty between the Allied and Associated Powers and Bulgaria[9] and the Convention between Greece and Bulgaria on mutual and voluntary migration of the minorities on either side, which mainly had a binding effect on the populations that were to be exchanged (Michailides 2003: 135), an important part of the Slav-speaking population lost Greek nationality. The fact that they left Greek territory entailed the loss of Greek nationality by the acquisition of the Bulgarian one and vice-versa (art. 5). The same measure of collective incorporation and exclusion of nationality was enacted in accordance with the Lausanne Treaty for the obligatory exchange of populations between Greece and Turkey. According to a decision of the Mixed Committee for Exchanges of the League of Nations, the measure's scope had been even extended to the exchangeable populations that resided abroad and had been naturalised there prior to the exchange.[10] The Convention on nationality between Greece and Albania, signed in 1926,[11] included provisions with respect to collective incorporation. The latter provided for the recognition of the Greek nationality for former Ottoman subjects that were born in Albania, but had acquired Greek nationality prior to the establishment of the Albanian state in 1913. Besides, it gave to the residents of Western Thrace, who had emigrated to that region from Albania, the possibility to opt for Greek or Albanian nationality.

The principle choices related to Greek nationality during the period from the expansion until the territorial integration of the Greek state, demonstrated an increasing awkwardness, as well as two key legislative or administrative concerns.

The first key concern was related to the ethno-cultural fortification of the persons meeting the criteria for acquiring Greek nationality. However, generous concessions to others that Greek legislation subordinates to the status of *allogenis* are found. These people were either initially related to the revolution or resided in Greece as asylum seekers, such as the Armenians and Caucasians.[12] The Constitution of 1927 provided for the acquisition of Greek nationality, 'without any other stipulation', by the monks of Mount Athos. The provision in question is still in force.[13] Besides, in the enacted legislation there are surviving facets of the 'honoris causa' naturalisations, regarding foreigners 'that have offered superior services to Greece or the naturalisation of whom may serve an interest of utmost importance to Greece'.[14]

The second key concern of the Greek administration, as expressed through its respective legislation on collective incorporation, clearly coincided with the related strategies of the neighbouring countries, which aimed at the definitive purge of potential internal enemies, i.e., national minorities. The relative provisions of the compulsory population exchange treaties from then on constituted a regrettable principle in international law, which has been intensely criticised by the Greek scholars in international law of that period (Seferiades 1928: 328).

The state's increasing discomfort as to nationality is related to the Greek emigration overseas. The law of 1856 provided for the loss of Greek nationality in case of naturalisation abroad. As of the end of the nineteenth century, the increasing flow of emigrants had as destination states in which ius soli was implemented (USA, Australia, Canada). Consequently, the legislation which stipulated the exclusivity of the Greek nationality resulted in its loss by the children of thousands of Greek emigrants to these states. In 1914, this situation was redressed by the Greek legislation. This movement caused paradoxical situations, since a large part of this population did not desire to breach their bonds with Greece. Furthermore, it was judged as detrimental to the nation, since it deprived the country of soldiers in a rather demanding historical juncture (Georgiadou 1941: 76). Law 120/1914 ruled that, from then on, an authorisation of the Greek government was required for the loss of Greek nationality. This provision is still in force. As a rule, Greek emigrants who have acquired foreign nationalities at birth following 1914 did not require the Greek government's authorisation. Therefore, they retained Greek nationality, as well, by virtue of being children of Greeks. This is the first massive example of acquisition of dual nationality in Greek history.

7.2.3 *Nationality during the Cold War*

This period schematically commences with the integration of the Dodecanese into Greece[15] and the end of Civil War in 1949 and extends to the period of the Cold War. Its main feature is withdrawal of nationality. This was a sanction reserved for citizens regarded as enemies. During the first century of the Greek state's existence, there was no comprehensive ideology with respect to the strategies of Greek nationality. Contrarily, during the Cold War period the policy related to nationality was marked by the endeavour of the Greek state to purge by any means the persons considered as 'unworthy' to be Greek. In parallel, the state was extremely reluctant to accept the acquisition of the Greek nationality by Greek citizens, who belonged to the Greek minorities in Albania and Turkey and had definitely returned to Greece. The state adopted this strategy, in order that specific minorities kept being reinforced. Moreover, the Greek state demonstrated – in a paradoxical way, attributed to its awkwardness – an extremely thrifty face towards any other category of Greeks of the Diaspora who desired to acquire the Greek nationality. This cautious practice against the naturalisation of the Greeks *homogenis* abroad was also visible concerning foreign spouses and the families of Greek nationals. This policy started changing hesitantly towards the end of the twentieth century.

Certainly, the measure of withdrawal of nationality had not been launched during that period.[16] Equally, it was exclusively reserved for national enemies and political dissidents as it had been in the course of that period.[17] The Civil War though, constituted a point of intersection with modern history, following which withdrawal of nationality was massively implemented. The citizens from whom nationality was withdrawn were either communists or members of minorities.

This practice was launched by a Decree in 1927.[18] It included a rule, which is held responsible for the negative publicity of the Greek law on nationality until today. '*Allogenis* Greek citizens, who have fled Greek soil and have no intention of returning, lose the Greek nationality. Minor children who emigrate with them lose also the Greek nationality at the same time their parents do. The intention not to return constitutes a real fact and may be presumed from any relative fact [...]. The Minister of Foreign Affairs examines the intention not to return, as well as any element related to this article ad hoc'. High-ranking administration officials admitted however that loss of nationality in this way 'does not politically constitute an institution worthy of being established [...] However, in a practical sense, it serves a national need of the highest importance' (Georgiadou 1941: 82). The replacement of art. 4 of the Decree of 1927 by art. 19 of the Code of Greek Nationality in 1955, and its regulatory fortification by way of the Constitution of 1975[19] and maintenance until 1998, clearly demonstrate its utmost national importance.[20]

Since 1940, the relative legislation did not concern only *allogenis*.[21] In the course of the German occupation, the collaborationist government adopted a new rule introducing the concept of the 'unworthiness' of someone to be a Greek citizen as a reason for withdrawal of nationality.[22]

The festive inauguration of this regrettable period of Greek nationality during the years of the Cold War took place in 1947 with the Resolution of 1947 by the Fourth Revisionary Parliament 'on the withdrawal of the Greek nationality from persons that are acting in an anti-national way abroad', which was maintained in force even following the enactment of the Code of Greek Nationality and ceased to be in force in 1962, however not retroactively.[23] The measure had been applied to over 56,000 Greeks who had departed for Eastern Europe during the years 1947-1949 (Centre of Planning and Economic Research 1978: 46), among whom were a respectable number of Slav-Macedonians (Kostopoulos 2000: 219). Acting similarly to the Italian fascists or by applying the Nazi German principle of withdrawal of nationality, the

Greek administration proceeded with en masse withdrawals of nationality under summary proceedings until the new Constitution of 1952 was put into force (Alivizatos 1979: 490).

However, even following the abolition of the Resolution, Greek legislation still disposed of a safe arsenal for the withdrawal of nationality from 'persons who were acting or had acted in an anti-national way'. The only – obviously fictitious – difference was that withdrawal of nationality was not binding any more, but at the administration's discretion.[24] In fact, the dictatorship did not need to invent new regulations, but only to tap into the already applicable law by force of its own Constitutional Act.[25]

Upon the restoration of democracy, those from whom nationality had been withdrawn, in compliance with the dictatorship's Constitutional Act, acquired it anew.[26] The reacquisition concerned however only those from whom nationality had been withdrawn according to the regime's Constitutional Act and not those from whom nationality had been withdrawn by normal regulatory means provided for by the Code of Nationality, during the dictatorship. These provisions, under art. 9 and 20 of the Code, were still implemented even following the restoration of democracy. It is worth noticing that a transitional provision of the Constitution of 1975 stipulated that 'Greeks, from whom nationality had been withdrawn by any means prior to the commencement of the Constitution's implementation, reacquired it following a judgement rendered by specific committees composed of judges, in accordance with the law'. However, no such committees ever convened nor has a related law ever been issued to date (Grammenos 2003: 202). In an attempt to limit the administration's discretion on issues related to the withdrawal of nationality the Constitution established after the dictatorship provided that 'withdrawal of nationality is permitted under the conditions and procedures prescribed by law'[27] if the Greek national undertakes anti-national service in a foreign country.

The history of Greek nationality has always lagged behind the overall political evolution. It is indicative that the Resolution of the Fourth Revisionary Parliament of 1947 was expressly abolished in 1985.[28] Even the first socialist government of 1981 did not examine the possibility of reacquisition of nationality and repatriation of the Slav-Macedonian political refugees. The express exclusion from repatriation of those who were not 'Greeks as to *genos*' currently constitutes the sole instrument in force that recognises, through exclusion, the existence of Slav-Macedonians in the country.[29]

All other ways of withdrawal of nationality had been abolished or enfeebled. Therefore, art. 19 of the Code of Greek Nationality dominated during the period following the downfall of the colonels' regime (1967-1974). According to this article 'it could be judged that *allogenis* that had fled Greek land without the intention to return, lost the Greek nationality'. As already mentioned, the article was also abolished later, in 1998,[30] after causing international condemnation and after having accomplished the 'national objective' for which it had been implemented. According to the administration, the number of people who had lost Greek nationality from the time the article had been put into force, in 1955, until its abolition, amounted to 60,000.[31] The practice of nationality withdrawal from members of minorities had as its objective to minimise, in terms of population, the minority of Thrace. This fact, combined with the important migratory flow towards Turkey and Western Germany has resulted in the level of the population being maintained at levels, similar to those existing in the period of the Lausanne Treaty (approximately 100,000).

At the time that Greek administration demonstrated its most repugnant face towards those who (were supposed to) constitute a threat, it was also inefficient to conduct negotiations 'as the mother-country' in order to maintain Greek nationality in Turkey. It compensated however for this inefficiency by an expression of generosity towards Greeks coming from Turkey: it subjected those from whom the Turkish nationality had been withdrawn to an extremely unique status of nationality, according to which the provision of a Greek passport was not equivalent to the conferment of national's status.[32] This situation resulted in a small, not calculable but not negligible either, number of persons subject to these categories of *homogenis* who still remained under this *sui generis* form of hostage. During the critical decades, the Greek state's stance was clear: 'no Greek nationality for *homogenis*'. The Greek state prefers to subordinate these people to the status of semi-nationality, in order to maintain the Greek minority in Turkey statistically alive, which was becoming weaker because of the harsh Turkish policies.

By the end of the 1970s, the issue of the Tsigans' statelessness was settled. An unknown number of them had never acquired Greek nationality, due to hindrances that the Greek state had attached to the 'Tsigans reluctance to cooperate with the competent Authorities'.[33] At the end of this decade a thriving percentage of Tsigans had Greek nationality through an innovative procedure of implementation of ius soli. Tsigans were considered as people of non-definable nationality, who were born in Greece and had consequently acquired Greek nationality *ex lege*.[34]

7.3 Recent developments and current institutional arrangements

7.3.1 Main general modes of acquisition of citizenship

7.3.1.1 Acquisition of citizenship by a Greek mother

The most important modification of the law of Greek nationality to date occurred in 1984 by virtue of Law 1438 'an amendment of the provisions of the Code of Greek Nationality and of the law on birth certificates'. The Law entailed major changes concerning the nationality status of Greek women, who were given the right to transfer their nationality to their children for the first time in Greek history. This law put into practice in the field of nationality the constitutional stipulation of 1975 for gender equality. The main amendments worth mentioning are the following:

- The generalisation of nationality acquisition to persons born either to a Greek father or mother. It should be noted, that up to then, only the children that were born out of wedlock or of whom the father was stateless acquired the nationality of a Greek mother.
- The reduction of the time limit for coming of age for those who that wanted to become naturalised, from 21 to eighteen[35] years, according to the new Civil Code.
- Civil marriage was considered valid according to the law 1250/1982. Until then, the non-Orthodox marriage of a Greek man to a foreign woman excluded his children from Greek nationality.
- The establishment of the principle of independency or individuality of nationality; until that time the existing principle was one of acquisition of nationality by marriage. The Greek law proceeded with a radical reform, in line with which 'marriage does not entail the acquisition or loss of Greek nationality'. This provision abolished the previous ones, according to which a Greek woman that was married to a foreign man would lose Greek nationality, unless she declared prior her intent to the contrary; conversely a foreign woman that was married to a Greek man would automatically acquire the Greek nationality, unless she had previously declared that she had no such intent.

Extreme enthusiasm, however, stemming from the political atmosphere of the first governance of the country by a socialist party resulted in Greek lawmakers interpreting the principle of independence of women's nationality in the most inflexible way, which was instituted in its absolute sense. As a result, the spouses of Greek citizens have been subjected for many years to the same status as others that had applied for naturalisation, without them disposing of any comparative advantage for the acquisition of Greek nationality by way of their marriage to a Greek man. This illogical situation was remedied in 1993, when it was ruled that 'marriage to a Greek person is also taken into consideration when the administration judges the application for naturalisation'.[36] Only in 1997,[37] did Greek law provide for the naturalisation of Greek foreign spouses by excluding the prerequisite of a period of prior stay in the country, in the case that a child had been born within the marriage in question. This generosity did not last long, since the new Code of Nationality that was passed at the end of 2004 added to the prerequisites for naturalisation of spouses the required lawful residence of three years in the country.[38]

In fact, the intention of the lawmaker in 1984, that is, the retroactive settlement of nationality issues related Greek women and their children, was not fully expressed. In that respect, the law of 1984 provided for a transitional period until the end of 1986 for the implementation of the provisions related to the acquisition of nationality both for the children that were born and for the women that had been married before its promulgation (8 May 1984). In the course of those two and a half years, Greek women and children who desired to acquire Greek nationality could do so by submitting a relevant declaration to the Greek authorities. Many people had, however, not been informed that a strict deadline existed. As a result, the time-limit lapsed with many of the eligible persons failing to avail themselves of the provision. Seventeen entire years were needed for the promulgation of Law 2910/2001 and for the abolition of the unrealistic, strict time-limit stipulated by the law of 1984. This resulted in a striking rise in the number of nationality acquisitions from 2001 on. The rise remains however invisible, as the Greek authorities cannot provide even elementary statistics on cases of nationality acquisition by way of this procedure.

This omission was not so important until the early 1990s, given that the acts of nationality acquisition via this procedure were scant. The fall of the regimes in Central and Eastern Europe, however, resulted in unanticipated situations for the country. An important number of persons, that in the meantime had acquired the nationalities of socialist states, had the opportunity to travel to Greece, which they considered as the country of their ancestors, as well as also to lawfully claim Greek nationality. As it was colourfully expressed, 'all of a sudden, everybody is looking for his Greek ancestor' (Baltsiotis 2004b: 316). This applied to the descents of second or third generation emigrants to the USA, Australia and Canada, who gradually discovered the comparative advantages offered by a nationality of an EU Member State, either by returning to Greece or – mainly – without. If we add to these large numbers, the so-called 'home-comers' from the former USSR (who will be discussed later on), it is clear that the 1990s posed new challenges to Greek nationality, faced by which it had to once again decide its course.

7.3.1.2 The (non-)naturalisation policy

It has been pertinently stressed that 'the non-naturalisation of *allogenis* foreigners constitutes a structural perception of the state, which is carefully adhered to' (Baltsiotes 2004a: 93). The naturalisation rate of foreigners is extremely low. Indicatively, from 1985 to 2003 approximately 13,500 persons acquired Greek nationality and in the period 1985-1997 fewer than 4,500. After the naturalisation of spouses was institutionalised, in deviation from the generally applicable rule requiring a stay of ten years in the country, the rates more than doubled. In 2001, the Greek state – aiming to impede the rise of applications for naturalisation, given that a decade had passed since a significant number of immigrants had arrived in the country – established[39] a naturalisation fee of 1,467 euros, with the aim of stemming the anticipated rise of naturalisation applications.[40]

The prerequisites of lawful prior residence in the country have been gradually and continuously increased over the years. Initially, the Greek law on nationality stipulated a three-year residency period following the application, as a necessary prerequisite of naturalisation. In 1968, the prerequisite of residence in the country changed: From then on, people who were already legal residents in Greece for eight years could apply for Greek nationality. In line with the law of 1993, the eight years became ten. Finally, in 2001, the prerequisite allowing residence in the country following submission of the application, to count towards the residency period, was abolished. The aim was obvious: to achieve the greatest possible bulwark against the increasing number of naturalisation applications.

In the 1980s, Greece gradually began to acquire the attributes of a modern capitalist society, into which the first immigrants flowed, mainly from Lebanon, Pakistan and Egypt. At the same time the phenomenon of mixed marriages became statistically visible. The nationality policy was reinforced with stricter regulations, so that the Greek state could face the oncoming immigrant wave defensively. In any case, nationality policy could not remain passive towards the overall evolution of social modernisation and state democratisation, which were mainly embarked upon by the first socialist government in 1981. The following paradox then became apparent: The regulatory prerequisites for the acquisition of Greek nationality became stricter, even though nationality politics became more extrovert. This attitude, which continued during the 1990s, did not suffice to change the profoundly xenophobic way in which any foreigner that desires to acquire Greek nationality is treated: as a menace to national homogeny. In the past, this fear was extended even to Greek *homogenis*, emigrants or political refugees. It was generally considered that since these persons had abandoned Greece, the state owed them nothing.

The country abstained from ratifying any international instruments that could introduce deviations from the absolutely rigid way in which the relevant policy was implemented. It was obvious that a potential ratification of the European Convention on Nationality of 1997 by Greece would influence the highly discriminatory treatment between *homogenis* and *allogenis* with regards to the acquisition of nationality issue (Papassiopi-Passia 2004: 36). Equally, it would influence a series of restrictions existing in the Greek legal order against naturalised foreigners. These restrictions, being mostly of a symbolic rather than a substantial nature, are indicative of the already mentioned phobia.[41]

7.3.1.3 The main mode of nationality withdrawal: art. 19 of the previous Nationality Code

The above-mentioned elements reflect a series of nationalist and authoritarian strategies, which were implemented in the country during the major part of the twentieth century – mainly after the Civil War (1946-1949). Equally, these strategies demonstrate Greece's position in the geo-political environment of the Cold War Balkans. It is no exaggeration to claim that Greece systematically encountered the issue of acquisition of Greek nationality by foreigners for the first time in the 1980s. Until then, the Greek administration exercised another practice with particular fervour: nationality withdrawal. As already mentioned, the regrettable measure of nationality withdrawal had reached its peak during the course of the Cold War. From 1960 it was restricted only to the Turkish minority in Thrace. This practice continued until 1998 when the infamous art. 19 of the Code of Greek Nationality, which stipulated the withdrawal of nationality for those leaving Greek soil without intending to return, was abolished.[42]

Art. 19 had severely been criticised by the country's legal community (Sitaropoulos 2004), given that it was prima facie unconstitutional. The Greek Constitution provides for the possibility of Greek nationality withdrawal 'only in case somebody has voluntarily acquired another nationality or in case he or she has entered into an anti-national service'.[43] During the beginning of the 1990s, the pressure put on Greece by international organisations, such as the Council of Europe and the OSCE, for the abolishment of this article was reinforced. However, according to the official records of discussions in Parliament, this article was only abolished when it was deemed that, if it continued in force, it would create more problems than it had already resolved (Anagnostou 2005). The abolition of art. 19 was not retroactive. Should the persons, from whom nationality had been withdrawn according to this article, desire to acquire nationality anew, they would have to follow the mode of naturalisation applicable to *allogenis* foreigners, without being subject to different regulations. In practice, the issue of nationality reacquisition was rather indifferent to the majority of the 47,000 people from whom nationality had been withdrawn, given that they no longer had ties to Greece. Most of them moved to Turkey or Germany. There still exist today, however, a number of people that has settled in Greece. The fact that there are individuals 'that have left Greek soil without the intention to return', who still remain in Greece is a paradox. Such a paradox can however be explained by the unrehearsed, arbitrary and maladroit way, in which the specific provision was implemented. In other words, there are many cases where nationality was withdrawn regardless of the fact that the individuals in question had never left the country. The case of a male person who lost his nationality according to Art.19, while serving in the Greek Army, is rather illustrative hereof (Kostopoulos 2003: 73).

In Thrace, there are still no less than 1,000 stateless persons of advanced age, members of the minority, who still hope to find justice. They constitute the remainders of a regrettable and very recent past of the history of Greek nationality.

7.3.2 Special categories and quasi citizenship

7.3.2.1 The procedure of 'definition' of the Greek nationality for homogenis

Nationality acquisition through the procedure of 'definition' has constituted an extremely important legal instrument for the Greek administration. The procedure of definition made it possible for the Greek administration to separate nationality acquisition by *homogenis* foreigners from the far stricter prerequisites for naturalisation by *allogenis* foreigners. Definition is based on a *sui generis* procedure of acquisition of Greek nationality from an ancestor, even when the ancestor has already passed away. The objective of this procedure is to determine a direct relationship between an ancestor that once held Greek nationality and the person applying for nationality to be granted on the basis of ius sanguinis. Quite often, this procedure is equivalent to nationality acquisition of whole – one or more – families, provided it is proved that a certain ancestor was a Greek citizen. Given that the provisions that put into practice the principle of gender equality in 1984 have been implemented retroactively, the right to acquire Greek nationality may also be established where Greek origin exists on the mother's side.

It must be noted, however, that there is no article in the Code of Greek Nationality that clearly defines the exact contents of the procedure for nationality definition. It is only stipulated that the Secretary General of the Region is mandated to issue the confirmatory acts for the definition (art. 21). However, it is not evident from any provision what exactly 'definition' is or what the related necessary prerequisites are. Naturally this deficiency may not be an imperfection of the law, but a conscious option of the lawmakers' not to submit the procedure of nationality definition to transparent legal limitations. The procedure is covered in detail in the relevant circulars of the Ministry of the Interior addressed to its services. Particular legislative lacunae are addressed by the executive power's regulatory acts. This is particularly true when it comes to assigning the *homogenis* status. The answer to the question 'who are the Greek *homogenis*?' has some historical constants, but a series of variables as well (Christopoulos & Tsitselikis 2003b: 87-89). The historical constant and limit is subordination to the orthodox *genos*: only Christian orthodox people may be *homogenis*. The variables mainly consist of a series of deviations that historical conjuncture dictates to the administration, according to international or domestic circumstances. The terms *homogenis* and *allogenis* are not defined as strict legal categories, but rather as flexible ideological concepts susceptible to change according to the political priorities of the times (Baltsiotes 2004a: 88). In this framework, their meaning is under continuous negotiation and confidential administrative consultation.

As a rule, *homogenis* are individuals of Greek origin and of Greek consciousness, as well. The case law of the Council of State reaches that conclusion, while examining the concept of (the opposite of *homogenis*), *allogenis*.[44] This relevant decision clarified two issues. First, that participation in the Greek nation is not determined on the basis of ethnic origin alone. Non-ethnic Greeks may also be part thereof, provided they assimilate. Second, a Greek national consciousness and a non-Greek identity are mutually exclusive (Stavros 1996: 119).

Consequently, a definition of *homogenis* could serve the needs of a given historical-political conjuncture, but it could not satisfy the respective needs of another period (Tsioukas 2005: 34). The perturbed history of Greek nationality could not bear a static definition of the term, in accordance with the latter of which, the quality of *homogenis* is attributed to citizens of certain countries or residents of certain regions that are of Greek descent. One of the numerous indicative examples is the following: Vlachs who migrated to Romania during the 1920s and 1930s constituted one of the target groups *par excellence* of the first legislative instruments on the withdrawal of Greek nationality from Greek *allogenis*. During the 1990s, the certification of an Albanian citizen of Vlach origin by the Greek consulate of Korce in South Albania was a necessary prerequisite for him or her to acquire a special *homogenis* identity card (Christopoulos & Tsitselikis 2003a: 33). This card proves that he or she belongs to the Greek ethnic group; it is also a prerequisite for the issuance of residence and working permits as well as for full access to special benefits for social security, health and education (Tsitselikis 2004: 7).

Based on the definition procedure, a sort of dormant nationality is established. This dormant nationality is formally entrenched when the person proves that his or her ancestor had been registered in the rolls of a municipality of the Greek state. The legal basis of Greek nationality derives from this registration. The related 'municipal roll certificates' constitute the legal presumption of Greek nationality. The local authorities may issue them following the submission of an application either via the Greek Consulates abroad, or directly to the municipality. Registration of the parents' marriage, as well as that of the interested party's birth in the rolls of the municipality or community of the Greek state constitutes a prerequisite for the issuance of the related certificates.

The *homogenis* that are able to produce such certificates of their ancestry follow a trouble-free and flexible procedure of definition for the acquisition of Greek nationality. Otherwise they have to follow the ordinary naturalisation procedure, but are exempted from the prerequisite of ten years lawful prior residence in the country and the 1,500-euro fee which normally applies. The authorities who handle the definition procedure are also different from those who deal with naturalisations. Naturalisations have always fallen within the mandate of the Ministry of the Interior and the related investigations have always fallen within the mandate of the respective Directorate of Nationality of the Ministry. On the other hand, the authority for nationality definition is particularly decentralised. In 1995,[45] the authority for issuing acts for nationality definition was transferred to the country's Prefects, while the related investigation remained with the Ministry's central services. In 1998,[46] the entire procedure, as well as prior investigation was transferred to the Regional Services. The Secretary General of the Region signs the decision for the acquisition of nationality. The very large number of definition applications submitted during the 1990s explains this initiative for decentralisation. Although it answers certain needs, many objections have been raised, as to if and to what extent the Regional Services are sufficiently staffed, in order to deal with the complicated issues regarding nationality definition that arise during the investigation (Grammenos 2003: 152 155).

It should be mentioned though that a number of cases of investigation for nationality definition remain unofficially within the mandate of the central services of the Ministry of the Interior, because of the particular 'national significance' that they present. This fact demonstrates the lack of trust – which in many cases is justified – in the judgement of the Regions.[47] These cases refer to:

- Turks of Thrace who have lost Greek nationality in various ways in the past.
- Slav-Macedonian political refugees who have not been considered 'Greeks with regard to *genos* and who have not reacquired Greek na-

tionality upon their repatriation', in accordance with the related ministerial decision of the first socialist government on 'Free repatriation and conferment of the Greek nationality to political refugees'.[48]

- The so-called fugitives in Bulgaria. These are mainly members of minorities of Bulgarian descent who fled Greek soil after the Second Balkan War until the outburst of the Civil War and had gone to Bulgaria.
- The Albanian muslims of Thesprotia (Chams) that were forced by the Greek National Army to leave Greece and go to Albania during the summer of 1944. Their nationality was withdrawn in a legally contestable mode by simple erasure from the municipality rolls.
- The Aromanian-Vlachs who began to migrate to Romania in the 1920s.
- Greek-Armenians, who directly migrated to the Republic of Armenia of the ex-USSR, and who were persecuted in Turkey during the 1920s.
- Greek Jews, who had begun to migrate to the land of the future Israel, even before the beginning of the Second World War.[49]

7.3.2.2 *The Greek Pontian 'homecomers' from the former USSR*

Sweeping changes have taken place since the end of the Cold War on the population map of Greece. The government estimates that almost 180,000 Pontian 'homecomers' from USSR countries reside permanently on Greek territory. By the end of 2003, almost 125,000 people had acquired Greek nationality, mostly through the definition procedure. According to the General Secretariat for Home Comers of the Ministry of Macedonia-Thrace, the majority of the *homogenis* from the former USSR come from Georgia (52 per cent), Kazakhstan (20 per cent), Russia (15 per cent), Ukraine (2 per cent) and Uzbekistan (2 per cent) (Ministry of Macedonia-Thrace 2000: 51). *Homogenis* that did not desire to acquire Greek nationality, mainly in order not to lose their former one,[50] have been provided the special *homogenis* identity card.

The Greek state uses the term 'homecoming' for Pontians coming from the states that succeeded the USSR, mainly Georgia and Kazakhstan, as well as for the Greeks of Marioupolis of the Ukraine. This term is neither ideologically neutral nor pragmatically valid. It originates from a fiction, an illusionary past. The term 'homecoming' illustrates more the peoples' expectance to escape poverty than their will to virtually 'return' to the home country. These people had never left Greece in order to come back to it. It is also characteristic that the Greek state persists in calling them '*homogenis* of Pontian origin' or 'Greek-Pontians'. On the contrary, the Greek public is more familiar with the term 'Russian-Pontians', which is rather derogatory.

The Greek state has shown extreme generosity towards the 'Greek-Pontians' regarding nationality. Most of these people were granted the Greek nationality under specific regulatory provisions, by means of a new summary mode of acquisition, later called 'specific naturalisation'.[51] Thousands of such 'specific naturalisations' have been registered 'as opposed to any other general or specific provision that prescribed the submission of a series of supporting documents'.[52]

7.3.2.3 The fluid status of the Greeks from Albania

Most of the migrants that came to Greece during the 1990s were Albanians. According to the National Census of 2001, Albanian immigrants represent more than half the total number of immigrants in Greece and amount to half a million.[53] According to reliable information from the Ministry of Public Order, approximately 200,000 of these where conferred with the status *homogenis* in accordance with the relevant Ministerial Decision.[54] The exact number is not known, since the Ministry of Public Order refuses to publicise it, invoking 'reasons of national security' (Baldin-Edwards 2005: 2).

A critical issue here is the Greek state's strategic choice to absolutely refuse Greek nationality to the Greeks from Albania. There is a fear that acquiring Greek nationality may cause the withdrawal of their Albanian nationality and consequently represent the definitive historical extinction or statistical death of the Greek minority in Albania. The Albanian Constitution does not prohibit dual nationality. Nonetheless, Greek-Albanian relations have been dogged by a serious lack of trust. In both states there survives residual, though ever decreasing, open irredentism towards each other. The endeavour for bilateral settlement, which was intensified in the summer of 2002 with a view to concluding a bilateral agreement between Greece and Albania, was not successful. Ever since, the issue is pending, but the complaints within the population of the Greek minority of Albania are growing.[55]

The only categories of Albanian nationals who have lately acquired Greek nationality have been the former holders of *homogenis* passports from Turkey and Albania. As of 2001, those individuals who were in a position to prove that an ancestor of theirs had Greek nationality in the past were able to acquire Greek nationality.[56] In 1998, the provision of a special *homogenis* identity card 'to the Citizens of Albania who are of Greek descent and live in Greece'[57] was opted for instead of conferment of the Greek nationality. The police authorities who conduct the investigation, in order to ascertain a person's Greek origin, provide these identity cards. The identity cards are valid for a three-year period, are renewable and are granted to the spouses and descendants of *homogenis*, as well.

This brief description demonstrates in the clearest possible way that a double standard exists regarding the policy for the acquisition of nationality by Greek *homogenis*. This policy has created numerous problems. The Greek state does not take into account the genuine will or capacity of these people to be integrated into the Greek society in any of the criteria for granting (or not) Greek nationality. The only criteria which have been put into practice constitute the results of obvious – although rarely admitted – political choices, mainly in the area of interstate relations or in the name of 'national commitment towards Greek brothers'. These criteria, however, generate obvious injustices, inequalities and impasses, which the Greek state has not yet managed to tackle.

7.3.3 *Institutional arrangements: The Greek law on nationality as an exceptional normative framework*

The Greek nationality law is par excellence a normative framework of multiple exceptions from the general rules governing the relationships between the administration and individuals. These exceptions originate from two provisions of the Code of Greek Nationality. According to art. 8, para. 2 of the Code, *the decision rejecting an application for naturalisation may not be justified*, whereas, as a general constitutional principle, all administrative acts unfavourable to the individual should be fully justified. The second provision prescribes that the articles of the Code of Administrative Procedure concerning the deadline for the administration's obligation to reply to the citizens' requests do not bind the administration 'in cases related to the acquisition, recognition or reacquisition of Greek nationality'.[58] The first exception entails the non-subordination of administrative acts or omissions related to nationality to any jurisdictional control. The second exception excludes any obligation to respond to individuals addressing their claims *in scripto* to the administration.[59] These two exceptional characteristics are the main reasons for the poor case law of Greek administrative justice on issues related to nationality loss or acquisition.

Without overstating the case, it is obvious that this regime of multiple exceptions dominating Greek nationality law flagrantly limits the possibility of effective juridical remedies and judicial control. These particular legislative provisions incorporate the consolidated view of the Greek administration that all tangible issues related to nationality do not pertain to the exercising of human rights and freedoms, but to the field of exercising sovereignty and protecting state interests. The limited jurisprudence of the Council of State, the country's highest administrative court, also proves the above-mentioned position. It therefore comes as no surprise that its case law is non-existent for cases of nationality acquisition. The Court's case law is also marginal regarding cases of nationality withdrawals.[60]

This perception, which is not a Greek inspiration or novelty, has largely contributed to the formation of a systemic maladministrative mentality of the Greek authorities on issues pertaining to nationality. This mentality is founded on the unlimited exercising of discretionary powers on issues related to nationality loss and acquisition. Dispensation from the general terms provided by the Code of Administrative Procedure allows the administration to keep naturalisation applications in the archives for years and years, even decades. The typical answer, which is given verbally by the Ministry's employees to the applicants, is that 'your file is under examination'. The discretionary power of the administration on such cases is, strictly speaking, infinite. It is also indicative that the first administrative document inviting the Ministry's staff not to abuse this discretion was the latest circular issued for the implementation of the new Nationality Code in January 2005.[61] An eminent professor of constitutional law who had been assigned by the socialist government prior to the 2004 elections as Minister of the Interior, declared in a conference: 'When I took over my post I requested an official briefing on nationality issues. It was then that I first heard about a verbal instruction by the former Minister. The instruction was that public servants should not proceed with any naturalisations of people from the Balkans' (Alivizatos 2005).

This verbally communicated policy has just as much to do with the content of the distinction *homogenis-allogenis* which encourages a differentiated treatment of foreigners on issues pertaining to nationality acquisition. Recognition of the *homogenis* status for a foreign national represents further privileged treatment as far as the procedure for acquiring nationality is concerned. Nevertheless, as we have already pointed out, the virtue of *homogenis* is extremely loose and flexible, dictated by what the Greek authorities consider as necessity, interest or threat at that specific moment. As a result, the policy of nationality acquisition or loss depends less on the law, and more on the Ministry's circulars and on the will and (overt or covert) motives of political leaders or high ranking administrative officials.

This phenomenon of *de facto* reversal of the hierarchy of legal norms – the circulars obtaining greater legal significance than the law – is familiar to the Greek administration and does not only refer to issues related to nationality. The larger the discretionary powers of the administration, the wider the normative framework covered by the ministerial circulars. One extreme, but indicative case is that of the Common Ministerial Decision on the 'definition of nationality of *homogenis* of Pontian origin from the USSR'[62] issued in the early 1990s, providing for the acquisition of Greek nationality by the Pontian 'homecomers' by summary procedure. This decision, which gave the green light to thousands of nationality acquisitions for the first time in Greek history since the population exchanges of 1923, was actually *contra legem* until 1993. At the time of its issuance, the mandatory law of 1940, which practically prohibited the acquisition of Greek nationality by this population group, was still in force.[63] It was only three years later that the law of 1940 was abolished.[64]

7.4 Conclusions

Nationality has never been on the political or even the academic agenda in Greece. There are specific reasons for this. On the one hand, the Greek state never felt safe enough to address nationality matters, considering the issue as *par excellence* 'nationally sensitive'. On the other hand, Greek society, was never really concerned with nationality matters, and reasonably so. The only occasion on which such matters became broadly known was the case of nationality acquisitions by the Greek Pontians of the former USSR. This issue preoccupied public opinion more because of its scandalous political nature than for any other reason. The Greek people showed their disdain for governments who 'create Greeks'[65] in order to collect votes.

Greek academia has very little to demonstrate in the field of nationality. Apart from limited literature related to private international law (Papassiopi-Passia 2004) or to former high-ranking civil servants of the Nationality Directorate of the Ministry of the Interior (Grammenos 2003), the disciplines of Greek legal, political science or sociology have made a limited contribution to the relevant research. Issues such as 'active', 'civic' or 'social' citizenship, which have recently preoccupied the policies and literature of other countries in the European Union, are simply not on the agenda in Greece (Tsitselikis 2004: 14).

At the outset of this century, the Greek state was highly defensive and phobic towards migration, which has had an impact on Greek policy on nationality loss and acquisition. It is commonly acknowledged today that 'it took more than five years for the Greek government to realise that immigrants were there to stay and the new phenomenon could not be managed only through stricter border control and massive removal operations' (Grobas & Triantafyllidou 2005: 5). A leading NGO in the field of human rights pointed out that 'the Greek legislator [...] considers migration, at the best of times, a historical accident, and at the worst, as a crime.'[66] As of the first year of its operation, the Greek Ombudsman has stressed that 'as in other European countries, the insistence of the Greek law on ius sanguinis (the so-called blood principle) generates many problems [...], not only for foreigners of non-Greek descent who settle permanently in Greece with the intention to integrate into Greek society or acquire Greek citizenship, but also for individuals of Greek descent seeking to acquire Greek citizenship or to have their citizenship recognised, as well as for stateless persons and persons of indeterminate citizenship' (Greek Ombudsman 1999: 28).

Towards the end of the twentieth century, the ius sanguinis principle starts being influenced by residence-based modes of nationality acquisition in a considerable number of European countries. To date, this fact does not seem to bother the Greek authorities. The new Nationality Code, which was adopted by the Greek Parliament at the end of 2004, does not even slightly move in the direction of adopting specific rules for nationality acquisition by individuals born and living in Greece. As a result, their naturalisation procedure is subject to the same – in practice stricter – rules as the generally applicable ones. For the foreign parents of children born in Greece, the lapse of a ten-year period suffices; children born in the country have to first come of age (i.e., eighteen years), unless, of course, they acquire nationality as unmarried minors, through their parents' naturalisation. This is an obviously introverted and weak-spirited legislative development: one (more) lost chance towards a perceptive and far-sighted planning, disengaged from out-of-date views and obsolete methods, at least as far as standards for human rights are concerned.

The Code was passed en bloc without any prior public consultation with relevant bodies, with an absolute majority of votes by the two big political parties. It is rather indicative that the Code was elaborated by the Ministry of the Interior during the previous socialist government and was brought into Parliament and passed – without the slightest amendment – by the new conservative government.[67]

The various aspects related to nationality loss or acquisition date back to the foundation of the modern Greek state. This model of state is based on the following combination: on the one hand, sovereignty of the Greek political community is founded on the recognition of the rights and freedoms of all, without discrimination. Yet, on the other hand, accession to nationality is ensured through the recognition of certain ethno-cultural characteristics, according to the priorities of the times.

Nevertheless, the abovementioned model has been going through a structural crisis due to the political conflict between the left and the 'nationaly-minded state' (*ethnikofron kratos*). This conflict dominated the Greek political scene during the major part of the twentieth century. In its longwinded culmination – from the beginning of the Civil War till the end of the dictatorship (1946-1974) – the Greek state went so far as to consider Greek communists were not (worthy to be) Greeks. Therefore, they were not entitled to Greek nationality.

Within this conflict, the Greek state has been threatened and triumphed, not by achieving a consensus, but by forcing the subordination of the majority of the Greek people. Apart from the Left, which was considered internal enemy number one until 1974, there remain considerable relics of national minorities, perceived collectively as the Trojan Horses of neighbouring irredentist nationalisms. After the fall of the dictatorship in 1974, the communists stopped being perceived as enemies, giving their place to individuals belonging to minorities. However, the appearance of a million migrants (particularly from Albania) during the last decade of the twentieth century has generated new suspicions. 'What will happen with a new Albanian minority in Greece?' is a common but often unmentionable fear.

In fact, the persistence of old attitudes is such, that the Greek state and society still consider themselves under a continuous state of threat, even if from an impartial point of view such a threat is non-existent.

According to the tradition of 1789, the Greek polity is indelibly sealed by the classical pattern of Jacobinism. Belonging to this polity signals the suppression of any mediatory body between the state and the individual with the sole exception of (one) nation (Wallerstein 2003: 655). Nevertheless, the Greek Jacobinism is *imperfect* (Christopoulos 2004b: 359-361). If in its traditional form this ideology sees the nation as the exclusive mediator between state and individual, the Greek version has an additional pretension: the interference of the (orthodox) *genos*.

The Greek political community resorts to assimilation strategies, because it cannot conceive of non-assimilated members. That has been the essence of the country's policy towards minorities all during the twentieth century. However, the Greek political community cannot conceive that some individuals are in position to be assimilated and, therefore, potentially entitled to Greek nationality. To put it simply: anybody can become French, as long as he or she is inspired by the ideals of the French revolution, nation, etc. For the Greek perception, Turks cannot become Greeks, unless they convert to Christianity.[68]

In concluding, we would argue that the abovementioned Greek model displays the symptoms of definite historical exhaustion. The major challenge of its redefinition has already matured. The reason for this is the recent massive migration phenomenon in the country. The structural contradiction of this model lies in that, on the one hand, it regards assimilation as an absolute condition for the social integration of migrants, while, on the other hand, it obstinately refuses Greek nationality to the overwhelming majority of these people, in the name of the pro-national and static category of the orthodox *genos*. In other words, adherence to the rights-oriented 1789 ideology is undermined by a purely ethno-cultural, ontological perception of the foundations of the political community. Of course, this is no Greek peculiarity. 'National citizenship – as an ideology and an institutional practice – has always embodied both of these components' (Soysal 1996: 17).

On the threshold of the twentieth century the Greek nationality finds itself facing new tormenting dilemmas and in quest of brave new inclusion strategies.

This is its inescapable point in time.

Chronological table of major reforms of Greek nationality law since 1945

Date	Document	Content of change
7 December 1947	Resolution XXVII of the Greek Parliament (Official Gazette A' 267)	Withdrawal of Greek nationality of Greeks living abroad, acting in an anti-national way.
1948	Law 517/1948 'on the nationality of the inhabitants of the Dodecanese'	Nationality of the inhabitants of the Dodecanese (the Dodecanese was annexed to the Greek territory in 1947).
20 September 1955	Greek Nationality Code: Legislative Decree 3370/1955 (Official Gazette A'258)	
22 July 1968	Emergence Act 481/1968 (Official Gazette A'164)	Prerequisite of 8 years of previous residence in the country for the naturalisation application (art. 3).
8 May 1984	Law 1438/1984 (Official Gazette A' 60)	Principle of gender equality in the field of nationality law and reduction of the age of majority from 21 to 18 years.
17 December 1989	Law 1832/1989 (Official Gazette A' 54)	Access to nationality for foreign female spouses of Greek nationals whose civil marriage abroad did not entail such acquisition under previous law (Art. 40, para.1 amended art. 7, para. 3 of Law 1438/1984).
6 April 1990	24755/6 4 1990 Common Ministerial Decision (Ministers of the Interior, Public Defence and of the Presidency of Government)	Special procedure for nationality acquisition by the 'Greeks of Pontian origin'.
23 April 1993	Law 2130/1993 (Official Gazette A' 62)	Specific status of nationality acquisition for the Greek repatriated *homogenis from the ex-Soviet Union and naturalisation of homogenis residing abroad; increase of legal residence to 10 years during the last 12 years or 5 years after the naturalisation application.*
15 June 1995	Law 2307/1995 (Official Gazette	Transfer to the Prefects of the

Date	Document	Content of change
	A'113)	authority to issue Acts for the definition of the Greek nationality (Art. 9, para. 1).
30 May 1997	Law 2503/1997 (Official Gazette A'107)	Naturalisation of spouses of Greek nationals. Exemption from the generally applicable rule of 10 years in the country (Art. 14, para.2).
22 October 1998	Law 2647/1998 (Official Gazette A' 237)	Transfer to the Secretary General of the Region of the authority to issue acts for the definition of the Greek nationality (Art. 1, para.1a) (Circular 69381/4396/6.2.1999).
25 June 1998	Law 2623/1998 (Official Gazette A' 139)	Abolition of art. 19 of the Greek National Code on withdrawal of the Greek nationality (Art. 9, para.14).
16 February 2000	Law 2790/2000 (Official Gazette A' 24) on the reinstatement of the situation of repatriated homogenis from the ex-Soviet Union.	Specific commissions providing opinion on the Greek origin of the homogenis; special *Homogenis identity card from ex-Soviet Union.*
2 May 2001	Law 2910/2001 (Official Gazette A' 91, 27.4) on the entry and residence of foreigners in the Greek territory.	Introduction of a fee of 1467 euros for the application for naturalisation; Abolition of transitory character of the Law 1438/1984. Regulation on gender equality as to reacquisition of nationality by women who had lost her nationality due to wedding Abolition of the prerequisite of five-year period of legal residence in the country after the naturalisation application is submitted.
1 May 2002	Law 3013/2002 (Official Gazette A' 102)	Abolition of the naturalisation fee for *homogenis; reacquisition of Greek nationality for a child born by a Greek mother who lost nationality due to recognition by a foreign father.*
24 December 2003	3207/2003 (Official Gazette A' 302)	Five years of residence for the naturalisation of athletes of the Olympic Greek national team (Art. 8, para. 13).
10 November 2004	Greek Nationality Code: Law 3284/ 2004 (Official Gazette A' 217)	Three years of legal residence in the country before the naturalisation application for the spouses of Greek nationals. Abolition of art. 32 of the Legislative Decree 3370/1955 which recognised as Greek

Date	Document	Content of change
		nationals, individuals registered in the Greek Consulates' records of the United Arab Republic till 1947.

Notes

1 Even earlier, as it is mentioned in the relevant chapter, in the so-called Revolutionary Constitutions of the 1820s.

2 See Ministry of the Interior, Circular 412, 19 December 1960 on the 'meaning of the terms *homogenis* and *allogenis* within the Greek Code of Nationality'. Forty years later, in another circular from the Ministry of the Interior providing relevant guidelines to the authorities with regard to the application of a new law, it is stated that a *homogenis* foreigner is 'a person not having the Greek nationality but, on the contrary, belongs to the Greek nation. In other words, it has to do with a foreigner with links to the Greek nation, in terms of language, religion, common tradition, and customs. All these criteria define someone as homogenis' (94345/14612/3-5-2001).

3 See retrospectively art. 4, para. 3 of the Constitution 1975-86-01, 7, para. 2 of the Constitution of 1968, 3 of the Constitution of 1952, 4 of the draft Constitution of 1958, 6 of the Constitution of 1927, 5 of the Constitution 1925, 3 of the Constitutions 1991 and 1864, where reference is made to the 'qualifications' of Greek citizens set out by the laws.

4 Sect. B 'On the General Rights of the residents of the Greek Territory', para. b: 'The indigenous residents of the Greek Territory that believe in Jesus Christ are Greek, and enjoy all political rights [...].' Para. d. 'The people coming from out of the country's borders residing or sojourning in the Greek territory are equal to the autochthonous residents before the law.' Para. e. 'The Administration has to be concerned with the issuance of a law on naturalisation of foreigners that desire to become Greek.'

5 Symbolically enfeebled, since the term 'residents of Greek territory' of the title of the relevant sect. B of the Constitution of 1822 was replaced by the term 'Greeks' in 1823.

6 A transitional provision sets out that a Greek is whoever has acquired nationality in line with the prior systems. It refers expressly to the acquisition of nationality by philhellenes, while from then on the law focuses on the father's nationality (Georgiadou 1941: 9).

7 Peace treaty between Greece and the Ottoman Empire of 22 November 1897, which was ratified by the law BΦIE' on 6 December 1897, Official Gazette, Issue no 181, 6 December 1897, p. 497.

8 Treaty between Greece and the Ottoman Empire of 1/14 November 1913, which has been ratified by the Law 79, Official Gazette, Issue no 229, 14 November 1913, p. 809.

9 14/27 November 1919, which has been ratified by the Law 2433, Official Gazette, Issue no 162, 23 July 1920, p. 1615. The treaty provides for the compulsory automatic acquisition of the Greek nationality by the Bulgarian citizens who were settled in Western Thrace before 1913. In that way, the *ipso jure* acquisition of nationality concerned exclusively the former Ottoman subjects of the annexed part who had acquired the Bulgarian nationality under the Treaty of Istanbul, in 1913. The Bulgarians that had settled in the region following 1913 were allowed to acquire the Greek nationality, though only upon the Greek government's authorisation.

10 Decision No 22 of 9 May 1924 of the Mixed Committee of the League of Nations. In this way the emigrants that visited Greece were treated as Greek on the part of the administration, so that their enlistment was ascertained. The situation ended in 1940, when, in terms of the related Mandatory Law 2280, their foreign nationality was retroactively recognised.

11 13 October 1926, ratified by the Law 3655 on 13 October 1928.

12 Art. 5 of the Decree of 12 August 1927 'on ratification and amendment of the Legislative Decree of 13/15 September 1926 'on amendment of provisions of the Civil Law'.

13 See art. 105, para. 1 of the Constitution in force.

14 See art. 17, para. 1,b of the Code of Greek Nationality.

15 The Italian citizens that were residing in Dodecanese on 10 June 1940 and their children that have been born subsequently acquire *ex lege* the Greek nationality, in accordance with a law (517/1948), which was issued for the implementation of the Paris Treaty between the Allies and Italy.

16 As already mentioned, in the course of rather unpredictable years for a newly-established state, even the Constitution of Trisina of 1827 had provided for the loss of nationality. Art. 29 thereof stipulates that 'any autochthonous or naturalised Greek residing in the Greek territory and enjoying citizen's rights, who prefers to resort to the protection of a foreign force, ceases to be Greek citizen'.

17 As a rule, loss and withdrawal of Greek nationality (regulated by the art. 17-21 of the Code of Greek Nationality) is incurred due to the acquisition of a foreign nationality and the express intent of the person, due to the assumption of service in a foreign state or due to adoption by a foreigner. It is of importance, though, to underline that even the expressed intention to renounce the Greek nationality, where the person has been naturalised abroad without prior authorisation, does not bind the Minister of the Interior to withdraw nationality.

18 Decree of 12 August 1927 on the ratification and amendment of the Legislative Decree 'on amendment of provisions of the Civil Law', 13/15 September 1926.

19 The transitional provision 111, para. 6 provided for the article being in force until its abolishment by law.

20 The target group of the legislation on the withdrawal of nationality from *allogenis* belonging to minority groups was gradually being differentiated: in the first stage, the main victims of withdrawal of nationality were ethnic Macedonians. In the following, and mainly due to the shrinking of the Greek minority of Istanbul and the invasion of the Turkish armament in Cyprus, the measure targeted the Turkish minority of Thrace.

21 Mandatory Law 2280/1940 (extensively in: Kostopoulos 2003: 56).

22 The term 'unworthiness' appears in the Law 580/1943 during the occupation period and is, in a very particular way, maintained in force after liberation, by virtue of a decision of the Ministerial Council in 1946.

23 By art. 1 of the Legislative Decree 4234/23.7.1962 'on regulation of issues concerning the country's safety'.

24 In line with art. 20, para. 2 of that time (currently 17) of the Code of Greek Nationality.

25 See art. 1 of the Constitutional Act /67 of the Constitutional Act of the regime 'on withdrawal of nationality of the persons acting in an anti-national way and on the confiscation of their property'.

26 Art. 10 of the Constitutional Act of 5/8-7/8/1974.

27 Art. 4, para.3, al. 2b of the Constitution. The norm implementing the constitutional provision is found in art. 17 (till 2004, art. 20) of the Nationality Code.

28 By art. 9 of the Law 1540/1985 'on regulation of the properties of political refugees'.

29 Joint Decision 106841/1983 of the Ministers of Interior and Public Order on 'Free repatriation and granting of Greek nationality to political refugees', in accordance with which 'all Greeks – by *genos* – who had fled abroad as political refugees in the course of the Civil War 1946-1949 and because of it, may freely return to Greece, even if their nationality had been withdrawn.'

30 By art. 9 of the Law 2623/98. Given that the abolition of art. 19 had no retroactive impact, the procedure for the re-acquisition of Greek nationality falls under the procedure for the naturalisation of *allogenis*.

31 According to a non-registered document of the Ministry of the Interior, Public Administration and Decentralisation addressed to the National Commission for Human Rights, dated 18 June 2003.

32 The Ministerial Council, after the fall of the colonels' regime, according to a decision classified as 'Top Secret' 'Issuing of special passports of *homogenis* to non-Greek citizens from Turkey and North Ipirus Act No 22, 1/3/1976' has affirmed that 'taking into consideration: that many *homogenis* that have been deprived of their ordinary passports [by the countries of origin] meet abroad insurmountable difficulties for their transfer, residence and right to work; that their naturalisation is not possible and that the passport does not always constitute full proof of citizenship, but refutable presumption of citizenship, decides: to provide Greek passports, the acquisition of which does not attribute the Greek citizenship: ... (a) to the *homogenis* from Turkey deprived of their Turkish citizenship. (b) The *homogenis* from Turkey residing in Greece more than five years without Turkish passport'. The difficulties encountered by any stateless citizen abroad seem absolutely reasonable. However, the Greek lawmakers realised that the naturalisation of these persons was not possible. At the same time they provided them with a Greek passport, which did not grant them Greek nationality. This attitude generated questions, at first sight. The well-known passport of the *homogenis* of Turkey and Albania (O.T.A.) established a third category of people who move between the status of citizen and the status of foreigner or stateless person. In line with the same Ministerial Decision, *homogenis* from Albania were subject to the same status, as well. However, the prerequisite of non-possession of the Albanian nationality did not exist for them, for the Albanian regime never used the measure of withdrawal of nationality en masse, as the Greek or the Turkish ones did.

33 General Order 212 of the Ministry of the Interior, dated 20 October 1978, on 'Regularisation of nationality of the Tsigans residing in Greece'. See also the General Order 81 of the abovementioned ministry, dated 12 March 1979.

34 Pursuant to art. 1 para. 2 of the Code of Greek Nationality, according to which: 'The Greek nationality is acquired at birth by any person that is born on the Greek territory, if this one does not acquire at birth a foreign nationality or is of unknown nationality.'

35 According to art. 127 of the Civil Code, as amended by the Law 1329/1983.

36 By art. 32 of the Law 2130.

37 By art. 12, para. 2 of the Law 2503.

38 See art. 5, para. 2a of the Law 3284.

39 By art. 58 of the Law 2910/2001.

40 A year later, *homogenis* are exempted from the obligation to pay the naturalisation fee, under an amending provision (by the art. 21, para. 3 of the Law 3013/2002).

41 Pursuant to art. 4, para. 4 of the recent Civil Servants Code (Law 2683/1999) 'whoever acquires the Greek nationality by naturalisation, may be appointed as a civil servant only one year following acquisition'. In the specific case, the period of one year has replaced the one of five years, which was the rule in the previous Code of 1977. A new restriction, of a three-year period, specifically applies to civil servants at

the Ministry of Foreign Affairs (art. 53 of the Ministry's Regulation), as well as to court clerks (art. 2, para. 2 of the Law 2812/2000). Finally, it is worth mentioning that a provision of 1977 ruling that '*allogenis* that have acquired the Greek nationality may not be appointed as notaries', was abolished in 2000 (art. 19, para. 1 of the Law 2830/2000).

42 By art. 9 of the Law 2623/1998.

43 Art. 4, para. 3 of the Constitution 1975/1986/2001.

44 '*Allogenis* Greek citizens of non-Greek descent are those, whose origin, distant or not, is linked to persons of a different nation; who by their actions and general conduct have expressed sentiments confirming the lack of a Greek national consciousness, in a way [that proves that] they cannot be considered as having assimilated into the Greek nation.' (Decision 57/1981)

45 By art. 9 of the Law 2307.

46 By art. 1 of the Law 2648.

47 In this regard, if the Regional authorities have evidence that the person requesting nationality belongs to certain population groups they forward the file to the competent Directorate of Definition of the Ministry of the Interior.

48 Joint Ministerial Decision 106841/29.12.1982 of the Ministers of the Interior and Public Order.

49 Under Act 621 of the Ministerial Council of 1949, Greeks, Armenians and Jews were losing Greek nationality through the provision of a one-way travel document to Israel and the USSR, after having declared in writing that they did not wish to return to Greece (see Baltsiotis 2004a: 90-92 and Kostopoulos 2003: 55).

50 It should be mentioned that the Nationality Code of Ukraine and Georgia provide for the loss of nationality in case of acquisition of another one.

51 Circular 7914/6330/2.3.2000 of the Ministry of the Interior on 'Acquisition of the Greek nationality by *homogenis* of ex-USSR'.

52 Circular 28700/11333/26.5.1993 of the Ministry of the Interior on 'Notification of provisions of the Law 2130/1993'.

53 According to the census results, 443,550 of the declared 796,713 immigrants are Albanians (Pavlou 2004: 373). Valid estimates show that their number has increased by almost 200,000, reaching one million (Baldwin-Edwards 2005: 4).

54 4000/3/10-/2001.

55 In fact, the Greek state is confronted with an impasse stemming from the incredibly large number of Albanian citizens who have been given the special *homogenis* identity card. As already mentioned, the number of Greek Albanians cannot exceed 100,000 people, even according to the most Greek-oriented statistical assessment (against the 60,000 that Albania recognises). However, the holders of these cards amount, as already mentioned, to double that number. The motives for this policy to provide the *homogenis* identity card to a large number of Christian Orthodox Albanians who have migrated to Greece can be questioned. The only thing certain is that the prospect that these people all acquire Greek nationality causes certain discomfort to the Greek authorities.

56 Until recently, there were people, descendants of Greek minority families from Albania born in the Greek territory during the 1940s, 1950s and 1960s; these people continued to have Albanian nationality, albeit they had no bonds at all with Albania nor had they ever visited it. We refer to the group of persons that has been already examined, the 'quasi-stateless people', according to the aforementioned Ministerial Decision of 1976 (see supra footnote 32). Before the Second World War, the borders between Greece and Albania were open. Many individuals moved from Greece to Albania either due to family bonds or due to professional or other activities. Therefore, at the decisive moment, after the Second World War, they did not expect

the abrupt political decision of the Albanian government to close the borders with Greece. As a result, a not insignificant group of people was blockaded in Albania. They only managed to leave for the first time in 1990. A similar thing has happened in reverse, for many members of the Greek minority of Albania that have been blockaded in Greece. These people have only started to acquire Greek nationality in 1999. Until then, they had been subordinated to the particular status of semi-citizenship, in accordance with the Secret Ministerial Decision of 1976.

57 It should be mentioned that proof of a person's Greek origin is sufficient for Greek law. National consciousness is not examined at all, as normally applies to other cases of *homogenis*; this confirms overtly the flexible nature of the quality of *homogenis*, which has been already analysed.

58 See art. 31 of the Code. The ordinary deadline provided for by the Code of Administrative Procedure (L. art. 5, para. 4 of Law 2690/1999) is sixty days.

59 The excuse for this is 'work pressure'. On this matter we would like to draw attention to the relevant circular of the Ministry of the Interior according to which 'the obligation of the public service to respond to the applicants within the time laid down by law, is not valid when it concerns issues related to Greek nationality. The necessity of such a regulation is obvious, since much more time is required for investigation and collection of data related to such cases in order to be in position to evaluate the applications.' See Circular .32089/10641, 26 May 1993 'Notification of provisions of the Law 2130/1993 on amendments of the articles of the Code of Greek Nationality and instructions for their implementation'.

60 Such judicial decisions concern mainly the undue implementation of the former art. 19 of the Code of Greek Nationality (Kostopoulos 2003: 64). A recent decision of the Council of State is worth mentioning (603/2003). This one revokes nationality withdrawal from individuals that were not notified in due time. The act of nationality withdrawal was revoked based on the principle of the so-called 'protected confidence' of citizens by the administration. The grounds were that the administration was, for example, not permitted to surprise an individual who had lived for thirteen years believing he was a Greek national by birth.

61 'Certainly, regarding uncomplicated nationality issues, when there is no need for investigation and when the civil servant has all the documents needed, the acts of the administration will be immediate, the applicant will be informed in due time and there will be no abuse of the provision in question'. Circular of the Ministry of the Interior /102744/2709, 28 January 2005.

62 24755/6.4.1990.

63 See art. 11 and 12 of the Mandatory Law 2280/1940.

64 By art. 23 of L. 2130/1993.

65 As stressed before, the pejorative term widely used for the nationality acquisitions of Pontian Greeks is the one of 'hellenopoiissis' i.e., 'made Greek'.

66 Hellenic League for Human Rights, Press Release 12/2000 on the occasion of the adoption of the new legislation on migration. See www.hlhr.gr.

67 The Code was voted against by the two political parties on the left, the Communist Party and the Left Coalition, their MPs expressing serious objections particularly regarding the naturalisation fees of 1,500 euros as well as the generally strict preconditions of the naturalisation procedure. None of them, however, contested the fundamental regulatory categories and concepts of the Greek nationality law, such as the preferential treatment of *homogenis*, etc.

68 That has been the case for a considerable number of muslims in the newborn Greek State in the nineteenth century: In order to acquire Greek nationality and reside in Greece, they converted to Christianity.

Bibliography

Alivizatos, N. (1979), *Les Institutions Politiques à Travers les Crises 1922-1974*. Paris: Librairie Générale de Droit et Jurisprudence.

Alivizatos, N. (2005), 'Keynote speech', paper presented at the conference 'History and juncture of the Greek nationality' organised by the Hellenic League for Human Rights, Athens, 16 February 2005.

Anagnostou, D. (2005), 'Deepening Democracy or Defending the Nation? The Europeanisation of Minority Rights and Greek Citizenship', *West European Politics* 28 (2): 335-357.

Argiros, A. (1996), *The Legal Regime of Home-comers*. Athens: National Foundation for the Rehabilitation of Homogenis and of Greeks Abroad [in Greek].

Baldwin-Edwards, M. (2005), *Statistical Data on Immigrants in Greece*. Athens: Mediterranean Migration Observatory.

Baltsiotis, L. (2004a), 'Nationality in the Cold War', in D. Christopoulos & M. Tsapogas (eds.), *1953-2003: Human Right's in Greece from the End of the Civil War till the End of the Change of Regime*', 81-98. Athens: Kastanioti publishing [in Greek].

Baltsiotis, L. (2004b), 'Nationality and Naturalisation in Greece of Migration', in D. Christopoulos & M. Pavlou (eds.), *Greece of Migration*, 303-337. Athens: Kritiki publishing [in Greek].

Bauböck, R. (1994), 'Changing the Boundaries of Citizenship. The Inclusion of Immigrants in Democratic Polities', in R. Bauböck (ed.), *From Aliens to Citizens – Redefining the Status of Immigrants in Europe*, 199-232. Aldershot: Avebury.

Centre of Planning and Economic Research (KEPE) (1978), *The population of Greece: Evolutions and assessments*, report of the Population Committee. Athens.

Christopoulos, D. (2004a), 'Nationality in the Era of Migration', in D. Christopoulos & M. Tsapogas (eds.), *1953-2003: Human Rights in Greece from the End of the Civil War till the End of the Change of Regime*', 99-109. Athens: Kastanioti publishing [in Greek].

Christopoulos, D. (2004b), 'Migrants in the Greek Political Community', in D. Christopoulos & M. Pavlou (eds.), *Greece of Migration*, 338-366. Athens: Kritiki publishing [in Greek].

Christopoulos D. & C. Tsitselikis (eds.) (2003a), *The Greek Minority of Albania*. Athens: Kritiki publishing [in Greek].

Christopoulos D. & C. Tsitselikis (2003b), 'Impasses in the Treatment of Minorities and Homogenis in Greece', *Jahrbücher für Geschichte und Kultur Südosteuropas* 5: 81-93.

Dimakis, I. (1991), *The Regime Change of 1843 and the Issue of Autochthonous and Eterochthonous Populations*. Athens: Themelio publishing [in Greek].

Dimoulis, D. (2001), 'Zwischen Frankreich und Deutschland. Volk, Staatsangehörigkeit und Staatsbürger im Griechischen Öffentlich-Rechtlichen Denken des 19. Jahrhunderts', in G. Kassimatis & M. Stolleis (eds.), *Verfassungsgeschichte und Staatsrechtslehre. Griechisch-deutsche Wechselwirkungen*, 87-137. Frankfurt: Klostermann.

Georgiadou, I. (1941), *The Greek Nationality*. Athens [in Greek].

Grammenos, S. (2003), *The Law of Greek Nationality*. Athens: Karanastasi publishing [in Greek].

Gropas R. & A. Triantafyllidou, 'Active civic participation of Immigrants, Greece', Country Report prepared for the project POLITIS funded by the European Commission, DG Research, *Key Action Improving the Socio Economic Knowledge Base* (unpublished).

Kokkinos, G. (1997), 'The Greek Constitutions and Nationality (1844-1927)', *Mnimon* 19: 78-89 [in Greek].

Kostopoulos, T. (2000), *The Forbidden Language*. Athens: Black List publishing [in Greek].

Kostopoulos, T. (2003), 'Nationality Withdrawals: the Dark Side of Modern Greek History', *Synchrona Themata* 83: 53-75 [in Greek].

Liakos, A. (2002), 'Identitta e Cittadinanza nella Grecia Moderna' in C. Sorba (ed.), *Cittadinanza. Individui, Diritti Sociali, Collettivita nella Storia Contemporanea*, 63-79. Rome: Publicazione degli Archivi di Stato.

Michailides, I. (2003), *Displacements of Slav-speaking populations (1912-1930). The war of statistics*. Athens: Kritiki Publishing [in Greek].

Ministry of Macedonia-Thrace (2000), *The Identity of Home-comers: Homogenis from the ex-Soviet Union*. Thessaloniki [in Greek].

Pantelis, A., S. Koutsoubinas & T. Gerozissis (eds.) (1993), *Texts of Constitutional History*, volume I. Athens: A. Sakkoulas publications [in Greek].

Papassiopi-Passia, Z. (2004), *Law of Nationality*. Thessaloniki: Sakkoulas publications [in Greek].

Pavlou, M. (2002), 'Greek State Policy from "Irredentism" to "Home-coming/Immigration": The Case of two Repatriated Kin Minority Groups', in European Commission for Democracy through Law (ed.), *The Protection of Minorities by their Kin-state*, 195-208. Strasbourg: Council of Europe publishing.

Pavlou, M. (2004), 'Annex', in D. Christopoulos & M. Pavlou (eds.), *Greece of Migration*, 367-402. Athens: Kritiki Publishing [in Greek].

Seferiades G. (1928), 'L'Échange de Populations', *Recueil des Cours de l'Académie de Droit International* 4: 307-439.

Sitaropoulos, N. (2004), 'Freedom of Movement and the Rights to a Nationality v. Ethnic Minorities: The Case of ex Article 19 of the Code of Greek Nationality', *European Journal of Migration and Law* 6: 205-223.

Soysal, Y. N. (1996), 'Changing Citizenship in Europe. Remarks on Postnational Membership and the National State', in D. Cesarani & M. Fulbrook (eds.), *Citizenship, Nationality and Migration in Europe*, 17-29. London: Routledge.

Stavros, S. (1996), 'Citizenship and the Protection of Minorities' in: K. Feather Stone & K. Yfantis (eds.), *Europe in Change – Greece in a Changing Europe*, 117-128. Manchester: Manchester University Press.

The Greek Ombudsman (1999), *Annual Report 1998*. Athens: National Printing House (also available under: www.synigoros.gr).

Tsioukas, G. (2005), 'Homogeneia and Nationality', *Synchrona Themata* 91: 32-38 [in Greek].

Tsitselikis, K. (2004), *Citizenship in Greece: Present Challenges for Future Changes*. www.kemo.gr.

Wallerstein, I. (2003), 'Citizens All? Citizens Some! The Making of the Citizen', *Comparative Studies in Society and History* 45 (4): 650-679.

8 Ireland

John Handoll

8.1 Introduction

Seen from the Irish constitutional perspective, persons born in the island of Ireland – whether in the 26 counties of Ireland or the six counties in the North (potentially part of a united Ireland) – to a parent who is an Irish citizen or entitled to become one, have the entitlement and birthright to be part of the Irish nation. This entitlement is also enjoyed by those otherwise qualified in accordance with law to be Irish citizens.

Since the establishment of the Irish Free State in 1922, Irish nationality policy and law has had to address the mechanisms of protracted divorce proceedings with Great Britain and its Empire/Commonwealth and the more intractable problems of partition, with Unionists in the North declining the route of a united Ireland in favour of continued membership of the six counties in the United Kingdom. Full ius soli citizenship for persons born in the six counties – albeit subject to a declaratory procedure – was introduced in 1956, and (albeit qualified in 2004) retained – initially as a constitutional entitlement of *all* persons born on the island of Ireland – as a crucial part of the British-Irish Agreement in 1998.

Following a 1998 constitutional amendment, persons born on the island of Ireland who had, or were entitled to, another nationality would become Irish citizens as from birth when they had done something that only an Irish citizen was entitled to do, such as applying for an Irish passport. This was principally designed to secure the right of people born in Northern Ireland, which is part of the United Kingdom, to take up Irish citizenship if they so wished, though it also originally applied to all those born on the island of Ireland (with a declaratory procedure introduced for children of diplomats and those born on Irish ships and aircraft). In order to avoid statelessness, a person born on the island of Ireland will, where he or she is not entitled to the citizenship of any other country, be an Irish citizen from birth.

In recent years, Ireland – at long last recognising its potential as the 'Celtic Tiger' – has become a country of immigration, attracting not only large numbers of expatriate Irish citizens and regular migrants for employment from other European states and third countries, but also asylum seekers and unlawfully-resident migrants. Fears, whether justified or not, that persons without a long-term connection with Ireland were seeking long-term residence rights with their Irish-born citizen children resulted in 2004 in a constitutional change restricting the constitutional ius soli entitlement to persons born in Ireland with at least one parent having, or entitled to have, Irish citizenship. In constitutional terms, the ius soli principle was subjected to the overriding ius sanguinis principle. Under legislation in force since the beginning of 2005, where a person is born on the island of Ireland to non-national parents (as defined), ius soli citizenship as from birth will be available only if a parent has been resident in the island of Ireland for three of the four years immediately preceding the person's birth. This residence condition will not apply where the Irish-born child is born to a British citizen or to a person with no restriction on residence in Ireland or Northern Ireland. There is no ius soli entitlement to citizenship for a child born in the island of Ireland one of whose parents was at that time entitled to diplomatic immunity in the State.

Persons born on the island of Ireland to an Irish citizen parent possess citizenship as from birth by virtue of their Irish descent. The relationship between the principles of ius soli and ius sanguinis is complex and, perhaps deliberately, ambiguous. Certainly as far as those born in the South are concerned, the dominant principle, reinforced by the recent constitutional change, has become that of ius sanguinis (for most, there is no question of having to do an act that only an Irish citizen can do). As far as the North is concerned, the principle of consent gives a certain priority to the ius soli principle, though those of a republican tradition can freely claim to be citizens by descent.

As a country of historic emigration, Ireland has had to address questions of the nationality status of those born outside the island. The ius sanguinis principle has been employed to give the children born abroad of an Irish citizen, himself or herself born in the island of Ireland, an automatic right of citizenship by descent. Where the Irish citizen parent has been born outside the island of Ireland, registration of birth is required (save where the parent is abroad in the public service): citizenship by descent may then be enjoyed, by registration, from generation to generation.

The ius sanguinis principle also applies to foundlings who are presumed, unless the contrary is proved, to have been born in the island of Ireland to at least one Irish citizen parent.

Ireland operated a system of post-nuptial citizenship by declaration for spouses of Irish citizens until its abolition in 2001, subject to transitional provisions which were to come to an end in November 2005.

This has been replaced by specific provisions on the naturalisation of spouses of Irish citizens.

Irish nationality may also be obtained by means of naturalisation at the absolute (though not entirely unlimited) discretion of the Minister for Justice, Equality and Law Reform. In addition to a general category of non-nationals who may apply for Irish citizenship through naturalisation, specific rules apply to the naturalisation of spouses of Irish citizens (replacing the previous system of post-nuptial citizenship by declaration), minor children of naturalised Irish citizens, persons of Irish descent or associations, refugees, stateless persons and persons who are or have been resident abroad on public service. It should be noted that the existence of the 'Irish Diaspora' has also led to a privileged naturalisation regime for those of 'Irish descent or Irish associations', though the operation of a controversial investment-based naturalisation regime based on 'Irish associations' has resulted in a very restrictive legislative definition of 'Irish associations' limited to family relations. The Irish President may grant citizenship as a token of honour to a person, or a child or grandparent of such person, who has done signal honour or rendered distinguished service to the nation.

A person granted a certificate of naturalisation is not required to give up any existing nationality (though the subsequent acquisition of another citizenship by a voluntary act other than marriage entitles the Minister to revoke the certificate, this clearly does not apply to a pre-existing other citizenship).

It should also be noted that where an adoption order is made, an adopted child who is not already an Irish citizen shall be one where the adopter, or one of the spouses of an adopting married couple, is an Irish citizen.

Nationality may be lost on grounds of renunciation. Nationality obtained through naturalisation may also be lost on grounds of: permanent residence abroad; voluntary acquisition (other than by marriage) of another nationality; failure in duty of fidelity to the nation and loyalty to the State; the possession of citizenship of a country at war with the State; or the provision of false information in procuring naturalisation. It is only the last ground that is likely to apply in the ordinary course of events. The fact of permanent residence abroad or the voluntary acquisition of another nationality are not easy to identify in the absence of effective registration and tracking procedures and no revocations on these grounds have been made, at least in recent times.

Citizenship will be taken never to have existed where a foundling first found in the State is subsequently found not to qualify for Irish nationality.

As seen above, the Irish-born children of British citizens enjoy the unconditional right of ius soli citizenship under 2004 legislation, in contrast to the Irish-born children of other non-nationals.

British citizens also enjoy the right to vote (but not to stand) in elections to the *Dáil* (the lower chamber of the National Parliament). This resulted from a constitutional change in 1984, to ensure that British citizens in Ireland were granted similar rights to those enjoyed by Irish citizens in the UK. The Electoral (Amendment) Act 1985 thus granted national level rights to British citizens and provided a mechanism (which has so far not been exercised) for granting rights to citizens of other EU Member States on a reciprocal basis.

It should also be noted that British citizens are not treated as 'non-nationals' for the purposes of immigration controls. There is no apparent legal basis for their expulsion.

8.2 Historical development

This section describes the main constitutional and legislative changes in Irish nationality law since the inception of the Irish Free State (*Saorstát Eireann*) in 1922.

In summary, the 1922 Constitution of the Irish Free State adopted a system of citizenship conferring citizenship on particular categories of persons domiciled within the jurisdiction of the Irish Free State at the time the Constitution came into operation and provided that the later acquisition and termination of citizenship was to be determined by law. For reasons largely associated with the relationship with British and other Commonwealth systems of citizenship, Irish nationality legislation was adopted only in 1935, with a minor amendment in relation to registration requirements in 1937.

The Irish Free State was succeeded by Ireland in December 1937. The 1937 Constitution conferred citizenship on citizens of the Irish Free State, with the entitlement of other persons to be determined by legislation. The 1935 Act remained in operation until 1956, when the Irish Nationality and Citizenship Act was passed. The 1956 Act, which forms the basis for current nationality legislation, was amended in 1986, partly to secure gender equality in post-nuptial citizenship arrangements, and in 1994, in relation to the registration of births outside Ireland.

In 1998, following the conclusion of the Good Friday Agreement, the Constitution was amended to make it clear that all those born in the island of Ireland had the entitlement and birthright to be citizens of Ireland. The recognition that persons born in Northern Ireland should be free to choose to become Irish citizens was reflected in changes made by 2001 legislation, which also replaced the declaratory post-nuptial citizenship regime with a naturalisation regime.

A perhaps unintended consequence of the liberal application of the ius soli rule to birth in the island of Ireland emerged with the increase of immigration into Ireland. Unlawfully resident migrants sought, initially with some success, rights of residence based on their relationship to Irish citizen children. An unknown number of heavily pregnant non-nationals arrived at points of entry into the State, shortly afterwards giving birth to Irish citizen children (a number regrettably died in the process). The *Chen* case (Judgement of 19 October 2004, not yet reported), decided by the European Court of Justice, addressed the question of the free movement rights of a child born of Chinese parents in Northern Ireland (and hence entitled to ius soli Irish citizenship) and her Chinese-national mother and made it clear that Irish citizen children born in the North and their carer parents could, where self-sufficient, enjoy rights of free movement in the UK. Such concerns, which many thought exaggerated or misplaced, resulted in an amendment to the Constitution in 2004 removing the *constitutional* entitlement to citizenship of those born in the island of Ireland where neither parent is an Irish citizen or entitled to be so. Subsequent legislation which came into effect on 1 January 2005 introduced a residence requirement to be satisfied by certain non-national parents before children born in the island of Ireland can benefit from ius soli citizenship and, amongst other changes, permits the naturalisation of minors and tightens up the conditions under which naturalisation can be granted on the basis of Irish associations.

8.2.1 Nationality and the Irish Free State

Although strong feelings of Irish nationhood clearly existed long before the establishment of the Irish Free State (*Saorstát Eireann*) in 1922, nationality law of the entire island of Ireland prior to that date was that of England and the United Kingdom (Parry 1957: 925).

Underpinning the fight for independence, there was a strong sentiment of an indigenous Irish people, whose 'sovereign and indefeasible' right to 'the ownership of Ireland and to the unfettered control of Irish destinies', had been usurped by a foreign people and government (1916 Proclamation of the Irish Republic). Those at the vanguard of the 1916 Rising saw nationhood as a tradition received from the dead generations of Irishmen and Irishwomen: Ireland's children – and by extension the children of these dead generations – were summoned, unsuccessfully for a while, to the flag.

The 1921 Anglo-Irish Treaty provided that Ireland should have the same constitutional status in the 'Community of Nations known as the

British Empire' as Canada, Australia, New Zealand and South Africa. It would thus have been open to it to follow the approach elsewhere in the Empire, with an overarching British subjecthood and the introduction of a local citizenship with purely domestic significance (Daly 2001: 378). Instead, the Irish Free State adopted a scheme of 'citizenship' (Parry 1957: 925), which put it on a problematic footing in relation to British nationality law, in particular concerning the relationship with the Six Counties of the North which had opted to remain in the Union.

Art. 3 of the Constitution of the Irish Free State (*Saorstát Eireann*) provided that: 'Every person, without distinction of sex, domiciled in the area of the jurisdiction of the Irish Free State (Saorstát Eireann) at the time of the coming into operation of this Constitution, who was born in Ireland or either of whose parents was born in Ireland or who has been ordinarily resident in the area of the jurisdiction of the Irish Free State (Saorstát Eireann) for not less than seven years, is a citizen of the Irish Free State (Saorstát Eireann) and shall within the limits of the jurisdiction of the Irish Free State (Saorstát Eireann) enjoy the privileges and be subject to the obligations of such citizenship: Provided that any such person being a citizen of another State may elect not to accept the citizenship hereby conferred; and the conditions governing the future acquisition and termination of citizenship in the Irish Free State (Saorstát Eireann) shall be determined by law.'

Art. 3 addressed the question of the Irish Free State's 'stock' of citizens at the time of its establishment. The territorial extent of the Irish Free State, within which these citizens had to be domiciled at the time the Constitution came into operation, was not defined in the article. The predominant view at the time appears to have been that Northern Ireland was not included (Ryan 2003: 148), so that there was no question of Northern Unionists having Irish Free State citizenship. However, in a 1933 judgement of one of the lower courts, it was held that, at the time of the coming into force of the Constitution, all of Ireland fell within the 'area of jurisdiction' of the Irish Free State.[1] Persons domiciled in that part of Ireland – the 'Six Counties' – that very shortly afterwards decided to remain as part of the UK were, for the purposes of Irish law, therefore treated as citizens of the Irish Free State. The privileges and obligations of Irish Free State citizenship could therefore be enjoyed by those in the North who wished it. It was not, in any practical way, foisted on those who did not: even if the possibility of electing out of citizenship applied to those domiciled in the North (Parry 1957: 926), there does not seem to have been a formal procedure for making such an election.

Legislation on the conditions governing the future acquisition and termination of acquisition was adopted only in 1935.

Supplementing art. 3 of the Constitution, the Irish Nationality and Citizenship Act 1935 recognised as 'natural-born' citizens those born in the Irish Free State on or after 6 December 1922 and those born outside the State after that date, whose fathers were, at the time of such birth, citizens of the Irish Free State. A registration requirement was imposed for those born on or after the passing of the Act (10 April 1935) outside the Irish Free State of a father himself born outside the Irish Free State (including in Northern Ireland) or a naturalised citizen. Persons born before 6 December 1922 in Ireland, or of parents born in Ireland, and not covered by art. 3 of the Constitution, would be deemed natural-born citizens upon taking up permanent residence in the Irish Free State or, if permanently resident outside the Irish Free State and not naturalised citizens of another country, upon registration.

There were detailed provisions on naturalisation, granted by the Minister 'at his absolute discretion', subject to compliance with conditions such as age, mental capacity, good character and periods of residence. Special provision was made in relation to naturalisation of a person, or a child or grandchild of a person, who had done signal honour or rendered distinguished service to the Irish nation, as well as of a minor with Irish descent or Irish associations. Certificates of naturalisation were to state the names of non-citizen children under the age of 21, who were – subject to the possibility of making a declaration of alienage on attaining that age – to enjoy the status of natural-born citizens. The Minister enjoyed absolute discretion to revoke a certificate of naturalisation in the case of fraud or misrepresentation, later criminal behaviour, absence of good character at the time of issue, ordinary residence outside the Irish Free State for a continuous period of more than seven years 'without maintaining substantial connection with' the Irish Free State or where the person concerned was a citizen of a country at war with the Irish Free State.

There were detailed provisions on post-nuptial citizenship. In certain cases, a citizen married to an alien would, where ordinarily resident outside the Irish Free State, lose his or her citizenship unless he or she lodged a declaration or election to retain such citizenship as his or her post-nuptial citizenship. In relation to aliens married to citizens, the ordinary residence condition for naturalisation was modified: a male alien could be naturalised on the basis of two years' ordinary residence in the Irish Free State, whilst a female alien was not required to satisfy any residence requirement.

In relation to loss of citizenship, it was provided that, in general, a citizen of the Irish Free State would lose his citizenship where, after reaching the age of 21, he became a citizen of another state. Those becoming a citizen of another state at birth or during his minority could make a declaration of alienage upon reaching the age of 21, unless such other citizenship had been previously lost.

An important provision, now largely of only historical significance, addressed the question of mutual citizenship rights between the Irish Free State and other countries.

The Act provided for the keeping of a 'foreign births entry book' in legations and consulates, as well as a 'Northern Ireland births register' and a 'foreign births register', in which to register the birth of a child outside the territory of the Irish Free State whose father was, on the day of such birth, a citizen of the Irish Free State. Provision was also made for the keeping of registers of nationals, to contain generally the names of persons temporarily or permanently resident outside the Irish Free State as well as the names of those whose right to be deemed a natural-born citizen of the Irish Free State was conditional on such registration.

Provision was made for the issue of certificates of nationality to any person who was a citizen, other than a naturalised citizen, of the Irish Free State.

The rupture with British nationality law was seen in provisions of the Act which repealed British nationality legislation, if and to the extent that it was or was ever in force in the Irish Free State. The same applied to the common law relating to British nationality. The possibility of imperial naturalisation was also excluded.

It was, finally, stated that every citizen of the Irish Free State, whether by virtue of art. 3 of the Constitution or under the Act, 'shall be such citizen for all purposes, municipal and international'.

8.2.2 The Irish Nationality and Citizenship Act 1956

8.2.2.1 The constitutional framework

The Irish Nationality and Citizenship Act 1956 (the '1956 Act'), amended in 1986, 1994, 2001 and the end of 2004, sets out the detailed legislative framework for Irish citizenship. It should be seen within the framework of arts. 2, 3 and 9 of the 1937 Irish Constitution, which has been amended in material respects in 1998 and 2004.

Art. 9 of the 1937 Constitution as originally worded provided:

'1.1° On the coming into operation of this Constitution any person who was a citizen of Saorstát Éireann immediately before the coming into operation of this Constitution shall become and be a citizen of Ireland.

2° The future acquisition and loss of Irish nationality and citizenship shall be determined in accordance with law.

3° No person may be excluded from Irish nationality and citizenship by reason of the sex of such person.'

From the inception of the 1937 Constitution, art. 2 stated that the 'national territory consists of the whole island of Ireland, its islands and the territorial seas'. In turn, art. 3 provided: 'Pending the reintegration of the national territory, and without prejudice to the right of the Parliament and Government established by this Constitution to exercise jurisdiction over the whole of the territory, the laws enacted by that Parliament shall have the like area and extent of application as the laws of Saorstát Éireann and the like territorial effect.'

Concerns that these provisions gave Ireland jurisdiction over Northern Ireland were given some credence by a 1990 Supreme Court judgement holding that art. 3 represented a 'legal claim of right' over Northern Ireland and that arts. 2 and 3 envisaged the 'reintegration of the national territory'.[2]

As will be seen, arts. 2 and 3 were radically recast as a result of the 1998 Good Friday Agreement, and art. 9 was qualified, in relation to the children of non-national parents, in 2004.

8.2.2.2 The 1956 Act

Legislation reflecting the requirements of art. 9.1.2° of the 1937 Constitution was adopted only in 1956, with the delay attributed by the Minister for Justice introducing the Bill to 'the war, and its aftermath, and all the attendant problems'.[3] It should be noted that, whilst the 1937 Constitution represented a clean break with the treaty-based concept of the Irish Free State (which was ostensibly based on the 1921 Anglo-Irish Treaty and which, after a crippling Civil War, the Republican *Fianna Fáil* party (in or out of government) sought progressively to undermine), the Republic was only declared in 1948 and Ireland left the Commonwealth in 1949 after the necessary UK legislation had been passed.

The 1956 Act brought in a number of important changes to the earlier regime. In terms of acquisition by descent, it was recognised that Irish citizenship could be derived from the mother as well as from the father: former concerns about the possession of dual or multiple nationality had decreased and – in relation to persons born abroad – it was 'determined that our nationality law should not be framed to exclude persons [...] who are of Irish stock'.[4]

A broader definition of Irish citizenship by birth included those born in the 'Six Counties' of Northern Ireland, though a person born in the Six Counties if not otherwise an Irish citizen could 'pending the reintegration of national territory' become a citizen from birth only by means of making a declaration of Irish citizenship. This declaratory procedure was intended to cover the 'limited category born in the Six Counties since 1922 who are of entirely alien parentage without any racial ties'.[5] It should be noted that making such a declaration did not have the effect of losing British nationality.

A new procedure of post-nuptial citizenship by declaration was introduced – in place of the former naturalisation requirement – for alien women on marriage to Irish citizens: no waiting period was required. This change, which reflected constitutional provisions relating to the family[6] did not extend to non-national *husbands* of Irish citizens, who had to apply for naturalisation. In practice, husbands of Irish citizens seeking naturalisation were required to reside in Ireland for two years, rather than the usual five years prescribed in the Act. This differential treatment (reflecting the position under the 1935 Act) was not, at the time, generally regarded as discriminatory and there appears to have been little criticism of it. Even 25 years later, a High Court Judge held that 'this diversity of arrangements' did not constitute 'a form of discrimination which is invidious and, therefore, prohibited by the Constitution': instead 'the distinction is more properly regarded as conferring a form of privilege on female aliens rather than being invidiously discriminatory against male aliens'.[7]

In relation to naturalisation, a new requirement that the applicant make a declaration of fidelity to the nation and loyalty to the State was introduced. The scope for granting a certificate of naturalisation on the basis of 'Irish descent or Irish associations' was widened, ostensibly to cover aliens joining the Defence Forces or required to spend part of their working year abroad:[8] however, in anticipation of difficulties which would emerge decades later (see sect. 8.2.5, below), one Deputy – Mr. Moran – suggested that 'if an Arab in Cairo drinks a glass of Irish whiskey it would qualify him for citizenship under this particular provision'.[9]

In relation to revocation of naturalisation, the absolute discretion of the Minister was removed and replaced by a requirement to give notice with reasons of any decision to revoke and to have the matter referred to a Committee of Enquiry upon application by the person concerned.

The provision in the 1935 Act that Irish citizenship should be lost on the voluntary acquisition of another citizenship was not repeated in the 1956 Act, reflecting reduced concerns about the consequences of dual or multiple nationality and the desire for a country of emigration not 'to disown our own flesh and blood'.[10] New provisions were introduced allowing for the voluntary renunciation of Irish citizenship by making a declaration of alienage where the person concerned had acquired, or was about to acquire, another citizenship.

8.2.2.3 *The 1986 amendments*

Reflecting international developments,[11] developments in other EC Member States and different attitudes in Ireland itself,[12] the Irish Nationality and Citizenship Act 1986 eliminated the different treatment of female and male spouses of Irish citizens in the obtaining of a declaration of post-nuptial citizenship. Sect. 8 of the 1956 Act was amended to cover both sexes, allowing men to make such a declaration. However, apparently reflecting concerns about 'bogus' marriages, the 1986 Act introduced a waiting period of three years before a declaration could be made, applying to non-national spouses of either sex. It was provided that the marriage had to be subsisting at the date of lodgement of the declaration and that the couple were living together as husband and wife. Equality between the sexes was also ensured in amended provisions removing the entitlement of married women under full age to renounce citizenship. Ireland was therefore able to delete the reservation it made to the UN Convention upon accession in December 1985.

The opportunity was taken to make other relatively minor amendments. The requirement to give one year's notice of an intention to apply for a certificate of naturalisation was abolished, on the grounds that it was not necessary and in practice had led to undue delay. Reflecting the desiderata set out in art. 34 of the Geneva Convention, the possibility for the Minister to dispense with the standard conditions for naturalisation was extended to refugees and stateless persons.

Finally, the operative date for citizenship of those citizens of Irish descent registered under sect. 27 of the 1956 Act was specified, with entitlement to citizenship only from the date of registration. This appeared to have been the intent in the 1956 Act, but unclear drafting had led to entitlement being recognised as from birth. This clarifying amendment appears to have been designed to address abuse by persons who had 'no real sense of identity with Ireland but for purposes of convenience decide to establish Irish citizenship in case they would need a second citizenship at a future date'.[13] This provision had the result of depriving the children of those entitled, who had been born before registration, from themselves enjoying an automatic entitlement to Irish citizenship subject to registration.

8.2.2.4 *The 1994 amendment*

The Irish Nationality and Citizenship Act 1986 contained transitional provisions allowing a six-month period, expiring on 31 December 1986, for persons to register under sect. 27 and continue to be entitled to citizenship as from birth. This resulted in a huge volume of applications, especially in Irish consulates in New York and Johannesburg, and it proved impossible to deal with many of these before the statutory deadline. This had the effect of depriving applicants of citizenship from birth even though the failure to meet the deadline was no fault of theirs. The Irish Nationality and Citizenship Act 1994 remedied this problem by providing that those who had applied for registration during the transitional period but had not been registered could be registered under sect. 27 of the 1956 Act and would be deemed to have been registered on 1 July 1986. Persons registered after 31 December 1986 were entitled to re-registration, with such re-registration deemed to have been made on 1 July 1986.

8.2.3 *North-South relations: The Good Friday Agreement and its consequences*

After the Nineteenth Amendment of the Constitution Act 1998, the new art. 2 of the Constitution provided: 'It is the entitlement and birthright of every person born in the island of Ireland, which includes its islands and seas, to be part of the Irish nation. That is also the entitlement of all persons otherwise qualified in accordance with law to be citizens of Ireland. Furthermore, the Irish nation cherishes its special affinity with people of Irish ancestry living abroad who share its cultural identity and heritage.'

Art. 3 of the Constitution was also replaced, with the new art. 3(1) providing: 'It is the firm will of the Irish nation, in harmony and friendship, to unite all the people who share the territory of the island of Ireland, in all the diversity of their identities and traditions, recognising that a united Ireland shall be brought about only by peaceful means with the consent of a majority of the people, democratically expressed, in both jurisdictions in the island. Until then, the laws enacted by the Parliament established by this Constitution shall have the like area and extent of application as the laws enacted by the Parliament that existed immediately before the coming into operation of this Constitution.'

These changes – described as '[a]rguably the most momentous changes to the Constitution' (Hogan & Whyte 2003: 68), resulted from the 1998 'Good Friday' Agreement, consisting of a Multi-Party Agreement between political parties in the North and a British-Irish Agreement between the UK and Irish Government. In order to secure political settlement in the North, the Irish Government agreed that, subject to a referendum approving the necessary changes, the Irish claim to territorial unity was abandoned. In the words of two eminent commentators on the Constitution, 'the focus of attention in the new provisions shifts from a definition of national territory to an attempt to define the nation by reference to its people' (Hogan & Whyte 2003: 71).

Art. 1(vi) of the British-Irish Agreement is of particular importance to Irish nationality policy, providing: 'The birthright of all the people of Northern Ireland to identify themselves and be accepted as Irish or British, or both, as they may so choose, and accordingly confirm that their right to hold both British and Irish citizenship is accepted by both Governments and would not be affected by any future change in the status of Northern Ireland.'

The term 'the people of Northern Ireland' was defined in the Annex as meaning 'all persons born in Northern Ireland and having, at the time of their birth, at least one parent who is a British citizen, an Irish citizen or is otherwise entitled to reside in Northern Ireland without any restriction on their period of residence'.

8.2.4 The 2001 amendments

The Irish Nationality and Citizenship Act 2001 replaced sects. 6 and 7 of the 1956 Act to reflect the changes following the Good Friday Agreement. It also replaced the system of post-nuptial declaration of citizenship for spouses of Irish citizens with special provisions for the naturalisation of such spouses. The opportunity was also taken to make a number of other changes in relation to the reckoning of periods of residence for the purposes of naturalisation (which had previously been addressed only by administrative practice), and the maintenance of the foreign births entry books and the central register. Last, but not least, the term 'alien' was replaced by the more human-sounding 'non-national' to describe all those who were not Irish citizens.

In relation to ius soli citizenship, the attribution of Irish citizenship from birth to 'every person born in Ireland' was replaced by a provision stating that '[e]very person born in the island of Ireland is entitled to be an Irish citizen'. The definition of 'Ireland' in the old legislation was replaced by the statement that 'a reference to the island of Ireland includes a reference to its islands and seas'. This approach was designed to respect the position of those in the North who did not wish to exercise that entitlement[14] as established in the British-Irish Agreement. In general, the entitlement could be evidenced by the doing of 'any act which only an Irish citizen is entitled to do', such as applying for an Irish passport or being registered to vote in Irish presidential elections.[15] It was no longer necessary for those born in the North to show their Irish parentage or, in the case of non-national parents, to make a declaration of citizenship. As a hostage to later fortune, the Irish legislature failed to limit the entitlement to citizenship of those born in the North to those with a parent who was British or Irish or otherwise entitled to reside there without restriction (a limitation which would have been consistent with the British-Irish Agreement).

For those who would otherwise be stateless, it was provided that a person born in the island of Ireland was an Irish citizen from birth where he or she was not entitled to the citizenship of any other country.

The new constitutional entitlement of persons born in the island of Ireland to be part of the Irish nation required the ending of exceptions to the application of the ius soli rule for children born to non-nationals entitled to diplomatic immunity in the State and to a non-national on a foreign ship or in a foreign aircraft. Such children would be Irish citizens upon declaration. Former Irish citizens, who had been born in the island of Ireland, who had made a declaration of alienage were to remain entitled to Irish citizenship and could by declaration take up citizenship from the date of such declaration.

In relation to ius sanguinis citizenship, a new and rather clearer provision essentially restated the existing law, but made it clear that the fact that a parent born in the island of Ireland had not at the time of a child's birth done an act that only an Irish citizen was entitled to do did not of itself exclude the child from the entitlement of ius sanguinis citizenship. Citizenship by descent could thus be claimed even where the parent entitled to be an Irish citizen had not obtained such citizenship by doing an act that only an Irish citizen could do.

The system of post-nuptial declaration by non-national spouses of Irish citizens was, subject to transitional provisions which lasted until November 2004, replaced by a naturalisation regime, stated to be in the 'absolute discretion' of the Minister, which required qualifying periods of residence in the island of Ireland, rather less onerous than those required under the ordinary naturalisation regime. This need for closer links with the island reflected the abuse of the declaratory procedure, with 'paid-for' marriages entered into in order to secure the passport of an EU Member State and the consequent rights of free movement.[16]

8.2.5 *'Passports for sale'*

Sect. 16(a) of the 1956 Act allows the Minister, if he thinks fit, to grant a certificate of naturalisation where the applicant is of Irish descent or Irish associations even where none or only some of the conditions for naturalisation in ordinary cases are not complied with.

In April 1989, the Irish Government approved a number of naturalisations based on investment and, around the same time, introduced an investment-based naturalisation scheme. A Statement of Intent was made available to interested persons setting out the conditions for naturalisation of investors. In 1994, Terms of Reference for an Advisory Group, to advise the Minister on such cases, were drawn up, changing the conditions for naturalisation and creating greater transparency. The scheme was abolished in April 1998, with the Minister for Justice initiating a review of the 1956 Act to see how it might facilitate investment and whether additional legislative measures would be warranted. A non-partisan Review Group was set up, consisting of representatives of various Government Departments, other public bodies and two independent experts from outside the public sector. The Report of the Review Group on Investment-Based Naturalisation was concluded in April 2000, but published only in August 2002: its summary of the operation of the scheme provides the basis for the discussion in this section. It should be noted that the scheme proved highly controversial and the issue has been debated in some detail in parliamentary debates on successive amendments to the 1956 Act. The debate was only laid to (temporary) rest by the 2004 Act, which made it clear that investment-based naturalisation could not be based on the concept of 'Irish associations'.

The Statement of Intent setting out the requirements for an investment-based naturalisation scheme was introduced around April 1989. This does not appear to have been a published document, but was made available to those who asked about the possibilities of such naturalisation. The Statement made it clear that, in applying sect. 16(a) of the 1956 Act, the Minister would regard an investor as having Irish associations and would dispense with the usual residence conditions where the investor had been resident in Ireland for two years, where the applicant had 'established a manufacturing or international services or other acceptable wealth and job-creating project here that is viable and involves a substantial investment by the applicant' and all other requirements of the Act had been complied with. Although no minimum amount of investment was specified, it appears that 500,000 Irish Pounds was usual. Between 1989 and 1994, 66 investors, and 39 spouses and minor children were naturalised on this basis. The Review Group stated that evidence of compliance with the provisions of the Statement 'is absent in many cases'. This conclusion is all the more disturbing since considerable flexibility was given to the Minister to determine whether the two-year residence requirement had been satisfied and whether there had been a 'substantial investment'.

The need for a more formal and transparent approach led to the drawing-up of Terms of Reference of an Advisory Group, advising the Minister on investment-based naturalisation cases, and these were applied to proposals from late-1994. The Terms of Reference required the applicant to purchase a residence in Ireland and retain it for at least five years, reside in Ireland for at least 60 days in the two years after naturalisation and to make an investment involving a net contribution of at least one million Irish Pounds for at least five years (or seven years in the case of a loan). From 1994 to the ending of the scheme,

40 investors, together with 24 spouses and children, were naturalised. It appears that compliance with the Terms of Reference was satisfactory.

In September 1996, the Government decided that no new applications would be accepted, unless and until new legislation was introduced, though existing applications would be dealt with. It appears that some new applications were made and existing ones amended. Finally, in April 1998, the scheme was abolished.

Although the Review Group concluded that 'the scheme had a significant impact on employment often in a context in which a high premium was placed on preserving jobs', it recognised that the scheme had attracted largely negative comment in the *Oireachtas* and the media in relation to individual cases and the whole idea of investment-based naturalisation in the context of the 'contrast between the allegedly unwelcoming attitude of the State to refugees, asylum-seekers and immigrants and its willingness to confer citizenship on wealthy persons who do not wish to reside in Ireland'.

The Review Group concluded that, given the current state of the Irish economy, it was neither appropriate nor necessary to re-introduce an investment-based scheme. A majority believed that the option of introducing such a scheme should be kept open, on a statutory basis and subject to strict rules, should there be a change in the economic or employment situation. An unidentified minority opposed retaining this option, partly on the grounds that such a scheme had not been introduced in other countries with developed economies. The Minister agreed with the majority conclusion, stating that *Oireachtas* approval would have to be obtained and making it plain that he had no plans to reintroduce such a scheme in the foreseeable future.[17] The Government followed this approach.

Despite the ending of the scheme and the assurances that it would not be reintroduced, it was felt that a loophole remained in the legislation, which would enable individuals to be naturalised on the basis of investment, or on the basis of a new scheme, based on the 'escape clause' of 'Irish associations'. In 2003, the Irish Nationality and Citizenship and Ministers and Secretaries (Amendment) Bill was introduced to close the loophole by requiring all applicants for investment-based naturalisation to satisfy the qualifying conditions in full. This Bill was withdrawn with the passing of the 2004 Act.

The Review Group had made it clear that it would be legally questionable to use the 'Irish associations' provision in sect. 16 of the 1956 Act as the basis for such a scheme since it was 'not clear that the link formed with the country [...] is sufficient to constitute Irish associations within the meaning of that section'. The possibility of re-employing sect. 16(i) was removed by an amendment made by the 2004 Act, which, going far further than was necessary to avoid the re-emergence of an investment-based naturalisation scheme, limited the claim of 'Irish associations' to 'persons related by blood, affinity or adoption' to a person who is, or was at the time of death, an Irish citizen or entitled to be an Irish citizen.

8.3 Recent developments and current institutional arrangements

8.3.1 Main general modes of acquisition and loss of citizenship

8.3.1.1 Political analysis

In June 2004, a Bill to amend art. 9 of the Constitution was passed by the people in a referendum. The resulting 27th Amendment of the Constitution Act was designed to remove the *constitutional* right to entitlement to Irish citizenship of persons born in the island of Ireland after the date of enactment of the Act who do not have, at the time of birth, at least one parent who is an Irish citizen or entitled to be an Irish citizen. Such persons are to be entitled to Irish citizenship only as provided by law.

The Government put forward the proposal for constitutional amendment to end the 'abuse' which permitted 'somebody with no real connections to Ireland, North or South to arrange affairs so as to give birth to a child in Ireland, North or South': it was pointed out that '[n]o other country in the world has a situation where citizenship can be acquired through this most tenuous of links with the country of citizenship and which carries with it such a wide range of free movement and other options for the citizen'.[18]

In the course of a rather acrimonious debate it had been argued that there was a considerable degree of 'citizen tourism', with non-nationals unlawfully resident in Ireland claiming residence rights on the basis of the birth of Irish citizen children and women in advanced stages of pregnancy coming to Ireland to give birth. This state of affairs had been encouraged by a generous reading of the 1990 judgment of the Supreme Court in the *Fajujonu* case,[19] where it was recognised that, where non-national parents had resided in Ireland for an appreciable time and had become a family unit together with children born in the State, the parents might be entitled to remain in Ireland by virtue of the residence rights of their Irish national children.

For a number of years after the *Fajujonu* case, non-national parents of Irish-born children were in practice permitted to remain, without much consideration of the circumstances in individual cases. In time, this approach was criticised by the Minister for Justice and others insofar as it appeared to give irregular migrants, failed asylum-seekers and persons whose application for asylum fell to be dealt with by another

Member State carte blanche to remain in Ireland where Irish-born children were involved. A more rigorous approach was taken by the Minister and endorsed by the Supreme Court in January 2003,[20] where a majority of the Court held that the constitutional right of the Irish citizen child to the company, care and parentage of his or her non-national parent was not absolute and unqualified, but rather had to be seen in the light of the Minister's obligation to consider whether there were grave and substantial reasons associated with the common good which required the deportation of the non-national parents (such as the fact of illegal residence). The majority judgments in the case – which recognised that the right of a child to the company of his or her parents could, where necessary, be enjoyed outside the State – led to a distinction being drawn between Irish citizen children of certain third-country nationals and Irish citizen children with at least one Irish citizen parent, with the latter enjoying unqualified rights of residence in Ireland with the company of their parent – the proposed constitutional amendment would clearly remove the *constitutional* basis for such an invidious distinction. There were, of course, strong alternative views that non-citizen parents should not be deported where this limited the full citizenship rights of their Irish citizen children and that the solution did not lie in limiting access to Irish citizenship but rather in accepting the consequences of existing citizenship rules for a relatively small number of persons. Even after constitutional amendment, such arguments continued to be advanced in the debate on the 2004 Irish Nationality and Citizenship Bill.

It also became relevant that, in May 2004, Advocate General Tizzano had delivered his Opinion in the *Chen* case, concluding that a child of non-national parents born in Northern Ireland and hence entitled to Irish citizenship and enjoying, through her parents, sufficient resources to ensure that she would not become a burden on the finances of the host state, was entitled as a matter of Community law to reside in Northern Ireland. The need to give that right useful effect, as well as the prohibition of discrimination on grounds of nationality in art. 12 of the EC Treaty, entitled the non-national mother to a long-term residence permit. It was, to say the least, potentially embarrassing to the Irish Government to retain a citizenship regime, with such Community law consequences in another Member State, especially where the right to the company of a parent had been rejected in Irish law. Indeed, as the Advocate General pointed out: '[i]n order to avoid such situations, the criterion [used by the Irish legislation for granting nationality] could have been moderated by the addition of a condition of settled residence of the parent within the territory of Ireland'.

In an Interpretative Declaration issued by the UK and Irish Governments in April 2004, the two Governments gave the legal interpretation that it was not their intention in making the 1998 Agreement that it should impose on either Government any obligation to impose citizenship on persons born in any part of the island of Ireland whose parents did not have sufficient connection with the island of Ireland. They therefore declared that the proposal to amend art. 9 accorded with the intention of the two Governments in making the 1998 Agreement and that the proposed change was not a breach of the Agreement or the continuing obligation of good faith in its implementation.

The June 2004 constitutional amendment represented for the persons concerned a return to the *status quo ante* the 1998 constitutional amendment reflecting the British-Irish Agreement. Any entitlement is dependent on legislation, rather than constitutional prescription.

8.3.1.2 *Acquisition of Irish citizenship*

The Irish Nationality and Citizenship Act 2004, signed into law on 15 December 2004, entered into effect on 1 January 2005. Prior to that date, all persons born on the island of Ireland, including those who had lost their *constitutional* entitlement in June 2004, were entitled to ius soli citizenship under sect. 6(1) of the 1956 Act. From 1 January, this right was made subject to special parental residence conditions applicable to a residual category of persons born of non-national parents, which are discussed below. It should be noted that persons born to a non-national *in Ireland* on a foreign ship or in a foreign aircraft are no longer able to exercise an entitlement to citizenship by declaration but are subject to the regime generally applicable to those born in Ireland.

The 2004 Act also introduced a number of other changes.

In relation to ius soli citizenship, it was provided that a person suffering from a mental incapacity would be able to have somebody do on his or her behalf any act that only an Irish citizen is entitled to do. The entitlement to Irish citizenship of a child of persons with a parent having diplomatic immunity in the State was limited to children of an Irish or British citizen, or of a parent entitled to reside in the State or in Northern Ireland without any restriction on his or her period of residence. The position of foundlings has been clarified by making it clear that a newborn child first found in the State will be deemed to have been born in the island of Ireland to parents at least one of whom is an Irish citizen, thus removing the risk of application of the rules relating to children of non-nationals. It was also made clear that a person born in an Irish ship or an Irish aircraft would be deemed to be born in the island of Ireland, remedying a drafting omission in the 2001 Act.

In relation to citizenship by descent, a provision in the 1956 Act which provided for the citizenship of a child born after the death of his father who was on the date of his death an Irish citizen, and which clearly offended against the principle of gender equality, was repealed, apparently on the basis that such an entitlement on a gender-neutral basis already existed in sect. 7 of the 1956 Act as amended in 2001.

In relation to naturalisation, the 1956 Act was amended to allow a minor born in the State to apply for naturalisation, with the application in fact made by the parent or guardian of, or a person *in loco parentis* to, that minor.

For the naturalisation of spouses of Irish citizens, an obvious anomaly was removed by providing that the requirement to intend to reside in Ireland after naturalisation did not apply to spouses of Irish citizens residing abroad in the public service. Such applicants were also to be able to count periods of residence outside Ireland in reckoning qualifying periods of residence.

In relation to the more flexible naturalisation regime available to applicants of 'Irish associations', it was provided that such associations would exist only in the case of a relationship 'by blood, affinity or adoption' to an Irish citizen or a person entitled to be an Irish citizen.

Provisions on reckoning the period of residence in relation to applications for naturalisation continued to exclude periods of unlawful residence, of education and study, and for the purposes of seeking asylum. They were amended to take account of provisions in the Immigration Act 2004 and changes in refugee law. In relation to the form of application for naturalisation, a provision penalising the making or giving of false or misleading information was repealed, but replaced by a more general provision on offences (see sect. 8.3.2.2).

Provisions on the obtaining of certificates of nationality have been supplemented by a provision enabling the Minister to revoke a certificate if satisfied that it was obtained by fraud, misrepresentation, or failure to disclose material information. The wording is similar, but not identical, to that applying to the power to revoke certificates of naturalisation.

Finally, the 1956 Act was amended by a provision penalising the knowing or reckless making of a declaration under the Act, or of a statement for the purposes of any application under the Act, which is false or misleading in any respect.

The Irish Nationality and Citizenship Act 1956 as it stands on 1 January 2005 prescribes three main modes for the acquisition of Irish citizenship: acquisition by ius sanguinis, acquisition by ius soli and naturalisation. Although the first of these is relatively straightforward, the position in relation to ius soli acquisition and naturalisation has become more complex over time and especially after the coming into force of the Irish Nationality and Citizenship Act 2004.

Applying the ius sanguinis principle, a person is an Irish citizen from birth if at the time of birth either parent was an Irish citizen or would, if alive, have been an Irish citizen (sect. 7 of the 1956 Act). This has become the primary basis for acquisition of most people born in Ireland since 2001 and for many in the North as well. This mode of acquisition, described as 'citizenship by descent', applies even where the parent concerned is at the time a person entitled to Irish citizenship but has not yet become one because he or she had not yet done an act that only an Irish citizen is entitled to do. Where the person concerned and the parent(s) from whom citizenship is derived were born outside the island of Ireland, conferment of Irish citizenship on the person concerned is conditional on registration of the person's birth under sect. 27 of the 1956 Act or on the parent being abroad in the public service at the time of the person's birth. Entitlement to Irish nationality amongst the 'Irish diaspora' can thus continue from generation to generation, provided that the chain is not broken by a failure to register.

The provision that every deserted newborn child first found in the State shall, unless the contrary is proved, be deemed to have been born in the island of Ireland to parents at least one of whom is an Irish citizen (sect. 10 of the 1956 Act), suggests that foundlings enjoy a form of ius sanguinis citizenship. Although many states may regard foundling citizenship conceptually as a variant of ius soli citizenship, this cannot be the case in Ireland, where ius soli citizenship is an entitlement which requires an affirming act to be done before it can be claimed.

The application of the ius soli principle has been somewhat complicated by the desire following the Good Friday Agreement to assure an entitlement to citizenship to all persons born in the island of Ireland, whether in the State or in Northern Ireland, which has now been qualified in relation to Irish-born children of third-country nationals having no real connection (on the basis of insufficient residence) with the island of Ireland.

On its face, ius soli citizenship applies to all persons born on the island of Ireland, subject to the above qualification. Though this is not explicitly stated in the constitution, or the legislation, it seems clear that ius sanguinis citizenship predominates over ius soli citizenship, so that those with ius sanguinis are Irish citizens without the need to do an act that only an Irish citizen is entitled to do. On this basis, it seems that ius sanguinis citizenship would predominate for births in Ireland and for significant numbers of births within the 'nationalist community' in the North. Ius soli citizenship, involving an entitlement which may or may not be exercised, is clearly relevant for those who are not of Irish descent and, paradoxically, for those in the North who would emphatically not see themselves as Irish and never do an act that only an Irish citizen is entitled to do.

A number of different categories of person enjoy ius soli citizenship subject to various conditions:

A. A person born in the island of Ireland who is not entitled to citizenship of any other country (and therefore would otherwise be stateless);
B A person born in the island of Ireland to parents at least one of whom was at the time of the person's birth a British citizen or a person entitled to reside in Northern Ireland without any restriction on his or her period of residence;
C. A person born in the island of Ireland to parents at least one of whom was at the time of the person's birth a person entitled to reside in the State without any restriction on his or her period of residence;
D. A person born on the island of Ireland where at least one parent is entitled to diplomatic immunity in the State, where at least one parent was at the time of birth an Irish citizen or entitled to be one, a British citizen or a person entitled to reside in the State or in Northern Ireland without any restriction on period of residence;
E. A person born in the island of Ireland who has made a declaration of alienage under sect. 21 of the Act; *and*
F. A person born on the island of Ireland on or after 1 January 2005, who does not qualify under A and is born of parents falling within a residual class of non-nationals not falling under B or C.

The 'island of Ireland' is not defined in the Act, but it is made clear that a reference to the island of Ireland includes a reference to its islands and seas (sect. 2(2) of the 1956 Act). A person born in an Irish ship or an Irish aircraft wherever it may be is deemed to be born in the island of Ireland (sect. 13 of the 1956 Act).

It should be noted that, in relation to categories B, C and D, the ius soli right will arise where the parent in question has died before the birth of the person concerned, provided that the parent has at the time of death the requisite nationality, entitlement to nationality or long-term resident status.

All persons falling within categories A to E are entitled without further conditions to be Irish citizens (sect. 6(1) of the 1956 Act).

Persons born in the island of Ireland who are not entitled to citizenship of any other country (category A) are citizens as from birth (sect. 6(3) of the 1956 Act). This applies to persons who would otherwise be stateless and the acquisition of Irish citizenship from birth is automatic.

A person born in the island of Ireland to a British citizen parent or to a (non-Irish citizen or British citizen) parent entitled to reside in Northern Ireland or the State without restriction on period of residence (categories B and C) will have ius soli citizenship from birth if he or she does any act that only an Irish citizen is entitled to do, or, if a minor or mentally incapable, such an act has been done on his or her behalf. There is no requirement that the parent has satisfied a minimum period of residence requirement. It is made clear that the fact that a person born in the island of Ireland has not, or has not done on his or her behalf, an act that only a citizen can do should not of itself give rise to a presumption that the person concerned is not an Irish citizen or is a citizen of another country.

A person born in the island of Ireland with at least one parent at that time entitled to diplomatic immunity in the State is entitled to ius soli citizenship only where at least one parent was at the time of birth an Irish citizen or entitled to be one, a British citizen or a person entitled to reside in the State or in Northern Ireland without any restriction on period of residence (category D).

Specific rules apply to a person born in the island of Ireland who has made a declaration of alienage under sect. 21 of the 1956 Act (category E). Such a person shall remain entitled to be an Irish citizen but shall not be one unless, in the prescribed manner he or she declares that he or she is an Irish citizen: such a person is an Irish citizen from the date of the declaration, rather than from birth (sect. 6(5) of the 1956 Act).

A person born in the island of Ireland *after 1 January 2005* of parents falling within a residual class of non-nationals (category G) is entitled to be an Irish citizen only if a parent of that person has, during the four years immediately preceding the person's birth, been resident in the island of Ireland for a period of three years, or periods the aggregate of which is not less than three years (sect. 6A(1) of the 1956 Act). There are specific provisions on establishing such residence.

Where a parent dies before the child's birth, the period between the former's death and the latter's birth is to be counted for the purposes of calculating a period of residence in the island of Ireland where the parent was, immediately before death, residing in the island of Ireland *and* the period of residence before death is reckonable for the purposes of sect. 6A (sect. 6B(1) of the 1956 Act).

Nationals of EU Member States (save the UK), other EEA Member States and the Swiss Confederation will, on making a statutory declaration of residence in Ireland for a stated period, be regarded as having been so resident unless the contrary is proved (sect. 6B(2) of the 1956 Act). A declaration of residence by such EU, EEA and Swiss nationals may also be made by a guardian (or person in *loco parentis*) of a minor child, by an authorised representative of a child suffering from a mental incapacity or by the child him- or herself upon reaching the age of eighteen (sect. 6B(3) of the 1956 Act). Such declarations are to be accompanied by such verifying documents (if any) as may be prescribed (sect. 6B(6) of the 1956 Act).

Periods of residence in the State are not to be reckonable in calculating a period of residence under sect. 6A where the non-national does not have permission to be in the State under sect. 5(1) of the Immigration Act 2004, where it accords with permission under sect. 4 of that Act to be in the State for education or study or where the non-national is entitled to remain in the State only as an asylum-seeker (sect. 6B(4) of the 1956 Act). Periods of residence in Northern Ireland will not be reckonable if the person concerned is not, during the entire period, a national of an EU Member State, another EEA State or the Swiss Confederation *and* residence in Northern Ireland during that period is not lawful under the law of Northern Ireland (sect. 6B(5)(a) of the 1956 Act). It will also not be reckonable where the same or similar conditions as set out in sect. 6B(4) in respect of reckoning residence in the State apply in Northern Ireland (sect. 6B(5)(b) of the 1956 Act).

Ireland operated a system of post-nuptial citizenship for spouses of Irish citizens until its abolition in 2001, subject to transitional provisions which come to an end in November 2005. This has been replaced by specific provisions on naturalisation of spouses of Irish citizens (see below).

Irish nationality may be conferred on a non-national by means of a certificate of naturalisation granted by the Minister for Justice, Equality and Law Reform (sect. 14 of the 1956 Act). All such grants are stated to be in the absolute discretion of the Minister. Specific sets of conditions for the issue of a certificate of naturalisation are set out for the general class of applicants (sect. 15 of the 1956 Act) and for spouses of Irish citizens (sect. 15A of the 1956 Act). The Minister is empowered to dispense with such conditions in relation to persons of Irish descent or associations, minor children of naturalised Irish citizens, persons who are or have been resident abroad in the public service, refugees or stateless persons.

The 1956 Act makes it clear that all person granted a certificate of naturalisation shall, from the date of issue and as long as the certificate remains unrevoked, be an Irish citizen (sect. 18(1) of the 1956 Act). A certificate is to be in the prescribed form and be issued on payment of the prescribed fee: notice of its issue is to be published in the *Iris Oifigiúil* (sect. 18(2) of the 1956 Act).

In relation to the general class of applicants, the Minister may, in his absolute discretion, grant a certificate of naturalisation if satisfied that the applicant satisfies a number of conditions for naturalisation (sect. 15 of the 1956 Act). The applicant must be of full age or, following the 2004 Act, be a minor born in the State (where the application is by a minor, the term 'applicant' will mean the parent, guardian or person *in loco parentis* to that minor). The applicant must also be of good character. The existence and outcome of criminal and civil proceedings against the applicant in Ireland or elsewhere must be disclosed and any such information – especially in the case of other than minor criminal offences – will be taken into account in the exercise of the Minister's discretion. Whilst questions of bankruptcy or heavy indebtedness have not in practice gone to the issue of good character, the Minister has frequently exercised his discretion in refusing an application on grounds of long-term dependence on the social welfare system. The applicant must have had one-year's continuous residence in the State immediately before the date of application and, during the eight years before that one-year period, must have had a total residence in the State amounting to four years. The applicant must intend in good faith to continue to reside in the State after naturalisation and must make (usually before a District Court Justice in open court) 'a declaration of fidelity to the nation and loyalty to the State'. It should be added that there are no requirements of linguistic competence or knowledge about Ireland.

In relation to non-national spouses of Irish citizens, the Minister may, in his absolute discretion, grant a certificate of naturalisation if satisfied that the applicant satisfies a number of conditions for naturalisation (sect. 15A of the 1956 Act). The applicant must be of full age (that is, over eighteen years) and of good character. Given the relative novelty of the regime, no real practice on 'good character' has yet developed, but it is thought that much the same approach would be taken as for naturalisation in general. He or she must have been married to the citizen for not less than three years, in a marriage recognised as subsisting under Irish law. The couple must be living together as husband and wife, and the citizen must submit an affidavit to that effect. The applicant must have had one-year's continuous residence in the State immediately before the date of application and, during the four years before that one-year period, must have had a total residence in the State amounting to two years. The applicant must intend to continue to reside in the State after naturalisation and must make (usually before a District Court Justice in open court) 'a declaration of fidelity to the nation and loyalty to the State'. The Minister may, in his or her absolute discretion, waive the conditions in relation to minimum period of marriage, residence in the State and intent to remain in the State 'if satisfied that the applicant would suffer serious consequences in respect of his or her bodily integrity or liberty if not granted Irish citizenship'. Where the applicant's spouse has been in public service, residence outside the island of Ireland is to count towards the required period of residence there and there is no requirement of intent to remain in the State (sect. 15A(3) and (4) of the 1956 Act). There are no requirements in relation to language or knowledge of Ireland.

The Minister enjoys the power, if he thinks fit, to grant an application in a number of cases, even though some or all of the conditions for naturalisation under sect. 15 of the 1956 Act are not complied with.

First, the conditions may be dispensed with where the applicant is of Irish descent or Irish associations, or where the applicant is a parent or guardian acting on behalf of a minor of such descent or associations (sect. 16(a) & (b) of the 1956 Act). The conditions most likely to be dispensed with are those relating to residence and the intent to reside in the State after naturalisation. Following the 2004 Act, a person will be of Irish associations if he or she is related by blood, affinity or adoption to a person who is, or is entitled to be, an Irish citizen, or if he or she was so related to a person who is deceased, who at the time or his or her death was, or was entitled to be an Irish citizen (sect. 16(2) of the 1956 Act). Whilst 'affinity' is not defined in the legislation, the Minister for Justice has asserted that it covers relationships by marriage, embracing the relationship between a spouse and the other spouse's blood relations.[21] A more generous approach than that adopted in sect. 16(2) may have been inspired by reference to art. 2 of the Constitution, stating that 'the Irish nation cherishes its special affinity with people of Irish ancestry living abroad who share its cultural identity and heritage'.

Second, the conditions may be dispensed with where the applicant is a naturalised Irish citizen acting on behalf of his or her minor child.

Third, where the applicant is or has been resident abroad in the public service.

Finally, the statutory conditions for naturalisation may be dispensed with where the applicant is a refugee within the meaning of the 1951 UN Convention and 1967 Protocol or is a stateless person within the meaning of the 1954 UN Convention.

There are provisions on calculating residence in relation to applications for naturalisation (sect. 16A of the 1956 Act). Periods of residence in the State are not to be reckoned where the non-national does not have permission to be in the State under sect. 5(1) of the Immigration Act 2004, where it accords with permission under sect. 4 of that Act to be in the State for education or study or where the non-national is entitled to remain in the State only as an asylum-seeker. This is not to apply to British citizens, as persons to whom the provisions of the Aliens Act 1935 do not apply by virtue of an order made under sect. 10 of that Act.

An application for a certificate of naturalisation is to be in the prescribed form and accompanied by such evidence, including statutory declarations, to support the application as the Minister may require (sect. 17(1) of the 1956 Act).

The Irish President may grant citizenship as a token of honour to a person, or a child or grandparent of such person, who, in the opinion of the Government, has done signal honour or rendered distinguished service to the nation (sect. 12 of the 1956 Act). A certificate of Irish citizenship shall be issued to the person concerned and he or she will be a citizen from the date of the certificate. Notice of issue is to be published as soon as may be in the *Iris Oifigiúil* (the official journal). This mode has benefited foreign sportsmen who have promoted Irish sport, art collectors, philanthropists and foreigners held hostage by terrorists.

Where an adoption order is made, under the Adoption Act 1952, the adopted child who is not already an Irish citizen shall be one where the adopter, or one of the spouses of an adopting married couple, is an Irish citizen (sect. 11 of the 1956 Act).

8.3.1.3 Loss of Irish citizenship

Nationality, however ascribed or acquired, may be lost on grounds of renunciation. Nationality obtained through naturalisation may also be lost on grounds of: permanent residence abroad; voluntary acquisition of another nationality; failure in duty of fidelity to the nation and loyalty to the State; the possession of citizenship of a country at war with the State; or the provision of false information in procuring naturalisation. Citizenship may be lost – or rather it will be taken never to have existed – where a foundling first found in the State is subsequently found not to qualify for Irish nationality.

An Irish citizen of full age who is or is about to become a citizen of another country and for that reason desires to renounce Irish citizenship may, if ordinarily resident outside the State, do so by lodging with the Minister for Justice, Equality and Law Reform a declaration of alienage in the prescribed manner: upon lodgement of such a declaration, or if not at that time a citizen of the other country when he or she becomes one, the individual concerned shall cease to be an Irish citizen (sect. 21(1) of the 1956 Act). In practice, the Department of Justice will, on lodgement, write to the person concerned to advise him or her of the consequences of the action and ask for return of the Irish passport. Such renunciation may not be made, except with the consent of the Minister, during a time of war as defined in sect. 28.3.30 of the Irish Constitution (sect. 21(2) of the 1956 Act).

A certificate of naturalisation may be revoked by the Minister for Justice, Equality and Law Reform where he is satisfied that one of a number of situations has arisen (sect. 19(1) of the 1956 Act). It should be stressed that Irish citizenship acquired by birth cannot be withdrawn.

First, that the issue of the certificate was procured by fraud, misrepresentation (whether innocent or fraudulent), or concealment of material facts or circumstances. No revocations on this ground appear to have been made. However, practice in relation to the previous system of declaratory post-nuptial citizenship suggests that the Minister will be prepared to revoke a naturalisation granted under sect. 15A of the 1956 Act if he comes to believe that the marriage was bigamous or the couple were not at the relevant time living together as a couple.

Second, that the person concerned has, by an overt act, shown him- or herself to have failed in his or her duty of fidelity to the nation and loyalty to the State.

Third, that, save in the case of a certificate issued to a person of Irish descent or associations, the person concerned has been resident outside the State, or in the case of spouses of Irish citizens naturalised under sect. 15A resident outside the island of Ireland, otherwise than in the public service, for a continuous period of seven years *and* without reasonable excuse has not during that period registered annually in the prescribed manner his or her name and a declaration of his or her intention to retain Irish citizenship (with an Irish diplomatic mission or consular office or with the Minister). The form is prescribed by the Irish Nationality and Citizenship Regulations 2002 and partly reflects the condition for naturalisation that the person concerned must intend in good faith to continue to reside in the State. It appears that this mode of loss is of little practical relevance, and no systematic checks on registration seem to be carried out.

Fourth, that the person concerned is also, under the law of a country at war with the State, a citizen of that country.

Finally, that the person concerned has by any voluntary act other than marriage acquired another citizenship. No revocations appear to have occurred in practice. There is no requirement to report acquisition of another citizenship.

The Act contains specific procedural safeguards for persons whose certificates the Minister intends to revoke. Before revocation, the Minister is to give notice in the prescribed form to the person concerned, stating the grounds for revocation and the right of that person to apply to the Minister for an inquiry as to these reasons (sect. 19(2) of the 1956 Act). Where application is made for an inquiry, the Minister is to refer the case to a Committee of Inquiry appointed by him, consisting of a chairman with judicial experience and such other persons as the Minister thinks fit, and the Committee is to report its findings to the Minister (sect. 19(3) of the 1956 Act).

8.3.1.4 *Statistical developments*

It has not proved possible to obtain detailed statistical data on the acquisition of citizenship through naturalisation or post-nuptial declaration. However, details are provided below of the numbers of individuals who have applied for naturalisation since 1985 and of those who have made post-nuptial declarations since 1997.

Table 8.1: Naturalisations, 1985 to 2004

Year	*Applications Received*	*Certificates Issued*	*Applications Refused*
1985	247	253	n/a
1986	378	271	n/a
1987	566	545	n/a
1988	415	333	n/a
1989	272	299	n/a
1990	373	179	n/a
1991	649	188	n/a
1992	474	150	n/a
1993	256	133	n/a
1994	284	175	n/a
1995	296	355	n/a
1996	348	226	n/a
1997	650	294	68
1998	588	352	31
1999	739	416	79
2000	1004	125	57
2001	1431	1012	8
2002	3574	1332	109
2003	3580	1664	179
2004	4074	1335	779

Source: Department of Justice 2005

Table 8.2: Post-Nuptial Declarations, 1985 to 2004

Year	*Declarations Received*	*Declarations Accepted*	*Declarations Refused*
1997	1052	1011	10
1998	1230	1217	5
1999	1242	1022	4
2000	1293	1018	4
2001	1502	1419	6
2002	1978	1485	4
2003	2369	2329	0
2004	2747	2449	1

Source: Department of Justice 2005

8.3.2 *Institutional arrangements*

8.3.2.1 *The legislative process*

The Department of Justice, Equality and Law Reform is the government department in charge of nationality matters.

The Minister is responsible for initiating change, including the sponsoring of bills.

Some basic principles of Irish nationality law are contained in the Irish Constitution. As seen above, certain provisions of the 2001 and 2004 Acts followed constitutional amendments. Proposals for amendment of the Constitution must be submitted by Referendum to the decision of the people (See arts. 46 and 47 of the Constitution), reflecting the people's 'right [...] in final appeal, to decide all questions of national policy, according to the requirements of the common good'.

The Irish Nationality and Citizenship Act 1956, and the 1986, 1994, 2001 and 2004 Acts amending the 1956 Act, are ordinary Acts of the *Oireachtas*, passed or deemed to have been passed by both Houses of the *Oireachtas* and signed and promulgated as law by the President.

It is difficult to give clear indications over time on the position taken by political parties in the legislative debate. This partly reflects the shift in the focus of the debate from 'nation-building', complicated by the desire to reintegrate Northern Ireland into Irish territory, to maintaining the integrity of the State as a state of migration. It also reflects the nature of coalition government, where two or more parties in Government may have to have regard to the policy expectations of coalition partners.

In perhaps overly simplistic terms, there has been a historical divide between those who supported the 1921 Anglo-Irish Treaty, and those who sought a complete break with the UK. This has had some influence on nationality policy and legislation. After a shattering civil war, the pro-Treaty *Cumann na nGaedhal* party (the predecessor of *Fine Gael*) held office between 1922-1933: nationality policy reflected the 1922 Constitution and, despite differences with the UK, continued to visualise Irish Free State citizenship in the overall context of the imperial nationality regime. A more 'independent' approach was taken by the *Fianna Fáil* Government which entered into power in 1932, which was reflected in the 1935 Act and its rupture with British nationality law (though this was accepted on the part of the British only in 1948). This approach continued until and after the 1956 Act, with an inter-party government in power between 1948 and 1957, followed by *Fianna Fáil* governments. In an era of nation-building, there were pronounced differences between the approach of the two main parties – the 'republican' *Fianna Fáil* and the more nuanced 'coexistential' *Fine Gael*. However, by 1998, there was a general (if not quite universal) consensus of parties North and South that the impasse with Northern Ireland should be resolved by means of the mechanisms set out in the Anglo-Irish Agreement.

A new divide has emerged between the current *Fianna Fáil*/Progressive Democrat coalition government, on the one hand, and major opposition parties. The coalition government has adopted an increasingly tough approach to immigration and asylum policy and, in this context, sponsored the 2004 constitutional change removing the constitutional ius soli entitled for children of non-nationals and the 2004 Act. This has been opposed by *Fine Gael*, Labour, the Green Party and *Sinn Fein*, as well as by a wide range of organisations active in the immigrant, refugee and human rights fields.

The High Court and the Supreme Court each enjoy the jurisdiction to determine the validity of any law having regard to the provisions of the Constitution. The constitutionality of Irish nationality law has been considered by the courts only twice, in relation to sect. 8 of the 1956 Act, as it stood before amendment by the 1986 Act, which differentiated between female and male spouses of Irish citizens in relation to a declaratory procedure for the acquisition of citizenship[22] and in relation to sect. 15 and 16 of the 1956 Act,[23] and in neither case were the constitutional claims seriously entertained. It should be noted that there is a presumption of constitutionality for Acts becoming law after the enactment of the 1937 Constitution and a constitutional claim can only be made if it is necessary to the protection of an individual's rights.

As seen above (sect. 8.3.1.1), there have been a number of Irish court cases concerning the right of non-national parents of Irish citizen children to remain in Ireland by virtue of their link with a citizen child. At the EU level, the *Chen* case vindicated the free movement rights of an Irish citizen child born in Northern Ireland, as well as the rights of the Chinese mother.

The Irish cases illustrate the links between immigration and citizenship policies. In the *A.O. & D.L.* case,[24] the majority of the Supreme Court subordinated any right of Irish citizen children to remain in the State with their non-national parents to the need for the Minister to preserve the integrity of and respect for the State's asylum and immigration laws. Although the formal rights of any Irish citizen to reside in the State were not questioned, an Irish citizen child with non-national parents required to leave the State would – if it was sought to maintain the unity family – also have to leave the State. Two minority judgments declined to follow this approach, refusing to recognise that there were no compelling reasons for the State's rights to prevail over those of the child and the family.

8.3.2.2 The process of implementation

The Minister for Justice, Equality and Law Reform enjoys wide powers under the Irish Nationality and Citizenship Act 1956 in relation to naturalisation and, to a lesser extent, the revocation of certificates of naturalisation. There are functional links between immigration and nationality in his Department: policy matters are addressed by the Immigration and Citizenship Policy Unit, whereas operational issues are dealt with by the Immigration and Citizenship (Operations) Division.

Certain tasks – in particular in relation to the registration of foreign births – are performed by the Department of Foreign Affairs and by embassies and consulates abroad.

Ireland is a unitary State. The implementation of nationality law is for the central authorities. No powers in relation to nationality law are granted to local authorities. The absence of statistics on the naturalisation of applicants according to their different groups of origin makes it difficult to comment meaningfully on whether there is a uniform or divergent implementation for such different groups. The author is not aware of ethnic or racial discrimination against any specific group or groups of applicants for naturalisation.

It is a different question whether the constitutional and legislative framework for nationality attribution or acquisition itself distinguishes between different groups. In relation to attribution, the constitutional change in 2004 removed the ius soli entitlement for those without an Irish citizen parent. It is clear that this change resulted from concerns about immigrants coming to Ireland specifically to avail themselves of the possibility of ius soli citizenship for their children: it is less clear that it reflected racial or ethnic discrimination. The 2004 Act conferred ius soli status on children born of British citizens or a non-national without restriction on residence in Ireland or Northern Ireland, without any additional requirement, but imposed a parental residence requirement for children of other non-nationals. Residence requirements are easier to establish in the case of nationals of other EU Member States, EEA Member States and Switzerland.

In relation to naturalisation, the general requirement of prior residence clearly disfavours those who have not been lawfully resident or who have come for purposes of study or to claim asylum. At least in recent years, there have been no outreach programs or the like, either encouraging immigrants in Ireland to naturalise or encouraging members of the Irish Diaspora to retain or reclaim citizenship. In the 1950s – at a time of significant emigration – an annual festival, *An Tóstal* (the Pageant), was introduced. Although it was designed to encourage emigrants and their descendants to visit Ireland (Daly 2001: 403), *An Tóstal* was mainly directed at promoting tourism. Now that Ireland has become a country of immigration, the focus is on attracting the workers that are needed and on tourists. Naturalisation is available and publicised to a certain extent, but it is not actively encouraged.

It is possible to appeal, by way of an application for judicial review, a refusal to grant a certificate of naturalisation, as well as a decision by the Minister to revoke a certificate of nationality.

The fact that a grant is expressed to be within the 'absolute discretion' of the Minister clearly reduces the possibility of successfully seeking judicial review of a decision to refuse a certificate of naturalisation.

It is well established that such an absolute discretion must be exercised in accordance with constitutional justice.[25]

In *Pok Sun Shun v. Ireland*,[26] it was held that, in considering whether to grant a certificate of naturalisation, the Minister was obliged to carry out the rules of natural justice and to adopt fair procedures. The Minister was not obliged to give the applicant a hearing, in the sense of disclosing information on file and giving him an opportunity to comment on it. Nor was he obliged to give reasons for the decision.

In *Mishra v. Minister for Justice*,[27] Kelly J. made it plain that the existence of an absolute discretion meant that the Minister could have regard to considerations of public policy which could have nothing to do with the circumstances of an individual application. Such discretion meant that the Minister did not automatically have to grant a certificate of naturalisation where the applicant had complied with the statutory criteria. The Minister was allowed to guide the implementation of discretion by means of a policy or set of rules, provided that this did not disable the Minister from exercising his discretion in individual cases. However, it was necessary to ensure that the consideration or application of a policy should not produce a result which was fundamentally at variance with the evidence of an applicant. The Minister had a policy of refusing naturalisation to foreign doctors temporarily registered with the Medical Council on the basis that they would leave the State upon naturalisation to work elsewhere on the basis of their newly-acquired citizenship. Since there was no evidence to support the assumption that the applicant would not continue to reside in the State, principles of constitutional justice and fairness required that the applicant be given an opportunity to clarify his position.

Kelly J. also confirmed that there was no obligation under the 1956 Act to give reasons for refusal of a certificate of naturalisation, although he suggested (without further explanation) that there might be circumstances where, even where there was no statutory right of appeal, natural justice or fairness required that reasons should be given.

In a 2003 Decision of the Information Commissioner,[28] the Commissioner decided that the Minister was required, under sect. 18 of the Freedom of Information Acts 1997 and 2003, to give an unsuccessful applicant a statement of reasons for the decision not to grant him or her a certificate of naturalisation. The Minister for Justice did not appeal this decision and appears to have accepted that reasons must now be given to unsuccessful applicants.

There are no known reported cases in relation to revocation, which reflects the fact that the procedure has not been employed, at least in recent times. The Minister enjoys a more limited discretion in this regard, in that he *may* revoke a certificate of naturalisation if satisfied of one of a number of matters and he would be bound (though this is not made completely clear in sect. 19 of the 1956 Act) to take due account of the report of the Committee of Enquiry. The courts would be able to intervene for the same reasons as for refusals to grant certificates of naturalisation.

There have been a couple of cases involving the purported withdrawal by the Minister of acceptance of the declaration of citizenship by spouses of Irish citizens under the former post-nuptial declaratory procedure. It was accepted in *Akram v. Minister of Justice*[29] that the Minister could determine that the lodging of a post-nuptial declaration was ineffective to confer Irish citizenship, on the basis that the marriage was not subsisting or that the couple were not living together. It was, however, necessary for the Minister to comply with the requirements of natural and constitutional justice. In *Kelly v. Ireland*,[30] it was made clear that, where a bigamous marriage was being alleged, the first marriage had to be strictly proved and that the Minister had the burden of proving that the marriage forming the basis for post-nuptial citizenship was a sham.

Mention should finally be made of attempts to prevent the making of false or misleading applications or statements by reinforcing the threat of criminal law sanctions. The 2004 Act repealed the provision prescribing relatively light sanctions which could be imposed by the courts for false or misleading statements or information given in relation to applications for naturalisation and replaced it by a more general provision applying to persons knowingly or recklessly making of a declaration under the Act, or of a statement for the purposes of any application under the Act, which is false or misleading in any respect. Summary conviction in the lower courts can result in a fine of 3,000 euros and/or imprisonment for up to twelve months, whilst more serious breaches resulting in conviction on indictment can result in a 50,000 euro fine and/or a prison sentence of up to five years. The possibility of imposing a five-year prison sentence means that such offences are treated as 'arrestable offences', which enables suspects to be arrested without warrant and questioned for up to 24 hours. If these powers are properly and effectively used, it should be possible significantly to reduce the cases of fraudulent applications.

8.4 Conclusions

Ireland, as an independent State, came into being in the early part of the twentieth century and has been in existence for less than 100 years. It has developed during this period from a State newly broken away from an 'occupying power', to a State that for most of the rest of the twentieth century had a problematic relationship with that power (which still rules over a portion of the island of Ireland) and then to a State that, with membership of the European Union, increasing wealth and a determination to heal the division between North and South, reached an accommodation with its former 'oppressor' and refocused its energies into creating a successful 'Celtic tiger' economy. Becoming a desirable country of immigration, remedying long periods of emigration and depopulation, it has been confronted with challenges of irregular migration and has taken controversial retrograde steps to counter certain of its effects.

Like all attempts to describe such developments in one short paragraph, the above is something of a caricature. Yet, Ireland has changed in fundamental ways during its brief existence and its nationality regime has changed with it. In this concluding section, it is intended briefly to show how changing conceptions of Irish nationality have reflected underlying beliefs in Irish identity and how, in a remarkable respect, a bold revision of the concept of Irish nationality has contributed to a new vision of Irish identity, which has the potential (though sadly not as yet the guarantee) of bridging the sectarian divide in the North of Ireland.

The central importance of the ius soli principle was seen at the inception of the Irish Free State. The new nationality was not limited to those of 'Irish stock', but, subject to a domicile or ordinary residence requirement, was extended to those who had been born, or whose parent had been born, in Ireland. Any other solution would doubtless have led to conflict and increased bloodletting, continuing the earlier troubles. The imminent Civil War was not principally between 'foreign' and 'indigenous' Irishmen and women, but between those who supported the 1921 Anglo-Irish Treaty and those who sought a cleaner break (though other factors doubtless played a part). Ius soli remained central to the definition of Irish nationality under the 1935 Act and, until recently, in the 1956 Act passed under the 1937 Constitution. The principle of ius sanguinis was initially a secondary, albeit important, one enabling those born outside Ireland of Irish parents to claim Irish nationality, in some cases by means of registration.

The issue was complicated by the Irish claim to territorial unity. As far as those born in Northern Ireland were concerned, the 1956 Act as originally drafted, envisaged a ius sanguinis entitlement for those born in the North of one or more Irish citizen parents, with a ius soli entitlement, exercised by means of declaration, to those born 'of entirely alien parentage without any racial ties'. The 1998 Good Friday arrangements, and the subsequent constitutional change, appeared to strengthen the ius soli principle, elevating it to a constitutional entitlement of all persons born on the island of Ireland to be Irish citizens. Such appearances were, however, deceptive. Those born of an Irish citizen parent, including a parent who has not done an act that only an Irish citizen can do, enjoy ius sanguinis citizenship, unqualified in the case of birth on the island of Ireland (whether North or South), but subject to a registration requirement if the child and the parent have both been born outside the island of Ireland. A person born in the North will be able to claim citizenship by descent or elect for ius soli citizenship by acting as only an Irish citizen can. A good number of those born in the North of 'loyalist' parents will not claim by descent and are unlikely to elect to exercise their entitlement: indeed, underlying the idea of such election is that it is the *choice* of the person concerned whether or not the election is made. Behind all the debate on ius soli citizenship, it is not to be forgotten that the ius sanguinis principle is the dominant one and is the basis for citizenship of most people born in the State since 1956, and many espousing the 'nationalist' tradition in the North. This importance has been confirmed, and capped, by the 2004 constitutional amendment.

Ius soli citizenship has also been central to the debate on immigration policy. For much of its existence Ireland was a country of emigration. With greater wealth, and a relatively relaxed immigration regime, Ireland has in recent years been a country of immigration, attracting regular and irregular foreign migrants and a large number of Irish national returnees. A generous application of the ius soli rule and a relaxed (or ineffectual) immigration regime led to increasing unplanned immigration. A possible – but by no means the only – solution was to tighten up the immigration regime and to recast the ius soli rule. In the event, this was just what happened.

The 1998 Good Friday arrangements and consequent changes in Irish nationality law benefited, perhaps unintentionally, increasing numbers of children born, not only in Ireland but also in the North, of foreign nationals, many of whom were irregular migrants. As early as 1990, an important signal had been given to new and would-be migrants by the Supreme Court, which held that the Irish citizen child of non-Irish nationals was constitutionally entitled to the company of his or her parents.

Insofar as this covered unsuccessful asylum seekers, together with those asylum seekers whose claim fell to be heard by another Member State under the Dublin regime, and other migrants in an irregular situation, this situation became increasingly unpalatable. The 1990 judgement was substantially reversed by the Supreme Court in 2003, with the unfortunate result that Irish citizen children of the foreign nationals themselves had a precarious residence status during their minority. This discrimination could only be avoided by removing the entitlement to Irish citizenship of such children born in the future.

Even after the 2003 judgement, heavily pregnant foreign nationals came to Ireland to give birth in the (by now vain) expectation that they would thereby obtain residence. This dilemma was largely resolved by the 2004 constitutional amendment, the consequent legislation subjecting the ius soli entitlement of children born of foreign nationals to a period of residence by the latter and measures taken to enable foreign parents of Irish citizen children to regularise their own residence position.

Although these changes were doubtless ungenerous, and found support from anti-immigrant sections of the population, it would – at least from the perspective of the national State – be wrong to regard them as racist or xenophobic in themselves. In the author's view at least, the Irish State was entitled, in accordance with its own constitutional traditions, to take a more restrictive approach to nationality attribution, and for that matter to strengthen immigration controls. As far as can be judged, nothing it has done is inconsistent with its international law obligations.

It was, nonetheless, regrettable that – as a result of the 2003 Supreme Court judgement – a divide was drawn between Irish citizen children of foreign nationals and citizen children born of Irish and other privileged parents. That divide (resisted by two Supreme Court judges) could have been removed by a courageous government and legislator prepared to tighten up immigration rules for future entrants without removing entitlement to citizenship from a vulnerable segment of Irish society. What happened was more predictable and less courageous. The fact that this represented a backward step, albeit one consistent with a coherent immigration policy, makes one fearful for the future.

It is significant, in this connection, that a trend towards ius soli – which is well suited to the needs of integrating migrants in an increasingly 'free-moving' world – has been qualified by a limitation of the *constitutional* right to ius soli citizenship to those who are Irish citizens by descent. From the constitutional perspective, an Irish identity that was, at the beginning of the State, defined by a link to the land and a conviction that Irish people as thus defined should have, in one way or another, control over Irish destinies, has over the years been replaced by a dominant blood-based conception of Irish identity as far as Ireland is concerned. This tendency, which was somewhat obscured by the constitutional changes following the Good Friday arrangements, was reaffirmed and capped by the constitutional revisions in June 2004.

Chronological table of major developments in Irish nationality law since 1945

Date	Development	Content of change
1956 (July)	Irish Nationality and Citizenship Act 1956	Principal legislative measure on nationality, implementing art. 9 of the Constitution.
1986 (July)	Irish Nationality and Citizenship Act 1986	Amended 1956 Act to remove gender inequality relating to post-nuptial citizenship.
1989	Introduction of Investment Based Naturalisation Scheme	Enabled naturalisation of significant investors on basis of Irish associations.
1994 (May)	Irish Nationality and Citizenship Act 1994	Amended 1956 Act to introduce new provisions on naturalisation of spouses of Irish citizens.
1998 (April)	Good Friday Agreement (UK/ Ireland)	Right of all people of Northern Ireland to be Irish or British, or both.
1998 (May-June)	Referendum and new art. 2 of the Irish Constitution	Entitlement of persons born on the island of Ireland to be part of the Irish nation.
2000 (April)	Report of Review Group on Investment Based Naturalisation	Review of investment-based naturalisation scheme.
2001 (June)	Irish Nationality and Citizenship Act 2001	Amended 1956 Act to introduce citizenship by birth in the island of Ireland. Replaced post-nuptial declaration for spouses with naturalisation regime.
2003 (January)	Supreme Court Judgement in L&O cases.	Denies right of Irish citizen child to have non-national parents remain in Ireland.
2003 (July)	New Government policy on non-national parents of Irish-born children	Initially restrictive policy, but slightly softened over time.
2003 (October)	Irish Nationality and Citizenship and Ministers and Secretaries (Amendment) Bill 2003	Designed to counter abuses of investment-based naturalisation scheme.
2004 (April)	Interpretative Declaration by the Irish and British Governments regarding the British Irish Agreement (4/04)	No obligation under Agreement where parent does not have sufficient connections with Ireland.
2004 (May)	Opinion of Advocate-General in Chen	Irish citizen child born in North and Chinese mother enjoy EU free movement rights.
2004 (June)	Referendum and amended art. 9 of the Irish Constitution	Removed constitutional entitlement to Irish citizenship of child born on the island of Ireland of non-national parents.

Date	Development	Content of change
2004 (October)	Judgement in Chen	Irish citizen child born in North and her Chinese mother enjoy EU free movement rights.
2004 (December)	Irish Nationality and Citizenship Act 2004	Amended 1956 Act to require parental residence requirement for citizenship of children of non-nationals, with specific exceptions.
2004 (December)	Irish Nationality and Citizenship Act 2004 (Commencement) Order 2004	Commenced 2004 Act.
2005 (January)	Irish Nationality and Citizenship Regulations 2005	Forms of declaration for citizenship purposes.
2005 (January)	Notice to non-national parents of Irish-born children, born before 1 January 2005.	Application form for residency.

Notes

1 *Re Logue* (1933) 67 Irish Law Times Reports 253, Circuit Court.
2 *McGimpsey v Ireland* [1990] 1 IR 110.
3 *Dáil Éireann Debates*, vol. 154, 29 February 1956.
4 Minister for Justice, *Dáil Éireann Debates*, vol. 154, 29 February 1956.
5 Ibid.
6 See art. 41 of the Constitution and Minister for Justice, *Dáil Éireann Debates*, vol. 154, 29 February 1956.
7 *Somjee v. Minister for Justice* (1981) Irish Law Reports Monthly 324.
8 Minister for Justice, *Dáil Éireann Debates*, vol. 154, 29 February 1956.
9 *Dáil Éireann Debates*, vol. 154, 29 February 1956.
10 Minister for Justice, *Dáil Éireann Debates*, vol. 154, 29 February 1956.
11 In particular, Resolution (77)12 of the Committee of Ministers of the Council of Europe on the Nationality of Spouses of Different Nationalities and the UN Convention on the Elimination of All Forms of Discrimination Against Women.
12 See Minister for Justice, *Dáil Éireann Debates*, vol. 364, 21 March 1986.
13 Minister for Justice, *Dáil Éireann Debates*, vol. 365, 30 April 1986.
14 Minister for Justice, *Seanad Debates*, 8 December 1999.
15 Ibid.
16 Ibid.
17 Minister of Justice, Press Release, 10 February 2002.
18 Mr. McDowell (Minister for Justice), *Dáil Éireann Debates*, vol. 583, No. 6, 21 April 2004.
19 *Fajujonu v. Minister for Justice* (1990), 2 Irish Reports 151.
20 *A.O. & D.L. v. Minister for Justice* (2003), 1 Irish Reports 1.
21 Minister for Justice, *Dail Debates*, 30 November 2004.
22 *Somjee v. Minister for Justice* (1981), Irish Law Reports Monthly 324.
23 *Pok Sun Shun v. Ireland* (1986), Irish Law Reports Monthly 593.
24 *A.O & D.L. v Minister for Justice* (2003), IR 1.
25 *East Donegal Co-Operative v. Attorney-General* (1970), Irish Reports 317, 341.
26 (1986) Irish Law Reports Monthly 593, High Court.
27 (1996) 1 Irish Reports 189, High Court.

28 Case 020353 – *Mr X and the Department of Justice, Equality and Law Reform.*
29 21 December 1999, High Court, unreported.
30 (1996) 3 Irish Reports 537, High Court.

Bibliography

Bacik, I., W. Binchy, C. Costello, O. Doyle, D. O'Connell & A. Reidy (2004), *The Citizenship Referendum: Implications for the Constitution and Human Rights.* Dublin: The Law School, Trinity College Dublin.

Daly, M. E. (2001), 'Irish Nationality and Citizenship since 1922', *Irish Historical Studies* 32 (127): 377-407.

Hogan, G. (2000), 'The British-Irish Agreement and the Irish Constitution', *European Public Law* 6 (1): 1-11.

Hogan, G.W. & G.F. Whyte (2003), *JM Kelly: The Irish Constitution.* 4th edition. Dublin: Lexis Nexis Butterworths.

O'Grady, J. P. (1989), 'The Irish Free State passport and the question of citizenship, 1921-4', *Irish Historical Studies* 26 (104): 396-405.

Parry, C. (1957), *Nationality and Citizenship Laws of The Commonwealth and The Republic of Ireland.* London: Stevens & Sons.

Ryan, B. (2003), 'The Ian Paisley Question: Irish Citizenship and Northern Ireland', *Dublin University Law Journal* 25: 146-176.

Ryan, B. (2004), 'The Celtic Cubs: The Controversy over Birthright Citizenship in Ireland', *European Journal of Migration and Law* 6: 173-193

9 Italy

Marta Arena, Bruno Nascimbene and Giovanna Zincone[1]

9.1 Introduction

Up to 2006 acquisition of the Italian nationality has been mostly rooted in family relationships. Family is one of the models of citizenship identified by Michael Walzer (1983) in his well-known typology. In the 'family' model, nationality and citizenship are reserved for members belonging to the national community by descent. In the Italian case, family ties in general, not just descent, play the main role as gatekeepers to nationality. *Ius sanguinis* (acquisition by descent) and *ius conubii* (acquisition by marriage) are the cornerstones of the 1992 Act, which represents the main current legislation on the subject. By comparison with prior legislation, especially the 1912 Act, which was previously the main legal instrument governing nationality, the 1992 Act reinforces the criteria inspired by the ius sanguinis principle, introducing a clearer *co-ethnic preference* for foreigners of Italian descent by way of: 1) a special temporary mass programme of reacquisition, and 2) a shorter period of residence in Italy for naturalisation compared to that which is applicable for other aliens. Acquisition by residence (*ius domicilii)* is made more difficult for foreigners of non-Italian descent and those not originating from EU countries; EU nationals are another (though slightly less) privileged category. *Area preference* for EU countries can also be considered a co-ethnic, family-model-oriented preference criterion. The EU is conceived by the legislator as a sort of extended public family which includes not only people of national origin (relatives), but also foreigners linked by special cultural and political elective affinities, and international legal bonds (a kind of in-laws).

Consistent with the family-oriented logic of the 1992 Act, acquisition by ius soli is also made more difficult, with new requirements that were not included in the 1912 Act. *Dual nationality* is definitively allowed by the 1992 Act, also to favour family ties. Since the 1975 and 1983 provisions, inspired by a gender equality principle, marriage to a foreigner has entitled both spouses to combine nationality by descent with nationality by spousal transfer, and to transmit their nationalities to their children.

We will now give a brief overview of these features of current Italian legislation and their impact on the chances of becoming Italian.

Most Italian nationals acquire their nationality by descent. There were only 13,444 naturalisations in 2003, and 11,934 in 2004. In contrast with these very low naturalisation figures, a large number of people of Italian descent living abroad were allowed to reacquire Italian nationality under a special provision included in the 1992 Act. They were 163,756 by the end of 1997.

Under the 1912 Act, Italian nationality could be lost by renunciation or by voluntarily opting to take the nationality of the country of immigration. The 1992 Act opened a window of opportunity for people of Italian descent living abroad who had lost their Italian nationality (or whose ancestors had lost theirs). This opportunity was further extended by postponing the deadline for application and including new categories of ethnic Italians. Furthermore, when Italian nationality is transmitted iure sanguinis, it is virtually impossible to lose it, since Italian legislation does not include expatriation as a cause of loss of citizenship, even after many generations. A large number of latent Italians have applied for an Italian passport, which gives them EU citizenship and entitles them to enter North American countries without a visa.

In addition, Italian expatriates, including those who have reacquired their nationality under the special 1992 provisions, have recently been granted the right to vote to elect their own representatives in special constituencies. The Italian Constitution (art. 51) granted even people of Italian descent not holding Italian nationality future opportunities for political rights: 'As far as admission to public office and elective positions are concerned, the law can equate Italians not belonging to the Republic with citizens'.

The family-oriented model views marriage as the other possible easy route to nationality, as an alternative to descent. In the last few years, about 87 per cent of naturalisations have been accorded by *ius conubii*. Very few requirements have to be complied with to obtain nationality by spousal transfer. Nationality can be acquired after six months of marriage if the couple is residing in Italy, or after three years if the couple lives abroad. This procedure is by entitlement (*beneficio di legge*), i.e., it does not depend on the discretion of the public authorities. The public authorities can only refuse the application if there are serious impediments such as a criminal record or evidence that the marriage is not genuine. The simplicity of this channel explains why this is by far the most common way for a foreigner of non-Italian descent to become an Italian citizen.

It is worth noting that women in Italy, as elsewhere, were granted citizenship before nationality. Art. 3[2] of the Italian Constitution asserted the principle of non-discrimination.[3] Women could then vote, but were still obliged to follow the legal status of their husbands as far as nationality was concerned. This contradiction was eventually resolved. Though in matters of nationality, equality of gender had to wait to gain ground, and to be embodied in International Conventions and Agreements. In Italy, women married to a national of another country were granted the right to retain their nationality in 1975, within the general Family Reform Act (no. 151, 19 May). This change was not due to the need to comply with international law, but to the need to follow the Constitutional Court's Ruling (no. 87 of 9 April 1975) which stated that loss of nationality for married women contravened art. 3 of the Constitution. In 1983, following a new Constitutional ruling (no. 30, 9 February 1983), a new Act (no. 123, 21 April) established the right for married women to transfer their nationality both to their children and to their foreign husband. The commentary on the Acts makes explicit reference to the Court's judgment and to the constitutional principle of gender equality. In the Italian case constitutional principles, rather than international treaties, seem to play a crucial role in supporting nationality reforms. After 1983, both spouses were given the opportunity to transfer their nationality to each other and to their children, but after the gender equality principle was integrated into the Constitution, which only came into force in 1948, the courts initially ruled out[4] the possibility that Italian nationality could be inherited by maternal descent by people born before 1948. However, more recent case law has extended the possibility of ius sanguinis by maternal descent even before 1948.[5] Under this legislation and interpretation, dual and multiple nationality have became unavoidable legal statuses.

In 1983, when introducing the possibility of acquisition by spousal transfer, the Italian law makers confirmed the general principle of prohibiting dual nationality. Children of parents of different nationalities were required to opt for one nationality within a year after coming of age. The subsequent 1986 Act provided that the deadline for this option was no longer the coming of age, but was postponed until approval of the forthcoming Nationality Act (as it was planned to include dual nationality in the reform). Therefore dual nationality has been allowed in practice since 1986 without restrictions, but the principle was not clearly established until the 1992 Act (art. 11).[6] This implies that acquisition of another nationality does not entail the loss of Italian nationality. Nonetheless, this principle does not apply when the person in question acquires the nationality of a country that signed and has still not withdrawn from the Strasbourg Agreement of 1963.

In comparison to the previous legislation, which adopted more universal criteria, the 1992 Act represents a step backwards towards a family-oriented model. Under the 1912 Act, all foreigners had to meet the general requirement of five years residence in Italy, except for first and second generation expatriates who could reacquire nationality after two years of residence.

The present Act increased the required period of residence for non-EU aliens to ten years before they are eligible to apply for naturalisation, while decreasing it to three years for aliens of Italian descent (with a third generation limit). A further reduction to two years was provided for aliens of Italian descent who were resident in Italy before coming of age. More generally, the family model favours not only blood relatives but also relatives by marriage. In fact, the assumption of cultural and political similarity also favours EU nationals, who benefit from a reduction in the residence period to four years. Most immigrants who are currently residing in Italy do not belong to EU countries. The percentage of EU nationals residing in Italy has decreased over time. At the end of 2001 they represented 10.8 per cent of the foreign residents; two years later, they were just 7 per cent of the total. The lower percentage of immigrants originating from EU countries is due to the large flows of immigrants from non-EU countries. However, this situation will change radically when Romania enters the EU in 2007 as Romanians are the largest nationality group among immigrants in Italy, and one of the most rapidly growing minorities.

In addition to rewarding foreign 'relatives and in-laws', the 1992 Act gives refugees and stateless persons the usual preferential treatment, allowing them to apply for naturalisation after five years of legal residence.

Consistent with the attitude of the 1992 Act, which gives priority to family ties as the main criterion for becoming Italian, both *ius domicilii* and ius soli were made more difficult ways of acquiring nationality by comparison with the provisions of the 1912 Act.

People of foreign parents who are born in Italy are granted the right to acquire Italian nationality at the age of eighteen by declaration if they can prove uninterrupted legal residence in Italy. Their residence in Italy must have been legal, and uninterrupted from birth to the age of eighteen. The 1912 Act did not require continuity or legality of residence. These are quite difficult requirements to comply with.

It is estimated that about 70 per cent of immigrants currently resident in Italy have been living in the country as undocumented residents (Blaugiardo 2005). In addition, many children of immigrants are likely to have spent long periods of time with their grandparents in their family's country of origin. According to the 2001 census, the total number of children of foreign resident parents born in Italy was just over 135,000. Roughly 3,000 people who had already reached the age of eighteen and kept their citizenship of origin must be added to this figure. In 2001, only 3,400 minors who were born in Italy of foreign parents were Italian nationals (Gallo & Paluzzi 2005). More generally speaking, the small number of naturalisations is also due to the extremely difficult procedure which is very discouraging.

To date, acquiring Italian nationality seems to be quite a difficult task, except for aliens who can rely on family ties with present or former Italian nationals (parents, a female or male ancestor, or a spouse). Furthermore, when transmitted iure sanguinis, Italian nationality can be retained abroad after many generations with no requirement.

9.2 Historical development

9.2.1 *From the Unity of Italy to the 1865 Civil Code*

Seven factors need to be taken into account to explain the shaping of the nationality legislation which was in force immediately after Italian Unification (these factors were not contemporaneous): 1) the Kingdom of Piedmont and Sardinia promoted the unification and transferred its legislation to the new State, albeit with some adaptations, 2) at the time of unification Piedmont already had a liberal regime, 3) the reigning house of Savoy, along with Piedmont and its capital Turin, had had especially strong ties with France, 4) Italy became a nation-state quite late; it was a nation in search of a state for a long time, 5) at the time that the national State was founded in 1861, unification was still incomplete, and there were lands which had yet to be freed (*irredente*) and people of Italian culture outside the borders of the new State, 6) the country had not yet experienced mass emigrations, although some emigration had already started, 7) before unification, Piedmont had already welcomed nationalist and liberal exiles, some of them were outstanding lawyers, who took part in the drafting of the Civil Code, which included the nationality regulations.

Piedmont was the driving force behind Italian Unification. This State, though geographically peripheral, was relatively modern in bureaucratic terms, and had already adopted a liberal constitutional regime. The ruling Savoy family used to have important dynastic ties with France, consolidated over the years by frequent marriages. In the past, their dominions were mainly situated beyond the Alps, and they only moved the capital from Chambéry to Turin in 1563. Turin is the only Italian city which was part of French territory during the French-Spanish War: from 1536 until the Cateau-Cambrésis Treaty (1559); then, during the last years of the Republic and the Empire, from 1802 to 1814 when, unlike the other Italian regions which became formally autonomous, Piedmont was incorporated into French metropolitan territory. The consequence of this direct and longer administration was 'a more radical transformation of the Piedmont departments', compared with other parts of Italy (Wolf 1973: 217). Unlike the restoration in the

Austrian dominions or the Kingdom of Naples, the restoration performed in Piedmont was very strict. However, after experiencing a direct French administration, the political culture had definitively changed.

Piedmont's policy legacy, its liberal regime, and its historical links with France are some of the factors that affected the pattern of nationality legislation immediately after Unification. These factors explain how nationality was first dealt with in the newly unified State, or rather the lack of specific regulation of citizenship as nationality, as the legal status of belonging to a state and being subjected to its laws, by comparison to citizenship as civil and political emancipation.

In some historical periods, some legal systems (such as the republican regimes at the end of the eighteenth century) only dealt with citizenship as civil and political emancipation, disregarding nationality which was considered as a natural bond with the territory and allegiance to the sovereign. The status of subject was assigned conventionally on the basis of permanent settlement, place of birth and descent. The same happened in the newborn Italy, which was influenced in this respect by various transfers from the legal culture of Republican France.

The Kingdom of Piedmont and Sardinia adopted a moderately liberal constitution in 1848, known as the Statuto Albertino after the sovereign Carlo Alberto. Art. 24 of the Statuto Albertino stated that 'all *regnicoli* [people of the Kingdom], whatever their title or status, are equal before of the law. Everyone has the same civil and political rights, and has access to civil and military office, apart from exceptions determined by law'. The term *regnicoli* implied that the population naturally belonged to the crown territories. Art. 24 was inserted in the section 'On the rights and duties of citizens', a collocation that was typical of seventeenth century constitutions, including the one in force in Piedmont during its republican French period.

Art. 24 was not intended to introduce a democratic principle of political rights, nor to establish universal (obviously male) political emancipation, as was the case with the laws introduced in France and Switzerland in the same year, 1848. The Statute was only intended to leave a moderate opening for future enlargement of the suffrage. The requirements giving entitlement to vote were laid down by ordinary laws, not by the Constitution. The electoral requirements were expected to be changeable, and adaptable to future social and political developments. Like other liberal regimes of the time, Italy imposed property and education restrictions in its suffrage, which were gradually relaxed, until universal male suffrage was introduced in 1912.

Like the Statuto Albertino, the Civil Code (the Codice Civile Albertino, which was promulgated on 20 June 1837 and came into force in

Piedmont and Liguria in 1838 and Sardinia in 1848) did not expressly deal with nationality, but with citizenship as political emancipation.

The code only took into consideration citizenship as nationality in cases of doubt or conflicts of sovereignty. It did this partly in order to take into account expatriate nationals and foreign spouses. It contemplated the possibility for children born abroad of emigrant fathers to become subjects and acquire the rights relating to this status by ius sanguinis (art. 19). A wife and children who were born subjects and emigrated with their father/husband benefited from all rights, even when the husband/father died; however, the children had to return to Italy to submit to compulsory military service within three years of coming of age if they wanted to keep their nationality (art. 38). A foreign woman who married a subject acquired his nationality by *ius conubii* (art. 21). Naturalisation was allowed by *ius domicilii* on application to the sovereign, to whom allegiance had to be sworn (art. 26). Ius soli was valid for children of long-term resident aliens. 'A child born in the sovereign state to a foreigner who has permanent domicile there is considered a subject.' The desire to stay permanently was interpreted as 'residence for an uninterrupted period of 10 years' (art. 24). Unlike the Napoleonic code, which made ius sanguinis a clear source of nationality and combined it with ius soli deferred until the age of majority, Piedmont, with its intellectuals and lawyers who knew what it was like to be a refugee or *émigré*, gave priority to the stable residence of the father as the criterion for enjoying ius soli.

The new State, founded in 1861, inherited the Statuto Albertino as its own constitution. The 'second-hand' constitution of unified Italy – as we have already underlined – reproduced a model of liberal and republican constitutions, and thus dealt with citizenship, as a political and civil emancipation, disregarding nationality, the *status civitatis*, i.e., the status of 'non-alien'. To sum up, in the newly unified Italy, the first legislation governing citizenship as nationality was already out of date as soon as it came into force, as there was no formal definition of who was entitled to nationality, apart from uncertain cases. It was simply assumed, according to custom, that a national was a person who had always been such, together with his descendants and wife.

Unlike other European countries, where the Napoleonic model of ius sanguinis was increasingly adopted, the Constitution and much of the legislation passed immediately after Unification, which was inherited from the Kingdom of Piedmont and Sardinia, did not specifically deal with nationality. This legal behaviour conflicted with the fact that Italy had finally become a nation-state, and might therefore have been expected to introduce a strong relationship between membership of the State and membership of the Nation. The Italian legislature tackled this incongruence in the Royal Decree of 15 November 1865, which introduced the new Civil Code. The model of citizenship adopted was in accordance with the legal culture of the nation as the foundation of the state, which was spreading throughout Europe and was then also dominant in Italy. Thus in the new Code, the acquisition of nationality was mainly regulated by the ius sanguinis criterion, which was considered a sufficient indicator of a shared belonging to the nation (Grosso 1997). Art. 4 states that '[a] child of a national is a national'. The Code integrated the ius sanguinis and *conubii* with a partial ius soli and, following the provisions already present in the Codice Albertino, made this opportunity dependent on the duration of the parents' residence (ten years) (art. 8). This mix of parents' *ius domicilii* and children's ius soli appeared later in the 1912 Nationality Act (art. 3), as well as in other European legal systems, but not in the current Italian one.

For the first time, the 1865 Code specified and regulated what was termed *piccola cittadinanza* ('lesser citizenship'), so defined in contrast with real 'citizenship', which included civil and political rights. The creation of 'lesser citizenship' was meant to pave the way for civil rights. These provisions were included in Section I 'On nationality and the enjoyment of civil rights', which in turn was included in Book One 'On persons'. The emancipation of nationality from civil and political citizenship was introduced at last.

Until 1861, Italy was a nation which, through the driving force of the Kingdom of Piedmont, was trying to turn itself into a state. In this context the adoption of preferential criteria for those who belonged to the nation without being part of the state can be fully understood. The Electoral Acts (1859, 1860), passed as an extraordinary measure (the procedure used at that time for many other acts) a few years before Unification, placed great emphasis on belonging. This law laid down as a condition for voting 'the possession of civil and political rights owing to birth or family relationships in the Royal States. However, those who do not belong to the Royal States by either of the criteria mentioned may, *if Italian,* partake of the right to vote, provided that they are naturalised by royal decree and have sworn an oath of loyalty to the King. Alien people may acquire the right to vote through naturalisation by Statute Law.' Thus the procedure for ethnic Italians was far simpler than for other aliens. The same very simple co-ethnic preferential procedure was included in the Electoral Act of 1895 and the Nationality Act reform of 1906.

As mentioned, the unification of the Italian State was still an incomplete process in 1861. Veneto and Venice were assigned to Italy in 1866 after Austria was defeated by the Prussians at Sadowa. Rome, the capital, was only conquered in 1870. There were still territories considered culturally Italian under Austrian rule: Trento and Trieste, Istria and Dalmatia. These were only acquired after the First World War, when the frontier was moved even beyond the 'linguistic border'. The process of unification was finally completed in 1924, with the acquisition of Fiume.

In view of the existence of 'Italians' in these territories outside the new kingdom of Italy, we might have expected to find strong provisions for co-ethnics in the 1865 Code and other legislation of the Italian legal system of the time. However, there is very little, apart from those quoted above. Little attempts were made to prevent the definitive loss of citizens because of emigration. Devices were introduced to prevent expatriates from losing Italian nationality, such as allowing dual citizenship, albeit informally. On the other side of the border the problem of regulating (Italian and other) immigrants' nationalities was also taken into account by the French legislation which, from 1851, made the acquisition of nationality by ius soli automatic and later increasingly binding. The 1865 Italian Code (art. 5) only stated that a child born on Italian soil to a father who had not lost his nationality by emigrating was Italian. The same principle also applied to children of emigrants born abroad of a father who had become a foreigner in the meantime, so long as the child came back to Italy and settled there.

9.2.2 *From 1865 to the Fascist period*

The 1865 legal framework was soon challenged by two factors: 1) mass emigration combined with the nationality laws of the receiving country, 2) colonial expansion. The decades following Unification saw 'the Great Emigration'. Italian emigration intensified in the 1890s and really exploded in the first decade of the twentieth century.[7] The initial previous emigration flows were often temporary and seasonal, like those going to neighbouring areas of the mountain economy in France and Switzerland. There was also a fairly substantial flow of seasonal emigrants (known as 'birds of passage') leaving the port of Genoa for Latin America. Nonetheless, it was only with the advent of steam navigation, which replaced sailing ships during the last decade of the nineteenth century, and the gradual economic modernisation of Italy and the displacement of people previously involved in agricultural activities, that mass permanent emigration took place.

The main countries to which Italians emigrated applied the ius soli, and even automatic naturalisation of residents. Brazil, in particular, included in its 1891 Constitution (art. 69) automatic naturalisation of all people resident on 15 November 1889, the day on which the Republic was proclaimed. Renunciation within six months was legally allowed, but strongly discouraged by the public authorities (Rosoli 1986; Lahalle 1990; Pastore 2004). According to 1865 Civil Code (art. 11 para. 2) Italy did not formally permit dual nationality. Children of emigrants born abroad and forcibly naturalised should have automatically lost their Italian nationality (Pastore 1999, 2001). In practice, Italian Governments used to give priority to art. 4 (ius sanguinis for children born abroad) and nationality could be lost only by an official act of renunciation (Vianello-Chiodo 1910). In these and other cases of loss, Italian nationality could only be regained through difficult procedures: a special Government authorisation. The lack of formal belonging could represent a reason for cultural alienation, a reason for estrangement from the country of origin, and a deterrent to repatriation. Millions of people left, and although a large percentage of them came back, the loss of population was nonetheless considerable.[8] There was also a fear that cutting the 'legal umbilical cord' with their native land could make emigrants less willing to send back precious remittances (Prato 1910). A serious deterrent that discouraged emigrants from returning was the existence of sanctions for those who had not performed their military service in the army. To remove this disincentive, a 1901 Act (no. 23 of 31 January) established that expatriates who had not complied with the duty of military service were no longer punishable after the age of 32. A subsequent Act (no. 217 of 17 May 1906) only introduced the requirement of six years of residence to apply for naturalisation (art. 1), reduced to four years for people who had served the State and three for those who had married an Italian woman or rendered special services to the country. In this context it is not surprising that the first major Act aimed at reforming the institution of nationality (no. 555 of 13 June 1912) was designed to encourage the repatriation of emigrants. It eliminated the requirement for special Government authorisation for the reacquisition of nationality, and replaced it with an automatic procedure. Two years of residence in Italy was sufficient to regain nationality (art. 9). The 1912 law reasserted the principle of ius sanguinis as a basic element of nationality, complementing it with the principle of ius soli in partial imitation of the French model: in our model, dual nationality was allowed to minors, and on coming of age they could choose, but were not obliged to opt for one nationality. The Italian Parliament accepted a trade off between tolerating dual nationality in exchange for keeping strong ties with its offspring abroad (art. 7). Dual nationality was tolerated for expatriates when the acquisition of the second nationality was automatic and inevitable, as in countries of immigration characterised by ius soli at birth. The treatment of dual nationality was thus not clearly decided, and for many emigrants, Italian nationality became a sort of 'spare nationality' (Quadri 1959: 323). In Italy, as in many other countries, dual nationality was a problem that proved difficult to solve in a definite, clear way and, as elsewhere, it later became the object of contradictory reforms. But before this could happen, Italy changed its nationality laws as a consequence of a series of crucial events, notably the rise and fall of Fascism.

One phenomenon affected citizenship, namely colonial expansion. It started before the advent of Fascism, it was strengthened by Fascism, and continued until its fall.[9] 1943. The Fascist Regime – as we will illustrate in the following paragraph – did not reform the main criteria of transmission of citizenship via ius sanguinis and ius connubii, neither did it change the elements concerning the ius soli when coming of age. The knotty problem of dual nationality was intentionally left unsolved. However it introduced strong discriminating criteria.

9.2.3 *From Fascism to the Constitution*

Three factors influenced the changes that took place during this period: 1) the continuation of colonial expansion, 2) the establishment of a repressive regime towards political opponents, 3) the racist and anti-Semitic attitude that became predominant within the Fascist movement, especially after the alliance with Nazi Germany. We will not deal with colonial expansion, since it did not have a direct impact on post-fascist legislation.

The March on Rome, as a result of which the fascists challenged the Government and persuaded the King to entrust Mussolini with the mandate of forming a new government, took place 28 October 1922. The regime imposed its authoritarian rule when Mussolini, in his speech of 3 January 1925, assumed 'historical and moral responsibility' for the murder of the MP Giacomo Matteotti, leader of a moderate socialist party. The regime was initially authoritarian, but not racist. The alliance with Nazi Germany led fascism to acquire a strong racist connotation and to pick on a group which was not originally its main target: the Jewish minority. The alliance began after Italy's annexation of Ethiopia in 1936, continued with the two countries' joint intervention in the Spanish Civil War, and was formalised with their adherence to the Anti-Comintern Treaty (6 November 1937). Previously, even if Mussolini, as an individual, may have indulged in some stereotypical judgements about Jewish people (Fabre 2005), this was not the official position of the regime. In 1932, in an interview with Emil Ludwig (Barberis 2004), Mussolini contrasted Fascism with Nazism, which was gaining ground at the time in Germany, stating that: 'anti-Semitism does not exist in Italy'; 'of course, a pure-blooded race does not exist, not even the Jewish one' and that 'fortunate mixes' are a source of 'the strength and power of a nation'; 'national pride does not need any race delirium'. Six years later, in 1938 (RDL, Regulation with the force of Royal Decree no. 1381, 7 September 1938), *Special Regulations towards Foreign Jews* were introduced. 'Art. 1 From the date of publication of this decree, foreign Jews may not take up permanent residence in the Kingdom, in Libya or in the Aegean Territories. Art. 2 For all the purposes of this decree anyone who was born of parents both belonging to the Jewish race is Jewish, even if he or she follows a religion other than the Jewish religion. Art. 3 Acquisition of Italian nationality by Jewish aliens after 1 January 1919 is revoked. Art. 4 Jewish aliens in the Kingdom of Italy, Libya or the Aegean Territories under Italian rule on the date of publication of the present decree, whose residence began after 1 January, 1919 shall leave the territory of the Kingdom of Italy, Libya and the Aegean Territories under Italian rule within six months of the publication of this Decree.' A later Decree (no. 1728 of 17 November 1938) introduced new *Regulations in Defence of the Italian Race.* This Decree prohibited Jews from owning property and barred them from many jobs. It also prevented Italian colonists from intermarrying with the inhabitants of the colonies.[10] In Art. 4 for the first time a co-ethnic principle is clearly stated in Italian legislation: the idea that foreigners of Italian descent are not real foreigners. The previous legislation, including the 1912 Act, had granted special opportunities to keep and reacquire Italian nationality to Italian expatriates and people who had themselves been citizens or had Italian citizens as ancestors, but not to persons who were Italian only by customs and culture. Before anti-Semitism, a strong racist element was introduced by a law on Italian East Africa (RDL, Regio Decreto Legge, Royal Decree no. 1019 of 1 June 1936): 'A person who is born in Italian East Africa of unknown parents is declared to be an Italian citizen if it can be reasonably inferred from his or her features and other traits that both parents are of white race'. The same law assigned the status of subjects to all inhabitants who were not Italian citizens or citizens of other states..

Even before it took on a clearly racist character, the Fascist regime had acquired authoritarian characteristics. During the Fascist period political rights were obviously neutralised by the complete lack of electoral competition. Fascism did not limit itself to the suppression of competition however, but also repressed opponents, imprisoning them, sending them into exile, beating them up, and even killing them. Many chose exile, but even then they were not safe from the punitive actions of hired fascist killers. The *status civitatis*, citizenship as simple nationality, was denied to exiles who did no more than publicly criticise the regime. The Exiles Act of 31 January 1926 (no. 108) was one of the repressive public measures used by Mussolini to establish the fascist regime. By this Act, those doing anything liable to 'cause a disturbance of the Kingdom, even if this does not amount to a crime', and those furthering 'the circulation of false information on the state abroad' were deprived of their nationality.

9.2.4 *From the Constitution to the 1992 Act*

The changes that took place during this period can be traced to the following factors: 1) principles established as a reaction to fascism and embodied in the new democratic constitution, 2) gender equality, 3) the need to regulate dual citizenship, and 4) the desire to reward emigrant communities and their descendants.

The provisions of the Italian Constitution, which came into force on 1 January 1948, can be considered as an attempt at providing an antidote to fascism. Thus it abolished loss of citizenship for political reasons (art. 22);[11] constitutional rules also prohibit discrimination on racial, religious, political, social or gender grounds (art. 3).[12] As already mentioned in the introduction, this article later served as the basis for a ruling of the Constitutional Court which forced reform of the nationality legislation in accordance with the principle of gender equality.

Cultural changes in family relationships, together with active feminist movements, form the background for nationality law reform in Italy, as elsewhere; this broad social shift was a phenomenon involving the whole western world. The fact that gender equality was embedded in international treaties was also influential. The 1957 UN Convention (which came into force in 1958) specified that women should not lose their citizenship as a result of marriage to a foreigner. In 1977, a resolution of the Council of Ministers of the Council of Europe (which came into force in 1983) recommended that people should be entitled to keep their nationality of origin and that both spouses should be entitled to transfer their citizenship to each other and transmit it to their children. However, Italy took action not as a consequence of obligations imposed by international treaties, but rather to comply with a ruling of the Constitutional Court: constitutional principles rather than international treaties seem to play a crucial role in supporting nationality reforms.[13]

Recognition of the principle of equality of gender accentuated an existing problem: dual citizenship. On this point, both international and Italian bodies hesitated. In the same year (1983), together with the possibility given to Italian women of transmitting their nationality to their children, minors holding dual nationality were required to opt on coming of age. However, this requirement was eliminated in 1986, when the deadline for opting in favour of one nationality was postponed until the approval of a new Nationality Act, and this, as has been described, definitively affirmed the principle of dual and multiple nationality. However, even before the 1992 Act, it was possible to keep Italian nationality if the other nationality was acquired unwillingly (for instance iure soli at birth). Furthermore the Italian Government had already accepted dual nationality with some states, for instance the State of San

Marino and signed bilateral agreements with some countries of Italian emigration to deal with problems connected with military service and voting (Giuliano 1965; Clerici 1977). This is the case, for example, with the Treaty between Italy and Argentina, concluded in Buenos Aires on 29 October 1971,[14] which exactly reproduced the agreement of 17 April 1969 between Spain and Argentina. This was a typical example of dissemination by imitation. The text of the agreement[15] made it possible to hold two different kinds of citizenship, although it attenuated the consequences by making the status of citizenship of the country where the citizen did not reside dormant , together with all the rights and duties connected with it, such as the right to vote and the duty to perform military service (Bariatti 1996; Pastore 1999 & 2001). Their Italian nationality, which had ceased because of the acquisition of nationality in Argentina, would take effect again as soon as they took up residence in Italy.

9.2.5 *Privileges for expatriates and ethnic Italians*

Co-ethnic criteria were already present in the 1948 Italian Constitution. Art. 51 allows the legislator to give citizenship rights (access to public office and elective bodies) to aliens of Italian culture and ethnicity even if they do not hold Italian nationality. The rules for retaining nationality can also be considered to favour co-ethnics: as mentioned, Italian expatriates were already allowed to retain Italian nationality under a dual nationality regime, under certain circumstances, by the 1912 Act, and this provision was later extended through bilateral agreements with some countries of emigration. Large numbers of people holding this kind of 'spare nationality' made use of this opportunity and applied (and are still applying) for an Italian passport (Menghetti 2002). The 1992 Act also introduced a programme allowing people who had nonetheless lost their Italian nationality (for instance, by opting for another nationality) to reacquire it. The window was due to stay open until 1994, but the deadline was then extended to 1995, and again to 1997. By taking advantage of this very easy procedure, 163,756 people have 'reacquired' Italian nationality according to the Italian Foreign Office. The same measure was extended for a five-year period (Statute no. 379 of 14 December 2000) to aliens of Italian descent living in territories which belonged to the Austro-Hungarian Empire before the end of the First World War[16] and then passed to the former Yugoslavia after the Second World War. A new Statute approved by the Italian Parliament in 2006 grants citizenship to Italian of national origins who were resident in the territories assigned to former Yugoslavia after the 1947 treaty, and to their descendants with no time limit, introducing language and cultural requirements.

9.3 Recent developments and current institutional arrangements

A new re-formulation of Italian nationality law was passed in 1992. Act no. 91 passed through Parliament on 5 February 1992,[17] and came into force six months later, in August. It was followed by Decree no. 572 of 12 October 1993: Rules for the Implementation of Act no. 91 of 5 February 1992, and Decree no. 362, 18 April 1994: Procedural Rules for the Acquisition of Nationality. Finally, Act no. 379 was passed on 14 December 2000. A new Statute amending article 17 of Act 91/92 of 1992 was passed on 6 February 2006.

The Italian policy in the nationality field as a whole, generally leans towards the individual bearing full responsibility for any act, without being required to passively submit to effects decided by law. A person wishing to acquire Italian nationality must state his or her purpose to the authorities, either by making a declaration or by following the naturalisation procedure. Even reacquisition and loss of nationality mostly comply with the same principle, and stem from a declaration.

Women are finally granted the full right to make decisions about their nationality. They no longer depend on their husband's nationality, and marriage does not cause them to lose their original nationality. Effectively, partly as a result of feminist pressure and in the wake of the judgements of the Constitutional Court in 1975 and 1983, Parliament brought the law into line with the idea of equality of gender. Starting with the Family Law Reform (Act no. 151 of 19 May 1975), the principles of equal treatment of men and women and non-discrimination (arts. 3 and 29) in the Constitution were given priority. When the new nationality legislation was passed, all these needs arising from the new ideas on women's roles were met.

People of Italian origin residing abroad enjoy special entitlement for obtaining Italian nationality easier and faster than other aliens. In the general mood of favour towards them, the Italian Government has recently adopted a new policy granting the right to vote to Italian nationals residing abroad. Special constituencies have been set up so that expatriates can stand for Parliament and the Senate. The Constitution was modified in order to achieve that reform, by means of a Constitutional Act (Constitutional Act no. 1 of 17 January 2000). Amending articles in the Constitution requires more than the simple majority needed to pass ordinary Acts. The rules of application have been laid down by an ordinary act, Act no. 459 of 27 December 2001.

9.3.1 *Main general modes of acquisition and loss of citizenship*

Act 91/92 was judged to be a step backwards when it was passed (Zincone & Caponio 2002). As a matter of fact that Act did not take into account that Italy had become a country of immigration, even though this was well established reality in the early 1990s when it was passed by Parliament. Its rules are deeply rooted in the previous legislation and in the traditional approach to modes of acquisition and loss of nationality.

As a mode of acquisition, the ius sanguinis criterion is still paramount, whereas the ius soli and *ius domicilii* have a merely residual place. People who migrated to Italy and were not born there have no certainty of obtaining Italian nationality, even if they are long-term residents (ten years are required), and whatever their employment status, as the acquisition of nationality still depends on a discretionary naturalisation procedure. In marked contrast, Act 91/92 introduced a detailed regulation for expatriates and their children who reside abroad but wish to retain or reacquire Italian nationality. These provisions scarcely seems appropriate considering current historical conditions, as large-scale emigration from Italy stopped at the beginning of the 1970s. Most of the defects in the Nationality Act clearly emerged with the immigration legislation of the late 1990s: Act no. 40 of 6/3/1998, as amended by Act no. 189 of 30/7/2002. Eventually Act 91/92 has turned out to be ill-suited for the acquisition of nationality by long-term documented residents, their children, refugees and asylum seekers. Such discrepancies are becoming increasingly serious as the number of second-generation immigrants grows. As a matter of fact, problems will need to be solved by a new reform of Act 91/92.

Loss of nationality occurs in the cases laid down by law. With the exception of articles 12.1 and 12.2 of Act 91/92, nobody can remain stateless, so loss of Italian nationality is only possible if the person will acquire, or still retains, another nationality. Loss normally stems from formal renunciation. It is automatic when it is applied by way of penalty. As a general rule since 1992, dual or multiple nationality has been allowed.

Like loss, reacquisition of Italian nationality generally depends on the initiative of the individual. In cases where it occurs automatically by law, it can always be refused by the person concerned by way of declaration.

9.3.1.1 *Political analysis*

In the paragraph devoted to the historical reconstruction of Italian nationality law, we have seen that the nationality legislation follows the historical course of the Italian political system, which in turn is immersed in the history of Europe: the birth of nation-states, military conflicts, with the consequent painful revision of borders, colonial invasions, the rise of totalitarian regimes, some with racist, and in particular anti-Semitic attitudes, the restoration of democratic regimes, fears of authoritarian relapses, emigrant and immigrant flows, and the slow process of inclusion of women.

However, European countries have not all followed the same historical path, and have not had the same relations between them. Italy achieved unification very late, with the result that its concept of state and citizenship were deeply rooted in the idea of nation. Italian nationalism was that typical of a small frustrated power which would have liked to become great but in fact only became aggressive (this was evident even before the advent of Fascism). In Italy, after the defeat in the war and the ruinous fall of fascism, nationalism became politically unpresentable for many years. Hence, after the Fascist period, it became discreet and concealed itself under the myth of emigration and gratitude to emigrants. This feeling is still present and is a cross-party feeling: while the right wing expresses its attachment to transplanted Italians, the left honours political exiles, farm labourers and factory workers. In the introduction we stated that the 1992 law was an objective step backwards in a context in which Italy was already dealing with immigration processes; an objective regression compared with the law passed during the liberal period before the First World War. In this paragraph we will try to understand the reasons for this step backwards and forecast the possible future developments.

How can the specific features of the 1992 Act be explained? The 1992 Act is a public decision, which was tardy and schizophrenic in content. Italy behaved as if it were a country of emigration[18] (Zincone & Caponio 2002), or a country of immigration that was beginning to experience an anti-immigrant backlash. Indeed, the law reinforces co-ethnic preferences and the criteria inspired by the ius sanguinis principle. However, unlike other European countries which have adopted and possibly reinforced strong co-ethnic criteria, Italy did not have a considerable number of its nationals unwillingly living immediately outside its borders. Italy had already clearly become a country of immigration. Immigrants had outnumbered emigrants since 1973. For this reason, the 1992 Act can be considered a delayed-action provision. The Act was passed only two years after another important Act (no. 39 of 28 February 1990) on the status of immigrants, which was openly pro-immigrant. The 1990 Immigration Act, passed some time before the Nationality Act, was immediately followed by the 'First National Conference on Immigration' (1990), in which the awareness of the political class that Italy had become a country of immigration, and the favourable[19] attitude of the same political class towards this phenomenon, clearly emerged. On the other hand, the introduction of the 1990 and 1992 Acts was not in tune with a public opinion which was starting to resist immigration but was prepared to extend citizen rights to immigrants,[20] including nationality. The political elite was not under pressure from voters, since although public opinion had started to worry about immigration (IRES 1992), this concern had not yet found an effective political voice. Although the predilection for immigrants of national origin is not at all exceptional in Europe, the timing of the co-ethnic legal option and the political unity of the consensus on the decision in Italy are relatively exceptional. 'The parliamentary debate and the legislative procedure that led to the passing of Statute 91/1992 are the result of systematic, long-term cooperation between all parliamentary forces' (Basili 2005a : 1). No trace of public debate can be found in the newspapers of the time (Ciccarelli 2005).

The 1992 Act was partly a measure which came into being as the result of a delayed-action mechanism, as it was the consequence of a promise made by the political class when Italy was (and still perceived itself as) a country of emigration.

The first reform project was presented in 1960 (Senate Bill no. 991 of 24 February), but it was especially during the First National Conference on Emigration (1975) that the promise of reforming the Nationality Act was strongly reasserted. During the debate in the Senate, a left-wing senator pointed out that the new regulations 'are part of the so-called emigration package that the Government has presented since the first conference on Italian emigration no less than fourteen years ago'[21].

Both he and other left-wing members of Parliament, though all in favour of the Act, realised that the Statute did not take into account the fact that Italy also had to face new problems connected with immigration. The bill was unanimously passed in any event. However, it was a delayed-action measure based on myths destined to last until the present day. Although it was already questioned from a scientific standpoint and also began to be questioned from a political standpoint, it continued and still continues to be dominant what Reyneri (1979) defined as 'the myth of productive return', namely the groundless hypothesis that emigrants would come back with human and financial capital capable of enriching the economy of the country.[22]

The impact of the myth was reinforced by the fact that Italian emigrants were actually coming back, partly because programmes to promote return from Germany and France, together with the Argentinean crisis, had had some effect. Regional governments, which had acquired autonomous decision-making powers since the 1970 regional reform (Statute no. 281), had already started to support policies in favour of return immigration (Pugliese 2002). The myth of productive return was and is still accompanied by the myth of '*L'altra Italia*' (The other Italy), namely the conviction that the Diaspora of immigrant descendants includes people who are still culturally very close to their homeland. This myth partially conflicts with the empirical evidence of studies of the

Italian diaspora (Bolzman, Fibbi & Vial 2003; Devoto 2005; Sollors 2005; Vegliante 2005). The hypothesis of another Italy outside the borders conceals the 'discreet nationalism', the reasons for which we have explained. Up to now, this purpose has still formed one of the two political lines present in the current reform proposals, the only approach that has generated nationality legislation in Italy at least till 2006.

An overview by Marzia Basili (2005 b) of the post-1992 bills and the bills that were present in the former Parliament shows two main political intentions.[23] The first aims at favouring long-term resident aliens, minors born or educated in Italy and at narrowing the gap between foreigners of Italian descent and nationals of non-EU countries. The second is designed to make it easier for foreigners of Italian descent to reacquire Italian nationality even if they still reside abroad. This second goal was advanced by reopening the deadline, which had been closed in 1997, and widening the categories of entitled ethnic Italians. These proposals were officially advanced on the basis that people of Italian origin would be more interested if they were given to the opportunity to vote for their representatives. We could suggest other, probably more decisive, reasons underlying applications for Italian nationality, such as the possibility of acquiring European nationality indirectly, together with all the rights connected to it (such as the possibility of residing, studying and working in the European Union), and the possibility of gaining access to the United States of America without a compulsory entry visa.

For the time being, the second political line, which favours foreigners of Italian origin, has had more success than the first, which aims at reducing discrimination against non-EU foreigners. The area of those entitled to reacquire Italian nationality has already been widened to include the former Austrian territories, through the Statute (no. 379 of 14 December 2000) mentioned earlier. This piece of legislation allows these people to acquire Italian nationality by simple declaration, even if they are living in a country other than Italy. The only exception is for those residing in Austria. Before the amendment, all these people were obliged to apply for naturalisation. It is important to note that Act no. 379 was passed by a centre-left Government without any opposition. Similarly, the centre-right Government has recently passed, without opposition, a new law (8 March 2006, no. 124) that modifies article 17 of the Nationality Law no. 91 of 5 February 1992. As mentioned above, this new law grants citizenship to people of Italian origin who were resident in the territories assigned to former Yugoslavia after the 1947 treaty, and to their descendants, without any time limit. In comparison with the 2000 provision, there are two novelties: 1) there are no time limits (5 years was the window of opportunity in 2000), 2) people who apply for nationality on the basis of this law must prove some proficiency in Italian and a basic knowledge of the Italian culture.[24]

Besides minor provisions such as the Minister's Decree of 26 May 2002, that established reciprocity with the other European countries that also allow dual nationality in specific cases, a consistent share of the bills presented before the present legislature called for the deadline for acquisition of nationality, which expired in 1997, to be reopened. These requests have mainly Italian-Argentineans in mind, as Argentina is a country which, more than others, is perceived as 'another Italy'. Another relevant stream of bills was aimed at reducing the residence period required for non-EU immigrants to submit applications for naturalisation, and at favouring minors. The latter were mainly presented by centre-left MPs.

However, the only serious past attempt at reform dates back to February 1999,[25] when Livia Turco, the Minister of Social Affairs,[26] drafted the Nationality Act reform with the cooperation of the Legal Department of the Ministry of the Interior and the Commision for Integration. Above all, the proposal was designed to favour minors, and was openly in tune with the then current trend in Europe. According to the proposal, immigrant parents could request that their child born in Italy acquire Italian nationality when he or she reached the age of five. The idea was to prevent children who were beginning compulsory schooling (which in Italy starts at the age of six) from still being foreigners, and from feeling and being perceived as different. It was also proposed[27] that parents should alternatively be required to have five years legal residence in Italy at the time of the application. According to the then recently passed Consolidated Act no. 386/1998, which governed the legal status of immigrants, a five-year residence period was considered the threshold for passing from the status of legal resident to the status of denizen. After five years of legal residence it was possible to apply for a permanent residence permit. The French system of dual ius soli for the third generation was included in the draft, as well as the already existing system of ius soli postponed until the age of eighteen, with the latter amended from the then current requirements of legal status at birth and continuity of residence in Italy. Relaxation of residence requirements, favouring minors, and dual ius soli were also the result of imitating[28] other European countries.

According to the plans of the centre-left Government, the five-year residence period was intended to become an important step on the way to integration, when access to local political rights, or even nationality, could begin. Unfortunately, under the last centre-left Government, neither the proposal to grant the right to vote in local elections nor the nationality reform were high on the agenda, and in fact they were left out. By contrast, similar proposals (local vote for non-EU residents and attenuation of the nationality law) have been put forward during the last centre-right government not only by the Catholic component of the coalition, which has traditionally been in favour of immigrants' rights, but also by Gianfranco Fini, Deputy Premier under the Second Berlusconi Government (2001-2005) and leader of *Alleanza Nazionale* (the National Alliance), a party reborn from the ashes of the old *Movimento Sociale Italiano* (Italian Social Movement), which in turn was openly nostalgic for the fascist regime. It is hard to explain the fact that the centre-left cooled towards citizenship rights for immigrants when at last some right-wing leaders took up the cause

Abandonment of the reform by the previous centre-left government can be seen as the result of these factors: 1) the relevance of specific actors within the informal decision-making process concerning immigration and immigrant rights, 2) a growing backlash by public opinion towards immigrants, believed to be too numerous, to include too many undocumented people, and to bring too much crime, 3) right-wing opposition which was using migration policies as an instrument of electoral competition, 4) the centre-left fear of losing this competition, which became more acute in the run-up to the regional elections in 2000 and the general elections in 2001 (Zincone 2006).

Among the informal actors taking part in the decision-making process concerning immigration and immigrants' rights a crucial role was played by an advocacy coalition in favour of immigrants and weak social strata (Zincone 1999). This coalition was made up of various associations with Catholic organisations being prominent. The attention of this lobby mainly focused on the most disadvantaged segments of immigrants, and on claiming basic rights for these people (amnesties for the undocumented, access to the national health service and education even for undocumented immigrants); its commitment to political and citizenship rights was less strenuous. This lobby, together with another powerful one (that of employers' associations) pushed for another goal: the expansion of legal migrant flows. This objective had far more support than granting immigrants the right to vote or Italian nationality. The power of these two lobbies was reinforced by the objective need for manpower and Italy's stagnant demography and aging population. The combined pressure of objective necessities and powerful actors made it impossible to give consistent answers to the demand from Italian public opinion to reduce or stop migration. To expel the undocumented immigrants and keep foreign criminals out are requests very hard to comply with in any country. In Italy, difficult circumstances underlie its geographical position and the extent of the black economy, in which undocumented migrants can find a job, pay back the money they owe for their 'journey' to Italy and the 'tourist' visa to enter the country, live on their own salaries and send remittances back home.

Moreover, several regularisation procedures were backed by the lobbies which protect the poor and weak, and by employers and families which enrol undocumented migrants for domestic labour and assistance to the elderly. All these factors contribute to irregular entries into Italy and illegal residence.

By contrast, Italian public opinion held different, differentiated attitudes towards immigrants and immigration. Pubic opinion was set against the arrival of new flows of immigrants though was prepared to grant rights to the documented immigrants already in the country.

Since the end of the 1990s, Italy, like other countries, has seen a tendency towards the rejection of immigration, and especially alarm about the arrival of illegal immigrants. However, public opinion was not against facilitating naturalisation or the acquisition of nationality by minors. A survey promoted by the Integration Commission, aimed at polling Italian public opinion on the possibility of reforming the nationality law along the lines recommended by the Ministry of Social Affairs and the Commission for Integration (i.e. reducing the residence period necessary before being able to apply for naturalisation, so as to favour minors who were born or educated in Italy), showed that the public was in favour of reform. 56 per cent of the sample was in favour of granting nationality within no more than five years, 69 per cent said they were in favour of simplified procedures for children of immigrants born in Italy, and 52 per cent were in favour of simplifying naturalisation for those who studied in Italy (ISPO Integration-Commission, Zincone 2000). Public opinion did not seem to consider co-ethnic preference as a valid criterion. Knowledge of the Italian language as an indispensable requirement was disregarded (62.1 per cent would have granted nationality regardless of linguistic skills). On the other hand, 80.9 per cent of the same sample was against increasing immigration quotas, while 68.4 per cent was against the entry of new immigrants even if business needed them. However, flows cannot be stopped, as they are objectively necessary and demanded by powerful lobbies. Under these circumstances, decisionmakers usually give 'false substitutes' for answers; since the required answer is not viable, the decision makers give another answer that could hopefully act as a substitute. In this case, since it is impossible to stop legal flows and hard to stem illegal entries, the response is to limit immigrants' rights. This is what the centre-left did in the period before the 2000 regional elections and the 2001 general election.

On the other hand, the centre-right contains both Catholic and free market components together with former post-fascists, who keep in close touch with communities of expatriates. It is not uniformly against immigrants, and retains a window of opportunity, if not quite open, at least half-open towards the advocacy coalition. The persistence of a half-open window, the persistence of objective demographic and man-power gaps, pressure by employers, and the need for solutions to these issues explain the reason why the migration policies worked out by the last centre-right government were not dramatically different from the ones devised by the left-wing parties.

The need to deal with electoral competition has led the past centre-left government to answer to 'impossible-to-meet-demands' with false substitutes. It turned down or limited the rights of long term resident immigrants. This explains why till 2006 there has been a considerable degree of continuity in the immigrant and immigration policies introduced to by the centre-left and centre-right, even though accompanied by strong parliamentary conflicts and clashes in public rhetoric (Zincone 2006). In the case of nationality laws the relative continuity is also matched by a lack of formal political confrontation, and consequently public debate on the issue.

9.3.1.2 *Statistical developments*

For this section we will refer to two sources: the national statistics agency ISTAT[29] and the Italian Ministry of the Interior. ISTAT has released a report (Gallo & Paluzzi 2005) on the acquisition of Italian nationality in the period 1991-2001, mostly focusing on 2001 census. The Ministry of the Interior has published data and statistics for the 1995-2002 period on its website.[30] Furthermore, the Ministry has provided our research pool with unpublished data on all acquisitions of nationality from 1985 to 21 March 2005.[31]

ISTAT collects data concerning both accepted and rejected applications. Conversely, the Interior Ministry only gives data about acquisitions, and we are not provided with information about the number of applications submitted and the percentage rejected.

Since 1986, the foreign population has tripled. Italy ranks fourth in the EU for number of aliens, after Germany, France and the UK.[32] According to the ISTAT data (Gallo & Paluzzi 2005), 84,551 aliens acquired Italian nationality in the period 1991-2001 (an average of 8000 per annum). The total rises to 153,421 in the span 1985-2005.[33] This survey covers acquisitions of Italian nationality by marriage (art. 5, Act 91/92) and by naturalisation resulting from long-term residence in Italy (art. 9, Act 91/92). In this paper, we have not taken other modes of acquisition into account, such as adoption or acquisitions of nationality by people of Italian origin, although they involve large numbers of people. What's more, we cannot break down the different modes of naturalisation embodied in art. 9.

With regard to the statistics for 1985-2005, it is clear that about 90 per cent of naturalisations stem from marriage. For this reason, the immigrant communities with the highest number of members becoming Italian are not the largest ones, but those most disposed to marry Italians. These include Romanians, Russians, people from the former Yugoslavia, Swiss and Dominicans (Gallo & Paluzzi 2005: 6, Table 2). By contrast, Albanians and Moroccans are not numerous among those acquiring Italian nationality by marriage, despite the size of their communities.[34]

Among those who obtained Italian nationality either by marriage or naturalisation in 1985-2005, women number 101,731, men only 51,690. Foreign men are less likely to inter-marry. So, in the same period, only 38,423 men became Italian by marriage, as against 95,267 women.

The low number of naturalisations is due to the difficulty in meeting the requirements, and particularly the required length of legal residence: ten years. Moreover, the procedures are slow. According to Gallo and Paluzzi's report, during the 1991-2001 period, just under 131,000 applications were submitted for naturalisation (an average of 12,000 per annum), while in 2000-2001 the number of applications doubled compared to the mid-1990s. In 2000-2001 the average was far more than 20,000 applications per annum, as against 10-11,000 applications per annum in 1995-1996. During the period 1991-2001, rejections of applications amounted to about 6 per cent, which is a little less than 1000 per annum. As can be seen from Gallo and Paluzzi's data (2005: 5, Table 1), the gap between the number of applications submitted and the number of naturalisations either achieved or rejected clearly suggests that a large number of applications are yet to be processed and are still lying in the archives. This suggestion is confirmed by data about the average waiting time to acquire Italian nationality (2.9 years in 2003; 3.8 in 2005; 3.2 in 2004).[35]

Recent regularisation policies have increased the number of immigrants holding a legal residence permit. However, this has not led to an increase in acquisitions of Italian nationality, which remains a very difficult goal to achieve.

9.3.2 *Special categories and quasi-citizenship*

In Italian law, nationality and citizenship overlap. This means that any national is granted all the civil and political rights embodied in citizenship. Conversely, the nationals of other countries are not entitled to political or civil rights. The only exception to that lays in art. 51.2 of the Constitution. It makes allowance for 'Italians not belonging to the Republic' to be 'equated' to citizens for some purposes, such as appointment to public or elective offices. Such a benefit can only be awarded by the discretion of the highest authorities, but these people remain aliens.

There is no category of people who are nationals but denied some civil and/or political rights. It is therefore only appropriate to refer to a quasi-citizenship status in case of foreign children under eighteen years. This status concerns the natural and legitimate children to a parent with lawful residence in Italy or who entered the country legally, and children who entered Italy unaccompanied by a parent. They have the same rights as Italian children, especially with regards to schooling, health, protection by the authorities, and access to any service and institution. They cannot be deported. Children who entered Italy illegally and alone (unaccompanied by a parent) may be repatriated provided that their families or the social assistance structures of the country of origin give sufficient guarantees of providing safety and care. All children are under the protection of a Special Committee (Committee for Foreign Children). Since the 2002 reform, they have been granted a special residence permit, even after coming of age, provided that they had entered the country before they were fifteen years old. In order to get such residence, they must have been following (or are going to follow or have completed) a two-year integration project, have a job and a suitable place to live. Numerous children have obtained residence in Italy through this channel.

To date no concept of citizenship of residence exists. Long-term residents holding a legal residence permit have no right to vote in local administrative elections, unless they obtain naturalisation. They are not eligible to hold public office.

9.3.3 *Institutional arrangements*

We will now single out all the various actors involved in the application and implementation of nationality law. We will explain the different types of procedures for acquiring Italian nationality, each of which features its own rules and practices.

9.3.3.1 *The legislative process*

Nationality matters are covered by a clause in favour of Parliamentary acts, so that any provision about nationality should be decided on or amended only through act of Parliament. The Government can only be vested with the power to make regulations in this area[36] by formal decision of Parliament, and cannot act by its own initiative. This issue stems from the extensive interpretation in case law, of art. 22 of the Constitution: 'No-one can be denied or lose Italian nationality for political reasons'. The Constitution does not require an extraordinary legislative process or more than a simple majority (50 per cent + 1) for legislation to be passed on nationality issues. Any amendment is therefore introduced by ordinary acts of Parliament. Otherwise, the procedural rules and rules for the implementation of acts fall within the competence of the Government, which issues them by decree. As a third step, the Ministry of the Interior deals by ordinance (or what might be called Minister's decree) with any administrative issue applying to civil service's or diplomatic offices' duties.

Proposals for reform and draft bills are often drafted and discussed by special Commissions made up of experts (professors, lawyers, civil servants and members of NGOs). These commissions are set up within the Government, the Ministries of Social Affairs and the Ministry of the Interior. As a result of this activities, Parliamentary Committees will be able to draw up bills and to present them in both Houses of Parliament when the time is ripe for reform.

Over the last decade, calls for reform have been made, especially by university researchers and professors, political actors (parties and politicians) and associations. The Constitutional Court has played a limited role. By contrast, in the 1980s its contribution was paramount in lobbying for gender equality. In 1975, the Constitutional Court (judgment no. 87 of 16 April 1975) stated that a woman's automatic loss of Italian nationality because of marriage to an alien, was unconstitutional. The Constitutional Court (judgement no. 30 of 28 January 1983) also ruled in 1983 that both mother and father should be able to pass Italian nationality on to their child by ius sanguinis. As they were not consistent with the Constitution, the prior rules could no longer have been applied since these judgments.

In this way, the Constitutional Court put forward guidelines for the Parliament, indicating the way it was expected to bring the law into conformity with the Constitution, and fundamental human rights. This was done with the legislative reform in 1975 (Family Law Reform), 1983 and 1992 (Nationality Law Reforms).

9.3.3.2 *The process of implementation*

The implementation of the provisions laid down in the Acts, involves governmental and ministerial activity. It is the Government's responsibility to issue decrees, with procedural rules to get the act come into force. Such decrees are technically issued by the President of the Republic.

The details are then tackled by each Ministry. In particular, the Ministry of the Interior is in charge of this task for matters of nationality. It is called on to solve any question which is unclear or that hinders administrative officials or diplomatic offices in current procedures related to acquisition, reacquisition or loss of Italian nationality. The Minister issues ordinances (or 'Minister's decrees') to specify precisely which documents are to be submitted, which conditions must be met, and to clarify the correct management of the procedure. It takes control over the cooperation among ministries and between the Ministry of the Interior and its local officials. Further explanations are provided in circulars or memos (*circolari*).[37] Regional and district authorities have no power to act in the field of nationality.

Applications for naturalisation must be submitted to the Prefect, who is a local authority, directly dependent on the central, ministerial power. Within this framework, the term 'local' refers to the lowest rank in the central and State authority's hierarchy, and does not apply to the local, decentralised management of decisions.

The Prefect collects all the documents required by law and correctly compiles the file to deliver to the Ministry of the Interior. The Minister receives the file and should decide the petition for naturalisation within 730 days. If the application is accepted, Italian nationality is bestowed by decree of the President of the Republic. If it is rejected, the procedure ends with a decree issued by the Ministry, stating that the petition has been rejected. The decree conferring Italian nationality has no effect unless the person to whom it relates, swears an oath of loyalty to the Italian Republic, and swears to observe the Constitution and the laws of the country. That is to be done within six months of the date of enactment of the decree.

The procedure is the same for acquisition by marriage. However, as such a decision is not a discretionary decision of the Ministry of the Interior, nationality will be definitely granted to the spouse when all conditions are met.

Declarations to acquire, reacquire or refuse Italian nationality must be made before the Registrar, who transcribes the declaration in the register and enters it in the register of births. If the person is residing abroad, the consulates take over this duty from the Registrar. The contents and conditions required by law must be checked by the Registrar when the declaration is made. The check will subsequently be repeated by the authorities specified in the Act, according to the type of declaration.

9.3.3.3 *Survey of practice*

Some of the main problems and doubtful questions arising in relation to current nationality procedures will be discussed below.

People under eighteen years born in Italy to non-Italian parents have no way of acquiring Italian nationality before the age of eighteen. Even though these children are likely to be more integrated into Italian society than people of Italian descent living abroad, the latter are clearly most favoured by the law relating to acquisition and reacquisition of Italian nationality.

The procedure for obtaining naturalisation lasts too long, and applicants are kept under excessive pressure.

Civil servants in the Prefect's offices (*Prefettura*), where applications have to be brought, are often unsuitable and not sufficiently qualified to cope with all stages of the procedure. In addition the Ministry of the Interior is responsible for deciding whether to confer Italian nationality or not. To make its decision, the Ministry takes a great deal of information into account, and processes all the documents delivered. It also gets opinions from the Police and Security Services,[38] which takes a long time. Evaluating this amount of information can take up to six years, although Decree no. 363 of 1994 (art. 3) sets the maximum time limit for completing the procedure at 730 days (two years).

The same applies to the acquisition of Italian nationality by marriage. Yet, as in this case the authority does not have discretionary powers, the applicant can at least be certain of the outcome of the procedure, however long it may last.

Long waits also occur in consulates abroad. Anyone who intends to apply for Italian nationality has to wait for a long time, before obtaining an appointment with the authorities. This is especially true in South American countries, where large communities of Italian emigrants live. They often apply for reacquisition of Italian nationality or directly for a certificate that proves they are already Italian, by ius sanguinis. Collecting all the documents, including very old birth certificates of parents or grandparents, stored in dusty archives in presbyteries,[39] is not always easy, and requires a great deal of time and care.

No specific financial criteria regarding the applicant's situation are mentioned as a condition for acquiring Italian nationality, either in acts and decrees, or among the administrative provisions. However, the documents which must be attached to the petition for naturalisation, include a certified copy of the income tax return for the three years preceding the application, or a certificate issued by the competent Direct Tax Office. In actual fact this factor carries a great deal of weight in the Interior Ministry's decision to accept the candidature for naturalisation. By the way, the financial situation of the applicant has already been checked throughout his or her residence period, as strict financial criteria had to be met to acquire legal (permanent or non-permanent) residence in Italy. As there is no parameter established by act or decree, the authorities have very wide discretion. In order to achieve a greater certainty of the law, associations, legal professionals and civil servants are calling for a rule to be laid down in an act or a decree.

Over the last two decades, marriages of convenience have become widespread, as few conditions need to be met in order to acquire Italian nationality by marriage. This phenomenon is likely to decrease rapidly, at least as far as Eastern Europeans are concerned, as their countries of origin join the EU.

A marriage of convenience occurs when both spouses agree not to abide by the obligations stated by law and not to exercise the rights embodied in the marriage. This must be done with the intention of contravening the rules on entry and residence of aliens in Italy.

This case is totally different from the one in which the Ministry of the Interior prevents the acquisition of Italian nationality by marriage, due to the fact that the applicant has been sentenced to one of the offences laid down by law (art. 6, Act 91/92).[40] Apart from the impediments set out in art. 6, the Act does not expressly mention any impediment to the acquisition of nationality. In particular, it does not express impediments about the suitability of the marriage. Nonetheless, the authorities have already turned down applications in such circumstances,[41] stating that the applicant could not prove her/his legal residence in Italy, because s/he did not abide by the rules and contravened Italian law.

Both Administrative Tribunals and Civil Courts have jurisdiction in nationality cases. Administrative Tribunals can quash a decision about acquisition, reacquisition or loss of nationality by the Ministry, on the ground of a procedural flaw. The Tribunal cannot replace the decision of the Ministry, so the person concerned is obliged to reapply in order to obtain a new decree. Most decisions by the Ministry are brought before Tribunals because of an excessive use of discretionary powers. Those applications had often been rejected due to public security issues or previous convictions.

The applicant can apply to the Civil Court for a judgment establishing his or her *status civitatis*, which means the possession (or non-possession) of Italian nationality by someone who claims to be already Italian.

Unfortunately, few cases have been brought before the Administrative Tribunals and Civil Courts, as the proceedings are slow and expensive. Moreover, in the case of an administrative judgment, the applicant has little interest in going on trial as far as, despite the decree quash, s/he would not obtain the Italian nationality and s/he woud have to reapply to the Prefect and/or the Ministry.

9.4 Conclusions

Until 2006, the Italian case was a clear example of path dependence, i.e., dependence on a model of intervention adopted in the past, whose features, instead of slowly weakening over time, were strengthened. Italy used to look to the past more and more often, behaving as if it were still mainly a country of emigration, and therefore interested in keeping and reacquiring Italian emigrants abroad as *pleno jure* members of its political community. The most important statute (no. 91/1992) governing the acquisition of nationality in Italy was inspired by the principles of ius sanguinis and co-ethnic predilection for foreigners of Italian origin. The legislation passed after the 1992 Act has extended the possibility of reacquiring Italian nationality, and extended citizenship rights for Italians resident abroad. We have explained this step backwards and outlined some of the main reasons behind it. For this purpose, it was important to describe the starting point. The first historical condition shaping the Italian approach to nationality was that of a late nation-state, a nation in search of a state. This explains the initial choice of the ius sanguinis principle, a choice that is also positioned within a nineteenth century European cultural legal framework moving in the same direction. Large-scale emigration flows from Italy led to reinforcement of the ius sanguinis principle, facilitating the recovery of lost nationality and the adoption of flexible measures regarding dual nationality. The 1992 Act specified these measures more clearly, establishing a right to dual nationality (which was previously restricted and ambiguous), and initiated large-scale reacquisition campaigns to re-Italianise the descendants of Italians abroad.

The fascist legislation had major effects on the legislation introduced by the Republic, in the sense that many features of the latter can be interpreted as a reaction and an attempt to prevent discriminatory measures in future. The Constitution which came into force in 1948 prohibited discrimination for political, racial and religious reasons, restoring liberal principles. It also introduced a prohibition on gender discrimination. However, gender equality was only actually implemented in the law after the mid-1970s, thanks to the activist feminist movements and as a consequence of rulings by the Constitutional Court. Up to 2006, the introduction of gender equality was the only departure from the accentuated path dependence, but this departure was so much determined by the time and the international context in which it took place that it cannot clearly be considered a distinctive national feature.

On the other hand, a specific feature needs to be explained, although it is not strictly Italian: the accentuation of co-ethnic preference even in the presence of large-scale immigration and drastic reduction of emigration flows. The first explanation that comes to mind is of a cognitive nature. Giving preference to co-ethnics is an expression of what we have called 'discreet nationalism'. Fascism had made explicit forms of nationalism unmentionable for a long time (though not forever), but both left and right wing could express nationalist feelings under the decent guise of gratitude towards Italian emigrants living abroad. Disguised nationalism and co-ethnic measures cannot be considered part of a backlash against immigrants' rights. They were introduced when the anti-immigration feeling and alarm at the arrival of illegal immigrants were gaining ground in public opinion, however these attitudes of public opinion did not concern immigrants' rights and had not begun to influence the behaviour of the political elite. In fact the 1992 Nationality Act was passed just after a very liberal pro-immigrant Act.

Later, when anti-immigrant backlash found political representation in part of the centre-right coalition, immigration became a contending electoral issue. This political change impeded reforms planned by the progressive parties. The centre-left would have liked to reform the law on nationality and grant the right to vote to immigrants, but was afraid that taking up the cause of immigrants would increase the risks of electoral defeat. Surveys showed that Italians were against the arrival of new flows and worried not only about the criminal component of immigration but also about the undocumented one. On the other hand, they were prepared to grant rights to the documented immigrants who were already present in the country. Since it was impossible to stop the flows, and reach the goal of blocking illegal entries and repressing criminal behaviour, the centre-left offered a 'false substitute' answer to the electorate: it put a stop to immigrants' rights.

Flows of migrants cannot be stopped simply because irregular and illegal flows are difficult to combat everywhere, even in the presence of bilateral agreements with the countries of origin and transit, because there is a lack of manpower available for certain jobs. Immigration has also been hard to stem in Italy because there are two powerful lobbies pressing for expansion of legal migrant flows and regularisation of irregulars: the immigrants advocacy coalition (mainly made up of Catholic organisations) and employers. The pressure from these lobbies is sufficient to make the party composition of the Government partly irrelevant, because both the main coalitions in Parliament include Catholic parties which represent a window of opportunity for the advocacy coalition, and both coalitions are sensitive to business needs. These factors (the persistence of objective factors and powerful actors) explain the relative continuity of policy between the past centre-left and the centre-right governments in such a divisive issue.

The convergence in policy is due to the fact that the centre-left used to move to the right out of a justified fear of being penalised by voters. It has behaved in accordance with political cycle theory. On the other hand, part of the right wing, Gianfranco Fini in particular, has proposed giving the vote to immigrants in local elections and reforming the nationality law, hoping in this way to realign themselves at the centre of the ideological axis and to have the chance of aspiring to the role of premier and being accepted into the most desirable European party families. However, until 2006 no one had viewed the reform of nationality as an overriding goal. Even more surprisingly, the main nationality reform (1992) was considered 'a minor law' (Clerici 1993), voted consensually at the end of the legislature. The subsequent reforms were aimed at making reacquisition of Italian nationality available to special categories of foreigners of Italian origin, and were passed by a large parliamentary majority.

A reform favouring the criteria of ius soli, *ius domicilii* and the first-and-a-half generation will be introduced by the centre-left coalition again in power. Nationality reform and local vote were included in the centre-left electoral platform. However until 2006, the left and right combined have worked to the sole advantage of foreigners of Italian descent, and for the moment they are likely to continue together in this direction, since both are afraid of offending people who could become nationals and their potential voters. After the 2006 national elections, the Centre left winning coalition can count on a very narrow majority, a majority that depends on the votes of the Senators elected abroad. It is consequently very doubtful that the co-ethnic attitude of the Italian legislation will change in the near future.

Chronological table of major reforms in Italian nationality law since 1945

Date	Document	Content of change
1 January 1948	Constitution (Costituzione della Repubblica Italiana)	
4 October 1966	Act n° 876	Reception of the Strasburg agreement for the reduction of cases of multiple nationality and on regulation of the obligatory military service in the national Army.
18 May 1973	Act n° 282	Agreement on nationality issues between Italy and Argentina.
19 May 1975	Act n° 151	Family Law Reform. Equality of treatment of men and women and non discrimination. Reacquisition of Italian nationality by those women who lost it according to the previous law because of their marriage to an alien (art. 219). (This rule was passed on to the art. 17.2, Act n° 91, 5 February 1992).
21 April 1983	Act n° 123 (Deleted)	Rules on Italian nationality.
15 May 1986	Act n°180	Amendment of the art. 5, Act n° 123, 21 April 1983.
5 February 1992	Act n° 91	New rules on Italian nationality. Complete re-statement.
12 October 1993	Decree (President of Republic) n° 572	Rules for the execution of the Act n° 91, 5 February 1992.
18 April 1994	Decree (President of Republic) n° 362	Rules of procedure for the acquisition of nationality.

Date	Document	Content of change
14 September 2000	Act n° 379	Acquisition of Italian nationality by people born in currently Italian areas, belonging in the past to the former Austro-Hungarian Empire
9 February 2006	Act n° Not yet published	Provisions regarding the acquisition of Italian nationality by people of Italian origin residing in the Republics of Slovenia and Croatia and their descendants. (Amendment to the art. 17, Act n° 91, 5 February 1992).

Notes

1 This report was planned with the following division of labour. Giovanna Zincone wrote the introduction, the historical development, the political analysis and the conclusions, part of the legal information used by Zincone was prepared by Marta Arena and Guido Tintori. Sect. 9.3: Recent Development and Current Institutional Arrangements was written by Marta Arena under the supervision of Bruno Nascimbene, incorporating some suggestions by Giovanna Zincone. Sect. 9.3.3.3 was written by Bruno Nascimbene.

2 'All citizens have equal social dignity and are equal before the law, without distinction by sex, race, language, religion, political opinion, personal or social conditions.'

3 The Italian Constitution was enacted on 27 February 1947, and came into force on 1 January 1948. Even before the Italian Constitution came into force, on 2 June 1946 women had voted in the referendum in which the Italian people were asked to choose between a Republic and a Monarchy.

4 For instance, Council of State opinion no. 105, sect. V, 15 April, 1983 was followed by a circular of the Ministry of the Interior k.60.1/5, 8 February 2001, both confirming 1 January 1948 as the starting date from which Italian women could transmit their nationality to their spouses and children. See also Court of Cassation judgment 6297, sect. I, 10 July 1996, and judgement no. 10086, 18 November 1996.

5 Court of Cassation judgment no. 15065, sect. I, 22 November 2000. In favour of retroactivity before 1948, see the judgement of the Turin High Court (Lucero case), 12 April 1999.

6 Even before that, the Italian Government had not only allowed but regulated dual citizenship through bilateral agreements. Even in 1992, dual nationality was mainly due to 'family reasons': 1) to make the Italian Nationality Act compatible with marriage to foreign partners, 2) to facilitate the reacquisition by aliens of Italian descent who had lost Italian nationality.

7 1,210,400 (1861-1870); 1,175,960 (1871-1880); 1,879,200 (1881-1890); 2,834,739 (1891-1900); 6,026,690 (1901-1910). Data processed by Guido Tintori from ISTAT figures.

8 Since the Unity of Italy, from 1861 to 1940, some 24 million Italians have emigrated; 26 if the century between 1876 and 1976 is considered. Although there are no fully reliable official statistics, estimates of the numbers who came back to Italy between

1876 and 1976 range from 33 per cent (Favero & Tassello 1978) to 50 per cent (Cerase 2001: 115f).

9 From 1549 to 1560 Italy had the fiduciary mandate on Somalia.

10 The most important articles of this 1938 Decree are as follows: 'Art. 1 The marriage of an Italian citizen of the Aryan race with a person of any other race is forbidden. Any marriage celebrated in contravention of this prohibition is void. Art. 2 The prohibition in art. 1 is reaffirmed and in addition, any marriage of an Italian with a foreigner must be previously approved by the Ministry of the Interior. Those disregarding this provision are liable to up to three months' imprisonment or a ten thousand lira fine. Art. 3 The prohibition in art. 1 is reaffirmed, and anyone holding a civil or military position in the Administration of the State, of the Organisations belonging to the National Fascist Party or under its control, in Districts Administrations, such as Municipalities, in state-controlled enterprises, Trade Unions and similar Administrations is forbidden to marry an alien. In addition to the penalties specified in art. 2, those contravening this prohibition will be dismissed and will lose their rank. Art. 4 For the purposes of arts. 1, 2 and 3, Italians not belonging to the Kingdom are not considered aliens.'

11 Art. 22: No-one can be deprived of his or her legal capacity, citizenship or name.

12 Art. 3: All citizens have the same social dignity and are equal before the law regardless of their sex, race, language, religion, political opinions, social and personal condition.

13 See sect. 9.3.3.3.

14 In Italy, it only came into force two years later, with Statute no. 282 of 18 May 1973.

15 *Accordo di cittadinanza tra la Repubblica italiana e la Repubblica argentina*: Statute no. 282, 18 May 1973.

16 In 1919, at the Conference of Paris, the regions of Trentino and Alto Adige (including Trieste) and Istria were incorporated into Italian territory.

17 All articles refer to the act or decree which follows them. Where no act or decree is cited, please see the act or decree which follows the article cited immediately above.

18 See the typology by Weil 2001.

19 Among the democratic parties, the only opposition came from the Republicans.

20 Also recent studies provide evidence that public opinion is reluctant to accept immigration flows, but inclined to grant nationality and political rights to immigrants (Bonifazi 1998 & 2005).

21 From the speech by Sen. Spetic (RC), Senate of the Republic, Assembly, 23 May 1991, see Basili 2005.

22 To quote a senior Interior Ministry official: 'I believe we cannot refuse to receive that invaluable human capital represented by the descendants of those people who took the hard decision to leave our country, honouring Italy by the value of their work and Italianness exported around the whole world' (Menghetti 2002: 6).

23 There is also a third policy line aimed at inserting criteria of integration and loyalty, but it is far less consistent at present. See, for instance, a bill presented by the Northern League which requires tests of both Italian and the local language and an oath of loyalty to the Italian Republic. Linguistic and loyalty tests are likely to be included in centre-left bills in the near future, due to increasing concern about the integration of Islamic minorities.

24 It is worth noting, though, that Statute no. 73 of 21 March 2001 had allocated special funds in order to promote the learning of the Italian language and culture among the Italian minorities in Croatia and Slovenia.

25 'Reforming Nationality Law', a meeting organised by the Ministry for Social Affairs and the Commission for Integration, 22 February 1999.

26 Inspired by progressive ideas she had already carried out an important reform of the legal status of foreigners in Italy together with Interior Minister Giorgio Napolitano (Statute no. 386 of 1998, known as the Turco-Napolitano Act).
27 In the official draft and bill, then presented in the Council of Ministers and in Parliament, the number of years of legal residence required became first eight, then seven.
28 According to Bendix (1964), this process led to the spread of legal institutions and rules from more advanced to less advanced political systems.
29 *Istituto Nazionale di Statistica* – National Statistics Institute.
30 www.interno.it.
31 These recent data had to be collected by us on parameters using an Excel program. We have made suitable aggregations.
32 Ibid.
33 As mentioned, we were given data until 20 March 2005.
34 See Graphics and Statistics by the Interior Ministry.
35 Courtesy of the Ministry of the Interior, Italian Department of Citizenship and Statistics – www.fieri.it.
36 In the Italian Constitutional system, some types of government decrees are extraordinary because they have the same force as a law passed by Parliament (*legge*). These are called *legge delega* (a law enacted by the Government under powers delegated by Parliament) or a *decreto legge* (Order of the Executive). The Constitution lays down the conditions whereby Parliament is entitled to delegate its legislative powers to the Government.
We use the general term 'act' to make the distinction from ordinary decrees (of implementation, entailing rules of procedure or performance of acts) which fall within the non-extraordinary executive jurisdiction of the Government.
37 H. Kelsen, the best-known positivist theorist, classified sources of law in a pyramidal order. In accordance with this hierarchical system, sources of Italian law are classified as follows:
First tier: Acts of Parliament; *Legge delega; Decreto legge* (these all have the same force)
Second tier: Government Decrees, issued by the President of the Republic
Third tier: Decrees issued by Ministries (D.M.).
In theory, administrative provisions (*circolari*) are not deemed to be a genuine source of law. They are documents delivered by each Ministry for the civil service to clarify its own duties. In reality, however, the application of sources of law depends heavily on these provisions, which are essential in order to understand the Italian legal system.
38 Such information is not provided in Statute 91/92. However, Art. 1.4 of Decree 362/1994 allows the Ministry of the Interior to request further documents in order to decide on naturalisation.
39 For a long time, it was the Catholic Church that acted on behalf of the Registry Office.
40 Council of State, sect. I, 22 May 2002, no. 1225/02.
41 Ministero dell'Interno, [PDF] *La cittadinanza italiana, Informazioni e dati sull'evoluzione delle naturalizzazioni, i controlli dei falsi matrimoni*, www.interno.it.

Bibliography

Ambrosini, M. & S. Molina (eds.) (2004), *Seconde generazioni. Un'introduzione al futuro dell'immigrazione in Italia*. Turin: Edizioni della Fondazione G. Agnelli.
Anderson, J. E. (1975), *Public Policy Making*. New York: Praeger.

Arena, S. (2004), *La Cittadinanza secondo la normativa italiana*. Bologna: Sepel.
Barberis, W. (2004), *Il bisogno di patria*. Turin: Einaudi.
Bariatti, S. (1996), *La disciplina giuridica della cittadinanza italiana*, vol. 2. Milan: Giuffrè.
Basili, M. (2005a), *Policy making sulla cittadinanza: l'approvazione della legge 91/92*, preparatory material for the MIUR research project 'Policy Making – Between Periphery and Centre, Between Member States and the EU, Between Formal and Informal Actors', Department of Social Sciences, University of Turin, FIERI.
Basili, M. (2005b), *Parliamentary Bills Synoptic Table*, preparatory material for the MIUR research project 'Policy Making – Between Periphery and Centre, Between Member States and the EU, Between Formal and Informal Actors', Department of Social Sciences, University of Turin, FIERI .
Bendix, R. (1964), *Nation-Building and Citizenship: Studies of our Changing Social Order*. New York: Wiley & sons.
Blangiardo, G. C. (2005), 'I processi di immigrazione: dall'illegalità alla regolarizzazione', in M. Livi Bacci (ed.), *L'incidenza economica dell'immigrazione*. Turin: Giappichelli.
Bolzman, C., R. Fibbi & M. Vial (2003), *Secondas-Secondos. Le processus d'intégration des jeunes adultes issus de la migration espagnole et italienne en Suisse*. Zurich: Seismo Editions.
Bonifazi, C. (1998), *L'immigrazione straniera in Itali*. Bologna: Il Mulino.
Bonifazi, C. (2005), 'Accettazione e rifiuto nelle opinioni degli italiani', in M. Livi Bacci (ed.), *L'incidenza economica dell'immigrazione*, Quaderno Cesifin 20, 87-117. Turin: Giappichelli.
Calvanese, F. (1983), *Emigrazione e politica migratoria negli anni Settanta*. Salerno: Pietro La veglia.
CARITAS (2003), *XIII Rapporto sull'Immigrazione*. Rome: Caritas – Idos.
CARITAS (2004), *XIV Rapporto sull'Immigrazione*. Rome: Caritas – Idos.
Cerase, F. P. (2001), 'L'onda di ritorno: i rimpatri', in P. Bevilacqua, A. De Clementi & E. Franzina (eds.), *Storia dell'emigrazione italiana. Partenze*, 113-125. Rome: Donzelli Editore.
Ciccarelli, S. (2005), *Profilo ragionato della rassegna stampa relativa alle leggi 40 del 1998 e 189 del 2002*, preparatory study for the MIUR research project 'Policy Making – Between Periphery and Centre, Between Member States and the EU, Between Formal and Informal Actors', Department of Social Sciences, University of Turin, FIERI.
Clerici, R. (1977), 'L'Italia e i nuovi accordi sul servizio militare', *Rivista di diritto internazionale privato e processuale*, 4: 741-776.
Clerici, R. (1993) *La cittadinanza nell'ordinamento giuridico italiano*. Padua: CEDAM.
Codini, E. & M. D'Odorico (eds.) (2004), *Per una nuova disciplina della cittadinanza. Quaderni ISMU*. Milan: ISMU.
Corsi, C. (2001), *Lo Stato e lo straniero*. Padua: CEDAM.
Devoto, F. J. (2005), 'Le migrazioni italiane in Argentina: il problema dell'identità, delle generazioni e del contesto', in M. Tirabassi (ed.), *Itinera. Paradigmi delle migrazioni italiane*, 309-339. Turin: Edizioni della Fondazione G. Agnelli.
Dunn, W. N. (1981), *Public Policy Analysis: An Introduction*. Prentice-Hall: Englewood Cliffs.
Fabre, G. (2005), *Mussolini razzista*. Milan: Garzanti.
Favero, L. & G. Tassello (1978), 'Cent'anni di emigrazione italiana (1876-1976)', in G. Rosoli (ed.), *Un secolo di emigrazione italiana 1876-1976*: 9-62. Rome: Centro Studi Emigrazione.
Gallo, G., & E. Paluzzi (2005), 'I cittadini italiani naturalizzati: l'analisi dei dati censuari del 2001, con un confronto tra immigrati di prima e seconda generazione', *Contributi ISTAT* 15: 1-21.

Giuliano, M. (1965), 'Sulla decorrenza dell'efficacia in Italia della sentenza straniera delibata e sulle conseguenze in tema di cittadinanza della delibazione di sentenza straniera di annullamento di matrimonio', *Rivista di diritto internazionale privato e processuale* 2: 307-311.
Giuliani, M. (1998), 'Sul concetto di "imprenditore di Policy"', *Rivista italiana di scienza politica* 28 (2): 357-378.
Grosso, E. (1997), *Le vie della cittadinanza*. Padua: Cedam.
Guglielman, P. & G. Zampaglione (eds.) (1995), *La cittadinanza*. Rome: Stamperia Nazionale.
Ham, C. & M. Hill (1984), *The Policy Process in the Modern Capitalist State*. Hemel Hempstead: Harvester Wheatheaf.
Hansen, R. & P. Weil (2001), 'Introduction: Citizenship, Immigration and Nationality: Towards a Convergence in Europe?', in R. Hansen & P. Weil (eds.), *Towards a European Nationality*, 1-23. London: Palgrave.
Howlett, M. & M. Ramesh (1995), *Studying Public Policy: Policy Cycles and Policy Subsystems*. Oxford: Oxford University Press.
IRES (1992), *Rumore. Atteggiamenti verso gli immigrati stranieri*. Turin: Rosenberg and Sellier.
Jenkins, W. I. (1978), *Policy Analysis. A Political and Organisational Perspective*. London: Martin Robertson.
Kingdon, J. W. (1984), *Agendas, Alternatives and Public Policies*. Boston: Brown and Co.
Lahalle, A. (1990) 'Les fonctions du droit dans l'intégration de la communauté italienne dans un pays d'immigration de peuplement (le Brésil) et dans un pays d'immigration de main d'oeuvre (la France)', Bulletin *Immigrés et justice* du Comité de Liaison des Associations Socio-Educatives de Contrôle Judiciaire (CLCJ) 23.
Menghetti, G. (2002), *Problematiche relative agli immigrati dall'Argentina*. www.interno.it.
Nascimbene, B. (2004a), 'Proposte di Riforma delle norme sulla cittadinanza', *Rivista di Diritto internazionale privato e processuale* 2: 555-564.
Nascimbene, B. (2004b), *Diritto degli stranieri*. Padua: CEDAM.
Parsons, W. (1995), *Public Policy: an Introduction to the Theory and Practice of Policy Analysis*. Cheltenham: Elgar.
Pastore, F. (1999), 'Droit de la nationalité et migrations internationales: le cas italien', in P. Weil & R. Hansen (eds.), *Nationalité et citoyeneté en Europe*, 95-116. Paris: La Découverte.
Pastore, F. (2001), 'Nationality, Law and International Migration: The Italian Case', in R. Hansen & P. Weil (eds.), *Towards a European Nationality. Citizenship, Immigration and Nationality Law in the EU*, 95-117. Basingstoke: Palgrave.
Pastore, F. (2004), 'Immigration in Italy Today. A Community out of Balance: Nationality Law and Migration Politics in the History of Post-Unification Italy', *Journal of Modern Italian Studies* 9(1): 27-48.
Prato, G. (1910), *Il protezionismo operaio*. Turin: Artigianelli.
Pugliese, E. (2002), *L'Italia tra migrazioni internazionali e migrazioni interne*. Bologna: Il Mulino.
Quadri, R. (1959), 'Cittadinanza', in A. Azava & E. Eula (eds.), *Novissimo Digesto Italiano*, vol. 3, 306–335. Turin: UTET.
Regonini, G. (2001), *Capire le politiche pubbliche*. Bologna: Il Mulino.
Reyneri, E. (1979), *La catena migratoria: il ruolo dell'emigrazione nel mercato del lavoro di arrivo e di esodo*. Bologna: Il Mulino.
Rokkan, S. (1970), *Citizens, Elections, Parties*. Oslo: Universitetsforlaget.
Rosoli, G. F. (1978), *Un secolo di emigrazione italiana*. Rome: Cser.
Sabatier, P. (1998), 'The Advocacy Coalition Framework: revisions and relevance for Europe', *Journal of European Public Policy* 5 (1): 6-38.

Sabatier, P. A. & H. C. Jenkins-Smith (1988), 'Special Issue: Policy Change and Policy-Oriented Learning: Exploring an Advocacy Coalition Framework', *Policy Sciences* 21: 123-278.

Sabatier, P. A. & H. C. Jenkins-Smith (eds.) (1993), *Policy Change and Learning. An Advocacy Coalition Approach*. Boulder: Westview Press.

Sollors, W. (2005), 'Contare le generazioni immigrate e 'sentirsi italiani'', in M. Tirabassi (ed.), *Itinera. Paradigmi delle migrazioni italiane*, 309-339. Turin: Edizioni della Fondazione G. Agnelli.

Tintori, G. (2006), 'Cittadinanza e politiche di emigrazione nell'Italia liberale e fascista. Un approfondimento storico', in G. Zincone (ed.), *Familismo legale. (Non) Diventare italiani*, 52-106. Bari-Rome: Laterza.

Vianello-Chiodo, M. (1910), *La cittadinanza del nostro emigrato. Della contemporanea attribuzione della cittadinanza di Stati diversi*. Rome: Cooperativa tipografica Manuzio.

Vegliante, J. C. (2005), 'Italiani in Francia: assimilazione e identità a seconda delle generazioni di immigrazione', in M. Tirabassi (ed.), *Itinera. Paradigmi delle migrazioni italiane*, 309-339. Turin: Edizioni della Fondazione G. Agnelli.

Walzer, M. (1983), *Spheres of Justice*. New York: Basic Book.

Weil, P. (2001), 'Access to Citizenship: A Comparison of Twenty-Five Nationality Laws', in A. T. Aleinikoff & D. Klusmeyer (eds.), *Citizenship Today. Global Perspectives and Practices*, 17-35. Washington, D.C.: Carnegie Endowment for International Peace.

Wolf, S. J. (1973), 'La storia politica e sociale', in AA.VV. *Storia d'Italia*, volume 3: Dal primo Settecento all'Unità, 5-508. Turin: Einaudi.

Zincone, G. (1999), 'Illegality, Enlightenment and Ambiguity: A Hot Italian Recipe', in M. Baldwin-Edwards & J. Arango (eds.), *Immigrants and the Informal Economy in Southern Europe*, 43-82. London: Frank Cass. (Also in *South European Society and Politics* 3.)

Zincone, G. (ed.) (2000), *Primo Rapporto sull'integrazione degli immigrati in Italia*. Commissione per le politiche di integrazione degli immigrati. Bologna: Il Mulino.

Zincone, G. (2001), 'Introduzione e sintesi. Utili, uguali, dissimili', in G. Zincone (ed.), *Secondo Rapporto sull'integrazione degli immigrati in Italia*, 17-84. Bologna: Il Mulino.

Zincone, G. & T. Caponio (2002), 'La nationalité en Italie – Une marche arrière et un parcours à contre-courant', in J. Reiller (ed.), *Nationalité et citoyenneté, nouvelle donné d'un espace européen*, 56-83. Paris: Centre d'Etudes et Prévisions.

Zincone, G. & T. Caponio (2005), *The Multilevel Governance of Migration*. www.imiscoe.org.

Zincone, G. (2006), 'The Making of Policies: Immigration and Immigrants in Italy', *Journal of Ethnic and Migration Studies* 32 (3): 347-375.

10 Luxembourg

François Moyse, Pierre Brasseur and Denis Scuto

10.1 Introduction

The main Luxembourgish legislation concerning the acquisition and loss of nationality is the law of 22 January 1968 about the Luxembourgish nationality (*nationalité luxembourgeoise*) (herafter 'LNL'). This law has been revised five times by the following laws:
- Law of 26 June 1970
- Law of 20 June 1977
- Law of 11 December 1986 (which introduces the equality between genders)
- Law of 24 July 2001
- Law of 1 August 2001

The Luxembourg jurisprudence and regulations on this subject are scarce.

The overall importance of determining the Luxembourg nationality lies in the fact that it confers to the individuals the rights of citizenship, which entail mainly the three following attributes: the electorate, the eligibility, the access to civil service employment. This last criterion has been shaken by the EC laws, as well as by the case law of the Court of Justice of the European Communities, which have largely limited the possibility for an EU member country to exclude citizens of other EU countries from becoming civil servants.

The main modes of acquisition and loss are determined as follows:
- Since 1940, the main criterion for the acquisition of the Luxembourg nationality is ius sanguinis. Ius soli intervenes only, in a very subsidiary way, in the establishment of Luxembourger *by origin*. In 2001, the ius soli gains some importance by the introduction of the art. 1, 3° of the LNL in the law of 24 July 2001: the Luxembourgish nationality is conferred to any child born in Luxembourg and who proves not to possess any other nationality.
- Until now, dual nationality is not tolerated according to the very restrictive rules entailed in art. 25 LNL. This may, however, change in the near future as we shall see later in this report.

- The main modes of acquisition of Luxembourgish nationality after birth are naturalisation and option. The main differences between these two modes are the following: The main criterion for naturalisation is the time of uninterrupted residence (five years) in the Grand Duchy immediately before the application. Option does not have the same residence criterion as it does not require an uninterrupted period of five years *immediately* prior to application. It does however require a period of residence of one year immediately before the application and an uninterrupted period of residence of five years any time before. Option adds new possibilities for acquiring the Luxembourgish nationality (foreigners acquiring the nationality of their spouse, children born in Luxembourg to a foreign national etc.). Naturalisation is decided by the legislative power (Chamber of Deputies), whereas option is submitted to the agreement of the Ministry of Justice.
- The barriers for ordinary naturalisation and option are rather high. On top of the classical conditions which are: age, regular residence (residence permit) and duration (five years), morality (absence of serious penal conviction or loss of civil rights) and sufficient integration, there are three supplementary requirements which are:
  1. proof that the applicant has lost his or her nationality of origin,
  2. that naturalisation must not be contrary to the obligations he or she has to fulfil towards the state he or she belonged to,
  3. that the applicant be sufficiently integrated which is proven by an active knowledge of the Luxembourgish dialect, which was instated as a language by law in 1984.
- According to the restrictive rule of art. 25 LNL, expatriates lose their Luxembourg nationality if, after residing twenty years abroad, they abstain from declaring their wish to retain their Luxembourg nationality.
- Gender equality as well as the equality of filiation (legitimate or natural child) has been introduced by the law of 11 December 1986.

Art. 4 LNL establishes two categories of nationals by distinguishing between the Luxembourger *by origin* and others. The ius soli is, in this case, of importance. The Luxembourgers *by origin* are those born in the Grand Duchy of Luxembourg before 1 January 1920, as well as their descendants. The legal consequences, however, are not of great importance and will be studied later in the report.

With regard to naturalisation and option, the town council has to motivate its advice regarding the conferrance of nationality to the applicant. This advice is however not binding.

This 'motivated' advice is given in a closed session. The content is therefore not public and the applicant has no way to challenge it. The criteria used in this advice are thus secret and discretionary.

The Members of Parliament take the final decision for naturalisations by way of law, whereas the Ministry of Justice is the competent institution in cases of option.

10.2 Historical development

Dividing history into four important phases may best outline the development of nationality law in the Grand Duchy of Luxembourg. These phases are:

1. the period of the French Civil Code (1803-1878)
2. the liberal period (1878-1934)
3. the phase of national restrictiveness (1934-1968)
4. the phase of hesitation between openness and distrust vis-à-vis foreigners (1968-2005)

These historical phases will be described hereunder one by one. It is unnecessary to retrace the historical developments of the nationality laws of Luxembourg prior to the period of the French Civil Code: indeed Luxembourg was not a sovereign country and thus, the historical developments in Antiquity or the Middle Ages are not specific to the Grand Duchy of Luxembourg.

Suffice to say that during these times, ius sanguinis was the rule. In Roman law, the following rule applied: '*Filius civitatem ex qua pater eius naturalem originem ducit, non domicilium, sequitur*', which can be translated as: the son follows the nationality of his father's origin, not of his domicile. In the Middle Ages, the period was ruled by what was called the ancient law (*l'Ancien droit*), which gave predominance to ius soli.

10.2.1 The period of the French Civil Code (1803-1878)

The French Revolution brought not only lasting changes within France itself, but in several countries of Europe, including Luxembourg. Indeed, French troops occupied Luxembourg (1795-1814), which became the *Département des Forêts* under Napoleonic rule. Napoléon Bonaparte's administrative changes have influenced the organisation of the country until today, including the introduction of the Civil Code of 1804.

The attribution of the Grand Duchy of Luxembourg as a personal territory to the King of the Netherlands, after the Vienna Congress in 1815, formed an intermezzo. The complex administrative situation of

Luxembourg cannot be retraced in just a few words. As a result of the Belgian revolution the big powers met in1831 in London and decided to create the Kingdom of Belgium.

However, while the Belgians accepted the splitting up of the Grand Duchy of Luxembourg (part of which is currently the *Province du Luxembourg* in Belgium), the Dutch King William I refused to recognise the treaty. The Belgian population controlled the whole country except the capital. Finally, a treaty was signed in London on 18 April 1839, the Grand Duchy of Luxembourg was split and the country as we know it today was born. In 1840, William II ruled the country as the King Grand Duc. New laws had to be established and the Civil Code was maintained.

The Civil Code introduced the system of ius sanguinis in place of ius soli, which was identified with the *Ancien Régime*. In these times, a person was attached to the soil of his lord of the manor. Nationality became the right of a person transmitted by lineal descent, from a father to his children. This transmission of nationality was reserved to the father, i.e., to the man, while the wife assumed the nationality of her husband.

After Luxembourg's independence, art. 9 of the Civil Code declared that 'a child born of a Luxembourgish father is a Luxembourger'. The birth on the national territory, though, was taken into consideration as an important item for the acquisition of the Luxembourgish nationality by a foreigner's child. It was stated that 'any person born from a foreigner in [the country of] Luxembourg may, during the year attaining his or her majority [of age], claim the quality of a Luxembourger'.

Access to the Luxembourg nationality by naturalisation is an individual right, done by a legislative act, which is enacted with caution and moderation. The will of the makers of the Constitution of 1848 was, as a sign of openness, to transform naturalised persons into fully-fledged Luxembourgers.

10.2.2 *The liberal period (1878-1934)*

During this period of time, two politicians and lawyers, who were both Ministers of Justice, influenced the spirit of the nationality law in a liberal and more open way, based on the principle of equality and on the importance given to social integration in the host country.

Paul Eyschen was the Director General of the Justice Department. He became Minister of Justice from 1888 to 1915 and introduced in 1878 the double ius soli: a person born in Luxembourg of a foreign father is a Luxembourger (in 1878: a foreign father, in 1890: a mother who was Luxembourgish originally and who became a foreigner by marriage).

The inspiration came from France, mainly form the law of 1851. Mr. Eyschen insisted on the importance of the influence of long term residence in the host country. He proposed that as soon as a person is born in Luxembourg, of parents who were themselves born in Luxembourg, this person should be considered as native. Indeed, he believed that when somebody has cut the ties with their country of origin and father and son have resided for a lengthy period in the Grand Duchy the son can be assumed to have acquired its habits, and the Luxembourg nationality should be granted for the benefit of the society. Thus the law foresaw that 'a child who grows up in Luxembourg and is born from a parent who has him- or herself grown up in Luxembourg is a Luxembourger'. Thus the grand-children of immigrants were Luxembourgers.

The second prominent personality was René Blum, a socialist M.P., who became the Minister of Justice between 1937 and 1940. He took an example from Belgian law and in 1926 introduced a draft bill which codified and modernised nationality law and which was adopted on 23 April 1934.

This law kept the system of double ius soli. It increased the possibilities for the acquisition of the Luxembourg nationality, while restricting cases of double nationality. In the name of freedom and the emancipation of women, it allowed the Luxembourg women to keep their nationality in case of marriage.

One of the reasons for adopting this law was to avoid forming national minorities. In a speech in Parliament Mr. Blum declared that 'in immigration countries like ours or in those countries with small numbers of births, which is also our case, the state should increase as much as possible the number of its nationals by assimilating all those who are born on national soil and thus we avoid the formation of colonies of foreigners in our country' (Blum 1939: 1062).

However, this continuity on the road of nationality law was to be disrupted by external influences, far removed from the world of politicians and lawyers inspired by the ideas of the French Revolution.

10.2.3 *The phase of national restrictiveness (1934-1968)*

This phase is characterised by national restrictiveness and by an interesting paradox. In the first place, the affirmation of Luxembourg's independence, which took place in the first half of the twentieth century, was done in opposition to Germany, as a powerful neighbour, which invaded the Grand Duchy twice, during both World Wars (1914 and 1940). In order to defend itself against the German plans of annexation, Luxembourg took over from its German neighbour the principles set out in the German nationality laws, based on an ethnic and cultural definition of the Luxembourger.

After 1933, when the German menace to the independence of Luxembourg became more and more tangible, the political parties, both right-wing or left-wing, insisted more and more on the concept of Luxembourgishness *(Luxembourgertum)* as a defence against Germanness *(Deutschtum)*.

This evolution resulted in the law of 9 March 1940 on Luxembourg nationality, which abrogated the double ius soli and instated ius sanguinis exclusively, even abolishing some possibilities of option, as introduced by the code civil and maintained afterwards by the laws of the nineteenth century.

At the time, the wife received the nationality of her husband. The possibility for a woman to keep her own nationality when marrying a foreigner was abolished. For the first time, the following wording appeared in the legislation: 'Naturalisation will be refused to a foreigner who does not justify sufficient assimilation.' This wording was to have a lasting influence later on.

Although this phase started in the 1930s this trend was already apparent since the beginning of the twentieth century. In fact, almost no foreigners were naturalised between 1914 and 1950.

This phase was also to have a lasting influence after 1945: the phantoms of the 1930s, the fear of spies and of traitors, of those who acquired the Luxembourgish nationality in order to better serve Germany and after 1945, the memory of the sufferings of the Second World War were key elements that would become the lenses through which nationality law would be viewed. These events led to the fourth phase.

10.2.4 *The phase of hesitation between openness and distrust vis-à-vis foreigners (1968-2005)*

The post-war laws kept the traces of all these events. Although the content of these laws will be analysed later, a quick summary of the evolution of nationality law will be made here in a historical perspective.

The law of 22 February 1968 reinstated the possibilities of option, while reinforcing the conditions of residence. The delay of fifteen years of residence for the acquisition of the Luxembourgish nationality (naturalisation), as introduced by the law of 1940, was retained in this law. Discrimination against women was also maintained. The double ius soli was kept outside the legislative reform. In 1966, the Minister of Justice, Pierre Werner, gave a speech, in which he showed that the influence of the war was still a characterising event. He said that 'many foreigners insufficiently assimilated in the country have only profited from the rights of citizenship to better serve their former fatherland

[...]. It does not appear wise to return to the combined laws of 1878 and 1890, which by their automatic mechanism do not allow the competent authorities to set aside the undesirables'[1].

Part of the discriminatory provisions against women were lifted by the law of 27 April 1977 approving the International Convention of the United Nations on the nationality of married women, which was signed on 20 February 1957, thus twenty years before. A transitory provision of the nationality law allows all Luxembourgish women who have lost their nationality of origin through marriage with a foreigner or through acquisition by the husband of a foreign nationality, without any manifestation of willingness from them, to recover their Luxembourgish nationality by a simple declaration at the municipality (*état civil*). This transitory provision lasted until the enactment of the law of 11 December 1986.

The law of 11 December 1986 brought equality to fathers and mothers regarding the transmission of nationality and allowed wider access to the Luxembourgish nationality, notably by offering the Luxembourgish nationality to the children if one of the parents held the Luxembourgish nationality, and by allowing acquisition by option of the Luxembourgish nationality by the foreign spouse, whether it be the husband or wife.

The attempt to diminish the residence requirement for eligibility for acquiring the Luxembourgish nationality from ten to five years which was introduced by the socialist Minister of Justice Robert Krieps, failed, particularly because of the criticism of the Council of State.[2]

The Council of State put forward the opinion that a long period of residence (ten years) presumed 'sufficient assimilation' to the Luxembourgish community. If the period of residence should be reduced, other criteria would be needed in order to assure 'sufficient assimilation'. Certainly the criterion regarding active knowledge of the Luxembourgish language should come into play.

However, the restriction regarding to the age needed to acquire the Luxembourgish nationality was lowered from twenty-five to eighteen years of age.

During the parliamentary debate, the arguments that had already been used by Minister René Blum in the 1930s surfaced once more, i.e., Luxembourg as a country of immigration and Luxembourg with a population with a small birth rate. Reference was made to a report, called the Calot report of 1978, a report on the demography in Luxembourg.[3] Everybody used his own interpretation of the report. The left-wing members of Parliament underlined the necessity to increase the number of naturalisations and options. The right-wing deputies declared that, due to the smallness of the country and the reduced Luxemboürgish population, the granting of the Luxembourgish nationality must be done with caution.

Just like in 1940 and in 1968, as well as in 2001, the political and demographic realities did not carry enough weight in the light of more nationalistic speeches and arguments. Questions were being asked about the necessary assimilation. Already in May 1939, Minister René Blum had challenged these arguments in vain. He asked the question, 'How can you prove that a foreigner is assimilated? Give me the symptoms of this adaptation', he cried out (Blum 1939: 1072).

In 1986, the politicians in charge of the question found, at last, the visible criteria: the knowledge of the languages of the country, especially the Luxembourgish language, which had been declared the official, national language, by way of a law in 1984.

The majority of the Council of State proposed to add, as a criterion for the refusal of nationality, the following words: '...if [the foreigner] cannot prove, notably by the way of certificates, to have sufficient knowledge of the Luxembourgish language'.[4] The Government decided however to follow the view of the minority of the Council of State, which was laid down in a supplementary opinion, and which refused to give a prohibitive and exorbitant character to these certificates, opting for a more pragmatic approach.

This opinion implied that the obligation to bring forth certificates proving the knowledge of Luxembourgish creates a supplementary obstacle, which is difficult to fulfil for some categories of citizens, especially manual workers. It was contradictory to the efforts made and the calls for a more active participation of foreigners in political life.

In general, after the war, two contradictory aspirations may be noted in the debates in Parliament, as well as in the laws themselves. On the one hand, there is a sincere will to facilitate access to the Luxembourgish nationality for foreigners who have resided in the country for a certain amount of time, either through naturalisation or through option. On the other hand, a majority of politicians continue to consider the legislation on nationality not as means of facilitating the entry of foreigners into Luxembourg's society, but as a means for checking if these foreigners are already sufficiently integrated.

This consideration became manifest in the law of 24 July 2001. While it facilitates the acquisition of nationality by naturalisation, by reducing the required residence period from ten to five years and by rendering it free of charge, at the same time law makes it more difficult to acquire the Luxembourgish nationality by stipulating that it will be refused to the foreigner 'who does not demonstrate sufficient integration, notably if he or she does not demonstrate sufficient active and passive knowledge of at least one of the [national] languages [...] (i.e., Luxembourgish, French, German) and if he or she does not have at least a basic knowledge of the Luxembourgish language, underscored by certificates and official documents'.

Thus the word *integration* has replaced the concept of *assimilation*, which was originally planned in the draft bill of 19 December 2000. It therefore took 60 years to change the formula introduced in 1940.

In its opinion, the Council of State developed the same arguments and objections as those contained in the separate opinion of 1985. However, in 2001, political reasons pushed the legislator to opt for a more restrictive or administrative access to nationality, at least in theory, by requesting the written and oral proof of the candidate's knowledge of the three national languages. Indeed a populist party (ADR) to the right of the main political party (Christian-social party), influenced the adoption procedure of the law on nationality (see sect. 10.3.1.3).

The government has not yet organised any official Luxembourgish language courses with a defined program or standard. Thus the criterion of knowledge of the Luxembourgish language is rather an arbitrary one.

In practice the applicant will be examined by a member of the town council in order to determine his proficiency in speaking and understanding the Luxembourgish language.

10.3 Recent developments and current institutional arrangements

10.3.1 Main general modes of acquisition and loss of citizenship

Since the Second World War, the Luxembourgish nationality policy has been characterised by a protectionist withdrawal into itself, trying to avoid the absorption by its powerful neighbours, especially Germany.

This protectionist attitude started to evolve with the legislation of 22 February 1968. Nowadays, Luxembourgish leaders wonder about the opportunity of a major reform of its legislation on nationality with the debate on the adoption of dual nationality.

Different factors may explain this debate about liberalisation and easing the conditions for the acquisition of nationality: the existence of an ever increasing foreign population, the essential role of foreign manpower in the economic development of the country and of the viability of the social security system, the dynamics of an ever deeper integration with the European Union.

10.3.1.1 Perspective on the main mode of acquisition of the Luxembourgish nationality

The main principle for the acquisition of the Luxembourgish nationality has always been ius sanguinis. The first version in the LNL of 1968 stated this principle in art. 1, 1° LNL as follows: 'a Luxembourger is: 1° the legitimate child born, even in a foreign country, of a father being Luxembourger at the date of his or her birth; the legitimate child born, even in a foreign country, of a mother being Luxembourger at the date of his or her birth and of a father being stateless'.

The law of 11 December 1986 brought two major reforms to the basic law of 22 February 1968 which provided in the modified art. 1, 1° that 'the child born, even in a foreign country, of a Luxembourgish national, provided that the filiation of the child is established before he or she turns eighteen and the parent is a Luxembourger at the moment the filiation is established'.

This version of the law of 11 December 1986 is the version in use nowadays in Luxembourg.

First, it establishes solemnly on the one hand the principle of equality of the children; it rejects the discrimination based on the circumstances of the birth and brings the adoptive filiation closer to the biological one. Second, the affirmation of the equality of gender leads to the rejection of any discrimination of women in the attribution of nationality.

The LNL of 1986 constitutes a real revolution in Luxembourg because, in addition to gender equality, it establishes the retroactivity of this new system for a period of eighteen years. Art. 44 provides that the new rules of the LNL, introduced in 1986 and contained in art. 1 and 2, apply 'even to the persons born before the coming into force of the law if these persons are not already, at this moment, eighteen years old' and 'even when the facts likely to lead to the acquisition of the Luxembourgish nationality occurred prior to this law coming into force'.

This rule of retroactivity also applies to adopted children.

When comparing the attitude of the Luxembourgish legislator to other European countries, one can identify some specificity on this matter. Generally, the historical context in Europe has shown that after the crisis of 1973 (the petrol shock), the goal of attaining 'zero immigration' has indeed failed.

Several other Member States of the European Union have reacted to immigrant settlement by opening up their doors to citizenship. The will to integrate the foreigners has often led to considering the acquisition of nationality as merely a station, though an important one, on the way to more comprehensive integration into the national society.

Although the conditions for acquisition of the Luxembourgish nationality have been eased, too, Luxembourg has remained firmly attached to ius sanguinis principles.

The inclusion of dual nationality in the governmental programme of 2004 may instill hope for an evolution that would change the views currently imbedded in the nationality law. It could push Luxembourg into the dynamics of the European Convention on Nationality signed by the Council of Europe in 1997. This Convention invites the states to find solutions in the area of multiple nationalities, while recognising that in this area, the interests of the states, as well as those of the individuals, must be taken into consideration.

The introduction of double nationality would then not be only a simple evolution. It constitutes a challenge, a unique occasion to modernise the nationality laws in a country, which today counts a percentage of foreigners of 40 per cent of the total population.

In a press conference in September 2004, Prime Minister Jean-Claude Juncker announced that at the end of 2006 the new law on double nationality would have been adopted. He said: 'Adopting the Luxembourgish nationality should not lead to break ones' autobiography'.[5]

The Ministry of Justice is in charge of writing this draft bill. It is not yet known whether the deadline will be met. No details have yet filtered out about the contents of the draft bill.

A parliamentary question was posed by MP Emile Calmes, on 8 March 2005.[6] The MP referred to the governmental declaration of 4 August 2004 which states that 'the legislation on nationality will be amended in order for the foreigners who wish to acquire the Luxembourgish nationality to do so without having to renounce their nationality of origin. The same possibility will be given to those Luxembourgers residing abroad and wishing to acquire the nationality of their country of residence'.[7]

The question referred to the probable date of adoption of such a law. The Minister of Justice Luc Frieden replied on 10 March 2005,[8] that the drafting will start in the second semester of 2005 and that the draft bill will hopefully be submitted to Parliament in the first half of 2006.

One must note that this governmental declaration continues, by stating that 'the acquisition of double nationality by option for second and third generation immigrants will be facilitated'.

However, it also states that 'in order to integrate those immigrants who wish to acquire the Luxembourgish nationality, courses on the Luxembourgish language and of culture and civic instruction will be set up *and rendered obligatory* for the candidates for naturalisation'.

From this declaration, it cannot be said that the trend toward a more open and flexible policy for the integration of foreigners through the introduction of double nationality is a very clear one. Double nationality will probably not solve the issue of the choice of policy between openness toward integration and a protective legislation.

Will it put some 'order into the Luxembourgish way of thinking', as Prime Minister Jean-Claude Juncker said in a speech held on 8 March 2002, when he spoke on migration at the invitation of the NGO ASTI?

It seems clear that the issue of nationality is to be seen in the wider context of the immigration policies of governments. As the topic analysed in this report is not the issue of immigration as such, these considerations were generally left out. However, one can argue that 'the moral and political grounds of double nationality will be judged according to the daily practice in migration matters' (Wey 2003).

10.3.1.2 *Statistics on the Luxembourgish population and the acquisition of nationality*

As mentioned in the first table on the state of the Luxembourgish population, the foreign population has constantly been growing since 1981 and currently amounts to 38.6 per cent of the resident population. This percentage appears to be rather high. However, the word 'foreigner' is no longer appropriate, considering that more or less 90 per cent of the non-Luxembourgers are European citizens. Thus, by defining only the 'non-EU' population as foreigners, it appears that Luxembourg has only 5 per cent of foreigners which is actually a rather small percentage.

The introduction of the Law of 24 July 2001 had a noticeable impact on the rate of naturalisation which climbed from 496 to 754 in 2002. However, this rate has to be put into perspective, considering that the rate of naturalisation was higher in 1995 (with 802) than in 2003 (with 785). The reason for the high rate in 1995 is unknown and has no connection to the enactment of laws.

10.3.1.3 *Restrictions on the acquisition of the Luxembourgish nationality*

The rules pertaining to the regulation of voluntary acquisition of nationality (through naturalisation and option) which are rather numer-

Table 10.1: State of the population in Luxembourg 1981, 1991, 2001-2004

Year	*1981*	*1991*	*2001*	*2003*	*2004*
Overall population (x1000)	364.6	384.4	439.5	448.3	451.6
Of whom: women	186.7	196.1	223	227.3	228.6
Luxembourgers	268.8	271.4	277.2	277.6	277.4
Foreigners (x1000)	95.8	113	162.3	170.7	174.2
Out of which: – Portuguese	29.3	39.1	58.7	61.4	63.8
– Italians	22.3	19.5	19	19	18.9
– French	11.9	13	20	21.6	21.9
– Belgians	7.9	10.1	14.8	15.9	16
– Germans	8.9	8.8	10.1	10.2	10.3
– British	2	3.2	4.3	4.7	4.6
– Dutch	2.9	3.5	3.7	3.6	3.6
– Other EU	10.6	6.6	9.2	9.7	9.6
– Other	-	9.2	22.5	24.6	25.5
Foreigners in %	...	29.4	36.9	38.1	38.6

Table 10.2: Statistics on naturalisation and option of Luxembourgish nationality by nationality by origin

Year	1980	1990	1995	1997	1998	1999	2000	2001	2002	2003
Total - Naturalisations and options										
All nationalities	489	748	802	749	631	549	684	496	754	785
German	125	97	70	60	44	41	50	45	47	50
Belgian	65	79	67	64	48	53	72	39	87	73
French	68	106	78	79	53	43	52	33	65	57
Dutch	21	30	15	17	15	11	14	13	11	17
Italian	124	191	209	192	149	94	157	105	119	120
Naturalisations										
All nationalities	213	199	270	302	184	253	224	207	356	344
German	50	17	21	18	20	16	14	15	18	19
Belgian	22	17	21	27	10	25	23	23	50	32
French	17	22	20	22	24	20	16	10	29	23
Dutch	10	1	2	3	3	9	7	7	6	5
Italian	62	23	51	77	47	42	43	46	51	36
Options										
All nationalities	276	549	532	447	447	296	460	289	398	441
German	75	80	49	42	24	25	36	30	29	31
Belgian	43	62	46	37	38	28	49	16	37	41
French	51	84	58	57	29	23	36	23	36	34
Dutch	11	29	13	14	12	2	7	6	5	12
Italian	62	168	158	115	102	52	114	59	68	84

Source: *Ministère de la justice*

ous and rigid, tend to slow down the process of access to the Luxembourgish nationality. These obstacles to acquiring the Luxembourgish nationality express a certain unwillingness on the part of the political leaders and the Luxembourgish population to integrate immigrants.

This mistrust towards foreigners could have its origins at the beginning of the twentieth century, Luxembourg having been invaded twice by the Germans. In order to improve its defence against the expansionist ambitions of this big neighbour it paradoxically took over the German principles on the matter of nationality, based upon an ethno-cultural definition of Luxembourg. Thus, left-wing as well as right-wing politicians focused on the notion of 'Luxembourgishness' (*Luxembourgertum*) as a rampart against 'Germanness' (*Deutschtum*).

In current times, as a member of the European Union, such a threat has completely vanished but the Luxembourgish attitude has not evolved to a similar extent. The small size of the country and the will to protect its economic advantage over its neighbours may explain this overcautiousness.

With the LNL of 2001 contradictory aspirations become manifest. This law aims at the liberalisation of the acquisition of the Luxembourgish nationality by naturalisation and option. As shown in the statistics above, this law has, from 2002 on, an impact on the number of acquisitions of Luxembourg's nationality by naturalisation and option: an increase of more or less 200 acquisitions of nationality in 2002 in comparison to 2001. This increase is however very relative because it constitutes the same result as ten years ago.

On the one hand, the LNL 2001 facilitates the conditions of acquisition by reducing the required period of permanent residence from ten to five years and by abolishing the charge for the acquisition procedure.

On the other hand, new obstacles are raised. The law refuses naturalisation or option if the applicant does not show proof of 'sufficient integration, particularly if he or she cannot prove to have a sufficiently active and passive knowledge of one of the languages stated in the law of 24 February 1984 [French, German and Luxembourgish] and a basic knowledge supported by certificates of the Luxembourgish language'.[9]

This nationalist restrictiveness in 2001 can be explained by a new important political factor: the arrival on the right of the conservative party (Social-Christian Party, CSV) of the Prime Minister, Jean-Claude Juncker, of a populist party, ADR, which decided to make the Luxembourgish language its battle horse. This party gained seven seats of the possible 60 at the general elections of 1999. The language criteria became a decisive issue because of the pressure of public opinion and fear of the electoral advance of the ADR. It is interesting to note that for the first time after the last World War, the law concerning the acquisition modes of nationality was not voted on unanimously. The majority, composed of the CSV, the liberals and the ADR, voted in favour, the socialists, the Green Party and the left-wing deputy voted against.

The obligation to prove knowledge of the Luxembourgish language is an additional obstacle which is particularly difficult for manual workers to fulfil in spite of all the services they have shown the Luxembourgish community during long years of economical maintenance of the country. The life of a manual worker essentially takes place in his work and with his family. It is natural that he speaks his native language with his family. It is also well known that the language used in Luxembourg at the workplace, especially on construction sites, in order to be able communicate between workers of different nationalities, is French. Therefore, it is very difficult for people already working for ten years in Luxembourg to learn an additional language which is not of great practical use. Thus, the language barrier represents a very effective and subtle threshold, one used by the Luxembourgish authority to reduce access to the Luxembourgish nationality and to prevent immigrants having recourse to public services.

Two other major restrictive factors have to be mentioned at the top of the list of classical conditions based on the age of the applicant, regular residence (residence permit) and duration (five years), morality (absence of serious penal conviction or loss of civil rights) and sufficient integration:

- Applicants have to prove that they have lost their nationality of origin.
- Naturalisation is refused to foreigners if it is contrary to the obligations they have to fulfil towards the state they belonged to.

The necessity to prove the renunciation of the former nationality appears to be a major obstacle to the liberalisation of access to the Luxembourgish nationality. Of course, these two conditions can be put aside if 'the applicant proves that he or she has asked the competent authority for either a certificate showing that he or she has no more obligations towards the state of origin and that it was impossible to obtain it within a time limit of one year from his or her request, or when the applicant is recognised by the Luxembourgish authority as a refugee,[10] or if he or she is a citizen of a state that does not permit the loss of nationality or permits it only after the acquisition of a new nationality'.[11]

Moreover, the Parliament, i.e., the Chamber of Deputies, in case of naturalisation, may in exceptional circumstances lay aside one or more of the conditions stated in art. 7, 2° to 6° LNL.

These conditions appear to be objective ones. However, one can ask oneself who will judge if the certificate establishes, in a satisfactory way, the loss of former nationality, or that it was impossible to obtain such a certificate?

10.3.1.4 Acquisition of nationality by marriage

Marriage to a Luxembourger, man or women, constitutes a particular category of option according to art. 19, 3° LNL. It is therefore of interest to study some statistics on mixed marriages in Luxembourg.

In 2000, the number of marriages between Luxembourgish nationals is 1,008 whereas the *international* marriages amount to 346 + 235 + 559 = 1,140. The birth rate of foreigners is higher than that of

Table 10.3: Marriages in Luxembourg

Husband	*Wife*	*1980*	*1990*	*2000*
Luxembourger	Luxembourger	1465	1369	1008
Luxembourger	Foreigner	218	296	346
Foreigner	Luxembourger	209	212	235
Foreigner	Foreigner	257	435	559

the Luxembourgers. The general birth rate in Luxembourg is positive thanks to these international marriages. No statistics are available on the exact number of people using the opportunity given by art. 19, 3° LNL.

10.3.1.5 Restrictions on retaining the Luxembourgish nationality

One of the most arguable rules is contained in art. 25 LNL which provides, in certain cases, for the automatic loss of nationality for certain categories of Luxembourgers who have committed no transgressions. This case must be distinguished from the withdrawal of nationality such as stated in art. 27 to 30 LNL, which applies to nationals who prove to be unworthy of keeping the Luxembourgish nationality.

The attitude of the Luxembourgish legislator is rather puzzling because most countries in the world try to protect their human patrimony. The reform of the LNL in 1986 accumulates scenarios for the loss of the Luxembourgish nationality in a country where the national population is stagnant. Eight cases of loss of nationality are provided for in art. 25.

Let us first point out one exception in art. 25 at the end, where it states that it is not applicable to persons working abroad in service of a Luxembourgish authority.

Thus, between 1986 and 2001, the doors open to losing the Luxembourgish nationality were much wider than those for gaining it. This is a very astonishing fact, considering the stagnation of growth of the national population in comparison to the large increase in the foreign population in Luxembourg.

The LNL of 1986 provides for the first time the possibility of losing the Luxembourgish nationality by voluntary renunciation (art. 25, 2°). This renunciation is in the form of a simple declaration recorded by the registry office, without judicial control or any witnesses. The only condition being that the applicant has to prove that he or she will not become stateless.

Art. 25, 1° LNL provides that the person who voluntarily acquires a foreign nationality, automatically loses his or her Luxembourgish nationality when he or she is older than eighteen years of age. This rule can be qualified as traditional as it has its roots in the *Code Napoléon,* the French Civil Code. The foundation of this rule is to avoid conflicts of nationality and is attached to the idea that an applicant to a foreign nationality is disinterested in his or her native country.

Art. 25, 4° LNL aims at Luxembourgish children who are adopted by foreigners. This rule provides that adopted children cease to be Luxembourgers, unless one of the adopters is Luxembourgish. There is no distinction made between adoption and fostering.

Art. 25, 5° LNL provides that a child whose filiation to a Luxembourgish parent failed to be established before he or she attains eighteen years of age, unless the other parent is Luxembourger, loses his or her Luxembourgish nationality. The LNL accepts here the risk that the child becomes stateless because it does not provide any alternative nationality, as for example, the residuary criterion of the ius soli in order to avoid at least that the children born in Luxembourg become stateless.

Art. 25, 6° LNL provides that children who are Luxembourgers because they are born in Luxembourg of unknown parents or found in Luxembourg, or who possess no other nationality because their parents are stateless, lose their Luxembourgish nationality if it is proven that they possess a foreign nationality before turning eighteen.

Art. 25, 7° refers only to Luxembourgers over eighteen who possess a foreign nationality, which means those with several nationalities. Ius soli and ius sanguinis are irrelevant in this case. It provides the most arguable rule because the target people will automatically lose their Luxembourgish nationality without their consent. Three different cases are envisaged:

a. A Luxembourger declares to a competent authority of a foreign state from which he or she possesses the nationality that he or she wants to keep this foreign nationality. The Luxembourger automatically loses his or her nationality by this declaration.
b. A Luxembourger in the same situation having not made any declaration, but getting a formal notice from the Luxembourgish Ministry of Justice that he or she must give up his or her foreign nationality; he or she must answer within two years, otherwise, he or she will automatically lose his or her Luxembourgish nationality at the end of these two years.
c. A Luxembourger has not, according to art. 35 LNL, declared the wish to keep the Luxembourgish nationality when the renouncement of a foreign nationality is impossible.

The above mentioned people are able to keep their nationality only in two specific cases:

a. If the target person does not get any formal notice from the Ministry of Justice. This case is indeed possible because no rules in the LNL oblige the Minister to deliver such notice.
b. If the target person has responded to the formal notice within the period of two years, which is only possible in the abovementioned case of art. 25,7°c.

The last scenario, according to art. 25,8° LNL, occurs when a Luxembourger, born in a foreign state and having the nationality of this foreign state, has lived since his or her eighteenth birthday and permanently during twenty years in this foreign state and has not declared, according to art. 35 LNL the desire to keep his or her Luxembourgish nationality. From the day of this declaration, a new time limit of twenty years occurs.

10.3.1.6 *The loss of the Luxembourgish nationality by lapse*

Art. 27 LNL provides that the Luxembourger who has not obtained his or her nationality through a Luxembourgish parent upon his or her birth, may be declared to have lost the Luxembourgish nationality, upon prosecution by the state prosecutor:

a. if he or she obtains the Luxembourgish nationality by false declarations, fraud or dissimulation of important facts;
b. if he or she seriously fails in his or her citizen's duty, for instance, by not paying the maintenance allowances due to divorce or bankruptcy. In practice, this point is hardly ever pursued;
c. if he or she exercises rights or fulfils national duties of foreign countries;
d. if he or she incurs, in Luxembourg or abroad, as the main culprit or as accomplice, a criminal sentence or imprisonment because of assassination, murder, theft, deceit, fraud, confidence trick, misappropriation of public funds, counterfeit, false testimony, subordination of witness or expert, indecent assault, rape, prostitution or corruption of young people, infringement of the art. 379 and 379bis of the penal code, gambling house, criminal association, abandonment of children, children snatching, bankruptcy, infringement of the legal rules concerning the internal and external security of the country, or for the attempt of any of these offences.

This rule is hardly applied nowadays and thus, is of no real significance.

10.3.2 *A special category of nationals: the Luxembourger by origin*

Art. 4 LNL of 24 July 2001 makes a distinction between two categories of nationals: the Luxembourger *by origin* and the other Luxembourger. The Luxembourgers born in the Grand Duchy of Luxembourg before the 1 January 1920, as well as their descendants, are labelled Luxembourgers *by origin*.

Art. 4, 2° states that 'the status of Luxembourgers by origin is sufficiently established by proof of possession of the Luxembourgish nationality deriving from the parent of the candidate whose nationality is the condition of its own. Proof to the contrary is possible'.

The legal consequences of this distinction are not very significant. More favourable conditions are granted to biological and adoptive children of a Luxembourgish adopter or parent for acquiring the Luxembourgish nationality (art. 19, 2°) as well as for the Luxembourger by origin to reacquire the Luxembourgish nationality (art. 26, al.1). The lapse of nationality only occurs for those persons who did not acquire the Luxembourgish nationality from a Luxembourgish parent at birth (art. 27, al.1). Thus, the lapse of nationality applies only to people becoming Luxembourgers by naturalisation or option.

It should be remarked that the number of cases whereby nationality lapses is extremely low, with the exception of the periods following the two World Wars. However, the psychological impact of such categories existing is in fact more severe than the effects thereof, giving the impression that there are two distinct kinds of nationals, each with different rights: the *true* Luxembourger and the imperfect nationals. Hopefully, this distinction which has nearly no consequences will be removed by the next reform.

10.3.3 Institutional arrangements

10.3.3.1 The administrative procedure to acquire nationality by naturalisation or option

A brief summary of the procedure of naturalisation according to art. 9 to 18 LNL:

- The naturalisation file is issued to the secretary of the town council where the applicant resides, following a request addressed to the Ministry of Justice. The target person submits a declaration to the registry office.
- The town council gives an advice with the grounds motivating it in a closed sitting. As the session is secret, the motivations of the advice are also secret. This procedure is rather non-transparent. There is obviously no way of appealing against this advice based on unknown motivations. The next reform should tackle this transparency issue in order to safeguard applicants' rights to appeal. The advice by the town council is not binding.
- A public inquiry is carried out.
- The file is submitted to the Council of State (*Conseil d'Etat*) and sent for decision taking to the Chamber of Deputies (legislative procedure).
- The procedure has been free of charge since the coming into force of the LNL of 24 July 2001 for all requests submitted after 1 January 2002. However, this is not a particularly large incentive for the applicant as the fees existing before 2001 were very low.

- The decision by the Chamber of Deputies, after promulgation by the Grand-Duke, is made known via administrative channels, i.e., by letter. The grounds for the decision is, as is the advice of the town council, secret. Hence, it is impossible to obtain statistics on the reasons for refusals.

It comes into force four days after publication in the official journal the *Mémorial A*.

The procedure of option in accordance with art. 23 and 24 LNL is quite similar to the one for naturalisation.

- The option file is personally issued to the secretary of the town council where the applicant resides. The target person submits a declaration to the registry office.
- The town council gives an advice with the ground motivating it in a closed sitting.
- A public inquiry is carried out.
- The Ministry of Justice takes a decision. The grounds motivating the decision are also secret.
- The procedure has been free of charge since the coming into force of the LNL of 24 July 2001 for all requests submitted after 1 January 2002.
- The decision of approval is made known via administrative channels, by letter.
- The declaration of option takes effect four days after its publication in the *Mémorial B*, the addendum of the official journal.

10.3.3.2 *The legislative process*

The rules concerning the acquisition or loss of the Luxembourgish nationality are, according to art. 9 of the Luxembourgish Constitution, settled by law. Thus, the Chamber of Deputies and the government may prepare draft legislative reforms. However, the Chamber of Deputies is the sole political body responsible for the enactment of laws.

There is no special majority required for matters of nationality law, a simple majority suffices.

There is no example of nationality law being subjected to judicial review by either the administrative or the constitutional court.

10.3.3.3 *The process of implementation*

The Ministry of Justice is competent to implement the nationality law and monitors its correct application. It publishes handouts explaining the procedure of acquisition for applicants. These handouts are available on the internet.[12] The government has no other campaigns to promote the acquisition of the Luxembourgish nationality. Luxembourgish civil society seems uninterested in the issue of nationality acquisition.

There are no campaigns in favour of the acquisition of the Luxembourgish nationality or of the integration of the foreign population other than by some few Luxembourgish NGOs.

10.4 Conclusions

Luxembourg is on the threshold of a major reform of its nationality law. Considering that nearly 40 per cent of the population living in the Grand Duchy of Luxembourg do not have the Luxembourgish nationality, there are large democratic and demographical issues.

The conservative party CSV which has the majority in the government and the Chamber of Deputies has put the reform of the nationality law on its political agenda and committed itself to adopting the principle of dual nationality as a way of resolving these issues which are particular to a small country like Luxembourg.

According to the statements of the Minister of Justice, Luc Frieden, this reform is expected to be enacted at the beginning of 2006.

The Luxembourgish legal system is traditionally hostile to dual or multiple nationalities. Its attachment to the principle of the uniqueness of nationality was founded on the desire to safeguard the national unity of a small country in close contact with countries granting their nationality according to more liberal criteria.

However, the national unity of Luxembourg has gradually changed due to the duality of its population: the natives and the foreigners. The challenge to the current political authorities is the necessity to promote the national unity *in ius* by, little by little, integrating the various groups of immigrants into the national community. These groups of immigrants de facto are already part of this community on an economical and social level through their harmonious integration, characterised in particular by a sufficiently long stay in the country and respect of its laws.

The rejection of the plurality of nationality, which was sensible in the past, nowadays frustrates the initial purpose. A more liberal attitude towards the plurality of nationality is precisely the way to protect national unity these days.

'A nation is a population with a common past and a common future', said the former French President Charles de Gaulle. This perspective makes it possible to appreciate the nation as an evolving phenomenon and, in particular, to surpass the concept of a nation based on ethnic criteria, naturally inclined to protect itself by withdrawing into itself and rejecting 'the others'. This perspective helps to focus, on the contrary, on the *elective* nation which constitutes an open community harmoniously integrating newcomers.

This dynamic perspective and the concept of an *elective* nation are not only the way to promote national unity, but also to prepare the way for European integration.

However, the general mentality of the Luxembourgish nationals is far from being inspired by this concept of an *elective* nation. An ever wider gap grows between the Luxembourgish politicians trying to tackle these issues of democracy and immigration and the Luxembourgish nationals who generally do not wish to integrate even other EU-nationals.

The increasing importance of the Luxembourgish language is one symptom of this general unwillingness to integrate the foreign population. Even the enactment of the dual nationality principle will probably lead to no significant change of this reticent mentality, because the acquisition of nationality does not constitute an effective way of integration in Luxembourg.

The average Luxembourger does not judge whether a person belongs to the nation based on his or her ID card, but, in practice, judges based on something more difficult to acquire than nationality, namely, perfect proficiency in speaking Luxembourgish.

Thus, the enactment of dual nationality will probably not be an adequate answer to the issue of immigration. Campaigns organised by the Luxembourgish state and especially by Luxembourgish NGOs to contribute to a mentality shift, appear, in this light, to be of major importance. Campaigns of these sorts are, however, at the moment of drafting this report, only initiated by very few NGOs in Luxembourg.

Chronological table of major reforms in Luxembourg's nationality law since 1945

Date	Document	Content of change
22 February 1968	Law on Luxembourgish nationality (Loi du 22 février 1968 sur la nationalité luxembourgeoise)	Ius sanguinis through the father.
22 February 1968	Law modifying the law on the Luxembourgish nationality *(Loi du 26 juin 1975 portant modification de la loi du 22 février 1968 sur la nationalité luxembourgeoise)*	Minimum residence requirement drops from 15 to 10 years.
11 December 1986	Law modifying the law of 22 February 1968 on the Luxembourgish nationality *(Loi du 11 décembre 1986 portant modification de la loi du 22 février 1968 sur la nationalité luxembourgeoise)*	Equality of gender and filiations (legitimate or natural child) in the determination of nationality by birth; easier conditions for naturalisation and option: minimum age is lowered from 25 to 18.
24 July 2001	Law modifying the law of 22 February 1968 on the Luxembourgish nationality *(Loi du*	Easier conditions for naturalisation and option: minimum of years of residence is lowered from 10 to 5;

Date	Document	Content of change
	24 juillet 2001 portant modification de la loi du 22 février 1968 sur la nationalité luxembourgeoise)	introduction of ius soli for children born in Luxembourg and having no other nationality.

Notes

1 See *Exposé des motifs du projet de loi n°63 [0](1232) portant modification et complément de la loi du 9 mars 1940 sur l'indigénat luxembourgeois, Compte-rendu des séances de la Chambre des deputes*, 1967-1968, p. 984f.
2 *Avis complémentaire séparé du Conseil d'Etat du 7 mai 1985 sur le projet de loi 2898/02 portant modification de la loi du 22 février 1968 sur la nationalité luxembourgeoise telle qu'elle a été modifiée dans la suite.*
3 *Rapport Calot sur la démographie du Luxembourg – passé, présent et avenir.*
4 See *Avis complémentaire séparé du Conseil d'Etat du 7 ai 1985 sur le projet de la loi 2898/02 portant modification de la loi du 22 février 1968 sur la nationalité luxembourgeoise telle qu'elle a été modifié dans la suite.*
5 See article in newspaper *La voix du Luxembourg*, 30 September 2004.
6 Question Nr. 345 of 8 March 2005, http://www.chd.lu/archives.
7 *Déclaration du Premier ministre Jean-Claude Juncker portant sur le programme gouvernemental*, 4 August 2004.
8 Answer to the question Nr. 345, http://www.chd.lu/archives.
9 Art. 7,4° and 22,3° LNL 2001.
10 According to the Geneva Convention of 28 July 1951.
11 Art. 7, al.2; art. 22, al.2.
12 See the site of the Ministry of Justice: http://www.mj.public.lu.

Bibliography

Blum, R. (1939), *Compte rendu des séances de la Chambre des Députés, 1938-1939*. Publication de la Chambre des Députés.

Calot, G. (1978), *Rapport sur la démographie du Luxembourg – passé, présent et avenir*. Luxembourg: STATEC.

Delpérée, F. & M. Verwilghen (2003), 'Citoyenneté multiple et nationalité multiple au Grand-Duché de Luxembourg', *Annales de Droit Luxembourgeois* 13: 61-220.

Goerens, J. & F. Delaporte, (1997), 'L'étranger dans la Cité', Rapport Luxembourgeois, *Journées luxembourgeoises de l'Association Henri Capitant*, 26-29 May.

Juncker, J.-C. (2002), 'Migrations: les enjeux! Défis pour l'économie et la cohésion sociale', paper presented at a conference organised by the NGO ASTI, Luxembourg, 28 March 2002.

Juncker, J.-C. (2004), 'Déclaration du Premier Ministre Jean-Claude Juncker portant sur le programme gouvernemental', 4 août 2004. www.gouvernement.lu.

Majerus, P. (1990), *L'Etat luxembourgeois*. 6th edition. Esch/Alzette: Editpress.

Scuto, D. (2005), 'Qu'est-ce qu'un Luxembourgeois? Histoire de la nationalité Luxembourgeoise du Code Napoléon à nos jours', *Forum* 244: 40-46.

Trausch, G. (ed.) (2003), *Histoire du Luxembourg. Le destin européen d'un petit pays*. Toulouse: Editions Privat.

Wey, C. (2003), 'Le consensus sociopolitique face à la politique d'intégration', *Ensemble* (ASTI) 71-72: 90-98.

11 The Netherlands

Ricky van Oers, Betty de Hart and Kees Groenendijk

11.1 Introduction

The first Dutch Nationality Act of 1892 introduced the principle of nationality acquisition *iure sanguini*, thereby putting a stop to the possibility of acquiring Dutch nationality by mere birth on Dutch territory. As of 1 July 1893[1], Dutch nationality was acquired through birth from a Dutch father. This was not the only gender discriminatory provision in Dutch nationality law. It also provided for automatic acquisition of Dutch nationality for foreign women marrying Dutch men and for loss of Dutch nationality in case a Dutch woman would marry a foreigner. Both regulations were abolished in 1964. It was, however, not until 1985 that the Dutch nationality regulations provided for acquisition of Dutch nationality through Dutch mothers.

Under current Dutch nationality law, the main mode of acquiring Dutch nationality still is by birth from a Dutch parent.[2] The Dutch Nationality Act 2003 however, also provides for acquisition of Dutch nationality *iure soli*, namely for second and third generation immigrants.[3]

Third generation immigrants automatically acquire Dutch nationality upon birth in the Netherlands from a parent whose main residence is in the Netherlands, provided this parent was also born in the Netherlands from a parent whose main residence was in the Netherlands at the time of his or her birth.[4] This double ius soli rule was introduced in Dutch law in 1953 and has undergone minor changes throughout the years.

In 1985, a right to opt for Dutch nationality was accorded to second generation immigrants that were born in the Netherlands and have been residing there since birth.[5] The 2003 Act accords an equal right to persons residing in the Netherlands from the age of four, and to six other categories of persons (art. 6 para. 1 sub b-h). Persons opting for Dutch nationality are not required to fulfil an integration requirement or to renounce their original nationality. This is what distinguishes the right of option from the naturalisation procedure. Before 1 April 2003, the option procedure consisted of a simple unilateral declaration that was free of charge. With the coming into force of the 2003 Act, a mayor may refuse to confirm the option declaration after a public order investigation. Furthermore, a fee of 132 euros is charged. Though the number of categories of persons that can profit from the option procedure has been increased, most categories face residence requirements. This way, the right of option, instead of forming a middle course between *ex lege* acquisition and naturalisation, has become a simplified form of naturalisation.

Access to Dutch nationality has also become harder for first generation immigrants since the 2003 Nationality Act came into force. Before 1 April 2003, immigrants who had lawfully resided in the Netherlands for five years or more, who had sufficient command of the Dutch language to communicate with others and had no serious criminal record were granted Dutch nationality (Groenendijk 2004: 111). As of 1 April 2003, the lawful residence in the Netherlands must have been uninterrupted for the entire five years prior to application. Furthermore, applicants are subjected to a strict naturalisation exam, which tests whether the applicant is sufficiently integrated into Dutch society. Compared to 2002, the number of applications for naturalisation in 2004 has decreased by 67 per cent.[6] Moreover, 50 per cent of all participants to the test did not pass the test, and could therefore not apply for naturalisation. During the twenty years preceding the 2003 Act, only 1-2 per cent of all applications were denied due to insufficient integration.[7]

Although the requirement to renounce the original nationality upon naturalisation was abolished in 1992, this condition was reintroduced in 1997. The 2003 Act exempts five categories of applicants from the requirement. The Manual for the application of the 2000 Nationality Act exempts another nine categories (Anon 2003: art. 9 para. 1 sub b, C. 4, 15). Currently, 62.7 per cent of all persons acquiring Dutch nationality through naturalisation keep their original nationality.[8]

While making it harder for first generation immigrants to acquire Dutch nationality, the possibilities for Dutch emigrants to retain their nationality have been enlarged. The 2003 Act provides a way to avoid automatic loss of Dutch nationality for dual nationals that spend ten years abroad.

Currently, the Dutch Centre-Right government has sent a proposal to allow for withdrawal of Dutch nationality from dual nationals guilty of (conspiring to) a terrorist act, to the Council of State for advice. Furthermore, the Minister of Alien Affairs and Integration, Verdonk of the conservative liberal VVD (people's party for freedom and democracy), has announced plans to delete certain categories of exceptions to the renunciation requirement.[9] Upon repeated requests in Parliament, she has announced the creation of a citizenship ceremony at the moment of naturalisation.

11.2 Historical development (1892-1985)[10]

11.2.1 1892-1953: The first Dutch Nationality Act

The first rules on Dutch nationality date from the nineteenth century. As of 1838, the Dutch Civil Code stipulated that everyone born in the Netherlands or in one of its colonies had Dutch nationality. The rule that accorded political rights to Dutch nationals came into force in 1850.[11] For the purpose of the 1850 Nationality Act, only persons born in the Netherlands or persons that descended from such persons were considered Dutch nationals; native inhabitants of the colonies were excluded from the scope of this Act.

In 1892, the two sets of nationality rules were replaced by one Dutch Nationality Act. The gender neutral ius soli acquisition was replaced by the gender specific ius sanguinis *a patre*. Since as of 1 July 1893,[12] Dutch nationality was acquired through Dutch fathers, it was important to decide who would be a Dutch national as of that day. The government decided not to attribute Dutch nationality, including political rights, to the 'native and assimilated inhabitants' of the colony of the Dutch East Indies. The notion of 'native and assimilated inhabitants' referred to the existing racial division of the population of the Dutch East Indies with, on the one hand, 'Europeans and assimilated' (mostly Christians) and, on the other hand, 'natives and assimilated' (mainly Arabs, Chinese, Mohammedans and pagans) (Heijs 1991: 24). A similar distinction did not apply in the other colonies. Because they were much smaller in number, the native inhabitants of Surinam and the Netherlands Antilles were allowed to retain their Dutch nationality.

An unwanted side-effect of the decision to exclude the native inhabitants of the Dutch East Indies from Dutch nationality was that the majority became stateless. Although the government continued to treat them as Dutch nationals, this offered no solution in international law. In 1910, the native population of the Dutch East Indies was offered a 'second rank' Dutch nationality, namely that of 'Dutch subject non-Dutch national'. After Indonesia's independence in 1949, the Dutch government would use the status of Dutch subject non-Dutch national to allocate citizens to Indonesia (see sect. 11.2.4).

Under the 1892 law, naturalisation was the only way for immigrants, who at that time were mainly Germans and Belgians, to obtain Dutch nationality. This was subject to the requirements of being of age, five years residence in the Netherlands or in one of the colonies and renunciation of the former nationality. This last requirement, which in practice had already applied since 1860, was applied strictly. Public order and financial requirements did not appear in the Act, but were applied in practice. If a man acquired Dutch nationality through naturalisation, his wife and children obtained it automatically. Naturalisation of foreigners took place by individual Act. Every application for naturalisation was decided upon in Parliament. The costs of a naturalisation procedure were fairly high.[13]

The 1892 Act provided for loss of Dutch nationality after ten years residence abroad without expressing the wish to remain Dutch at the municipality of the last place of residence or at a Dutch consulate. Ten years after the Act came into force, Parliamentary discussions mainly focussed on re-naturalisation of former Dutch nationals that had forgotten to make the necessary statement (Heijs 1995: 75).

This changed in 1914. After the First World War broke out, the number of applications for naturalisation rose considerably. The Minister of Justice saw no need for preventing the naturalisation of long-term immigrants that had successfully assimilated into Dutch society. Although the regular naturalisation policy was said to be applied, naturalisation rates dropped. In 1915, only 23 persons obtained Dutch nationality through naturalisation, a number that had not been that low since 1872. Nevertheless, for some Members of Parliament, mainly liberals and members of the Anti Revolutionary Party (ARP), Dutch naturalisation policy was still too tolerant. They stressed the importance of an emotional tie to the Netherlands and saw the practical application in the implementation of naturalisation guidelines. A request for naturalisation had to be turned down if an applicant was not considered to feel sufficiently connected with the Netherlands (Heijs 1995:83).

The interest in acquiring Dutch nationality increased further in the 1920s (Heijs 1995: 84). This rise can be explained by the tighter labour market policy that linked the right to work and reside in the Netherlands to the possession of Dutch nationality.

Due to the economic crisis and the political situation in Germany, the number of applications for naturalisation grew fast in the 1930s, from 414 applications in 1929 to 1,648 applications in 1933.[14] During the crisis years, economic interests had an impact on naturalisation policy. The protection of the labour market and public funds caused the policy to become more restrictive. In 1933, the Catholic Minister of Justice instructed his Department to intensify the investigation into the applicant's background and motives for naturalisation (Heijs 1995: 90). In the second half of the 1930s, this inquiry was extended further. Applicants were required to fill out detailed questionnaires, so-called 'Staten van Inlichtingen', that contained questions regarding the applicant's motives for naturalisation, the applicant's education, membership of a political party, whether he was known to be a spy, whether he was likely to become a burden on the Dutch state in the future, etc.[15] A residence requirement of fifteen, instead of the statutory period of five years was applied in practice (Heijs 1995: 91). Applicants were not informed of the progress of their application or of the reasons for a denial.

It was not only applicants who were sparsely informed of the naturalisation procedure. Parliament was rarely involved in matters concerning the naturalisation policy and was only informed of important policy changes after it took the initiative to ask questions. Most applications passed Parliament without discussion (Heijs 1995: 93).

On 10 May 1940, the Netherlands were drawn into the Second World War. Soon afterwards, the Dutch Parliament stopped assembling and Queen Wilhelmina and her Ministers fled to London. The naturalisation of aliens came to a standstill (Heijs 1995: 107). The naturalisation of married women, however, remained under discussion. Alterations of Dutch nationality law that followed these discussions will be treated later on in this overview (see sect. 11.2.3).

In the post war years, the Netherlands had to cope with poverty, housing shortage and high birth-rates. The Dutch government actively promoted the emigration of Dutch citizens. Large numbers of Dutch citizens moved to Canada, Australia and elsewhere. The Netherlands became a country of emigration.[16]

Naturalisation policies remained restrictive. Feelings of suspicion regarding the motives for naturalisation prevailed and the thorough inquiry of these motives and the applicant's background that had been introduced in the 1930s was still applied (Heijs 1995: 109). The primary question was whether Dutch interests might be damaged by the naturalisation, while the assimilation of the applicant was a secondary concern. For several years, naturalisation rates were low. The ideal of the nation-state, one that expects a loyal attitude of members of the Dutch nation towards the Dutch population and State, greatly influenced the naturalisation practice during this period.

Behaviour during the war became an important criterion for naturalisation. Priority was given to persons who had been actively involved in the Resistance during the war and to men who fought in the allied armies. For these people, naturalisation was free of charge. Priority was also given to persons whose naturalisation would serve the country's social, cultural or economical interests.[17]

Another issue in the post-war years was the naturalisation of Germans. The first Dutch government after the War made plans to expel all Germans living in the Netherlands. Because of fierce opposition by the allied forces occupying Germany, these plans did not materialise. In 1946, the first post-war naturalisations took place. Germans who had shown good moral behaviour were not excluded.[18]

11.2.2 1953-1975: A period of liberalisation

In 1953, a process of liberalisation started with the introduction in the 1892 Act of automatic acquisition of Dutch nationality for immigrants of the third generation. A legitimate child acquired Netherlands nationality if it was born to a parent who had residence in the Netherlands at the time of the child's birth where this parent was born to a mother residing in the Netherlands at the time of birth of her child (de Groot 1996: 552).[19] One of the reasons for introducing this rule was the presence in the border region of large numbers of Belgians that were born in the Netherlands, but did not hold Dutch nationality (Heijs 1995: 115). Large numbers of Dutch nationals found themselves in a similar position on the other side of the border. The new ius soli-provision, which would apply to many more than merely the Belgian inhabitants of the border area, was defended with the argument that third generation immigrants in fact belonged to the Dutch community. The third generation was assumed to have integrated in Dutch society and was no longer required to individually prove that they fulfilled the conditions for naturalisation.

The provision, which had retro-active effect until the coming into force of the 1892 Act, was likely to create cases of dual or multiple nationality. This did not concern the Dutch government. It attached greater value to the equal treatment of individuals who could only be distinguished from Dutch nationals in a legal sense. Another argument was the lowering of the administrative burden (Heijs 1995: 135-136).

The liberalisation also included first generation immigrants. In 1953, the first naturalisations of former Dutch nationals that had served in a German army took place through ministerial decision. In the years thereafter, the possibilities for naturalisation outside Parliament were extended. In 1954, the governor of Surinam was attributed the authority to naturalise Indonesians living in Surinam. In 1958, the Crown was authorised to naturalise minor children whose father had deceased and whose mother possessed Dutch nationality[20] and in 1962 the government was authorised to naturalise former inhabitants of New Guinea (Heijs 1995: 137). The last and most important extension of the possibilities of naturalisation by Royal Decree took place in 1976, where this new naturalisation procedure was made available to persons having a strong connection with the Netherlands (see later on in this paragraph).

Under the influence of the ratification of several treaties, naturalisation was more and more perceived as a right, especially for refugees and stateless persons.[21] In an unpublished White Paper concerning naturalisation in 1965, the Socialist Minister of Justice stated that naturalisation of permanent residents in the Netherlands should be promoted and that it was no longer necessary that every single naturalisation served specific Dutch interests.[22] Still, naturalisation of assimilated immigrants was in the Dutch public interest, since it would prevent problems relating to ethnic minorities, and those who were not likely to adapt to Dutch norms and values were not eligible for naturalisation.[23]

The necessity of addressing every single application for naturalisation individually in Parliament was questioned. Naturalisation took place by Act, which meant that Parliament was involved in each individual application, but the applications were rarely the subject of discussion (Heijs 1995: 143). The denial of an application was exceptional. From 1955 until 1964 less than 2 per cent of the applications were refused. At the beginning of the 1970s, less than 0.5 per cent of the applications were refused.[24]

After a long debate between the Secretary of State for Justice (ARP) and the Parliamentary Commission for Naturalisation, it was agreed that the legal position of applicants ought to be improved and that the naturalisation procedure had to be simplified. The Secretary based his arguments on the abovementioned unpublished White Paper on naturalisation dating from 1965. He stated that the views on nationality had considerably changed during the past decades (Heijs 1995: 161). With the incorporation of the right to a nationality in the Universal Declaration of Human Rights, a process of liberalisation of the naturalisation policy had started. Also, the number of naturalisations had risen and the number of denials had dropped. According to the Secretary of State, it was no longer necessary to treat nine out of ten naturalisations in Parliament. These political and practical arguments led to a partial amendment of the 1892 Act in 1976 (Heijs 1995: 162). In that year, it was decided that as of 15 March 1977, certain categories of applicants for naturalisation could be awarded Dutch nationality upon a simple decision by the Minister of Justice instead of by Act.[25] The latter procedure used to be long and complicated. A large number of authorities had to be consulted and consensus had to be reached in both houses of Parliament.[26] Generally, the procedure took 2 years or more (Groenendijk & Heijs 2001: 149). Under the new procedure, applications had to be made to the Queen's Cabinet, who then forwarded them to the Ministry of Justice. The procedure of naturalisation by ministerial decision was simpler, because the request was not treated in Parliament. The official investigation was also more limited; it was generally only the police that undertook a short inquiry. In case of a denial of the application by the Minister, there was a possibility for appeal.[27]

The new procedure applied to applicants having a strong connection with the Netherlands. The Dutch government considered second generation immigrants, former Dutch nationals and former Dutch subjects and non-Dutch nationals, as applicants having such a connection with the Netherlands.[28] However, proposals from the Parliamentary Commission for Naturalisations in 1972 to grant second generations Dutch nationality upon birth in the Netherlands or allowing them to opt for Dutch nationality upon coming of age were too far-reaching for the Secretary of State (Heijs 1995: 163).

The process of liberalisation of Dutch nationality law continued with the publication in 1977 of a circular specifying the conditions for naturalisation.[29] The requirements laid down in the 1892 Act were interpreted and specified in considerable detail. For the larger part, they had already been applied in practice for many years. The main reason why the Dutch government had not published the conditions previously was that it did not want to commit itself to obeying its own rules. A further reason was that the government wanted to refrain from giving applicants a handle to oppose a negative decision (Heijs 1995: 169). However, appealing to a negative decision in a Court was still not possible.

The publication of the conditions made clear that naturalisation no longer was a favour, but more and more was perceived as a right, not only for applicants with a strong connection with the Netherlands, but also for applicants to be naturalised by Act. Three requirements had to be fulfilled by every applicant.

The first was that there may not be any objection against the applicant residing in the Netherlands for an indefinite period of time. This condition was to prevent the naturalisation policy from interfering with the admission policy. Another condition was the social integration of the applicant in Dutch society. Integration was assumed to have taken place, if he was both able to speak and understand the Dutch language and had assimilated in Dutch society. Immigrants who still felt mainly connected to the country of origin were not considered to have assimilated completely, even if they had been accepted by their surroundings (Böcker, Groenendijk & de Hart 2005). This was assessed on the basis of a short interview by an official of the (alien) police. Minor children and female spouses of the applicant and former Dutchmen were not required to have integrated. The third condition was that the applicant constituted no threat to the public order.

The liberalisation translated into rising naturalisation numbers in the period between 1975 and 1984. Whereas in 1976, 4,201 immigrants had acquired Dutch nationality, this number rose to 13,179 in 1984, peaking in 1982 with 19,728 acquisitions. Most naturalisations concerned immigrants from the former colony of Surinam. Although the numbers of immigrants from Turkey and Morocco had grown between 1975 and 1984 from 50,000 to 155,000 (Turkish) and 115,000 (Moroccan), naturalisation numbers of these groups remained low.

Only 975 Turkish and 516 Moroccan nationals were naturalised during those ten years (Heijs 1995: 208).

11.2.3 1936-1985: Equality between men and women

The 1892 Nationality Act stipulated that the status of women was determined by the status of their husband. This meant that foreign women marrying a Dutch national automatically acquired Dutch nationality, whereas Dutch women lost their nationality upon marriage with a foreign husband. The Act also stipulated that during marriage, women could not independently re-apply for Dutch nationality. On the other hand, women would acquire Dutch nationality automatically if their husband was granted it through naturalisation. Re-obtaining or renouncing Dutch nationality independently was only allowed after dissolution of the marriage after death or divorce (de Hart 2006: 8). Children acquired Dutch nationality as descendants of a Dutch father if born in wedlock or acknowledged or legitimised after birth.

The main arguments subsequent Christian-Democratic governments used to defend this discriminatory policy was the protection of the 'unity of the family', the principle that prescribes the same nationality for the members of a family. At the same time, it was felt that marriage with a foreigner illustrated the alienation of the woman in question from Dutch society.

The first amelioration in the legal position of married women and their children took place in 1936, subsequent to the Hague Convention on 'Certain questions relating to the Conflict of Nationality Laws' of 1930.[30] A foreign woman who married a Dutch national still automatically acquired Netherlands nationality but a Dutch wife who married a foreigner or a stateless person did not automatically lose her Dutch nationality.[31] She retained her nationality if she could not acquire a foreign nationality by marriage. A child of a Dutch mother and a stateless father acquired the Dutch nationality of its mother if it was born in the Netherlands.[32] In principle a married wife still followed the nationality of her husband, but one exception was made: if the husband lost his Dutch nationality, the wife kept her Dutch nationality, if otherwise she would become a stateless person.[33]

The outbreak of the Second World War led to a temporary breach in the concept of the unity of the family. The government wanted to put a stop to the uncontrolled access of German women marrying Dutch men and to protect Dutch women who had married a German national from expulsion. A Royal Decree of 22 May 1943 stipulated that Dutch women who had married a national from a country with which the Netherlands had no diplomatic relations would not lose their nationality. Similarly, German women who had married a Dutch husband after 9 May 1940 did not acquire Dutch nationality.

In 1950, it was decided that German women marrying Dutch men could again acquire Dutch nationality, if they had either resided in the Netherlands for one year, or had been married for at least five years. Dutch women would lose their Dutch nationality upon marriage with a German again as of 1953 (de Hart 2006).

In 1964, as before in 1936, implementation of international law was the main reason to introduce more equality in Dutch nationality law. In that year, the Dutch Nationality Act was revised when the New York Treaty on the Nationality of Married Women of 1957 entered into force.[34] This treaty laid down the independent status of a married woman in nationality law. As a result of the revision of Dutch nationality law a foreign wife of a Dutch national did not automatically acquire the Dutch nationality of her husband anymore; however she could acquire this status by a simple option declaration.[35] A Dutch woman who married a foreigner or a stateless person kept her nationality, even in cases where she acquired her husband's nationality by operation of the law.[36] A transitory regulation was created to provide for equality for the women who had married a foreign national before 1964. During the period of one year, these women could re-acquire Dutch nationality by lodging a simple declaration, if they were still married and had not acquired another nationality voluntarily. After the transitional period of one year, a woman could only make this declaration after she had been resident in the Netherlands for at least one year. Of all the women that re-acquired their Dutch nationality in the first year, 40 per cent retained their husband's nationality (de Hart 2006). The objections of the Dutch government against dual nationality were made subordinate to the equality principle.

Another alteration was the termination of joint naturalisation for married couples. As of 1964, both spouses had to individually meet the naturalisation requirements.

Gender inequality was abolished on 1 January 1985. As of that date, children acquire Dutch nationality at birth when either parent is Dutch.[37] The 1984 Nationality Act also provides for the same procedure of acquisition of Dutch nationality for foreign men and women married to Dutch nationals: as of 1 January 1985, both have to rely on naturalisation if they want to acquire Dutch nationality. Before that date, foreign women married to Dutch men were able to simply lodge a declaration of option. Instead of according a similar right of option to foreign men marrying Dutch women, the government decided to subject the foreign women to the naturalisation procedure. The fear of marriages of convenience lay behind this decision (de Hart 2006). In this context, Jessurun d'Oliveira spoke of 'good women suffering under bad men' (Jessurun d'Oliveira 1977).

11.2.4 1949-1975: Dealing with the colonies

To conclude, a few words need to be dedicated to the naturalisation policies concerning the inhabitants of Indonesia and Surinam, two former colonies of the Netherlands. When these colonies became independent, the status of the inhabitants of the former colonies occupied the minds in Parliament for several years.

After the independence of Indonesia in 1949, it was decided that the 70 million Dutch subjects, non-Dutch nationals, would become Indonesian nationals and lose their former status. The 250,000 Dutch nationals who were accorded the right to opt for Indonesian nationality were strongly encouraged to do so by the Dutch Government. Eventually, only 13,600 Indonesian Dutch opted for Indonesian nationality. Later on, many of these persons would regret their decision to opt for Indonesian nationality. They became known as the '*repenters*' who, according to various Members of Parliament, needed to be admitted to the Netherlands. Following Parliamentary attention to this group and to the non-acknowledged Indonesian children with a Dutch father, the so-called social Dutch, the immigration policy concerning these groups became more lenient. This, however, did not count for the policy concerning their naturalisation. It was not until 1960 that the Ministry of Justice embarked on a more liberal policy concerning the naturalisation of the *repenters* and the social Dutch. As of 1960, it was mostly Indonesians that acquired Dutch nationality through naturalisation. Previously, German immigrants had always formed the largest group.

When Surinam became independent in 1975, it was harder to legally determine which citizens belonged to Surinam and which did not, since the status Dutch subject, non-Dutch national, did not apply in this country. Using the indirect criteria of 'country of birth' and 'country of residence', it was decided that Dutch nationals living in Surinam on 25 November 1975 obtained Surinamese nationality. This provision did not apply to first generation Dutch nationals of European origin. A right to opt for Dutch nationality was accorded to the second generation of Dutch nationals of European origin. Hence, only Dutch nationals of Surinamese origin and Dutch nationals of Asian origin (the descendents of immigrants from the former Dutch and British East Indies) (Heijs 1991: 35) acquired the new Surinamese nationality. The 1975 Allocation Agreement stipulated that acquisition of Surinamese nationality entailed the loss of Dutch nationality. Dutch nationals of Surinamese and Asian origin did not receive a right of option for Dutch nationality.

The 1975 Agreement, despite the absence of a legal distinction between natives and Europeans, had the same effect as the 1949 Agreement with Indonesia. Most white Dutch nationals living in Surinam retained their Dutch nationality (or were allowed to opt for it), whereas the non-white Dutch nationals lost this nationality (Heijs 1991: 35). The restriction of immigration played a much larger role in the realisation of the 1975 Agreement than it did at the coming about of the Agreement of 1949. Whereas immigration only became an issue after Indonesian independence, due to the deterioration of relations between Indonesia and the Netherlands, the Dutch government wanted to put a stop to immigration coming from Surinam shortly after its independence. This intention of the Dutch government was only partially realised. Whereas at the time of Surinam's independence 100,000 Surinamese Dutch nationals lived in the Netherlands (Reubsaet 1982), their number had grown to 244,000 by 1990. Ten years later, 300,000 persons living in the Netherlands were born in Surinam or had a parent born in Surinam, while only 10,000 of them had Surinamese nationality.[38]

11.3 Recent developments and current institutional arrangements

11.3.1 Political analysis

11.3.1.1 Introduction: integration policies

In order to understand developments of nationality law, it is relevant to describe Dutch integration policies, which have had a profound impact since the 1980s. Dutch integration policies have shifted from what has been called a 'pacesetter of multicultural policies' (Vermeulen & Penninx 2000: 3) to a more assimilationist approach (Joppke & Morawska 2003:2). In the 1950s and 1960s, the Netherlands was a country of emigration. The Dutch government did not concern itself with developing a policy concerning the influx of newcomers, mainly because their stay in the Netherlands was considered as temporary.[39] In the 1970s, the policy was two-fold, since it both aimed at integration, and at the return of immigrants to their home-countries. Since the immigrant stay in the Netherlands was still considered to be temporary, 'integration with preservation of cultural identity' was the policy's motto.

In 1979, the Scientific Council for Government Policy (WRR) published its influential report *Ethnic Minorities*, advising the government to accept the fact that most immigrants would stay permanently in the Netherlands, and to develop a policy aimed at equal participation of minorities in society.

The starting point was the improvement of the settled immigrants' legal position. The government mentioned two ways in which the differences in legal status between Dutch nationals and immigrants could be diminished. The first was by naturalisation. The restrictive Dutch immigration policy justified a generous naturalisation policy (Heijs 1995: 180). The second way was by diminishing the differences between Dutch nationals and non-Dutch nationals in laws and policies, where these differences were no longer justified. Hence, in the 1980s many initiatives were taken to improve the legal position of immigrants and to stimulate naturalisation (de Hart 2005: 6). The new Dutch Nationality Act, which came into force on 1 January 1985, was mentioned as being of 'special importance' for the new minorities' policy.[40]

In the 1990s, a shift from a 'minorities' policy' to an 'integration policy' took place. The government developed a new approach, with emphasis on the need for integration of individual immigrants. Providing immigrants with the instruments for a fuller participation in society had replaced the 'caring' approach of the 1970s and 1980s (Entzinger 2003: 73). The focus was on the obligations of individuals. The term 'active citizenship' was introduced to re-emphasise the responsibility of each individual for his or her place in society. The 1998 Act on the Civic Integration of Newcomers, by introducing so-called newcomer programs, requires individual immigrants to take obligatory language and societal knowledge courses.[41]

During the same period, the integration of immigrants became a subject of public debate. The idea emerged that immigrants had been treated too liberally, that they had been 'pampered' without imposing obligations. Several years later events led to an atmosphere of increasing tension and the idea that the integration of immigrants into Dutch society had failed. This development was triggered by the publication in 2000 of an influential article entitled 'The Multicultural Tragedy' (*Het multiculturele drama*) by Paul Scheffer, a publicist and prominent member of the Socialist PvdA, followed by the events of 9/11, the rising influence of the populist politician Pim Fortuyn, his murder in May 2002, and finally the murder of cineaste Theo van Gogh on 2 November 2004. Integration was no longer to be stimulated, but a requirement for non-western Dutch immigrants of foreign descent, now generally referred to as 'muslims' (de Hart 2005: 7). The current policy is the opposite of the minorities' policy of the 1980s, in which the idea prevailed that a strong legal position would contribute to immigrants' integration. In the current policy, admittance, a secure legal residence and Dutch nationality are regarded as remuneration for integration. The Minister of Alien Affairs and Integration (Conservative Liberals) regularly refers to acquisition of Dutch nationality as 'the first prize'.[42] Currently, naturalisation is the crown on the completed integration process.

In the following, we will describe how the changed thinking on integration influenced Dutch nationality law.

11.3.1.2 *Acquisition of Dutch nationality for first generation immigrants*

On 1 January 1985, a new Dutch Nationality Act came into force, replacing the former 1892 Act.[43] The minorities' policy, introduced in the early 1980s, clearly influenced the final text of the new Act. Strengthening the legal position of non-Dutch minorities was a central element of this policy. Under the new Act, the procedure for acquiring Dutch nationality through naturalisation was simplified and applicants for naturalisation were given the possibility of appealing negative decisions. With the coming into force of the 1984 Act, naturalisation became more a right than a favour.

An example of this transformation was the codification in the Act of the conditions for naturalisation. The new nationality Act stipulated that, in order to be eligible for naturalisation, an applicant must

- Be at least eighteen years of age;
- Have been granted a residence permit in the Netherlands by the immigration authorities for a purpose not limited in time;
- Have resided in the Netherlands for at least five consecutive years prior to the application;
- Not constitute a danger to public order, public morals, public health or the security of the Kingdom;
- Have made an effort to renounce his or her foreign nationality, unless renunciation cannot be demanded.

The conditions for naturalisation mentioned in the new Act hardly differ from the conditions that were published in 1977.

11.3.1.3 *Integration and dual nationality: an impossible combination?*

The determination of the 1984 Nationality Act and the ratification of the Council of Europe Convention on the Reduction of Cases of Multiple Nationalities took place on the same day.[44] Though the Convention aimed at reducing the number of cases of dual nationality, the new Dutch nationality Act generated many cases of dual nationality. As of 1 January 1985, Dutch nationality could be acquired from the father and the mother. The government did not consider this amendment in contradiction to the objective of preventing multiple nationality, because it gave more weight to the principle of gender equality (de Hart 2006: 16).

Under the 1984 Act, second generation immigrants were given the possibility of acquiring Dutch nationality by lodging a simple, unilateral declaration. This so-called option procedure did not require renunciation of the original nationality. The third generation-provision, in force since 1953, was retained. It would also create its share of dual nationals. Nevertheless, the Dutch government explicitly expressed itself to be against multiple nationality in case of naturalisation (de Hart 2004: 151).

Though fiercely opposed by left-wing parties, who used as a main argument the incompatibility of the requirement with the goal of making nationality acquisition easier as incorporated in the new minorities' policy, the renunciation requirement was incorporated in the 1984 Act. However, persons from whom renouncing their original nationality could not reasonably be expected were exempted from the requirement.[45]

These exceptions were already laid down in the circular that was published in 1977.[46] Renunciation was not required if the laws of the country of origin did not allow it (for example Morocco, Greece, Iran and most countries in Eastern Europe), if it could not reasonably be expected that the applicant contacted the authorities of his country of origin (refugees), or in case renunciation would cause disproportional (moral or financial) damage. Since retention of the original nationality largely depends on laws and practices in the country of origin, Jessurun d'Oliveira spoke of a 'shuffling of lottery balls' (Jessurun d'Oliveira 1991).

The dual nationality of Dutch emigrants abroad was also addressed during the Parliamentary discussion of the 1984 Act. According to the Government, automatic loss of Dutch nationality upon spending ten years abroad was justifiable, since the connection of these Dutch nationals with the Netherlands would be either very weak or non-existent (de Hart 2005: 18). Automatic loss of Dutch nationality provided for a correction of the growing number of dual nationals under the new Act. Equality between immigrants and emigrants also was used as an argument at the expense of dual nationality for Dutch nationals living abroad. In 1983, an article by Mackaay, a Dutch lawyer living in Canada, concerning the advantages of dual nationality for emigrants was published in the largest weekly for lawyers in the Netherlands (Mackaay 1983). Following this article, hundreds of letters were sent to Parliament and the Ministry of Justice by Dutch emigrants with dual nationality. The campaign failed to convince a majority in Parliament. Motions allowing for dual nationality for emigrants and immigrants put forward by left wing parties were rejected. As of 1 January 1985, Dutch nationality was lost automatically after ten years of residence abroad.[47]

At the end of 1989, the discussion concerning the renunciation requirement has revived. This was mainly due to the Scientific Council for Government Policy's (WRR 1989) report on 'Alien Policy' (*Allochtonenbeleid*). In this report, the Council restated that integration required improvement of the immigrant's legal position and, hence, naturalisation should not be made more difficult than strictly necessary (de Hart 2005: 20). The Council recommended allowing dual nationality for immigrants.

Initially, the Lubbers III government (Socialists and Christian Democrats, 1989-1994) turned down the Council's advice.[48] Subsequently, pressure was applied in the Second Chamber to abolish the renunciation requirement. Outside of the Second Chamber, immigrant organisations spoke out against the renunciation requirement. The IOT, the national body of Turkish organisations, actively lobbied for the abolishment of the renunciation requirement. The fact that Turkish men could give up Turkish nationality only after fulfilling their military obligations explains the Turkish interest in abolishment of the requirement (Groenendijk & Heijs 2001: 159).

In May 1991, the government sent the Memorandum 'Multiple nationality and voting rights for aliens' to the Lower House.[49] In this Memorandum, the government observed that a change in the perception of dual nationality had taken place (Bedem 1993: 33). It acknowledged that allowing for dual nationality might serve the realisation of the government's strive for integration and participation in society.[50] The government proposed to abolish the requirement. The Memorandum represented a compromise between the parties forming the coalition government. Where the Christian Democrats gave up their objections against the possibility of retention of former nationality, the Socialists gave up their wish to extend voting rights for non-national residents to the national level.

The government's proposal caused a division in the Second Chamber. The conservative liberals and the small right wing parties condemned the acceptance of dual nationality (de Hart 2004: 153). The Christian Democratic Party was internally divided. The Socialists and small left wing parties were clear proponents of dual nationality. They stressed that globalisation and migration had changed the world, creating the possibility of having a connection with several countries. They also claimed that dual nationality would promote integration (Böcker et al. 2005).

At the end of 1991, a compromise between proponents and opponents of the renunciation requirement was reached. In a motion formulated by Socialists and Christian Democrats, the latter could read a confirmation that the renunciation requirement still existed, but would in future be applied more leniently, whereas according to the former, the motion provided for a choice by the immigrant himself whether or not to retain his former nationality.[51] The motion was adopted by a majority of the Second Chamber. Pending the required amendment of the nationality legislation, the Christian Democratic Minister of Justice, with the Second Chamber's consent, used his statutory discretion to abolish the renunciation requirement in November 1991.[52] The new policy only applied to immigrants. Dutch nationals that acquired another nationality or emigrants with dual nationality that spent ten years abroad would still lose their Dutch nationality.

The measure was a success, since it led to a dramatic increase in the number of naturalisations, in particular among Turks, Moroccans and refugees. We will discuss the effects of the abolishment, and later the reintroduction of the renunciation demand in sect. 11.3.2.1.

In February 1993, a Bill was introduced to formalise the practice of allowing for dual nationality for immigrants and extend it to Dutch nationals. The discussion in Parliament in the years that followed mainly focussed on dual nationality for immigrants.

According to the Christian Democrats and Conservative Liberals, the rise in the number of naturalisations clearly showed that naturalisation had become too easy. In their opinion, naturalisation should not be seen as means for integration, but as a crown on the completed integration procedure (Böcker et al. 2005). Socialists, Progressive Liberals and Green Left still advocated dual nationality, seeing it as a means to further integration.

In 1995, the Parliament was flooded with letters from Dutch nationals living abroad. Since ten years had passed after the coming into force of the 1984 Nationality Act, the first Dutch emigrants had automatically lost their Dutch nationality as a consequence of their residence abroad. In the letters, the emigrants pleaded for the possibility of dual nationality. Both left- and right-wing parties favoured dual nationality for emigrants, albeit for different reasons. The Conservative Liberals spoke out for dual nationality of Dutch emigrants, stating that it should be left to the receiving country whether or not to allow for dual nationality. The main argument of the Christian Democrats was that dual nationality could be allowed for Dutch emigrants since they did not pose an integration issue. Left-wing parties spoke out for the Dutch emigrants mainly as an argument to also allow for dual nationality for immigrants. In their opinion, allowing for dual nationality for emigrants was not compatible with objecting to dual nationality for immigrants.

Despite renewed doubts concerning the abolishment of the renunciation requirement, the bill that allowed for dual nationality for both immigrants and emigrants passed the Second Chamber in 1995. In Senate, the right-wing majority rejected the government's attempt to codify the abolition of the renunciation requirement. In 1996, the Secretary of State of the Justice department decided to withdraw the Bill.

In 1997, the requirement for applicants to renounce foreign nationality was reintroduced. A circular laid down the exceptions that were larger in number than the exceptions that applied to the renunciation demand before 1992.[53] They applied to the majority of the immigrants that applied for naturalisation (de Hart 2004: 157).

In February 1998, a new Bill on Dutch nationality was proposed.[54] In this Bill, the renunciation requirement was retained. During the Parliamentary discussion of the Bill, the major political parties developed a more restrictive attitude towards naturalisation in general, especially concerning the required knowledge of Dutch language and society. Christian Democrats and Conservative Liberals claimed that most immigrants had been obtaining Dutch nationality for pragmatic reasons rather than as a sign of loyalty to the Netherlands. Eventually, the Christian Democrats voted against the bill, arguing that the requirements for naturalisation should be even stricter. Conservative Liberals and the small Christian parties criticised the large number of exceptions to the renunciation requirement. They wondered what was left in practice of the legal obligation to renounce one's nationality upon naturalisation (Groenendijk & Barzilay 2001: 54).

Finally, the bill was approved in 2000 and it came into force on 1 April 2003.[55] It still allowed dual nationality in many cases, but made access to Dutch nationality more difficult. By then, discussions regarding the integration requirement had led to the addition of a strict language and society test as a condition for naturalisation.

While making it harder for first generation immigrants to acquire Dutch nationality, the possibilities for Dutch emigrants to retain their nationality have been enlarged. Dutch nationality is no longer lost automatically after spending ten years abroad (art. 15 para. 3 and 4 DNA 2000). Those who lost Dutch nationality this way were given the possibility to re-acquire it under easier conditions (art. V para. 1 DNA 2000). Furthermore, Dutch nationals that apply for the nationality of their partner are allowed to keep their nationality (Art. 15 para. 2 sub c DNA 2000).

Recently, the Minister of Alien Affairs and Integration (Conservative Liberals) has submitted a Bill trying to combat dual nationality. It includes elimination of two legal exceptions to the renunciation requirement, both stemming from the Second Protocol of the Strasbourg Convention, namely the exception for second generation immigrants (born or having resided in the Netherlands for five years before reaching majority) and foreign spouses or partners of Dutch nationals. The Minister claimed that introduction of the renunciation requirement for the categories mentioned was not contrary to the European Convention on Nationality, since other articles in the Dutch Nationality Act provided for easy access to Dutch nationality for these groups.[56]

A further proposal the Government made concerning dual nationality, was to withdraw Dutch nationality from dual nationals that have been convicted for terrorist acts. In a letter sent by the Government to the Second Chamber on 10 November 2004, following the murder on the Dutch film maker Theo van Gogh the week before, the Memorandum that preceded the Bill which includes the measures to restrict dual nationality was mentioned as one of the measures to combat terrorism.[57] In the eyes of the Dutch government, reducing dual nationality is an instrument in the fight against terrorism. Meanwhile, the Council of State has already given advice concerning a proposal for withdrawing Dutch nationality in case of conduct seriously prejudicial to the vital interests of the State.

11.3.1.4 Second and third generation: supposed integration?

In the past twenty years, not only the renunciation requirement has been the subject of political debate. Nationality acquisition by second and third generation immigrants also gave rise to discussion in Parliament. In the original bill for a new Dutch Nationality Act in 1981, the clause on automatic acquisition of Dutch nationality for third generation immigrants, in force since 1953, was not included.[58] In the government's opinion, the simple fact of birth in a country did not justify automatic acquisition of that country's nationality. According to the Government, the assumption that birth in a country generated feelings of connection with that country was superseded.[59]

Two years later, the Government revised its opinion. In the memorandum of reply, the Secretary of State for Justice (CDA) stated that retention of the double ius soli provision was desirable, since it would strengthen the legal position of third generation immigrants in the Netherlands.[60] This change of direction was closely connected to the minorities' policy set out in the governmental White Paper on minorities, which was published a few months later.

However, the government did not intend to retain the third generation provision in its old form. Instead, it proposed to afford the right of option, to be exercised upon coming of age, or earlier by the child's legal representatives. The government, supported by Moluccan lobby organisations, did not want to impose Dutch nationality. But the strong lobby of the NCB, the Dutch Centre for Immigrants, had a major influence on the Parliamentary debate concerning the third generation-provision (Groenendijk & Heijs 2001: 159). They could however not convince Parliament to allow for automatic acquisition of Dutch nationality for second generation immigrants.[61]

Eventually, after the adoption, by large majority, of a Christian Democrat/Liberal amendment, the third generation-provision was maintained in its original form. The third generation was expected to integrate in Dutch society automatically hence justifying acquisition of Dutch nationality at birth.

According to the current Dutch government, the primary goal of the Dutch Nationality Act of 2000, that came into force on 1 April 2003, is to assure that anyone who, either because of birth, because of integration in Dutch society or because of other reasons possesses a sufficiently strong tie with the Netherlands, and fulfils the other conditions for acquisition of Dutch nationality, has the right to fully participate in Dutch society and to this end acquire Dutch nationality. Another aim is to promote the exclusive possession of Dutch nationality, as a means to promote integration.[62] The third generation provision shows that these goals are not always reconcilable. Though the clause can well be defended using the first goal, the same provision is responsible for creating cases of dual nationality, hence clashing with the second goal of the new Nationality Act. Still, the provision is retained in the Act.

During the discussion on the budget for the Ministry of Justice on 3 November 2003, MP Sterk (Christian Democrats), supported by Nawijn (MP for the Centre Right List Pim Fortuyn) and Hirsi Ali (Conservative Liberals), proposed a motion requesting that government no longer allow for dual nationality for the third generation (3 November 2003, Tweede Kamer 2003-2004, 29 200 VI, no. 81). In the motion, the third generation of immigrants is referred to as *allochtones*, though the automatic acquisition of Dutch nationality is not questioned. The motion was not passed by the Government.

As of 1 January 1985, not only third generation immigrants, but also second generation immigrants could profit from favourable conditions when applying for Dutch nationality. In 1983, under the influence of the minorities' policy, which aimed at reinforcing the long-term immigrants' legal position in order to further integration, the government proposed to grant the right of option to the second generation. Since 1976, this category had benefited from an accelerated procedure of naturalisation by ministerial decision.

Parliament received the government's proposition positively, and the 1984 Nationality Act, in addition to the retained third generation provision, provided for the right of option for the second generation. As of 1 January 1985, those born on Dutch territory were granted the right to opt for Dutch nationality between the ages of 18 and 25, under the condition that they had been residing on Dutch territory since birth.

The option procedure differed in many ways from the traditional acquisition of nationality through naturalisation. Contrary to the naturalisation procedure, the option procedure was a unilateral declaration by the applicant, without further conditions. There was no obligation to renounce the former nationality and no public order or integration requirement. Whilst during the naturalisation procedure it was evaluated for each individual applicant whether feelings of loyalty and connection towards the Dutch state existed, these feelings were presumed to exist in the option procedure. However, Parliament and Government shared the opinion that these feelings were not strong enough to provide for acquisition of Dutch nationality at birth, as was the case for the third generation.

In practice, the right of option for second generation immigrants proved to be less important than MPs expected at the time. Most immigrant children acquired Dutch nationality upon naturalisation of their parents.

In the amended Dutch Nationality Act, in effect since April 2003, the number of categories of persons that can acquire Dutch nationality by option is extended from two to eight.[63] The right of option is also introduced for second generation immigrants that have been lawfully residing in the Netherlands since the age of four (art. 6 para. 1 sub e). Furthermore, the maximum age of 25 for lodging a declaration of option has been cancelled. The 2000 Act also offers a possibility for children to share in the acquisition of Dutch nationality through the right of option by their parents. At first sight, this legislation is favourably disposed towards persons interested in acquiring Dutch nationality through the right of option. However, it also puts up important barriers.

For persons eligible for acquisition of Dutch nationality through the right of option, simply lodging a declaration is no longer enough. Under the new Act, the mayor may refuse confirmation in case of 'serious suspicions that the person constitutes a threat to public order, public decency or the safety of the Kingdom' (art. 6 para. 3).

In the Manual for the application of the Dutch Nationality Act, it is specified what has to be understood by 'serious suspicions that the person constitutes a threat to public order, public decency or the safety of the Kingdom'. It appears that this ground of refusal is to be interpreted in the same way as it is in the case of a naturalisation.[64] This means that if an applicant has been convicted for a crime that has been sanctioned in a certain way, within the four years preceding application, the request for Dutch nationality will be denied. It also means that a serious suspicion that an applicant has committed such a crime will lead to a refusal to confirm the option procedure. According to the Manual, there is a 'serious suspicion' if, for example, the applicant's case is still pending before a criminal Court or the prosecution has not yet started. Another difference between the old and the new option procedure is that under the new Act, most categories of optants have to have lawful residence in the Netherlands.[65] Some categories are even required to have had a certain period of habitual residence before making the declaration. The old act did not stipulate such conditions. Moreover, whereas the option procedure for Dutch nationality was free of charge before 1 April 2003, as of that date, a fee of 132 euros has to be paid.

Currently, the right of option no longer constitutes a middle course between *ex lege* acquisition and naturalisation. It can be seen as a simplified form of naturalisation. The option procedure and the naturalisation procedure show more similarities than differences (Dekker 2003: 126). The two main differences are the absence of the integration requirement and renunciation requirement.

11.3.1.5 *Integration and the first generation: the language and integration-requirement*

Integration into Dutch society has always been a condition for naturalisation. Before 1985, integration was mentioned as a condition for naturalisation in the instructions for naturalisation.[66] According to these instructions, the applicant should have 'a reasonable knowledge of the Dutch language' and be 'assimilated into Dutch society'.[67] In the bill for the 1984 Nationality Act, the requirements for naturalisation were explicitly codified. By mentioning the integration requirement as the first condition for naturalisation, the Dutch government wanted to show that in its opinion, integration was the most important requirement (art. 7 proposition 1984 Act). At the same time, the Dutch government made clear that 'integration' is not the same as 'assimilation'. These notions had been synonymous for quite some time in the naturalisation policy, but ever since the White Paper on Minorities had characterised Dutch society as multicultural, with room for minorities to enjoy their own culture, the term assimilation was no longer applied. Where 'assimilation' was easily associated with unilateral and total adaptation to the Dutch society by the immigrant, 'integration' was considered to be compatible with the goals of the White Paper (Heijs 1995: 193).

During the discussion of the bill, practically all parties objected to the integration requirement, albeit for different reasons. Small left wing parties feared that the vagueness of the requirement would lead to legal insecurity and inequality.[68] Since they had an 'instrumentalist' view on naturalisation, and saw acquisition of Dutch nationality as a condition for integration rather than the other way round, they favoured abolishment of the integration requirement altogether. To this end, several left-wing MPs put forward an amendment.[69]

Although a large majority in Parliament criticised the vagueness of the integration-requirement, they thought a total abolishment of the condition too far-reaching. With the Secretary of State they shared the opinion that 'the circumstance that a precise and sound definition, applicable under all circumstances, is hard to find' was no reason to waive the integration requirement.[70] Most MPs had an 'emotional' vision concerning naturalisation. In their view, a certain number of years of residence in the Netherlands was not enough for conferring Dutch nationality. A certain feeling of connection to Dutch society had to exist. Both the renunciation requirement and the integration requirement safeguarded this connection (Heijs 1995: 22).

In order to overcome the vagueness of the integration requirement, Christian Democratic and Conservative Liberal MPs proposed to incorporate conditions for integration in the Act. In an amendment, they in fact codified the criteria from the old 1977 instructions on naturalisation. Their amendment was adopted. In the 1984 Act, integration in Dutch society was defined as having a reasonable knowledge of Dutch language and having been accepted in Dutch society.[71]

In practice, after 1985, only the language test was used to judge whether an applicant fulfilled the integration requirement. If the language-requirement was fulfilled, it was assumed that applicant maintained contacts with Dutch nationals. Only in the case of bigamy would sufficient language skills not suffice for a positive judgement on integration (Heijs 1995: 195). The language requirement was considered fulfilled if the applicant was able to make the application for naturalisation on his or her own and if he or she could have a conversation about common and daily affairs.

The Manual on the application of the Dutch Nationality Act mentioned illiterates, persons with limited education and the elderly as categories of persons that were to be treated flexibly when it came to knowledge of the Dutch language. Though the Manual provided guidelines for civil servants in charge of determining whether applicant sufficiently spoke and understood Dutch, at the same time it raised new questions. What, for example, had to be understood by 'flexible treatment' or by 'limited education'?

In research conducted in 1988, it appeared that not all civil servants were informed of the policy concerning the language requirement (Heijs 1988). The language test was not applied uniformly in all municipalities. In more than 10 per cent of the cases, not only speaking and understanding, but also reading and writing Dutch was tested (Heijs 1988: 51). Failing the language test was the most important ground for refusal of applications for naturalisation. However, less than 5 per cent of applications were refused (Heijs 1995: 58).

The content of the integration requirement again arose during the discussion of the 1998 bill to amend the 1984 Nationality Act.[72] This bill aimed at a limited relaxation of the renunciation requirement (see earlier in this section). Apart from specifying the language requirement, it did not alter the integration requirement.[73] During the bill's discussion in Parliament, the major conservative political parties developed a more restrictive attitude towards naturalisation. The integration requirement especially was subjected to heavy criticism. The larger conservative parties frequently used the term 'loyalty'. The Christian Democrats, for example, expressed the opinion that, in order for an applicant to be eligible for naturalisation, he had to feel Dutch. Dutch nationality was something to be proud of and should not become a throw-away or consumption article. Christian Democrats, Conservative Liberals and the small Christian parties insisted on a stricter integration requirement (de Hart 2004: 28).

In February 2000, the Conservative Liberals and Christian Democrats proposed an amendment that aimed at requiring a higher proficiency of the Dutch language upon naturalisation, and at testing the applicant's knowledge of Dutch society. At the same time, the Progressive Liberal D66 proposed an amendment to lay down the rules concerning applicant's reading and speaking skills and knowledge of Dutch polity in a Decree.[74] When it became clear that a majority in Parliament was in favour of a stricter integration requirement, the secretary of State decided to alter the bill for the new Nationality Act: A Decree would specify to what extent applicants for naturalisation are required to command Dutch language and polity.[75] In the explanatory memorandum, the Secretary spoke of 'oral and written' knowledge of Dutch language and knowledge of Dutch polity and society.

After the new Dutch Nationality Act entered into force 1 April 2003, a Royal Decree provided for a naturalisation exam consisting of two parts: firstly a societal knowledge test and secondly a test of the ability to read, write, understand and speak the Dutch language.[76]

This shift to a naturalisation exam requiring sufficient knowledge of Dutch society and sufficient oral and written knowledge of the Dutch language can be explained by the shift in Dutch integration policy, that became more assimilationist (de Hart 2005: 4). Integration was no longer to be stimulated but a requirement, and it was to this end that the new naturalisation exam was introduced.

The integration requirement was not the only requirement that was made stricter by the 2000 Act. Following the linking of the Nationality Act to the 2000 Aliens Act,[77] as of 1 April 2003, applicants for naturalisation must have been lawfully residing in the Netherlands during the entire five years immediately prior to application. Furthermore, the lawful residence must have been uninterrupted.[78]

In addition to these stricter conditions for naturalisation, the possibilities of losing Dutch nationality are extended. A new provision, providing for the possibility of losing Dutch nationality following fraud or concealment of a material fact, has been introduced in the 2000 Act. Contrary to the other provisions dealing with loss of Dutch nationality, statelessness does not stand in the way of a withdrawal of nationality under the new provision. In 2004, 55 persons lost Dutch nationality on the basis of this new article.[79]

In order to understand the barrier that is thrown up by the new naturalisation exam and the influence it might have had on the number of naturalisations in 2003 and 2004, we will examine the content of the exam in more detail. Applicants need to have passed the naturalisation exam before they can apply for naturalisation.

The computerised exam consists of two parts. Part I is the so-called Societal Orientation (SO) test. In 45 minutes, the applicant is required to answer by computer 40 multiple choice questions concerning polity, employment, income and financial matters, residence, health care, transport and traffic. Only if the applicant passes the SO test, will he or she be allowed to take part in the language test.

The second part takes about four hours and examines whether the applicant can sufficiently speak, understand, read and write Dutch. The applicant is required to make himself or herself understandable in Dutch. What he writes down or tells has to be comprehensible for others.[80] The level of the language test in the naturalisation exam is the same as the level that is pursued in the integration program offered to newcomers after their arrival in the Netherlands.

The costs of the naturalisation test are 90 euros for the SO test and 165 euros for the language test. Applicants first have to pay the costs for the SO test before they take part in this part of the exam. Once they have passed the Societal Orientation test, they will have to pay for the language test, after which they are allowed to take part in the second half of the naturalisation exam. In addition to the costs that are charged for the exam, the applicant will also be charged a fee for the naturalisation application (348 euros). Hence the total costs are 603 euros.

The content of the naturalisation exam is not published and the government offers no possibilities to prepare for the exam. As the leader of the project to introduce the exam explained at a seminar on the amended Nationality Act in March 2003: 'One cannot study to be Dutch, one has to feel Dutch.' The brochure from the Ministry of Justice concerning the naturalisation exam mentions that the courses offered to immigrants by the municipality in which they reside, are helpful to acquire the necessary knowledge, but do not guarantee a positive outcome of the naturalisation exam. In case the applicant did not take part in the official integration course, the brochure suggests that he or she uses his or her knowledge gathered in practice, or during courses and trainings. If applicants fail the test, they can retake it after waiting for half a year.

The following categories of immigrants are exempted from the test: Moluccans, who, on the basis of the Act of 9 September 1976 are treated as Dutch nationals (see sect. 11.3.3) applicants who master Dutch language at secondary school level, who have obtained the integration certificate after successful completion of the statutory integration course provided for by the Act of 1998 or who have formally been exempted by the municipal authorities from taking part in this integration course due to sufficient knowledge of Dutch language.

Applicants that suffer from a medical or language impediment may be totally or partially released from the test. If an applicant wants to rely on a medical impediment such as deafness, blindness, speech defects or a mental obstruction for (partial) exemption of the naturalisation exam, he or she will have to submit a doctor's certificate. The IND will decide whether the applicant's claim for exemption is granted.

The local educational centre (ROC) of Amsterdam is in charge of claims for exemption on the basis of language impediments. The centre will analyse the applicant's ability to learning Dutch within five years. On the basis of this feasibility study, the ROC Amsterdam will advise the IND whether total or partial exemption should be granted or not. The applicant is charged 200 euros for the feasibility study.

Applicants suffering from an impediment are required to take those parts of the naturalisation exam that they are able to. Persons suffering from blindness, dyslexia or illiteracy, for example, could in general still take the parts that did not require reading ability. In practice, however, the SO test and the speaking and understanding part of the language test also required reading skills. Consequently, the applicants who were not able to read were exempted from the complete exam. This practice did not comply with the objectives in the Royal Decree on the naturalisation exam. Hence, the Minister of Alien Affairs and Integration (Conservative Liberals) has provided the possibility of taking parts of the test by phone. This way, persons who have problems reading, or using a computer, such as rheumatics, or having other physical impediments, can still take parts of the exam.[81] The telephonic test has not yet been put into use, due to technical defects.

In order to surround the moment of acquisition of the Dutch nationality with more decorum, several MPs have insisted on the creation of a citizenship ceremony. In December 2004, Conservative Liberals put forward a motion, stating that loyalty and commitment to the Dutch society may be expected of new Dutch nationals and that special attention ought to be paid to their rights and duties as Dutch nationals on the memorable moment of acquisition of Dutch nationality. The motion was supported by a majority in Parliament. The Minister of Alien Affairs and Integration, who repeatedly referred to acquisition of Dutch nationality as the 'first prize' in the integration process, declared to be very willing to pursue the course charted by Parliament. On 24 August 2005, the first citizenship ceremony took place in The Hague. The

Minister of Alien Affairs and Integration welcomed 30 new Dutch nationals by presenting them with the Dutch flag and a copy of the Dutch Constitution. 24 August is meant to become 'naturalisation day'.

11.3.2 *Statistical developments*

In examining statistics concerning the acquisition of Dutch nationality, two developments in the numbers of acquisitions and applications for naturalisation stand out. The first is related to the abolishment and reintroduction of the renunciation requirement, the second to the introduction of the naturalisation test.

11.3.2.1 *Effects of the abolishment and reintroduction of the renunciation requirement*

We have seen that the renunciation requirement has had its share of attention over the past few decades. In order to examine the actual effects of the (abolishment of) the renunciation requirement, one can compare the numbers of naturalisations prior to the abolishment of the renunciation requirement in 1991 with the number of naturalisations between 1991 and 1997, when the requirement was reintroduced. Since categories of applicants are exempted from the renunciation re-

Table 11.1: Numbers of naturalisations in the Netherlands from 1985 to 2003: Did the (absence of the) renunciation requirement affect the number of naturalisations?

Year	*Number of naturalisations*
1985	16,000
1986	12,000
1987	10,000
1988	7,000
1989	27,000
1990	12,000
1991	27,000
1992	34,000
1993	40,000
1994	47,000
1995	68,000
1996	79,000
1997	56,000
1998	56,000
1999	58,000
2000	46,000
2001	43,000
2002	42,000
2003	25,000

Source: Central Bureau of Statistics

quirement, a closer look should also be taken at the actual number of applicants that had to renounce their original nationality.

The renunciation requirement for naturalisation was abolished in 1991. In the 1990s, the number of naturalisations rose considerably. An average of 50,000 persons per year acquired Dutch nationality through naturalisation, compared to 19,000 persons per year in the 1980s. This rise of naturalisations can partially be explained by the abolishment of the renunciation requirement.[82] In 1996, the number of acquisitions of Dutch nationality by naturalisation reached an absolute peak with 78,731. It is possible that applicants for naturalisation were anticipating the re-introduction of the renunciation requirement. Whatever the reason may have been, the number of acquisitions by naturalisation in 2001 was slightly lower than 43,000 (Böcker et al. 2005).

If the effects of the re-introduction of the renunciation requirement are examined per group of immigrants, the results differ significantly. The effects on the naturalisation behaviour of the Turks were considerable. In 1992, the naturalisation quota among this group of immigrants rose to 20 per cent and subsequently dropped to 5 per cent in 1999-2001 (Böcker et al. 2005). The re-introduction of the requirement hardly had any effect on the quota of naturalisations among Moroccans. The difference in the effect of the renunciation requirement on the two groups of immigrants can be partially explained by the nationality regulations in the countries of origin (Böcker et al. 2005). According to Moroccan nationality law, it is almost impossible to renounce Moroccan nationality, whilst the Turkish nationality law does provide for this possibility.[83] In her struggle against dual nationality, the Minister of Alien Affairs and Integration (Conservative Liberals) officially requested the Moroccan government in December 2004 to alter the Moroccan nationality law, so as to provide for a possibility for Moroccan Dutch to renounce their Moroccan nationality (www.novatv.nl, broadcast 7 December 2004).

Two other large groups of immigrants, refugees and EU citizens, are hardly affected by the reintroduced renunciation requirement. This can be explained by the exemption of the renunciation requirement of the first category and by the low tendency towards naturalisation of the second (Böcker et al. 2005).

The renunciation requirement is used as an extra criterion for integration. In the eyes of the Dutch government, an applicant can only be considered fully integrated if he or she is prepared to have Dutch nationality as his or her unique nationality. Consequently, dual nationality constitutes an impediment for integration. But how many immigrants actually have to renounce their nationality when they apply for Dutch nationality?

On 1 January 1998, a year after the reintroduction of the renunciation requirement, more than 600,000 persons in the Netherlands held another nationality next to their Dutch nationality. In 2003, their number had grown to almost 900,000 persons (statline.cbs.nl). In 63 per cent of all naturalisations, the applicant is allowed to retain his or her former nationality. In half of these cases (32 per cent), dual nationality is allowed because legislation in the country of origin does not allow for renunciation of nationality. In the rest of the cases, the Dutch Nationality Act and the Manual on its application provide for exceptions to the renunciation requirement. Refugees make up 16 per cent of the total of applicants that is allowed to retain their original nationality, spouses of Dutch nationals account for 12 per cent of the total and the second generation constitutes 2 per cent. The Minister of Alien Affairs and Integration has proposed to no longer exempt second generation immigrants and spouses of Dutch nationals from the renunciation requirement.

It should be noted that the growing number of dual nationals in the Netherlands cannot only be explained by the fact that groups of applicants are exempted from the renunciation requirement. Children born from mixed marriages often have multiple nationalities and persons acquiring Dutch nationality by the right of option are not required to give up their original nationality.[84] This also counts for third generation immigrants that automatically acquire Dutch nationality upon birth in the Netherlands.

11.3.2.2 *Effects of the introduction of the naturalisation exam*

The possible effect of the 2003 Nationality Act and the new naturalisation exam becomes clear when examining the following table.

Table 11.2: Effects of the introduction of the naturalisation exam in the Netherlands

Year	*2000*	*2001*	*2002*	*2003*	*2004*
Number of applications	36,780	32,520	38,685	36,965	19,340

Source: IND

The total number of applications in 2002 was 38,685, whereas there were 19,340 applications in 2004.[85] However, one must remember that before 2003, minors that applied for naturalisation together with their parents were not separately registered. If the number of applications for naturalisation in 2004 is considered excluding minors, 12,761 applications remain.[86] This means a decrease by 67 per cent compared to 2002.

In the first year the new nationality act was in force, 4007 persons presented themselves for the naturalisation exam, but only 60 per cent (2,429 persons) paid for the first part of the exam and subsequently took part in it.[87] Of the 1724 persons that passed the social orientation exam, only 1213 persons paid the 165-euro fee in order to take the language exam. One may conclude that the fee charged for the naturalisation exam possibly has a negative effect on the number of naturalisations.

In the first year the naturalisation exam was held, roughly half the candidates (53 per cent) passed the complete exam. Prior to 1 April 2003, only 1-2 per cent of all applications were turned down because of insufficient integration. One can conclude that the introduction of the naturalisation test has had drastic consequences. Despite the impressive decline in the number of applications for naturalisation and the strong rise in the percentage of applicants who fail to meet the integration requirement, several conservative MPs asked whether it would be possible to push up the language test one level. Although the Minister promised to examine this, she warned that only few immigrants, notably the highly educated, would be able to naturalise.[88]

11.3.3 *Quasi citizenship*

In the Netherlands, in 1976, a quasi-citizenship status was accorded to former inhabitants of the Moluccas, one of Indonesia's archipelagos. When this country became independent in 1949, the Moluccans struggled for autonomy. In 1951, because of the war situation, some 12,500 former inhabitants of the Moluccas who had served in the Dutch colonial army were transported to the Netherlands with their families and demobilised shortly after their arrival. Both the Dutch government and the Moluccans, who were waiting for the independent South Moluccan Republic (RMS) to be established, were convinced that the Moluccan residence in the Netherlands was temporary and no measures were taken to promote the integration of Moluccan immigrants into Dutch society. However, in the 1970s, the Moluccan archipelago still formed an integral part of Indonesia. The number of Moluccans in the Netherlands had grown to 30,000 persons. Most of them still believed in the future foundation of an independent Moluccan Republic, and did not wish to obtain Dutch nationality.[89] At the same time and without any regrets, most Moluccans had lost Indonesian nationality because of the new Indonesian Nationality Act of 1958. As a result, most Moluccans in the Netherlands had become stateless.

In the 1970s, many Moluccans started to feel unhappy with the lack of attention from the Dutch government towards the creation of the RMS. They were also disappointed in the moderate course followed by the exiled Moluccan government. In order to force the Dutch government to conduct a more active policy, seven Moluccan youngsters hijacked a train in 1975. Partly due to this and other violent actions and previous promises, the Dutch government decided to improve the situation of the Moluccans.[90] It offered the Moluccans (almost) equal rights to Dutch nationals, without making them Dutch nationals. The rights were incorporated in the 1976 Act on the position of Moluccans, which entered into force on 9 September 1976.[91] The Act applied to Moluccans, brought to the Netherlands by the Dutch government in 1951 or 1952 and resident in the Netherlands on 9 September 1976, while not in possession of the Dutch nationality. It also applied to the children of these Moluccans, provided they were resident in the Netherlands on 9 September 1976.

Though the Act considerably improved the legal position of the Moluccans residing in the Netherlands, they faced problems when they wanted to travel abroad. In their newly obtained passports, the words 'Nationality: Dutch' had been crossed out and the passage 'will be treated like a Dutch national on the basis of the law of 9 September 1976, Staatsblad 476' had been added. Many countries continued to require visas. A solution to this problem was offered in 1991, when the Dutch government declared that all stateless Moluccans were Dutch nationals in the sense of the Passport Act. From that time on, they were given regular Dutch passports.

In 1976, some 30,000 Moluccans received the 'quasi-citizenship' status. Because of large-scale naturalisation and acquisition of Dutch nationality by the second and third generation, nowadays only a small number of Moluccan inhabitants of the Netherlands still have the status, probably less than 1000 persons.

There is a second status that might be qualified as quasi-citizenship. In 1990 a rule was adopted that foreign nationals after twenty years of lawful residence in the Netherlands could no longer be expelled on the grounds of public order. Under the Aliens Act 2000 an additional protection against expulsion was provided: after twelve years a residence permit can no longer be withdrawn for having provided incorrect information. The permanent residence permit of a foreign national with twenty years of residence in the Netherlands can only be withdrawn on grounds of national security or because the immigrant has taken up residence abroad.[92] Thus, these denizens have almost full protection against expulsion, a protection that may be even better than the protection granted to EU nationals under the 2004 Directive on the freedom of movement and residence of EU nationals within the Union.[93]

11.3.4 *Institutional arrangements*

11.3.4.1 *The legislative process*

Currently, regulations concerning loss and acquisition of Dutch nationality are incorporated in the Dutch Nationality Act. The Dutch Constitution contains no provisions relating to Dutch nationality.

In case the Dutch Nationality Act is amended, the normal legislative procedure is followed. This means that, after the Council of State is consulted for advice, a normal majority is necessary in both Chambers of Parliament before the Act can be adapted.

Royal Decrees and Ministerial regulations are used to provide more information concerning the provisions of the Act, for example concerning the naturalisation test[94] and the fees of naturalisation and the right of option.[95] A Manual on the application of the Dutch Nationality Act is available for those in charge of applying the provisions of the Act. After the coming into force of the 2003 Nationality act, a total of three Royal Decrees and two Ministerial regulations are applied to determine in a more detailed manner the regulations concerning acquisition and loss of Dutch nationality. Before the coming into force of this Act, the legal provisions were complemented by the provisions of only one Royal Decree, which concerned the fees for naturalisation, the option procedure being free of charge. One may conclude that applicants for naturalisation and the option procedure may have a harder time finding exactly what their rights and obligations concerning nationality acquisition are. One may also conclude that the Dutch central authorities want to strengthen their influence on the implementation of the provisions of the Act.

11.3.4.2 *The process of implementation*

Important changes in the procedure of nationality acquisition occurred with the coming into force of the 1984 Dutch Nationality Act. As of 1 January 1985, all naturalisations took place by Royal Decree. This was a compromise between the burdensome and archaic naturalisation by Act of Parliament and a simple ministerial decision, which was proposed by the government in its first draft of the 1985 Nationality Act. Another important change in the procedure was the transfer of the inquiries regarding the fulfilment of the conditions for naturalisation from the Aliens Police to the local authorities. As of 1 January 1988, the mayor was required to advise the Ministry of Justice whether an application for naturalisation should be granted or not. In practice this meant that a municipal civil servant had a conversation with the applicant and asked the Alien Police for information concerning applicant's residence status and conduct. Subsequently, in 1994, the Ministry had embarked upon an experiment in several cities whereby applications for naturalisation were filed directly with the civil registrar of the municipality, in which the applicants live, for preliminary investigation and registration.[96] In 1998, it was decided to extend this procedure to all applications in all municipalities. This alteration has considerably accelerated the procedure. As of 1998, most applications are dealt with within one year, which is the period prescribed by the 1984 Nationality Act (Groenendijk & Heijs 2001: 150). The new procedure also provided for an appeal against a negative decision on the application for naturalisation with the District Court.

A short comment needs to be made about these changes in procedure that are to the benefit of the applicant for naturalisation. In 1993, the Directorate of Private Law, a small section which handled and decided applications for naturalisation, was integrated with the large Directorate for Aliens Affairs to form a new agency: the Immigration and Naturalisation Service (IND). Though both Directorates had always formed part of the same Ministry of Justice, they clearly had a different perspective as to their tasks and to the official view regarding immigrants and their place in Dutch society. Whereas in the Naturalisation Section the predominant view for decades was that naturalisation of long-term resident immigrants was in the interest of Dutch society, the Directorate for Alien Affairs primarily perceived itself as the country's gatekeeper. When the departments were integrated in 1993, approximately 25 civil servants were active in the Naturalisation Service, compared to 900 in the Directorate for Aliens Affairs. It is not hard to imagine which of the two perspectives prevailed after the fusion. Later on it was to become clear that though until 1992 there had been a clear liberalisation of Dutch nationality law, after 1993, a series of restrictive measures had been introduced (Groenendijk 2004: 111-112).

As has been mentioned before, civil servants of the municipality were responsible for checking whether an applicant fulfilled the language and integration requirements under the 1984 Act. Discrepancies in the execution of this task were one of the reasons behind the introduction of the uniform and objective naturalisation exam on 1 April 2003.

11.4 Conclusions

If Dutch nationality law and policy as of 1892, the year in which the first nationality Act came into force, were to be described in terms of 'restrictive' and 'liberal', an evolution from restrictive to liberal and back to restrictive can be noted. An explanation for this evolution can be found in the influence that was exercised by the ideal of the nation-state and the government's minorities' policy. Both have been influenced by the actual size of migration and the prevailing attitude towards immigrants.

Ideas concerning membership of the Dutch nation and ideas concerning the protection of Dutch interests, both inherent in the ideal of the nation-state, have constantly marked nationality law and policy (Heijs 1995: 217). The nation-state ideal presupposes one homogenous people, a community in which individuals feel narrowly connected and collectively and loyally cooperate for the preservation and development of their State. The interest of the 'own' population prevails above the interests of aliens. There is a clear difference between 'them' and 'us' and nationality is far more than merely a legal status. In the ideal of the nation-state, nationality is considered as the membership of the state, a proof of the fact that one belongs to the national community or ones own people (Heijs 1995: 9). In order for aliens to acquire the nationality of the state, it has to be guaranteed that the alien has started to belong to the nation to a certain extent. Whether nationality is granted, subsequently also depends on external factors, such as demographical, economical, social or political factors.

Furthermore, the government's policy concerning minorities has had an important influence on Dutch nationality law as of the first half of the 1980s. Before that time, the government did not develop a coherent minorities policy, since it assumed that the immigrants' residence in the Netherlands was temporary. The policy concerning the integration of minorities first exercised a liberal influence on Dutch nationality law, supposing that a strong legal status of immigrants would contribute to a speedy integration. Later on, the integration policy started exercising a more restrictive influence on nationality law. Nowadays, naturalisation is seen as the crown on a completed integration, the 'first prize' in the integration contest.

From 1892 until 1953, the ideal of the nation-state had exercised a restrictive influence on Dutch nationality law and policy. With the coming into force of the first Dutch Nationality Act in 1892, Dutch nationality could no longer be acquired automatically upon birth in the Netherlands. Acquisition of Dutch nationality upon birth from a Dutch father became the main mode of gaining Dutch nationality. Birth from a Dutch parent was seen as a better guarantee for the future development of feelings of loyalty and commitment to the Dutch state than mere birth on Dutch territory. Hence, ideas concerning membership of the Dutch nation have played an important role in the choice for acquisition at birth iure sanguini.

The link between membership of the Dutch nation and the legal rules and policy is more explicitly present in the case of acquisition of Dutch nationality through naturalisation (Heijs 1995: 220). Whether an applicant is eligible for naturalisation is examined in each case on the basis of several conditions. The idea of membership of the Dutch nation, of feeling connected to Dutch society, has always played a role in naturalisation policy.

The ideal of the nation-state exercised an influence of exclusion on the naturalisation policy in the first half of the last century. Especially in the 1930s, the attitude towards immigrants that wanted to acquire Dutch nationality was one of suspicion. Since it was suspected that applicants applied for Dutch nationality out of self-interest without possessing a strong emotional tie to the Netherlands, the requirements for naturalisation were severe. In the first years after the war, the naturalisation policy remained restrictive.

In 1953, a process of liberalisation of Dutch nationality law commenced. In that year, an element of acquisition of Dutch nationality iure soli was reintroduced in Dutch nationality law: third generation immigrants would automatically acquire Dutch nationality upon birth in the Netherlands. According to the Dutch government, these immigrants only differed from 'real' Dutch nationals from a legal viewpoint. Feelings of loyalty towards the Dutch people and order were assumed to be present, which justified automatic attribution of Dutch nationality. The ideal of the nation-state started exercising an inclusive influence.

The process of liberalisation also had an effect on the naturalisation policy. In the 1950s, the possibilities of naturalisations without Parliamentary interference were extended. This development culminated in 1976, providing for extra-parliamentary naturalisation for persons having a strong connection with the Netherlands, such as second generation immigrants and former Dutch nationals. The process of liberalisation continues when the conditions for naturalisation were made public in 1977.

The new Nationality Act of 1984 made acquiring Dutch nationality simpler for first and second generation immigrants and remained unaltered for those of the third generation. The naturalisation procedure was simplified and for second generation immigrants the possibility to opt for Dutch nationality was introduced. The option procedure consists of lodging a unilateral declaration to the authorities, without public order and integration requirements. It is assumed that feelings of loyalty and commitment towards the Netherlands exist among these immigrants; consequently, it was no longer necessary to examine whether this was so in each individual case. In the new Act, the third generation provision was retained. Third generation and, to a slightly lesser extent, second generation immigrants were perceived as members of the Dutch nation. As of 1 January 1985, acquisition of Dutch nationality iure soli applied to both generations.

The new minorities' policy, which was adopted in 1983, had an important influence on the content of the 1984 Act. With the adoption of an official minorities policy, the government for the first time acknowledged that the residence of most immigrants in the Netherlands was permanent. To prevent ethnic minorities from permanently being part of the weaker groups in society, integration policy had to be intensified. The starting point of the new minorities policy was improvement of the legal position of settled immigrants. This goal could be achieved through naturalisation. The new Dutch Nationality Act was mentioned as being of 'special importance' for the new minorities policy.

The wish to provide easier access to Dutch nationality for long-term immigrants in order to improve their legal position lay behind the discussion concerning the renunciation requirement. In the new 1984 Act, this requirement, which demands that applicants for naturalisation give up their original nationality, was upheld. After extensive parliamentary debate during the first years after the Act came into force, it was decided in 1991 to abolish this condition for naturalisation. In the opinion of a majority in Parliament naturalisation should not be made more difficult than strictly necessary.

The suspension of the renunciation requirement marked the end of the process of liberalisation of Dutch nationality law and policy. When a bill was introduced in 1992 to formalise the practice of not applying the renunciation requirement, the Conservative Liberals and Christian Democrats expressed renewed doubts concerning the abolished requirement. They did not interpret the increase in the number of naturalisations as a success of the new policy, but rather as the creation of a possibility of access to Dutch nationality for persons with a very weak bond with the Netherlands. In their opinion, persons wishing to retain their original nationality cannot feel sufficiently connected to the Netherlands and should therefore not be offered the possibility to become a member of the Dutch nation. In 1997, the renunciation requirement was reintroduced. Views concerning nation-membership started to exercise a restrictive influence on nationality law and policy.

When a bill providing for an adaptation of the Nationality Act was introduced in 1998, several political parties started expressing a more restrictive attitude towards naturalisation. In particular, the Christian Democrats kept stressing the importance of feelings of loyalty towards the Dutch nation in order to become a Dutch national. Discussions concerning the language and integration requirement eventually resulted in the creation of the strict naturalisation exam. In a new Nationality Act that came into force on 1 April 2003, access to Dutch nationality was also made harder since new barriers in the option procedure were put up and the residence requirement was made more severe. The stricter requirements for acquisition of nationality can be linked to a change in the Dutch integration policy. When consensus on the policy as applied in the 1980s had broken down during the 1990s, a shift took place from a minorities policy to an integration policy which focussed on obligations of individuals and introduced the term 'active citizenship'. During the same period, integration started playing a role in the public debate. The publication of Scheffer's influential article '*The Mulitcultural Tragedy*', the events of 9/11, the rise of the populist politician Pim Fortuyn and the murder of cineaste Theo van Gogh led to an atmosphere of increased tension between immigrants and *autochthons* or the indigenous population. The idea emerged that integration of *allochtones* or immigrants, now often referred to as 'muslims', was no longer to be stimulated but demanded. The current policy, in which naturalisation is seen as the crown on a completed integration, is the opposite of the minorities policy conducted in the 1980s. During these years, facilitating the naturalisation policy was seen as a means to increase immigrant participation in society at large. Immigrants, who had lawfully lived in the Netherlands for five years or more, who had sufficient command of the Dutch language to communicate with others and wanted to acquire Dutch nationality, should be granted that nationality, unless the applicant had a serious criminal record. Nowadays, long-term residence in the Netherlands is no longer considered to imply integration. A high degree of loyalty towards Dutch society is expected from applicants, who are subjected to a strict computerised naturalisation exam in order to test whether they have sufficiently integrated. Naturalisation is no longer seen as an instrument for integration, but rather, as already mentioned, as the crown on a completed integration process.

With the coming into force of the 2000 Act, becoming a full member of the Dutch nation has become far less easy. The low numbers concerning application for naturalisation and the high percentage of denials have not yet led to protests in Parliament. Plans to reduce the number of exceptions to the renunciation requirement and to deprive persons guilty of (conspiring to) a terrorist act of Dutch nationality show that Dutch nationality law will continue to develop in a more restrictive direction in the years to come.

Chronological table of major reforms in Dutch nationality law since 1945

Date	Document	Content of change
27 December 1949	Treaty on the allocation of citizens between the Kingdom of the Netherlands and the Republic of the United States of Indonesia (Overeenkomst betreffende de toescheiding van staatsburgers	Independence of Indonesia: Agreement on the allocation of nationality to the inhabitants of Indonesia.

Date	Document	Content of change
	tussen het Koninkrijk der Nederlanden en de Republiek der Verenigde Staten van Indonesië)	
27 May 1953	Act of 15 May 1953 (entry into force 27 May 1953; with retroactivity from 1 July 1893)	Introduction of the 'double ius soli'-provision: A legitimate child acquires Dutch nationality if it is born to a parent with residence in the Netherlands at the time of the child's birth and the parent was born to a mother residing in the Netherlands at the time of his or her birth.
1 March 1964	Act of 14 November 1963	Dutch women marrying foreign men keep their nationality, even if they acquire another nationality by marriage; foreign women marrying citizen men no longer automatically acquire Dutch nationality; they are granted a right of option; termination of joint naturalisation of foreign married couples. As of 1964, both spouses have to individually fulfil the naturalisation requirements.
25 November 1975	Treaty on the allocation of citizens between the Kingdom of the Netherlands and the Republic of Surinam (Overeenkomst betreffende de toescheiding van staatsburgers tussen het koninkrijk der Nederlanden en de Republiek Suriname)	Independence of Surinam; Agreement on the allocation of nationality to the inhabitants of Surinam.
15 March 1977	Act of 8 September 1976	Act of 1892 amended for the last time; possibility for naturalisation by ministerial decree in stead of by Act for persons with a strong connection to the Netherlands; textual change of the renunciation requirement; possibility of alteration and determination of name upon naturalisation.
10 March 1977	Circular of Ministry of Justice	Specifying the conditions for naturalisation and exceptions to renunciation requirement.
1 January 1985	New Dutch Nationality Act of 19 December 1984 (Rijkswet op het Nederlanderschap)	Equal treatment of men and women (most important aspect of the incorporation of this principle in the law is that children born after 1 January 1985 also acquire Dutch nationality through the mother); all naturalisations by Royal Decree rather than by Act;

Date	Document	Content of change
		right to opt for Dutch nationality for migrant children born on Dutch territory; automatic loss of Dutch nationality for dual nationals born in country of other nationality and residing in that country for an uninterrupted period of ten years after majority.
1 January 1985	Act approving the ratification of the Strasbourg Treaty on the Reduction of Cases of Multiple Nationality	Ratification of Strasbourg Treaty on the Reduction of Cases of Multiple Nationality.
1 January 1992	Memorandum of 20 December 1991	Dutch government by ministerial memorandum decides to no longer apply renunciation requirement.
20 August 1996	Act of 15 May 1996	Ratification and entry into force of second protocol Strasbourg Treaty on the Reduction of cases of Multiple Nationality.
9 July 1997	Circular	Re-introduction of renunciation requirement (with exceptions).
21 December 2000	Act approving the ratification of the European Convention on Nationality; adoption of new Dutch Nationality Act (Rijkswet op het Nederlanderschap; entry into force on 1 April 2003)	Act approving the ratification of the European Convention on Nationality, which came into force in the Netherlands on 1 July 2001.
1 February 2001		Entry into force transitional provision V para. 2 which provides for the re-acquisition of nationality for persons who under the 1985 Act had lost Dutch nationality following a long-term residence abroad (in force until 1 April 2003).
1 April 2003	Coming into force of Act of 21 December 2000 amending Dutch Nationality Act of 1985	Amended Nationality Act provides for: language and integration test as a condition for naturalisation; adaptation Nationality Act to Aliens Act; children born out of wedlock out of a Dutch father and migrant mother no longer automatically acquire Dutch nationality after acknowledgement after birth; abolishment of the rule that dual nationals born in country of other nationality and residing in that country for an uninterrupted period of ten years after majority automatically lose Dutch nationality.

Notes

1 The day the 1892 Act came into force.
2 Art. 3 para. 1 Dutch Nationality Act (DNA) 2003.
3 Act of 21 December 2000, *Staatsblad* 618, amended by Act of 18 April 2002, *Staatsblad* 222. Come into force 1 April 2003. The *Staatsblad* is the Dutch Bulletin of Acts and Decrees.
4 Furthermore, the child is required to have main residence in the Netherlands at the time of birth (art. 3 para. 3 DNA 2003).
5 Art. 6 para. 1 sub a Act of 19 December 1984, *Staatsblad* 628.
6 Source: Immigration and Naturalisation Service (IND).
7 Source: IND.
8 Letter from the Minister of Alien Affairs and Integration to Parliament, Tweede Kamer 2003-2004, 28 689, no. 19.
9 Memorandum Multiple Nationality and Integration, Tweede Kamer 2003-2004, 28 289, no. 19.
10 This part of our study primarily relies on E. Heijs 1995.
11 The right to vote and the right to hold public office.
12 The day on which the 1892 Act came into force.
13 After extensive debate, it was decided to charge 100 guilders.
14 *Bijlagen Handelingen EersteKamer* (Appendices Proceedings Upper House), 1931-1932, IV, no. 78a, p. 10 en 1934-1935, no. 41a, p. 1.
15 In 1935 it becomes clear that Dutch nationality is only granted if it is more or less certain that the applicant will also be employed in the future.
16 It is not until 1961 that the Netherlands experiences its first net immigration since 1945 (Groenendijk & Heijs 2001).
17 Because of the shortage of qualified staff, priority is for instance given to primary school teachers. Persons conducting business of importance to the Netherlands can also obtain Dutch nationality with priority (Heijs 1995: 110).
18 E.g., the taking part in the Resistance, joining the Dutch armed forces, helping the persecuted, etc. (Heijs 1995: 115).
19 Before 1953, the *third generation* or *double ius soli* rule only applied to stateless children.
20 Act of 16 July 1958, *Staatsblad*, 1958, no. 342.
21 The Refugee Convention that entered into force in the Netherlands in 1956 prescribes that naturalisation of refugees should be facilitated as much as possible. The UN Convention relating to the Status of Stateless Persons, which entered into force in the Netherlands in 1962, prescribes the same for stateless persons.
22 Provided to Eric Heijs by F. Th. Zilverentant, expert on nationality law at the Justice Department.
23 In this context, he explicitly refers to applicants who have committed a crime in the past, Germans that voluntarily joined the German army, applicants that live in concubinage and homosexuals.
24 *Bijlagen handelingen Tweede Kamer* (Appendices Proceedings Tweede Kamer), 1971-1972, 11799, no. 1, p. 2
25 Act of 8 September 1976, *Staatsblad* 1976, no. 465.
26 Before deciding on naturalisation, the ministry consulted several authorities on the applicant's motives for naturalisation, his or her knowledge of the Dutch language, social behaviour, criminal record, political activities and financial situation. As a rule, the ministry received information on each applicant from the Advocate General, the public prosecutor, the local police, the internal security agency, and the governor of the province and the mayor of the municipality in which the applicant was living. In

most cases, the applicant was interviewed by the police and the municipal civil registrar, and sometimes by the public prosecutor as well. If the ministry, on the basis of these consultations, considered that there were no obstacles to the naturalisation of the applicant – which was the outcome of the large majority of cases – a bill was sent to Parliament.

27 Though an application for naturalisation by Act was rarely denied before 1976, the applicant did not have any legal remedy against this decision.

28 Mostly Surinamese nationals who had settled in the Netherlands after Surinam's independence, Indonesian 'repenters' who had not yet acquired Dutch nationality (see sect. 11.2.4) former Dutch nationals who had fought in the German army during the Second World War and Moluccan immigrants.

29 *Hoofdafdeling Privaatrecht afdeling Nationaliteit en Burgerlijke Staat* (Main Department Private Law department Nationality and Civil Status), 10 March 1977, *Staatscourant* (Government Gazette) 27 April 1977, no. 81, p. 4.

30 Act of 21 December 1936, *Staatsblad* 209; *LNTS* 179: 89.

31 Art. 5 Nationality Act 1892 (1936).

32 Art. 2 sub c Nationality Act 1892 (1936).

33 Art. 5 Nationality Act 1892 (1936); de Groot 1996: 551.

34 Act of 14 November 1963, *Staatsblad*, 467, in force on 1 March 1964; *Tractatenblad* (Bulletin of Treaties), 1965, 218.

35 Art. 8 Nationality Act 1892 (1963).

36 Art. 8a Nationality Act 1892 (1963); de Groot 1996: 552.

37 In case a child is born out of wedlock to a Dutch father and a foreign mother, he or she will acquire Dutch nationality *ex lege* after acknowledgement or legitimation (art. 4 par. 1 and 2 DNA 1985).

38 Source: Central Bureau of Statistics (CBS).

39 Report Commission Blok, Tweede Kamer 2003-2004, nos. 8-9, p. 28.

40 *Bijlagen Handelingen Tweede Kamer*, 1982-1983, 16 102, no. 21, p. 92.

41 Act of 9 April 1998, *Staatsblad* 1998, no. 261; de Hart 2005: 7.

42 Tweede Kamer 29200 VI, no. 7, p. 3 (November 2003), Hand. Tweede Kamer 10 December 2003, p. 2486, Tweede Kamer 27083, no. 63, p. 15 (June 2004) en Hand. Tweede Kamer 2 September 2004, p. 6075 en 6096.

43 Act of 19 December 1984, *Staatsblad* 628.

44 *Tractatenblad* 1974, 4; *Aanvullend Protocol en Protocol tot wijziging* (Additional Protocol and Change Protocol), 24 November 1977, *Tractatenblad* 1981, 45 en 46; *Goedkeuringswet* (Approval Law), *Staatsblad* 1984, 627.

45 Art. 9 para. 1 sub b Dutch Nationality Act 1984.

46 Hoofdafdeling Privaatrecht afdeling Nationaliteit en Burgerlijke Staat (Main Department Private Law Department Nationality and Civil Status), 10 March 1977, *Staatscourant* 27 April 1977, p. 4.

47 Since Dutch nationality law only allowed for loss of Dutch nationality in case this would not leave a person stateless, only dual nationals were affected by the provision.

48 Tweede Kamer, Bijlagen II, 1989-1990, 21 132, no. 9, p. 43.

49 Tweede Kamer 1990/91, 21 971, no. 14. For comments on the Memorandum see Jessurun d'Oliveira 1991.

50 Tweede Kamer 1990-1991, 21 971, no. 14.

51 Tweede Kamer 1991/92, 21 971, no. 19; Böcker et al. 2005.

52 Circular of Secretary of State of Justice of 20 December 1991, *Migrantenrecht (Migrant Law)* 1992, p. 62.

53 *Staatscourant* 9 July 1997, no. 128, p. 7.

54 Tweede Kamer 1997-1998, 25 891 (R 1609), no. 2.

55 Act of 21 December 2000 (*Staatsblad* 618) amended by the Act of 18 April 2002 (*Staatsblad* 222).
56 Letter from the Minister of Alien Affairs and Integration to the Second Chamber, Tweede Kamer 2003/2004, 28 689, no. 19, p. 3.
57 Letter of 10 November 2004 from the Ministers of Home Affairs and Kingdom Relations to the Second Chamber, 5319045/04, p. 9 and 16.
58 Tweede Kamer 1981, 16 947, (R 1181), nos. 1-2.
59 *Bijlagen Handelingen Tweede Kamer*, 1981, 16 947, no. 3 p. 11.
60 *Bijlagen Handelingen Tweede Kamer*, 1982-1983, 16 947, no.7, p.8.
61 As a compromise between automatic acquisition and naturalisation, these immigrants were given a right to opt for Dutch nationality.
62 Tweede Kamer 2003-2004, 28 689, no. 19, p. 5.
63 Under the 1984 Act, persons born in the Netherlands could acquire Dutch nationality by option upon coming of age. In case a person born in the Netherlands was stateless, he could opt for Dutch nationality already after three years (art. 6 para. 1 sub a and b).
64 Handleiding voor toepassing Rijkswet op het Nederlanderschap 2003, art. 6 para. 3, C.3, p. 1.
65 Except for children legitimised or acknowledged by a Dutch national (art. 6 para. 1 sub c) and children put under joint custody of a Dutch national and a non-Dutch national (art. 6 para. 1 sub d).
66 Circular of 23 March 1979, altered 27 January 1981, *Staatscourant* 21.
67 Art. 1 of the instructions for naturalisation, *Staatscourant*, 2 April 1979, no. 65, p. 11.
68 Pacifist Socialist Party (PSP), Communist Party the Netherlands (CPN), Political Party Radicals (PPR).
69 Amendment Van Es c.s., *Bijlage Handelingen Tweede Kamer*, 1983-1984, 16947, no. 29.
70 Memorandum in reply, *Bijlage Handelingen Tweede Kamer*, 1982-1983, 16947, no. 7, p. 2.
71 In the case of residence in the Dutch Antilles, of the language spoken on the island of residence (art. 8 para. 1 sub d Dutch Nationality Act 1984).
72 Tweede Kamer 1997-1998, 25 891 (R 1609), no. 2.
73 Whereas the 1984 Act required 'a reasonable knowledge of Dutch language', the article in the proposition demanded 'a sufficient knowledge of Dutch language necessary for social intercourse'.
74 Amendment Dittrich (D66), Tweede Kamer 1999-2000, 25 891, no. 26.
75 *Vijfde nota van wijziging* (Fifth Memorandum of Amendment), Tweede Kamer 1999-2000, 25 891 (R 1609), no. 33.
76 Decree on the naturalisation exam, *Staatsblad* 2002, 197.
77 Act of 23 November 2000, *Staatsblad* 495, 7 December 2000.
78 The residence requirement for children that want to rely on their parent's naturalisation to acquire Dutch nationality also became stricter. For information on the linking of the Aliens Act and the Dutch Nationality Act see Groenendijk 2003.
79 Source: IND.
80 IND, *Monitor Naturalisatietoets*, second edition, 1 April 2003-30 September 2003.
81 Tweede Kamer 2004-2005, 27 083 and 29 543, no. 66.
82 Other possible explanations for the rise of the number of naturalisations are the high level of immigration, especially of asylum seekers in the early 1990s, and the policy of decentralisation, applied since 1988.
83 Impossibility of renunciation because of nationality law in country of origin constitutes an exemption from the renunciation requirement. In 1996 and 2001, all

Moroccans acquiring Dutch nationality by naturalisation kept their Moroccan nationality (source: CBS).

84 In 2002, 20,422 children born in the Netherlands acquired more than one nationality at birth. In most cases, the other nationality was the Moroccan nationality (5,256) or Turkish nationality (4,992) (Memorandum Multiple Nationality and Integration, Tweede Kamer 2003/2004, 28 689, no. 19, p. 6.).

85 Since the new rules came into force halfway 2003, 2004 offers a better picture of the effects of the 2003 Act than 2003.

86 Source: IND.

87 Rapportage Naturalisatie; Trends in naturalisatie 1999-2003 en naturalisatietoets (Naturalisation Report; Trends in Naturalisation 1999-2003 and Naturalisation Test), INDIAC, p. 21.

88 Tweede Kamer 2004-2005, 29 800 VI, no. 101, p. 34.

89 At most 25 per cent had obtained Dutch nationality (*Appendices Proceedings Tweede Kamer*, 1974-1975, 12839, no. 6, p. 6).

90 In 1959, Minister of Social Work Klompé had already pleaded for a more active participation of the Moluccans in Dutch society. In 1971, the same Minister promised to improve the legal position of the Moluccans residing in the Netherlands.

91 *Staatsblad* 1976, 468.

92 Art. 22 Aliens Act 2000 and art. 3.86(7)(c), 3.97 and 3.98 Aliens Decree 2000.

93 Art. 28 of Directive 2004/38/EC, OJ 2004 L 229/35.

94 Decree of 15 April 2002, *Staatsblad* 2002, 197, Regulation of 13 March 2003, *Staatscourant* 2003, 57.

95 Decree of 17 June 2002, *Staatscourant* 2002, 325.

96 Together handling about 80 per cent of all applications (Groenendijk & Heijs 2001: 149).

Bibliography

Anon (2003), *Handleiding voor toepassing Rijkswet op het Nederlanderschap*. Den Haag: SDU.

Bedem, R.F.A. Van den (1993), *Motieven voor naturalisatie; Waarom vreemdelingen uit diverse minderheidsgroepen wel of niet kiezen voor naturalisatie*. Arnhem: Gouda Quint.

Böcker, A., K. Groenendijk & B. de Hart (2005), 'De toegang tot het Nederlanderschap. Effecten van twintig jaar beleidswijzigingen', *Nederlands Juristenblad* 80 (3): 157-164.

De Groot, G.R. (1996), 'Netherlands Nationality Law', in B. Nascimbene (ed.), *Nationality Laws in the European Union*, 545-589. London/Milan: Butterworths/Giuffrè Editore.

De Groot, G.R. & K. Saarloos (2004), 'De valkuil van de Rijkswet op het Nederlanderschap', *Migrantenrecht* 7: 252-258.

De Hart, B. (2004), 'Debates on Dual Nationality in the Netherlands', *IMIS Beiträge* 24: 149-162.

De Hart, B. (2005), 'Multiple Nationality, Integration and Terrorism; Political and Public Debates on Dual Nationality in the Netherlands', paper presented at the conference Dual Citizenship-Democracy, Rights and Identity in a Globalising World, Toronto, 17-19 March 2005.

De Hart, B. (2006), 'The Morality of Maria Toet; Gender, Citizenship and the construction of the nation-state', *Ethnic and Migration Studies* 32 (1): 49-68.

Dekker, J. (2003), 'Optierechten nieuwe stijl', *Migrantenrecht* 4/5: 126-132.

Entzinger, H. (2003), 'The Rise and Fall of Multiculturalism: The Case of the Netherlands', in C. Joppke & E. Morawska (eds.), *Toward assimilation and citizenship, immigrants in liberal nation-states*, 59-86. New York: Palgrave Macmillan.

Gelauff, M. (2003), 'De gewijzigde Rijkswet op het Nederlanderschap in hoofdlijnen', *Migrantenrecht* 4/5: 112-119.

Groenendijk, K. & R. Barzilay (2001), *Verzwakking van de Rechtspositie van toegelaten vreemdelingen (1990-2001)*. Utrecht: Forum.

Groenendijk, K. & E. Heijs (2001), 'Immigration, Immigrants and Nationality Law in the Netherlands, 1945-98', in R. Hansen & P. Weil (eds.), *Towards a European Nationality: Citizenship, Immigration and Nationality Law*, 143-172. New York: Palgrave.

Groenendijk, K. (2003), 'De toegenomen koppeling van de RwNed aan de Vw: meer barrières en minder integratie', *Migrantenrecht* 4/5: 148-157.

Groenendijk, K. (2004), 'Legal Concepts of Integration in EU Migration Law', *European Journal of Migration and Law*, 6 (2): 111-126.

Heijs, E. (1988), *Selectie bij naturalisatie: de rol van taalkennis als eis voor het Nederlanderschap*. Dissertation, Catholic University of Nijmegen.

Heijs, E. (1991), 'Nederlanderschap in de Nederlandse Koloniën: Regulering van immigratie vanuit de koloniën door nationaliteitsbeleid in Nederland', *Recht der Werkelijkheid* 12 (2): 21-42.

Heijs, E. (1995), *Van vreemdeling tot Nederlander; de verlening van het Nederlanderschap aan vreemdelingen 1813-1992*. Amsterdam: Het Spinhuis.

Jessurun d'Oliveira, H.U. (1977), 'Nederlanders, wie zijn dat?', *Nederlands Juristenblad* 24: 589-597.

Jessurun d'Oliveira, H.U. (1991), 'Het 'meerdere', een regeringsnotitie over meervoudige nationaliteit', *Nederlands Juristenblad* 43: 1734-1741.

Jessurun d'Oliveira, H.U. (2004), 'Alweer plannen om de afstandseis bij naturalisatie uit te breiden', *Nederlands Juristenblad* 43: 2232-2238.

Joppke, C. & E. Morawska (eds.) (2003), *Toward assimilation and citizenship, immigrants in liberal nation-states*. New York: Palgrave Macmillan.

Makaay, E. (1983), 'Verlies van het Nederlanderschap voor emigranten', *Nederlands Juristenblad* 58: 1319-1322.

Reubsaet, T.J.M. (1982), *Surinaamse migranten in Nederland, deel I, Het beleid van de rijksoverheid van 1965-1979: uitgangspunten, doelstellingen en middelen*. Nijmegen: Instituut voor toegepaste sociologie.

Ringeling, A.B. (1978), *De beleidsvrijheid van ambtenaren; Het spijtoptantenprobleem als illustratie van de activiteiten van ambtenaren bij de uitvoering van beleid*. Alphen aan den Rijn: Samson.

Scheffer, P. (2000), 'Het multiculturele drama', *NRC Handelsblad* 29 January 2000.

Vermeulen, H. & R. Penninx (2000), *Immigrant Integration: The Dutch Case*. Amsterdam: Het Spinhuis.

12 Portugal

Maria Ioannis Baganha and Constança Urbano de Sousa[1]

12.1 Introduction

The Nationality Law in force until 2006[2] foresees a mixed system for acquisition of nationality at birth, placing greater emphasis on a ius sanguinis concept of nationhood to the detriment of an imperial tradition of ius soli. It therefore goes against the Portuguese tradition of favouring ius soli, dating back to the seventeenth century and continued by the 1959 Act, which foresaw automatic and *ex lege* acquisition of Portuguese nationality by the children of a Portuguese or foreign father (or Portuguese or foreign mother, when the father was stateless, of unknown nationality or unknown) born in Portuguese territory.

The Portuguese legal framework is very tolerant of dual nationality. Portugal has not signed any international conventions aimed at avoiding dual nationality. The 1981 Nationality Act has shaken off the principle that a person should only have one nationality, and that the acquisition of a foreign nationality should lead to the loss of Portuguese nationality (Ramos 1994: 136). Furthermore, access to Portuguese nationality is never subject to the loss of the foreign nationality that the person in question may hold, which means that the two may co-exist. The 1981 Nationality Act merely sets out rules to resolve conflicts when dual nationality occurs. Thus, should a person hold both a foreign and Portuguese nationality, only the latter is taken into consideration by Portuguese law (art. 27 of the Nationality Act).

Naturalisation depends on a discretionary decision made by the Portuguese Minister of Home Affairs. Applicants, who meet the respective legal requirements for naturalisation, do not have a subjective right. Even if a foreign national meets the requirements for naturalisation, the Government may, merely based on one's own interests, deny him or her the right to Portuguese nationality.

Art. 14 of the Constitution sets out that 'Portuguese citizens who temporarily or habitually reside abroad shall enjoy the protection of the State in the exercise of their rights, and shall be subject to such duties as are not incompatible with their absence from the country.'[3] The fact that a Portuguese citizen lives abroad in no way undermines these rights. His or her descendants are Portuguese at birth, if they declare that they wish to be Portuguese or if the birth is registered in the Portuguese register of births. In addition, a foreign spouse has the right to opt for Portuguese nationality, should he or she have been married for at least three years, but there are legal bases for the Portuguese State to oppose it. If Portuguese residents abroad are registered with the consulate for electoral purposes, or are in Portuguese territory, they can vote and stand for parliamentary and presidential elections. For local elections they must be registered on the electoral lists. They also enjoy special representation in Parliament by electing four members.[4]

People who have acquired Portuguese nationality after birth enjoy the same status as those who acquired it at birth, except for eligibility to hold office as President of the Republic. Art. 122 of the Constitution sets out that, only citizens of Portuguese origin, i.e., who acquired Portuguese nationality at birth, are eligible as President of the Republic. On the other hand, they enjoy more favourable arrangements as far as military duties are concerned in that they are excused from national service should they acquire Portuguese nationality upon their eighteenth birthday or later (art. 38, Law 174/99).

Nationals of Lusophone countries living in Portugal enjoy a quasi-citizenship status with wide-ranging rights as far as political participation and access to public office are concerned, from which other foreign citizens are excluded. Art. 15 (3) of the Constitution sets out that 'Citizens of Lusophone countries may, provided there is reciprocity, be granted rights not otherwise conferred on aliens, except the right to become President of the Republic, President of the Parliament, Prime-Minister, President of the Supreme Courts, and to serve in the armed forces and the diplomatic service.' Currently, the terms of reciprocity have been met by Brazil. Brazilian citizens who have been living in Portugal for over three years and have the status of equal political rights, enjoy practically the same rights as the Portuguese (with the said exceptions), without losing their Brazilian citizenship and without needing to acquire Portuguese citizenship. In particular, they have access to non-technical posts in the civil service, can be elected to Parliament, as mayor, or serve as Government ministers. This status enables Brazilian citizens to fully exercise their political rights, and notably to vote and stand for election in local, regional and general elections, with the exception of noting or standing for election in presidential elections. However, this movement towards a concept of citizenship that is disengaged from nationality goes beyond the special status of Brazilians or the inherent status of EU citizens (which implies the right to vote and stand for election in local and European Parliament elections). According to art. 15 (4) of the Constitution, any alien who resides in Portugal has the right to vote and be elected in local government elections, provided that there is reciprocity, i.e., that a Portuguese national can also vote or be eligible in the alien's country of nationality.

12.2 Historical development of Portuguese nationality law

12.2.1 *The roots of Portuguese nationality law: the 1603 Ordinations of King Philip*

The 1603 Ordination ordered by King Philip (compilation of legislation) led to the first legal arrangements on nationality (Title LV of the Second Book). Only acquisition of nationality at birth was regulated, establishing a mixed system giving prevalence to ius soli. Children with a Portuguese father (ius sanguinis *a pater*[5]) were only Portuguese if they were born in Portugal (both ius soli and ius sanguinis); if they were born abroad they were not Portuguese unless the father (or mother, if the child was illegitimate) was in the King's or Crown's service.

On the other hand, pure ius soli was not present either, since the legitimate children born in Portugal to a foreign father were only Portuguese if the father had been living in the Kingdom for ten years and had property there (Ramos 1992: 7-13; Gonçalves 1929: 511).

With the rise of liberalism, arrangements on nationality were enshrined in the monarchical constitutions of the nineteenth century.

12.2.2 *Nationality law in the monarchical constitutionalism of the nineteenth century*

The 1822 Constitution signed on 23 September marked the beginning of Portuguese constitutionalism and stayed in force until June 1823, when the counter-revolutionary movement for restoring absolute monarchy decreed its obsolescence (Canotilho 2003: 128). In 1836, following the liberal revolution in September, the 1822 Constitution was restored.

Regarding acquisition of nationality at birth the 1822 Constitution keeps the mixed system inherited from the Ordinations of King Philip, although it gave a predominant role to ius sanguinis *a pater* (Ramos 1992: 15). Thus, according to art. 21 (I) and (II), children born in Portugal to a Portuguese father (or a Portuguese mother if they were illegitimate) were considered Portuguese. In comparison to the previous legislation a more important role was given to ius sanguinis, since the children of a Portuguese father (or the illegitimate children of a Portuguese mother) who were born outside Portugal were considered Portuguese, provided they met one condition: that they took up residence in Portugal.[6] At the same time, the scope of ius soli was reduced, since children born to a foreign father in Portugal were only considered Portuguese if they met two conditions: namely that they lived in Portugal and upon reaching the age of majority declared that they wanted to be Portuguese (art. 21 (V)). The fact that art. 21 (III) considered children of unknown parents found in Portugal to be Portuguese was not a concession to ius soli, but rather a measure against statelessness (Ramos 1992: 21). Lastly, art. 21 (V) grants Portuguese nationality to freed slaves. This could be considered as acquisition at birth, since, legally speaking, the slave was only 'born' and became a person, when freed (Ramos 1992: 22).

Regarding the acquisition of nationality after birth, art. 21 (VI) of the 1822 Constitution foresaw discretionary naturalisation. Naturalisation could only be granted to foreign adults living on Portuguese soil. In addition to these requirements, foreigners (unless they were children of a Portuguese father who had lost Portuguese nationality) had to meet one of the following conditions: being married to a Portuguese woman; or having acquired a trading, farming or industrial establishment in Portugal; or having performed relevant services to the nation.

Art. 23 foresaw two grounds for loss of Portuguese nationality: naturalisation in another country and the acceptance, without government permission, of employment, honour or pension from a foreign government.

The 1826 Constitutional Charter, in force for two short periods (1826 to 1828 and 1834 to 1836), was restored in 1842 and remained in force until the republic was declared in 1910. It kept the mixed system of acquisition of nationality at birth, though it placed greater emphasis on ius soli, since it considered all those born on Portuguese soil to be Portuguese.[7] Ius sanguinis continued to be subject to residence in Portugal. The child of a Portuguese father (or the illegitimate child of a Portuguese mother) was only Portuguese if the father lived in Portugal. Ius sanguinis was only sufficient criterion if the father was abroad on the Crown's service. In such cases, the acquisition of Portuguese nationality was not subject to any conditions.

The only way foreseen in the Charter to acquire nationality after birth was naturalisation, with art. 7 (2) referring to ordinary law to set the conditions for conferment. The Decree of 22 October 1836 foresaw three requirements for a foreign citizen to be naturalised: age of maturity; two years' residence[8] (unless descended from a Portuguese) and the ability to acquire means of subsistence (art. 1). Unlike the 1822 Constitution, the Charter does not mention the acquisition of nationality by foundlings (encompassed by the broad scope of ius soli) and freed slaves.

Concerning the loss of nationality, art. 8 foresaw, in addition to the causes listed in the 1822 Constitution, in loss as a consequence of banishment.

The 1838 Constitution stayed in force until 1842, when the 1826 Constitutional Charter was restored. During this period, ius sanguinis clearly dominated nationality law. Art. 6 (I) of the 1838 Constitution stated that the child of a Portuguese father was Portuguese, whether the child was born in Portugal or not (ius sanguinis *a pater*). Two new features were brought in concerning ius sanguinis *a mater*: on the one hand, an illegitimate child born to a Portuguese mother was Portuguese if born in Portugal; if the child was born abroad it was only Portuguese if it took up residence in Portugal. On the other hand, ius sanguinis *a mater* became relevant for legitimate children, since the child born to a Portuguese mother and a foreign father would be Portuguese if he or she was born in Portugal and did not declare a preference for the other nationality. Like the 1822 Constitution, the 1838 Constitution also granted Portuguese nationality to foundlings[9] and to freed slaves. Lastly, art. 6 (VI) foresaw naturalisation as a means of acquiring Portuguese nationality after birth, referring to the ordinary law for the relevant requirements.[10]

As for the loss of nationality, art. 7, like art. 8 of the 1826 Constitutional Charter, set out three causes: criminal conviction which meant loss of citizenship; naturalisation in a foreign country; acceptance without government permission of an honour or reward from a foreign government.

12.2.3 *The 1867 Civil Code: mixed system with prevalence of ius soli*

The 1867 Civil Code adopted a mixed system of acquisition of nationality at birth, with prevalence being given to ius soli, although it was of less influence than in the Charter (Ramos 1992: 30). This solution was imposed by the principle of constitutionality which was the determining criterion set out in the 1826 Constitutional Charter in force at the time (Ramos 1994: 117).

Art. 18 stated that children born on Portuguese soil to a Portuguese father (or illegitimately to a Portuguese mother) were Portuguese. In addition, children born in Portugal to a foreign father (who is not in Portugal on his country's service) were Portuguese, unless they declare that they were not.[11] This possibility of opting for the father's nationality by expression of intent by the person in question (if over the age of majority) or by the legal agent (if under age) reduced the weight of ius soli (Ferreira 1870: 40; Gonçalves 1929: 518), compared to the Constitutional Charter (which did not foresee such a possibility). Lastly, all those who were born on Portuguese soil to unknown parents or parents of unknown nationality were also deemed Portuguese.

The Civil Code also embodied ius sanguinis *a pater*: children born abroad to a Portuguese on the Crown's service were considered Portuguese (art. 18 (5)). Ius sanguinis was still conditional in other cases, since children born abroad to a Portuguese father (or illegitimately to a Portuguese mother)[12] would only acquire Portuguese nationality at birth should they take up residence in Portugal or declared (personally if an adult or via their legal agent if under-age) that they wanted to be Portuguese (art. 18 (3)).[13] In this case, acquisition of Portuguese nationality via ius sanguinis depended upon a tacit choice (taking up residence in Portugal) or an expression of intent, and took effect from birth (Gonçalves 1929: 523).

The Civil Code foresaw two cases of acquiring nationality after birth, specifically *ex lege* acquisition of Portuguese nationality by a foreign woman who marries a Portuguese man and naturalisation via a discretionary Government act,[14] provided the foreign national met the following legal requirements set out in art. 19:[15] specifically, 1) having reached the age of maturity; 2) having a means of subsistence; 3) having lived on Portuguese soil for at least three years;[16] 4) having a clean criminal record proved by a police record from the country of origin and in Portugal; 5) having performed all military duties in the country of origin.

Art. 22 of the Civil Code foresaw four ways of losing nationality. In all of these cases, the same provision foresaw its reacquisition, which meant that the legislator of 1867 did not foresee loss of nationality as definitive (Ramos 1992: 35). The first cause of loss of Portuguese nationality was naturalisation in another country. The effects of loss of nationality did not encompass the wife and children, who would only lose their nationality should they declare that they wanted to follow the nationality of their husband or father. Those who had lost their Portuguese nationality through naturalisation in a foreign country could reacquire it by taking up residence in Portugal and expressing their wish to reacquire it. This was *ex lege* reacquisition, although it was subject to these two legal requirements. The second *ipso jure* cause of loss of nationality was accepting, without the government's permission, public office, pension or honour from a foreign government. Unlike the previous case, the Civil Code only foresaw reacquisition via a discretionary Government act, which shows the legislator's particular contempt for this form of loss of nationality. The third cause for loss of nationality was expulsion by judicial decision. This was merely a temporary loss, in that it was only valid whilst the conviction had effect. Once the sentence had been served, the person in question automatically and *ex lege* reacquired Portuguese nationality. Lastly, the Civil Code brought in a new form of *ex lege* loss of nationality: the marriage of a Portuguese woman to a foreign man (unless she did not acquire the nationality of her husband as a result of the marriage, in which case she would keep her Portuguese nationality). The woman would reacquire Portuguese nationality should the marriage be dissolved, provided she took up residence on Portuguese soil and made an expression of intent.

12.2.4 *Law 2098 of 29 July 1959: mixed system with prevalence of ius soli*

As for the acquisition of nationality at birth, the 1959 Act kept the traditional mixed system, with greater emphasis on ius soli (Proença 1960: 21; Ramos 1996: 601). In fact, according to art. I of the 1959 Act, Portuguese nationality was acquired *ex lege* and automatically by those born on Portuguese territory (ius soli), specifically by the child of a Portuguese father (or Portuguese mother, should the father be stateless, unknown or of unknown nationality),[17] the child of a stateless or unknown father or of unknown nationality, and the child of a foreign father (or a foreign mother, should the father be stateless, unknown or of unknown nationality) if the parent was not in Portugal in his or her country's service.[18] For the purpose of acquiring Portuguese nationality via ius soli, foundlings were presumed to have been born in Portugal.

Ius sanguinis only determined *ex lege* granting of Portuguese nationality to the children born abroad to a Portuguese father or mother[19] if the parent was abroad in the service of the Portuguese state (art. II). This was the only case in which ius sanguinis independently and automatically determined acquisition of nationality at birth. Apart from this case, ius sanguinis was only relevant for acquiring nationality at birth by declaration, which was a non-automatic mode of acquiring nationality, because, in addition to depending on the fulfilment of legal requirements it could be prevented by Government opposition (a new feature of the 1959 Act). The legal requirements were linked to will (declared or presumed) of those in question. Or, to be more precise, children born abroad to a Portuguese parent not in the service of the Portuguese state could only acquire Portuguese nationality if they a) declared that they wished to be Portuguese, b) registered in the Portuguese Register of Births, and c) voluntarily took up residence in Portuguese territory made official by a declaration of residence at the Central Registry Office (art. IV and V of the 1959 Act). However, even if they met these requirements, the Government had the right to oppose and thus prevent Portuguese nationality from being granted. So obtaining Portuguese nationality in these cases was no longer considered an absolute right.[20]

A foreign woman who married a Portuguese man would acquire her husband's Portuguese nationality *ex lege*, unless she declared that she did not want to be Portuguese and could prove that her own country's legislation would not strip her of her original nationality (art. X of the 1959 Act).

As to discretionary naturalisation, the 1959 Act contained the same arrangements as the 1867 Civil Code, as amended by the 1910 Decree, and foresaw naturalisation as a way of acquiring Portuguese nationality after birth, although it made it subject to more conditions, such as decent moral and social behaviour and knowledge of the Portuguese language. In addition, it continued to be a discretionary act of the Government.[21] In order to make naturalisation easier for those foreigners with a true link to the Portuguese community, art. XIII waived the residency and language requirements for the descendants of Portuguese citizens. These requirements could also be waived by the Government for foreign citizens who married Portuguese women, or those who had performed or been called on to perform notable service for the Portuguese state. Lastly, art. XVII gave the Government extraordinary powers to grant naturalisation, with no further requirements, to those foreigners who came from communities with Portuguese ancestors and who wished to become part of the Portuguese community. The foreign citizens who were to benefit mainly from this arrangement were those from countries like Brazil, which was historically linked to Portugal as a former colony.

Art. XVIII (a) and (c) of the 1959 Act foresaw five grounds for the loss of Portuguese nationality. Only the first three led to automatic loss of nationality without the need for the person concerned to declare his or her intent, whilst the last two were tantamount to renunciation which required an expression of intent from the person concerned.

- Portuguese nationality was lost when a Portuguese citizen voluntarily acquired a foreign nationality. The aim was to avoid dual nationality. Acquiring a foreign nationality through naturalisation imposed by the State of residence did not lead to the automatic loss of Portuguese nationality, but could lead to it on the basis of a Government decision (art. XIX).
- Accepting public office or performing military service in a foreign state could also lead to losing Portuguese nationality (*ex lege*), if the Portuguese citizen did not hold the nationality of the other state in question as well, and did not leave office or service by the deadline set by the Portuguese Government. The 1959 Act brought far-reaching changes compared to the 1867 Civil Code, which considered not only holding public office in a foreign state, but also accepting any honour, pension or reward from a foreign state as grounds for losing Portuguese nationality. In view of the development of international relations this precept was considered to be too severe, which was why the 1959 Act removed it (Proença 1960: 105).

- The marriage of a Portuguese woman to a foreigner automatically led to her losing her Portuguese nationality, unless she did not acquire her husband's nationality as a result of the marriage or declared, prior to the wedding, that she wished to keep her Portuguese nationality. Furthermore, she would not lose her Portuguese nationality if she rejected her husband's nationality, provided that the national law of her husband's country allowed it (art. LX).
- Citizens born on Portuguese soil who declared that they no longer want to be Portuguese lose their Portuguese nationality provided they held another nationality. This provision was aimed above all at children born to foreign parents and who had acquired Portuguese nationality through ius soli, as well as their parents' foreign nationality through the effects of ius sanguinis. This was a case of voluntary loss of Portuguese nationality, since it depended on an expression of intent made by the person in question or by his legal agent if the person was under-age (art. XVIII (d)).
- Those on whom Portuguese nationality had been conferred, or who had acquired it by an expression of intent made by their legal agent, also lose Portuguese nationality if they declare that they did not wish to be Portuguese and proved that they held another nationality. As in the previous case, this was voluntary loss of nationality, which was only admissible if the person in question held two nationalities. In this case, however, the legislator focused more on the Portuguese born abroad who had acquired Portuguese nationality through ius sanguinis on the basis of a declaration made by their legal agent (art. XVIII (e)).

In all of the above cases (except (2)), the legislator not only considered the wishes of the person in question, but also the general interest in avoiding statelessness since renunciation only led to the loss of Portuguese nationality if the person in question held another nationality, and would therefore not become stateless.

Following a decision taken by the Cabinet, the Government could furthermore decree loss of Portuguese nationality in the following three situations: 1) when a Portuguese with dual nationality only behaves like a foreigner; 2) when such a person has been convicted for a crime against external security; 3) or has engaged in illicit activities to the benefit of the foreign country or its agents and against the interests of the Portuguese state (art. XX).

Based on the assumption that the loss of Portuguese nationality was open to remedy, the 1959 Act, like its predecessor, foresaw ways in which nationality could be reacquired. Those who had lost their Portuguese nationality for having acquired a foreign nationality through naturalisation, could reacquire it provided they met the following two premises: they took up residence in Portugal and expressed their intent to reacquire Portuguese nationality. These requirements applied to Portuguese women who had lost Portuguese nationality through having married a foreigner, allowing them to reacquire Portuguese nationality following dissolution or annulment of their marriage. Moreover, those persons who had lost Portuguese nationality because of a renunciation made before they came of age, by their legal agent, could reacquire it when they came of age, should they be residing in Portugal and express this intent. In both cases, meeting these requirements implied *ex lege* reacquisition (without the authorities' involvement), and thus represented a true right for the persons concerned (art. XXII). In addition, the Government could decide that citizens who had lost Portuguese nationality by Government decision, could reacquire it. Unlike the above situations, this required a discretionary act by the Government.

12.2.5 *Decree Law 308-A/75 of 24 June 1974: the effects of de-colonisation on Portuguese nationality*

The process of de-colonisation triggered by the Portuguese Revolution (25 April 1974), led to the creation of five new African countries: Cape Verde, Guinea Bissau, São Tomé e Principe, Angola and Mozambique. Decree Law 308/75 of 24 June 1975 sought to solve the impact of the creation of these new states on Portuguese nationality. (This item of legislation was repealed by Law 113/88, of 29 December 1988.) The Decree Law governed the issue of losing or retaining Portuguese nationality by those people who had been born or were living in the Portuguese overseas territories that had gained independence.

It was assumed that these persons would acquire the nationality of the new state. The Decree Law thus merely stipulated that Portuguese nationality would be retained by those persons who had not been born overseas but were living there (art. 1), in addition to those who, despite having been born in the territory of the colonies, had maintained a special connection with mainland Portugal by having been long-term residents there (art. 2). All those not covered by one of the situations that enabled them to keep Portuguese nationality would lose it *ex lege* (art. 4).

This legislation raised many doubts as to how it should be interpreted and implemented and has generated many case laws, right up to the present day. It has also been criticised by legal thinkers, in particular, because it led to the *ex lege* loss of Portuguese nationality by thousands who had been born or had settled in the newly-independent overseas territories without considering their wishes and their effective links to Portugal. Furthermore, it fostered statelessness, whenever those concerned did not acquire the nationality of the new state (Ramos 1976: 340; Jalles 1984: 188; Santos 1993: 443).

12.2.6 *Law 37/81 of 3 October 1981: mixed system giving prevalence to ius sanguinis*

In 1981, a new law (Law 37/81) was adopted in Portugal. As this law will be analysed in detail in Chapter 3, in this chapter we shall from a historical perspective only focus on the differences vis-à-vis earlier legislation, and the amendments made in 1994 and 2004.

In many ways, the 1981 Law breaks away from earlier legislation, although it did retain some principles, such as avoiding statelessness and the individual's will in determining nationality. The breaks must be understood in the context of the 1976 Constitution, which came in the wake of the revolution of 25 April 1974 that restored democracy to Portugal. Although the Constitution only considered those foreseen in law and international conventions as being Portuguese (art. 4), it contains a series of rules and principles that restrict the legislator's sphere of action with regard to acquisition and loss of nationality.

The first break with the previous legislation (which foresaw prevalence of ius soli) concerns acquisition of nationality at birth. This was changed to a mixed system, in which greater importance is attached to the role of ius sanguinis and ius soli is restricted. The acquisition of nationality by the children of Portuguese born abroad (that is, through ius sanguinis) no longer depends on criteria linked to residence in Portugal. A mere expression of intent or registration of the birth in the Portuguese civil register became sufficient. In addition, since ius soli was no longer considered an autonomous criterion, major changes were made concerning the children of foreigners born in Portugal. In order to prove that the birth in Portugal was not merely by chance, acquisition of nationality through ius soli became dependent on an expression of intent and the parents having lived in Portugal for a period of not less than 6 years (Ramos 1996: 610).

Secondly, the 1976 Constitution enshrined the principle of non-discrimination towards children born out of wedlock (art. 36 (4)) and imposed an end to discrimination between women and men and legitimate and illegitimate children (Ramos 1994: 115; Ferreira 1987: 8). The 1981 Act implemented these provisions regarding acquisition of nationality at birth. Thus, ius sanguinis *a mater* is made fully equal with ius sanguinis *a pater*, and all cases of parentage are treated in the same way. In addition, achievement of the principle of equality (art. 13) and banning discrimination between spouses (art. 36) required changes to the Nationality Act in order to bring an end to the effects of marriage on women's acquisition or loss of nationality. The new Nationality Act provided for equality between men and women in acquisition after birth as a result of marriage. Marriage to a Portuguese man or woman no longer resulted in acquisition of nationality, but became just one of the grounds for voluntary acquisition of Portuguese nationality. The 1981 Act thus enshrined the principle of nationality being separate form marriage (Ramos 1996: 622).

A third break from previous legislation is linked to the arrangements for loss of nationality, which became exclusively voluntary. This was grounded in the principle of regarding the right to citizenship as an individual's basic right and brought an end to the loss of citizenship for political reasons or as a punishment (art. 26 (1) and 30 (4) of the Constitution). This curtailed any automatic loss of nationality (*ex lege*), imposed by a decision from the administrative authorities or the involuntary loss of Portuguese nationality (Miranda 1998: 120). Loss of nationality could no longer be used by the state as a means of punishing the individual for not having a link to the Portuguese community or for not having been loyal to the state. Instead, it became the exclusive domain of the individual's will, in addition to requiring a situation of dual nationality in order to avoid statelessness (Ramos 1994: 129).

The 1981 Act also introduced complete tolerance towards dual nationality. On the one hand, acquisition of Portuguese nationality no longer relied in any way on renouncing ones foreign nationality. On the other, acquisition of a foreign nationality no longer resulted in the loss of Portuguese nationality, as was the case under previous legislation.

Lastly, the 1981 Act brought about profound changes concerning the right of appeal. The principle of effective jurisdictional protection of people's rights (art. 20 of the Constitution) and the nature of nationality as a basic right required that appeals on matters pertaining to Nationality Law be lodged with the courts (Ramos 1992: 214). Under the terms of the 1959 Act, appeals concerning the acquisition, loss or reacquisition of nationality could be lodged with the Minister of Justice – an administrative authority – whose decisions could be appealed in the Supreme Administrative Court. The 1981 Act made the Lisbon Court of Appeal the instance for appealing against any and all acts pertaining to the acquisition, loss or reacquisition of Portuguese nationality – that is to say, a jurisdictional body.

12.2.6.1 *Law 25/94 amending Law 37/81: restricting foreigners' access to Portuguese nationality*

Immigration to Portugal, particularly illegal immigration, increased significantly in the 1990s, leading to the first amendment of the 1981 Act by Law 25/94 of 19 August 1994. The aim was to make it more difficult for foreigners to obtain nationality at birth (via ius soli) and after birth (particularly through marriage or naturalisation).

Firstly, the grounds for the child born to foreign parents in Portugal became more restrictive making it difficult for immigrants' children to obtain Portuguese nationality. On the one hand, the law required not only that the parents have Portugal as their habitual place of residence but that they also hold a residence permit. This aimed at not only excluding the children of illegal immigrants from obtaining nationality, but also those who were in Portugal legally, but on the basis of a different permit, such as a work permit or permit of stay[22] (which since 2001 covers a large percentage of foreigners living in Portugal). Furthermore, Law 25/94 introduced a distinction between those foreigners from Lusophone countries and others keeping the minimum period of residence at six years for the former, but increasing it to ten years for the latter.

In addition, the arrangements for acquiring Portuguese nationality through marriage to a Portuguese citizen were amended. Firstly, the legislator required a minimum period of three years of marriage for the spouse of a Portuguese citizen to acquire Portuguese nationality. Furthermore, the opposition by the state could now be founded on the applicant's failure to prove an effective link to the Portuguese community. Prior to 1994, the Public Prosecutor had to prove the applicant's obvious lack of integration into the Portuguese community in order to successfully oppose the acquisition of nationality through marriage. Since this proof was difficult to obtain the 1994 legislator transferred the burden of proof making it the foreign applicant's duty to prove the link, which became one of the premises for acquiring nationality.

12.2.6.2 *Framework Law 1/2004: the reacquisition of Portuguese nationality*

In order to eradicate the effects of earlier legislation on emigrant communities, Framework Law 1/2004 of 15 January introduced major changes to the reacquisition arrangements: firstly, it removed the possibility for reacquisition to be opposed and established *ex lege* acquisition, whenever the loss of nationality had not been registered. Secondly, reacquisition was made retroactive to the date of loss, allowing the children of emigrants born abroad to acquire Portuguese nationality via ius sanguinis.

12.3 Recent developments and current institutional arrangements

The acquisition, loss and reacquisition of Portuguese nationality is regulated by Law 37/81 of 3 October, as amended by Law 25/94 of 19 August and by Framework Law 1/2004 of 15 January (1981 Nationality

Act). This Act is supplemented by Decree Law 322/82 of 12 August, amended by Decree Law 253/94 of 20 October and Decree Law 37/97 of 31 January (Nationality Regulation).

12.3.1 *Main general modes of acquisition and loss of citizenship*

12.3.1.1 *Political analysis*

Following the Revolution of 25 April 1974, the Portuguese Colonial Empire collapsed. Clarifying which of the ex-colonies' nationals and residents could keep Portuguese nationality was made more urgent given that the 1959 Nationality Act, which was then in force, stated that all those born on Portuguese territory had the right to Portuguese nationality and to move to the Portuguese mainland.

Decree Law 308-A/75 of 24 June established which of those born or residing in the ex-colonies would retain or lose Portuguese nationality. Once the problem that arose with de-colonisation and retaining Portuguese nationality had been resolved, the 1959 Nationality Act remained in force until 1981 despite the fact that, to a certain extent, it contradicted the 1976 Constitution.

Law 37/81 of 3 October aimed not only at achieving consistency between the Nationality Act and the Constitution,[23] at introducing the principles of non-discrimination[24] and of a fundamental right to nationality,[25] but also at profoundly reforming the acquisition of nationality at birth. Breaking with a centuries-old tradition the new law gave prevalence to ius sanguinis over ius soli (which alone no longer conferred Portuguese nationality).[26]

If the need to make the Nationality Act consistent with the 1976 Constitution warranted consensus amongst the political parties with parliamentary representation, the same cannot be said regarding the prevalence of ius sanguinis over ius soli; regarding access to Portuguese nationality for emigrants and their descendants; or regarding the reacquisition of nationality by those who had surrendered it voluntarily.

The relegation of ius soli as a criterion for the acquisition of nationality at birth and the greater importance attached to ius sanguinis are the result of the political and historical context at that time. Portugal's decrease in size and its return to being a European state after the decolonisation process in the 1970s, as well as the wish to move closer to European tradition in this domain, led the legislator of 1981 to reduce the role of ius soli. Furthermore, the strong flow of emigrants out of Portugal through the 1960s required greater importance to be given to ius sanguinis as a means of preserving Portuguese nationality for the children of emigrants and a substantial human resource for the state (Miranda 1998: 108; Ramos 1994: 117; Jalles 1984: 178).

The Government, at the time a centre-right coalition (the Democratic Alliance), upheld the principle of ius sanguinis.[27] The Socialist Party (PS), whilst in agreement with the new Law that favoured access to nationality for emigrants and their descendants, that is to say the principle of ius sanguinis, also defended the continuation of ius soli.[28] The nationality problems resulting from decolonisation and postcolonial immigration and the lack of access to Portuguese nationality by an increasing number of children born in Portugal of Lusophone African origins did not appear to warrant the intervention of any other Members of Parliament.

Clearly what was on the political agenda at the time was emigration. Whilst immigration had grown at an annual rate of 13 per cent between 1975 and 1980 (Baganha & Marques 2001: 15), it was not a subject that interested the majority of Portuguese politicians. They did not appear to be interested in the impact on nationality that the prevalence of ius sanguinis over ius soli could have on the descendants of immigrants who had settled in Portugal. It was this new perception of Portugal as a small European territory and an emigrant population estimated at more than four million people that led the main political forces, both those in power and in the opposition, to pass a law that had as a key objective to facilitate the right to Portuguese nationality of emigrants and their descendants spread around the world.

After debate and general approval the bills on nationality submitted by the Government, the PS and the independent Social Democratic party (ASDI) were forwarded to the Commission for Constitutional Affairs where a new text was agreed upon which endeavoured to organise the three documents. In this way Law 37/81 of 3 October was approved by all political parties represented in Parliament.[29] However, the legislators' concern in facilitating the acquisition of Portuguese nationality by all members of the communities of Portuguese descent across the world, went even further. It allowed for dual nationality and reacquisition of nationality by all those who had lost it through previous legislation, or as a result of voluntary acquisition of a foreign nationality or due to marriage.

In 1994, the Nationality Act underwent a first amendment with Parliament's approval of Law 25/94 of 19 August, based on a proposal submitted by the Social Democratic majority Government. This proposal should be examined in the light of this Government's overall political activity that proposed more restrictive policies regarding foreigners, as is clearly evident in the 1993 Immigration Act (Decree Law 59/93 of 3 March) that was much more restrictive than the previous one, both in terms of foreigners entering and staying in Portugal. It was now a case of completing the legal framework regarding foreigners not of Portuguese descent by restricting their right to nationality. These amendments were supported by the main political powers with parliamentary representation.

Whilst in the 1981 Nationality Act debate, the legislator's concern and the political agenda was how to facilitate a right to Portuguese nationality for Portuguese emigrants across the world, what concerned the Government in 1994 was how to stem the growing number of immigrants acquiring Portuguese nationality as well as various scandals related to fictitious marriages. The debate centred entirely on restrictions that should be placed on foreigners' rights to nationality. Once the Government's proposal had been cleansed of a few spurious attempts at xenophobia, the main political parties – the governing Social Democratic Party (PSD), the Centre Social Democratic – Popular Party (CDS-PP) and the Socialist Party (PS) voted in favour, whilst all the parties to the left of the Socialist Party (PS), voted against.[30]

Based on a proposal by the majority centre-right Government the 1981 Nationality Act was amended once again in 2004[31] with regard to nationality reacquisition. This Government bill and the one presented by the PS on the same issue were both approved, whilst the projects presented by the Left Block (BE) and the Greens, aimed at making more profound changes to the Nationality Act, were rejected.

Profiting from its overall majority in Parliament the Government approved the Framework Law 1/2004 of 15 January, which changed the provisions for nationality reacquisition for women who had previously lost the right to Portuguese nationality due to marriage, and those who had lost it when they voluntarily acquired a foreign nationality. The objective was to facilitate reacquisition of nationality for emigrants who had lost Portuguese nationality automatically as result of previous legislation and also to redress the negative impact which Law 2098 of 1959 had had on Portuguese communities abroad, since it went against the real wishes of emigrants who continued to feel part of Portugal without actually being Portuguese nationals and without being able to pass their nationality on to their children.

Neither the original version of the Nationality Act of 1981, nor the new wording of 1994, nor the minor changes in 2004, raised heated debates or political divisions. Quite the opposite: from 1981 until today this Act has reflected a broad and consensual understanding amongst the main political powers about who is, and who should be, Portuguese.

According to the Nationality Act, the following acquire nationality at birth *ex lege*:

- The child of a Portuguese (mother or father) who was born on Portuguese territory or on territory under Portuguese administration (art. 1 (a));[32]

- The child of Portuguese descent (mother or father) who was born abroad, if the parent was serving the Portuguese State (art. 1 (a) *in fine*);
- A person born on Portuguese territory who does not have any other nationality (art. 1 (d)).[33]

In all of these cases of extraterritorial ius sanguinis and acquisition by foundlings and stateless children, the persons concerned are of Portuguese origin, under the simple terms of the law, as long as the following is stated in the births register: the Portuguese nationality of either of the parents (or no mention of foreign nationality of the parents); when born abroad, a statement that the mother or father were serving the Portuguese state on the date of birth; or a statement that no other nationality is held (art. 1 of the Nationality Regulation).

The Nationality Act also provides arrangements for voluntary acquisition at birth (by option/ by declaration and/or registration):

- if the child of a Portuguese mother or father born abroad declares (in person or through a legal agent) that he or she wants to be Portuguese or that the birth is registered at the Portuguese registry office (art. 1 (b));[34]
- if the child of foreigners born in Portugal meets at the time of birth the following three requirements (art. 1 (c)): (1) the parents have lived in Portugal with a valid residence permit[35] for at least six or ten years, depending, respectively, on whether they come from a country where the official language is Portuguese or from another country, (2) the parent is not in Portugal serving his or her own state, and (3) they make a declaration that they wish to be Portuguese.

Different from *ex lege* acquisition, in these two cases the acquisition is voluntary since it always depends on the applicant's expression of intent. But once this statement has been made, and when the other legal requirements have been met, the acquisition of nationality works automatically in accordance with the law and cannot be prevented by the state as is the case with acquisition after birth by declaration (Ramos 2001: 219)

In the first case, acquisition is through ius sanguinis, but this is not enough on its own to determine the conferment of Portuguese nationality. If the birth is abroad, it is not enough for the child to have a Portuguese father or mother in order to obtain Portuguese nationality at birth, rather the applicant must declare in person or through a legal agent that he or she wishes to be Portuguese. An explicit declaration registered at the Central Registry Office or a tacit declaration resulting from registration of the birth at the consulate at the place of birth or at the Registry Office is sufficient (art. 6 of the Nationality Regulation). The Portuguese nationality of a child of a Portuguese born abroad is proven by registration of that declaration or by the registration of birth at the Portuguese registry (art. 21 (2) of the Nationality Act).

In the second case, nationality acquisition is through ius soli, despite the fact that this alone is not enough to confer nationality on children born in Portugal to foreign parents. This is because acquisition depends not only on the wishes of the individual – as is the case with ius sanguinis – but also on the parents' situation (they cannot be in Portugal serving their State), the length of time the parents have resided in Portugal, as well as their residence status (not all residence statuses are valid, for example, a work permit or permit of stay are not eligible).

Despite the fact that nationality acquisition is voluntary in both of these cases, it is a form of acquisition at birth. On the one hand, the requirements for acquisition have to be verified at birth. On the other hand, if Portuguese nationality is established after birth, and as a consequence the declaration is made later, the acquisition has a retroactive effect (*ex tunc*), without affecting the validity of legal relationships already established on the basis of another nationality (art. 11 of the Nationality Act). However, the provisions for nationality acquisition are only considered relevant if the descent of the child is established before he or she comes of age (art. 14 of the Nationality Act).

Acquisition of nationality after birth only takes effect when the respective legal requirements have been met, in other words, *ex nunc* (art. 12 of the Nationality Act). The Act foresees three ways of acquiring nationality after birth: *ex lege* in case of adoption, by declaration based on a legal entitlement in case of filial and spousal transfer of nationality and by discretionary naturalisation. Acquisition of nationality after birth does not occur automatically in any of these cases. It depends on non-opposition from the state (for acquisition after birth through adoption or personal wish) or a discretionary Government act (for acquisition through naturalisation).

- Acquisition through filial or spousal transfer: There are two cases in which the Nationality Act provides for the right of foreigners to voluntarily acquire Portuguese nationality by declaration in order to assure the national unit of the family:
  - filial transfer of nationality: Minors or disabled children with a mother or father who acquires Portuguese nationality (for example, by naturalisation) can acquire Portuguese nationality by declaration (art. 2).[36]
  - spousal transfer of nationality: A foreigner who has been married for more than three years to a Portuguese national can acquire Portuguese nationality by declaration made by virtue of marriage (art. 3 (1)).

In neither of these cases, is the acquisition of nationality automatic, as this is subject to other conditions: that the Public Prosecutor does not oppose, or should he have opposed acquisition, that the Court of Appeal or the Supreme Court of Justice consider such opposition to be unfounded (arts. 9 and 10).

Since 1994 applicants (a foreigner married to a Portuguese national or whose father or mother acquired Portuguese nationality) have had to prove a true link to the national community by documentary evidence, testimony or by another legally permitted means (art. 22 (1) (a) of the Nationality Regulation).

- Acquisition by adoption. 'A child fully adopted by a Portuguese national acquires Portuguese nationality' (art. 5). This is an ex lege acquisition, with no need for an expression of intent: all that is required is that the registration of the birth of the child in question clearly states that he or she was adopted by a Portuguese national (art. 13 of the Nationality Regulation). However, as in previous cases, this acquisition is not automatic in the case of adoption, for it also depends on non-opposition by the Public Prosecution Service, or on a Court decision that such opposition is unfounded.[37]
- The final means of acquisition after birth considered by the law is naturalisation. Naturalisation depends, above all, on an expression of intent, since naturalisation can only be conferred following an application to the Portuguese Home Office (art. 7 (1) of the Nationality Act and art. 15 (1) of the Nationality Regulation). Yet, the foreigner's intent is not enough, for legal requirements which allow the Government to confer Portuguese nationality by naturalisation also have to be met. According to art. 6 (1) of the Nationality Act, the Government can only grant Portuguese nationality by naturalisation if the following requirements are met: The person in question must:
  - be of age or emancipated according to Portuguese law;[38]
  - have resided in Portugal or in another territory under Portuguese administration, with a valid residence permit for a period of six or ten years depending on whether he or she comes from a country where the official language is Portuguese or from another country;
  - have sufficient knowledge of the Portuguese language;
  - demonstrate proof of true integration in the national community;
  - be of good repute;
  - have a means of subsistence.

Foreigners who have held Portuguese nationality, who are descendants of Portuguese, are members of communities of Portuguese origin, or who have provided some form of service to the Portuguese State are exempt from fulfilling some of the legal naturalisation requirements, specifically those related to residence (period of residence and residence permit), knowledge of the Portuguese language and integration in the Portuguese community (art. 6 (2)).

Whilst legal requirements have to be checked, naturalisation is a discretionary concession whereby the Government grants Portuguese nationality to a foreigner through a decree of the Minister of Home Affairs. The Government is free to exercise this discretionary power and a foreigner does not have a subjective right to naturalisation even if he or she fulfils the legal requirements, as naturalisation can be denied for reasons of convenience (Ramos 1992: 163).

Naturalisation is subject to registration at the Civil Registry Office (art. 18 (1) (c) of the Nationality Act) and only becomes valid as from this date (art. 12 of the Nationality Act).

The legal arrangements for loss of nationality are influenced by the 1976 Constitution which states that nationality is a fundamental right of an individual (art. 26 (1)) and forbids the loss of nationality for political reasons (art. 26 (4)) or as a consequence of serving a prison sentence (art. 30 (4)). These constitutional principles and the general principle that no one can be deprived of their nationality arbitrarily influenced the legislators regarding the laws governing loss of nationality. Loss of nationality has to be defined in law and cannot be determined by the acts of public authorities (Ramos 1994: 114; Ferreira 1987: 8). Loss of Portuguese nationality is also not possible if the citizen in question becomes stateless (Jalles 1984: 172).

Unlike its predecessor, the 1981 Nationality Act is underpinned throughout by these principles, as it does not foresee any *ex lege* loss of Portuguese nationality or due to state intervention. Art. 8 of the Nationality Act only foresees loss of nationality when it is the individual's own free will and as long as he or she has another nationality. In other words, in Portugal, the state cannot impose loss of nationality even as a result of the acquisition of another state's nationality (as was the case in Portugal until this law came into force). Neither is the mere wish to renounce nationality sufficient. In order to avoid situations of statelessness the applicant must hold the nationality of another state.

Nullity of a registration of birth (in cases of *ex lege* acquisition at birth) or the registry of nationality acquisition after birth based on falsehood (arts. 89 and 91 of the Civil Registry Code) are not treated in the same light as loss of nationality. It is this registration that proves Portuguese nationality. If the registration is based on a false declaration (for example, the child was not of a Portuguese citizen, but, as a result of an error or false documents was registered as being the child of a Portuguese citizen and, therefore, Portuguese), the Public Prosecutor can appeal at any time to the Lisbon Court of Appeal to declare its nullity and order its cancellation (art. 25 of the Nationality Act). Since the declaration of nullity of the registration upon which nationality was granted has retroactive effects one does not classify this in legal terms as a loss of nationality, but rather as non-acquisition of nationality. As the person in question never held Portuguese nationality, one cannot legally refer to loss of nationality.

These cases are extremely rare and normally refer to Decree Law 308-A/75 that determines the *ex lege* loss of Portuguese nationality to citizens from Portuguese ex-colonies who did not fulfil the requirements to hold Portuguese nationality. Given the difficulties in enforcing this law, there were cases when, due to an administrative error, certain people saw their nationality registration recorded as valid whereas, according to the law, they had lost it. In these cases, when the citizen in question cannot be blamed for false registration, the Courts consider the declaration of nullity as invalid because it amounts to an abuse of the law.[39]

This is not the case when false registration is due to a citizen's own actions, for in such cases the declaration of nullity and cancellation of the registration operates retroactively and withdraws Portuguese nationality from the person in question (legally, it is as if nationality had never been acquired).[40]

Those who have lost Portuguese nationality as a result of renouncing it by means of a declaration made when they were not legally autonomous can reacquire it by declaration when they come of age (and, are therefore legally autonomous to exercise this right). Reacquisition is not automatic with the declaration but depends on it not being legally contested within a period of one year, based on the principles we have previously discussed. If it is contested, then a court must declare it unfounded (art. 4 of the Nationality Act).

The other two situations are linked to the legal arrangements for loss of nationality, which were in force until 1981.

Art. 30 of the Nationality Act, as amended by Framework Law 1/2004 of 15 January allows women who lost Portuguese nationality due to marriage to reacquire it by means of a declaration. Reacquisition of nationality has become easier in that it is no longer subject to non-opposition by the Public Prosecutor and the interested party need not prove integration into the Portuguese community. Furthermore, reacquisition is effective retroactively from the date of loss of nationality that allows children who were born after this date to acquire Portuguese nationality of origin by declaration.

Art. 31 of the Nationality Act, as amended by the Framework Law 1/2004, allows for the reacquisition of Portuguese Nationality by all those who lost it when they acquired another nationality. So long as there is no definitive registration of loss of nationality, reacquisition is *ex lege* but allows the applicant to oppose it by declaring that he or she does not want to be Portuguese. Only when there is definitive registration of loss of nationality is an expression of intent required stating the wish to reacquire nationality. The reacquisition of nationality in these cases is no longer subject to non-opposition by the Public Prosecutor and becomes effective from the date of acquisition of the foreign nationality (and therefore from the date of loss of Portuguese nationality), without affecting the validity of previously established legal implications based on another nationality. The intention was to consider as of Portuguese origin the children of emigrants who were born after the loss of Portuguese nationality resulting from the 1959 Law. Without this retroactive effect, they would have to be considered foreigners, with their only chance of becoming Portuguese being by means of naturalisation or marriage to a Portuguese citizen. This new arrangement allows for children who were born after the automatic loss of Portuguese nationality by their parent, to acquire nationality of origin if they state that they want to be Portuguese or if they register their birth at the Portuguese Civil Registry, in accordance with the terms of art. 1 (1) (b) of the Nationality Act.

12.3.1.2 *Statistical development of acquisitions*

Statistical information on nationality acquisition only started to be published in 1994 and even then only partially. In fact in 1994, 1995 and 1998, only the total number of acquisitions by means of naturalisation was published. These statistics are only broken down into naturalisation and other modes of acquisition, which is insufficient for a more profound analysis of this topic to be carried out.

Bearing in mind these limitations and also by using an unpublished work covering information on the acquisition of nationality through marriage and naturalisation (Oliveira & Inácio 1999), we can partially rebuild the series of nationality acquisitions between 1985 and 2003. From what was said, one can deduce that the aforementioned series (Table 12.1) is a conservative estimate for the period between 1985 and 1994 and for the years 1995 and 1998.

Table 12.1 indicates that the total annual number of nationality acquisitions is generally low, never above 2,000 during the period examined. Over five-year periods we can see that the annual average was 740 nationality acquisitions between 1985 and 1989; 1,314 between 1990 and 1994; and 1,173 between 1999 and 2003.

In other words, there seems to have been a substantial increase in the number of nationality acquisitions from the 1980s to the 1990s. According to Oliveira and Inácio (1999), this increase was largely due to the acquisition of Portuguese nationality by Chinese citizens during

Table 12.1: Acquisition of nationality in Portugal 1985-2003

	Total	*Naturalisation*	*Other*
1985	875	42	833
1986	476	17	459
1987	76	25	51
1988	861	21	840
1989	1,412	37	1,375
1990	846	65	781
1991	1,139	61	1,078
1992	1,706	78	1,628
1993	1,177	115	1,062
1994	1,704	81	1,623
1995	1,413		
1996	1,154	532	622
1997	1,364	661	363
1998	519	519	
1999	946	286	660
2000	721	126	594
2001	1,082	295	787
2002	1,369	225	1,144
2003	1,747	552	1,195
total	20,587		

Source: 1985-1994: Oliveira 1995-2003: National Institute for Statistics (INE)

the transition period for the handing over of Macao to China. It is worth noting that the average annual number of nationality acquisitions drops slightly from 1999 to 2003 in comparison to the average for 1990-1994.

Table 12.1 also indicates that the series is erratic and difficult to analyse, although during the last three years for which we have information, there seems to be an upward trend. This growth, as is shown on Table 12.2, results mainly from nationality acquisition by other means (a category that is mainly composed of nationality acquisitions by marriage to a national).

As can also be seen in Table 12.2, nationals of countries where the official language is Portuguese (ex-colonies in Africa and Brazil) are the largest group to seek nationality acquisition, as well as being the largest immigrant communities in Portugal.

Also worth noting is the high level of nationality acquisitions by Venezuelan citizens. In this case, the claim to Portuguese nationality can be explained by the large number of Portuguese descendants living in that country as well as the serious social and economic crisis that the country is going through, which probably makes Portuguese nationality acquisition more appealing.

Although the foreign population in Portugal has been growing continuously since 1985, nationality acquisition has not grown at the same

Table 12.2: Acquisition of Portuguese nationality by naturalisation, other modes and by previous nationality

Former nationality	*1994**	*1995**	*1996*		*1997*		*1998***	*1999*		*2000*		*2001*		*2002*		*2003*	
	Nat.	*Nat.*	*Nat.*	*Other*	*Nat*	*Other*	*Nat.*	*Nat.*	*Other*	*Nat.*	*Other*	*Nat.*	*Other*	*Nat.*	*Other*	*Nat.*	*Other*
Angola	55	76	40	17	45	11	56	37	25	17	25	29	36	22	60	68	76
Cape Verde	129	169	70	10	86	7	159	75	42	36	33	148	80	53	218	144	226
Guinea Bissau	44	43	23	4	16	–	67	24	13	16	11	37	18	25	48	21	17
Mozambique	29	30	15	4	21	5	56	23	14	5	5	11	13	1	26	25	31
São Tomé	21	18	10	–	12	–	28	8	7	5	2	14	6	10	24	29	29
Total (ex-colonies in Africa)	**278**	**336**	**158**	**35**	**180**	**23**	**366**	**167**	**101**	**79**	**76**	**239**	**153**	**111**	**376**	**287**	**379**
EU	27	45	21	23	18	29	13	14	28	1	24	–	27	2	43	9	53
Others Europe	19	24	11	8	15	3	6	2	9	–	7	2	12	1	15	5	25
Canada	39	76	49	20	54	38	4	27	43	11	44	5	49	22	43	29	39
USA	67	164	64	56	86	117	7	32	59	4	60	8	82	22	86	29	65
Brazil	176	235	120	121	204	92	46	22	164	22	153	33	250	43	302	114	229
Venezuela	266	431	77	334	68	363		9	210	1	185	1	161	17	204	28	283
Other/stateless	99	102	32	25	36	38	77	23	46	8	46	7	53	7	75	51	122
Total	**971**	**1,413**	**532**	**622**	**661**	**703**	**519**	**286**	**660**	**126**	**595**	**295**	**787**	**225**	**1,144**	**552**	**1,195**

Source: INE

* No information about other modes of acquisition

** No reference to Venezuela

Table 12.3: Acquisitions of Portuguese nationality as a percentage of the foreign resident population

Year	*Percentage*
1985	1.10%
1986	0.55%
1987	0.08%
1988	0.91%
1989	1.40%
1990	0.79%
1991	1.00%
1992	1.38%
1993	0.86%
1994	1.08%
1995	0.84%
1996	0.67%
1997	0.78%
1998	0.29%
1999	0.49%
2000	0.35%
2001	0.48%
2002	0.57%
2003	0.70%

Sources: Table 12.1 and Foreigners and Borders Service (SEF)

rate. In fact, as can be seen in Table 12.3, nationality acquisitions as a percentage of the foreign population residing legally have been falling since 1997.

As mentioned, the figures on nationality acquisition are incomplete, making analysis difficult. We can however, reach two conclusions: (1) For the period examined, the percentage of foreigners that acquired Portuguese nationality never surpassed 1.5 per cent of the total foreign population residing legally in Portugal. For the majority of years the rate was below 1 per cent; (2) The figures are erratic not allowing for generalisations regarding behavioural trends, although the last three years show an upward trend.

12.3.2 *The quasi-citizenship status of the nationals of countries having Portuguese as the official language*

12.3.2.1 *Political analysis*

Decolonisation did not have a great impact on the Nationality Act, in the sense that it did not lead to a different mode of nationality acquisition for the citizens of these countries. As is the case with other foreigners, they can acquire nationality in the regular ways provided for by the law, although some aspects of acquisition were made easier.

Thus, the period of residence required for nationality acquisition by ius soli or naturalisation is shorter (six years) than that required of foreigners who do not come from a Lusophone country (ten years).

In terms of citizenship, however, decolonisation had an enormous impact as it contributed to the creation of a privileged status for nationals of Lusophone countries characterised by the conferral of a series of rights regarding political participation that previously had only been given to Portuguese nationals. A common language and history among Lusophone countries was the determining factor for maintaining mutual privileged ties, which was also established as a fundamental principle in Portuguese Foreign Policy (art. 7 (3) of the Constitution). These ties led to the creation of a Lusophone status of citizenship enshrined in art. 15 (3) of the Constitution, which has its origins in the 1971 Convention between Portugal and Brazil.

Lusophone citizenship differs from European citizenship. On the one hand, it allows for various political rights to be exercised, not only at a local but also at a national level, as well as access to public offices which are not predominantly of a technical nature. On the other hand, and contrary to European citizenship, Lusophone citizenship, as it exists today in relation to Brazilians, does not provide any right to entry and permanent residence in Portuguese territory nor to diplomatic protection in another country.

On 7 September 1971, the Convention on Equal Rights and Obligations between Portuguese and Brazilians was signed with regards to the special bonds between Portugal and Brazil and the large community of Portuguese settlers in Brazil. This Convention created a true Luso-Brazilian citizenship status, giving Brazilian nationals with a Portuguese residence permit broad political rights. They were denied access, though, to the following positions: President of the Republic, Member of Parliament, Member of the Government, judge of the Supreme Court, diplomatic representative and officer in the armed forces.

In order to make provisions for this Convention, art. 15 (3) of the 1976 Portuguese Constitution gave citizens of Lusophone countries, through international agreement and reciprocity, rights that other foreigners did not have, with the exception of access to higher positions in the government of the country including its autonomous regions, service in the armed forces and the diplomatic corps. In view of the decolonisation process and the ties with African countries that had achieved their independence, the Constitutional Legislator chose not to restrict the quasi-citizenship status to Brazilians, but made it available to all the nationals of the new states (although only Brazil met the reciprocity condition).

In 1988, Brazil went a step further in strengthening Luso-Brazilian citizenship: art. 12 of the new Brazilian Constitution provides the Portuguese with permanent residence in Brazil and the same rights as a Brazilian if there is reciprocity for Brazilians in Portugal. The only exceptions are, for holding the positions of President and Vice-President of the Republic, Speaker of the Federal Parliament, President of the Federal Senate, judge of the Supreme Federal Court, positions in the diplomatic corps and officers in the armed forces.

In response to demands by Brazilians who enjoyed fewer rights in Portugal than those that the 1988 Brazilian Constitution provided for the Portuguese, the Treaty of Friendship on equal rights was signed in 2000, strengthening the Luso-Brazilian citizenship status created by the 1971 Convention. Furthermore, the 2001 constitutional review reworded art. 15 (3) allowing the law to confer on citizens of Lusophone states with permanent residence in Portugal, broad citizenship rights that are not conferred on other foreigners, as long as reciprocity conditions are met. The only exceptions are access to 'positions of President of the Republic, Speaker of the Portuguese National Parliament, Prime Minister, President of the Supreme Courts and service in the Armed Forces and Diplomatic Corps'.

The re-wording of art. 15 (3) of the Constitution was a decisive step in creating the citizenship of the Community of Lusophone countries with a very broad range of political rights. The citizens of these countries who live in Portugal can achieve the same citizenship status as the Portuguese, as long as the same is provided for the Portuguese living in their countries. In particular, they can vote at local and national levels as well as be elected as Members of Parliament without having to acquire Portuguese nationality. They also have access to certain professions such as to that of judge or police officer, amongst others, which entail exercising public authority. In other words they enjoy the same political rights without having to acquire Portuguese nationality. As the reciprocity clause is only in place in relation to Brazil currently only Brazilians enjoy this quasi-citizenship status.

Decree Law 154/2003 and the Treaty of Friendship create two legal statuses for Brazilians with a residence permit in Portugal which are conferred by the Home Office upon application by the interested party: the status of equal rights and obligations and the status of equal political rights.

The status of equal rights and obligations allows Brazilians to enjoy the same rights as a Portuguese citizen, especially to hold positions in the civil service that are not predominantly technical (for example a judge or a policeman). A Brazilian with this status is only prevented from having the right to diplomatic protection and from holding political positions, serving in the Armed Forces or diplomatic corps (arts. 15 and 16 of Decree Law 154/2003). Brazilians who only have a general status of equal rights and obligations (without equal political rights) may vote and stand for elections in local elections in accordance with art. 15 (4) of the Constitution.

The equal political rights status allows a Brazilian to exercise full political rights, specifically voting and standing for election in local, regional and legislative elections (art. 19 of Decree Law 154/2003) with the exception of voting and standing in presidential elections (Costa 2000: 197). This status is only conferred on Brazilians who have previously or simultaneously acquired the status of equal rights and obligations (art. 2 (1) of Decree Law 154/2003) and as long as they have lived in Portugal with a residence permit for at least three years (art. 17 of the 2000 Treaty of Friendship and art. 5 (2) of Decree Law 154/2003).

The equal rights status does not imply loss of nationality of origin and is dependent on the acquisition of a residence permit, as Brazilian citizens, just like any other foreign nationals, do not have the right to enter and remain on Portuguese territory. Moreover, they are subject to the immigration laws that allow the State to control and limit the entry and stay of foreigners. But once legally resident in Portugal they can apply for this quasi-citizenship status, holding it for as long as they hold a residence permit. This status becomes extinct if the Brazilian citizen loses nationality or no longer holds a residence permit (due to expulsion or because it was withdrawn from him or her).

Citizens of Lusophone countries who do not have an equal political rights status and who reside in Portugal have the right to vote and stand in local elections if there is reciprocity.

These political rights are also conferred on other foreigners but the period of residence required by law before being able to exercise them is longer. In other words, the residence requirement for nationals of Lusophone countries to exercise political rights is shorter than for citizens of all other countries. Therefore, according to art. 2 (1) (c) of the Framework Law 1/2001 (the law that governs the election of members of local authorities) the nationals of Lusophone states who have lived in Portugal for more than two years can vote in local elections. In order to stand for local government they must have resided in Portugal for more than four years (art. 5 (1) of the Framework Law 1/2001). At present Brazilian citizens (even without equal political rights status) and Cape-Verdians enjoy these rights.

Unlike other foreigners (even those who have active and passive electoral capacity in elections for local authorities), the nationals of Lusophone states can also participate in local referenda (art. 35 of the Framework Law 4/2000).

The move towards a concept of citizenship that is disengaged from nationality goes beyond the privileged status of nationals of Lusophone countries or inherent status of EU citizen (which implies the right to vote or stand for election in local and European Parliament elections).

Any alien who resides in Portugal has the right to vote and stand for local elections if the reciprocity condition has been met (art. 15 (4) of the Constitution). The right to vote in local elections is conferred on them if they have held legal residence for more than three years (art. 2 (1) (d) of the Framework Law 1/2001) and they are eligible if they have resided legally in Portugal for more than five years, as long as they are nationals from countries that give the same entitlements to Portuguese nationals.

Other foreigners who have held a residence permit in Portugal for more than five years can be elected to local government bodies as long as they are nationals of countries where reciprocity conditions are met and where eligibility is conferred on the Portuguese that reside there (art. 5 (1) (d), Framework Law 1/2001).

12.3.2.2 *Statistical evolution of the stock of quasi-citizens*

Foreign citizens resident in Portugal who have the right to vote in local elections, on a reciprocal basis, are the aliens from Brazil, Cape Verde, Argentina, Chile, Estonia, Israel, Norway, Peru, Uruguay and Venezuela. Those from Brazil, Cape Verde, Peru and Uruguay can also be elected in local elections. Of the nationalities mentioned above, only Brazil and Cape Verde have numerically significant populations residing in Portugal. The statistical evolution of the stock of legal residents from these two nationalities is as follows:

Table 12.4: Brazilians with equal rights, equal political rights, or both statuses

Year	*Equal rights and obligations status*	*Equal political rights status*	*Both equal rights and obligations and equal political rights status*	*Total*
1993	349	32	34	415
1994	1,289	64	93	1,446
1995	582	41	65	688
1996	413	44	52	509
1997	568	48	79	695
1998	321	45	48	414
1999	737	54	185	976
2000	779	27	122	928
2001	751	3	81	835
2002	625	59	29	713
2003	455	2	47	504
2004	475	10	38	523

Source: SEF, unpublished data

Table 12.5: Stock of quasi-citizens in Portugal 1985-2003

Year	*Total of foreign residents*	*Cape Verde*	*Brazil*	*Total quasi-citizens*	*Quasi-citizens in % of total*
1985	79,594	24,959	6,804	31,763	40%
1990	107,767	28,796	11,413	40,209	37%
1995	168,316	38,746	19,901	58,647	35%
2000	207,607	47,216	22,411	69,627	34%
2003	250,697	53,858	26,561	80,419	32%

Source: SEF, Statistics, several years

The nationals from Cape Verde and Brazil represent a sizable share of the total foreign resident population. In fact, during the period considered they represented more than one third of the resident foreign population. This share has however systematically decreased since 1985, essentially due to the fact that the annual growth rates of the residents from Cape Verde are below the annual growth rates of the total resident foreign population.

12.3.3 *Institutional arrangements*

12.3.3.1 *The legislative process*

Since 1976 the legislative process on acquisition, loss and reacquisition of Portuguese nationality increased Parliament's exclusive competence, as it took on the form of a Framework Law (art. 166(2) of the Constitution).

Framework laws are general parliamentary laws that, as is the case for other laws, require a general vote, a vote on each individual article, and a final overall vote, as well as promulgation by the President of the Republic in order to enter into force. They are laws of increased importance (art. 112 (3) of the Constitution) as they are always Parliament's exclusive domain, they have to be voted on article-by-article in the plenary (not the committee) and the final vote must be passed by an overall majority of the sitting members of Parliament (and not just by those who are in the Chamber at the time of the vote) (Canotilho 2003: 750). Regarding the legislative proceedings there are no specifics on this matter. Members of parliamentary groups or the Government can submit proposals or bills on the nationality law.

12.3.3.2 *The process of implementation*

In Portugal, only central authorities are competent to implement nationality law. Firstly, all acts related to acquisition and loss of nationality are subject to registration, which is centralised at the Central Registry Office (in Lisbon). Secondly, the authorities play a decisive role in acquisition after birth. Acquisition by filial and spousal transfer or by adoption can be prevented by legal proceedings taken by the Public Prosecutor in the Lisbon Court of Appeal. The acquisition of nationality by naturalisation depends on a discretionary decision by the Home Office.

The role of embassies and consulates is merely instrumental as they solely receive declarations for acquisition and forward them to the Central Registry in Lisbon (art. 17 of the Nationality Act).

The effectiveness of all activity related to granting, acquisition and loss of nationality depends on its registration.

Declarations required for granting the Portuguese nationality by ius sanguinis are subject to registration when the birth registry abroad is not transcribed into the Portuguese civil registry. The same goes for acquisition by ius soli (descendants of foreigners born in Portugal), nationality acquisition after birth (marriage and filial transfer), as well as naturalisation and the declaration of loss of nationality (art. 18 (1) of the Nationality Act). All these declarations should be present at the Central Register of Nationality under the authority of the Central Registry Office (art. 16 of the Nationality Act). Acquisition of nationality after birth by expression of intent (spousal and filial transfer) or through naturalisation, as well as the loss and reacquisition of nationality are proved by this register (art. 22 (1) of the Nationality Act). This registration is made upon request by the parties concerned (art. 18 (2) of the Nationality Act) and is attached to their birth record (art. 19 of the Nationality Act and art. 35 of the Nationality Regulation). Only after this registration has been made can the person in question claim their right to Portuguese nationality (or, otherwise, that he or she has ceased to be Portuguese).

The acquisition of nationality at birth for the descendants of Portuguese born in Portugal or abroad (if their father or mother are serving the Portuguese State or if their birth was registered at the Portuguese civil registry), of those born in Portugal without a nationality (or foundlings), as well as of those that were fully adopted by Portuguese nationals, is proven by the birth record at the civil registry (art. 21 and 22 (2) of the Nationality Act and art. 1 and 13 of the Nationality Regulation).

Registration therefore plays a key role within the system of nationality law: on the one hand it allows the Portuguese State to know who their nationals are, and on the other hand it allows those concerned to prove their Portuguese nationality (Ramos 1992: 206; Reis 1990: 48).

The Registrar of the Central Registry Office has broad-ranging powers in the domain of nationality. Firstly, he or she must issue an opinion on any nationality-related issues, specifically if they have been submitted by the consulates, in the case of doubt regarding the Portuguese nationality of those that they wish to enrol or register at the consulate (art. 23 of the Nationality Act). Secondly, he or she can issue Portuguese nationality certificates upon application, although the validity of these can always be refuted when no nationality registration exists (art. 24). Thirdly, the Registrar of the Central Registry Office must inform the Public Prosecutor of any facts that could lead to opposition to the acquisition of nationality after birth, by declaration or adoption (art. 22 (3) of the Nationality Regulation). Finally, it is his or her responsibility to declare the legal non-existence of a nationality registration when the signature of the employee who should have signed it is missing, to cancel it and to rectify any irregularities in the registration, as long as they are not based on doubts about the registered nationality (art. 36 (2) of the Nationality Regulations).

The registration of nationality or of the facts that determine conferment of nationality of origin must follow the rule of law, and is only valid if the legal requirements for acquisition of Portuguese nationality are met. If these requirements are not met, registration can be declared null and void by the Lisbon Court of Appeal and will be cancelled as a result. This is not legally a case of loss of nationality but rather a case of non-acquisition as the nullity declaration has retroactive effect and therefore, legally, the person in question never actually acquired Portuguese nationality (as the legal requirements for acquisition were never met).

The acquisition of nationality after birth, by marriage, filial transfer or adoption is not automatic although it is a right of those who fulfil the legal requirements. This is because the state can prevent it by taking legal proceedings (Ramos 1986: 287).

The legal procedures of opposition aim at preventing persons deemed 'undesirable' or without any link to Portugal from acquiring Portuguese nationality, in the case where the foreigner has the right to this acquisition. According to art. 9 of the Nationality Act, opposition can only take place when there are indications of the existence of the following grounds:

- The applicant's failure to prove any real link to the national community;[41]
- Committing a crime which carries a prison sentence of over three years according to Portuguese Law;
- The performance of public[42] duties or non-compulsory military service for another state.

Opposition to acquisition of Portuguese nationality is a special legal proceeding that may be initiated by the Public Prosecutor within a year of the fact on which the nationality acquisition after birth was based. Once a year has lapsed without opposition from the Public Prosecutor, the right to opposition expires and acquisition becomes definitive. The

Lisbon Court of Appeal is responsible for declaring or rejecting an opposition (art. 10 (1) of the Nationality Act and art. 23 of the Nationality Regulations).

In almost all cases, the opposition proceedings are intended to prevent the acquisition of Portuguese nationality by a foreigner married to a Portuguese and are based on the lack of integration into the national community. Since 1994 it is not sufficient for a foreigner to have been married to a Portuguese for three years and to declare that he or she wishes to be Portuguese. The interested foreigner has to prove a feeling of belonging to the Portuguese community, demonstrated by real efforts, such as knowledge of the Portuguese language and local habits, friendships with Portuguese, residence in Portugal (which is not a necessary condition), social habits, economic or professional integration, and interest in the country's history or present.[43]

These are just some of the criteria used by the courts to prove a link with the Portuguese community although there is no fixed formula for such determination. Sometimes it is sufficient for the applicant to have Portuguese children and to demonstrate that they want to learn Portuguese, without demand for actual knowledge of the Portuguese language or residence in Portugal.[44] On other occasions, case law adopts a restrictive approach, not considering sufficient the fact that the foreigner is married to a Portuguese citizen, has Portuguese children, lives and works in Portugal, speaks Portuguese, has knowledge of Portuguese history, etc. Instead there is a demand for proof – although what proof is not disclosed – of a feeling of psychological and sociological belonging to the national community[45] or a demonstration that the person in question participates in Portuguese culture; as if they were members of the Portuguese community deciding against the application to nationality in case of any doubt regarding the link.[46]

Nationality acquisition by virtue of naturalisation depends on a discretionary decision by the Portuguese Minister for Home Affairs. Applicants who meet the requirements for naturalisation do not have a subjective right.[47] Even when a foreigner meets the requirements the Government is free to decide whether to grant naturalisation or not, merely based on its own interest (Ramos 1992: 167). This discretionary decision itself cannot be contested through the courts. A negative decision can only be subject to a judicial appeal limited to verification of the legal requirements foreseen by the law.

The naturalisation proceedings are of an administrative nature and begin with an application by the foreigner to the Portuguese Minister of Home Affairs.

A foreigner can be exempted from the legal residence requirement and the Portuguese language skill requirements and from the need to prove a link with the national community, if he or she has already held

Portuguese nationality, is considered to be of Portuguese descent, is a member of a community of Portuguese ancestry or has carried out relevant services for the Portuguese state.

The proceedings end with a decision by the Minister of Home Affairs to grant or refuse the application. The granting of naturalisation is published in the Official Journal (Diário da República), 2nd series (art. 19 of the Nationality Regulation) and only takes effect when registered at the Conservatory for Central Registrations.

The enforcement of the Nationality Act can lead to doubts and litigation and is subject to the principles of the rule of law. For this reason, the Nationality Act has a system of judicial appeal against any act concerning the acquisition and loss of the nationality. Both the interested person and the Public Prosecutor have the right to appeal the decisions made by authorities in matters of nationality. It is the competence of the Lisbon Court of Appeal (civil jurisdiction, 2nd instance) to hear appeals on any acts related to Portuguese nationality (art. 26 of the Nationality Act and art. 38 (3) of the Nationality Regulation).

Exclusive competence for the civil courts in nationality litigation was introduced by the 1981 Law that removed all competences previously held by the administrative courts.[48] Attributing all competences to the Lisbon Court of Appeal on any matter related to the acquisition or loss of nationality is an attempt to ensure consistency in the interpretation and enforcement of the Nationality Act (Ramos 1992: 215). Its decisions can be appealed in the Supreme Court of Justice.

An appeal can be made at any time (it is not subject to any deadline) by the applicants themselves or by the Public Prosecutor (art. 25 of the Nationality Law and art. 38 (2) of the Nationality Regulation). For example, a ground for appeal could be the decision by the Registrar at the Central Registry Office to refuse to register nationality acquisition after birth while the applicant is entitled to it (because he or she has met all the requirements and the Public Prosecutor has not opposed it or opposition was ruled unfounded by the Court of Appeal).

12.4 Conclusions

The Nationality Act considers children born abroad of Portuguese parents as being of Portuguese origin if they declare their wish to be Portuguese, but does not consider children born in Portugal to foreigners as being of Portuguese origin unless the aforementioned requirements are met. This clearly demonstrates the lawmakers' choice of mixed criteria, in which ius sanguinis predominates (Ramos 1992: 141) and represents a departure from ius soli, which up until the 1980s dominated the Portuguese nationality law.

Making the acquisition of nationality by children who are born to foreigners in Portugal subject to a period of residence formalised by a residence permit (and no other permit of stay or work permit) further restricts the ius soli principle. This may have been acceptable in the 1980s when Portugal was still predominantly a country of emigration, but today, with the huge increase in the number of immigrants that settle in our country, it appears to be inappropriate. This is because it does not take into account how well integrated a foreigner is, which is not determined by whether he or she is in Portugal legally or what kind of permit his or her parent holds. Instead, it is based on formal, administrative requirements. This could be considered unfair and contrary to the principle of effective nationality since it makes nationality acquisition dependent on facts that are wholly detached from a person's desire to become Portuguese which is reflected by his integration into the Portuguese community. It is not uncommon that immigrants who are in illegal situations (because they do not hold any form of residence permit) or who do not hold a residence permit, have children who were born and grew up in Portugal, learned Portuguese as their mother tongue, feel that Portugal is their country and want to be Portuguese, yet nationality is refused to them because their parents do not have a residence permit.

The integration of immigrants in our country and the need to avoid the negative impact on social cohesion that such a restrictive regime of nationality acquisition can have on foreigners who are born in Portugal suggests that in granting nationality greater importance should be attached to the ius soli criteria.

In the case of acquisition of nationality after birth by virtue of marriage to a Portuguese national the state's right of refusal if the foreigner cannot prove a link to the Portuguese community can result, in specific cases, in disregard of the principle of one family, one nationality. This is due to the fact that the law does not define specific criteria that allows for proof of this link, resulting in disparities between the relevant courts as far as grounds for opposition are concerned, and result in an undesirable situation of legal uncertainty. Sometimes it is considered sufficient that the foreigner is married to a Portuguese, has Portuguese children and makes an effort to learn Portuguese, in order to prove the link with the national community, with no demand for proof that the person in question lives and works in Portugal. On other occasions, residence in Portugal, professional integration, and the existence of Portuguese children, reasonable knowledge of the Portuguese language and even knowledge of the political and historical reality are not enough for establishing this link. Rather a feeling of psychological or sociological belonging to the national community is demanded, making it practically impossible (given the lack of means of proof) for the foreigner to prove this and implying the refusal of Portuguese nationality. The double standard of Portuguese case law and the lack of an objective legal framework that allows for proof of a person's link to the national community is a source of legal uncertainty that is incompatible with the principle of preserving family unity in matters of nationality.

Given that access to nationality by the state where a foreigner resides is an important means of integration in the society that receives him or her, it should be facilitated for all those that have a link to the Portuguese community. One of these means is naturalisation. Yet in Portugal this method of integration has always been under-valued and is seen as a mere discretionary right of Government (and not as a foreigner's right). Portugal has opted, instead, to ensure the principle of general legal equality of immigrants with Portuguese nationals, enshrined in art. 15 (1) of the Constitution.[49] According to this constitutional provision 'Aliens and stateless persons temporarily or habitually resident in Portugal shall enjoy the same rights and be subject to the same duties as Portuguese citizens.'[50]

As foreseen by our legislation, naturalisation is an administrative act that allows for the exercising of discretionary powers by the administration. Such a procedure is unsuitable given the social reality of the country, which has become a country of immigration. In fact, there has been a significant increase in the number of foreigners who have settled in Portugal with their private and family lives centred here. Despite the broad scope of the constitutional principle of equality between foreigners and the Portuguese, the majority of foreigners who live in Portugal continue to be deprived of important citizenship rights (either because the reciprocity condition has not been met or because certain rights are reserved exclusively to nationals by the constitution and the law), which excludes them from the community in which they live. Within this context naturalisation should be an important means of integration in the society that receives the immigrant. Therefore, we can question the suitability of the naturalisation arrangements – that provide the Government with a large margin of discretionary power in granting nationality – in view of a new social reality characterised by increasing multi-culturalism. In order to promote the integration of immigrants and social cohesion, it would be more suitable to establish a subjective right to naturalisation for the resident foreigner, as long as certain legal requirements are met, with the administration exercising a restricted power rather than a discretionary one.

In July 2005, the Socialist government introduced a proposal in Parliament for a new Nationality Law, which was approved in February 2006. When it comes into force (after approval by the President of the Republic and publication in the *Official Journal*), this law will introduce profound changes in the Portuguese Nationality Law by extending the ius soli criteria and liberalising naturalisation. The main changes are:

- introduction of *ex lege* acquisition of Portuguese nationality for the third generation of immigrants born in Portugal (double ius soli);
- improvement of ius soli acquisition of nationality by declaration: access to nationality at birth for all persons born and living in Portugal if, at the moment of birth, one of the parents has legally resided in Portugal for five years (irrespective of the legal title);
- a subjective right to naturalisation after birth for minor children born in Portugal (irrespective of their legal residence status), if one of their parents has been a legal resident for the last five years or if the minor has concluded the first four years of mandatory schooling;
- introduction of a subjective right to naturalisation for immigrants after six years of legal residence in Portugal under the further conditions of knowledge of the Portuguese language and a clean criminal record. Naturalisation no longer requires proof of means of subsistence or other proofs of integration apart from language skills;
- discretionary naturalisation of illegal immigrants born in Portugal who have lived there for more than ten years;
- acquisition of nationality by the non-married partner of a Portuguese national;
- the new law no longer differentiates between nationals of Lusophone countries and others (the same period of residence is required);
- transfer of the competence on naturalisation from the Ministry of Home Affairs (and the Aliens and Borders Service) to the Ministry of Justice.

This greater emphasis on ius soli and the conception of nationality as a right of those with a strong link to the Portuguese community are positions defended by all the parties represented in Parliament. Hence, a large majority of Parliament approved the new Nationality Law, which will recover the very old tradition of ius soli.

Chronological table of major reforms in Portuguese nationality law since 1945

Date	Document	Content of change
29 July 1959	Nationality Act (Law 2098) (Lei da Nacionalidade)	Mixed system with predominance of ius soli. Broad regulation of loss of nationality, especially i.a. *ex lege loss by voluntary acquisition of another nationality.*
1976	Portuguese Constitution (Constituição da República Portuguesa)	Recognises nationality as a human right and stipulates a restrictive rule on loss of nationality (rules out loss on political grounds or as an effect of criminal conviction).
24 June 1975	Decree Law 308/75 (abrogated by Law 113/88 of 29 December 1988)	Regulates the impact, of the decolonisation and the building of new states, on the Portuguese nationality.
3 October 1981	Nationality Act (Law 37/81) (Lei da Nacionalidade)	Mixed system of acquisition at birth with predominance of ius sanguinis.
19 August 1994	Law 25/94 (amended the Law 37/81)	Introduced restrictions in the acquisition of nationality by ius soli and in the rules for acquisition after birth (spousal transfer and naturalisation).
15 January 2004	Organic Law 1/2004 (amended the Law 37/81)	Establishes a more favourable regime for the reacquisition of nationality by those expatriated Portuguese who lost their nationality before 1981 due to a marriage with an alien or voluntary naturalisation.
17 April 2006	Organic Law 2/2006	Double ius soli for third generation; ius soli for second generation if one parent has 5 years residence; naturalisation of foreigners born in Portugal who have resided (legally or illegally) in the country for the last ten years; general entitlement to naturalisation after 6 years if clean criminal record and Portuguese language skills; no more naturalisation privileges for Lusophone citizens.

Notes

1 Translated by Gary Mullender.

2 Law 37/81 of 3 October, as amended by Law 25/94 of 19 August and by Framework Law 1/2004 of 15 January.

3 One of these duties is to perform military service, for which special arrangements are in force for emigrants. According to art. 38 (3) of Law 174/99 (Military Service Act), expatriates who have permanent residence abroad are not obliged to perform military service.

4 According to art. 12 (4) and 13 (3) of Law 174/99 (Parliamentary Elections Act), expatriates who are registered as voters are divided into two constituencies: one that covers European states and the other that represents all non-European countries. Each constituency elects two members for the Parliament.

5 Ius sanguinis *a mater* was only relevant if the child was illegitimate. Discrimination against nationality being passed on by the mother influenced Portuguese law until 1976, when the Portuguese republic enshrined the principle of spousal equality and equality of children born in and outside wedlock (art. 36 of the Constitution).

6 Residence in Portugal was not required if the father (but not the mother) was abroad on the Crown's service, in which case *ius sangunis* was fully applicable.

7 This prevalence to ius soli is due to the influence of the Brazilian constitution, which was its source of inspiration (Ramos 1992: 63).

8 The period of residence could be shortened or dispensed with should the foreign citizen meet one of the following conditions: being married to a Portuguese woman; being politically pursued for his defence of the representative system; having built or improved a road in Portugal; having made a considerable capital investment in banking, commerce or industry; having established himself as an industrialist or trader; having performed relevant services; or having performed acts which benefited Portuguese citizens (art. 4).

9 This was not a concession to ius soli, but a measure to prevent statelessness.

10 The 1836 Decree was applicable.

11 Should the statement declining Portuguese nationality have been made by the minor's legal agent, he can withdraw it when he comes of age (art. 18 (2)).

12 The Civil Code kept the traditional limitation of ius sanguinis *a mater* to illegitimate children.

13 The possibility of making this declaration instead of meeting the residence condition (not foreseen in the 1826 Charter), however, places greater emphasis on ius sanguinis.

14 The Minister of Justice was the competent authority for granting or refusing naturalisation.

15 Prior to the amendments made in 1910, the only requirements of foreign citizens were that they had reached the age of maturity; had means of subsistence and had lived on Portuguese soil for at least one year. Foreign citizens of Portuguese descent did not necessarily have to fulfil these requirements provided they took up residence in Portugal. This provision aimed to facilitate access for Brazilian nationals. (Ferreira 1870: 13).

16 The period of residence was not required of a descendant of Portuguese citizens who had taken up residence in Portugal. Foreign citizens married to Portuguese women and those who had performed notable services for the nation could also be exempted from this condition (art. 19-2).

17 In these cases, acquisition occurs via the conjunction of ius soli and ius sanguinis.

18 Such a reference in the birth register excludes the presumption that Portuguese nationality has been acquired on the basis of having been born in Portugal (art. 2 of the 1960 Nationality Regulation).

19 Under the 1867 Civil Code, only extraterritorial ius sanguinis *a pater* was relevant.

20 The government's right of opposition (which did not exist in earlier legislation) did not apply to ius soli acquisition, which was *ex lege* and automatic.

21 Thus, through a decree from the Portuguese Minister for Home Affairs, the Government could grant nationality through naturalisation to foreign applicants who met all the following requirements, set out in art. XII: 1) being of age; 2) being able to make a living; 3) having a record of decent moral and social behaviour; 4) having complied with the laws on military recruitment in their country of origin; 5) having an adequate knowledge of the Portuguese language; 6) having lived on Portuguese soil for at least three years.

22 Different from residence permits, a permit of stay (*autorização de permanência*) excludes the holder from voting or applying for naturalisation in Portugal.

23 All political parties represented in Parliament agreed on the need to make the Nationality Act compatible with the new Constitution.

24 The 1981 Act eradicated any form of discrimination between men and women or children born in or out of wedlock.

25 The concept of nationality as a fundamental right clearly influences the 1981 Nationality Act. On the one hand, it reinforces the role of individual intent when determining nationality, in that nationality acquisition of Portuguese children born abroad (ius sanguinis), children of foreigners born in Portugal (ius soli) as well as after birth (filial and spousal transfer) now depend on a declaration of intent by the person in question (Ramos 1992: 119). On the other hand, as explained above, it decisively influences the legal provisions for the loss of nationality, which now depend on a declaration of intent by the person concerned.

26 The reason for this change was defended by the centre-right majority in the following way: [At the end of the Empire, Portugal was] 'a small territory with strong migratory phenomena' (speech by Fernando Condesso from the PSD, a party that was part of the majority that supported the Government. In Parliamentary Debates, Diary of the Assembly of the Republic 80. 1981: 3178).

27 Parliamentary Debates, Diary of the Assembly of the Republic 80. 1981: 3162f.

28 Parliamentary Debates, Diary of the Assembly of the Republic 80. 1981: 3184.

29 With the exception of art. 8, 29 and 30 that received negative votes from the Portuguese Communist Party (PCP), the Portuguese Democratic Movement/ Democratic Electoral Commission (MDP/CDE) and from the Portuguese Democratic Union.

30 Parliamentary Debates, Diary of the Assembly of the Republic 80, 1994: 2618.

31 The Government was supported by a centre-right majority based on a coalition of the PSD with the CDS-PP.

32 Acquisition of Portuguese nationality through the joint effect of ius soli and ius sanguinis (territorial ius sanguinis).

33 As explained above, the primary purpose is to prevent statelessness rather than to introduce ius soli, since ius soli is only applied to prevent the person in question from being left without a nationality (Ramos 1992: 132; Jalles 1984: 179).

34 This declaration can be made at any time, specifically if the person is of age. However, the child of a Portuguese parent can only acquire nationality if the descent is established when the child is a minor (art. 14 of the Nationality Act).

35 Prior to 1994, only habitual residence was required, with or without a residence permit.

36 This declaration should be made by the child or, when disabled, by the legal guardian (art. 10 (1) of the Nationality Rules).

37 There are no known judicial decisions of opposition to the acquisition of Portuguese nationality by a foreigner adopted by a Portuguese.

38 Emancipation before the age of majority can be achieved through marriage.

39 See the 29 January 2004 Court of Appeal sentence. All rulings mentioned are published on www.dgsi.pt.

40 See the Supreme Court of Justice ruling of 18 December 2003.
41 Prior to Law 25/94 a basis for opposition was 'the obvious lack of any real link to the national community'. It was the Public Prosecutor's responsibility to prove this.
42 Portuguese case-law adopts a restricted interpretation of the concept of 'exercise of public duties', only considering relevant the duties that imply a relationship of political trust, which could lead to grounds for doubts that the foreigner who wants to acquire Portuguese nationality will be loyal to the Portuguese state (ruling by the Supreme Court of Justice of 25 February 1986). In addition, holding public office of a political nature is not sufficient grounds either, the Public Prosecutor has to prove that because of these duties the foreigner in question is undesirable. In this sense, the ruling by the Supreme Court of Justice of 11 April 1998 considered that the fact that a foreign applicant for nationality was Minister of Construction and Housing in Angola for a short period of time was not sufficient ground for opposition. This is because the grounds for opposition do not have to be seen as preventive but merely as indications of 'undesirability', with the responsibility of proving the undesirability resting with the Public Prosecutor.
43 See, amongst many others, the ruling by the Lisbon Court of Appeal dated 17 October 2002, as well as the ruling by the Supreme Court of Justice dated 11 February 2004.
44 In this sense, the ruling by the Lisbon Court of Appeal dated 16 October 2003.
45 See the ruling by the Lisbon Court of Appeal dated 2 February 1999 and 17 December 1998.
46 See the ruling by the Supreme Court of Justice dated 7 January 2004.
47 In this sense, the ruling by the Supreme Court of Justice dated 26 February 2004.
48 In terms of the 1959 law, the first instance of appeal was administrative (and not judicial), leaving decisions on nationality to the Ministry of Justice. Its decisions could be appealed in the Supreme Administrative Court.
49 The principle of equality however is not absolute, since art. 15 (2) of the Constitution provides exceptions and allows the law to establish others: 'Paragraph 1 (equality principle) does not apply to political rights, to the performance of public functions that are not predominantly technical or to rights and duties that, under this Constitution or the law, are restricted to Portuguese citizens.' Nevertheless, the CPR itself has introduced exceptions to these exclusions by granting the citizens of Lusophone countries with permanent residence in Portugal all political rights, on a reciprocal basis, with the exception of holding the office of President, Speaker of the Parliament, Prime-Minister, President of the Supreme Courts, serving in the armed forces and diplomatic corps (art. 15 (3) of the CPR) and granting all foreign citizens resident in Portugal the right to vote and be elected in local elections, on a reciprocal basis (art. 15 (4) of the CPR).
50 Translation taken from the English version of the Portuguese constitution published on the site of the Assembleia da República, www.parlamento.pt.

Bibliography

Baganha, M. I. & J. C. Marques (2001), *Imigração e Política: o Caso Português*. Lisboa: FLAD.

Canotilho, J. J. Gomes (2003), *Direito Constitucional e Teoria da Constituição*. Coimbra: Almedina.

Canotilho, J. J. Gomes & V. Moreira (1993), *Constituição da República Portuguesa Anotada*. Coimbra: Coimbra Editora.

Costa, P. M. Abreu da Silva (2000), 'A participação dos portugueses não residentes e dos estrangeiros residentes nas eleições portuguesas', *Documentação e Direito Comparado* 81/82: 180-216.

Ferreira, A. (1986), 'A atribuição da nacionalidade portuguesa e a sua prova', *Tribuna da Justiça* 24: 8-13.

Ferreira, A. (1987), 'A atribuição da nacionalidade portuguesa e a sua prova', *Tribuna da Justiça* 25: 7-10.

Ferreira, J. Dias (1870), *Código Civil Portuguez, Annotado.* Lisboa: Imprensa Nacional.

Gonçalves, L. da Cunha (1929), *Tratado de Direito Civil.* Coimbra: Coimbra Editora.

Jacinto, O. (2004), *Atribuição, aquisição e perda da nacionalidade portuguesa.* www.conservadoresdosregistos.pt.

Jalles, I. (1984), 'Nationalité et statut personnel dans le droit de la nationalité portugaise', in M. Verwilghen (ed.), *Nationalité et statut personnel. Leur interaction dans les traités internationaux et dans les législations nationales*, 169-193. Brussels: Bruylant.

Miranda, J. (1998), *Manual de Direito Constitucional*, Tomo III. Coimbra: Coimbra Editora.

Oliveira, C. & A. Inácio (1999), *Nacionalizações em Portugal (1985-1996).* Lisboa, SociNova, Working Paper 11.

Proença, J. Gonçalves de (1960), *Comentário à nova Lei da Nacionalidade.* Lisboa: Edições Ática.

Ramos, R. M. Moura (1976), 'Nacionalidade e descolonização (Algumas reflexões a propósito do decreto-lei n.º 308-A/75, de 24 de Junho)', *Revista de Direito e Economia* 2: 331-362.

Ramos, Rui Manuel Moura (1983), 'La double nationalité d'aprés le droit portugais', *Boletim da Faculdade de Direito* 59: 181-211.

Ramos, R. M. Moura (1986), 'Oposição à aquisição da nacionalidade Portuguesa', *Revista de Direito e Economia* 12: 273-299.

Ramos, R. M. Moura (1992), *Do Direito Português da Nacionalidade.* Coimbra: Coimbra Editora.

Ramos, R. M. Moura (1994), 'Nacionalidade', in J. P. Fernandes (ed.), *Dicionário Jurídico da Administração Pública*, 103-137. Lisbon: Atlântida.

Ramos, R. M. Moura (1996), 'Le droit portugais de la nationalité', in B. Nascimbene (ed.), *Nationality Laws in the European Union*, 599-627. Milan: Giuffrè Editore.

Ramos, R. M. Moura (2001), 'Migratory Movements and Nationality Law in Portugal', in R. Hansen & P. Weil (eds.), *Towards a European Nationality. Citizenship, Immigration and Nationality Law in the EU*, 214-229. Hampshire: Palgrave Publishers.

Reis, A. Ferreira dos (1990), *O registo, a prova e o contencioso da nacionalidade.* Porto: Elcla Editora.

Santos, A. Marques dos (1986), 'Reconhecimento em Portugal de um casamento celebrado na China por cerimónia privada e seus efeitos em matéria de atribuição da nacionalidade portuguesa aos filhos havidos desse casamento', *Revista Jurídica* 7: 39-81.

Santos, A. Marques dos (1993), 'Nacionalidade e efectividade', in *Estudos em memória do Professor Doutor João Castro Mendes.* Lisboa: Lex.

13 Spain

Ruth Rubio Marín

13.1 Introduction

As a country with an emigration tradition, the main mode of automatic acquisition of nationality in Spain is *ius sanguinis,* even though the system also contains ius soli elements. Spain embraces an unqualified ius sanguinis in favour of those born of a Spanish mother or father who become nationals regardless of whether they are born in Spain or outside of Spain (art. 17.1. of the Civil Code, henceforth CC). Automatic access to nationality is also guaranteed for those born in Spain but only if at least one of the parents was also born in Spain (double ius soli) (art. 17.1 b) CC) or if the person would otherwise become stateless (either because both parents are stateless or because none of their citizenships is passed on to the child via ius sanguinis) (art. 17.1.c) CC). Finally, automatic acquisition of Spanish nationality through filial transfer is also provided for in the case of adoption, for those persons younger than eighteen years adopted by a Spaniard, from the moment of adoption (art. 19.1 CC).

With regard to the modes of *non-automatic acquisition* the Spanish system distinguishes between four modes: by option; by discretionary naturalisation (called *carta de naturaleza*); residence-based acquisition and by 'possession of status.' Acquisition by option only requires the target person to express his or her will. It provides for people who have a special link to Spain including: those who are or have been subject to the *patria potestas* of a Spaniard (art. 20.1.a) CC) (for instance, the children of a naturalised immigrant); those whose (natural or adopted) father or mother was a Spaniard at birth, born in Spain (art. 20.1 b) CC) (for instance, the children of Spanish emigrants who lost the Spanish nationality); those for whom descent from a Spaniard or birth in Spain is established after they turn eighteen years of age (20.1.c) CC in connection to art. 17.2) and finally, those cases of adoption where the adopted person is eighteen or older (20.1.c) CC in connection to art. 19.2).

Non-automatic acquisition through naturalisation includes acquisition by discretionary conferral called (*carta de naturaleza*) and other forms of entitlement based conferrals. The latter can be either purely residence based, or hinge on both residence as well as other criteria. Typically, the Spanish school labels all of these as acquisition by residence. Regarding the acquisition by discretionary conferral the Spanish legal order simply allows for this possibility when extraordinary circumstances concur. No definition is given as to what 'extraordinary circumstances' means. It is the target person who has to apply for it and he or she may be successful or not depending on the full discretion of the Government (art. 21.1 CC).

What is commonly identified as acquisition by residence refers to a mode of acquisition that entitles the applicant to Spanish nationality conferred by the Department of Justice upon application (art. 21.2 CC). If the requirements are fulfilled, the target person is indeed entitled to nationalisation but the government may deny nationality if the public order or national interests so dictate. The legal system provides for a general residence requirement of ten years of uninterrupted, legal and prior residence and also provides for shorter residence requirements for specific groups (art. 22 CC). These include: refugees (five years); nationals of Latin American countries, Andorra, Philippines, Equatorial Guinea, Portugal or Sephardic Jews (two years) and finally a set of categories in which only one year of residence is required. The latter include: those born in Spain; those who had a right to acquisition by option but did not exercise it in due time; those who have been subject for at least two consecutive years to guardianship of a Spanish citizen or institution; those who at the time of application have been married for at least one year to a Spaniard; the widow or widower of a Spaniard if they were not separated at the time of the death of their spouse, and those born outside of Spain whose father or mother, grandfather or grandmother were Spaniards by birth.

Common requirements for acquisition by option, discretionary naturalisation and residence based acquisition include: an oath of loyalty to the King and obedience to the Constitution and the laws; renunciation of prior nationality and registration in the Civil Registry (art. 23 of the CC). Moreover, residence based acquisition by entitlement requires proof of good civic conduct and sufficient integration into Spanish society. Some nationals are exempt from the renunciation requirement. They form the class of nationals for whom dual citizenship is legally accepted. This class includes nationals from Latin American countries, Andorra, Philippines, Equatorial Guinea, and Portugal (art. 23.b and 24.1).

Finally the Spanish legal order provides for the possibility of acquisition based on possession of status for people who in good faith have enjoyed and used the Spanish nationality for at least ten years under a title which they thought was legitimate (art. 18 CC).

As for the loss of Spanish nationality, the Spanish Constitution of 1978 (art. 11.2) determines that Spaniards 'by origin' cannot be deprived of their nationality.[1] Therefore, when regulating the modes of loss, the Spanish Civil Code distinguishes between two main modes. One refers to voluntary loss and the other one to involuntary loss. The latter does not apply to those who are Spanish by origin.

There are four possibilities for voluntary loss (art. 24 CC). First, for those who are emancipated,[2] live in a foreign country on a regular basis and have voluntarily acquired another nationality, except when the second nationality is one of a Latin American country or that of Andorra, the Philippines, Equatorial Guinea or Portugal. Loss can be prevented through declaration at the Civil Registry. Secondly, Spanish nationality can be lost by those emancipated Spaniards who live abroad on a regular basis and make exclusive use of another nationality which was attributed to them when they were minors. Here again the loss can be prevented through declaration of the wish to retain the Spanish nationality at the Civil Registry. Third, Spanish nationality can be voluntarily relinquished by those emancipated persons living abroad regularly as long as they have another nationality. Finally, the Spanish legal order provides for the loss of Spanish nationality for those who were born and live abroad and are descendants of Spaniards who were also born abroad as long as the country of residence recognises them as nationals and unless within three years of coming of age or becoming emancipated they do not declare their intent to retain their Spanish nationality at the Civil Registry.

Involuntary loss (art. 25 CC), on the other hand, occurs in three instances. Firstly, if naturalised nationals make exclusive use for three years of the nationality they relinquished when acquiring the Spanish nationality. Secondly, if a naturalised alien voluntarily joins the military or takes up political office in a foreign country in contravention to the express prohibition by government. Thirdly and finally, when it be legally proven that a person acquired nationality through falsity or fraud.

As for the reacquisition of nationality (art. 26 CC) the main condition, other than the expression of will, is that the person be a legal resident in Spain. Emigrants and their descendants are exempt from this requirement and the Ministry of Justice can exempt others from it in the case of exceptional circumstances. As for those who lost the Spanish nationality involuntarily reacquisition is subject to the discretion of government.

Whereas this is the general regime, Spain has traditionally considered nationals of some countries as forming part of a joint cultural community and acknowledges a certain historical debt towards other communities. Certain expressions of these considerations are still to be found in Spanish nationality law. The two main ones include the shortening of the time of residence required in order to naturalise and the toleration of dual nationality. As for the former, whereas the general residence requirement for naturalisation through residence is ten years, two years is enough for nationals from Latin American countries, Andorra, the Philippines, Equatorial Guinea, and Portugal and for Sephardic Jews. As far as the toleration of dual nationality is concerned, since the 1950s Spain has had a tradition of signing bilateral agreements with several Latin American countries recognising the system of dormant/active nationality. Since 1990, it has modified the Civil Code to exempt nationals from Latin American countries, Andorra, the Philippines, Equatorial Guinea and Portugal from the requirement of giving up their prior nationality when acquiring the Spanish nationality (art. 23 b CC in relation to art. 24.1 CC).

The Constitution entrusts the regulation of nationality exclusively to the central state (art. 149.1.2 of the Constitution). Spain has never passed legislation exclusively focused on nationality and has ruled on nationality through the Civil Code, which only dedicates a few articles to it. A crucial role in this is played by the General Directorate of Registries and Notaries (*Dirección General de los Registros y del Notariado*), an administrative body which falls under the Justice department and deals with civil status and nationality. This body has been in charge of producing administrative guidelines which have been essential for interpreting the vague legislation. This body is also in charge of deciding on acquisition and loss of nationality. Its decisions can be appealed either to a civil court or to an administrative court. Both the administrative decisions by the General Directorate and the judicial decisions, especially those by the Supreme Court have also become a rich, yet dispersed, and not always consistent, source of interpretation of the nationality law.

13.2 Historical development

13.2.1 *Spanish nationality law: the Civil Code of 1889*

The regulations on Spanish nationality in their contemporary form date back to the origins of our constitutionalism in the early nineteenth century (Fernández Rozas 1987). Indeed, it became a common trend for the several constitutions that Spain enacted in that period, starting with Spain's first constitution of 1812, to briefly address the question of the acquisition of Spanish nationality and the rights and duties of foreigners in Spain.[3] All of these constitutions regulated the matter briefly, delegating the responsibility of expanding the regulatory framework into laws that, for the most part, were never enacted. The first legislative attempt to define the main traits of Spanish nationality in a more comprehensive manner occurred in 1889 when the Civil Code was passed. Until today the Civil Code has remained the locus of Spain's nationality regulations. Given that the code can only contain a few provisions dedicated to nationality, precedents set by the administrative body responsible for deciding on the conferral or denial of nationality, the judicial decisions overseeing such decisions as well as administrative regulations have been essential in supplementing the legislation.

Data on migration flows which was first collected in the early 1880s (although by then large scale migration had been occurring for many years) show that at the end of the nineteenth century, recorded emigration flows were going in two main directions: one, of temporary migration to Algeria (at the time a French colony in need of European workers) and another one to Latin America, mostly to Argentina, Brazil and Uruguay. After its independence, Cuba became the second destination for Spanish emigrants after Argentina.

The 1889 Civil Code devoted twelve articles to the nationality issue. The brevity of this regulation allowed for a large degree of judicial discretion in its application. The rules were criticised by legal scholars who complained about their deficient technical value, especially when compared to other systems in force at the time (Fernández Rozas 1987: 70). Nonetheless, this regulation has remained the backbone of Spanish legislation on nationality until our days.

The main characteristics of the nationality system embodied in the 1889 Civil Code have been described as 'a strong component of ius sanguinis, a relatively generous application of ius solis and a rather naïve application of the principle of naturalization by residence' (Moreno Fuentes 2001: 124). To these one could also add the prevalence of the principle of legal unity of the family (Fernández Rozas 1987: 72).

Regarding ius sanguinis, which has remained stable until today, the Civil Code provided that persons born from a Spanish father or mother would be Spanish even if they were born outside of Spain (art. 17.2 of the 1889 Civil Code). This ensured that Spaniards who, at the end of the century, were emigrating mostly to Latin America (especially, Argentina and Uruguay) could pass on their nationality to their descendants. This allowed Spain to maintain links with its emigrants and their descendants. Moreover, since during the 1860s and 1870s Spain had signed agreements with many of these countries implicitly accepting dual nationality, there were a large number of cases of dual nationals among the expatriates.[4] However, to avoid the perpetuation of generations of Spanish nationals living abroad without any connection to Spain, a concern that was partly triggered by the participation of the descendants of Spanish emigrants or *criollos* in the struggles for independence of the American colonies (Moreno Fuentes 2001: 124), art.

26 of the Civil Code required all Spanish emigrants who wanted to maintain their Spanish nationality in those countries who, by virtue of their residence considered them to be their nationals, to register themselves as well as their spouses and descendants at the Spanish embassy or consulate.

Women and men were treated equally under art. 17.2 of the Civil Code and thus could both pass their nationality on to their children. However, according to art. 22 of the Civil Code, a Spanish woman who married a foreigner would automatically assume his nationality to ensure the legal unity of the family. She would only be able to recover Spanish nationality if the marriage was dissolved. Similarly, a foreign woman automatically became naturalised when she married a Spanish man. This meant that although in theory, and through the application of ius sanguinis, women could pass on their nationality to their descendants, this was only the case when they were single mothers. As for the children, it was foreseen that until they became of age, or emancipated, they would have the nationality of their parents (art. 18 CC), which meant, unless these were children born out of wedlock, their father's.

As for the application of ius soli, art. 17 of the Civil Code provided that all those born in Spanish territory would be Spanish. However, art. 18 and 19 toned down this apparently generous ius soli regime by requiring the foreign parents of a Spanish-born child, or the child, after reaching the age of majority, to declare a willingness to acquire Spanish nationality and giving up their previous one in order to actually enjoy the benefit of Spanish nationality. Thus, more than strictly ius soli, this represented what has been named a *facultas soli* (Moreno Fuentes 2001: 125; Fernández Rozas 1987: 71). Even if conceptualised as a 'privilege' or 'extraordinary benefit' (Castro y Bravo 1952) this still allowed for relatively easy naturalisation of second generations. Nothing was added to address the concerns of the third generation.

As for naturalisation, the Civil Code contemplated naturalisation by discretionary granting (*carta de naturaleza*) (art. 17.3 CC) or acquisition by residence (art. 17.4CC). The requirements for the former were not further specified, other than the mandatory renunciation of prior nationality, swearing loyalty to the Constitution and registering in the Civil Registry (art. 25 CC). As for the latter, the provision simply stated that all those who had become residents of any locality in the monarchy would be Spanish, but added nothing as to how to define residence, the length of residence or the way of certifying it. In 1916, a law was passed introducing the requirement of ten years residence before qualifying for naturalisation, which has remained the general rule. That law already provided for shorter residence requirements in some cases such as when a man married a Spanish woman, or somebody started or developed an industry in Spain, owned an industry or business, or rendered a special service to the country.

As far as the loss of the nationality was concerned, the Civil Code foresaw that the Spanish nationality would be lost through acquiring a foreign nationality, accepting employment in a foreign government or joining the military forces of a foreign country without royal authorisation (art. 20 of the Civil Code). However, nationals who lost their nationality because of naturalisation abroad could recover it, were they to come back to Spain and declare their willingness to do so at the Civil Registry (art. 21). Those who instead lost their nationality for accepting employment in a foreign government or joining the military forces of a foreign country without royal authorisation would not be able to recover Spanish nationality without royal authorisation (art. 23). Finally those who were born in a foreign country from a Spanish father or mother who lost their Spanish nationality as a result of their parents losing theirs could also recover it by expressing their willingness to do so upon coming of age, at the Civil Registry or at the Consulate (art. 24).

13.2.2 *Spanish nationality under the Second Republic (1931-1939): a failed attempt of reform*

Spain's Second Republic was proclaimed in 1931. Its values were embodied in the 1931 Constitution which had a short life since the Republican regime was interrupted by the Civil War which broke out in 1936 and lasted until 1939. It was followed by over 40 years of dictatorship under Franco. In terms of migration patterns, the world economic crisis of the late 1920s had a strong impact on Spanish migration patterns (Moreno Fuentes 2001: 121). Many migrants decided to return and those who considered migration as an exit option found less and less countries willing to accept them. The political upheaval as a result of the proclamation of the Republic followed by civil war and then dictatorship stopped work related migration but forced over a million people into exile, mostly to France and Latin American countries.

Taking the most progressive European legislation as a reference (mostly the French nationality statute of August 1927) the reforms introduced by the Constitution of 1931 represented an attempt to radically transform the nationality regime. In spite of its brief life the regulation is worth mentioning because many of the characteristics of today's nationality legislation can be traced back to the Constitution of the Second Republic. Due to the brevity of the Republican period, however, the set of regulations laid down in the 1931 Constitution was, for its part, mostly not developed into comprehensive laws. The interpretation given to it, when applied by government and the courts, was just as progressive and this jurisprudence has also contributed to today's regime.

Among the main objectives of the new nationality rules were to better protect Spanish emigrants abroad (especially in view of the increasingly non-assimilationist policies of receiving countries) (Alvarez Rodríguez 1990:173-189); to increase the Spanish population and to consolidate the idea of a 'community of Hispanic nations' (Moreno Fuentes 2001: 126; Fernández Rozas 1987: 73).

One of the ways to achieve this was by making the application of ius sanguinis even more generous. Another way was to explicitly regulate dual nationality with countries belonging to the Ibero-American community (Moreno Fuentes 2001: 126).[5] Thus, the new constitution exempted Spanish expatriates from the requirement of registering at an embassy or consulate to avoid losing their nationality. Henceforth, a Spanish national would lose his or her nationality when acquiring a second one only if that acquisition was fully voluntary and it was not acquisition of the nationality of an Ibero-American country. Children of Spanish nationals abroad would also acquire the Spanish nationality by descent regardless of whether the country of residence granted them its nationality. On the other hand, children born in Spain of foreign parents would have a right to choose unless they were born from unknown parents, in which case they would automatically acquire the Spanish nationality (arts. 23.2 and 23.3 of the 1931 Constitution).

In accordance with the egalitarian spirit of the Republican regime the new law tried to eliminate all kinds of gender discrimination and women who married foreigners would no longer lose their nationality. This fully ensured women's equal chances to pass on their nationality to their children regardless of their marital status. Women would only acquire an option to acquire the nationality of their spouses through marriage (art. 23.4 of the 1931 Constitution)

The procedures for naturalisation by residence were also clarified in the only piece of nationality legislation that was enacted under the 1931 Constitution. While the original ten-year residence requirement was maintained, in the spirit of strengthening the relations with the nations with whom Spain considered to have historical ties, the residence requirement was reduced to only two years if the foreigner came from one of the Hispano-American republics, Portugal, Brazil or the Spanish protectorate in Morocco.

As for the loss of the Spanish nationality, it was foreseen as a consequence of accepting employment in a foreign government if that entailed exercising public authority or of joining the military forces of a foreign country without state approval (art. 24.1 of the 1931 Constitution). Nationals who voluntarily acquired another nationality would also lose the Spanish nationality (but without this having an automatic impact on their descendants' nationality) (art. 24.2 in the 1931 Constitution). The Constitution provided that on the basis of reciprocity and as determined by law nationals of Portugal, Hispano-America, including Brazil, residing in Spain could naturalise without losing their nationality of origin. The Constitution also mentioned that in those same countries Spanish nationals could acquire a second nationality without losing the Spanish one, as long as those countries allowed for this and regardless of reciprocity (art. 24.2 of the 1931 Constitution).

13.2.3 *Franco's regime and the 1954 and 1975 reforms*

In 1938 the Republican constitution was invalidated and the 1889 Civil Code was fully re-established as the main legislative framework governing nationality. After that a major reform did not take place again until 1954. The main aim of this reform was to introduce clarity to a system which had become complex and full of minor regulations, mostly administrative.[6]

The changes introduced in the Civil Code through the 1954 legislation were consistent with changes in Spain's emigration patterns. The emigration to Latin America was ending and being replaced by temporary migration, mostly by men, to European countries rebuilding their economies after the war. The main destinations now included Germany, Switzerland and the Benelux. There was the assumption that this newer form of migration would be temporary and thus the 1954 legislator did not expect it to have any implications for nationality issues. This explains why the focus remained on expatriates in Latin America and on the question of the number of generations that would be allowed to pass on their Spanish nationality while abroad. Reviving the spirit of the old Civil Code, the legislator decided now that third-generation emigrants had to register at a Spanish embassy or consulate for them to retain their Spanish nationality, to avoid the perpetuation of expatriates without real connection to Spain (art. 26 of Civil Code as amended by the 1954 statute). First and second generations remained exempt from the registration requirement.

The 1954 reform picked up the idea of establishing dual nationality treaties with the countries of the Ibero-American community of nations. Although, as we saw, the idea was originally put forward in the Constitution of the Second Republic it fitted well with Franco's ideology which embraced the narrative of Spain's continuation of the long lost Spanish Empire of glorious times (Moreno Fuentes 2001: 141). In fact the preamble of the 1954 reform stated that Spain shared a 'spiritual mission' with countries with which 'for well-known reasons that transcend all kinds of contingencies it is inextinguishably linked' (Lete del Río 1984). Thus, the new art. 22 of the reformed Civil Code provided that Spanish nationals who voluntarily acquired the nationality of another country would automatically lose their Spanish nationality, except when the country belonged to the Ibero-American community of nations or the Philippines, if the relevant bilateral agreements had been signed between Spain and the country in question. Indeed, between the 1950s and 1960s, Spain signed twelve of those agreements giving legal expression to a widely spread de facto reality and providing a framework for its regulations.

Another novelty of the 1954 reform was that it rendered slightly more flexible the requirements to access nationality, by introducing for the first time double ius soli to ensure that the third generation of foreigners living in Spain would gain automatic access to nationality (art. 17.3 CC). The requirements were strict, however: both parents had to have been born in Spain and reside in Spain at the time the child was born. The idea was to avoid the perpetuation of generations of foreigners living permanently in Spain.

Access to nationality through naturalisation by residence was also made slightly easier in some respects. Although the ten years residence requirement was retained as a general rule, the period was reduced to two years in the case of a foreign man marrying a Spanish woman. Borrowing from the Second Republic legislation, two years was also the rule for nationals of the Ibero-American community and the Philippines. On the other hand the concept of public order became a tool to exercise greater political scrutiny over the naturalisation process, allowing the Ministry of Justice a tremendous amount of discretion. Art. 20 simply provided that the Spanish nationality could be denied for reasons related to public order.

As for the loss of Spanish nationality, the regulation remained practically unchanged except for the addition of the possibility to lose the Spanish nationality as a punishment for a criminal offence (art. 23.2).

One of the most regrettable aspects of the reform was its going back to some of the more regressive aspects of the old Civil Code, including the discrimination against women who, in the name of the legal unity of the family, would again lose their nationality if they could acquire that of their husbands when they married (23.3). Foreign women marrying Spanish men would on the other hand acquire Spanish nationality automatically (art. 21). Only one exception was foreseen, namely for the sake of avoiding statelessness: women could keep their nationality and pass it on to their children to avoid statelessness (art. 17.2). The blunt discrimination was only tackled in the partial reform to the Civil Code which took place in 1975 and symbolised the late regime's attempt to seem more democratic.[7] After the 1975 reform, marriage stopped being a sufficient condition for either losing or acquiring Spanish nationality. However, Spanish women could still pass their nationality on, though only when the children were not accorded that of their father.

13.2.4 Spain's transition to democracy and to a country of net immigration: the 1978 Constitution and the 1982 reform

After Franco's death in 1975, Spain entered upon a new democratic path. The current Constitution, which was approved on 6 December 1978 epitomises the result of this transition. Together with Spain's embracement of democracy the relevant framework for our purposes needs to take into account two further phenomena: the return migration that took place during the transitional period and the beginning of the transformation process of Spain into a net recipient of migratory flows.

During 1974-77 the migratory balance of Spanish nationals shifted for the first time with nearly 300,000 emigrants returning from abroad. This phenomenon of course had a high political profile and left its visible traces in the new Constitution (Moreno Fuentes 2001: 130). At the same time, in spite of Spain's severe economic crisis at the beginning of the 1980s, the new Spain, a main attraction for foreign investment, started generating jobs at the very top and bottom of the occupational scale. These jobs were partly taken by foreigners. From less than 50,000 in 1975, the number of foreigners rose gradually to about 250,000 in 1995.[8] Initially, immigrants from Latin America were clearly the majority but they were soon matched by the rapidly growing number of immigrants from Africa, mostly the Maghreb. People from Asia (China and Philippines) also started to increase their presence. Moreover, from the late 1980s onward, Spain also began to receive large numbers of asylum seekers, due to refugee crises in Eastern Europe, former Yugoslavia and Sub-Saharan Africa.

The 1978 Constitution, breaking with our constitutional tradition, does not purport to offer a more or less comprehensive regulation of nationality. In fact art. 11.1 refers the matter to further legislation providing that the Spanish nationality is acquired, kept and lost according to the laws. The Constitution does however define a set of basic principles. Art. 11.2 states that Spanish nationals 'by origin' cannot be deprived of their nationality whereas art. 11.3 authorises Spain to sign dual nationality agreements with Ibero-American countries as well as with other countries that have or have had special links with Spain. The same provision recognises that with regards to those countries, Spanish nationals can naturalise without losing their nationality of origin. The existence of a historical community of Ibero-American nations, dating back to the 1931 Second Republic, has thus been preserved in the Spanish Constitution. As mentioned, the return of Spanish emigrants was also taken into account in the drafting of the new

Constitution which, in its art. 42 (in the Chapter on Leading Social and Economic Principles) provides that: 'the State shall protect the social and economic rights of Spanish workers abroad, and enact a policy to facilitate their return.' These are the only provisions that make explicit or implicit reference to nationality. However, other clauses, such as the one which prohibits discrimination on the grounds of sex, have naturally had an impact on the matter as well.

The first reform of nationality legislation of the new democratic regime took place in 1982, when the numbers of foreign nationals living in Spain was still rather small and Spain was far from being generally perceived as a country of immigration.[9] The 1982 reform retained the basic traits of Spanish nationality legislation[10] adapting it to the constitutional mandates. For instance, consistent with the constitutional prohibition of discrimination on the grounds of sex (art. 14 in the Constitution) the law finally removed all types of discrimination against women regarding both their access and their right to pass on their nationality to their descendants (see art. 17.2 CC as reformed by the 1982 Statute). However, the opportunity was not seized to change the regulation in depth. It was clear that changing Spanish nationality legislation was not perceived as a priority in the new democratic venture and when the government presented its bill to be discussed in parliament, only the Communist party challenged it in depth yet with little success.[11] Indeed the matter also had a low political profile in public opinion and the law passed almost secretly during the summer of 1982.

One of the main characteristics of the new regulation, other than the removal of all forms of sex discrimination, was the systematic distinction between nationals 'by origin' and those with 'derivative nationality', a distinction with relevance for the purpose of acquisition and more importantly for the loss of the Spanish nationality (arts. 22.2, 23.4 and 24 CC). The 1978 Constitution had indeed foreseen that Spanish 'by origin' could only lose their nationality voluntarily and the 1982 legislative reform made a strict interpretation of this. True, the reformed Code still stated that the voluntary acquisition of another nationality could imply the loss of Spanish nationality but several exceptions made even this rule inapplicable in practice. For one thing the acquisition of the nationality of one of the Ibero-American community of nations, plus Andorra, Equatorial Guinea or, for that matter, any other country with whom Spain had signed a bilateral agreement of dual nationality would not imply the loss of Spanish nationality. Also, nationals would not lose their Spanish nationality if they stated that the acquisition of another nationality was the result of their emigration to that country (art. 23 of the Civil Code as reformed by the 1982 legislation). The underlying reason behind this new provision was the aim of protecting emigrants living in countries with which Spain did not have bilateral agreements.[12] The other possibilities of loss (loss because of committing certain crimes, for falsity or fraud in the acquisition, for voluntarily joining the military forces or exercise of public office in a foreign nation without governmental authorisation) were only reserved for nationals who were not so 'by origin' (art. 24 CC).

For the rest, ius sanguinis was still maintained as the central mode of acquisition and the registration requirements at the embassy or consulate as requirement for the retention of nationality were now removed. Ius soli was rendered slightly more flexible by allowing the double ius soli rule to apply even if only one of the foreign parents (and not both) had also been born in Spain and by removing the requirement of residence of the parents in Spanish territory at the time of birth, again mostly as a way of avoiding the perpetuation of foreigners living in Spain (art. 17.4 CC). Other novelties were the inclusion of automatic acquisition of nationality by minors adopted by a Spaniard (art. 18 CC) whereas in the previous legislation adoption was only an instance of privileged naturalisation by residence (two year residence requirement) and the restriction of access by option.

Some changes were made to the residence-based acquisition mode. The rule, ten years of residence, was once again retained but the affinity based privileged reduction to two years was expanded to cover not only nationals from the Ibero-American community but also from Andorra and Equatorial Guinea. In recognition of its historical debt to Sephardic Jews, expelled from the Spanish Kingdom in 1492, the legislator included the community of Sephardic Jews into the privileged group. For those married to a Spanish national one year of residence would be sufficient, as well as for those born from a Spanish parent who had lost his or her nationality and those born in Spanish territory. While trying to facilitate the incorporation of second generations, the Spanish legislator thus departed from the option of *facultas soli*, or naturalisation by option of second generations.

13.3 Recent developments and current institutional arrangement

13.3.1 *Political Analysis*

By the middle of the 1980s, the presence of immigrants in Spain started to increase dramatically confirming the process of gradual transformation of Spain into a net recipient of migratory flows rather than a country of net emigration. In 1985, the first law systematically regulating all immigration issues was passed, representing the 'end of a period of laxity in Spanish border control and the beginning of a process of regulating immigrants who were living in Spain without proper legal status' (Moreno Fuentes 2001: 133). In 1985 Spain also joined the EC becoming the gatekeeper of the EC's southern border.

In spite of this radical transformation, the Spanish regulation on nationality has not been significantly modified since the mid 1980s, and the reforms that it has been subject to (in 1990, 1993, 1995 and, most recently, in 2002) have still prioritised the concerns about former expatriates who lost their nationality and their descendants, over those of immigrants for whom access to nationality is an opportunity for integration. In 1990 the socialist government of the day led a reform of the Civil Code on nationality matters[13] and, for the first time, the incorporation of immigrant populations was debated in parliament. However such debate had little impact on the reforms actually undertaken. The reforms were mostly aimed at solving some of the problems of applicability and interpretation of the Civil Code after the 1982 reform, as the law candidly recognised. Two later reforms, one in 1993 and one in 1995 were very limited and focused exclusively on recovery of the Spanish nationality by expatriates and its transmission to their descendants.[14]

The most recent reform of the Civil Code by Statute 36/2002 of 8 October, was passed both soon after and just before a series of consecutive major reforms of Spanish immigration law, triggered by Spain's changing immigration patterns.[15] It declares that its main purpose is to facilitate the retention, recovery and transmission of Spanish nationality by Spanish emigrants in accordance with the constitutional imperative expressed in art. 42. Since at least the mid-1990s, several bills have been discussed in parliament. To those proposed by the conservative party (Popular Party, PP), the party in government from 1996 to 2004, one must add those put forward by the Socialist Party, (PSOE), the main party in the opposition and the 'United Left' (*Izquierda Unida*), a smaller party to the left of PSOE. The last bill presented by the 'Popular Party' (*Partido Popular)* was the one that, with small modifications, became law. As we shall see, unlike those of the other political parties, the PP bill paid virtually no attention to the question of the integration of immigrants through facilitated acquisition of the Spanish nationality.[16]

Other than in the fulfilment of the constitutional mandate, Statute 36/2002 justifies the reform that it embodies by the need to satisfy the many requests expressed by numerous descendants of Spanish emigrants themselves. In October of 2000, a motion had been passed in Congress, in plenary session, on the need to undertake measures to improve legally and economically the situation of Spanish emigrants. The motion had been influenced by the findings of a report presented to the Social Policy and Employment Commission in Congress on the situation of expatriates as well as that of immigrants and refugees in

Spain.[17] The report had recommended legislation to facilitate acquisition of nationality by descendants of emigrants and the recovery of nationality by emigrants themselves but also measures to avoid the marginalisation of foreigners. It expressed the concern that relegating foreigners in Spain to the status of second-class citizens would create the objective conditions for virulent racism and xenophobia. Unfortunately, only the first set of recommendations was followed.

In 2003, the Socialist Party presented a new bill which was rejected once again. The bill endorsed measures similar to those the Party has been defending for the last number of years with the integration of immigrants in mind. Moreover, the bill was also sensitive to the requests of a group that has become more and more active in civil society, those who went into exile during the dictatorship, and their descendants, as well as the so-called children of the war (*niños de la Guerra*),[18] all of whom have been demanding the reinstatement of Spanish nationality and its extension to their direct descendants, however remote, as a form of reparation.[19] Since March 2004, the Socialists have been in power. However, to my knowledge, they have not yet pushed for a concrete reform of nationality legislation that would endorse the various reforms that the Party has embraced for the past decade.

13.3.2 *Main general modes of acquisition and loss of citizenship*

13.3.2.1 *Acquisition of nationality*

Spain does not have a specific nationality law. The regulation on nationality is still contained in the Civil Code as well as in other procedural norms, mostly in the Statute and Executive Decree on the Civil Registry.[20]

Following the tradition that is predictably becoming more and more controversial as Spain turns into a country of immigration (see, for all, Lara Aguado 2003), the Spanish regime still distinguishes between 'nationality by origin' (*nacionalidad originaria*) and 'derivative nationality' (*nacionalidad derivativa*). Whereas the former used to refer, and still does for the most part, to instances of automatic acquisition or acquisition at birth, the latter was usually reserved for non-automatic and acquisition after birth. Currently the Spanish legal system still refers to these two modes of acquisition although it contemplates a few instances in which 'nationality by origin' is not acquired at the moment of birth and requires application. The major practical implication is that 'nationals by origin' enjoy a set of prerogatives from which those who have a 'derivate nationality' have been excluded. These prerogatives include: the capacity to be the King's tutor (according to art. 60.1 in the Spanish Constitution); the right not to be deprived of Spanish nationality against one's will (according to both art. 11.2 of the Spanish

Constitution and art. 25 of the Civil Code) and the possibility to retain Spanish nationality when acquiring the nationality of a certain set of countries with which Spain has special historical and cultural ties (according to art. 11.3 of the Spanish Constitution and art. 24 of the Civil Code).

The main mode of automatic acquisition of nationality in Spain is still ius sanguinis, even though the system also contains ius soli elements. Spain embraces an unqualified ius sanguinis in favour of those born of a Spanish mother or father who will become national 'by origin' regardless of whether they are born in Spain or outside of Spain (art. 17.1. CC).

Moreover, automatic access to nationality 'by origin' is guaranteed to those who are born in Spain but only if at least one of the parents was also born in Spain (double ius soli) (art. 17.1 b) CC) or the person would otherwise become stateless (either because both parents are stateless or because none of their citizenships is passed on to the child via ius sanguinis) (art. 17.1.c) CC). Automatic acquisition 'by origin' through filial transfer of nationality for the case of adoption is also contemplated for those foreigners under eighteen years who are adopted by a Spaniard, from the moment of adoption (art. 19.1 CC). This was reformed in 1990. Before that, acquisition 'by origin' was only recognised if at the time of birth of the adopted person one of the adopting parents was a Spaniard as well.

There have been voices both in the political and in the academic arena claiming the need to embrace further elements of ius soli in view of the increasing immigrant population. Thus, the various bills submitted over the last decade before the 2002 reform and again in 2003 by the socialist party include the recognition of Spanish nationality for those born in Spain from foreign parents if at least one of them is a legal permanent resident at the time of birth. United Left's (*Izquierda Unida*) proposals did not even require legal residence but only de facto permanent residence.

As for *non-automatic acquisition* Spain has traditionally distinguished, and still does, between two modes: by option and by naturalisation (the latter can be divided into two sub-modes: discretionary naturalisation (called in Spain *carta de naturaleza*) and residence-based acquisition). To these, a third mode was added in the 1990 reform and is still present: acquisition by 'possession of status'.

Acquisition by *option* is a privileged form of acquisition recognised in favour of people with special links to Spain who only have to express their will in due time and form (through either a declaration or petition) to acquire Spanish nationality (Lete del Río 1994: 27). To this day, there are four types of beneficiaries. The first one refers to those who are or have been subject to the 'parental authority' (*patria potestas)* of a

Spaniard (art. 20.1.a) CC).[21] This provision was reformed in 1990. Before that, it referred to people being subject to either 'parental authority'(*patria potestas)* or guardianship. After the reform the latter will only enjoy privileged residence-based entitlement (one year residence). Thus the children of foreigners who naturalise in Spain will acquire a right to Spanish nationality by option for being or having been (if they are of age) under the 'parental authority' (*potestas)* of a Spanish citizen. The parent first has to become a Spanish national though, so that his or her descendants can then acquire the option (Marín López 2002: 2859-2882).

The second group entitled to nationality by option are those whose (natural or adopted) father or mother was Spaniard 'by origin' born in Spain (art. 20.1 b) CC), without time limit and regardless of their age and place of residence. This possibility was introduced in the latest legal reform on nationality in 2002. It is aimed at allowing the children of those Spanish emigrants who had lost their nationality at the time their children were born to acquire Spanish nationality. This option had already been introduced in the 1990 reform through a transitory provision, but it was only valid for three years after the 1990 statute came into force. At the time, the legislator justified it as a way of 'solving the last negative consequences of a historical process – the massive emigration of Spaniards – which is unlikely to reoccur'. The provision provided that the applicant who exercised his or her right of option should be legally residing in Spain, although this requirement could be waived by government. Then a 1993 reform again opened up this possibility, through a transitional provision, for those exercising it before January 1996, in order to reach those beneficiaries dispersed throughout the world, especially those living in rural areas and for whom accessing information might be more difficult. The 1995 reform extended this option until 7 January 1997. Finally, the 2002 reform incorporated the possibility (to be exercised as of 9 January 2003) without subjecting it to time limits of any sort and removing the requirement of residence in Spain by the applicant. The legislator specified that in doing so it was fulfilling the mandate of art. 42 in the Constitution, as facilitating the retention and transmission of Spanish nationality was a way of protecting Spanish emigrants. It recognised having accepted in this regard the many claims presented to the 'Emigration Council' (*Consejo de la Emigracion)* by emigrants over the years.[22] Even as reformed, the provision has been subject to criticism by those who believe that the two restrictions implicit in it are unjustified (Lara Aguado 2003). First, the restriction, among the reference persons, to those who are Spanish 'by origin', which means that the children of a naturalised immigrant who emigrates losing his Spanish nationality in the process would not be able to benefit from this option. Second, the restriction implicit in the requirement that the reference person, the father or the mother, must have been Spaniards *born in Spain,* which is a way of limiting the possibility of option to the children of the first generation of Spanish emigrants, maybe for no other reason than to accept those whose numbers would be enough to fulfil Spain's labour needs (Rubio & Escudero 2003: 126).

The third group of persons entitled to nationality by option, since the 1990 reform, are those for whom descent from a Spaniard or birth in Spain as triggering factors have been established after they turned eighteen (20.1.c) CC in connection to art. 17.2). Prior to the reform, acquisition was automatic regardless of the age of the person and this could entail granting Spanish nationality to an adult who might not have had any ties with Spain when the triggering factor (birth in Spain or descent from Spaniard) was established. This was considered excessively intrusive. For similar reasons, the right of option is also recognised in those cases of adoption where the adopted person is eighteen or older ((20.1.c) CC in connection to art. 19.2 CC). Such right was again introduced in the 1990 reform. Before that, adoption only opened the path to acquisition when the adopted person was a minor.

Exercising this option, except in the case of those whose mother or father was Spanish by origin born in Spain, is subject to a time limit – basically, until the person turns twenty, for those subject to 'parental authority' (*patria potestas)* of a Spaniard, except when the person cannot be considered emancipated at the age of eighteen in accordance with the law of his or her nationality, in which case the person can exercise the option during the two years following emancipation. The time frame is also two years after adoption or determination of descent or place of birth.

The procedure is described in arts. 226 to 230 of the Civil Registry Executive Decree. Basically the request has to be formulated at the Civil Registry of either the place of birth or place of residence of the person in question or at a consular or diplomatic office if the person resides abroad. In any event a copy will be sent to the judge in charge of the Registry of the place of birth of the person or the Central Registry if the person was born abroad as it is there that the acquisition of nationality needs to be inscribed. After the relevant documents have been presented the person in question will exercise the option, which will only come into effect fully after he or she relinquishes his or her prior nationality (if necessary), swears loyalty to the king and the constitution (if he or she is fourteen or older) and records it in the Registry. In case the procedure is not successful an appeal can be submitted to the General Directorate of Registries and Notaries (DGRN) and, failing that, the person in question can appeal via the judiciary by addressing the issue to a civil court.

Non-automatic acquisition through naturalisation includes acquisition by discretionary conferral, traditionally called *carta de naturaleza,* and other forms of entitlement based conferrals, either purely residence-based or focusing on both residence and other additional criteria. The Spanish legal school has traditionally placed all of these under the common label of naturalisation by residence even though in some instances the period of residence required is very short.

Regarding acquisition by discretionary conferral, the Spanish legal order simply allows for this possibility when 'extraordinary circumstances' concur in the target person, who has to apply for it and may be successful or not depending on the full discretion of the Government, who can grant it through a Royal Decree (art. 21.1 CC). In practice, the set of interpretations of what those 'exceptional circumstances' are has ranged from an interest in spreading the Spanish language, good soccer, and the belonging to some international brigades during the Spanish civil war (Rubio & Escudero 2003: 126). The survival of this mode has been subject to constant criticism by the legal school as such broad discretion is said to contradict the spirit of the Constitution (Espinar Vicente 1986: 108). On the other hand, its usefulness in allowing the gaps and deficiencies of the existing legal order to be filled and overcome has also been recognised (Abarca Junco & Pérez Vera 1997: 176).

What is commonly known as residence-based acquisition by the Spanish legal school, which we will call naturalisation by residence, refers to a mode of acquisition that entitles the applicant to 'derivative' Spanish nationality conferred by the Department of Justice and requires individual application (art. 21.2 CC). Although once the target person fulfils the required legal conditions he or she is entitled to acquire nationality, the system still allows for some discretion. The relevant provision explicitly states 'that the Spanish nationality is (also) acquired through residence in Spain, under the conditions specified in the following provision, and is conferred by the Department of Justice which can deny it on justified grounds related to public order or national interest.' According to the Supreme Court and the legal school, granting nationality is not simply a matter of right. Rather, once the person qualifies according to the law, the state is authorised to check that the necessary requirements have been fulfilled and that in view of the general interest the granting is indeed justified. On the other hand, it is the specific denial of nationality that needs to be justified on specific public order or national interest grounds, not the conferral to which the person is in principle entitled once he or she fulfils the necessary legal requirements (Morán del Casero 2002: 453).[23]

As for the conditions that the target person must satisfy, the legal system contemplates a requirement of ten years of continual, uninterrupted, legal and prior residence and then provides for shorter residence requirements for specific groups (art. 22 CC). This general ten year requirement, which comparatively speaking makes Spain fall into the category of the more demanding countries in terms of naturalisation requirements, has survived the various reforms up to this day and has been subject to constant criticism. The bills presented by the Socialist and the United Left groups during the last decade have advocated a reduction of the general residence requirement to five years. The United Left has also proposed that the ten-year residence requirement be left only for those instances in which either the legality or the continuous nature of residence cannot be proven.

There are however quite a few groups of applicants who are placed in a faster track. The list has been changing and gradually expanding. Refugees only have a residence requirement of five years.[24] Nationals of Latin American countries, Andorra, the Philippines, Equatorial Guinea, Portugal or Sephardic Jews only have a requirement of two years. In the nationality reform proposals discussed during the last decade, both Socialist and the United Left parties suggested that it would be convenient to reduce the five-year requirement for refugees to two and to extend this option in favour of stateless persons as well (see also Rubio & Escudero 2003: 129).

Finally, there is a category for which only one year of residence is required which includes several groups. The requirement applies to those born in Spain which means that although no ius soli exists for the second generation, one year of legal residence is sufficient for the children of immigrants born in Spain to apply for derivative nationality (legally represented by their parents) if they do not acquire it otherwise. One year of residence is also sufficient for those who had a right to option subject to a time limit but, for some reason, did not exercise it in due course. Included in this fast track are also those who have been subject for at least two consecutive years to the guardianship of a Spanish citizen or institution. Those who at the time of application have been married for at least one year with a Spaniard are also covered. In case that the reference person is somebody who has naturalised it is required that he or she be both married and Spaniard for at least a year before he or she can have his or her spouse apply for Spanish nationality. Not included are partners in civil unions, regardless of their sexual orientation, something which the Socialist proposals have been meaning to amend. The widow or widower of a Spaniard, if at the time of the death of the spouse they were not separated, is also entitled to gain Spanish nationality through the one-year residence track. Finally those born outside of Spain whose father or mother, grandfather or grandmother was Spaniard by origin. Notice that in reality if the mother or father, besides having been Spaniards by origin, were born in Spain, their children would not need to reside in Spain as they could simply access nationality through option.

This provision has been subject to only relatively minor changes since the mid-1980s. The inclusion for the first time of refugees in the faster track residence based acquisition was brought about by the 1990 reform which, in this respect, resurrected a 1982 communist proposal. Minors and non-emancipated persons were also included among those who could gain residence-based nationality when duly legally represented, through the 1990 reform. The requirement that spousal transfer through one-year residence take place only if at the time of application the applicant has been married for at least one year with the national and both are not *de iure* or *de facto* separated was again introduced by the 1990 reform. Previously, having been married, even if the marriage was dissolved at the time of application, was sufficient to qualify. The 1990 legislator changed this to avoid sham marriages. Also a vestige of the 1990 nationality reform was the addition of the widow or widower to the fast track list. Finally, the addition of the grandchildren of former Spaniards was a result of the 2002 reform and its attempt to facilitate recovery of the Spanish nationality by former expatriates and its transmission to their descendants. Before that, the provision only referred to the parents, not to the grandparents and hence excluded the third generation.

In the past decade, victims and descendants of victims of the civil war and Franco's political regime who had to go into exile have been mobilising around the possibility of recovering Spanish nationality when it was lost as a result of such exile. The new socialist government of Zapatero (himself the grandson of somebody executed during the civil war) seems receptive to this and similar claims. Indeed even before the Socialists came to power in March 2004 they had already echoed this concern in the 2003 socialist reform bill, which includes among those who should have a one-year residence-based entitlement to nationality all direct descendants (however distant) of people who went into exile as a result of the war or Franco's dictatorship up until 1975.

There has been some dispute as to the how 'legal and uninterrupted residence' is to be interpreted for the purpose of satisfying the residence requirements. As for 'uninterrupted' residence, a decision by the Supreme Court (decision of 19 September 1998) has been crucial to the interpretation by defining that short trips abroad do not interrupt residence as long as the person keeps his or her life centred in Spain.

More difficult to determine is what 'legal' residence means, other than the obvious exclusion of people who are in the country in contravention of the legal system. There are several possible interpretations. According to the most restrictive one, the requirement needs to be interpreted in the light of immigration legislation, because such legislation distinguishes between three situations (stay, temporary residence, and permanent residence). The claim is that only residence, strictly speaking, qualifies be it temporary or permanent (see, for instance, Pérez de Vargas 2003: 4075; Palao Moreno 2001: 52; Diez Picazo 2003: 295). This interpretation also used to be frequently embraced by the Supreme Court.[25] Part of the doctrine and the DGRN, at times, have sustained that the legal residence concept in the Civil Code is independent from that in the immigration legislation altogether which means that as long as the residence is not in contravention to the legal order (for instance disobeying some expulsion order) it qualifies for naturalisation purposes regardless of the type of permit under which the person lives in Spain (see for all, Diez del Corral 2001: 412-414).[26] More recently, the Supreme Court has also occasionally embraced this interpretation.[27] Finally, some scholars defend an intermediate position: although the concept of residence has to be interpreted in the light of the immigration legislation, once the person has technically speaking achieved the status of legal *resident* the other periods of time that the person has spent in the country legally can also be taken into account (see, for all, Pretel Serrano 1994). The 2002 reform was a wonderful opportunity for the legislator to finally clarify this question. However, the response was once again ambiguous. The provision was not changed and still makes reference to 'legal residence'. However, in the explanatory introduction to the statute the legislator explicitly mentions the need to interpret residence as *effective* and points to the interpretation offered by the Supreme Court in its decision of 19 November 1998, a decision which makes reference to the person's intent to integrate into the Spanish society. Thus, more and more the belief is that, actual residence (as long as it is legal) and the consolidation of effective ties with Spain is what counts for the purpose of naturalisation (Lara Aguado 2003: 6).

Common requirements for acquisition both through option and naturalisation (whether through discretionary or residence-based entitlement) include: oath of loyalty to the King and obedience to the Constitution and the laws; renunciation of prior nationality and registration in the Civil Registry (art. 23 of the CC). Moreover, residence-based naturalisation requires proof of good civic conduct and sufficient integration into Spanish society. Some of these requirements call for further specification.

Since the 1990 reform, some nationals have been exempted from the requirement to renounce prior nationality. They form the class of nationals for whom dual citizenship is legally accepted. This class includes nationals from Latin American countries, Andorra, the Philippines, Equatorial Guinea and Portugal (art. 23.b and 24.1 CC). In recognition of the stronger ties with the EU it has been proposed that nationals from other EU countries should not be asked to give up their nationality when naturalising in Spain either (Lara Aguado 2003). Aware that such a condition constitutes a hurdle in the process of naturalisation and hence of integration of immigrants the 1993 socialist bill proposed removing this requirement altogether.

'Good civic conduct' is an indeterminate concept. To show good civic conduct, the petitioner will be asked to present certificates of proving lack of criminal record or of good conduct issued by both the Spanish authorities and the authorities of the country of origin. Moreover, the DGRN may refer itself to the Department of the Interior to check the conduct of the applicant, especially where it relates to the fulfilment of obligations regarding his or her entrance and residence in Spain. Be that as it may, the Supreme Court has decided that the requirement of good conduct needs to be interpreted in the light of the constitutional order, which means the need to check whether the conduct infringes the norms regarding the exercising of rights and duties in the constitution and other international instruments.[28] As for the relevance of the existence of a criminal record which has been deleted, there is nothing specified, however the case law of the Supreme Court seems to favour the interpretation of the irrelevance of such records unless the seriousness of the criminal conduct is such that a different result should be embraced.[29]

As for 'sufficient social integration' into Spanish society (art. 22.4 CC), the law does not specify what this means either. Art. 220 of the Decree on the Civil Registry (*Reglamento del Registro Civil*) requires applicants to declare whether they know Castilian or any other Spanish language, and any other circumstance showing adaptation to the Spanish culture and Spanish life style (studies, social service in the community, etc.). The provision also refers to the need to show sufficient means of subsistence in Spain. Ultimately, it is the judge in charge of the Civil Registry who will informally interview the applicant and decide whether in the applicant's view this requirement has been fulfilled. The religious belief of the applicant cannot be taken into account in making such judgement.[30]

Procedurally speaking, the person in question will formulate his or her request to the judge in charge of the Civil Registry of his or her domicile who will speak for or against the conferral and send the application to the DGRN, which by delegation from the Department of Justice has to decide within one year of the application. After that the person can appeal the decision in the administrative judicial system (21.2 CC). If the DGRN decides affirmatively, the applicant will have to go to the Civil Registry of his or her domicile within 180 days to ratify the intention to become a Spanish national and swear loyalty to the King and allegiance to the Constitution and the laws.

Since the 1990 reform the Spanish legal system has incorporated the possibility of acquisition by 'possession of status' for people who in good faith have possessed and used the Spanish nationality for ten years (art. 18 CC) on the grounds of a title validly inscribed at the Civil Registry, even if it turns out that the title was not valid after all. This mechanism is a way to avoid sudden and drastic changes in the nationality of a person. Consistent with the idea of reducing the general residence requirement from ten to five years, the 2003 socialist bill proposes to reduce to five years also the residence period required for acquisition by 'possession of status'. Although not necessarily fulfilling the tasks that it was intended to, a retroactive application of this provision has recently been allowing people born in Equatorial Guinea and in the Sahara, during the period that these were Spanish colonies, and who are now living and working in Spain, to regularise their employment situation in the absence of the necessary documentation (García Rubio 1992: 980-991).

The Civil Code contemplates the possibility of recovery of lost nationality. Given that the political debate thus far has mostly centred on the effects of emigration, nationality recovery has actually been a relatively high profile issue. According to art. 26.1 CC the main condition for recovering the Spanish nationality (however it was acquired), other than the expression of will and the registration thereof in the Civil Registry, is that the person be a legal resident in Spain. However, emigrants and their children are clearly given preferential treatment in that they are exempt from the residence requirement. At their discretion and in exceptional circumstances the Department of Justice may grant other exemptions from the residence requirement.

This mode of reacquisition has been subject to changes in all the reforms that have occurred since 1982. Until the 1990 reform, one year of residence immediately prior to the petition was required. Emigrants who could supply proof of their condition could be exempted from this requirement by the Department of Justice. The 1990 reform changed this to require legal residence in Spain at the time of petition only, providing that for emigrants *and their children* this requirement could be waived by government. Other people would be exempted from the residence requirement only under very exceptional circumstances. The 1995 reform then exempted emigrants from the residence requirement. The legislator at the time justified this by arguing that the exemption procedure was long and burdensome and resulted almost always in the exemption being granted anyway. Finally the 2002 reform also exempted children of emigrants from the residence requirement. Until the 2002 reform it was also necessary for nationals to give up their other nationality, although since the 1990 reform the legislator had already exempted nationals from Latin American countries, Andorra, Philippines, Equatorial Guinea and Portugal from this requirement. The requirement was removed altogether in 2002.

Apart from the loss and possible recovery of nationality due to emigration the other instance of recovery of lost nationality that deserved some attention was that of Spanish women who lost their nationality through marriage to a foreigner. The 1995 law reforming the Civil Code on the matter of recovery of nationality contained a transitional provision (transitional provision 2) providing that a Spanish woman who had lost her nationality because of marriage to a foreigner before the 1975 statute came into force abolishing this practice, could recover it under the same conditions as emigrants and their descendants (i.e., requirement of legal residence that could be waived by the government, declaration of intention, registration in the Civil Registry and, until the 2002 reform, renunciation of prior nationality).

Finally, one important caveat needs to be added for the case whereby nationality was lost involuntarily. Indeed, under art. 26.2 CC when loss of nationality has occurred involuntarily and has been applied to persons who were not nationals 'by origin' (who are the only ones who can lose the Spanish nationality in this way) then reacquisition is subject to the discretion of government. This provision is also the result of previous reforms. Prior to the 2002 reform, this additional requirement of discretionary governmental authorisation also applied to those who had lost their Spanish nationality by not having fulfilled their mandatory military or civil service obligations, unless they were 40 years or older (50 years or older, until the 1995 reform). The 1990 reform was the first one that introduced an exemption from the need for governmental authorisation for those who had not performed their military or civil service but were older than 50. After the abolishment of mandatory military service or alternative social civil service in 2001 this restriction no longer made sense.[31]

13.3.2.2 *Loss of nationality*

The Spanish Constitution of 1978 (art. 11.2) determines that Spaniards 'by origin' cannot be deprived of their nationality. This is probably the most relevant distinction between nationals 'by origin' as opposed to those with 'derivative' nationality, and although some scholars have criticised it (Lara Aguado 2003), it is a distinction embedded in the constitution itself. Other than this constitutional distinction, the modes of loss are also regulated in the Spanish Civil Code. There are two main modes of loss of Spanish nationality. One refers to voluntary loss and the other one to involuntary loss. The latter does not apply to those who are Spanish by origin.

As far as voluntary loss is concerned there are four possibilities (art. 24 CC) of which none are valid when Spain is at war (art. 24.5 CC).

First, for those who are emancipated, live abroad on a regular basis and have voluntarily acquired another nationality, except when the second nationality is one of a Latin American country or that of Andorra, the Philippines, Equatorial Guinea or Portugal. The loss in this instance can be prevented by way of submission of a declaration to the Civil Registry (24.1 CC). This provision has been changed in both the 1990 and the 2002 reforms. Before the 1990 reform the provision provided that the nationality would not be lost if the person could prove at the Consular Registry that the acquisition of a foreign nationality was related to emigration. This was a way to protect those who emigrated to a country with which Spain did not have a dual nationality agreement. In the 1990 reform the possibility of retaining Spanish nationality was removed. Thus, three years after the newly acquired nationality, the Spanish nationality would be lost. Finally, in 2002, the provision was amended again to introduce the option to retain the Spanish nationality by declaring a desire to do so at the Civil Registry, a declaration that must take place within three years of the acquisition of the new nationality.

Secondly, Spanish nationality can be lost voluntarily by those emancipated Spaniards who live abroad on a regular basis and make exclusive use of another nationality which was attributed to them when they were minors. This mode of loss was introduced in the 1990 reform. Here again and since 2002, the loss can be prevented by declaring the wish to retain Spanish nationality at the Civil Registry (24.1 CC).

Third, emancipated nationals who live abroad regularly can freely relinquish their Spanish nationality as long as they have another nationality (24.2 CC). This mode was amended in 1990. Before that, this option was foreseen only for those who enjoyed another nationality since they were minors. After emancipation they were given the option of relinquishing the Spanish nationality. Unlike now, it was not required that they live abroad.

Finally, setting some constraints to the perpetuation of generations of expatriates abroad, since the 2002 reform the Spanish legal order provides for the loss of nationality for those who were born and live abroad, descendants of Spaniards who were also born abroad, as long as the country of residence provides them with its nationality and as long as within three years of becoming of age or becoming emancipated they do not declare the intent to keep their Spanish nationality, at the Civil Registry (art. 24.3 CC).

Involuntary loss (art.25 CC) can occur in three instances. The first was only introduced in the 2002 reform and only occurs when naturalised nationals make exclusive use for three years of the nationality they renounced when acquiring Spanish nationality (art. 25.1 a). Secondly, involuntary loss can occur when the naturalised alien voluntarily joins the military or takes up a political office in a foreign country in contravention of express prohibition by government (25.1 b), something which is rather interesting at a time in which Spain not only allows but actually promotes the recruitment of foreigners into its professional army (Rubio & Escudero 2003: 126). Finally, loss can occur when through a judicial decision it is determined that the person acquired the nationality through falsity or fraud (25.2 CC). The 2002 reform specified that this loss would not affect third parties acting in good faith. Until 2002, the Civil Code also contemplated the possibility of loss of nationality by naturalised aliens as a result of a criminal conviction. Indeed, until 1995, the criminal code punished with the loss of nationality those committing a crime against the external security of the state. This possibility was first removed from the criminal code in 1995 and so this mode of loss became practically ineffective since then. In 2002 it was removed from the Civil Code altogether.

13.3.2.3 *Statistical developments*

To my knowledge no systematic and comprehensive effort to produce the sort of statistical data that would be relevant for the purpose of assessing the impact of different legislative reforms of nationality legislation, on naturalisation rates, has ever been undertaken. There are no thorough statistical data in Spain on nationality of origin and mode of acquisition. There is also a general lack of studies analysing naturalisation tendencies. Below we present the data we have nevertheless been able to gather.

One can observe that naturalisation patterns were rather erratic until 1996 when from 8,443 they started increasing systematically, at a rate of approximately 3,000 per year (with the exception of the drop in 2000), reaching 26,556 in 2003 but rarely exceeding a global naturalisation rate of 2 per cent and thus lying in general below the European average (Izquierdo 2004: 30).

Moreover, there are significant differences between the naturalisation rates of immigrants from different continents and countries. So, if we focus on the time span between 1998 and 2003 we can observe that naturalisations of immigrants from Latin America (mostly from Ecuador, Peru, the Dominican Republic and Colombia) and Africa (mostly from Morocco and Algeria and more recently from Senegal and Nigeria) represent about 80 per cent of the total. Europeans (mostly from Great Britain, Germany, France and Portugal and only more recently from Eastern Europe), who remain even today the largest source of foreign residents, have systematically shown a very low interest in naturalisation (accounting only for at most 10 per cent of the total number of naturalisations). The differences between that percentage and the higher percentages of previous years (34 per cent in 1985 or 20 per cent in

Table 13.1: Number of foreigners who have been granted Spanish nationality by year and country of origin since 1985[32]

	Europe				*Africa*	*America*	*Asia*	*Australia, Oceania*	*Stateless, Unknown*	*Total*
	Total	*EU15*	*Eastern Europe*	*Other Europe*						
1985	1,252	1,173	49	30	230	1,775	415	7	30	3,709
1986	1,037	968	28	41	1,694	1,865	480	7	38	5,121
1987	1,247	1,162	26	59	5,051	2,155	575	4	45	9,077
1988	1,211	1,153	39	19	3,440	2,898	652	2	55	8,258
1989	915	843	43	29	2,168	2,234	448	2	35	5,802
1990	1,120	992	73	55	1,852	3,315	743	5	44	7,079
1991	665	570	63	32	586	2,019	511	4	34	3,819
1992	869	776	59	34	771	2,812	780	2	28	5,262
1993	1,386	1,208	114	64	1,315	4,447	1,181	5	77	8,411
1994	1,020	792	175	53	1,227	4,432	1,070	3	50	7,802
1995	730	564	112	54	1,060	4,165	761	3	37	6,756
1996	816	619	150	47	1,030	5,532	1,028	5	22	8,433
1997	1,005	744	210	51	1,471	6,382	1,424	2	27	10,311
1998	1,329	987	284	58	2,150	8,249	1,400	5	44	13,177
1999	1,410	1,041	286	83	2,880	10,368	1,671	3	52	16,384
2000	1,009	697	260	52	2,578	7,146	1,225	1	40	11,999
2001	1,348	866	390	92	3,826	9,846	1,677	3	44	16,744
2002	1,533	938	540	55	4,325	13,883	2,014	5	50	21,810
2003	1,574	832	670	72	8,517	14,418	1,992	5	50	26,556
In per cent										
1985	34%	32%	1%	1%	6%	48%	11%	0%	1%	100%
1986	20%	19%	1%	1%	33%	36%	9%	0%	1%	100%
1987	14%	13%	0%	1%	56%	24%	6%	0%	0%	100%
1988	15%	14%	0%	0%	42%	35%	8%	0%	1%	100%
1989	16%	15%	1%	0%	37%	39%	8%	0%	1%	100%
1990	16%	14%	1%	1%	26%	47%	10%	0%	1%	100%
1991	17%	15%	2%	1%	15%	53%	13%	0%	1%	100%
1992	17%	15%	1%	1%	15%	53%	15%	0%	1%	100%
1993	16%	14%	1%	1%	16%	53%	14%	0%	1%	100%
1994	13%	10%	2%	1%	16%	57%	14%	0%	1%	100%
1995	11%	8%	2%	1%	16%	62%	11%	0%	1%	100%
1996	10%	7%	2%	1%	12%	66%	12%	0%	0%	100%
1997	10%	7%	2%	0%	14%	62%	14%	0%	0%	100%
1998	10%	7%	2%	0%	16%	63%	11%	0%	0%	100%
1999	9%	6%	2%	1%	18%	63%	10%	0%	0%	100%
2000	8%	6%	2%	0%	21%	60%	10%	0%	0%	100%
2001	8%	5%	2%	1%	23%	59%	10%	0%	0%	100%
2002	7%	4%	2%	0%	20%	64%	9%	0%	0%	100%
2003	6%	3%	3%	0%	32%	54%	8%	0%	0%	100%

Sources: 1985-1995: National Institute of Statistics (*Instituto Natcional de Estadística, www.ine.es*); *1996-2003: Secretary of State for Immigration and Emigration (Secretaria de Estado de Inmigración y Emigración, extranjeros.mtas.es).*

1986) is thus more related to the increase of other sources of migrants and their naturalisation rates than to a significant change in the low disposition to naturalise among Europeans.

Although immigrants from Latin America (nowadays the second largest source following closely that from European countries) and from African countries (nowadays the third largest source) have added up to 80 per cent of all naturalisations, there are significant differences between the two. Thus, whereas the naturalisation of immigrants from African countries has ranged between 12 per cent and 32 per cent between 1996 and 2003, that of citizens from Latin America has ranged from 54 to 66 per cent in the same time span. Although some of the differentiation may be accounted for by demographic variations in the yearly flux of immigrants from different regions, and different intentions regarding permanent settlement (Izquierdo 2004: 30), the different naturalisation regimes that apply to each group may also explain some of the difference. The highest hurdles for naturalisation thus far have been the excessively long period of required residence (ten years) and the need to relinquish one's prior nationality. Naturalisation is, however, facilitated for nationals from Latin America who are granted the privilege of a shorter residence requirement (two years) and do not have to renounce their nationality of origin.

Some data support this interpretation.[33] Moroccans are by far the largest group of foreign residents. In 1997, the total resident population of Moroccans was 77,189 and there were 1,056 naturalisations of Moroccans (a ratio of 1.37 per cent). That same year, the three Latin American countries with the largest populations in Spain were, in this order, Argentina (with 18,246 residents), Peru (with 18,023) and the Dominican Republic (with 17,845). The naturalisation ratio for Argentineans was then 7.5 per cent, for Peruvians 6.4 per cent and for Dominicans 7 per cent). Similarly, in the year 2000, there were 161,870 Moroccans living in Spain and only 1,921 were naturalised (1.18 per cent). The three largest groups from Latin American countries were Peruvians (with a naturalisation ratio of 5.4 per cent), Dominicans (6.53 per cent), and Cubans (5.39 per cent).

On the other hand, it seems that over the last years the difference in naturalisation rates between Latin Americans and Northern Africans has been decreasing (in 1996, Africans accounted for only 12 per cent of total naturalisations and Americans for 66 per cent whereas in 2003 the difference has shrunk to 32 per cent and 54 per cent respectively). It is not clear yet whether the main reason behind this has to do with demographics (many of the African immigrants might have satisfied the ten-year residence requirements only more recently) or other changes related to immigrants' settlement projects or attitudes in the receiving society. It seems that during the 2000-2004 Aznar government there was an attempt to favour immigration from Latin America, which was seen as more culturally attuned than that from Africa and this may have encouraged Africans to opt for naturalisation as a way of ensuring a secure residence. However, precisely because of this we might see an increase in the overall naturalisation of Latin Americans in the coming years, especially resulting from the more recent influx of Colombians and Ecuadorians. This would reflect the shift in Spain's receiving policies (Izquierdo 2004: 30) but also the increasingly polarised perceptions about the culturally defined 'other' when it comes to the assessment of naturalisation requirements that refer to the assimilation of immigrants into Spanish society.

13.3.3 Special Categories

Together with the general regime on nationality one should also note the existence of a special regime for nationals of certain countries or cultures with which Spain is said to have either a historical debt, special ties of cultural affinity or a logical combination of the two. The special treatment is limited to two features. One is the shortening of residence time required to naturalise and the other one the existence of a conventional and/or legal regime of dual nationality.

As we saw, Spain's general residence requirement for residence-based naturalisation is ten years. Two years is, however, sufficient for nationals of Latin American countries, Andorra, the Philippines, Equatorial Guinea, Portugal or Sephardic Jews.[34] In the nationality reform proposals discussed lately, both the socialist and the United Left parliamentary groups have suggested the convenience of extending this option in favour of nationals of the EU, the descendants of the Moors (who were expelled in similar ways as the Sephardic Jews) and the people from the Sahara for the circumstances under which Spain abandoned the then Spanish province (Lara Aguado 2003: 7). This would thus expand the circle of persons to whom Spain acknowledges a historical debt or with whom it recognises special ties.

As for tolerance of dual nationality (see Aguilar Benítez de Lugo 1996), starting in the 1950s Spain signed a series of dual nationality covenants with many Latin American countries, recognising an affinity in traditions, culture and language.[35] Strictly speaking these treaties did not recognise two nationalities but rather created a system of active/dormant nationality which meant that the two nationalities were never active at the same time. In general (although there are slight variations), these treaties provide that the exercising of rights, diplomatic protection, the granting of passports and all other social, civil and employment rights will be ruled by the legal system of the country in which the person resides. The same applies to military obligations.

Being a national of one of the countries does not entail automatic acquisition of the Spanish nationality. Rather, the person still has to fulfil all the applicable legal conditions (arts. 22 and 23 of the Civil Code) with the one single exception of Guatemala where the two-year residence requirement is automatically waived.

The 1978 Constitution echoed this tradition. Indeed, art. 11.3 in the Constitution authorises Spain to sign dual nationality agreements with Ibero-American countries as well as with other countries that have or have had special links with Spain. The same provision recognises that with regards to those countries, Spanish nationals can naturalise without losing their nationality of origin.

In spite of the constitutional sanctioning, the practice has been discontinued and practically replaced with a system of legal, as opposed to conventional, dual nationality, starting in 1990 when the Civil Code was amended to allow for dual nationality of nationals from Latin American countries, Andorra, the Philippines, Equatorial Guinea and Portugal to acquire Spanish nationality through residence (art. 23.b and 24.1). Consistent with this, Spanish nationals voluntarily acquiring the nationality of those countries do not lose their Spanish nationality (24.5). Also, from 1990 onwards, those applying for the recovery of Spanish nationality were exempted from relinquishing to their prior nationality if that nationality was the nationality of one of those countries. This comparative advantage became moot in 2002 when the renunciation requirement was removed altogether for those applying for the reacquisition of their lost nationality.

13.3.4 *Institutional arrangements*

The Spanish Constitution of 1978 breaks with Spain's constitutional history in that it does not purport to set the rules for nationality issues. Art. 11.1 of the Constitution refers the matter to further legislation when it says that 'the Spanish nationality is acquired, kept and lost according to the laws'. Although Spain is a quasi-federal country with seventeen so-called Autonomous Communities, each with legislative powers, the Constitution entrusts the regulation on nationality exclusively to the central state (art. 149.1.2 of the Constitution). The Constitution distinguishes between several types of legislation. Some matters, mainly those of 'constitutional nature' (i.e., legislation on constitutional rights or on the country's political institutions and system) are subject to regulation by organic law (art. 81 of the Constitution). Such legislation requires an absolute majority in Congress, which represents a high degree of political consensus among the parliamentary parties. Because nationality legislation is referred to in art. 11 and has not been included under art. 81 there is a general understanding that it need not be covered by organic laws and in fact it has not been (Pérez Vera 1984: 230-240).

Unlike most of its European counterparts Spain has never had legislation exclusively focused on nationality. Rather, as we have seen, it has consistently ruled on nationality through the Civil Code. Dedicated to many other subject matters the nationality rules in the Civil Code are contained in just eleven of the 1976 provisions in the Code. If one adds to these the five procedural provisions contained in the Legislation on the Civil Registry we have a total of sixteen legal provisions dedicated to this subject matter. Needless to say, administrative regulations and guidelines have been necessary to fill in the legislative gaps (see Carrascosa González & Sánchez Jiménez 2002). This practice has been criticised for not respecting the constitutional mandate that nationality be regulated by *law* (Fernández Rozas 1987: 90), especially in view of the fact that many of these guidelines (such as those of 1983 after the 1982 legal reform) have been restrictive in nature. The General Directorate of Registers and Notaries (*Dirección General de los Registros y del Notariado)*[36] (DGRN) produces such administrative guidelines.

The DGRN is the main administrative body in charge of deciding on the acquisition and loss of nationality. In those cases where there is virtually no discretion involved (such as acquisition by option) so that what is asked for is technically speaking an act of *ex lege* declaration (and not a decision strictly speaking) the procedure is instantiated in front of the judge in charge of the Civil Registry where the applicant's birth is recorded or his or her place of residence if the applicant was born in Spain, but if the procedure is not successful an appeal may be submitted to the DGRN within 30 days. After that the judicial path is open to the applicant and he or she can submit their case to a civil court. In the case of acquisition by residence a decision is taken, within one year of the application, by the DGRN, acting in the name of the Ministry of Justice. Every six months the official bulletin publishes a list with the names of those persons who have acquired nationality by residence. If the application is denied the person in question can appeal the decision to the administrative judicial order (21.2 CC). The decisions of the DGRN, together with those of the judges who eventually get to revise them, and especially those of the Supreme Court (which, in the Spanish system are the only ones which are granted value of legally binding precedent) have also become a rich yet diverse and not always consistent source of interpretation of the nationality law. In view of the increasing foreign population and hence the increasing importance of access to nationality as a source of integration it seems more and more compelling that there be a piece of legislation specifically dedicated to regulating nationality.

Moreover, one needs to take into account that the judges in charge of the several Civil Registries (49 in Spain, one in each of the main provinces plus a Central Registry in Madrid) as well as consular and diplomatic offices abroad all apply the nationality legislation so that there is space for diverging interpretations. For instance, it is the judge of the Civil Registry of the place of residence of the applicant who will interview the applicant for residence-based naturalisation and thus decide, in principle, whether he or she is of good moral character and is sufficiently integrated into Spanish society. While in the past only a minimum knowledge of Spanish was tested in an informal interview and societal integration was evaluated based on responses to very simple questions (such as whether the applicant has friends in Spain, the kinds of activities that they and their children do, the things they like or dislike about the Spanish culture), the DGRN is now insisting that the judges of the Civil Registries start asking more specifically about Spanish democratic institutions or history.

13.4 Conclusions

In almost every aspect of its nationality regime Spain has always looked to the past. Since the nineteenth century it has relied on brief constitutional references and the Civil Code as a locus of regulation without fully embracing the public law dimension of the subject. With some changes, the substance of this law also portrays Spain's self-image as a net sender and/or receiver of migration. It still very much favours ius sanguinis over ius soli, it still asks foreigners to reside in Spain for ten years and give up their prior nationality before they can acquire a Spanish one. The transformation of Spain into a net receiver of migration flows has not yet changed Spain's historical view of the matter. The focus has been, at least since the 1978 Constitution was enacted, that of trying to remedy past wrongs. Indeed, up to this day the only politically salient matter has been how to attend to the needs of those who were forced to emigrate because of rough socio-economic conditions of the past and, as a result of that, have lost their Spanish nationality or seen their descendants lose theirs. More recently another wound of the past is crying for justice, namely that of the people who, as a result of the civil war or Franco's dictatorship, had to leave the country with similar consequences for themselves and their descendants in terms of loss of nationality.

Over the past decade the challenges of the present are pressing for a forward looking nationality regime. The increasing presence of immigrants renders the issue of nationality as a key to integration more pertinent than ever. In this regard, certain reforms of the nationality legislation seem most relevant. One would be the expansion of ius soli to allow people born in the country to acquire Spanish nationality, at least if it can be shown that the parents are permanently settled in Spain or to allow them to opt for Spanish nationality once they turn of age if they were born in Spain. Another obvious one would be reducing the period of residence required for naturalisation from ten to five years as a rule.

There is one domain in which demands of the past and the present, each valid in its own terms and considered separately, clash when they come to be perceived jointly. It is the privileged treatment that certain nationals are receiving vis-à-vis others. Taking numbers into account, one may divide the immigrant population into two large groups: one, formed by immigrants from Latin America, and one formed mostly by Moroccans as well as other people coming from Africa and Asia. The former is provided a much easier path to inclusion through nationality. Beyond the rhetoric of cultural affinity one could make the argument that there is a reparations-based claim on the part of Latin American countries due to Spain's history of conquest and exploitation in the new world. On the other hand, the exclusion of the largest non-European foreign population from this faster track to integration, namely Moroccans, is worrisome, not least because of the religious and cultural overtones that such exclusion is doomed to have in our times. Neither the argument concerning cultural ties (much of Spain was under muslim rule for over seven centuries) nor the argument of historical wrongs can sufficiently justify the differentiation (think of the inclusion of descendants of Sephardic Jews among the privileged group in contrast with the exclusion of the Moors who were also expelled from Spain at the end of the fifteenth century).

Probably the best way out of this conundrum is to bring the two closer by redefining and making the rules for inclusion more flexible altogether, avoiding at the same time any bias in the degree of symbolic recognition. Once again, expanding ius soli, shortening the general residence time for naturalisation, and maybe also giving up the rule requiring prior renunciation of nationality altogether would be the best way to advance towards the right balance. Moreover, in the midst of the construction of a European polity, nationals from other European Union Member States (still the largest foreign population in Spain) should not be left out of the fast track option. However, including them while leaving Moroccans out would only sharpen the distinctions that already prevail, fuelling the perception of cultural bias.

Avoiding bias and prejudice is not only going to be essential in shaping forward looking nationality legislation but also in ensuring its fair application. Legal certainty will prove to be essential and will require putting legislation in the place thus far occupied by administrative guidelines and precedents set by the courts and administrative bodies. Also, vague clauses, such a 'general interest', 'public order', 'sufficient social integration' and 'good civic conduct', for the most part loosely and generously interpreted in the past, will require concretisation as the question of the naturalisation of immigrants gains political profile, as it will presumably do over the next decade, unless we let nationality become the new gate for exclusion that it has become in other countries with a longer tradition of immigration.

Chronological table of major reforms in Spanish nationality law since 1945

Date	Document	Content of change
15 July 1954	Statute of July 1954 (Ley de 15 / 1954 sobre reforma del Código Civil en materia de nacionalidad)	Reform of the Civil Code on matters of nationality.
31 May 1974	Decree 1836/1974 (Decreto 1836/ 1974)	Reform of the Civil Code.
2 May 1975	Statute 14/1975 (Ley 14/1975 sobre reforma de determinados artículos del Código Civil sobre la situación jurídica de la mujer casada)	Reform of the civil and commercial code, pertaining to married women's legal statues.
1978	Spanish Constitution (Constitución Española)	
13 July 1982	Statute 51/1982 (Ley 51/1982 de modificación de los artículos 17 al 26 del Código Civil)	Reform of nationality legislation in the Civil Code: gender equality; expansion of ius soli; reinforcement of dual nationality.
17 December 1990	Statute 18/1990 (Ley 18/1990 sobre reforma del Código Civil en materia de nacionalidad)	Reform of nationality legislation in the Civil Code: easier naturalisation of political refugees; reinforcement of dual nationality; reacquisition of nationality; acquisition by possession of status.
23 December 1993	Statute 15/1993 (Ley 15/1993 por la que se prorroga plazo para ejercer la opción por la nacionalidad espanola)	Reform of nationality legislation in the Civil Code: extension of period of amnesty for reacquisition of Spanish nationality.
2 November 1995	Statute 29/1995 (Ley 29/1995 por la que se modifica el Código Civil en materia de recuperación de nacionalidad)	Reform of nationality legislation in the Civil Code: reacquisition of Spanish nationality.
23 November 1995	Organic Statute 10/1995 (Ley Orgánica 10/1995 de reforma del Código Penal)	Reform of the criminal code: removal of loss of nationality because of criminal offence.
8 October 2002	Statute 36/2002 (Ley 36/2002 de modificación del Código Civil en materia de nacionalidad)	Reform of nationality legislation in the Civil Code: reacquisition of Spanish nationality; reinforcement of dual nationality.

Notes

1 Traditionally, Spanish citizenship law has distinguished between 'nationality by origin' (*nacionalidad originaria*) and 'derivative nationality' (*nacionalidad derivativa*). Whereas the former used to refer, and still does for the most part, to instances of automatic acquisition and acquisition at birth, the latter was usually reserved for non-automatic and acquisition after birth. Currently the Spanish legal system still refers to these two modes of acquisition although it provides for instances in which 'nationality by origin' is not acquired at the moment of birth and requires application.

2 Typically, emancipation comes either upon achieving majority, at eighteen, when a minor marries, with consent of those exercising *patria potestas*, or with judicial authorisation, see art. 314 of the CC.

3 All of the following Spanish constitutions made some reference to Spain's nationality regime: the Constitution of 1812; that of 1837 which inspired the regime that would then be reproduced by the Constitutions of 1845, 1869 and 1876 ultimately influencing the 1889 Civil Code legislation.

4 In the first third of the nineteenth century the American colonies of Spain gained independence with the exception of Cuba and Puerto Rico who gained independence in 1898. In the 1850s and 1860s Spain signed treaties of peace, cooperation and recognition with its former American colonies which laid down the preferential treatment to be given to Spanish migrants in those countries in terms of the ability to settle, as well as the possibility of gaining the nationality of the host country without automatically losing their Spanish nationality (Moreno Fuentes 2001: 120).

5 This idea of an Ibero-American community of nationals in which dual nationality would be tolerated anticipated a policy introduced in the 1950s, when a series of dual nationality agreements were established between Spain and several Latin American countries.

6 Statute of 15 July 1954 which was developed by a Decree of 2 April 1955.

7 Reform of the Civil Code by the Statute of 2 May 1975 specifically concerned the nationality of married women and was developed by the Internal Order of the General Directorate of Registries and Notaries of 22 May 1975.
Around the same time some legal measures were also enacted to guarantee residents of some former Spanish colonies in Africa a right to option for Spanish nationality (Royal Decree 2978/1977 for Equatorial Guinea independent since 1968; Treaty of 4 January 1969 by which Ifni was returned to Morocco and the Royal Decree 2258/1976 regarding the end of the Spanish administration over the Sahara). However the many administrative hurdles and the fact that some of these measures were enacted only many years after independence made them relatively useless.

8 Moreno Fuentes 2001, citing sources of *Anuario de Migraciones*, 1997, Madrid: Ministerio de Asuntos Sociales, 1998.

9 This reform was enacted by the Statute 51/1982 of 13 July and was developed by the Instruction of the DGRN of 16 May.

10 See Statute 51/1982 of 13 July, modifying arts. 17-26 of the Civil Code.

11 The Communist Party insisted that nationality in Spain should stop being regulated through the few provisions in the Civil Code dedicated to it and, following the example of other European countries, should instead be the object of a special statute dedicated exclusively and in much more depth to its regulation.

12 Another way to protect emigrants and thereby respect the constitutional mandate to do so, was to foresee, for the first time, that they could recover Spanish nationality, had they lost it, with exemption from the otherwise general requirement of being residents in Spain (art. 24.4 II of the Civil Code).

13 Statute 18/1990, of 17 December, modifying the civil mode in matters of nationality, which was developed by the Instruction of General Directorate of Registries and Notaries (*Dirección General de los Registros y del Notariado*, henceforth DGRN) of 20 March 1991.
14 See Statute 15/1993 of 23 December and Statute 29/1995 of 2 November modifying art. 26 of the Civil Code on the recovery of the Spanish nationality.
15 Organic Statute (*Ley Organica*) 4/2000 of 11 January on rights and freedoms of foreigners, reformed first by Organic Statute 8/2000 of 22 December and most recently by Organic Statute 14/2003 of 20 November.
16 See the 'Official Parliamentary Journal' (*Boletín Oficial de las Cortes Generales*, henceforth BOCG): Bills presented by the 'Federal Parliamentary Group of the United Left' (*Grupo Parlamentario Federal de Izquierda Unida*) on the amendment of nationality law: BOCG, 'Congress of Members of Parliament' (*Congreso de los Diputados*), VI Legislatura, Serie B, 7 December 1998, num. 261-1 and later, BOCG, Serie B, 26 October 2002, num. 168-1. Bills presented by the Socialist Group in Congress (*Grupo Socialist del Congreso*) on the amendment of nationality law: BOCG, 'Congress of Members of Parliament' (*Congreso de los Diputados*), VI Legislatura, Serie B, 22 February 1999, num. 278-1 and later, BOCG, Serie B, 9 March 2001, num. 115-1. After the 2002 nationality reform was passed, the socialist group presented another bill, namely, BOCG, 'Congress of Members of Parliament' (*Congreso de los Diputados*), VII Legislatura, Serie B: proposición de Ley, 28 February 2003, num. 305-1. As for the bills presented by the Popular Party Parliamentary Group (*Grupo Parlamentario Popular*) these were: BOCG, 'Congress of Members of Parliament' (*Congreso de los Diputados)*, VI Legislatura, Serie B, 10 May 1999, num. 303-1 and later, BOCG, Serie B, 16 March 2001, num. 122-1. This last bill was the one approved with only small changes.
17 See BOCG of 27 February 1998.
18 This is the popular name given to about 3000 children who, between 1937 and 1938, were evacuated from Spain by the Republican government to several countries, mostly to the Soviet Union. The loss of the civil war in 1939, the immediate breakout of the Second World War and the Cold War never allowed these children to return to their families in Spain.
19 To set this in perspective, one should bear in mind that the Spanish Parliament did not pass a unanimous resolution condemning the Franco regime until 20 November 2002, that is 27 years after Franco's death. A group called *Morados* was formed in 2002 at the initiative of a group of young Mexicans who are descendants of Spanish people who went into exile. Relying mostly on the internet, they have helped organise all those in similar situations in other countries to push forward a request for Spanish nationality for the children and grandchildren of Spaniards who went into exile.
20 Statute on the Civil Registry (*Ley del Registro Civil)*, of 8 June 1957 and Executive Decree of 14 November 1958.
21 The Spanish Civil Code provides that non-emancipated children are under the *potestas* of both the mother and the father. This *patria potestas* is exercised jointly by both the father and the mother unless they are separated in which case the person with whom the child lives will, in principle, exercises the *potestas*. See art. 154 and 156 CC.
22 The Emigration Council is a consultative body ascribed to the Ministry of Employment and Social Affairs, General Directorate for the Regulation of Migration: *Direccion General de la Ordenacion de la migraciones*. For years it has articulated the claims of Spanish expatriates and emigrants and their descendants.
23 See also Supreme Court decision of 1 July 2002.
24 Probably in fulfilment of art. 34 of the UN Convention of 28 July 1951, which Spain signed in 1978, which refers to the duty of states to facilitate and accelerate the

possibility for refugees to acquire their nationality as well as simplifying the procedures as far as possible.

25 See, further, decision of 19 September 1988.

26 See also Resolution of the DGRN (*Resolución de DGRN*) 1 of 27 November 2001 (BIMJ), num. 1910: 412-414.

27 See for instance, Supreme Court, decision of 23 May 2001, allowing a foreign student to count all of the time legally and effectively spent in Spain regardless of the technicalities of the student's permit under the immigration legislation.

28 See decision by the Supreme Court of 12 May 1997, 2 June 1998, and 16 March 1999.

29 See decisions of the Supreme Court for 19 December 2002; 5 November 2001; 12 March 2002 and 5 October 2002.

30 See Supreme Court decision of 24 October 2001.

31 It was abolished by the Royal Decrees 247/2001 of 9 March and 342/2001 of 4 April.

32 This table includes numbers of acquisitions by residence (entitlement) and by discretionary naturalisation in exceptional circumstances. Statistics on acquisitions by option (persons whose descent from a national is established after minority; persons born in Spain whose descent from a foreign national born in Spain is determined after minority; persons under patria potestas of a Spanish national; persons aged eighteen and above adopted by a Spanish national; persons with a parent who was born in Spain and was originally a Spanish national) or declaration (reacquisition by Spanish nationals 'by origin') have never been produced.

33 Anuario Estadístico de Extranjería, Ministerio de Interior extranjeros.mtas.es/es/general/DatosEstadisticos_index.html.

34 According to the instruction of the DGRN of 16 May 1983 one can prove one's condition as a Sephardic Jew through one's family name, family language as well as other indicia, the belonging to the Sephardic Jewish religion being only one of them.

35 These include those signed with Chile (24 May 1958), Peru (16 May 1959), Paraguay (15 June 1959), Nicaragua (15 June 1961), Guatemala (28 July 1961), Bolivia (12 October 1961), Ecuador (4 March 1964), Costa Rica (8 June 1964), Honduras (15 June 1966), Dominican Republic (15 March 1968), Argentina (14 April 1969), Colombia (27 June 1979).

36 This administrative body is ascribed to the Justice department and is divided into two sub-directorates, one dealing with civil status and nationality and the other one with notary public and property.

Bibliography

Abarca Junco, P & E. Pérez Vera (1997), in Pérez Vera et al. (eds.), *Derecho Internacional Privado*, vol. 1, 3rd edition. Madrid: Universidad de Educación a Distancia.

Aguilar Benítez de Lugo, M. (1996), 'Doble Nacionalidad', *Boletín de la Facultad de Derecho* 10-11: 219-262.

Alvarez Rodríguez, A. (1990), *Nacionalidad y Emigración*. Madrid: La Ley.

Carrascosa González, J. & M. A. Sánchez Jiménez (2002), *Legislación sobre Nacionalidad y Extranjería Comentada y con Jurisprudencia*. Madrid: Colex.

Castro y Bravo, F. de (1952), *Derecho civil de España. Derecho de la persona*, vol. 2. Madrid: I.E.P.

Diez del Corral Rivas, J. (1991), 'Comentario al art. 22 CC', in *Comentarios del Código Civil* vol. 1, 202-203. Madrid: Ministerio de Justicia.

Díez-Picazo, L. (2003), *Sistema de Derecho Civil I*, 11th edition. Madrid: Tecnos.

Espinar Vicente, J.M. (1986), *Derecho Internacional Privado. Derecho Internacional Privado Español*, vol. 2: *La nacionalidad*. Granada: Comares.

Fernández Rozas, J.C. (1987), *Derecho Español de la Nacionalidad*. Madrid: Tecnos.

García Rubio, M.P. (1992), 'Consolidación de la nacionalidad española', *Anuario de Derecho Civil*: 980-991.

Izquierdo, A. (2004), 'Cambios en la Inmigración a Resultas de la Política Restrictiva del Gobierno Español', *CCIS, Working Paper* 109.

Lara Aguado, A. (2003) 'Nacionalidad e Integración Social: a propósito de la Ley 36/2002 de 8 de octubre', *La Ley* 24 (5694): 1-11.

Lete del Río, J.M. (1984), *La nueva regulación de la nacionalidad*. Madrid: Editorial Civitas.

Lete del Río, J.M. (1994), 'La adquisición de la nacionalidad por opción', *Actualidad Civil* 1: 27.

Marín López, A. (2002), 'La adquisición de la nacionalidad española por opción en la reciente doctrinal registral', *Boletín de Información del Ministerio de Justicia* 16 (1925): 2859-2882.

Morán del Casero, J. (2002) 'Procedimientos sobre nacionalidad española', in F. González Navarro (ed.), *Procedimientos administrativos especiales*, vol II, 453-490. Madrid: Escuela Nacional de Adeministración Pública.

Moreno Fuentes, F. J. (2001), 'Migration and Spanish Nationality Law', in R. Hansen & P. Weil (eds.), *Towards a European Nationality. Citizenship, Immigration and Nationality Law in the EU*, 118-142. New York: Palgrave.

Palao Moreno, G. (2001), *Nacionalidad y extranjería*. Valencia: Tirant lo Blanch.

Pérez de Vargas Muñoz, J. (2003), 'Nacionalidad y extranjería: algunos aspectos civiles', *Boletín Informativo Ministerio de Justicia*, 15 de diciembre 2003: 4072-4101.

Pérez Vera, E. (1984), 'Artículo 13', in A. Villaamil (ed.), *Comentarios a las leyes políticas*, vol. 2, arts. 10 a 23, 230-240. Madrid: Edersa.

Pretel Serrano, J.J. (1994), 'La adquisición de la nacionalidad española en la Ley 18/1990, de 17 de diciembre', *Jornadas sobre nacionalidad y extranjería*. Centro de Estudios Registrales.

Rubio C. & M. Escudero (2003) 'Nacionalidad y ciudadanía: una relación a debate', *Ciudadanía e Inmigración, Anales de la Cátedra de Francisco Suárez* 37: 105-155.

14 Sweden

Hedvig Lokrantz Bernitz and Henrik Bernitz

14.1 Introduction

The Instrument of Government *(regeringsformen)*, which is the fundamental law that lays down the basic principles by which the Swedish State is governed, states in Chapter 8 art. 2 that provisions relating to Swedish citizenship are laid down in law. The provisions are found in the Swedish Citizenship Act (2001: 82). This law, however, gives no information concerning the particular legal effects of national citizenship; these must instead be sought in other parts of Swedish legislation. The Swedish Citizenship Act merely concerns the acquisition and loss of citizenship, as well as procedures.

For a long time the ius sanguinis tradition has been predominant in Sweden, however it was expressly stated for the first time in the Citizenship Act of 1894. Since then, nationality reforms have taken place in 1924, 1950 and 2001, and ius sanguinis has remained the principal rule, even though the principle of domicile gained importance through the Citizenship Act of 2001. Since 1979, by an amendment to the Citizenship Act of 1950, a child acquires Swedish citizenship at birth if its mother is Swedish. It does not matter if the child is born in Sweden or abroad, or whether it is born in wedlock or not. If the mother is foreign, automatic acquisition is however possible through a Swedish father if the child is born in Sweden or born in wedlock.

Even though many provisions of the Act of 2001 are based on old traditions and are a product of continuous legal development, the act has in several aspects entailed a new attitude and is a consequence of the modernisation of society. The acceptance of dual citizenship and the emphasis on the principle of domicile belong primarily here. Another innovation is that the law is not based on Nordic cooperation. Instead, the law is based on the European Convention on Nationality from 1997.

As to the issue of dual citizenship, Sweden previously had, like many other countries, a negative attitude which was reflected in its national legislation. Sweden has, however, through the Citizenship Act of 2001 changed its attitude to a positive one. Dual citizenship is fully accepted, in every situation. Much of the development in this area is related to the reduced significance of national citizenship for an individual's status in the state, as Sweden has increasingly been equalising the rights of citizens and foreigners. A Swedish citizen, who is a dual citizen, is practically always considered a Swede, and the fact that the person also has a foreign citizenship is normally ignored when Swedish law is applied.

There are no categories of citizenship, or any quasi-citizenship in Sweden. Every Swede (born a Swede or naturalised, male or female) has the same legal position, and the same rights and duties. This is also the case with expatriates (they have, for example, the right to vote for Parliament). However, a person who has completely lost contact with Sweden, i.e., a person who is born abroad and who has never lived in Sweden or been in Sweden under circumstances that indicate a link with the country, normally loses his or her citizenship according to statutory limitations at the age of 22. The loss also includes his or her children, unless the other parent still holds Swedish citizenship and the child also derives Swedish citizenship from him or her. This is the only way that Swedish citizenship can be lost involuntarily.

Swedish citizenship has, since the late nineteenth century, been dealt with in Nordic cooperation. Sweden has however abandoned this cooperation through the Swedish Citizenship Act of 2001. Nevertheless, Nordic citizens (i.e., citizens from Denmark, Finland, Norway and Iceland) still enjoy benefits compared to people originating from other countries. Apart from facilitated naturalisation, a Nordic citizen can acquire Swedish citizenship by notification. Acquisition of Swedish citizenship by notification is a simplified, formal procedure whereby a person can become a Swedish citizen if he or she satisfies certain legal requirements. A person who meets the legal requirements cannot be denied citizenship. As a consequence of the increased importance of the principle of domicile the possibility of notifications was extended to embrace new groups through the Citizenship Act of 2001. One of the objectives was to encourage the integration of immigrants.

A person who does not fulfil the legal requirements for acquisition by notification has to apply for naturalisation to become a Swedish citizen. Sweden has, for a very long time, had a rather high proportion of acquisition of citizenship among long-term resident immigrants. The barriers for naturalisation are not very high in Sweden compared to many other countries. Instead, the possibilities of appling for naturalisation are rather generous. Since the 1920s, the rules on naturalisation have basically remained unchanged, and amendments made have often weakened the conditions for naturalisation (Sandesjö & Björk 2005: 180). The former requirement that an applicant should have enough means to support him- or herself was, for example, abolished in 1976. The former language requirement was also abolished during the

1970s. Some requirements have however been sharpened, for example the proof of identity requirement and the good conduct requirement.

When the Citizenship Act of 1950 came into force, men and women were already given an equal position under nationality law. Except for the fact that citizenship is acquired at birth if the mother is Swedish but not necessarily if only the father is Swedish, there are no other gender inequalities in any mode of acquisition or loss of citizenship. The possibility to acquire Swedish citizenship through marriage was abolished by the law of 1950, but if an applicant is married to a Swede or living in conditions resembling marriage with a Swede exemptions may be granted from the requirements for naturalisation (in most cases the period of domicile).

14.2 Historical development

14.2.1 Early historical developments and the Royal Ordinance of 1858

During early historical periods, from the Middle Ages to the sixteenth century when the nation-state became an important concept, every person living permanently in Sweden was considered a Swede, whether born in the country or not (Lokrantz Bernitz 2004: 73). Franchise, as well as marriage to a Swedish woman, was enough to prove a true and permanent immigration. From the sixteenth century onwards, the king had, in practice, the right to naturalise foreigners and grant Swedish citizenship, but the differences between citizens and foreigners were not always significant. During the seventeenth and eighteenth centuries, Swedish nationality law began developing. A Swedish citizen was then a person born in the country and whose parents were Swedish, and a person from a foreign country who had his permanent residence in Sweden. From the beginning of the nineteenth century a formal naturalisation of foreigners was demanded.

In 1809, a new Instrument of Government was enacted. It contained some of the first expressions of a modern nation-state in Sweden. Naturalisation was however not clarified, and a new provision, regulating naturalisation of foreign men, was therefore introduced in the Instrument of Government in 1856-57. The provision was specified in a royal ordinance of 1858 on regulations and conditions for foreign men to be registered as a Swedish citizen,[1] and this ordinance was the first true nationality law in Sweden. The scope of the ordinance was however rather limited, as the provisions only dealt with naturalisation of foreign men (Lokrantz Bernitz 2004: 75). Nevertheless, this early ordinance already stated that a person, who applied for naturalisation, had to prove that he was no longer the subject of a foreign state.

Apart from the regulations on naturalisation in the ordinance of 1858, Swedish citizenship was still not codified and other means of acquisition and loss were decided in case law and administrative practice. The case law was however neither integrated nor uniform and the need for codification became more and more obvious, not least because of Sweden's growing international relations. At the end of the nineteenth century and the beginning of the twentieth century Sweden had turned into an emigration country, and between 1850 and 1930 almost 1.2 million people left Sweden to settle in other parts of the world, mostly in North America. It was not until the end of the nineteenth century however that firmer nationality rules were developed. In the 1890s, a Nordic cooperation on nationality developed.

14.2.2 *The Citizenship Act of 1894*

In Sweden, Nordic cooperation resulted in the law of 1894 on the acquisition and loss of (Swedish) citizen's rights.[2] This law was, in principle, a codification of rules already existing in practice. In only two aspects did the law contain new rules; automatic acquisition of citizenship on the grounds of socialisation, and the loss of citizenship for persons who had been domiciled abroad for an extended period, and their possibility to recover citizenship by resuming residence in the country. The royal ordinance of 1858 still applied and contained the provisions on naturalisation.

As mentioned above, the ius sanguinis principle was expressly laid down in the Citizenship Act of 1894 for the first time, but the principle had already been generally accepted in customary law for some time. According to sect. 1 of the Act, a child born in wedlock acquired Swedish citizenship by birth through its father. For children born out of wedlock the mother's citizenship was however determinative.

A novelty, introduced by the law of 1894, concerned socialisation-based acquisition of citizenship. Foreigners (men and unmarried women) born and since birth resident in the country, acquired Swedish citizenship automatically at the age of 22, unless the person renounced the citizenship and proved that he or she had a foreign citizenship (sect. 2). If a man acquired citizenship according to this rule, the acquisition also included his wife and children.

The citizenship of a married woman was dependent on her husband's citizenship. A woman who married a Swedish man automatically acquired Swedish citizenship (sect. 3). This also included any child of theirs born before their marriage and who had not reached the age of majority. A Swedish woman who married a foreigner lost her Swedish citizenship, whether or not she acquired her husband's citizenship (sect. 6). The same applied for the couple's unmarried children.

Dual citizenship was not accepted in the law of 1894 and consequently, a Swede who acquired a foreign citizenship lost his Swedish citizenship, no matter where he was resident (sect. 5).

Loss of Swedish citizenship was also stated for men and unmarried women who had been living abroad for ten years (sect. 7). Unless the stay abroad was part of official employment citizenship was lost if the person in question did not make a statement that he or she wished to retain Swedish citizenship. Such a statement had to be renewed every ten years. If a man lost his citizenship according to this provision then the loss also included his wife and children. A person, who had lost his or her Swedish citizenship by residing abroad, could recover it by simply resuming residence in Sweden. It was, however, on condition that the person had not acquired a foreign citizenship in the meantime (sect. 8). The rule was supplemented in 1909 with a provision laying down that a Swede who had become a citizen of a foreign state, with which Sweden had an agreement, would be considered as losing the foreign citizenship upon returning permanently to Sweden. As a consequence, the person recovered his Swedish citizenship. Due to the emigration from Sweden, such agreements had already been concluded with the US (where 97 per cent of the Swedish emigrants settled) in 1869 and with Argentina in 1885 (Lokrantz Bernitz 2004: 155).

14.2.3 *The Citizenship Act of 1924*

In 1924, a new Citizenship Act on the acquisition and loss of Swedish citizenship[3] came into force, and just like the previous Act, it was a product of Nordic cooperation.

Unlike the law of 1894, the title of the new Act included the expression 'citizenship' (the previous law had used the expression 'citizen's rights'), as 'citizenship' was considered as indicating that the legal relationship between the individual and the state not only included rights but also duties.

Contrary to the Act of 1894, the new Citizenship Act contained provisions on naturalisation, and the royal ordinance of 1858 was thus repealed. According to sect. 5, a foreigner who had reached the age of 21, who had been residing in the country for five years, who was known to lead a respectable life and who could support his family, could be naturalised. If the applicant could not prove the loss of his or her foreign citizenship, it was laid down as a condition that such proof should be provided within a certain period of time. Exceptions to the requirements of naturalisation were possible if it was for the benefit of the country, if the person had formerly held Swedish citizenship or if there were other special reasons for granting citizenship. Exemptions were however neither granted from the good conduct requirement, nor from the support requirement (Fahlbeck, Jägerskiöld & Sundberg 1947: 96).

Apart from the rules on naturalisation the provisions on acquisition laid down in the former Act of 1894 remained basically unchanged. The right to recover Swedish citizenship by resuming residence in the country was however limited to those who had acquired Swedish citizenship by birth, but later lost their citizenship (sect. 4). The re-acquisition was automatic.

The most important novelties in the law of 1924 concerned loss of citizenship. In the previous Citizenship Act, loss of Swedish citizenship due of the acquisition of a foreign nationality had not been dependent on the person's habitual residence. According to the Act of 1924 a person who acquired a foreign citizenship only lost his Swedish citizenship if he took up residence in the other country (sect. 8).

Loss of citizenship for people permanently residing abroad was also fundamentally altered. Instead of losing his or her Swedish citizenship after ten years abroad, as the law of 1894 had provided, a Swedish man or unmarried woman lost Swedish citizenship at the age of 22 if he or she was born abroad and never had been domiciled in Sweden (sect. 9). The loss could however be avoided if permission to retain citizenship was granted. The political reason behind this change of attitude was the fact that a true affinity with the country was now regarded as essential for citizenship, and families living abroad should not be allowed to retain their Swedish citizenship for generations if they had lost every link with the country.

14.2.4 *The Citizenship Act of 1950*

After the Second World War a review of the Nordic countries' nationality laws was considered necessary and the Nordic cooperation was resumed. In Sweden, this resulted in a new law in 1950 on Swedish citizenship.[4] The law of 1950 was based on three major principles: the ius sanguinis tradition, the wish to avoid statelessness, and the fact that double citizenship should be avoided (Sandesjö & Björk 2005: 25). The Act resembled the previous nationality laws in many ways, but there were also some major changes. One of the most important changes concerned the position of married women. Before the law of 1950 a married woman had been dependent on her husband, and changes in the husband's nationality also affected his wife. Now married women were given an independent position; if a foreign woman married a Swedish man this had no other effect on her nationality than facilitating her acquisition of Swedish citizenship, and if a Swedish woman married a foreigner she kept her Swedish citizenship.

Concerning the issue of children, the original wording of the Citizenship Act of 1950 did not introduce any major changes, and children born in wedlock still acquired the father's citizenship (sect. 1). It was already noted in the legal history of the Act (*traveaux preparatoires*) however that the application of the principle of equal rights of man and woman would imply that a child born in wedlock would acquire Swedish citizenship if the mother was Swedish. As most other countries still upheld the principle of the father's citizenship being determinative, a logical consequence of a change in Sweden would, however, have been a large number of persons holding dual citizenship. As avoiding dual citizenship was one of the main principles of the Act, acquisition through the mother was not introduced at this stage (Bellander 1996: 645). During the following years the issue was discussed upon several occasions, but it was not until 1979 that the law was altered (again in Nordic cooperation). Since 1979, a child acquires Swedish citizenship by birth primarily through its mother, whether it is born in wedlock or not. One of the reasons for finally changing the law was the fact that the former provision had become old-fashioned, as the equality of opportunities between men and women had increased in many different areas (Sandesjö & Björk 1996: 43). Other countries had already altered their nationality laws in this direction. Another reason was that immigration had increased, and many Swedish women married foreign men with the result that their children did not acquire Swedish citizenship.

In 1950, another novelty introduced was the privileged position given to other Nordic citizens. Negotiations between the Nordic countries preceded the law aimed at placing Nordic citizens on an equal footing, as far as possible. Facilitated naturalisation and the possibility of acquiring citizenship through notification were therefore introduced for Nordic citizens (sects. 6 and 10).

As to the issue of naturalisation, the period of required domicile was initially set to seven years (compared to five years in the Act of 1924), but, apart from this, the major principles of naturalisation remained unchanged in the new Act (sect. 6). Over the years the provision was however amended several times, and in 1976 the period of domicile was set to two years for Nordic citizens and five years for other foreigners. At the same time the requirement that an applicant should be able to support him- or herself and his or her family was abolished. The facility to grant exemptions was extended by the Act of 1950 to cover all naturalisation requirements (Sandesjö & Björk 1996: 95).

Other major changes in Swedish nationality law introduced by the Act of 1950 concerned acquisition through notification for people recovering their Swedish citizenship and for persons who had grown up in Sweden. Concering recovery, the re-acquisition of Swedish citizenship was no longer automatic. Instead, a notification was required (sect. 4). Recovery was however still limited to people born in the country, and the applicant still had to prove that he or she had lost his or her foreign citizenship. As to those who had grown up in the country acquisition was no longer automatic, instead a notification was required (sect. 3). According to the original wording of the provision, a person born in Sweden, who had reached the age of 21 but not yet 23 and who had been domiciled in Sweden uninterruptedly, had an unconditional right to become a Swedish citizen by notification. In 1969, the period of domicile was reduced, and the former condition that the person had to be born in Sweden was abolished. The amendments were a consequence of the Swedish ratification of the UN Convention on the Reduction of Statelessness. In 1979, a new Section (sect. 2a) on notification was introduced because of new provisions in Swedish family law on custody of children. According to sect. 2a a child, who had not acquired Swedish citizenship by birth or by the marriage of its parents, acquired Swedish citizenship through the father by notification if the father was a Swedish citizen at the time of the child's birth, and had custody or joint custody of the child.

Another amendment to the Act, made in 1972, was also related to changes in family law. In family law, adopted children had been given a status equal to the status of other children whenever kinship was required in Swedish law. To avoid dual citizenship an exception was made, however, regarding citizenship. A new sect. 13a was introduced in the Citizenship Act, stating that only if the father or mother adopted a child of their own then the provisions on acquisition or loss because of the mother's or the father's acquisition or loss would apply to the adoptee.

14.2.5 *The Instrument of Government of 1974*

Like most other democracies, Sweden has a written constitution which sets out the rules for political decision-making. Instead of one document, Sweden has four fundamental laws. One of them is the Instrument of Government (*regeringsformen*) which serves as a basis for how Sweden is ruled. According to Chapter 2 art. 7, no citizen who is domiciled in the realm or who has previously been domiciled in the realm may be deprived of his or her citizenship. The provision aims at protecting both citizens living in the country, as well as citizens who have left the country.

The prohibition was first introduced in the Swedish legal system by the present Instrument of Government which came into force in 1974. The prohibition against denationalisation has however not always been an evident feature of Swedish law. In the preparatory work on the Act of 1950 a provision was suggested that would have made it possible to deprive naturalised persons who had committed serious crimes, of their citizenship. The suggested regulation did not correspond to any similar provision in earlier Swedish nationality laws. The Act of 1950 was a product of Nordic cooperation, and the suggestion should be read in the light of bad conditions in the other Nordic countries during the Second World War (in which Sweden did not participate). The suggested provision was however never enacted, as the Council of Legislation considered it being in conflict with the Constitution.

The issue of denationalisation has since then been discussed upon several occasions. In 1994, a Committee of Inquiry examined the possibility of introducing a provision to make it possible to withdraw citizenship from persons who had acquired citizenship by giving false information when applying for naturalisation. The committee concluded that even if it be somewhat offensive that the State cannot apply this effective instrument, the disadvantages of using it would have such ramifications that deprivation of citizenship should not be introduced. The main argument against deprivation was the fact that it would create two kinds of citizenship; one that could never be withdrawn, and one that could. This would put people born as Swedes in a better position, and the important principle of the equality of all before the law would not apply. Family related problems, as well as problems connected to the execution of the decisions were also focused on. Instead of introducing a possibility of deprivation of citizenship, in 1999 Parliament codified the requirement that a person applying for naturalisation must provide proof of his or her identity. This requirement had, until then, been part of case law and administrative practice.

Recently, the issue of denaturalisation has been on the agenda again, and a Commission of Inquiry has submitted a report in 2006 that recommends the introduction of denationalisation.

14.3 Recent developments and current institutional arrangements

14.3.1 Main general modes of acquisition and loss of citizenship

During the fifty years that the Citizenship Act of 1950 was in force, Swedish society changed in substantial ways. The general development placed foreigners domiciled in Sweden on an equal footing with Swedish citizens in a growing number of areas. The principle of domicile thus gained importance, and citizenship correspondingly lost significance. The society also became more and more internationalised, and people lived, worked and studied abroad in a manner that was not predictable in 1950. In 1995, Sweden also joined the EU. Over the years immigration has increased. In 1950, the number of foreign citizens living in Sweden was about 123,000. In 1997, there were about 522,000. The emigration of Swedish citizens was also substantial. Between 1960 and 1997 the net emigration was about 135,600 persons. Some principles of the Act of 1950 consequently lost importance. A modernisation and adjustment to new circumstances was considered necessary, and a new Citizenship Act came into force on 1 July 2001.

Ius sanguinis, as well as the wish to avoid statelessness, have remained main principles of Swedish nationality law. The wish to avoid statelessness remains pertinent, and many provisions in the new Act expressly emphasise the importance of this principle.

Contrary to previous citizenship acts, the Act of 2001, however, fully accepts dual nationality. The reasons previously cited against dual citizenship, such as national security reasons, difficulties with diplomatic protection and problems with military service are today viewed as less significant. There were several reasons for the change of attitude. Apart from the increased importance of the principle of domicile and the internationalisation of Swedish society, the personal advantages were considered very important as people often are truly and genuinely connected to more than one country (Lokrantz Bernitz 2004: 262). Swedish expatriates played an important role in the acceptance of dual citizenship, and had a big influence on the debate preceding the acceptance. In the legal history of the Act, the advantages in practical life of having dual citizenship were also focused on, for example the possibility to visit one's native country without applying for a visa, and the possibility to work and live in both countries without special permission. Keeping the original citizenship was also considered as making it easier for people who were planning to return to their native countries. By enjoying the security and advantages of Swedish citizenship while retaining his or her native citizenship, a person would also, according to the legal history of the Act, feel more at home in Sweden and integrate more quickly into Swedish society. The fact that dual citizenship was already rather common in Sweden due to exemptions granted to the provisions of the Act of 1950, was also an important reason for the new Swedish attitude.

There are three main possibilities for acquiring Swedish citizenship: automatically, by notification, and by application for naturalisation.

Among those who acquire Swedish citizenship automatically are children who acquire citizenship by birth (Citizenship Act, sect. 1). According to the main principle, a child acquires Swedish citizenship by birth if the mother is a Swedish citizen, whether the child is born in Sweden or not. If the mother is an alien, the child can however in some circumstances acquire Swedish citizenship automatically by birth through a Swedish father. As in the Act of 1950, a child acquires Swedish citizenship automatically by birth if the father is a Swedish citizen and married to the child's mother. In the Act of 2001, a new provision, based on ius soli, has also been introduced, stating that a child acquires Swedish citizenship automatically by birth if the father is Swedish citizen and the child is born in Sweden. The reason for giving ius soli increased importance was Sweden's ratification of the European Convention on Nationality, and also the aim to treat children born out of wedlock equally to those born in wedlock (Sandesjö & Björk 2005: 47). The same rules apply if the father has deceased prior to the birth. If there is a risk that Swedish citizenship might be in doubt, then a declaration may be issued on application (sect. 21). Since 2005, a child born from artificial insemination acquires Swedish citizenship at birth if the child has a foreign mother who is legally registered for partnership or cohabiting with a Swedish woman, and the child was born in Sweden.

Automatic acquisition of the father's Swedish citizenship is also the case when the parents get married after the birth of the child (sect. 4). When a Swedish man marries a woman who is an alien, any child of theirs that was born before their marriage and has not acquired Swedish citizenship by birth becomes a Swedish citizen, if the child is unmarried and under eighteen years of age. Also foundlings discovered in Sweden are automatically considered Swedish citizens until indication to the contrary is discovered (sect. 2). This is, however, not an expression of ius soli, but a rule of presumption, as the other rules on acquisition in the Citizenship Act determine the citizenship if the child's origin is discovered.

Some adopted children also acquire Swedish citizenship automatically, namely children adopted in Sweden or in another Nordic country, and children adopted by virtue of a foreign adoption decision approved or otherwise legally valid in Sweden (sect. 3). Automatic acquisition of citizenship for adopted children was first introduced in 1992 by an amendment to the Act of 1950. According to that provision, children adopted in Nordic countries acquired citizenship automatically, while children adopted by virtue of a non Nordic adoption decision valid in Sweden had to apply for naturalisation (Sandesjö & Björk 2005: 55). In the Act of 2001 this restriction has been abolished.

As mentioned above, the principle of domicile has gained much importance in Sweden, as it is often considered better in the light of the new structures of society than the principle of nationality. Belonging to Swedish society through long-term residence is generally believed to create a strong link between the individual and the state. New provisions, extending the possibilities of foreign children grown up in the country to acquire citizenship by notification were thus introduced through the Act of 2001.

There are four categories that can use the facilitated procedure of notification: children who have not acquired Swedish citizenship automatically, and whose father was Swedish upon the birth of the child, children who have grown up in Sweden and fulfil the residence requirement, persons who reacquire Swedish citizenship, and Nordic citizens.

Regarding children who have not acquired Swedish citizenship automatically, but who have a Swedish father (sect. 5), the procedure of notification supports the intention that a true relationship between the child and the father should exist, as only the father can submit the notification.

As to people who grew up in Sweden, three different groups can take advantage of the procedure of notification: stateless children born in Sweden (sect. 6), other children holding a permanent residence permit and who have been domiciled in Sweden for at least five years (three years if the child is stateless) (sect. 7), and young persons who have reached the age of eighteen but who are not yet twenty (sect. 8). The intention of the provision on stateless children is to fulfil Sweden's international obligations regarding statelessness. The child must be stateless since birth, domiciled in Sweden and hold a permanent residence permit. For stateless children, as well as other children grown up in the country, a notification has to be submitted by the child's guardian. As to young persons aged between eighteen and twenty, notification is possible if the person has a permanent residence permit and has been domiciled in Sweden since the age of thirteen (fifteen if the person is stateless). A political objective is to give young adults the possibility to choose for themselves whether they want to become Swedish citizens upon reaching the age of majority. As concerns recovery of Swedish citizenship by notification (sect. 9), a permanent residence permit is required as well as a certain period of domicile (a total of ten years before reaching the age of eighteen and domicile in Sweden for the preceding two years). As concerns notifications submitted by Nordic citizens (sect. 18), domicile in Sweden for the previous five years is required. The person must also have acquired his or her Nordic citizenship by a means other than application and not have been sentenced to imprisonment during the required period of domicile in Sweden. A person who has lost his or her Swedish citizenship and has thereafter continuously been a citizen of a Nordic country may recover Swedish citizenship by notification if he or she becomes domiciled in Sweden (sect. 19).

When an alien becomes a Swedish citizen by notification, his or her unmarried children who are under the age of eighteen and domiciled in Sweden also acquire Swedish citizenship if the alien has sole custody of the child or joint custody with the other parent and that parent is a Swedish citizen (sect. 10). If the parents become Swedish citizens at the same time and if they share custody, the child also acquires Swedish citizenship.

Aliens who cannot use the procedure of notification can apply for naturalisation (sect. 11). There are several criteria that the applicant must fulfil. First, the person has to provide proof of his or her identity. This requirement has been tightened up due to the increasing number of aliens arriving in Sweden without identity documents. Second, the applicant must have reached the age of eighteen. The applicant must also have a permanent residence permit and have been residing uninterruptedly in Sweden for the past five years (two years if the person is a Nordic citizen, and four years if the person is stateless or a recognised refugee). There is also a good conduct requirement. Naturalisation of an adult does not automatically include his or her children. Instead it shall, in the decision concerning naturalisation, also be decided whether or not the applicant's unmarried children shall acquire Swedish citizenship (sect. 13).

There are several possibilities for granting exemptions from the requirements for naturalisation mentioned above. According to sect. 12, applicants who have formerly held Swedish citizenship and persons who are married to a Swedish citizen or living in conditions resembling marriage with a Swedish citizen may be naturalised even if they do not meet all requirements. Exceptions can also be made if there are other special reasons for granting Swedish citizenship. There is also the possibility for an applicant who cannot provide proof of identity to become naturalised if he or she has been domiciled in Sweden for at least the previous eight years and can give the authorities reason to believe that the stated identity is correct. The political intention is to afford people the possibility to apply for Swedish citizenship, even if they originate from countries where it is difficult or perhaps impossible to acquire identification documents.

Sweden does not, contrary to many other countries, have any language requirements. Language requirements have never been provided for Swedish citizenship acts, however, in administrative practice knowledge of the Swedish language was required until the late 1970s (Lokrantz Bernitz 2004: 145). The question of reintroducing language requirements has since then been debated upon several occasions and seems to be a sensitive issue. It was for example examined in the report of the Commission of Inquiry and in the Government bill preceding the Citizenship Act of 2001. The reintroduction of language requirements was also a big and highly debated issue in the electoral campaign in the parliamentary election of 2002. The Liberal Party made this proposal to increase the 'Swedishness' of the naturalised Swedes. The main arguments against language requirements have been concerns about integration and justice as well as the difficulties in determining and documenting levels of knowledge.

As to loss of citizenship, a decision regarding citizenship is viewed in Sweden as being a favourable administrative decision which means that a decision on citizenship can never be annulled. A naturalised Swede is allowed to retain citizenship even if citizenship was acquired, for example, through fraud, through false information or by threat. In case B637/89 the Court of Appeal (*Svea hovrätt*) concluded, in a case concerning narcotics crimes, that a decision on naturalisation regarding a man who had acquired his citizenship through false identity was not a nullity. As already mentioned there is a provision in the Instrument of Government stating that no citizen who is domiciled in Sweden or who has previously been domiciled in Sweden may be deprived of his or her citizenship. Introducing denaturalisation has, however, been suggested in 2006.

As Sweden has now fully accepted dual citizenship, only two possibilities of losing Swedish citizenship remain in the Citizenship Act: loss after statutory limitation and release.

According to sect. 14 in the Citizenship Act a person loses his or her Swedish citizenship automatically after the statutory limitation at the age of 22 if the person was born abroad, has never been domiciled in Sweden and has never been in Sweden under circumstances that indicate a link with the country. People with no ties to Sweden are thus not considered entitled to retaining Swedish citizenship. A person who risks losing his or her citizenship can however apply for permission to retain it, an application that may be turned down by the authorities if the link to Sweden is considered insufficient. The loss of citizenship does not apply if it would result in the person becoming stateless.

Someone who for any reason does not wish to keep his or her Swedish citizenship may be released from it on application (sect. 15). If the person is not already a foreign citizen release shall be conditional on the acquisition of citizenship in another country within a certain period of time.

14.3.1.1 *Political analysis*

Swedish politics is to a high degree based on consensus and negotiations. A large majority in Parliament has often backed major decisions. Since the 1930s, the Social Democratic Party (*Socialdemokraterna*), supported by the trade unions (*LO*), has been the dominating political force in the country.

The parties represented in the Swedish Parliament are divided into two separate political blocks, the ruling socialist/green block and the more market-oriented right-of-centre block (non-socialist block). The left-of-centre block, formed by the Social Democrats, together with the

Left Party (*Vänsterpartiet*) and the Green Party (*Miljöpartiet*), have been in the majority in the Parliament since 1994, when they replaced the right-of-centre government headed by Prime Minister Carl Bildt. Since then, Göran Persson, party leader of the Social Democrats, has been prime minister of Sweden.

The right-of-centre block which forms the opposition is composed of four non-socialist parties. Since the 1980s, it has been dominated by the Swedish conservatives, the Moderate Party (*Moderata Samlingspartiet*). The second largest party in the right-of-centre block is the Liberal Party (*Folkpartiet*), who achieved a strong election result in the last Parliamentary elections in 2002. Two smaller parties, the Centre Party (*Centern*) and the Christian Democrats (*Kristdemokraterna*) also represent non-socialist alternatives.

On matters concerning immigration, there has been an alliance between the Social Democrats and the Moderates, which in practice has been decisive for the Swedish policy in this area. Today however, this alliance seems weaker than before and it can be assumed that the existing order will be challenged in the future.

With the exception of the electoral period between 1991 and 1994, when the New Democracy party (*Ny Demokrati*) was represented in the Parliament, there has not been any party represented in the Swedish Parliament that could be labelled 'populist'. There seems to be a consensus in Sweden that populist parties should be avoided, and any attempt would probably fail to reach the public through the media. In this respect the political landscape in Sweden differs from that of if its neighbours, Norway and Denmark. This may be one of the reasons why the issue of immigration is less prominent in the Swedish political debate than in neighbouring countries.

Swedish immigration policy is based on the country's international commitments on refugees. A large proportion of immigration into Sweden consists of family reunification. There are at present very few possibilities for labour-related immigration into Sweden (except for Nordic and EU citizens). This has not however always been the case, as immigration into Sweden during the first decades after the Second World War, like in many other Western European countries, was based on the need for people who could fill up the increasing demand for labour caused by the expansion of Swedish industry. Some of those immigrants arrived in groups organised by the Swedish labour market authorities, but mostly they arrived by themselves. In the public debate there are today strong voices for an increase of labour-related immigration, not least to cope with demographic changes. There are however, at this point in time, no propositions to allow more labour-related immigration though ministers in Government have voiced a need for such a change.

In Sweden there is little difference in practice between a citizen and a foreigner who holds a permanent residence permit. There is, for example, no discrimination as to the right to use social welfare systems. Acquiring citizenship is, at large, often a question on how long a person has been in the country, and there is little added value in becoming a citizen. In many ways it is more a question of practicalities.

One of the few substantial differences between being a Swedish citizen and being a permanent resident in Sweden is, however, the right to vote for Parliament. The general view is that naturalised Swedes vote less frequently than native-born Swedes. This has been a source of concern for a long time as Sweden has one of the highest records of participation in elections in the world. In the public debate there is, however, no or very little discussion on which party potentially 'gains' from immigration, i.e., wins the immigrant's vote.

In Sweden, the politically sensitive issues on immigration are connected to permanent residence and the criteria that should apply for this, and are therefore dealt with on a level prior to the actual question of citizenship and naturalisation. The requirements for naturalisation, for example the proof of identity requirement laid down in the Citizenship Act, however, form an extra barrier. The focus on permanent residence, and the fact that citizenship historically has been a low-key issue in Sweden, is probably the reason why citizenship is not widely debated.

The legal conditions for acquiring a permanent residence permit in Sweden are rather strict. About half the immigration into Sweden is attributed to family reunification. Swedish policy on family reunification is liberal, but only for the immediate family (primarily spouses, cohabitants, and children). For other relatives the regulations on family reunification seldom apply. Family reunification is, however, not directly connected to citizenship, but rather to a permanent residence permit.

Traditionally, the focus of Swedish policy regarding immigrants has been on integration. The intention has not been that the immigrants should cut their ties with their native countries. The Swedish policy is reflected, for example, in the so called 'home language' policy, where children with immigrant parents are encouraged to preserve linguistic ties with their countries of origin by attending publicly funded language courses where the children learn their native language. The Government's immigration policy is therefore two-sided, both helping immigrants to preserve links to their country of origin and at the same time also helping them integrate into Swedish society. Of the two, integration is surely the most predominant issue in the public and political debate.

As to different groups of immigrants, the only group that enjoys a specific position according to Swedish nationality law is other Nordic citizens. As mentioned above this has been the case for a long time, and the advantageous regulations were transferred to the new Citizenship Act of 2001 without any political opposition or particular debate. Apart from Nordic citizens, other more generally defined groups such as stateless children, have, as already mentioned, been given certain benefits. Another generally defined group, for which a specific regulation applies, comprises those who do not fulfil the good conduct requirement for naturalisation. It is worth noting that this requirement applies mainly to those who have committed crimes during their time in Sweden.

None of the political parties represented in the Swedish Parliament has any outspoken policy concerning either the increase or decrease of the number of naturalisations. A factor like fulfilment of the legal criteria of whether the person in question has a strong enough link to the country, is, however, considered important.

There are today no specific political or social goals regarding naturalisation in Sweden, apart from fulfilling the countries international commitments on refugees. As already mentioned, the political battleground on matters of immigration and nationality is focused on permanent residence, and it is difficult to specify any major political battle lines on either nationality law or citizenship. An exception is the Green Party that can be said to have a more liberal view than the majority in Parliament. The Green Party wants to introduce a new basis for acquisition of citizenship in Sweden based on the birthplace of the child, i.e., a child born in Sweden would automatically qualify for citizenship (ius soli). The Green Party supports the current Social Democratic government (however it is not in the coalition), but its own support base is between six to eight per cent of the voters.

Those in the political sphere who are concerned with questions related to nationality law normally focus on the problems relating to integration, whether 'being Swedish' should be more closely related to citizenship and whether the relationship between rights and responsibilities should be more prominent. So far this has not resulted in any major political proposals.

The review of Swedish nationality law that resulted in the new Citizenship Act of 2001 was not provoked by any major political debate, but should merely be seen as a wish to modernise the nationality law and put it in line with the changes that had occurred in Swedish society because of immigration and internationalisation. Practical considerations dominated and the political debate preceding the new legislation was more of a technical nature than a wish to use the nationality law in a wider debate, for example, on the meaning of 'being Swedish'.

All political parties in the Swedish Parliament sponsored the current Citizenship Act and backed the legislative package. The only exception, which also gave rise to a major debate and political battle, concerned the acceptance of dual citizenship. The Moderate Party did not support the new attitude towards dual citizenship and voted against the new proposal on this particular point. The problems foreseen and the political arguments against dual citizenship concerned the question of how to deal with and protect citizens abroad, especially persons running into trouble in the other country of which he or she is also a citizen. The political majority in Parliament, however, found that the benefits of allowing people to have dual citizenship outweighed the problems and disadvantages. The Moderate Party also argued for a stricter regulation on how to deal with people with a criminal record applying for citizenship. The new Citizenship Act was however adopted without any difficulties.

The new Act was not triggered by external pressure such as, for example, adaptation to international law. The ratification of the European Convention of Nationality however implied some changes to the Swedish attitude towards nationality law. Nor was the new Act provoked by any legal disputes. As Sweden does not have a constitutional court the Act was not blocked by any legal decisions. The reasons for enacting a new Citizenship Act were purely dictated by the need for a modernisation of Swedish nationality law.

Likewise, when, prior to the decision in Parliament on the new Citizenship Act, relevant referral bodies were invited to put forward their comments and suggestions on the proposed law, there was little opposition. The immigrant organisations were on the whole pleased with the proposed amendments. Nor was there any real public debate regarding the new Citizenship Act. This does not, however, mean that the new legislation was enacted by stealth, but rather that the Swedish construction, where focus lies on permanent residence instead of citizenship, leaves little room for debate and consequently little public or political interest in the law governing citizenship. In contrast to many other countries not even the question of naturalised terrorists seems to be of public interest. When, for example, a Swedish citizen of foreign origin was held by the US at the Guantanamo Base accused of terrorism, the general view in Sweden was that the Swedish government should help him. It is generally considered that control should be carried out at an earlier stage, already when the application for naturalisation is evaluated, and the records of the Swedish Security Service are therefore sometimes consulted before approval.

A current political topic is, however, the need for special ceremonies to be arranged for people who have been granted Swedish citizenship. This kind of ceremony has not previously been part of Swedish tradition, but has now been introduced at a municipal level throughout the country, including the City of Stockholm. It has generally been the right-of-centre parties that proposed the introduction of such ceremonies. The ceremonies can be seen as a political wish to demonstrate the value of citizenship as something stronger and more important than permanent residence.

As citizenship is rarely discussed in Sweden, many Swedes have an unclear view of the concept of citizenship and of the rights that citizenship entails. Many Swedes believe, for example, that being a Swedish citizen entitles the person to welfare-security rights also outside of Sweden. This was, for example, noted on New Year 2005 with respect to the tsunami catastrophe, where the general view was that the Swedish government and other authorities did not fulfil their obligations towards the Swedish citizens involved as they did not come to their rescue in the way that many citizens had expected.

With respect to the abovementioned, a Commission of Inquiry has in 2006 examined future possible amendments to the Citizenship Act. Although the content of the report lies beyond the scope of this study, the work of the commission is worth mentioning, as the need for an evaluation reflects problems with the current legislation. The commission has focused on the question of denaturalisation, an issue that has arisen as the result of murders committed in the name of honour, and officials taking bribes at the Swedish Migration Board (*Migrationsverket*). The murders in the name of honour gave rise to an intense public debate, but this debate has not primarily focused on citizenship issues. The officials taking bribes had granted citizenship to people with a criminal record who would otherwise have failed to qualify for naturalisation. This highlighted the need for an evaluation of whether it should be possible to withdraw citizenship based on incorrect decisions. Such a provision can, however, only be introduced if the Instrument of Government is first amended. The Commission of Inquiry has also examined whether people, who have acquired citizenship by submitting false information about their identity, for example, should be considered as having acquired citizenship on false pretences and therefore risk losing their citizenship. The Commission has suggested an amendment that would make denationalisation possible. The introduction of denationalisation would be something radically new in Swedish nationality law and will surely spark intense debates.

The new Citizenship Act has however achieved its intended effect of modernising the nationality law, and most political parties seem pleased with the result. One of the most important goals was to make it easier to acquire Swedish citizenship for children who grew up in the country and for those who wanted to keep their foreign citizenship. An increase in the number of acquisitions within those groups has been noted. Apart from the aspects that the above-mentioned Commission of Inquiry is dealing with, the general spirit of the Swedish nationality law is not disputed. Most people seem to agree on the fact that the new Citizenship Act fits the reality of Sweden today.

14.3.1.2 *Statistical developments*

The First World War, in combination with immigration restrictions in the US, slowed down the emigration from Sweden that had been going on since the middle of the nineteenth century. Sweden then turned into an immigration country, and since 1930 immigration has annually exceeded emigration, except for a number of years in the 1970s. During the Second World War many refugees from Germany and other Nordic countries immigrated to Sweden. After the war most of them returned to their native countries, but quite a few also remained in Sweden. During the first decades after the war, labour immigrants from other parts of Scandinavia, as well as countries such as Yugoslavia, Greece, Italy and Turkey dominated. In the late 1960s, Parliament decided that immigrants should have their residence permits approved prior to entering the country, and thus immigration became regulated. Permits were only given if the country was considered in need of the particular kind of foreign labour that the person could provide. People from other Nordic countries, who have had the right to reside and work wherever they like within the Nordic area since 1951, were exempted, and Nordic immigration increased. During the 1960s, and the first half of the 1970s about 50,000 Finns and 11,500 Norwegians became Swedish citizens. There was also an increase in immigration from non-Nordic countries because of family unification. During the 1970s the Swedish immigration policy became more restrictive. Foreigners who had their ordinary residence in Sweden were however encouraged to naturalise. The number of naturalisations thus increased during the 1970s as a consequence of the immigration that had taken place during the 1960s. The tendency to naturalise differed, however, between various groups of people. While many refugees from Hungary, Czechoslovakia and Poland naturalised, labour immigrants from Southern Europe were less willing to naturalise (Widgren 1980: 30). In the 1980s, the numbers of asylum seekers from countries like Iraq, Lebanon and Turkey increased, and in the 1990s new zones of conflict, like the collapse of Yugoslavia, brought many people to Sweden. About 100,000 Yugoslavs (mostly Bosnians) found a new home in Sweden. In July 2005, the Swedish population comprised about nine million inhabitants. About half a million of these were foreign citizens. Since 2000 the total number of residence permits granted has been between 45,000 and 50,000 per year.

In 2004, about 50 per cent of the immigrants originated from non-European countries and about 20 per cent from Nordic countries.

Table 14.1: Swedish Population Statistics 1960-2004

	1960	*1970*	*1980*	*1990*	*2000*	*2004*
Total population	7,497,967	8,081,229	8,317,937	8,590,630	8,882,792	9,011,392
Foreign citizens	190,621	411,280	421,667	483,704	477,312	481,141
Foreign citizens in %	2.5	5.1	5.1	5.6	5.4	5.3
Inhabitants born abroad	299,879	537,585	626,953	790,445	1,003,798	1,100,262
Total number of acquisitions of citizenship	8,452	11,539	20,833	16,770	43,474	28,893
whereof men					21,319	13,307
women					22,155	15,586

Source: Statistics Sweden (*Statistiska centralbyrån, SCB*); *www.scb.se*

About 14,400 Swedish citizens returned to Sweden, and about 20,500 Swedish citizens emigrated.

Concerning the issue of naturalisations, it is difficult to get an accurate figure of the total number of naturalisations per year before the new Citizenship Act came into force in 2001. The reason is that acquisition, according to the previous Citizenship Act of 1950, was often conditional, and the applicant would have to prove within two years that he or she had been released from his or her former nationality. The objective was to avoid dual citizenship. If the applicant fulfilled the condition, he or she became a Swedish citizen on the day that proof was provided, but the examination of the requirements for naturalisation as well as the decision of approval were already completed when the conditional citizenship was approved (Sandesjö & Björk 1996: 118). It is, however, clear that the number of persons acquiring Swedish citizenship has increased over the decades, and between 1960 and 2004 the number increased more than three times. Since 2001, the number of women acquiring Swedish citizenship has exceeded the number of men by between 2,000 and 3,000 per year. The high number of acquisitions in 2002 is explained by the fact that during that year the Swedish Migration Board was given extra means to reduce the waiting time for the examination of applications.

The acceptance of dual citizenship is estimated to have increased the number of acquisitions of citizenship. There has, however, been no political campaign encouraging foreigners to acquire Swedish citizenship, as dual citizenship could involve some major disadvantages for the individual such as problems related to military service. On the contrary, Swedish authorities issue information about the problems that can be caused by having dual citizenship.

Table 14.2: Naturalisation matters decided and approved naturalisations in Sweden 2001-2004

	2001	*2002*	*2003*	*2004*
Matters decided[5]	23,676	24,852	21,138	17,394
Approved naturalisations (adults)	19,845	21,893	18,032	15,109

Source: Swedish Migration Board (*Migrationsverket*). *www.migrationsverket.se.*

To arrive at the total number of naturalisations (i.e., adults and children) approximately 50 per cent should be added to the figures in Table 14.2. In 2004, the total number of children (0-17 years) acquiring Swedish citizenship was 9,763.

The number of refusals of naturalisation is rather limited. This can partly be explained by the generous Swedish attitude towards naturalisation and also by the possibilities for granting exemptions from the naturalisation requirements. Another explanation could of course be the fee (1,500 Swedish kronor in 2005, which is about 160 euros), which deters people from taking a chance and applying even if they know that they do not fulfil all requirements.

The number of notifications per year has steadily increased since the mid-1990s. The Citizenship Act of 2001 made new groups of persons eligible to submit notifications, and it is very likely that the number of naturalisations within those groups has decreased since 2001. The total number of approved notifications for non-Nordic citizens in 2004 was 1,218. The extended possibilities for notification in the Citizenship Act of 2001 have not, however, increased the number of notifications as much as expected.

As to Nordic citizens, an increase in the number of approved acquisitions of citizenship can be noted in 2003, which can probably be explained by the new Citizenship Act of Finland coming into force accepting dual citizenship. The number of Finns acquiring Swedish citizenship increased from 1,561 in 2002 to 2,816 in 2003. A similar

Table 14.3: Refusals of naturalisation and reasons for refusal in Sweden 2001-2004

Reason for refusal	*Year*			
	2001	*2002*	*2003*	*2004*
Unclear identity	818	791	1,199	658
Period of domicile too short	462	606	481	356
Has not led or cannot be expected to lead a respectable life	907	969	791	683
Other reasons for refusal	4	116	153	193
Total number of refusals	2,291	2,482	2,624	1,890

Source: Swedish Migration Board (*Migrationsverket*). *www.migrationsverket.se.*

increase can be noted for Icelanders. The number of Icelanders acquiring Swedish citizenship increased from 39 in 2002 to 118 in 2003. The total number of Nordic citizens acquiring Swedish citizenship in 2003 was 3,639 (compared to 2,292 in 2002). In 2004, the number of acquisitions of citizenship was 3,681. This includes both naturalisations and notifications.

The number of refused notifications is increasing. One reason might be that the legal requirements are not always known to the applicant. Another reason might be that the fee for submitting notifications is rather low, in 2005 just 175 Swedish kronor (475 for Nordic citizens), and the applicant does not lose much by applying even if he or she knows that all requirements are not fulfilled.

As to the issue of loss of citizenship after a statutory limitation has expired, the loss is automatic, but the person may, as mentioned, apply for permission to retain Swedish citizenship before he or she reaches the age of 22. In 2004 there were 372 such applications and 315 of those were approved. Only two cases were refused. As to the issue of release of citizenship, 105 matters were decided in 2004. 37 of those were immediately approved, whereas 54 matters were approved on condition that the applicant prove, within a year, that he or she had acquired a foreign citizenship.

14.3.2 *Institutional arrangements*

14.3.2.1 *The legislative process*

Before the Government (*regeringen*) submits a proposal to the Parliament (*riksdagen*), the various alternatives available are examined by an assigned Commission of Inquiry, composed of politicians, experts or officials. The Commission of Inquiry presents its recommendations in a report published in Swedish Government Official Reports (*SOU, Statens offentliga utredningar*). This report is referred to various municipalities, agencies and organisations for consideration. The Government then adopts a position on the recommendation and on the proposals from the referral bodies. Within the Swedish Government, the Ministry of Justice handles matters of nationality.

The Government submits a proposal to the Parliament in the form of a Government bill (*proposition*). Members of Parliament have the right to introduce proposals to the Parliament, based on a Government bill, in the form of a private member's motion (*motion*). A Government bill is normally sent to the Council of legislation (*lagrådet*), which examines whether the proposed law is in conflict with legislation already existing. Characteristic for Sweden is that the legal history, especially reports from Commissions of inquiry and Government bills, have a great influence on the interpretation of legislation, especially in areas where there have been very few court decisions.

Proposals made by the Government are tabled once in the Chamber and then referred to a committee. The committees are composed of Members of Parliament (proportionally to the size of the parties in the Chamber), and carry out much of the work in Parliament (Strömberg & Lundell 2004: 40). Practically all proposals must be considered by a committee. There are, for the moment, sixteen committees, each responsible for different subjects. The committees shall deliver reports on all matters which have been referred to them, and which have not been withdrawn. A committee report is submitted to the Chamber and normally tabled twice at meetings of the Chamber before settlement. Questions concerning citizenship have been moved from the committee dealing with the labour market (*Arbetsmarknadsutskottet*) to the committee on social insurance (*Socialförsäkringsutskottet*). The change was made for practical reasons, namely to create a more even workload between the committees, however it also coincided with the shift in Swedish immigration policy that occurred when labour-related immigration decreased.

The Swedish Citizenship Act is an ordinary law, which means that amendments, as well as new nationality laws, are decided by Parliament according the normal procedure laid down in the Instrument of Government. Votes taken in the Parliament constitute a decision if more than half of those voting concur.

The Government is responsible for the implementation of new laws and may adopt provisions relating to the implementation by means of a statutory instrument. The statutory instrument (2001: 218) concerns citizenship.

As mentioned above, there is no such thing as a constitutional court in Sweden. The establishment of a constitutional court has been discussed upon several occasions, but rejected as being an unfamiliar element in Swedish legal culture (Warnling-Nerep, Lagerqvist Veloz Roca & Reichel 2005: 165). There is no possibility of trying the legal applicability of a provision without referring to an actual case. If a court or other public body finds that a provision conflicts with a rule of fundamental law or other superior statute, or finds that a procedure laid down in law has been disregarded in any important respect when the provision was made, the provision may not be applied. The result of the investigation can, however, never be the annulment of a provision, but only a ruling that the provision in question is not applicable in the actual case. Provisions approved by Parliament (laws) or by Government (statutory instruments) shall be waived only if an error is manifest. Such an investigation has never, as far as known, been made in a matter related to citizenship.

14.3.2.2 *The process of implementation*

Matters concerning naturalisation are examined by the Swedish Migration Board (*Migrationsverket*) (Citizenship Act sect. 22). Anyone may apply for naturalisation and if they fulfil the conditions citizenship is normally granted. There is however a certain allowance for discretion in the assessment, though it may not be arbitrary and must be applied in accordance with fixed criteria. Many of the refusals for naturalisation are based on unclear identity. The identification documents required in administrative practice are an original of the applicant's national passport or other original photo identification papers issued by an authority in the applicant's native country. The papers must be of decent quality and not have too simple a format. There must be no doubt that they are genuine and have been properly issued. If an applicant has neither a passport nor identification papers it is nevertheless sufficient if a spouse or an immediate family member, who has become Swedish citizen by proving his or her identity with a national passport or identification paper from his or her native country, verifies the applicant's identity.

The requirement of good conduct has been tightened up over the years. A person who has committed a crime in Sweden can still become a Swedish citizen, but waiting periods have been introduced in administrative practice. The waiting periods serve as guiding principles but individual control and examination is always carried out. If the applicant, for example, has been sentenced to imprisonment for one month, he or she can normally become Swedish citizen no sooner than four years after the crime. If the applicant has been sentenced to imprisonment for one year he or she can become a Swedish citizen no sooner than seven years after the crime. Marks on a person's record, such as unpaid taxes, fines or child support, can also cause an application to be rejected.

As mentioned earlier, exemptions may be granted from the naturalisation requirements. Most frequent in administrative practice are exemptions from the residence requirement (Sandesjö & Björk 2005: 126). For instance, a person can obtain Swedish citizenship after only three years in Sweden if he or she has been the spouse or cohabitant of a Swedish citizen for at least two years. Exemptions from the residence requirement can also be granted for emigrants returning to Sweden, people employed on Swedish ships and people living abroad who have been married to a Swedish citizen for at least ten years and who do not live in their native country. Exemptions are less frequent for the other naturalisation requirements. Exemptions from the age requirement are, however, sometimes granted. A child with either a mother or a father who is a Swedish citizen can, for example, obtain Swedish citizenship independently if the parents submit an application. Exemptions from the requirement of a permanent residence permit are rare. Exemptions could, however, be granted, for example, if a person who has lost his or her Swedish citizenship after statutory limitation has expired applies for naturalisation. Exemptions from the good conduct requirement are normally not granted.

An application for naturalisation is made on a special form and a fee must be paid. Normally the application is then examined within a year. A matter considered being of particular importance requiring guidance regarding the application of the Citizenship Act could, before 2006, be forwarded to the Government for examination (sect. 25) and the Government should then normally consult the Aliens Appeals Board (*Utlänningsnämnden*) before deciding. The Government could also forward the matter to the Board for decision. This section has now been repealed.

The Swedish Migration Board examines matters on notification if they concern people originating from non-Nordic countries (sect. 22). Notifications submitted by citizens of Denmark, Finland, Iceland and Norway are examined by the county administrative board (*länsstyrelsen*) in the county where the person is registered as resident.

Release from citizenship and applications concerning permission to retain citizenship to avoid automatic loss after statutory limitation has expired, are examined by the Swedish Migration Board. In administrative practice, applications for permission to retain citizenship are rarely refused. Normally, applications from the first generation born abroad are granted, while applications from subsequent generations are granted only as long as the ties with Sweden have not been completely severed. Many applications are also approved even though the person in question does not risk losing his or her citizenship after statutory limitation expires. The reason is the wish to avoid confusion as it has turned out that many such applicants do not understand why their applications are not examined.

Normally only the person directly affected by a decision (and his or her legal representative) has the right to appeal. Decisions on notifications were, before an amendment in 2006, appealed to a public administrative court (sect. 26). Leave to appeal was required for appeals to an administrative court of appeal. Decisions made by the Swedish Migration Board in matters concerning naturalisation and loss of citizenship were appealed to the Aliens Appeals Board (sect. 26). In 2004, the Aliens Appeals Board decided in 1,057 appealed matters. 33 per cent of those were approved. On average, the handling of an appeal took 198 days.[6] A decision by the Aliens Appeals Board was final and could not be appealed (sect. 26). Since 2006 decisions on notifications and naturalisations are appealed to special migration courts.

A security matter, i.e., a matter in which the National Police Board has recommended to the Swedish Migration Board that an application should be rejected on grounds concerning the safety of the realm or public safety, is appealed to Government (sect. 27). The National Police Board may also appeal a decision in a security matter if the decision goes against the Board's recommendation.

The institutional order is intended to counteract any divergent implementation and application of the rules. Prohibitions of discrimination and unfavourable treatment because a person belongs to a minority group by reason of race, colour, or ethnic origin, also intend to guarantee a uniform application. To secure a uniform application in practice, the Swedish Migration Board has special meetings every week (or every second week) where application matters and administrative practice are discussed. There are also internal guidelines and manuals. The Swedish Migration Board has however occasionally been accused of subjectivity, and, as mentioned, there have been cases of individual officials granting citizenship after taking bribes.

As to the issue of notifications, the examination leaves no room for discretionary powers. Those who meet the legal requirements have an unconditional right to become citizens and citizenship can consequently not be denied. All requirements have to be met by the date that the application arrives at the Swedish Migration Board or at the county administrative board.

One of the reasons for the lack of case law related to nationality law is the fact that naturalisation has been exempt from judicial review for a long time in Sweden, as the decision by the Aliens Appeals Board was final. Before 2006 it was not possible to refer matters concerning naturalisation to the courts. The only possibility to have a naturalisation case tried in court was if relief for substantive defects (an action of exceptional character) was granted by the Swedish Supreme Administrative Court. There are only a handful of such cases. These cases, however, provide very little guidance as the Supreme Administrative Court has not established any fixed guidelines. The court had a standing locution regarding the right to a judicial appeal of a decision by the Aliens Appeals Board.

As of 31 March 2006 the institutional order has been changed and decisions by the Swedish Migration Board and the county administrative boards are now appealed to special migration courts (located at three different county administrative courts). A decision by a migration court may be appealed to a migration court of appeal. This change has come about despite earlier rejections by Government. However, pressure from immigration organisations and other political parties represented in Parliament brought the change forward. The reason for the amendment has not been criticism of the previous institutional order regarding citizenship but the fact that the Aliens Appeals Board has ceased to exist as appeals in other matters concerning aliens and immigration were transferred to migration courts. The new institutional order intends to fulfil the principle of legal certainty and legal protection of the individual, as well as making the process more transparent.

14.4 Conclusions

In Sweden there has been an obvious change of attitude regarding the importance of citizenship, and during recent years a weakening of the concept of citizenship has occurred.

In early history, citizenship was not codified and ordinary residence in Sweden was enough to consider a person loyal to the country. Anyone who immigrated permanently became a citizen, and those who emigrated lost their citizenship. In the nineteenth and twentieth century citizenship became strictly regulated, and it was carefully specified who belonged to the Swedish population and who did not. It became more difficult to acquire citizenship for those who were not descended from Swedes and acquisition of citizenship through naturalisation or recovery was periodically restricted. One explanation for this policy might be that Sweden was an emigration country during a substantial part of this period.

Today, with Sweden being an immigration country, there is a more liberal attitude towards citizenship. The intention of the new Swedish Citizenship Act of 2001 was to effectively fulfil the principle of legal certainty and legal protection of the individual. The extension of the possibilities to submit notifications, the rather generous provisions on naturalisation, the acceptance of dual citizenship, and the prohibition against denaturalisation all indicate that Sweden has a generous attitude towards the individual. Acquisition of citizenship is viewed as a part of the integration process, and an aim of the new Act was to strengthen the status of citizenship as a part of integration.

As an example of the generous Swedish attitude towards the individual applicant one may point to the fact that knowledge of the Swedish language is not required. One reason, for instance, is that language requirements are considered unfair, as some groups of people would have trouble learning a new language. According to the legal history of the Citizenship Act of 2001, the Swedish policy in this area is based on the idea that the immigrant has his or her own responsibility to learn the Swedish language, and that the immigrant is expected to do his or her best on the basis of own individual qualifications. Swedish authorities are primarily responsible for organising language courses, and the question of language fluency is therefore the task of the educational system. All necessary measures are thus taken prior to the question of naturalisation. In the majority of cases, however, a person seeking naturalisation is assumed to have sufficient knowledge of Swedish society and the Swedish language through the requirement of a certain period of residency for naturalisation.

Nor does Sweden require any oath of loyalty to the country. The oath was already abolished in the law of 1924, and today an oath would probably be hard to combine with the objectives for allowing dual citizenship.

An alien's status in Sweden is very similar to that of a Swedish citizen, and to a large extent Swedes and foreigners have the same rights. The development in Sweden as to increasingly giving equal rights to citizens and foreigners reflects a clear change in the view of the core and idea of citizenship. In many contexts the concept of domicile has taken over the role of citizenship. Much of the development in Sweden depends on new international relationships, but also on a revised view of the rights of the individual. The Swedish concept of citizenship may have its background partly in the country's view on its status in the world. Additionally, it may also depend on the good living conditions that the country offers its inhabitants. The absence of war in modern times, the endeavours for equality and considerations of integration are other important factors. A review of provisions in Swedish legislation in which citizenship is required as a qualifying criterion for rights or other legal consequences shows that these provisions are few in number. One of the most important rights reserved for citizens is, as already mentioned, the right to vote in elections for Parliament. In general, however, only a few constitutionally protected rights are reserved for citizens, like, for example, the right to enter the country and the prohibition against deportation. In other legislation citizenship is primarily required for holding important public offices; it can however be maintained that the requirements concerning Swedish citizenship for employment in the public service are considerably fewer than those permissible in EU law. Most other EU Member States have more far-reaching requirements.

Another illustrative example of the Swedish attitude towards citizenship is the fact that Swedish law lacks any definition as to who is a 'citizen'. Nor does the law define the actual concept of 'citizenship'. This can be compared, for example, to the new Finnish Nationality Act from 2003 which expressly defines the concept of citizenship. One can also make a comparison to the United States where in a number of cases the Supreme Court has set out the fundamental central principles and definitions. There are also important decisions of the German Constitutional Court. One explanation for the lack of a definition can be that for a long time the Swedish population was easy to distinguish and citizenship was viewed as something obvious, and therefore not considered in need of a legal definition. Another basic explanation can be that issues of citizenship have for a long time been exempt from judicial review. One central sub-issue here is naturally the requirements for naturalisation. As already mentioned, judicial review is, however, possible from 2006.

To conclude: citizenship in Sweden is not a big political issue. The parties represented in Parliament more or less agree on the citizenship policy. The generous Swedish attitude towards the individual and the equalising of citizens' and foreigners' rights are therefore likely to continue.

Chronological table of major reforms in Swedish nationality law since 1945

Date	Document	Content of change
1 January 1951	Swedish Citizenship Act (1950:382) (lagen (1950:382) om svenskt medborgarskap).	New citizenship act. Swedish Citizenship Act (1924: 130) repeated.
1 January 1951	Ordinance (1950:614) on citizenship (medborgarskapskungörelsen (1950:614)).	Provisions regarding the implementation of the Citizenship Act (1950:382).
1 January 1951	Ordinance (1950:664) on the application of sect. 10 in Swedish Citizenship Act (1950:382) in relation to Denmark and Norway (Kungörelsen 1950:664 angående tillämpningen i förhållande till Danmark och Norge av 10 § lagen den 22 juni 1950 (382) om svenskt medborgarskap).	
1 January 1969	Law 1968:704: Amendment to the Citizenship Act (1950:382).	Facilitated acquisition by notification. 'Domiciled uninterruptedly' for certain periods sufficient; new provisions on ordinary residence for Nordic citizens; certain matters could be forwarded to the Government for decision.
8 February 1969	Ordinance (1969:6) on the application of sect. 10a-c in Swedish Citizenship Act (1950:382) (Kungörelsen om tillämpning av 10 § a-c i lagen den 22 juni 1950 (nr 382) om svenskt medborgarskap)	New ordinance concerning Nordic citizens. Ordinance (1950:664) on the application of sect. 10 in Swedish Citizenship Act (1950:382) in relation to Denmark and Norway repealed.
1 July 1969	Ordinance (1969:235) on citizenship (medborgarskapskungörelsen (1969:235)).	New ordinance regarding the implementation of the Citizenship Act (1950:382). Ordinance (1950:614) on citizenship repealed.
1 January 1972	Law 1971:881: Amendment to the Citizenship Act (1950:382).	Normally no automatic citizenship effects because of adoptive parent's

Date	Document	Content of change
		acquisition/loss.
6 March 1974	Law 1974:152: Instrument of Government (Regeringsformen).	New fundamental law. Instrument of Government of 1809 repealed.
22 July 1975	Ordinance (1975:608) on the requirement of Swedish citizenship for access to certain offices. (Förordning (1975:608) om krav på svenskt medborgarskap för tillträde till vissa statliga tjänster).	New ordinance.
1 January 1977	Law 1976:871: Amendment to the Instrument of Government.	Prohibition against denationalisation extended to citizens previously domiciled in Sweden.
1 January 1977	Law 1976:469: Amendment to the Citizenship Act (1950:382).	A child born after a divorce acquires the mother's citizenship; automatic acquisition for children whose parents become citizens by notification; requested domicile for naturalisation: two years (Nordic citizens), five years (other aliens); naturalisation requirement concerning support abolished; period of domicile for notification five years for Nordic citizens; changes in parent's citizenship have effects on own adopted children.
1 January 1978	Ordinance (1977:819) on the application of a certain provision in Citizenship Act (1950:382) (förordningen om tillämpning av viss bestämmelse i lagen (1950:382) om svenskt medborgarskap).	New ordinance concerning sect. 10b on notification for Nordic citizens.
1 July 1979	Law 1979:139: Amendment to the Citizenship Act (1950:382).	Automatic acquisition by birth through mother instead of father; acquisition of citizenship through Swedish father possible by notification; child does not lose citizenship because of parents' marriage; loss because of dual citizenship acquired by birth.
1 January 1985	Law 1984:682: Amendment to the Citizenship Act (1950:382).	Changes primarily related to responsible authorities.
1 July 1991	Law 1991:501: Amendment to the Citizenship Act (1950:382).	Minor changes related to national registration.
1 January 1992	Law 1991:1574: Amendment to the Citizenship Act (1950:382).	Government may grant naturalisation for the benefit of the country; in naturalisation decisions children's acquisition shall be decided on; specification of matters that may be forwarded to the Government; new provisions on

Date	Document	Content of change
		declaration of a person's citizenship; appeal: decisions by Swedish Immigration Board appealed to Aliens Appeals Board; determination of authorities that can demand information from social welfare boards.
1 January 1992	Ordinance 1991:1576: Amendment to the Ordinance (1969:235) on citizenship.	Minor changes.
1 July 1992	Law 1992:392: Amendment to the Citizenship Act (1950:382).	Automatic acquisition on adoption for some children; extended group of adoptee affected by the parents' acquisition/loss.
1 May 1994	Law 1994:143: Amendment to the Citizenship Act (1950:382).	Minor administrative change.
1 April 1995	Law 1995:11: Amendment to the Citizenship Act (1950:382).	Change of institutional order.
1 July 1995	Law 1995:774: Amendment to the Citizenship Act (1950:382).	Good conduct requirement for naturalisation extended to future expectations; most decisions by Aliens Appeals Board may not be appealed.
1 July 1996	Law 1996:633: Ordinance (1975:608) on the requirement of Swedish citizenship for access to certain offices.	Repealed the ordinance.
1 July 1997	Law 1997:195: Amendment to the Citizenship Act (1950:382).	Automatic acquisition on adoption if the adoption decision is valid; parent's acquisition/loss entail citizenship effects if adoption decision is valid.
1 October 1998	Law 1998:321: Amendment to the Citizenship Act (1950:382).	Minor changes regarding the responsible authorities.
1 January 1999	Law 1998:1453: Amendment to the Citizenship Act (1950:382).	Proof of identity requirement for naturalisation codified; exemptions from identity requirement for naturalisation possible after eight years of domicile.
1 July 2000	Law 2000:298: Amendment to the Citizenship Act (1950:382).	Swedish Immigration Board becomes Swedish Migration Board.
1 July 2001	Law 2001:82: Swedish Citizenship Act (2001:82) (Lagen (2001:82) om svenskt medborgarskap).	New citizenship act. Swedish Citizenship Act (1950:382) repealed.
1 July 2001	Ordinance on Citizenship (2001:218) (medborgarskapsförordningen (2001:218).	Provisions on the implementation of the Citizenship Act of 2001. Ordinance (1969:235) on citizenship repealed. Ordinance (1977:819) on the application of a certain provision in Citizenship Act (1950:382) repealed.

Date	Document	Content of change
1 July 2001	Law 2001:82: Swedish Citizenship Act (1924:130) (lagen den 23 maj 1924 (nr 130) om förvärvande och förlust av svenskt medborgarskap).	Sect. 13 (1) on recovery of citizenship repealed.
1 May 2005	Ordinance (2004:294) with instructions for the Swedish Migration Board (förordningen (2004:294) med instruktion för Migrationsverket).	New Ordinance.
1 July 2005	Law 2005:451: Amendment to the Citizenship Act (2001:82).	Automatic acquisition for some children born after insemination introduced; possibility to notification introduced for some children born after insemination
31 March 2006	Law (2005: 722): Amendment to the Citizenship Act (2001: 82).	New institutional orders appeal to special migration courts.

Notes

1 Kungl. förordning den 27 februari 1858 (nr 13) angående ordningen och villkoren för utländsk mans upptagande till svensk medborgare.
2 *Lag den 1 oktober 1894 (nr 71) om förvärvande och förlust av medborgarrätt.*
3 *Lag den 23 maj 1924 (nr 130) om förvärvande och förlust av svenskt medborgarskap.*
4 *Lagen (1950:382) om svenskt medborgarskap.*
5 An authority can decide on a matter by approving or rejecting it, but it can also refuse the matter if there are formal mistakes, remove it if the applicant withdraws the application, or transfer it if the applicant has turned to the wrong authority.
6 Alien Appeals Board (*Utlänningsnämnden*); statistics: www.un.se.

Bibliography

Bellander, I. (1996), 'Le droit Suédois de la nationalité', in B. Nascimbene (ed.), *Nationality Law in the European Union*, 629-671. London: Butterworths.

Fahlbeck E., S. Jägerskiöld & H G.F. Sundberg, (1947) *Medborgarrätt*. Helsingfors: Institutet för offentlig och internationell rätt.

Lokrantz Bernitz, H. (2004), *Medborgarskapet i Sverige och Europa Räckvidd och rättigheter (Nationality and Citizenship in Sweden and the European Union)*. Uppsala: Iustus Förlag.

Sandesjö H. & K. Björk (1996), *Medborgarskapslagen med kommentarer*. Stockholm: Publica.

Sandesjö H. & K. Björk (2005), *Nya medborgarskapslagen med kommentarer*. Stockholm: Norstedts juridik.

Strömberg H. & B. Lundell (2004), *Sveriges författning*. Lund: Studentlitteratur.

Warnling-Nerep, W., A. Lagerqvist Veloz Roca, & J. Reichel (2005), *Statsrättens grunder*. Stockholm: Norstedts juridik.

Widgren J. (1980), *Svensk invandrarpolitik*. Lund: LiberLäromedel.

15 United Kingdom

Ann Dummett

15.1 Introduction

British nationality law defines six types of legal nationality. These are British Citizenship (BC), British Overseas Territories Citizenship (BOTC – formerly called British Dependent Territories Citizenship or BDTC), British Overseas Citizenship (BOC), British Subjects (BS), British Protected Persons (BPP) and British Nationals (Overseas) (BNO). By far the largest category is British citizenship. This status is the only one which confers right of residence and entry in the UK, together with EEA freedom of movement.

The main mode of acquisition of British nationality has always been by birth to anyone (except foreign diplomats) on the national territory. This ancient ius soli rule had for seven centuries made a child of any parentage a national whether the parent was legally present or not, and had the important effect of assimilating into nationality the children of successive alien immigrants.

Since 1 January 1983, a child born on the national territory is a British citizen only if a parent is a citizen or 'settled' under immigration law, that is, having been given indefinite leave to remain without any conditions of stay. If a parent subsequently becomes a citizen or settled, the child has a right to registration. Foundlings on the national territory are citizens, and children born stateless there, or who have lived there for ten years, are entitled to registration.

The national territory now encompasses the United Kingdom itself and the Islands (Channel Islands and Isle of Man) together with the Overseas Territories (i.e., British colonies), whose inhabitants then living, perhaps 200,000 in all, if they were already British Overseas Territories Citizens, automatically became British citizens on 26 February 2002. It should be noted that all these territories have restrictive immigration laws, so that many inhabitants and their children do not qualify for either BOTC or British citizenship, not being 'settled' under local laws.

Whereas the ius soli rule originated in English common law, ius sanguinis rules have always been statutory. There has always been additional, exceptional provision for children born to some, but not all, British nationals outside the national territory. Today, a person classified as a 'citizen by descent' cannot automatically pass on British nationality to a child born outside the national territory except under certain conditions (see sect. 15.3).

At the end of 2004, a child born outside the national territory was a British citizen if either parent was a British citizen otherwise than by descent. An illegitimate child was a citizen only if the mother was a citizen: however an Act of 2002 will make an illegitimate child eligible through the father when sect. 9 comes into force. Meanwhile, the Home Secretary will usually register as a citizen a child whose parents are unmarried.

The Home Secretary has discretion to register any minor child of any parentage wherever born. Registration is the term used instead of naturalisation for the granting of citizenship when the applicant is a minor. It is also used for resumption of citizenship by adults after renunciation, and for BOCs, BSs and BPPs acquiring British citizenship. Formerly, registration was used for wives of citizens and for Commonwealth-country citizens acquiring British status: these uses have been phased out. Generally, registration is easier and cheaper than naturalisation, but the term describes several different processes.

Naturalisation of settled persons has recently been made more difficult and expensive in practice. An applicant needs five years' residence or five years' designated service, good character, knowledge of the English, Welsh or Scottish Gaelic language, knowledge of the way of life in Britain and an oath of allegiance to the Queen to be taken at a citizenship ceremony. Decisions are at the discretion of the Home Secretary and there is a limited appeal against refusal. A spouse needs only three years' residence to qualify.

The UK has always tolerated plural nationality (except for some limitations between 1870 and 1948).

Expatriates have the right to return and reside at any time. Their spouses and children, if not British citizens, have to qualify under immigration law. Certain rights in the UK, e.g., health care and access to financial help with university education, depend on residence and not on citizenship. Voting in Parliamentary elections is possible to many but not all expatriates provided they register to vote.

Except where European Community law provides otherwise, European Community nationals have no special privileges in the UK: they can be naturalised only on the same basis as all other aliens. Commonwealth-country citizens likewise now have no special access.

Although some of his functions are fulfilled in the Overseas Territories by the local Governor, the Home Secretary effectively has power over all nationality decisions under the legislation.

British citizenship can be renounced in order to obtain another nationality, and there is an entitlement, to be used once only, to resume it. Naturalised and registered citizens may be deprived of their status if they obtained it by fraud, misrepresentation or concealment of a material fact. Under the Nationality, Immigration and Asylum Act 2002, the Home Secretary may deprive *any* citizen of the status if he is satisfied that the person has done anything seriously prejudicial to the vital interests of the UK or an overseas territory (provided the person would not then become stateless). There is an appeal, but not to an ordinary court.

The Home Secretary may not discriminate on racial or religious grounds in his nationality functions.

There is no constitutional basis in UK law for citizens' rights; these depend on statutory provisions made separately from nationality laws, with one exception. The British Nationality Act 1981 specified that British citizens have 'right of abode' in the UK.

15.2 Historical development

15.2.1 The thirteenth century to 1608

'There is not, and never has been, any domestic concept of British nationality as such', wrote Professor Clive Parry, Fellow of Downing College, Cambridge (1957: 5). There is still some truth in this remarkable observation, for in 1981 the British government refused to insert in the major British Nationality Act of that year any definition of a British national. The Minister introducing the measure in the House of Lords said, 'The concept of British national is not something known to our domestic law'. Very reasonably, Viscount Simon objected, 'I do not understand how there can be anything called "British nationality" unless there are people who enjoy it'.

Lord Trefgarne replied that an amendment to the Bill, proposed by Lord Geddes and supported by some members of all parties in the House of Lords, defining the holders of all three of the proposed new 'citizenships' in the Bill as British nationals, 'would serve only to generate confusion'. It would 'raise expectations among the less well informed which in the event could not be realised'. It would 'imply some sort of eventual immigration commitment in the minds of some less informed people. That is the principal difficulty which we face'.[1] The Geddes amendment narrowly lost, by 102 votes to 105.

International law clearly requires that a state may not deny entry to its own nationals. Since such denial had been happening for nearly twenty years in 1981, and the government intended to continue it under a new set of labels, there had to be a pretence that the United Kingdom was abiding by international law. Therefore it was not possible to define the particular people it wanted to exclude as 'nationals', although that is undoubtedly what they were on the international plane.

This kind of fiction was possible because of the extraordinarily confused history of British nationality, a history that began with the concept of the 'subject' in mediaeval times. Although it is an anachronism to call mediaeval subjecthood a nationality, I shall have to call it one because of the continuous use up to 1948 of the term 'subject' to denote persons belonging to the country.

English, then British, history has been the story of a land and not of a people. Birth on or association with the land has always been the primary rule for acquiring nationality. Provision for ius sanguinis and for naturalisation has always been secondary, though both types of acquisition also go back to the middle ages. There was significant immigration to England in the mediaeval period of craftsmen and traders from France, Italy, Germany and the Low Countries, and the children of these aliens became subjects under the ius soli rule, as did the children of more numerous immigrants in later centuries.

The original rule of ius soli was a feudal one. A person born on any lord's land was that lord's subject and owed him allegiance. From the fact of birthplace arose rights and obligations on the part of both lord and subject. By the end of the thirteenth century it had become established that birth in the king's 'ligeance' made a person the king's subject, and the term 'ligeance' denoted both a tract of land and loyalty to the king (Pollock & Maitland 1952). From the king's point of view, a subject was a person who could provide military service and also be taxed. Those born outside the ligeance were aliens born. However, one should not suppose a hard-and-fast distinction between subjects and aliens that served for all purposes. The most important attribute of a subject in lawyers' eyes was the capacity to hold land in England, and for this reason disputes about who was a subject and who was not were for over four centuries concerned with property and inheritance.

In 1204, King John of England seized the lands of all those Norman barons who had not returned to England by a given date and who held English lands: war with the king of France then continued intermittently until 1244, when King Louis of France insisted that all those living in France must choose between him and Henry III of England. Traditionally, these events are supposed to be the origin of the common-law rule that only subjects could hold land in England. But the law was not consistently applied.

English common law was a customary law, 'common' in the sense of applying throughout the realm but also in the sense of being rooted in shared assumptions. It was not written in any code, but was developed by judicial decisions on the basis of unwritten assumptions. These were supposed, in turn, to rely on immemorial usage but in fact lawyers and judges had an important role in their formation. The common law is both conservative and flexible. It looks back to judicial precedent, but it also provides room for interpretation. 'Its roots', wrote C. K. Allen in 1927, 'strike deep into the soil of national ideals and institutions' (1939: 66).

The events of the early thirteenth century still have modern consequences. When King John lost his Norman possessions, he retained the Channel Islands. The islands, though constitutionally separate from the United Kingdom for some purposes, notably in their separate tax regimes and their relationship with the EEA, are for nationality purposes part of the United Kingdom, and birth there makes one a national.

Similarly, the Isle of Man is constitutionally separate from the United Kingdom but not for nationality purposes. It was granted by the Scottish Crown to earls of Derby in the fifteenth century and later to the dukes of Atholl. It was brought under the British Crown's administration in 1765.

The common law made no distinction between the different origins of aliens. For example, it barred aliens from sitting on juries empanelled to try English defendants or to hear civil cases between English parties, but from an early date alien merchants were given a jury composed half of Englishmen and half of aliens, to ensure them of impartiality. However, the alien jurors could be of any country or language, the principle evidently being that all these foreigners were the same. The half-tongue jury rule was confirmed in a statute of 1353: remarkably, it was confirmed again several times, the latest occasion being in 1825.

In the thirteenth century, King John's Great Charter (Magna Carta) had given alien merchants the right to come and go freely in and out of the kingdom. Subjects also had this right, of course, but the royal prerogative overrode the rights of some subjects and aliens together when Jews were expelled from England in 1290, not to return (officially at least) until 1656.

From the late-thirteenth century onwards, the king began to issue letters patent under his prerogative power to make certain aliens into denizens. This was an intermediate status between subjects and aliens, similar to the ancient Greek status of metic. It gave permission to hold land (but not to inherit it or bequeath it to children born before endenisation). The attributes of endenisation varied over the centuries, and it became very rare from the early-nineteenth century onwards.

The earliest example of naturalisation was the grant made to Elyas Daubeny in 1295 of the right to be heard in all royal courts *ut Anglicus* and to be taken and reputed as *Anglicum purum*. The grant was made by the king acting alone. From then on, there were occasional Acts of Parliament conferring naturalisation on certain individuals: these continued until the nineteenth century, when in 1844 Parliament provided for naturalisation by the executive power of the Home Secretary, after which legislation to naturalise individuals became very unusual.

In 1351, the statute *De Natis Ultra Mare* was passed, naming a list of individuals who had been born beyond the sea, out of the ligeance of the king, providing that they could all inherit property on the same terms as those born within the ligeance.[2] They were all children of the king or of fathers in the king's service. The statute furthermore added that *all* children born beyond the sea whose fathers and mothers were at the faith and ligeance of the king of England, and provided that the mothers had gone outside the realm with the permission of their husbands, could inherit, i.e., that they were subjects. ('Ligeance' is here used in the sense of allegiance rather than of a tract of land.)

The wording of the statute provided endless disputes over the next four centuries about which children born abroad were subjects and which were not, also about through how many generations born abroad subjecthood could pass. It was variously interpreted. But the statute had one permanent, clear consequence: birth abroad to a person in Crown service has always made a British national, however the parent's nationality was acquired. (Until 1983, the parent concerned had to be male.)

A rare example of theoretical discussion of the nature of allegiance and of subjecthood is found in Calvin's Case.[3] King James VI of Scotland had become James I of England, but the two kingdoms remained separate. J. Mervyn Jones calls the judgment 'the pure milk of the common law' (1947). It established certain doctrines which lasted a long time. Allegiance was to the person of the king, not to the kingdom. Allegiance was indelible: it could not be shaken off. Subjects were under the king's obedience, and he would protect them. The loyalty of the subject was due to the king by the law of nature and the law of nature was part of the law of England. Annexation of territory by the king made the inhabitants his subjects. Aliens within the kingdom owed a local allegiance, unless they were diplomatic servants of another ruler.

The case arose from the question, whether persons born in Scotland before James became king of England (the *antenati*) were subjects in England or not. The court decided they were not. But the *postnati*, born in Scotland after James's accession to the English throne, were subjects in England.

Incidentally, the case confirmed toleration of plural nationality, quoting from the thirteenth-century English jurist Bracton, who had considered the case of a knight who owed allegiance to two different lords.

15.2.2 *Religion and nationality*

Between 1529 and 1540, King Henry VIII made himself head of both church and state in England, by a series of Acts of Parliament. Church and nation were to be one. English nationalism became and remained for a long time fiercely anti-Catholic.

In 1570, the Pope excommunicated Queen Elizabeth and declared that her subjects were freed from their allegiance to her. In 1580, Parliament legislated to make any attempt to convert the queen's subjects to the Roman Catholic faith a treasonable offence. Priests made by the See of Rome since her reign were to be banished from the kingdom, and if they re-entered they were to be executed. These measures affected the rights of subjects as well as aliens.

Under James I, religious tests were incorporated in naturalisation law. An Act of 1609 required anyone becoming naturalised by private Bill to take the oath of supremacy (i.e., of royal supremacy over the Church) and to have taken the Anglican communion. Later, when new modes of naturalisation were introduced in order to encourage immigration between 1660 and 1714, the religious tests were still imposed. Endenisation survived until the nineteenth century, because it imposed no religious tests.

Conformity to the Church of England was enforced systematically, down to parish level in England and Wales. However in Ireland, which was ruled as a separate kingdom by English monarchs, the population remained stubbornly Catholic. Elizabeth I demanded uniformity of worship in 1560: forty years of war between England and the Irish rebels followed. James I settled Protestant landowners from Scotland and England in Ulster, on the ground that Catholic landowners had committed treason and forfeited their rights. The Irish rebelled in 1641 against the Ulster settlers and massacred great numbers of them. In revenge, in 1649, the English Protestant revolutionary leader, Oliver Cromwell, led an army into Ireland and in turn massacred many civilians, and in 1652 the English Parliament required forfeiture of the lands of almost every Irish landlord.

Irish immigration into England and Scotland has continued for economic reasons from the early centuries up to the present day, and many people in both countries have some Irish ancestry. Except in Elizabeth I's reign, when it was strictly limited in order to keep out potential subversives, Irish immigration has never been controlled. It has been too economically useful.

In 1662, a new measure, to encourage skilled craftsmen and in particular French Huguenot refugees, provided that skilled artisans could be naturalised after spending three years engaged in their trades in England, and from 1708 to 1710 a Foreign Protestants' Naturalisation

Act allowed any alien to become naturalised after taking the oaths of supremacy and allegiance and receiving Anglican communion.[4] These persons had also to declare before a court their support for the Protestant succession to the throne.

Jews had been re-admitted to England in the revolutionary period of the seventeenth century, and their children became British subjects by ius soli. Some became friends of princes: it was a Rothschild who brought the first news of the battle of Waterloo to the king in 1815.

The Dutch, although Protestants, who came while William of Orange was king, were unpopular in England, and a section was incorporated into the Act of Settlement 1701 prohibiting naturalised and endenised subjects from being Privy Councillors, MPs or Crown servants. These and other disabilities on naturalised subjects remained until 1844. The Act also prohibited any English king from being, or marrying, a Catholic, a provision which is still law today. (There is no such prohibition on any other religion.)

Disabilities on dissenting Protestants were relaxed from the early eighteenth century, but Catholics were not emancipated until 1829.

15.2.3 *Britain and the United Kingdom*

Wales was annexed to the English Crown in 1284 and later assimilated into England by Acts of Parliament in 1536 and 1542.[5]

James VI of Scotland, who became king of England also in 1603, wanted the two kingdoms to be united, but Parliament refused and an Act of Union between England and Scotland was not made until 1707.[6] The United Kingdom of Great Britain was then born, the basis of British nationality.

Kings of England had long been lords of Ireland, which had suffered English invasion as early as 1172, and which had been treated as a colony by successive monarchs. Ireland had its own Parliament, which in 1634 passed a statute to naturalise resident Scots, including those who had been born before 1603 in Scotland and who were therefore at the time aliens in England. In *Craw v. Ramsey* an English court decided that naturalisation did not make a person a subject in England, because legislation was effective only within the territory over which the legislator had authority.[7] But a person naturalised in England was a subject in Ireland, because Ireland was subordinate to England: it had been 'conquered and subjugated'.

This decision was to have very large consequences in the British empire overseas.

By an Act of Union passed in 1800, Ireland became in 1801 part of the United Kingdom. Irish demands for Home Rule were a major factor in British politics from then on. Just before the First World War, a

Home Rule Bill was at last passed in Britain, but its implementation was suspended because of the war. Violent revolt in Ireland followed, ruthlessly put down by the British army. At a general election in 1918, the nationalist Sinn Fein party carried all the southern counties, and set up a republican government there. In 1920, Britain, refusing to recognise the republic, established two Home Rule parliaments, one in the south and one in Ireland's Protestant north. Armed conflict continued, and eventually an Irish Free State was recognised in the south, while the six northern counties remained part of the United Kingdom. In 1937 the Irish in the south proclaimed national sovereignty and renamed the country Eire. In 1949, Eire declared herself the Republic of Ireland.

At Westminster, the British Parliament recognised the Republic and declared that Ireland had left the Commonwealth but was not a foreign country. Under the Ireland Act 1949, rules of law referring to the monarch's dominions would continue to apply *as if* the Republic were part of those dominions.[8] So Irish citizens retained the rights of British subjects in Britain, including political rights. By a reciprocal arrangement, British subjects held rights in Ireland. This system still holds. The Irish have gained further rights in Britain as a result of European Community law, notably in exemption from some provisions of British immigration law on the admission of relatives.

The Ireland Act also provided that Irish citizens born before 1949 could opt to remain British subjects by making a simple declaration, thus becoming dual nationals.

15.2.4 *Naturalisation and plural nationality*

Parliament's power to naturalise aliens by legislation directed at individuals was cumbersome. The Aliens Act 1844 empowered the Home Office (which already issued certificates of endenisation) to naturalise a resident alien by a simple procedure on presentation of a character reference.[9] The oath of allegiance must be taken and a fee paid. This Act also in part removed restrictions on aliens' holding land. The purpose was to encourage naturalisation at a time when immigrants were beneficial to industry and trade.

The Naturalisation Act 1870 removed all remaining restrictions on alien landholding, provided for naturalisation at the Home Office's discretion after five years' residence or Crown service, and allowed renunciation of British nationality for persons acquiring another nationality.[10] The Act was however restrictive and confused in some respects. A woman, upon marrying an alien, was to lose her British status while an alien woman became British, upon marrying a British husband. Since British authorities could not tell other countries who should acquire their nationality, some married women became stateless. Any subject being voluntarily naturalised in a foreign country and not being under a disability was to lose Britishness. Thus the 1870 Act initiated the only period in the history of British nationality when plural nationality was limited, and the position was not fully rectified until 1948.

15.2.5 *The British Empire*

It cannot be emphasised enough that British nationality law has often been imprecise and uncertainly applied. The history of nationality in the British Empire exhibits many muddles and contradictions, which had somehow to be sorted out in the twentieth century.

At first, around 1600, there was no problem about the status of people in the overseas colonies: those who had left England for the new lands were subjects, and the common law followed them to make all colonial-born children (except children of slaves and of American Indians) into subjects by ius soli. The colonies were part of the monarch's common-law dominions. However, the territories were left to run themselves in many respects. The governing authorities in the colonies soon took new powers upon themselves, including the power to naturalise. There was little or no religious discrimination in colonial naturalisations, so Catholics, Jews and Quakers could become local subjects. This enabled them to hold land. But such naturalisations took effect only in the colony concerned: someone naturalised in Virginia was a subject there but an alien in Pennsylvania. He was also an alien in England itself: following the judgement in *Craw v.* Ramsey legislation was effective only in the territory over which the legislator had authority.[11]

The empire grew in size and complexity in the eighteenth and nineteenth centuries, by treaty or by annexation. Some territories had native rulers: here the British regarded inhabitants not as subjects but as British Protected Persons; e.g., in several hundred princely states in India. BPP status originated in 1815, with British protection of the Ionian Islands. It was created under the royal prerogative. In practice, there was little difference between the treatment of subjects and of BPPs in the countries concerned, and internationally both were recognised as fully British. In 1945 there were about 100 million BPPs in the world, and about 400 million British subjects.

BPP status was occasionally granted to individuals, but mainly it was acquired by birth in a 'protected' territory, e.g., in the Malay states, which had their own Sultans. It was also bestowed on inhabitants of countries mandated to British rule by the League of Nations after the First World War (e.g., Palestine, Iraq, Tanganyika; the Iraq mandate ended in 1932). Some later remained under British administration as

United Nations trust territories. A British Nationality and Status of Aliens Act 1943 provided that the child of a British subject born in a protected territory was a subject.[12] BPP emigrants did not have the same right of transmission to children, but if their children were born within the common-law dominions of the Crown they would be subjects by ius soli. Children born in other protected territory would be BPPs.

It would be a mistake to suppose that this complex system was always applied with precision in practice. 'There must be a multitude of persons', wrote Sir Francis Piggott, 'who cannot say with certainty whether they are British subjects or not' (1907: Preface).

From the mid-nineteenth century onwards, Canada, Australia, New Zealand and South Africa were granted a large degree of autonomy, and from around 1900 began to control immigration, particularly by Indians and Chinese, many of whom were British subjects from other parts of the empire. Those who came had few citizenship rights after arrival. A British Nationality and Status of Aliens Act 1914 created an Imperial Certificate of Naturalisation valid anywhere in the empire but local certificates continued to be issued.[13] However, all subjects from any part of the empire had right of entry to the UK.

Pride in the expansion of empire made British governments happy to create as many British nationals in the world as possible. Ius sanguinis was extended indefinitely for children of British subjects, born abroad, in Acts of 1918 and 1922, e.g., in Argentina.[14]

The civic and political rights of subjects varied enormously from one territory to another, but all of them exercised the full rights of a subject if they came to the United Kingdom. This is why Commonwealth citizens still, today, vote and stand for office in the UK. BPPs however were in domestic law aliens under British protection and had no such rights.

15.2.6 *The British Nationality Act 1948*

The British Nationality Act 1948 made fundamental changes in British nationality law, as countries of the empire on every continent of the world moved toward independence.[15]

Britain tried to retain subjecthood as a nationality of the empire. The challenge to British rule had first succeeded in Ireland (see sect. 15.2.3). Then in 1946, Canada, already virtually independent, decided to assert her own citizenship internationally and issue her own passports. As a result, the British government responded by convening a group of legal experts to decide what changes must be made to the imperial system in general.

At the same time, Indian independence, after a long struggle, had become inevitable. In haste, the sub-continent was divided into two new states, India and Pakistan, in 1947. India soon rejected the Queen as Head of State, declaring itself a republic.

The foundation of subjecthood, and also the link which had bound together the empire and was now supposed to bind the Commonwealth of Nations as a voluntary association of countries, was allegiance to the monarch. This was an idea which British politicians found hard, after seven centuries, to reject. They had become accustomed too to defining Britishness in terms of imperial and not merely national identity. So the British Nationality Bill, which they drew up in 1948, retained subjecthood as in theory a nationality of the whole empire, within which there were to be separate citizenships, explaining that nationality (subjecthood) was to be the genus, citizenship the species. Other countries were expected soon to become independent, but all would be linked together in the Commonwealth. Within the overall scheme there would be a single citizenship of the United Kingdom and Colonies. As each colony became independent, its inhabitants would change this status for the citizenship of a new state.

All subjects would continue, as before, to have the right of entry to the UK and the rights of the subject (voting etc.) there. It would have been politically unthinkable at the time to remove these rights from persons anywhere in the empire: imperial troops had fought for Britain in the Second World War, and British people's pride and sense of identity were still bound up with empire. However one unfortunate result was that the new status of citizen of the UK-and-Colonies (CUKC) had no rights attached to it: only the opportunity (it was not even a right) to be granted a British passport. For anything else, the British had still to rely on being subjects.

From the beginning, the scheme was unworkable. There were Hindu-muslim riots in India and Pakistan; about two million people fled from one country to the other to escape massacre, and hundreds of thousands of these failed to obtain citizenship in either country. According to the British Nationality Act 1948, they should have been transformed then into CUKCs when these countries' citizenship schemes took effect. Taking effect meant being incorporated in British law in either a statute or an Order in Council, and in this sense the citizenship laws of India, Pakistan and Ceylon (Sri Lanka) never took effect. Although in practice the new states' laws were recognised, the British subjects omitted from their provisions became known as 'British subjects without citizenship of any Commonwealth country' (BSWCs). The number of people in this category has never been known with accuracy. A few were of British descent, their families having lived and worked in India for generations. The Home Secretary had discretion to register most of such persons as CUKCs if they applied before January 1950, which some failed to do.[16]

Another group of BSWCs consisted of Irish citizens who were British subjects immediately before 1 January 1949 and who gave written notice to the Home Secretary that they claimed to remain British subjects. Most of the people concerned were resident in Britain.

The status of British Protected Persons remained unchanged. They were mentioned in the Bill only to be excluded from the expression 'alien' in the Aliens Restrictions Acts.

These secondary issues apart, the main scheme of the Bill could not succeed because it failed to recognise the reality that new states' citizenships were also new states' nationalities. Internationally, no country regarded an Indian citizen/British subject as anything but an Indian national. Moreover, once the new states declared themselves republics, as many did, allegiance to the monarch could no longer be the basis of their status in British law. It was agreed in 1949 that the Queen should be Head of the Commonwealth, a courtesy title with no constitutional implications. But what now was subjecthood?

For the future the Bill provided that a person would become a subject if he or she had citizenship of any Commonwealth country. The terms 'British subject' and 'Commonwealth citizen' were to be interchangeable in law. This was a gesture towards republicans in India and elsewhere who understandably resented the word 'subject'. But people in Britain never came to think of themselves as 'Commonwealth citizens', though that was what they were under the 1948 Act.

Persons becoming naturalised in the UK and in the colonies still had to take the oath of allegiance to the Queen, although allegiance was no longer the basis of subjecthood or of the new CUKC status: both were now to be determined by statutory definition.

The new law attracted very little attention. Its one newsworthy aspect was to return rights to married women. British women who married aliens would retain their British nationality. And alien women marrying British men would have the choice, whether to retain their alien nationality or exercise the right to register as CUKCs without any residence qualification, a right available even if the women were divorced or widowed.

The main provisions of the new law on citizenship of the UK-and-colonies (CUKC) used elements of both ancient and modern law concerning subjecthood:

- since the mediaeval period, the basic rule of ius soli, tolerance of plural nationality, citizenship for children born abroad to English (then British) parents, also of parents in Crown service;
- since the nineteenth and early twentieth centuries, executive decisions on naturalisation, conditions for naturalisation including five

years' residence and evidence of good character, and sufficient knowledge of the English language.

There was provision for the renunciation and resumption of UKC citizenship. Persons from Commonwealth countries were to have privileged access to CUKC through registration: twelve months' residence in the UK was the only condition and no fee was to be charged. As Commonwealth citizens/British subjects retained free entry to the UK, this condition was a very easy one to fulfil.

15.2.7 *Immigration and nationality*

In the nineteenth century, alien entry and stay were completely uncontrolled, in line with liberal, free-trade theory, and many foreign revolutionaries took advantage of this, Marx and Lenin being among the best-known. However, after the assassination of Tsar Alexander II in 1881, and many subsequent anarchist and revolutionary murders elsewhere in Europe, the British authorities became nervous about aliens as potential subversives. At the same time, new racial theories had gained intellectual popularity: in Britain there were claims that the 'Teutonic' British were intrinsically superior to Latin races, and religious anti-Jewish prejudice was transformed into racial anti-Semitism.

In 1905, an Aliens Act, directed chiefly against poor Jews from Eastern Europe fleeing persecution, placed control of alien entry with the Home Office, the government department responsible for security and policing. Official policy from then on was suspicious and restrictive towards entrants, and a large discretion was written into the law, which made differential treatment of individuals possible. The consequences have lasted up to the present.

Strong anti-German feelings in the following years helped to produce the Aliens (Restriction) Acts of 1914 and 1919. After 1917, the government was very frightened of communism and between the world wars almost all alien immigrants were admitted only temporarily. For example, in 1927, 412,686 aliens were given permission to land, while 409,925 departed. Despite pressure to admit refugees, only 55,000 European Jews were admitted between 1933 and 1939.

In 1939, 239,000 aliens lived in Britain, 80,000 of these being refugees (a group including many east Europeans admitted before 1914 who had been refused naturalisation or not applied for it). In 1920, without referring back to ministers, the Permanent Secretary (chief official) at the Home Office trebled the naturalisation fee to ten British Pounds, a sum equivalent to many weeks' wages for the lowest-paid workers, who included pre-war Jewish immigrants. It was Home Office practice (not written into legislation) that Jews must be resident fifteen years and not just the statutory five before being considered for naturalisation. John Pedder, a Home Office civil servant, wrote in 1924, 'Slavs, Jews and other races from central and eastern parts of Europe [...] do not readily identify themselves with this country' (Dummett & Nicol 1990: 154).

After the Second World War, the authorities were still reluctant to admit aliens even though Britain was suffering a severe labour shortage and needed massive reconstruction of houses and factories. By 1951, there were only 429,000 aliens in a total population of about 48 million. This figure included about 16,000 European Voluntary Workers (displaced persons) who had been admitted annually *outside* the provisions of the Aliens Acts. Even this small number drew hostility from some trade unions and newspapers.

Alien immigration was far too small to meet the demand for labour, and from the late 1940s onwards immigrants from West Indian and African colonies and then from the independent countries of India and Pakistan began to arrive in search of work. As 'British subjects' under the 1948 British Nationality Act, they were free to do so.

The Labour government (1945-51) did not want 'coloured' immigration, and used some administrative means to discourage it (Dummett & Nicol 1990: 177 ff.). Conservative ministers in the 1950s discussed how they could limit it without excluding immigrants 'of good type' from the white Dominions. Race and colour dominated the immigration debate. In 1962, a Conservative government, under pressure from local Conservative associations, passed a Commonwealth Immigrants Act to control the entry of all Commonwealth citizens (i.e., all British subjects under the 1948 Act) unless they had been born in the UK or Ireland or held passports issued by the UK or Irish governments.[17] The result was that CUKCs from colonies became subject to control, as did citizens of independent Commonwealth countries.

The 1962 Act and Rules gave a large discretion to Immigration Officers, who used it to admit most white Commonwealth applicants freely and to refuse many Asians, Africans and West Indians.

The Bill in Parliament was attacked not on the grounds that Britain was denying entry to her own citizens but with the claim that it was against the Commonwealth ideal and was racially discriminatory. Alien immigration had become much less controversial. During the 1960s, three times as many alien work-permit holders were admitted annually as were 'Commonwealth' work-voucher holders. In practice, though not in law, it was often easier for these aliens to bring their dependants in than for Commonwealth immigrants, who theoretically had some entitlement to be joined by wives and children under sixteen. It was obvious how the Home Office was using its discretion in immigration policy, but the use of discretion in naturalisation policy could not be known because this process was secret.

There were minor British Nationality Acts in the next few years. The BNA 1964 facilitated renunciation and resumption.[18] The BNA (no. 2) 1964 made registration possible as CUKCs for children born stateless abroad with a British parent (this usually meant the mother of an illegitimate child).[19] The BNA 1965 enabled alien wives of British subjects without citizenship of any Commonwealth country to become BSWCs.[20]

There is a hidden intention in the first BNA 1964: it provided for resumption of CUKC in countries which had become independent only by persons who had a qualifying connection with the UK itself – a connection which in effect applied to people of UK ancestry and excluded people of Indian descent in the newly-independent East African countries.

The East African countries of the empire all had sizeable minorities of Indian descent, forming a middle class of business-people, civil servants, teachers, bank workers etc. between the white minority which ran the country and the large African majority. With independence, the Indians were afraid they would be deprived of their positions by the new African governments. Some opted for citizenship of the new countries concerned; others thought they would play safe by retaining CUKC status after independence – then, if things went wrong, they could go to Britain. Their passports would be issued on behalf of the UK government and they would therefore be free of entry control. Things did go wrong in Kenya, where the new government imposed severe disabilities on non-citizens, who found themselves suddenly forbidden to work. Several thousand came to Britain. The Labour government in power at the time panicked and rushed a Bill through Parliament in only five days to deny entry to the 'Kenya Asians' as they were called. CUKCs had no right of entry to any colony except the one with which they had connections. Kenya was no longer a colony. With entry to the UK barred, these CUKCs (and subsequently others in newly independent territories) had nowhere to go under the Commonwealth Immigrants Act 1968.[21]

Ministers argued that they were not denying but delaying entry, and set up a voucher system, a queue for admission, which allowed only a small trickle of persons to come each year. CUKCs who tried to travel from Kenya were turned back at British ports and turned back again when returned to Kenya. Eventually, many were imprisoned upon arrival in Britain and after a time freed and allowed to stay. Every effort was made to discourage their coming.[22] Racial origin was not named in the law; the device used was a qualifying connection with the UK:

the person or at least one of his or her parents or grandparents must have been born, naturalised, registered or adopted in the UK.

It became very difficult for immigration officials in other countries to determine who was returnable to the UK and who was not: possession of a passport was not enough.

Within the UK there were two distinct sets of controls: one for aliens and one for British subjects and Commonwealth citizens. The Conservative government, which took power in 1970, produced the Immigration Act 1971, designed to combine both systems in one. Persons called patrial would be free of control.[23]

Patrial	**Non-patrial**, subject to control
CUKCs born, registered, adopted or naturalised in the UK (some registrations and adoptions excepted)	All aliens
CUKCs with parent or grandparent as above	British Protected Persons
CUKCs who had been ordinarily resident in UK for at least 5 years at any time	CUKCs whose status derived from colonies
Any CUKC woman married to a CUKC man	Commonwealth-country citizens not qualifying as patrial (i.e., most of them)
Commonwealth-country citizen with a parent born in UK	
Commonwealth citizen woman married to a patrial	

When the Immigration Rules were published, they made clear that there would be privileged access for persons with a British-born grandparent, decisions to be made at discretion. Several million white citizens of independent Commonwealth countries were thus effectively freed of controls.

15.2.8 The British Nationality Act 1981

Patriality had become a quasi-nationality, and the situation was so confusing that it soon became clear that a thorough overhaul of British nationality law was needed. The Labour and Conservative parties, and several independent bodies, produced plans for a new system. The most radical but least regarded came from AGIN (the Action Group on Immigration and Nationality), which proposed right of entry for all those with some existing form of *de lege* British nationality. By this time, most former colonies had become independent and the number of colonial citizens had shrunk. But the great stumbling block for even comparatively liberal-minded politicians was Hong Kong, where it was estimated there were about 2.6 million CUKCs of Chinese origin (the rest of the population consisting mainly of immigrants from the People's Republic of China). The Labour government did nothing.

In 1979 a Conservative government returned to power, having promised in its manifesto that it would introduce a new British Nationality Act 'to reduce future sources of immigration'. When it produced its draft measure, more than one newspaper described it as a new immigration Bill. The government's original proposals, set out in a White Paper of July 1980, drew heavy condemnation. *The Scotsman* newspaper commented: 'They do not define British nationality as having any meaning [...]. British nationality is to have no rights attached to it whatever: The idea that it should do so is specifically rejected by the White Paper.' (12 July 1980)

The Economist said: 'It is taken for granted that the aim of a new law should be to limit in the future the numbers of people in the world eligible to enter and live in the UK. This aim however is not to be fulfilled, because the proposals would leave untouched the right of several million patrial Commonwealth citizens (mostly white people) to come here and settle [...]. In short, the proposals would create a disguised racial Immigration Act rather than a true Nationality Act. [The measure] demonstrates the increasingly racial loading of the concept of British citizenship'. (2-8 August 1980)

The main plan was to re-label existing categories in immigration law as types of British nationality thus:

Patrial CUKCs	British citizens
Patrial British subjects without citizenship	British citizens
Non-patrial Colonial CUKCs	British Dependent Territories Citizens

Non-patrial CUKCs in former colonies	British Overseas Citizens
Non-patrial BSWCs	British subjects
British Protected Persons	British Protected Persons

The last three were designed to die out, as there was virtually no provision for transfer to children.

There had been no formal consultations with other Commonwealth countries on the proposed changes. Even more surprisingly, the White Paper never mentioned the European Economic Community, although the UK was already a member, and the EEC rules on movement of persons were already in operation: the consequences for immigration as a whole were obvious.

The government yielded to a few objections, but only on minor points. The British Nationality Act 1981 remains the main basis for the present law.[24]

The only legislative change made before 1985 was the British Nationality (Falkland Islands) Act, which actually emphasised the racial character of the main scheme. Mrs. Thatcher had gone to war with Argentina in 1982 over the sovereignty of this British colony, which was very small, with fewer than 2,000 inhabitants, but which mattered greatly to Argentinean national feeling.[25] The inhabitants were all white, being mostly the descendants of Scottish shepherds. Dependent Territories' Citizens under the 1981 Act, they were made full British citizens in 1983 as a victorious gesture.

The British Nationality Act 1981 has been slightly amended with new provisions concerning Hong Kong, which was returned to China in 1997. The Regulations have also been changed on several occasions. Some major changes were made in the Nationality, Immigration and Asylum Act 2002,[26] but these are not yet all in force, and by the end of 2004, no dates had been set for commencement on some important points (see sect. 15.3.1.3).

The most controversial clause in the 1981 Bill was a limitation on the ancient ius soli rule. This was opposed by the churches, the Labour, Liberal and SDP parties in Parliament, and many NGOs. Only a child with a British citizen parent or settled parent would become a British citizen by birth in the UK. Other children would have to rely on a parent's non-British nationality or else be stateless. There were however complicated provisions for registration of children not born citizens. 'Settled' meant being ordinarily resident and not subject to any restrictions under immigration law, and a parent who became either a citizen or settled after the birth was entitled to register a child already born in the UK. There was a separate provision for registration of stateless children. Until 1981 only a birth certificate in the UK had been needed to prove a child's citizenship; from commencement date onwards (1 January 1983) a new bureaucracy had to be satisfied. This reflected the government's aim of reducing future immigration. In future, some children born in the UK would be alien or stateless, and would lack right of abode.

The new system was a classic example of the Home Office's approach. The purpose of the new law was to limit immigration rather than to deal with nationality itself, and so the means chosen were a complicated collection of provisions to reduce the number of people eligible to pass on nationality and with it the right of abode to their descendants. Yet liberal objections must be met: hence the elaborate provisions for registration – for which many potential applicants would fail to apply. The same motives underlay the creation of two alternative 'citizenships': British Dependent Territories Citizenship (BDTC) and British Overseas Citizenship (BOC), both carrying the name of Britishness to satisfy liberals and traditionalists, but conferring no right of entry to Britain.

Before the 1981 Act came into force, there had been various statutory provisions enabling British people with a UK connection to pass on their citizenship to children born outside the UK. These were now replaced by rules intended to limit citizenship by descent mainly to the first generation born abroad. But again there had to be exceptions. The long-standing rule that children born to parents in Crown service abroad would be nationals was preserved: it was therefore possible that a 'citizen by descent', born abroad, could pass on citizenship to a child born abroad if he or she was a diplomat or serving in the armed forces. Again, when that child grew up, he or she would be able to pass on citizenship if in Crown service abroad at the time of the birth. The new rules on descent included mothers as well as fathers for the first time. British citizens in European Community service were added to Crown servants, provided they had been recruited in an EC country. Certain other groups were included under the heading of 'designated service' abroad: e.g., employees of the British Council and the Commonwealth War Graves Commission. Subsequently, new regulations made under Order (a procedure authorised in the main Act) have added other forms of designated service, including some commercial employment.[27] Thus, an elaborate system was set up which failed to satisfy everyone. There was no retrospective provision for children already born abroad to British mothers. The rules on designated service appeared arbitrary to some people.

The system also provided that a parent who did not qualify to pass on citizenship by descent under the main scheme (e.g., a British journalist, a citizen by descent, with an alien wife, becoming a father while working abroad) was entitled to register a child as British if certain conditions were satisfied: if the parent in question had ever lived in the UK continuously for three years without more than 270 days' absence up to the time of the birth or was present in the UK three years before the application for the child's registration. The child would be a citizen by descent. No citizen by descent was entitled to become a citizen other than by descent.[28] The Home Secretary was given the power in sect. 3 (1) to register any minor child of any parentage and any birthplace at discretion.

The 1981 Act repeated earlier naturalisation rules: five years' residence, the last year being free of immigration control; good character; a language test in English, Welsh or Scottish Gaelic (the last two to appease Welsh and Scottish nationalism). The language test consisted of an interview with a police officer: if the applicant and the officer could understand each other's speech, all was well.

Registration was to become a process used mainly for minors. Its use as privileged access for Commonwealth citizens and for wives of British citizens was cut off by the 1981 Act after a transitional period.

The 1981 Act provided for renunciation and resumption (on one occasion only) by entitlement, with discretion for the Home Secretary to allow resumption more than once. Normally, renunciation occurs when a British citizen acquires another nationality in a country which does not permit dual nationality.

The 1981 Act provided for deprivation of nationality if a naturalised or registered citizen had obtained citizenship by fraud, misrepresentation or concealment of a material fact. The Act further provided that a naturalised or registered citizen could be deprived if he or she was disloyal to the Queen, or had assisted an enemy in time of war or had in the last five years been sentenced to at least twelve months' imprisonment in any country. There was a possibility for appeal to a committee appointed by the Home Secretary and including a person of judicial experience (sect. 40). Only about a dozen people were ever deprived under this particular rule.

15.3 Recent developments and current institutional arrangements

15.3.1 *Regulations of acquisition and loss of nationality*

15.3.1.1 *British Overseas Territories Act 2002*[29]

In 2002, the colonies, already renamed British Dependent Territories, were again renamed British Overseas Territories. These territories are very varied: the Cayman Islands are a tax haven for the rich, the British Antarctic Territory has no inhabitants except scientists and penguins, while Diego Garcia in the Indian Ocean has become an American airbase, all its citizens forcibly removed to Mauritius and forbidden to return.[30] Most colonies have Governors appointed from the UK. After 1947, most colonies were granted independence in a series of Acts of Parliament and Orders in Council, and their new governments established various forms of citizenship, some generous and some restrictive.

There were three colonies which could not be granted independence: Gibraltar because by the Treaty of Utrecht 1713 it must be returned to Spain if Britain left; Hong Kong because by a series of treaties most of the colony (Kowloon and the New Territories, which were integrated into one with the Crown colony of Hong Kong) was on lease from China due to end in 1997; and the Falkland Islands because their sovereignty was disputed with Argentina.

A citizen from the United Kingdom had no right to enter any colony, nor had a citizen from one colony the right to enter any other. Only a 'belonger', differently defined in each colony, had the right to enter the territory concerned. Citizenship of the UK and Colonies was hardly ever mentioned in the dependencies' laws. The inhabitants who 'belonged' were universally described as 'British subjects' who fulfilled certain conditions unrelated to the citizenship established in the British Nationality Act 1948. A child born outside the colony to a belonger parent was usually considered a belonger only if he or she had parents domiciled or ordinarily resident there. Moreover, a colony's Governor often had powers to withdraw belonger status.

Under Community law Gibraltar, as a European territory for which a Member State was responsible, was included in EEC freedom-of-movement rules. Special provision for Gibraltarians was written into the British Nationality Act 1981, sect. 5, entitling them to be registered as British citizens on application. Colonial CUKCs there had been excluded from the right to enter the UK under the Commonwealth Immigration Acts, and in 1971 the government had had to consider how to reconcile their position with Community law. A unilateral Declaration was hurried out in December 1972 just before the 1971 Immigration Act came into force on 1 January 1973. It specified that British nationals for Community purposes would be patrial CUKCs, patrial BSWCs and persons who, or whose fathers, had been born, registered or naturalised in Gibraltar. Exactly the same groups were specified in a new Declaration late in 1982; only the names had been changed: British citizens, British Subjects one of whose parents had been born, adopted, registered or naturalised in the UK, and certain BDTCs connected with Gibraltar.

The 1981 Act established a British Dependent Territories Citizenship (BDTC) for all the colonies, with no effective change to the existing regime of belonger status. Colonial citizens have never been represented in the Westminster Parliament, and so in the debates on the 1981 Bill they had to rely on the few members for British constituencies in the Commons, and few members of the Lords, who took a special interest in their affairs, to speak up for them. Lobbyists from Hong Kong tried hard to get their special problems recognised. The colony was of enormous economic and financial importance.

Bit by bit, the British government made a few concessions in the following years. In the 1985 agreement for the return of Hong Kong to China, it was agreed that Hong Kong BDTCs could apply for a new status called British National (Overseas) – BNO, available on application up to 1 July 1997. This was not a citizenship but a name to put on a travel document, to facilitate business travel. BNOs have to naturalise in order to become BCs. Then the Hong Kong Act 1990 provided that British citizenship could be granted to 50,000 people in certain specified categories who were considered necessary to Hong Kong's future.[31] (This was to persuade them not to abandon Hong Kong for other countries.) The Hong Kong (War Wives and Widows) Act 1996 entitled Hong Kong women whose husbands had fought in the Second World War to register as BCs.[32] The British Nationality (Hong Kong) Act 1997 belatedly entitled those Hong Kong citizens not eligible for any other nationality after the handover in July 1997 to register as BCs.[33] Most of these people were of Indian ethnic origin: their families had often lived in Hong Kong for generations.

All the inhabitants of Chinese ethnic origin were already Chinese citizens under the law of the People's Republic. Those who had been BDTCs numbered barely half the territory's population, the rest of the Chinese ethnic population having been immigrants from the People's Republic.

Once Hong Kong had reverted to China, the British government could consider the situation of other BDTCs, who totalled fewer than 200,000 persons. Action was not swift, but eventually the British Overseas Territories Act was passed in 2002.[34] It provided that all BDTCs alive on commencement day (1 April 2003) were to be British citizens and also British Overseas Territories citizens. This 'domestic double nationality' allowed the persons concerned right of entry to the UK itself as well as to the overseas territory of residence; as before, it conferred no rights in the other dependencies. Persons connected with the sovereign military bases of Akrotiri and Dhekelia in Cyprus would not become BCs unless they had a connection with some other dependency. But BCs from the UK still had no right of entry to any overseas territory.

After commencement of the BOTA 2002, acquisition of British citizenship in the overseas territories was brought into line with the rules for the United Kingdom concerning birthplace, adoption, descent etc.[35] But to be 'settled' is a status very hard to obtain in the overseas territories: and their children can therefore seldom benefit from the ius soli rule and acquire local citizenship.

15.3.1.2 *The Nationality, Immigration and Asylum Act 2002*[36]

Nationality may come first in the title of this measure, but 89 per cent of the text is on immigration and asylum. The main purpose of the Bill was to deal with these two issues. In Parliament, the debates rarely touched upon the nationality provisions, which are an odd mixture. Some of them can be summarised as tidying up the existing law. Sects. 5 to 15 are broadly in this category: some provide a measure of sex equality (on resumption, rights for fathers of illegitimate children, and children born to British mothers abroad between 1961 and 1983), while sect. 11 defines unlawful residence, sect. 14 makes minor changes concerning Hong Kong, sect. 8 removes an age limit for registering stateless children born in the UK and sect. 10 provides for regulations on the 'right of abode', which still exists for Commonwealth-country citizens who held it before 1983. Sect. 12 provides that BOCs, BSs and BPPs are entitled to registration as British citizens wherever in the world they are living, not only in the UK as under the 1981 Act. But the provision is not quite as liberal as it seems: many people in the categories affected have died off; the applicant must have no other nationality, the citizenship acquired is 'by descent' (i.e., not usually transferable), a fee must be paid, and many possible beneficiaries have no means of learning about the new rule.

The main changes in the 2002 Act concern naturalisation and deprivation of citizenship.[37] There is a new emphasis on the value and importance of British citizenship: A citizenship ceremony becomes obligatory; applicants must show 'sufficient knowledge' of life in Britain, and the oath is altered to require a commitment to democratic values and fulfilment of a citizen's duties. The new ceremony, organised at County Council level under Home Office guidelines, has proved popular. But the barriers to naturalisation have been made much higher, especially for spouses, who must now take a language test and a test of 'knowledge of life in the UK'. Arrangements for these tests have been chaotic and in early 2005 were still not finalised. The standard required in English must be equivalent to ESOL (English for Speakers of Other Languages) Entry Three, a very much higher standard than the old police interview test. This can be waived for reasons of age or disability or at discretion, but otherwise is certain to affect many adversely. The 'life' test will eventually be merged with the language test. Attendance at a 'life in the UK' course is to be made compulsory. Tests, courses and ceremonies must all be paid for, adding significantly to the cost of naturalisation. The total cost to an applicant can be over 400 British Pounds.[38]

The avowed aim is 'to develop among migrants and the settled population a stronger sense of social participation and shared values' (Home Office, 'Controlling our Borders', February 2005). This is in line with the Blair government's drive for conformity to values laid down from above, seen in many aspects of social policy. It must be said that the values in naturalisation policy include celebration of Britain's ethnic diversity.

Sect. 8 provides that, although the Home Secretary may still discriminate on grounds of ethnic or national origin in immigration policy, he may no longer do so in his nationality functions.

The most important change in 2002 concerns deprivation of citizenship. Added to the 1981 clause is a long and confusing section (sect. 4) providing that the Home Secretary can deprive *any* citizen if he is satisfied that the person has done anything seriously prejudicial to the vital interests of the UK or an overseas territory, provided the person would not thereby become stateless. There is an appeal to an immigration adjudicator, unless the Home Secretary says his decision was taken wholly or partly in reliance on information which in his opinion should not be made public in the interests of national security, of the UK's relations with another country, or otherwise in the public interest. There may then be an appeal to the Special Immigration Appeals Commission.

Undoubtedly, the political motivation behind the 2002 Act's provisions making naturalisation harder and deprivation easier was anxiety following the attack on New York's twin towers in September 2001.

15.3.1.3 Party politics and nationality

The two major parties in Britain, Labour and Conservative, have held power alternately since 1945 as follows:

1945-1951	Labour	BNA 1948
1951-1964	Conservative	Commonwealth Immigrants Act 1962; BNA 1964
1964-1970	Labour	BNA (No. 2) 1964; BNA 1965; Commonwealth Immigrants Act 1968
1970-1974	Conservative	Immigration Act 1971
1974-1979	Labour	
1979-1997	Conservative	BNA 1981; Hong Kong Acts 1985 to 1997
1997-2004	Labour	British Overseas Territories Act 2002; Nationality, Immigration and Asylum Act 2002

Policy on nationality has followed a more or less continuous line regardless of which party has been in power. Both main parties have since 1962 seen nationality as *instrumental* in achieving the ends of immigration policy. Immigration has been the primary concern, nationality only secondary. As explained above, there has never been a clear political theory of the nation of the kind taken for granted in continental Europe nor is there a fundamental, constitutional law to satisfy. This has meant that nationality policy can easily be manipulated to serve ends outside itself. Public opinion has always taken nationality for granted, and frequently has no idea what rights it does or does not confer.

The Labour Party Green Paper (discussion document) issued in 1975 was in almost every respect similar to the Conservative proposals on nationality in 1972: both proposed cutting off existing nationals with an 'overseas' status and denying entry to the UK, and ignored the question of substantive rights attached to citizenship (Dummett & Nicol 1990: 241-242 and notes). Both parties have had very similar attitudes to immigration when in power. The similarity has been somewhat obscured in the public eye by divisions of opinion *within* political parties; part (though not all) of the Labour left being more liberal and one wing of the Conservatives very restrictive. These internal differences have largely disappeared under the influence of power and, probably, under that of the permanent officials in the Home Office.

In theory, civil servants do not advance their own opinions and simply serve whatever government is in power. In practice, the officials are far more knowledgeable in their respective fields of policy than their temporary political masters. In such a highly complicated area as nationality, therefore, they play a decisive role in providing ministers with information and suggestions and in formulating legislation and the rules under which it is administered. Highly important here is the very large discretion written into British nationality law: legislation is so designed that the Home Office officials can take their own decisions on a large range of cases, seldom reviewed by the courts.

A second strand of policy has been a series of small, liberal adjustments yielding to outside non-party lobbying: some advances in sex equality (1981 and 2002), concessions on Hong Kong in the 1990s, improved rights for colonial citizens (British Overseas Territories Act 2002). It often takes some time for these amendments to be introduced: there was already active lobbying for all of these causes in 1981, but only sex equality had some recognition (and that only partial) then. The right for the three least privileged groups of British nationals (BSs, BOCs and BPPs) to register as British citizens was called for in 1981 but not introduced until a significant number in all categories had either died off or managed to acquire some other nationality.

15.3.2 *Institutional arrangements*

15.3.2.1 *The legislative process*

The United Kingdom has no single-document constitution serving as a fundamental law which ordinary legislation has to satisfy. Parliament can therefore do what it likes in legislating on nationality/citizenship.

The process is as for other legislation: a bill is prepared by a government department (always the Home Office in this matter), 'read' three times in the House of Commons and three times in the House of Lords, and then submitted for royal assent, which is a mere formality and never withheld.

The first reading in each House is a simple announcement, a bill having been published. At second reading, there is a debate in the relevant House. The House will then go into committee for detailed scrutiny, clause by clause, of the bill. It then returns to the House concerned for third reading. Amendments are generally made at committee stage, and others may be added for discussion at third reading. At every stage, decisions are made by a simple majority of votes.

By convention, a bill with constitutional implications normally has its committee stage in the whole House of Commons, but the government has control of business; the government of the time decided that the highly important 1981 British Nationality Bill should go to a small committee instead. On these small committees, the political parties are represented in proportion to their strength in the whole House. In the case of a tied vote, the Chairman of the committee must give his or her casting vote to the government side. (In the full House of Commons, the Speaker is under the same obligation to support the government.)

Some bills are initiated in the House of Lords: there are then three readings in that House, followed by three in the Commons. A bill returns after three readings in both places to the House where it was initiated if there have been changes to it in the most recent stage. Usually, the House of origin accepts these changes, but if the Commons have the final say they may undo some of the Lords' amendments. The guiding principle is that the Commons, being elected, has a superior right to that of the unelected Lords to take decisions.

The composition of the House of Lords is peculiar. It still includes the descendants of hereditary peers, some of whose titles go back many centuries. It also includes two Church of England archbishops and 24 bishops, whose right to be there goes back to the middle ages. But many members now are 'life peers', appointed for public service and unable to transmit their titles to heirs. Many life peers are former members of the Commons.

Members of Parliament almost invariably vote as the party Whips tell them to do. The party in power has usually an absolute majority in the Commons (and therefore on its committees) and unless the government decides to accept an amendment that amendment can rarely succeed. Outside pressure sometimes persuades the government to accept some concessions, which are then presented in government wording and usually have only limited effect. In 1981, the churches objected to many parts of the British Nationality Bill, but succeeded in wringing only minor concessions from the government.

Voting in the House of Lords is less dependent on party affiliation than in the Commons. There are some 'crossbench' peers who vote independently, and even the party members will sometimes go against their own Whips. However, the Lords' powers have been limited by a series of Parliament Acts since 1910. If their amendments are not to the government's taste, they can be voted down when a Bill makes its final return, after the Lords' consideration of the measure, to the full House of Commons.

The timing of the whole process is in the hands of the government. Clearly there is little hope of substantial change to the main principles of a government Bill, once it has been introduced, and even less hope of total rejection.

There is no constitutional court to carry out judicial review of a bill. The process of judicial review is, however, often used for individual cases concerning application of the law once it has been passed.

15.3.2.2 *The process of implementation*

The Home Office, a central government bureaucracy, implements nationality law. No local or regional body has the power to make decisions. In the Overseas Territories the Governor has the power, but applications in foreign countries go through the British embassies to the Home Office in London. The Home Office also has the responsibility for issuing passports, and for immigration law and its administration, also for the police and part of the intelligence services.

Decisions on nationality 'by grant', that is by naturalisation and registration, are routinely made by officials. If nationality is refused, an appeal can be made to the Home Office itself, when senior officials will reconsider applications. Otherwise, like all administrative decisions, they can be judicially reviewed. The Home Office says it has no record of how many judicial reviews there have been in recent years, though some have been successful. Before 1997, the Home Office did not have to give reasons for refusal, though in fact it would tell an applicant if failure to meet the residence requirements was a reason. In 1997, Mohammed al Fayed succeeded in persuading the Court of Appeal that the Home Office must behave reasonably and fairly, informing an applicant of reasons so that he would know what to do to re-apply.[39] The NIAA 2002 provided that reasons must be given, reversing the position in the BNA 1981.

In 2003, 44 per cent of applications were granted on the basis of residence, 30 per cent to spouses, and almost 24 per cent to minor children. Grants totalled 124,315, the highest figure ever recorded. Applications from the European Economic Area (including Gibraltar) were only one per cent of the total, with the rest of Europe accounting for 14 per cent. The largest group of applicants were from India, Pakistan and various African countries. Total applications have risen steadily year-by-year since 1993 from just under 50,000 to 124,315 in 2003. In 2003, the largest number of refusals (3,005) were on the ground that residence requirements had not been fulfilled, the second largest (1,280) because of delays by the applicant in replying to enquiries. 740 refusals were on the ground that good character requirements had not been met. The Home Office says that this figure includes refusals of persons considered a threat to national security, but we cannot know how many were refused on this ground, nor whether the evidence in any case was of a kind which would satisfy a court.

The Home Office does not keep stock statistics of resident foreign nationals. Its estimate that 61 per cent of foreign-born people who had been in the UK for six years or more in 2002 were British citizens is admittedly only approximate; it presumably includes those foreign-born people who are British at birth. The Organisation for Economic Co-operation and Development estimated in 2003 that the total UK population was 59.3 million, with the stock of foreign nationals at 2,865 million or about 4.8 per cent of the total. This estimate was based on the Labour Force Survey (a sample survey which omits anyone not in work), UNHCR, the International Passenger Survey, the Home Office statistical bulletin and the Control of Immigration statistics (which record inward flows). Immigration to the UK comes from every continent; the main source countries since 1999 have been India and the USA.

Despite the quantity of information put out by the Home Office on the process, policy remains in many respects secret. However, advisers agree that there is no evidence of discrimination for or against any particular group.

There is no public outreach program to encourage naturalisation. Government policy appears to encourage it by stressing, since 2002, the positive value of being a citizen, but in practice over the same period it appears that procedures have been tightened. Alarm over terrorism, after July 2005, will probably increase scrutiny, especially as one of the London bomber suspects had been naturalised after lying about his former nationality.

15.4 Conclusions

Why is British nationality law so different from the laws of other states? First, the UK does not have the same theory of the nation that has taken hold elsewhere since 1789. England had its revolution too early and too inconclusively for it to have any lasting effect. The views expressed in the mid-seventeenth century by Levellers and others were thoroughly modern and democratic, claiming that governments derived their powers from the consent of the governed and that all men were equal as sons of Adam. But there was no theory of the nation as an organic whole of which nationals were members, no identification between a 'nation' in the sense of a particular people and the 'state' which gave form to their organisation. English demands for freedom and representation were highly individualistic. Later on, in the eighteenth and nineteenth centuries, British radicals were never asking for a new type of nation, but for new laws and forms of representation in the nation they already had and took for granted.

This nation was then and still is a somewhat vague concept. It has moved from being 'England' to 'Britain' to 'the United Kingdom' to the empire (sometimes described a hundred years ago as 'Greater Britain beyond the seas') and then more uncertainly to a United Kingdom as one member of the Commonwealth of Nations. The UK itself consists of three and a half *historic* nations; England, Wales and Scotland have separate national consciousnesses, while Northern Ireland is regarded as British by its Protestant inhabitants and Irish by Catholics.

Secondly, to understand British nationality law today, one must bear in mind:

- its ancient roots in English common law,
- the persistence of backward-looking habits of mind in its making up to and including the twentieth century,
- the UK's lack of a modern, single-document constitution comparable to those of other countries,
- the uncertainty and confusion of the law in the former British empire,
- the failure to deal clearly with legal change when the empire came to an end,
- British governments' obsession with immigration since 1945,
- the modern dominance of the Home Office over legislation, administration and nationality policy generally, to the exclusion of other government departments and, for the most part, of the judiciary.

These characteristics are evident in the preceding sections of this report.

The system is now on a statutory basis, with legislation followed by frequent statutory instruments and general regulations made under the legislation's powers. Very small details are defined: for example, the number of women entitled to register as British citizens under the Hong Kong War Wives and Widows Act 1996 was probably not more than 50, and one adviser mentioned it to me as 'half a dozen'. Within the main Acts there are numerous exceptions, qualifications and references back to other legislation. The structure as a whole, with its division into five types of nationality, two of which overlap, plus the peculiar status of British (Overseas) National, is excessively complicated. It rests on ambiguous policy aims. One aim has been to curtail non-white immigration from the old empire through the means of nationality law rather than immigration law itself. This was the main purpose in 1981. But there has also been a desire to appear in a good light, to seem at least to be alive to old obligations and at the same time to be modern, for example by providing measures of sex equality. The bureaucratic habits of the officials in the Home Office who prepare new laws for the parliamentary draughtsmen make for close attention to every possible detail and the stopping of every possible loophole, however small. And they always begin from the existing structure of the moment, which for centuries has been over-complicated, and try to incorporate the general requirements of their political masters in the scheme (often adding, it should be said, some ideas of their own). The underlying policy appears to be a desire to restrict the number of British nationals in the world. The close limitation on citizenship by descent for children born abroad, and the unprecedented limitations on ius soli in the 1981 Act, confirm this view of policy. It is the exact reverse of the policy in the first half of the twentieth century, which was expansive.

On the other hand, naturalisation for people already in the UK is in fact increasing; recent sex equality provisions in 2002 will have a slightly expansive effect on transmission, and the granting of British citizenship to BOTCs in the overseas territories has increased the number of British citizens in the world by about 200,000. These measures have a very small effect on overall numbers: the two last-named are political gestures to satisfy lobbyists while the new procedures in naturalisation are part of the government's policy to encourage 'integration' and a more definite idea of citizenship than has been common up to now. Citizenship has never had the strong meaning that it has in most other countries. It has been regarded as a personal quality: being law-abiding, a good neighbour and a participant in community affairs. It has not been related to a concept of legal nationality; indeed, the Citizens' Advice Bureaux found all over the country advise aliens (including asylum seekers) and nationals alike. The government's present policy is intended to make all residents identify with the UK and its interests.

Very few people in the UK think of themselves as European citizens. The general impression conveyed by the media, and not corrected by most politicians, is that the European Union is something outside the UK and which keeps interfering with the UK's freedom of action. 'Brussels' is often mentioned as a hostile power. Although some 30 per cent of voters vote for the European Parliament, the character of European institutions is hardly known to the majority of the population. People who have travelled in other European countries have a more positive though not always better-informed view. There are pro-Europeans and anti-Europeans in both major political parties: only the Liberal Democrats are consistently pro-European.

Thus the UK's sense of nationhood is inward-turned. No longer imperial and not yet fully European, it still looks to the past for a belief in national greatness. But there are of course many conflicting attitudes among politicians, journalists and the population at large. Opinion-forming is centred in London, which in some ways is like a small, separate country, and which is now thoroughly multi-racial and proud of this fact. It contains highly successful people whose ancestry derives from the old empire as well as from a wide variety of foreign countries, European and non-European. Throughout the country, ethnic minorities are highly visible in public services at every level (e.g., senior and junior doctors, nurses, technicians and cleaners in the Health Service; teachers including school Heads; transport workers) and in private industry and services. While some parts of London and many other cities contain very poor people of immigrant descent and experience racist attacks, abuse and discrimination, it is generally accepted these days that racism is unBritish. Much hypocrisy of course results. There is still racism in fact. There would undoubtedly be more if we had not had strong legislation against racial discrimination since 1976.

Hostility to muslims has become a serious matter in recent years. But – perhaps because of widespread British indifference to religion and suspicion of talking about a national culture – muslims can be British; girls can wear the headscarf at school and at work. Perhaps the vagueness and oddity of the British sense of nationhood can be an advantage in social life if not in law. We must hope that reaction to the London bombings will not destroy the positive achievements of recent decades.

Chronological table of major reforms in British nationality law since 1945

Date[40]	Document	Content of change
1948	British Nationality Act	UK-and-Colonies citizenship created within imperial British subjecthood.
1949	Ireland Act	Irish citizens to be treated as if British subjects.
1962	Commonwealth Immigrants Act	Colonial CUKCs and Commonwealth-country citizens subjected to UK entry control.
1964	British Nationality Act	Facilitated renunciation and resumption for some CUKCs.
1964	British nationality Act (No. 2)	Entitled stateless children of a British parent to register.
1968	Commonwealth Immigrants Act	CUKCs of colonial origin in independent countries subjected to entry control.
1971	Immigration Act	Creation of patriality (right of abode) as test for entry.
1972	Unilateral Declaration attached to the British Treaty of Accession to the EC	Defined which British nationals had freedom-of-movement rights: patrial CUKCs, patrial BSWCs and persons born or with fathers born in Gibraltar.
1981	British Nationality Act	Creation of British citizenship and three other 'citizenships'.
1981	East African Asians Case, 3 EHRR 76	A group of East African CUKCs complained to the European Commission on Human Rights in Strasbourg of degrading treatment by the British government. They were unable to use the Fourth Protocol of the ECHR as the UK had refused to ratify it. The Commission declared their case admissible, but it never proceeded to the Court.
1982	Unilateral Declaration revising the terms but not the content of the earlier Declaration attached to the British Treaty of Accession to the EC	British citizens, Dependent Territories' Citizens from Gibraltar and BSWCs with right of abode in the UK.
1985	International agreement between UK and People's Republic of China	Creation of British Nationals (Overseas).
1990	Hong Kong Act	50,000 Hong Kong residents to be registered as British citizens.
1997	British Nationality (Hong Kong) Act	Entitled non-Chinese Hong Kong citizens to register.
1997	R. v. Secretary of State for Home Department *ex parte Fayed*	Home Secretary must give reasons for refusal of naturalisation. Incorporated in NIAA 2002.
2000	Race Relations (Amendment) Act (RRA 2000)	Permitted Home Secretary to discriminate on grounds of ethnic or national origin in naturalisation.
2001	R. v. Secretary of State for Home Department ex parte Ullah	In principle, citizen by descent cannot upgrade status.

2002	British Overseas Territories Act (BOTA 2002)	BDTCs renamed BOTCs and given British citizenship also.
2002	Nationality Immigration and Asylum Act (NIAA 2002)	Withdrew permission accorded to Home Secretary under RRA 2000.

Notes

1 See Parliamentary Debates, House of Lords, 13 October 1981 for all the foregoing quotations.
2 25 Edw. 3, St. 1 (St. 2).
3 1608, 7 co. Rep, 1.
4 1708, 7 Anne c. 5.
5 1536, 28 Hen. 8. c. 3 (Wales); 1542, 34 and 35 Hen. 8. c. 26 (Laws in Wales).
6 6 Anne c. 14.
7 1669, Vaugh. 274, 124 ER 1072.
8 12, 13 and 14 Geo. 6, c. 41 (Ireland).
9 7 and 6 Vict, c. 66 (Aliens).
10 33 and 34 Vict. C. 14 (Naturalisation).
11 1669, Vaugh. 274, 124 ER 1072.
12 6 and 7 Geo. 6, c. 14.
13 4 and 5 Geo. 5, c. 17.
14 8 and 9 Geo. 5, c. 38 and 12 and 13 Geo. 5, c. 42.
15 11 and 12 Geo. 6, c. 56 (British nationality).
16 An Act extending this period for registration was passed in 1958, see 6 and 7 Eliz. 2, c. 10 (British Nationality) s. 3(1)(B).
17 10 and 11 Eliz. 2, c. 21.
18 Eliz. 2, c. 22.
19 Eliz. 2, c. 54.
20 Eliz. 2, c. 34.
21 Eliz. 2, c. 9.
22 A group of East African CUKCs complained to the European Commission on Human Rights in Strasbourg of degrading treatment by the British government (*East African Asians Case*, 1981, 3 EHRR 76). They were unable to use the Fourth Protocol of the ECHR as the UK had refused to ratify it. The Commission declared their case admissible, but it never proceeded to the Court.
23 Eliz. 2, c. 77.
24 Eliz. 2, c. 61.
25 1983, Eliz. 2, c. 6.
26 Eliz. 2, c. 41.
27 British citizenship (Designated service) (Amendment) Order 1987, No. 611.
28 *R. v. Sec. of State for Home Department ex parte Ullah* (2001).
29 See also British Overseas Territories (Amendment) Regulations S.I. no. 539 2003.
30 There is some minor provision for their nationality problems in the BOTA 2002, sect. 6.
31 1990 Hong Kong selection scheme Order S.I. 1990 no. 2292.
32 Eliz. 2, c. 41.
33 Eliz. 2, c. 20.
34 Eliz. 2, c.8.

35 2003 Adoption (Intercountry Aspects) Act 1999, (Commencement No. 9) Order 2003 No. 362 (c. 22).
36 See the NIAA (Commencement no. 9) Order, S.I. no. 2298, 2004 (c. 124), giving commencement dates for different sections of the Act.
37 2003 British Nationality (General) Regulations, S.I. No. 548, 2003.
38 Full details of the procedure are excessively complicated (they can be found at www.ind.homeoffice.gov.uk).
39 *R. v. Sec. of State for Home Department ex parte Fayed.*
40 The dates given for these Acts follow standard British usage, but do not indicate on what day their provisions, separately or as a whole, came into force. Some NIAA provisions, for example, are not yet in force at the time of writing. For more information concerning commencement dates on specific provisions see the detailed answers on selected modes of acquisition of nationality for the EU-15 at www.imiscoe.org/natac.

Bibliography

Allen, C. K. (1939), *Law in the Making.* 3rd edition. Oxford: Oxford University Press.

Dummett, A. & A. Nicol (1990), *Subjects, Citizens, Aliens and Others.* London: Weidenfeld & Nicolson.

Fransman, L. (1998), *Fransman's Nationality Law.* 2nd edition. London: Butterworth.

Jones, M. (1947). *British Nationality Law and Practice.* Oxford: Oxford University Press.

Parry, C. (1957), *Nationality and Citizenship Laws of the Commonwealth and of the Republic of Ireland.* London: Stevens.

Piggott, F. (1907), *Nationality including Naturalisation.* Volume I. London: William Clowes.

Pollock, F. & F. Maitland (1952), *History of English Law.* 2nd edition. Cambridge: Cambridge University Press.

List of contributors

Marta Arena, FIERI, Torino
marta_arena_tos@yahoo.fr
Maria Ioannis Baganha, Department of Economics, University of Coimbra
mbaganha@fe.uc.pt
Rainer Bauböck, Institute for European Integration Research, Austrian Academy of Sciences, Vienna
Rainer.Baubock@oeaw.ac.at
Henrik Bernitz, consult JKL, Stockholm
henrik.bernitz@jklgroup.com
Pierre Brasseur, Freelance Researcher, Luxembourg
pierrebrasseur@gmx.fr
Dimitris Christopoulos, Department of Political Sciences, Panteion University of Athens
christopoulos@synigoros.gr
Dilek Çinar, Research Affiliate, European Centre for Social Welfare Policy and Research
cinar@euro.centre.org or dilek.cinar@univie.ac.at
Betty de Hart, Centre for Migration Law, Radboud University of Nijmegen
B.deHart@jur.ru.nl
Ann Dummett, Oxford
fon/fax: 0044 1865 558 698
Eva Ersbøll, Danish Institute for Human Rights, Copenhagen
eer@humanrights.dk
Jessica Fagerlund, Freelance Researcher, Oslo
jessica_fagerlund@yahoo.no
Marie-Claire Foblets, Department of Law and Anthroplogy, Catholic University Leuven
Marie-Claire.Foblets@ant.kuleuven.ac.be
Kees Groenendijk, Centre for Migration Law, Radboud University of Nijmegen
C.Groenendijk@jur.ru.nl
Kay Hailbronner, Department of Law, University of Konstanz
Kay.Hailbronner@Uni-Konstanz.de

John Handoll, William Fry Solicitors, Dublin
John.Handoll@williamfry.ie
Hedvig Lokrantz Bernitz, Department of Law, Stockholm University
hedvig.lokrantz-bernitz@juridicum.su.se
Sander Loones, Freelance Researcher, Leuven-Oostduinkerke
sander.loones@dofi.fgov.be
François Moyse, AS-Avocats, Brussels
f.moyse@as-avocats.com
Bruno Nascimbene, Law Department, University of Milano and FIERI, Torino
info@nascimbene.com
Bernhard Perchinig, Institute for European Integration Research, Austrian Academy of Sciences, Vienna
Bernhard.Perchinig@oeaw.ac.at
Ruth Rubio Marín, Department of Constitutional Law, University of Sevilla
rrubio@us.es
Denis Scuto, Faculty of Humanities, Arts and Educational Science, University of Luxembourg
denis.scuto@education.lu
Alexis Spire, Centre for Administrative Political and Social Studies, University of Lille
alexis.spire@libertysurf.fr
Constança Urbano de Sousa, Law Department, Autonomous University of Lisbon
constanca@universidade-autonoma.pt
Ricky van Oers, Centre for Migration Law, Radboud University of Nijmegen
r.vanoers@jur.ru.nl
Harald Waldrauch, 1/30 Beach Road, Bondi Beach, 2026 NSW, Australia
harald.waldrauch@gmx.at
Patrick Weil, Centre for Social History of the Twentieth Century, Sorbonne, Paris
Patrick.Weil@univ-paris1.fr
Giovanna Zincone, FIERI, Torino
fieri@fieri.it